Understanding Operating Systems

Fourth Edition

Ida M. Flynn, University of Pittsburgh

Ann McIver McHoes, Carlow University

THOMSON

COURSE TECHNOLOGY

Australia • Canada • Mexico • Singapore • Spain • United Kingdom • United States

Understanding Operating Systems,
Fourth Edition

Ida M. Flynn
Ann McIver McHoes

Senior Product Manager: Alyssa Pratt	Senior Marketing Manager: Karen Seitz	Cover Designer: Laura Rickenbach
Executive Editor: Mac Mendelsohn	Associate Product Manager: Mirella Misiaszek	Compositor: Pre-Press Company, Inc.
Developmental Editor: Deb Kaufmann	Editorial Assistant: Jennifer Smith	Printer: Quebecor, Taunton
Production Editor: Dusty Friedman, The Book Company	Senior Manufacturing Coordinator: Trevor Kallop	

ISBN 0-534-42366-3

Dedicated to Ida Moretti Flynn in celebration of her life and her devotion to the art of teaching.

AMM

Contents

Appendixes

Preface

We believe that operating systems can be understood and appreciated by anyone who uses a computer. So we wrote a book that explains this very technical subject in a not-so-technical manner, putting the concepts and theories of operating systems into a format that readers can quickly grasp.

For those new to the subject, this text demonstrates what operating systems are, what they do, how they do it, how their performance can be evaluated, and how they compare with each other. Throughout the text we describe the overall function and tell readers where to find more detailed information, if they so desire.

For those with more technical backgrounds, this text introduces the subject concisely, describing the complexities of operating systems without going into intricate detail. One might say this book leaves off where other operating systems textbooks begin.

Of course, we've made some assumptions about our audiences. First, we assume our readers have some familiarity with computing systems. Second, we assume they have a working knowledge of an operating system and how it interacts with its users. We recommend (although we don't require) that readers be familiar with at least one operating system. In a few places we found it necessary to include examples using Java or pseudocode to illustrate the inner workings of the operating systems but, for readers who are unfamiliar with computer languages, we've added a prose description to each example that explains the events in more familiar terms.

Organization and Features

This book is structured to explain the functions of an operating system regardless of the hardware that houses it. The organization addresses a recurring problem with textbooks about technologies that continue to evolve—that is, constant advances in the subject matter make the textbook immediately outdated. To address this problem we've divided the material into two parts: first, the theory of the subject—which does not change much—and second, the specifics of operating systems—which change quickly and evolve with the technology. Our goal is to give readers the ability to apply the topics intelligently, realizing that, although a command, or series of commands, used by one operating system may be slightly different from that of another, their goals are the same and the functions of the operating systems are also the same.

Although it is more difficult to understand how operating systems work than to memorize the details of a single operating system, understanding general operating system concepts is a longer-lasting achievement. Such understanding also pays off in the long run, because it allows one to adapt as technology changes—as, inevitably, it does. Therefore, the purpose of this book is to give users of computer systems a solid background in the components of the operating system, their functions and goals, and how they interact and interrelate.

Part One, the first twelve chapters, describes the theory of operating systems. It concentrates on each of the "managers" in turn and shows how they work together. Then it introduces network organization concepts, security, ethics, and management of network functions. Part Two examines actual operating systems, how they apply the theories presented in Part One, and how they compare with each other.

The meat of the text begins in Chapters 2 and 3 with memory management because it is the simplest component of the operating system to explain and has historically been tied to the advances from one operating system to the next. We explain the role of the Processor Manager in Chapters 4, 5, and 6, first discussing simple systems and then expanding the discussion to include multiuser systems. By the time we reach device management in Chapter 7 and file management in Chapter 8, readers will have been introduced to the complexities of large computing systems. Chapters 9 and 10 introduce terms and concepts related to networking and Chapters 11 and 12 discuss security, ethics, and some of the tradeoffs that designers have to make to satisfy the needs of users.

Each chapter includes learning objectives, key terms, and a research topic. For our more technically-oriented readers, the exercises at the end of each chapter include problems for advanced students. Please note that some advanced exercises assume knowledge of matters not presented in the book—but they're good for those who enjoy a challenge. We expect readers from our more general audience will cheerfully pass them by.

In an attempt to bring the concepts closer to home, throughout the book we've added real-life examples to illustrate abstract theory. However, let no one confuse our conversational style with our considerable respect for the subject matter. The subject of operating systems is a complex one and it cannot be covered completely in these few pages. Therefore, this textbook does not attempt to give an in-depth treatise of operating systems theory and applications. This is the overall view.

Part Two describes the MS-DOS, Windows, and UNIX and Linux operating systems and how each applies the theories discussed in Part One. The structure of each chapter is similar so that each operating system can be roughly compared with the others. We have tried to include the advantages and disadvantages of each. Again, we must stress that this is a general discussion—an in-depth examination of an operating system would require details based on its current standard version, which can't be done here. We strongly suggest that readers use our discussion as a guide, a base to work from, when comparing the pros and cons of a specific operating system and supplement our work with research that's as current as possible.

The text concludes with several reference aids. Terms that are important within a chapter are listed at its conclusion as key terms. The extensive end-of-book Glossary includes brief definitions for hundreds of terms used in these pages. The Bibliography can guide the reader to basic research on the subject. Finally, the Appendices feature several helpful learning tools including a guide to acronyms, a translation table showing a few comparable operating system commands, a comparison of graphical user interfaces, the ACM Code of Ethics, a list of significant innovators, and a timeline of operating system developments.

Not included in this text is a discussion of databases and data structures, except as examples of process synchronization problems, because they do not relate directly to operating systems. We suggest that readers begin by learning the basics as presented in the following pages before pursuing these complex subjects.

Changes to the Fourth Edition

This edition features two new chapters—Security and Ethics (Chapter 11), and System Management (Chapter 12). While our previous editions covered some of this material in a single chapter, the time has come to emphasize system security, ethics, system monitoring, and patch management. Security and system management information changes daily, so the information presented in these pages offers a good beginning point for students interested in the subjects. For the latest research, we suggest readers visit the Web pages mentioned in those chapters.

To help learners structure their readings, every chapter now begins with learning objectives. And we've also incorporated several references to wireless technology even though that subject is too vast to do justice to in these pages.

In several chapters throughout the text, Linux case studies are included to illustrate the theory presented in that chapter. For example, at the conclusion of Chapter 3 on memory management, we have a case study discussing Linux memory management. The material in each case study is optional so readers can choose to review it or not, depending on their interest in the Linux operating system.

Throughout the text, we've added discussions of threads, cache memory, updated illustrations, and anecdotal information about current operating systems.

Chapter 7 on device management has been extensively revised to reflect the technology most current at the time of this writing including a more in-depth discussion of RAID and optical discs such as CDs and DVDs. With the industry's legendary speed in hardware improvements, it isn't surprising that this chapter is the most dynamic in Part One and will be the first to go out of date. We encourage readers to supplement our text with the most current industry literature for up-to-date device management theory.

Chapter 13 discusses MS-DOS, a historically significant, yet persistent operating system that students can still see via many Windows operating systems.

Chapter 14 discusses Windows operating systems with an emphasis on Windows XP.

In Chapter 15 UNIX and Linux are discussed in tandem. Our integration of the two should provide readers with an adequate framework in which to compare these two very similar systems that have come to be rivals in the marketplace.

In the Appendixes, we've added a list of innovators who have received the Kobayashi award from the Institute of Electrical and Electronics Engineers (IEEE) as well as a comprehensive timeline featuring highlights of operating systems evolution. Both additions may help readers gain a wider perspective of the subject.

Other changes throughout the text are editorial clarifications, a more readable page layout, expanded captions, improved illustrations, and the most current information on the operating systems presented in Part Two.

A Note for Instructors

The following supplements are available when this text is used in a classroom setting:

Electronic Instructor's Manual. The Instructor's Manual that accompanies this textbook includes additional instructional material to assist in class preparation, including Sample Syllabi, Chapter Outlines, Technical Notes, Lecture Notes, Quick Quizzes, Teaching Tips, and Discussion Topics.

Distance Learning. Course Technology is proud to present online test banks in WebCT and Blackboard to provide the most complete and dynamic learning experience possible. Instructors are encouraged to make the most of the course, both online and offline. For more information on how to access the online test bank, contact your local Course Technology sales representative.

PowerPoint Presentations. This book comes with Microsoft PowerPoint slides for each chapter. These are included as a teaching aid for classroom presentations, either to make available to students on the network for chapter review, or to be printed for classroom distribution. Instructors can add their own slides for additional topics that they introduce to the class.

Solutions. Selected solutions to Review Questions and Exercises are provided on the Teaching Tools CD-ROM and may also be found on the Course Technology Web site at **www.course.com**. The solutions are password protected.

This text has a modular construction. Chapters 2 through 12 are the core of the book; Chapter 1 may be assigned as preliminary reading or may be covered in the introductory lecture. The order of presentation in a classroom does not need to follow the table of contents in sequence. Other than Chapters 2 and 3, and Chapters 4 and 5, which are best understood when they are presented in that order, an instructor can present the chapters in any order. Chapter 6 may be omitted for less technical audiences. If you don't want to explore networks, skip Chapters 9 and 10. We encourage you to include Chapters 11 and 12 in your class material as security and system management have become increasing crucial for operating systems administrators. In addition, instructors have the option of integrating one or all of the operating systems described in Part two depending on the individual's preferences, the course direction, and time availability.

Acknowledgments

Special thanks go to Roger Flynn of the University of Pittsburgh, Terri Lennox of Westminster College, Charles R. Woratschek of Robert Morris University, Eleanor Irwin, Karen Esch, Mary Puthawala, Ed Hayes, and Annette Anderson for their assistance and encouragement.

Our gratitude goes to all of our friends and colleagues, particularly those at the University of Pittsburgh, who were so generous with their encouragement, advice, and support. Special thanks also to those at Course Technology, Brooks/Cole, and PWS Publishing who made significant contributions to all four editions of this text, especially Alyssa Pratt, Deb Kaufmann, Kallie Swanson, Mike Sugarman, and Mary Thomas Stone. In addition, the following individuals made a key contribution to this edition: Shawn Day, Chris Scriver, Susan Whalen, and Dusty Friedman.

We deeply appreciate the comments of the reviewers who helped us refine this edition:

Gary Heisler, Lansing Community College
Janet Kourik, Webster University
Nipul Patel, Purdue University

and to the many readers and instructors who have helped us with all four editions, we thank you.

Ida M. Flynn

Ann McIver McHoes
mchoes@acm.org

Part One

Operating Systems Theory

Part One, the first twelve chapters of the book, is an overview of operating systems—what they are, how they work, what their goals are, and how they achieve those goals. Each chapter covers a primary part of the operating system, beginning with the management of main memory and moving on to processors, devices, files and networks. Finally, Chapters 11 and 12 explore system security issues, system management, and the interaction of the operating system's components.

Although this is a technical subject, in our discussions we try to include the definitions of terms that might be unfamiliar to you. However, it isn't always possible to describe a function *and* define the technical terms while keeping the explanation clear. Therefore, we include a Key Terms section with definitions at the end of each chapter, and an extensive Glossary at the end of the book for your reference. Items listed in the Key Terms sections and Glossary are shown in **boldface** the first time they appear in the text.

Throughout the book we keep our descriptions and examples as simple as possible to introduce you to the system's complexities without getting bogged down in technical detail. Therefore, be aware that for almost every topic explained in the following pages, there's much more information that can be studied. The goal is to introduce you to the subject, and to encourage you to pursue your interest using other texts or primary sources if you need more detail.

In Part Two, we look at specific operating systems and how they apply the theory described in Part Two.

Chapter 1

Introducing Operating Systems

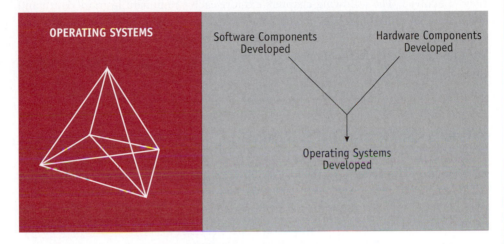

"I think there is a world market for maybe five computers."
—Thomas J. Watson *(1874–1956; chairman of IBM 1949–1956)*

Learning Objectives

After completing this chapter, you should be able to describe:

- The basic role of an operating system
- The major operating system software subsystem managers and their functions
- The types of machine hardware on which operating systems run, and give at least one example of an operating system for each of the following: PDAs, microcomputers, minicomputers, mainframes, workstations, and supercomputers
- The differences between the following types of operating systems: batch, interactive, real-time, hybrid, and embedded
- Multiprocessing and its impact on the evolution of operating system software
- System architecture trends in current operating systems

To understand the operating system is to understand the workings of the entire computer system, because the operating system manages each and every piece of hardware and software. This text explores what operating systems are, how they work, what they do, and why.

This chapter briefly describes how operating systems work and how, in general, they've evolved. The following chapters explore each component in more depth and show how its function relates to the other parts of the operating system. In other words, you see how the pieces work harmoniously to keep the computer system working smoothly. Note: throughout this text, **boldface** type indicates terms that are defined in the glossary.

What Is an Operating System?

Let's begin with a definition: What is an **operating system**? To put it in the simplest terms, it's the executive manager, the part of the computing system that manages all of the hardware and all of the software. To be specific, it controls every file, every device, every section of main memory, and every nanosecond of processing time. It controls who can use the system and how. In short, it's the boss.

Therefore, when the user sends a command, the operating system must make sure that the command is executed or, if it's not executed, must arrange for the user to get a message explaining the error. This doesn't necessarily mean that the operating system executes the command or sends the error message—but it does control the parts of the system that do.

A computer system consists of **software** (programs) and **hardware** (the physical machine and its electronic components). Operating system software falls in a broad category of software. Other categories can include utility software and application software, (programs such as word processors or media players that perform specific tasks for users). The next two sections describe the components of operating system software, and the machine hardware on which it runs.

Operating System Software

The pyramid shown in Figure 1.1 is an abstract representation of an operating system and demonstrates the interrelationships of its major components.

The base of the pyramid shows the four essential managers of every operating system: the **Memory Manager**, the **Processor Manager**, the **Device Manager**, and the **File**

(figure 1.1)

This model of a non-networked operating system shows four sub-system managers supporting the User Command Interface.

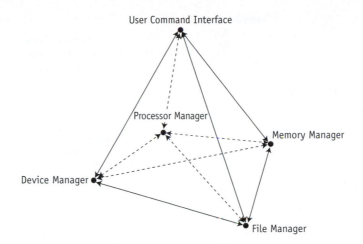

Manager. In fact, these managers are the basis of all operating systems and each is discussed in detail throughout the first part of this book. Each manager works closely with the other managers and performs its unique role regardless of which specific operating system is being discussed. Network functions were not always an integral part of operating systems; they were normally mounted over existing operating systems. Hence, we haven't identified a separate corner in the pyramid but have incorporated the chapters related to these functions under the heading of operating systems.

On the other hand, the **User Command Interface,** from which users issue commands to the operating system, is the component that is unique to each operating system and is very different from one operating system to the next—sometimes even between different versions of the same operating system. (For your convenience, Figure 1.1 is repeated inside the front cover showing the chapters in which each component is discussed.)

Regardless of the size or configuration of the system, each of the subsystem managers, shown in Figure 1.2, must perform the following tasks:

• Monitor its resources continuously
• Enforce the policies that determine who gets what, when, and how much
• Allocate the resource when it's appropriate
• Deallocate the resource when appropriate

For instance, the Memory Manager is in charge of **main memory,** also known as RAM. It checks the validity of each request for memory space and, if it is a legal request, the Memory Manager allocates a portion that isn't already in use. In a multi-user environment, the Memory Manager sets up a table to keep track of who is using which section of memory. Finally, when the time comes to reclaim the memory, the Memory Manager deallocates memory.

A primary responsibility of the Memory Manager is to preserve the space in main memory occupied by the operating system itself—it can't allow any part of it to be accidentally or intentionally altered.

The Processor Manager decides how to allocate the **central processing unit (CPU)**. An important function of the Processor Manager is to keep track of the status of each process. A process is defined here as an instance of execution of a program.

The Processor Manager monitors whether the CPU is executing a process or waiting for a READ or WRITE command to finish execution. Because it handles the processes' transitions from one state of execution to another, it can be compared to a traffic controller. Once the Processor Manager allocates the processor, it sets up the necessary registers and tables and, when the job is finished or the maximum amount of time has expired, it reclaims the processor.

Conceptually, the Processor Manager has two levels of responsibility. One is to handle jobs as they enter the system and the other is to manage each process within those jobs. The first part is handled by the Job Scheduler, the high-level portion of the Processor Manager, which accepts or rejects the incoming jobs. The second part is handled by the Process Scheduler, the low-level portion of the Processor Manager, which is responsible for deciding which process gets the CPU and for how long.

The Device Manager monitors every device, channel, and control unit. Its job is to choose the most efficient way to allocate all of the system's devices, printers, terminals, disk drives, and so forth, based on a scheduling policy chosen by the system's designers. The Device Manager makes the allocation, starts its operation, and, finally, deallocates the device.

The fourth, the File Manager, keeps track of every file in the system including data files, assemblers, compilers, and application programs. By using predetermined access policies, it enforces restrictions on who has access to which files. The File Manager also controls what users are allowed to do with files once they access them. For example, a user might have read-only access, read-and-write access, or the authority to create and delete files. Also, the File Manager allocates the resource by opening the file and deallocates it by closing the file.

However, it is not enough for each manager to perform its individual tasks. It must also be able to work harmoniously with every other manager. Here is a *simplified* example. Let's say someone types a command to execute a program. The following major steps must occur in sequence:

1. The Device Manager must receive the electrical impulses from the keyboard, decode the keystrokes to form the command, and send the command to the User Command Interface, where the Processor Manager validates the command.

2. The Processor Manager then sends an acknowledgment message to be displayed on the video monitor so the user realizes the command has been sent.

3. When the Processor Manager receives the command, it determines whether the program must be retrieved from storage or is already in memory, and then notifies the appropriate manager.

4. If the program is in storage, the File Manager must calculate its exact location on the disk, pass this information to the Device Manager, which retrieves and sends the program on to the Memory Manager, which must find space for it and record its exact location in memory.

5. Once the program is in memory, the Memory Manager must track its location and progress as it is executed by the Processor Manager.

6. When the program has finished executing, it must send a finished message back to the Processor Manager.

7. Finally, the Processor Manager must forward the finished message back to the Device Manager, which displays it on the video monitor for the user to see.

Although this is an oversimplified demonstration of a complex operation, it illustrates the incredible precision required by the operating system. Remember, no single manager could perform its tasks without the active cooperation of every other part.

Operating systems with networking capability have a fifth essential manager called the Network Manager that provides a convenient way for users to share resources while controlling users' access to them. These resources include hardware (such as CPUs, memory areas, printers, tape drives, modems, and disk drives) and software (such as compilers, application programs, and data files). By adding the fifth manager to create a networked operating system, we create a five-sided pyramid. The base for the pyramid is shown in Figure 1.3 and described in detail in Chapter 9.

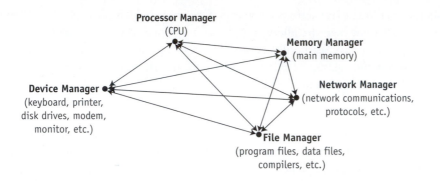

(figure 1.3)

Networked systems have a Network Manager that assumes responsibility for networking tasks while working harmoniously with every other manager.

Machine Hardware

To appreciate the role of the operating system, we need to understand the essential aspects of the computer system's hardware, the physical machine and its electronic components including memory chips, input/output devices, storage devices, and the central processing unit (CPU).

Main memory is where the data and instructions must reside to be processed.

I/O devices, short for input/output devices, include every peripheral unit in the system such as printers, disk drives, CD drives, magnetic tape devices, keyboards, DVD players, modems, and so on.

The CPU, the central processing unit, is the brains, with the circuitry (sometimes called the chips) to control the interpretation and execution of instructions. In essence, it controls the operation of the entire computer system, as illustrated in Figure 1.4. All storage references, data manipulations, and I/O operations are initiated or performed by the CPU.

Until the mid-1970s, computers were classified by capacity and price. A **mainframe** was a large machine—in size and in internal memory capacity. The IBM 360, introduced in 1964, is a classic example of an early mainframe. The IBM 360 model 30, the smallest in the 360 family, required an air-conditioned room about 18 feet square to house the CPU, the operator's console, a printer, a card reader, and a keypunch machine. The CPU was five feet high and six feet wide, had an internal memory of 64K (considered large at that time), and a price tag of $200,000 in 1964 dollars. Because of its size and price at the time, its applications were generally limited to large computer centers belonging to the federal government, universities, and very large businesses.

The **minicomputer** was developed to meet the needs of smaller institutions, those with only a few dozen users. One of the early minicomputers was marketed by Digital Equipment Corporation to satisfy the needs of large schools and small colleges that

(figure 1.4)

A logical view of a typical computer system hardware configuration illustrating the role of interfaces and key functions common to microcomputer systems. Computers with network access also require a network interface. The tower holds the Central Processing Unit, the Arithmetic and Logic Unit, registers, cache, and main memory, as well as controllers and interfaces shown within the dotted lines.

began offering computer science courses in the early 1970s. (The price of its PDP-8, (Peripheral Device Processor-8) was less than $18,000.) Minicomputers are smaller in size and memory capacity and cheaper than mainframes. Today, computers that fall between microcomputers and mainframes in capacity are often called midrange computers.

The **supercomputer** was introduced primarily for government applications needing massive and fast number-crunching ability to carry out military operations and weather forecasting. Business and industry became interested in the technology when the massive computers became faster and less expensive. A Cray supercomputer is a typical example with six to thousands of processors performing up to 2.4 trillion floating point operations per second (**teraflops**). Today, supercomputers are used for a wide range of tasks from scientific research to customer support and product development. They're even used to perform the intricate calculations used to create animated motion pictures. And they help oil companies in their search for oil by analyzing massive amounts of data (Stair, 1999).

The **microcomputer** was developed for single users in the late 1970s. Tandy Corporation and Apple Computer, Inc. were the first to offer microcomputers for sale to the general public. Tandy targeted the small business market and Apple aimed for the elementary education market. These early models had very little memory by today's standards—64K was the maximum capacity. Their physical size was smaller than the minicomputers of that time, though larger than the microcomputers of today. Eventually, microcomputers grew to accommodate software with larger capacity and greater speeds. The distinguishing characteristic of a microcomputer is its single-user status.

The most powerful microcomputers used by commercial, educational and government enterprises are called **workstations**. Typically, they're networked together and are used to support engineering and technical users who perform massive mathematical computations, computer-aided design (CAD), or other applications requiring very powerful CPUs, large amounts of main memory, and extremely high-resolution graphic displays to meet their needs.

Since the mid-1970s rapid advances in computer technology have blurred the distinguishing characteristics of early machines: physical size, cost, and memory capacity. The most powerful mainframes today have multiple processors coordinated by the Processor Manager. Simple mainframes still have a large main memory, but now they're available in desk-sized cabinets. Minicomputers look like microcomputers, and the smallest can now accomplish tasks once reserved for mainframes.

Networking is an integral part of modern computer systems and has become a permanent feature in the most recent entries in the computer market: personal organizers, personal digital assistants (PDAs), palmtop computers, and hand-held Web browsers. Although they were relatively rare before 1996, the rapid development of the Web has provided means for delivering information to a mobile society creating a strong market for such equipment. Their capabilities vary from storing addresses, to-do lists, memos and e-mail messages, to supporting PC-type applications such as spreadsheets and personal financial management, to collecting data at a manufacturing site, to collecting your signature when a courier asks you to sign for a package. Hand-held devices are lightweight, can operate remotely on battery power, can fit in a coat pocket, and make it easy to exchange data with a desktop PC, which saves time when data is uploaded into a computer system.

At one time computers were classified by memory capacity; now they're distinguished by processor capacity. We must emphasize that these are relative categories and what is large today will eventually become medium-sized and then small sometime in the near future.

In 1965, Intel executive Gordon Moore observed that each new processor chip contained roughly twice as much capacity as its predecessor, and each chip was released within 18-24 months of the previous chip. He concluded that the trend would cause computing power to rise exponentially over relatively brief periods of time. Now known as Moore's Law, the trend has continued and is still remarkably accurate and forms the basis for industry forecasts. The Intel 4004 chip in 1971 had 2,300 transistors while the Pentium II chip twenty years later had 7.5 million, and the Pentium 4 Extreme Edition processor introduced in 2004 had 178 million transistors.

Many operating systems have been written for use on multiple platforms and others are written to operate on one specific type of computer. Table 1.1 lists several popular operating systems and the platforms they can manage.

<table>
<tr><td>**(table1.1)**</td><td>**Platform**</td><td>**Operating System**</td></tr>
<tr><td rowspan="7">*A brief list of platforms and some of the operating systems available to run them. (listed in alphabetical order)*</td><td>Microcomputers</td><td>Linux, Macintosh, MS-DOS, Windows 2000/XP</td></tr>
<tr><td>Minicomputers</td><td>Linux, IBM OS/400, OpenVMS Alpha, UNIX</td></tr>
<tr><td>Mainframe computers</td><td>IBM OS/390, UNIX</td></tr>
<tr><td>Supercomputers</td><td>IRIX, UNICOS</td></tr>
<tr><td>Workstations</td><td>HP-UX, Sun Solaris, UNIX</td></tr>
<tr><td>Networks</td><td>Linux, NetWare, UNIX, Windows Server 2003</td></tr>
<tr><td>PDA</td><td>Palm OS, Windows CE</td></tr>
</table>

Types of Operating Systems

Operating systems for computers large and small fall into five categories distinguished by response time and how data is entered into the system: batch, interactive, real-time, hybrid, and embedded systems.

Batch systems date from the earliest computers, which relied on punched cards or tape for input when a job was entered by assembling the cards into a deck and running the entire deck of cards through a card reader as a group—a batch. Present-day batch systems aren't limited to cards or tapes, but the jobs are still processed serially, without user interaction.

The efficiency of the system was measured in **throughput**—the number of jobs completed in a given amount of time (for example, 30 jobs per hour) and turnaround was measured in hours or even days. Today it's uncommon to find a system that is limited to batch programs.

Interactive systems (also called time-sharing systems) give a faster turnaround than batch systems but are slower than the real-time systems we'll talk about next. They were introduced to satisfy the demands of users who needed fast turnaround when debugging their programs. The operating system required the development of time-sharing software, which would allow each user to interact directly with the computer system via commands entered from a typewriter-like terminal.

The operating system provides immediate feedback to the user and response time can be measured in minutes or seconds, depending on the number of active users.

Real-time systems are the fastest and are used in time-critical environments where data must be processed extremely quickly because the output influences immediate decisions. Real-time systems are used for space flights (Figure 1.5), airport traffic control, high-speed aircraft, industrial processes, sophisticated medical equipment, distribution of electricity, and telephone switching. A real-time system must be 100 percent responsive 100 percent of the time. Response time is measured in fractions of a second, but this is an ideal not often achieved in the field.

Although in theory it's possible to convert a general-purpose operating system into a real-time system, in practice the overhead of general-purpose systems is so large that real-time performance can't be achieved. Therefore, most real-time work requires operating systems that are specially designed to meet real-time needs.

Hybrid systems are a combination of batch and interactive. They appear to be interactive because individual users can access the system via terminals and get fast response, but such a system actually accepts and runs batch programs in the background when the interactive load is light. A hybrid system takes advantage of the free time between

Courtesy of NASA

(figure 1.5)

Computer interface box for the Apollo spacecraft (1968). The guidance computer had few moving parts and no vacuum tubes making it both rugged and compact. The development of this computer inspired technological breakthroughs that led the way for integrated circuit boards.

demands for processing to execute programs that need no significant operator assistance. Many large computer systems are hybrids.

Embedded systems are computers placed inside other products to add features and capabilities. For example, you find embedded computers in household appliances, automobiles, digital music players, elevators, and pacemakers. In the case of automobiles, embedded computers can help with engine performance, braking, and navigation. Several projects are under way to implement "smart roads," which would alert drivers in cars equipped with embedded computers to choose alternate routes when traffic becomes congested.

As you can see from these examples, operating systems for embedded computers need to be very different from each other and also from that of a general computer system. Each one is designed to perform a set of specific programs, which are not interchangeable among systems. This permits the designers to make the operating system more efficient and utilize the computer's limited resources, such as memory, to their maximum.

Before a general-purpose operating system, such as Linux, can be used in an embedded system, the system designers must select which components, from the entire operating system, are needed in that particular environment. The final version of this operating system will include only the necessary elements; any unneeded features or functions will be dropped. Therefore, operating systems with a small kernel (the core portion of the software) and with other functions that can be mixed and matched to meet the embedded system requirements will have potential in this market.

Brief History of Operating Systems Development

The evolution of operating system software parallels the evolution of the computer hardware they were designed to control. Here's a very brief overview of this evolution.

1940s

The first generation of computers (1940–1955) was a time of vacuum tube technology and computers the size of classrooms. Each computer was unique in structure and purpose. There was little need for standard operating system software because each computer's use was restricted to a few professionals working on mathematical, scientific, or military applications, all of whom were familiar with the idiosyncrasies of their hardware.

A typical program would include every instruction needed by the computer to perform the tasks requested. It would give explicit directions to the card reader (when to begin, how to interpret the data on the cards, when to end), the CPU (how and where to store

13

the instructions in memory, what to calculate, where to find the data, where to send the output), and the output device (when to begin, how to print out the finished product, how to format the page, and when to end).

The machines were operated by the programmers from the main console—it was a hands-on process. In fact, to debug a program, the programmer would stop the processor, read the contents of each register, make the corrections in memory locations, and then resume operation. The first bug was a moth trapped in a Harvard computer, as shown in Figure 1.6.

To run programs, the programmers would have to reserve the machine for the length of time they estimated it would take the computer to execute the program. As a result, the machine was poorly utilized. The CPU processed data and made calculations for only a fraction of the available time and, in fact, the entire system sat idle between reservations.

In time, computer hardware and software became more standard and the execution of a program required fewer steps and less knowledge of the internal workings of the computer. Compilers and assemblers were developed to translate into binary code the English-like commands of the evolving high-level languages.

Rudimentary operating systems started to take shape with the creation of macros, library programs, standard subroutines, and utility programs. And they included device driver subroutines—prewritten programs that standardized the way input and output devices were used.

These early programs were at a significant disadvantage because they were designed to use their resources conservatively at the expense of understandability. That meant that many programs used convoluted logic that only the original programmer could understand, so it was nearly impossible for anyone else to debug or change the program later on.

(figure 1.6)

Dr. Grace Hopper's research journal from her work on Harvard's Mark I computer in 1945 included the remains of the first computer "bug," a moth that had become trapped in the computer's relays causing the system to crash. The term is still in use today.

1950s

Second-generation computers (1955–1965) were developed to meet the needs of a new market—businesses (figure 1.7). The business environment placed much more importance on the cost effectiveness of the system. Computers were still very expensive, especially when compared to other office equipment (the IBM 7094 was priced at $200,000). Therefore, throughput had to be maximized to make such an investment worthwhile for business use, which meant dramatically increasing the usage of the system.

Two improvements were widely adopted: Computer operators were hired to facilitate each machine's operation, and job scheduling was instituted. Job scheduling is a productivity improvement scheme that groups together programs with similar requirements. For example, several FORTRAN programs would be run together while the FORTRAN compiler was still resident in memory. Or all of the jobs using the card reader for input might be run together, and those using the tape drive would be run later. Some operators found that a mix of I/O device requirements was the most efficient combination. That is, by mixing tape-input programs with card-input programs, the tapes could be mounted or rewound while the card reader was busy.

Job scheduling introduced the need for control cards, which defined the exact nature of each program and its requirements. This was one of the first uses of a **job control language** (**JCL**), which helped the operating system coordinate and manage the system's resources by identifying the users and their jobs and specifying the resources required to execute each job.

The following is an example of a simple program (set-up for the DEC-10 computer)

$JOB (insert user number)   < identify job and user

$PASSWORD (insert user password)   < positively identify user

$LANGUAGE (indicate compiler needed) < specify resource
[source deck]

$DATA   < identify resource
[data deck]

$EOJ   < identify end of job and release
                                        resources

But even with batching techniques the faster second-generation computers allowed expensive time lags between the CPU and the I/O devices. For example, a job with 1600 cards could take 79 seconds to be read by the card reader and only 5 seconds of CPU time to assemble (compile). That meant the CPU was idle 94 percent of the time and actually processing only 6 percent of the time it was dedicated to that job.

Eventually, several factors helped improve the performance of the CPU. First, the speed of I/O devices like tape drives, disks, and drums gradually became faster.

Second, to use more of the available storage area in these devices, records were blocked before they were retrieved or stored. (Blocking means that several logical records are grouped within one physical record.) Of course, when the records were retrieved, they had to be deblocked before the program could use them. To aid programmers in these blocking and deblocking functions, access methods were developed and added to object code by the linkage editor.

Third, to reduce the discrepancy in speed between the I/O and the CPU, an interface called the control unit was placed between them to perform the function of buffering. A buffer is an interim storage area that works like this: as the slow input device reads a record, the control unit places each character of the record into the buffer. When the buffer is full, the entire record is quickly transmitted to the CPU. The process is just the opposite for output devices: the CPU places the entire record into the buffer, which is then passed on by the control unit at the slower rate required by the output device.

If a control unit has more than one buffer, the I/O process can be made even faster. For example, if the control unit has two buffers, the second buffer can be loaded while the first buffer is transmitting its contents to or from the CPU. Ideally, by the time the first has been transmitted, the second is ready to go, and so on. In this way, input, or output time is cut in half.

Fourth, in addition to buffering, an early form of spooling was developed by moving off-line the operations of card reading, printing, and card punching. Although it's used

(figure 1.7)

The IBM 650 Magnetic Drum Data Processing System Machine, introduced in 1954, was the first mass-produced computer.

Courtesy IBM Archives

today as a noun, "spool" is an acronym that stands for Simultaneous Peripheral Operation On-Line. For example, incoming jobs would be transferred from card decks to tape off-line. Then they would be read into the CPU from the tape at a speed much faster than that of the card reader. A spooler works the same way as a buffer but, in this example, it's a separate off-line device while a buffer is part of the main computer hardware.

Also during the second generation, techniques were developed to manage program libraries, create and maintain data files and indexes, randomize direct access addresses, and create and check file labels. Several standard file organization techniques were developed such as sequential, indexed sequential, and direct access. With these techniques in place, standardized mini-programs called macros relieved programmers of the need to write customized open and close routines for each program.

Timer interrupts were developed to allow job-sharing, and to protect the CPU from infinite loops on programs that were mistakenly instructed to execute a single series of commands forever. A fixed amount of execution time was allocated to each program when it entered the system and was monitored by the operating system. If any programs were still running when the time expired, they were terminated and the user was notified with an error message.

During the second generation, programs were still run in serial batch mode—one at a time. The next step toward better use of the system's resources was the move to shared processing.

1960s

Third-generation computers date from the mid-1960s. They were designed with faster CPUs, but their speed caused problems when they interacted with the relatively slow I/O devices. The solution was **multiprogramming**, which introduced the concept of loading many programs at one time to share the attention of a single CPU.

The first multiprogramming systems allowed each program to be serviced in turn, one after another. The most common mechanism for implementing multiprogramming was the introduction of the interrupt concept, which is when the CPU is notified of events needing operating systems services. For example, when a program issues an I/O command, it generates an interrupt requesting the services of the I/O processor and the CPU is released to begin execution of the next job. This was called **passive multiprogramming** because the operating system didn't control the interrupts but waited for each job to end an execution sequence. It was less than ideal because if a job was CPU-bound (meaning that it performed a great deal of nonstop processing before issuing an interrupt), it would tie up the CPU for long periods of time while all other jobs had to wait.

To counteract this effect, the operating system was soon given a more active role with the advent of **active multiprogramming**, which allowed each program to use only a preset slice of CPU time. When time expired, the job was interrupted and another job was allowed to begin execution. The interrupted job had to wait its turn until it was allowed to resume execution later. The idea of time slicing soon became common in many time-sharing systems.

Program scheduling, which was begun with second-generation systems, continued at this time but was complicated by the fact that main memory was occupied by many jobs. The solution was to sort the jobs into groups and then load the programs according to a preset rotation. The groups were usually determined by priority or memory requirements—whichever was found to be the most efficient use of resources.

In addition to scheduling jobs, handling interrupts, and allocating memory, the operating systems had to resolve conflicts whenever two jobs requested the same device at the same time.

Few major advances were made in data management during this period. Library functions and access methods were still the same as in the last years of the second generation. The operating system for third-generation machines consisted of many modules from which a user could select; thus the total operating system was customized to suit its user's needs. The most frequently used modules were made core resident, and those less frequently used resided in secondary storage and were called only when they were needed.

1970s

After the third generation, during the late 1970s, computers had faster CPUs, thus creating an even greater disparity between their rapid processing speed and slower I/O access time. The first Cray supercomputer, shown in Figure 1.8, was released in 1976. Multiprogramming schemes to increase CPU use were limited by the physical capacity of the main memory, which was a limited resource and very expensive.

A solution to this physical limitation was the development of **virtual memory**, which took advantage of the fact that the CPU could process only one instruction at a time. With virtual memory, the entire program didn't need to reside in memory before execution could begin. A system with virtual memory would divide the programs into segments and keep them in secondary storage, bringing each segment into memory only as it was needed. (Programmers of second-generation computers had used this concept with the roll in/roll out programming method, today called overlay, to execute programs that exceeded the physical memory of those computers.)

At this time there was also growing attention to the need for data resource conservation. Database management software became a popular tool because it organized data

(figure 1.8)

The Cray I supercomputer, introduced in 1976, boasted 8 MB main memory and a world-record speed of 160 million floating-point operations per second. Its circular design meant that no wire was more than four feet long.

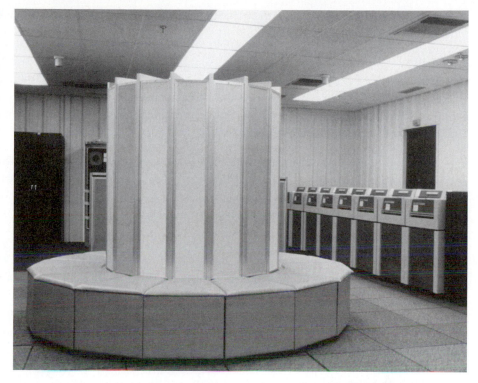

in an integrated manner, minimized redundancy, and simplified updating and access of data. A number of query systems were introduced that allowed even the novice user to retrieve specific pieces of the database. These queries were usually made via a terminal, which in turn, mandated a growth in terminal support and data communication software.

Programmers soon became more removed from the intricacies of the computer, and application programs started using English-like words, modular structures, and standard operations. This trend toward the use of standards improved program management because program maintenance became faster and easier.

1980s

Development in the 1980s dramatically improved the cost/performance ratio of computer components. Hardware was more flexible, with logical functions built on easily replaceable cards. It was also less costly, so more operating system functions were made part of the hardware itself, giving rise to a new concept—**firmware**, a word used to indicate that a program is permanently held in ROM (read only memory), as opposed to being held in secondary storage. The job of the programmer, as it had been defined in previous years, changed dramatically because many programming functions were being carried out by the system's software, hence making the programmer's task simpler and less hardware dependent.

Eventually the industry moved to **multiprocessing** (having more than one processor), and more complex languages were designed to coordinate the activities of the multiple processors servicing a single job. As a result, it became possible to execute programs in parallel, and eventually operating systems for computers of every size were routinely expected to accommodate multiprocessing.

The evolution of personal computers and high-speed communications sparked the move to distributed processing and networked systems enabling users in remote locations to share hardware and software resources. These systems required a new kind of operating system—one capable of managing multiple sets of subsystem managers, as well as hardware that might reside half a world away.

With network operating systems, users generally became aware of the existence of many networked resources, could log in to remote locations, and could manipulate files on networked computers distributed over a wide geographical area. Network operating systems were similar to single-processor operating systems in that each machine ran its own local operating system and had its own users. The difference was in the addition of a network interface controller with low-level software to drive the local operating system, as well as programs to allow remote login and remote file access. Still, even with these additions, the basic structure of the network operating system was quite close to that of a standalone system.

On the other hand, with distributed operating systems users could think they were working with a typical uniprocessor system when in fact they were connected to a cluster of many processors working closely together. With these systems, users didn't need to know which processor was running their applications or which devices were storing their files. These details were all handled transparently by the operating system—something that required more than just adding a few lines of code to a uniprocessor operating system. The disadvantage of such a complex operating system was the requirement for more complex processor-scheduling algorithms. In addition, communications delays within the network sometimes meant that scheduling algorithms had to operate with incomplete or outdated information.

1990s

The overwhelming demand for Internet capability in the mid-1990s sparked the proliferation of networking capability. The World Wide Web, conceived in a paper by Tim Berners-Lee, as shown in Figure 1.9, made the Internet accessible by computer users worldwide, not just the researchers who had come to depend on it for global communications. Web accessibility and e-mail became standard features of almost every oper-

(figure 1.9)

Mockup of a page from a 1989 proposal by Tim Berners-Lee that illustrates his revolutionary "linked information system." Based on his research, he designed the first World Wide Web server and browser, making it available to the general public in 1991.

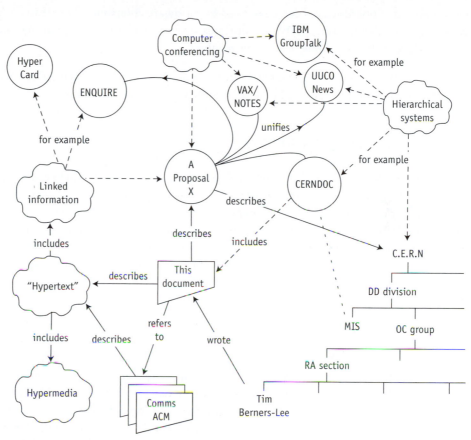

ating system. However, increased networking also sparked increased demand for tighter security to protect hardware and software.

The decade also introduced a proliferation of multimedia applications demanding additional power, flexibility, and device compatibility for most operating systems. A typical multimedia computer houses devices to perform audio, video, and graphic creation and editing. That can require many specialized devices such as a microphone, digital piano, musical instrument digital interface (MIDI), digital camera, digital video disc (DVD) drive, compact disc (CD) drives, speakers, additional monitors, projection devices, color printers, and high-speed Internet connections. They also require specialized hardware (such as controllers, cards, busses) and software to make them work together properly.

Multimedia applications need large amounts of storage capability that must be managed gracefully by the operating system. For example, each second of a 30-frame-per-minute full-screen video requires 27 megabytes of storage unless the data is compressed in some way. To meet the demand for compressed video, special-purpose chips and video boards have been developed by hardware companies. One standard, called digital video interface (DVI), compresses video at a 150:1 ratio, enabling one hour of video to be stored in less than one gigabyte.

What's the effect of these technological advances on the operating system? Each advance requires a parallel advance in the software's management capabilities.

Current Operating Systems

The 1980s marked the end of a clearly delineated evolution of operating system design. With the 1990s, new design features and even new operating systems were introduced to accommodate the surge of imaginative developments in hardware devices and software applications. Primary design features of current operating systems are based on the needs of users, who have come to expect support for multimedia applications, Internet and Web access, as well as client/server computing. Computer systems help to provide these services with increased CPU speed, high-speed network attachments, and an increased number and variety of storage devices.

System Architecture

One area showing a great deal of improvement is the system architecture of operating systems—the way their components are programmed and organized, specifically the use of **object-oriented design** and the reorganization of the operating system's nucleus, the **kernel**. The kernel is the part of the operating system that resides in memory at all times, performs the most essential operating system tasks, and is protected by hardware from user tampering.

Early operating systems were designed as a comprehensive single unit, as shown in Figure 1.10. Therefore, their kernel was very large and included all the functions of an operating system, such as memory allocation, process scheduling, device allocation and networking. This type of architecture made it cumbersome and time consuming for programmers to add new components to the operating system, or to modify existing ones, which is necessary to keep up with hardware or application software improvements and innovations.

Most recently the nucleus, or kernel, has been limited to a few essential functions, such as process scheduling and memory allocation, while all other functions, such as device allocation, are provided by special processes, which are treated as regular applications by the kernel. This approach makes it easier to add new components or modify existing ones and works well in distributed systems.

Object-oriented design was the driving force behind this new organization of the kernel. Objects are self-contained modules (units of software) that provide models of the

(figure 1.10)

Early operating systems were loaded in their entirety into main memory. (a) Modern object-oriented systems load only the critical elements into main memory (b) and call other objects (c) as needed.

real world and can be reused in different applications. By working on objects, programmers can modify and customize pieces of an operating system without disrupting the integrity of the remainder of the system. In addition, using a modular, object-oriented approach can make software development groups more productive than was possible with procedural structured programming.

Threads

Process handling, which addresses the way in which processes are executed to maximize the system's efficiency and satisfy users' needs, is also an area that has benefited from research and development efforts. One of the biggest improvements can be seen in the implementation of threads, multiprocessing, and distributed systems,

To explain the concept of threads we must first introduce the concept of a process or task. A process has two characteristics:

• It requires space in main memory where it resides during its execution although, from time to time, it requires other resources such as data files or I/O devices.

• It passes through several states (such as running, waiting, ready) from its initial arrival into the computer system to its completion.

In modern operating systems, multiprogramming and virtual memory dictate that processes be swapped between main memory and secondary storage during their execution. With conventional processes (also known as *heavyweight* processes), this swapping results in a lot of overhead. That's because each time a swap takes place, all process information must be saved to preserve the process's integrity.

A **thread** (or *lightweight* process) can be defined as a unit smaller than a process, which can be scheduled and executed. Using this technique, the heavyweight process, which owns the resources, becomes a more passive element, while a thread becomes the element that uses the CPU and is scheduled for execution. Swapping threads is less time consuming than swapping processes because there is less information to be saved. Some operating systems support multiple processes with a single thread, while others support multiple processes with multiple threads. This topic will be explored further in Chapter 6, "Concurrent Processes."

Many software packages implement multithreading, meaning that the application is typically carried out as a separate process with several threads of control. For example, a word processor may have a thread that accepts user input, another that checks the spelling of the words, and a third that automatically archives the document at specified intervals. Alternatively, a Web browser may have one thread that displays images and another that accepts input from the keyboard. Multithreading is also used to increase responsiveness in a time-sharing system, to increase resource sharing, and decrease overhead.

Multiprocessing Configurations

Threads are used extensively in distributed systems where the benefits of multithreading are further increased by the cooperation of multiple processors with each thread running concurrently on a different processor.

Symmetric multiprocessing, a type of multiprocessing, is available on many operating systems. This allows for several CPUs to process multiple jobs at the same time. The CPUs are independent of one another, but each has access to the operating system, which resides in main memory, and they share memory as well as secondary storage devices. So, if a system has five processors, it could run up to five jobs simultaneously, as shown in Figure 1.11. With this arrangement, synchronization of all five CPUs must be closely monitored to avoid conflicts, such as if two or more CPUs were erroneously assigned to run the same program. Synchronization is a topic of Chapter 6.

Another type of multiprocessing, asymmetric multiprocessing, continues to evolve as microprocessors become less expensive and more powerful. In this case some operating systems functions are assigned to subordinate processors, which take their instructions from the main CPU. For example, in a system with only one processor, disk

(figure 1.11)

This symmetric multiprocessing system with five processors can run five jobs independently at the same time.

Storage Devices

scheduling and program calculations are all managed by the CPU. However, if a second processor is added to the system and assigned responsibility only for disk scheduling, then, upon request from the main CPU, this subordinate microprocessor executes its own algorithm to handle the requests for disk access. This multiprocessing configuration allows the main CPU to handle more processes. The algorithms used in handling disk queues will be presented in detail in Chapter 7, "Device Management."

Distributed Processing

Historically, data processing was carried out using a centralized model, which means that all processing took place in a single location or facility. Decentralization of the data processing function came about with the advent of microcomputers, even though they originally were designed as standalone computers. Early microcomputer configurations allowed for processing devices to be placed at remote locations but did not provide for their connection. In the 1980s PCs were connected to computer networks to share printers and modems. By the mid-1990s, with the introduction of the Internet and the Web, network connectivity became an essential component of a PC. Most modern operating systems for microcomputers include a Web browser as well as e-mail, remote login, and file transfer capabilities.

The rush to network PCs gave impetus to the concept of **distributed processing**, where processors are placed at remote locations and are connected to each other via telecommunication devices. These systems are different from symmetric multiprocessing systems because they do not share memory. Each processor has its own local memory, and computers communicate with each other through telephone lines or high-speed busses. Users of a distributed operating system perceive the computing environment as a single, transparent system rather than a collection of individual computers interconnected with a network.

One benefit of distributed processing is that computations can be dispersed among several processors. A second is that the overall capability of the computer system is maximized by balancing the efficiency of each individual computer system. For example, a chain of department stores can have a mainframe computer at headquarters, where the bulk of processing takes place, but still have access to inventory data that's maintained on systems in remote locations, and the bulk printing takes place at the mailing center.

Conclusion

In this chapter, we looked at the overall function of operating systems and how they have evolved to run increasingly complex computers and computer systems. Of course, we've only seen the general picture—an overview of the hardware and the role of the operating system software. In the following chapters, we'll explore in detail how each segment of the operating system works, as well as its features, functions, benefits, and costs. We'll begin with the part of the operating system that's the heart of every computer: the module that manages main memory.

Key Terms

batch system: a type of system developed for the earliest computers that used punched cards or tape for input, which were entered in a "batch."

central processing unit (CPU): the component with the circuitry, the "chips," to control the interpretation and execution of instructions.

Device Manager: the section of the operating system responsible for controlling the use of devices. It monitors every device, channel, and control unit and chooses the most efficient way to allocate all of the system's devices.

embedded system: a dedicated computer system, often small and fast, that resides in a larger physical system such as jet aircraft or ships.

File Manager: the section of the operating system responsible for controlling the use of files.

firmware: software instructions or data that are stored in a fixed or "firm" way, usually implemented on Read Only Memory (ROM).

hardware: the physical machine and its components, including main memory, I/O devices, I/O channels, direct access storage devices, and the central processing unit.

hybrid system: a computer system that supports both batch and interactive processes.

interactive system: a system that allows each user to interact directly with the operating system via commands entered from a keyboard.

kernel: the primary part of the operating system that remains in random access memory and is charged with performing the system's most essential tasks, such as managing main memory and disk access.

main memory: the memory unit that works directly with the CPU and in which the data and instructions must reside in order to be processed. Also called *primary storage* or *internal memory.*

mainframe: the historical name given to a large computer system characterized by its large size, high cost, and high performance.

Memory Manager: the section of the operating system responsible for controlling the use of memory. It checks the validity of each request for memory space and, if it's a legal request, allocates the amount needed to execute the job.

microcomputer: a small computer equipped with all the hardware and software necessary to perform one or more tasks.

minicomputer: a small to medium-sized computer system, also called a midrange computer.

multiprocessing: when two or more CPUs share the same main memory, most I/O devices, and the same control program routines. They service the same job stream and execute distinct processing programs concurrently.

multiprogramming: a technique that allows a single processor to process several programs residing simultaneously in main memory and interleaving their execution by overlapping I/O requests with CPU requests.

network: a system of interconnected computer systems and peripheral devices that exchange information with one another.

object-oriented: A programming philosophy whereby programs consist of self-contained, reusable modules called objects, each of which supports a specific function, but which are categorized into classes of objects that share the same function.

operating system: the software that manages all the resources of a computer system.

Processor Manager: a composite of two submanagers, the Job Scheduler and the Process Scheduler, which decides how to allocate the CPU.

real-time system: an extremely fast computing system used in time-critical environments that require immediate decisions, such as navigation systems, rapid transit systems, and industrial control systems.

software: a collection of programs used to perform certain tasks. Software falls into three main categories: operating system programs, compilers and assemblers, and application programs.

supercomputer: the fastest, most sophisticated computers made, used for complex calculations.

thread: a portion of a program that can run independently of other portions. Multithreaded applications programs can have several threads running at one time with the same or different priorities.

workstation: A desktop computer attached to a local area network that serves as an access point to that network.

Exercises

Research Topics

1. Write a one-page review of an article about operating systems appearing in a recent computing magazine or academic journal. Be sure to cite your source using standard citation format as demonstrated in the bibliography of this text. Give a summary of the article including the primary topic, information presented, and the author's conclusion. Give your personal evaluation of the article, including the author's writing style, use of jargon, facets that made the article interesting to you, and its relevance to your own experiences.

2. Give at least two reasons why a regional bank might decide to buy six server computers instead of one supercomputer.

3. Select one of the following professionals: an insurance adjuster, a delivery person for a courier service, a newspaper reporter, a doctor (general practitioner), or a manager in a supermarket. Put forward a theory about how that person might use a hand-held computer in their work.

Exercises

4. Name five current operating systems and the computers or configurations each operates.

5. Name the five key concepts about an operating system that you think a user needs to know and understand.

6. Explain the impact of the evolution of computer hardware with respect to the evolution of operating systems software.

7. Explain the fundamental differences between interactive, batch, real-time, and embedded systems.

8. List three situations that might demand a real-time operating system and explain why.

9. Give an example of an organization that might find batch-mode processing useful and explain why.

10. List three tangible (physical) resources of a computer system

11. Briefly compare active and passive multiprogramming.

Advanced Exercises

12. Compare the development of two operating systems described in Part Two of this text including design goals and evolution.

13. Draw a system flowchart illustrating the steps performed by an operating system as it executes the instruction to back up a disk on a single-user computer system. Begin with the user typing the command on the keyboard and conclude with the display of the result on the monitor.

14. Identify the clock rates or processors that use 8 bits, 16 bits, 32 bits and 64 bits. Discuss several implications scheduling the CPU in a multiprocessing system.

15. In a multiprogramming and time-sharing environment, several users share the system simultaneously. This situation can result in various security problems. Name two such problems. Can we ensure the same degree of security in a time-share machine as we have in a dedicated machine? Explain your answers.

16. Give an example of an application where multithreading gives improved performance over single-threading.

17. If a process terminates, will its threads also terminate or will they continue to run? Explain your answer.

18. If a process is suspended (put on "wait" by an interrupt), will its threads also be suspended? Give an example.

Chapter 2 | Memory Management: Early Systems

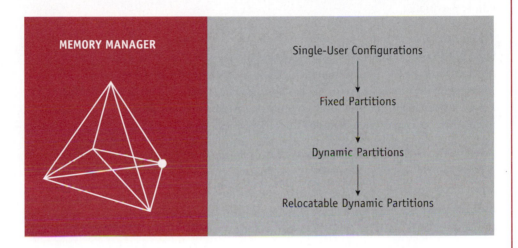

MEMORY MANAGER

Single-User Configurations

↓

Fixed Partitions

↓

Dynamic Partitions

↓

Relocatable Dynamic Partitions

"*Memory is the primary and fundamental power, without which there could be no other intellectual operation.*" —Samuel Johnson *(1709–1784)*

Learning Objectives

After completing this chapter, you should be able to describe:

- The basic functionality of the three memory allocation schemes presented in this chapter: fixed partitions, dynamic partitions, relocatable dynamic partitions

- Best-fit memory allocation as well as first-fit memory allocation schemes

- How a memory list keeps track of available memory

- The importance of deallocation of memory in a dynamic partition system

- The importance of the bounds register in memory allocation schemes
- The role of compaction and how it improves memory allocation efficiency

The management of main memory is critical. In fact, from a historical perspective, the performance of the *entire* system has been directly dependent on two things—how much memory is available and how it is optimized while jobs are being processed.

This chapter introduces the Memory Manager and four types of memory allocation schemes: single-user systems, fixed partitions, dynamic partitions, and relocatable dynamic partitions.

These early memory management schemes are seldom used by today's operating systems but they are important to study because each one introduced fundamental concepts that helped memory management evolve, as shown in Chapter 3, "Memory Management: Virtual Memory," which discusses memory allocation strategies for Linux. Information on how other operating systems manage memory is presented in the memory management sections in Part Two of the text.

Let's start with the simplest memory management scheme—the one used in the earliest generations of computer systems.

Single-User Contiguous Scheme

The first **memory allocation scheme** worked like this: Each program to be processed was loaded in its entirety into memory and allocated as much contiguous space in memory as it needed. The key words here are *entirety* and *contiguous*. If the program was too large and didn't fit the available memory space, it couldn't be executed. And, although early computers were physically large, they had very little memory.

This demonstrates a significant limiting factor of all computers—they have only a finite amount of memory and if a program doesn't fit, then either the size of the main memory must be increased or the program must be modified. It's usually modified by making it smaller or by using methods that allow program segments (partitions made to the program) to be overlaid. (To overlay is to transfer segments of a program from secondary storage into main memory for execution, so that two or more segments take turns occupying the same memory locations.)

Single-user systems work the same way. Each user is given access to all available main memory for each job, and jobs are processed sequentially, one after the other. To allocate memory the operating system uses a simple algorithm (step-by-step procedure to solve a problem):

Algorithm to Load a Job in a Single-User System

1 Store first memory location of program into base register (for memory protection)
2 Set program counter (it keeps track of memory space used by the program) equal to address of first memory location
3 Read first instruction of program
4 Increment program counter by number of bytes in instruction
5 Has the last instruction been reached?
    if yes, then stop loading program
    if no, then continue with step 6
6 Is program counter greater than memory size?
    if yes, then stop loading program
    if no, then continue with step 7
7 Load instruction in memory
8 Read next instruction of program
9 Go to step 4

Notice that the amount of work done by the operating system's Memory Manager is minimal, the code to perform the functions is straightforward, and the logic is quite simple. Only two hardware items are needed: a register to store the base **address** and an accumulator to keep track of the size of the program as it's being read into memory. Once the program is entirely loaded into memory, it remains there until execution is complete, either through normal termination or by intervention of the operating system.

One major problem with this type of memory allocation scheme is that it doesn't support multiprogramming (discussed in detail in Chapter 4, "Processor Management"); it can handle only one job at a time. When they were first made available commercially in the late 1940s and early 1950s, these single-user configurations were used in research institutions but proved unacceptable for the business community—it wasn't cost effective to spend almost $200,000 for a piece of equipment that could be used by only one person at a time. Therefore, in the late 1950s and early 1960s a new scheme was needed to manage memory.

The next design used partitions to take advantage of the computer system's resources by overlapping independent operations.

Fixed Partitions

The first attempt to allow for multiprogramming was to create **fixed partitions** (also called **static partitions**) within the main memory—one partition for each job. Because the size of each partition was designated when the system was powered on, each partition could only be reconfigured when the computer system was shut down, reconfigured, and restarted. Thus, once the system was in operation the partition sizes remained static.

A critical factor was introduced with this scheme: protection of the job's memory space. Once a partition was assigned to a job, no other job could be allowed to enter its boundaries, either accidentally or intentionally. This problem of partition intrusion didn't exist in single-user contiguous allocation schemes because only one job was present in main memory at any given time so only the portion of the operating system residing in main memory had to be protected. However, for the fixed partition allocation schemes, protection was mandatory for each partition present in main memory. Typically this was the joint responsibility of the hardware of the computer and the operating system.

The algorithm used to store jobs into memory requires a few more steps than the one used for a single-user system because the size of the job must be matched with the size of the partition to make sure it fits completely. Then, when a block of sufficient size is located, the status of the partition must be checked to see if it's available.

Algorithm to Load a Job in a Fixed Partition

```
1 Determine job's requested memory size
2 If job_size > size of largest partition
    Then reject the job
        print appropriate message to operator
        go to step 1 to handle next job in line
    Else
      continue with step 3
3 Set counter to 1
4 Do while counter <= number of partitions in memory
  If job_size > memory_partition_size(counter)
  Then counter = counter + 1
  Else
    If memory_partition_size(counter) = "free"
      Then load job into memory_partition(counter)
        change memory_partition_status(counter) to "busy"
        go to step 1 to handle next job in line
    Else
      counter = counter + 1
    End do
```

5 No partition available at this time, put job in waiting queue

6 Go to step 1 to handle next job in line

This partition scheme is more flexible than the single-user scheme because it allows several programs to be in memory at the same time. However, it still requires that the *entire* program be stored *contiguously* and *in memory* from the beginning to the end of its execution. In order to allocate memory spaces to jobs, the operating system's Memory Manager must keep a table such as Table 2.1 showing each memory partition size, its address, its access restrictions, and its current status (free or busy) for the system illustrated in Figure 2.1. (In Table 2.1 and the other tables in this chapter, K stands for kilobyte, which is 1,024 bytes. A more in-depth discussion of memory map tables is presented in Chapter 8, "File Management.")

(table 2.1)

A simplified fixed-partition memory table with the free partition shaded.

Partition Size	Memory Address	Access	Partition Status
100K	200K	Job 1	Busy
25K	300K	Job 4	Busy
25K	325K		Free
50K	350K	Job 2	Busy

As each job terminates, the status of its memory partition is changed from busy to free so an incoming job can be assigned to that partition.

(figure 2.1)

Main memory use during fixed partition allocation of Table 2.1. Job 3 must wait even though 70K of free space is available in Partition 1 where Job 1 only occupies 30K of the 100K available. The jobs are allocated space on the basis of "first available partition of required size."

The fixed partition scheme works well if all of the jobs run on the system are of the same size or if the sizes are known ahead of time and don't vary between reconfigurations. Ideally, that would require accurate advance knowledge of all the jobs to be run on the system in the coming hours, days, or weeks. However, unless the operator can accurately predict the future, the size of the partitions are determined in an arbitrary fashion and they might be too small or too large for the jobs coming in.

There are significant consequences if the partitions' sizes are too small; larger jobs will be rejected if they're too big to fit into the largest partitions or will wait if the large partitions are busy. As a result, large jobs may have a longer turnaround time as they wait for free partitions of sufficient size or may never run.

On the other hand, if the partition sizes are too big, memory is wasted. If a job does not occupy the entire partition, the unused memory in the partition will remain idle; it can't be given to another job because each partition is allocated to only one job at a time. It's an indivisible unit. Figure 2.1 demonstrates one such circumstance.

This phenomenon of partial usage of fixed partitions and the coinciding creation of unused spaces within the partition is called **internal fragmentation**, and is a major drawback to the fixed partition memory allocation scheme.

Dynamic Partitions

With **dynamic partitions**, available memory is still kept in contiguous blocks but jobs are given only as much memory as they request when they are loaded for processing. Although this is a significant improvement over fixed partitions because memory isn't wasted within the partition, it doesn't entirely eliminate the problem, as illustrated in Figure 2.2.

As shown in Figure 2.2, a dynamic partition scheme fully utilizes memory when the first jobs are loaded. But as new jobs enter the system that are not of the same size as those that just vacated memory, they are fit into the available spaces on a priority basis. Figure 2.2 demonstrates **first-come first-served** priority. Therefore, the subsequent allocation of memory creates fragments of free memory between blocks of allocated memory. This problem is called **external fragmentation** and, like internal fragmentation, it lets memory go to waste.

In the last snapshot, (e) in Figure 2.2, there are three free partitions of 5K, 10K, and 20K—35K in all—enough to accommodate Job 8, which only requires 30K. However they are not contiguous and, because the jobs are loaded in a contiguous manner, this scheme forces Job 8 to wait.

Before we go to the next allocation scheme, let's examine how the operating system keeps track of the free sections of memory.

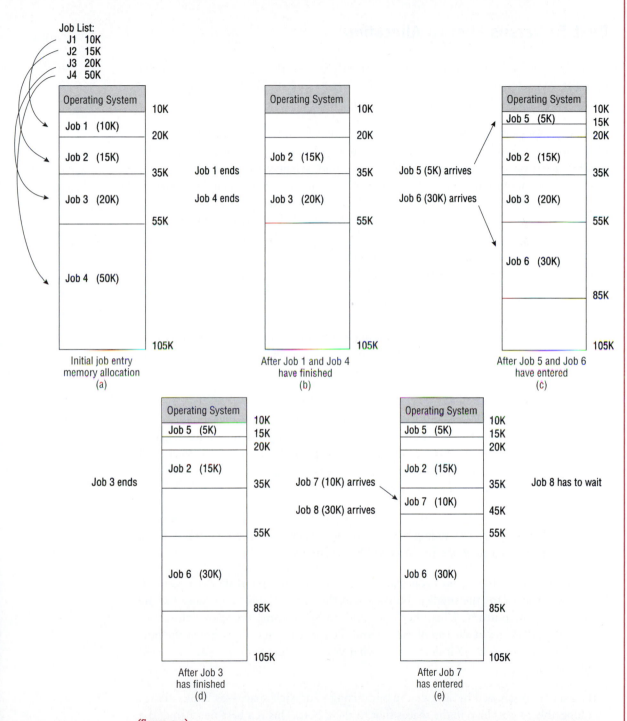

(figure 2.2)

Main memory use during dynamic partition allocation. Five snapshots (a-e) of main memory as eight jobs are submitted for processing and allocated space on the basis of "first come, first served." Job 8 has to wait (e) even though there's enough free memory between partitions to accommodate it.

Best-Fit Versus First-Fit Allocation

For both fixed and dynamic memory allocation schemes, the operating system must keep lists of each memory location noting which are free and which are busy. Then as new jobs come into the system the free partitions must be allocated.

These partitions may be allocated on the basis of **first-fit memory allocation** (first partition fitting the requirements) or **best-fit memory allocation** (least wasted space, the smallest partition fitting the requirements). For both schemes the Memory Manager organizes the memory lists of the free and used partitions (free/busy) either by size or by location. The best-fit allocation method keeps the free/busy lists in order by size, smallest to largest. The first-fit method keeps the free/busy lists organized by memory locations, low-order memory to high-order memory. Each has advantages depending on the needs of the particular allocation scheme—best-fit usually makes the best use of memory space; first-fit is faster in making the allocation.

To understand the trade-offs, imagine that you've turned your collection of books into a lending library. Let's say you have books of all shapes and sizes, and let's also say there's a continuous stream of people taking books out and bringing them back—someone's always waiting. It's clear that you'll always be busy, and that's good, but you never have time to rearrange the bookshelves.

You need a system. Your shelves have fixed partitions with a few tall spaces for oversized books, several shelves for paperbacks, and lots of room for textbooks. You'll need to keep track of which spaces on the shelves are full and where you have spaces for more. For the purposes of our example, we'll keep two lists: a free list showing all the available spaces, and a busy list showing all the occupied spaces. Each list will include the size and location of each space.

So as each book is removed from its shelf, you'll update both lists by removing the space from the busy list and adding it to the free list. Then as your books are returned and placed back on a shelf, the two lists will be updated again.

There are two ways to organize your lists—by size or by location. If they're organized by size, the spaces for the smallest books are at the top of the list and those for the largest are at the bottom. When they're organized by location, the spaces closest to your lending desk are at the top of the list and the areas farthest away are at the bottom. Which option is best? It depends on what you want to optimize: space or speed of allocation.

If the lists are organized by size, you're optimizing your shelf space—as books arrive, you'll be able to put them in the spaces that fit them best. This is a best-fit scheme. If a paperback is returned, you'll place it on a shelf with the other paperbacks or at least with other small books. Similarly, oversized books will be shelved with other large books. Your lists make it easy to find the smallest available empty space where the book can fit. The disadvantage of this system is that you're wasting time looking for the best space. Your other customers have to wait for you to put each book away, so you won't be able to process as many customers as you could with the other kind of list.

In the second case, a list organized by shelf location, you're optimizing the time it takes you to put books back on the shelves. This is a first-fit scheme. This system ignores the size of the book that you're trying to put away. If the same paperback book arrives, you can quickly find it an empty space. In fact, any nearby empty space will suffice if it's large enough—even an encyclopedia rack can be used if it's close to your desk because you are optimizing the time it takes you to reshelve the books.

Of course, this is a fast method of shelving books, and if speed is important it's the best of the two alternatives. However, it isn't a good choice if your shelf space is limited or if many large books are returned, because large books must wait for the large spaces. If all of your large spaces are filled with small books, the customers returning large books must wait until a suitable space becomes available. (Eventually you'll need time to rearrange the books and compact your collection.)

Figure 2.3 shows how a large job can have problems with a first-fit memory allocation list. Jobs 1, 2, and 4 are able to enter the system and begin execution; Job 3 has to wait

(figure 2.3)

Using a first-fit free scheme, Job 1 claims the first available space. Job 2 then claims the first partition large enough to accommodate it, but by doing so it takes the last block large enough to accommodate Job 3. Therefore, Job 3 (indicated by the asterisk) must wait until a large block becomes available, even though there's 75K of unused memory space (internal fragmentation and unused memory). Notice that the memory list is ordered according to memory location.

Job List:

Job number	Memory requested
J1	10K
J2	20K
J3	30K*
J4	10K

Memory List:

Memory location	Memory block size	Job number	Job size	Status	Internal fragmentation
10240	30K	J1	10K	Busy	20K
40960	15K	J4	10K	Busy	5K
56320	50K	J2	20K	Busy	30K
107520	20K			Free	
Total Available:	115K	Total Used:	40K		

even though, if all of the fragments of memory were added together, there would be more than enough room to accommodate it. First-fit is fast in allocation, but it isn't always efficient.

On the other hand, the same job list using a best-fit scheme would use memory more efficiently, as shown in Figure 2.4. In this particular case, a best-fit scheme would yield better memory utilization.

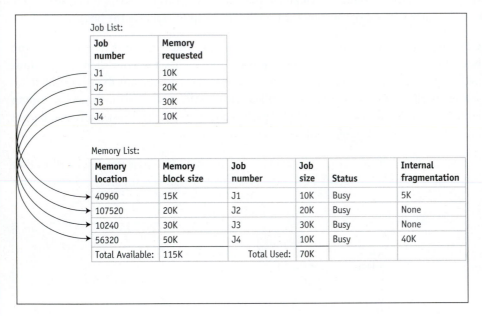

Job List:

Job number	Memory requested
J1	10K
J2	20K
J3	30K
J4	10K

Memory List:

Memory location	Memory block size	Job number	Job size	Status	Internal fragmentation
40960	15K	J1	10K	Busy	5K
107520	20K	J2	20K	Busy	None
10240	30K	J3	30K	Busy	None
56320	50K	J4	10K	Busy	40K
Total Available:	115K		Total Used:	70K	

(figure 2.4)

Best-fit free list. Job 1 is allocated to the closest-fitting free partition, as are Job 2 and Job 3. Job 4 is allocated to the only available partition although it isn't the best-fitting one. In this scheme all four jobs are served without waiting. Notice that the memory list is ordered according to memory size. This scheme uses memory more efficiently but it's slower to implement.

Memory use has been increased but the memory allocation process takes more time. What's more, while internal fragmentation has been diminished, it hasn't been completely eliminated.

The first-fit algorithm assumes that the Memory Manager keeps two lists, one for free memory blocks and one for busy memory blocks. The operation consists of a simple loop that compares the size of each job to the size of each memory block until a block is found that's large enough to fit the job. Then the job is stored into that block of memory, and the Memory Manager moves out of the loop to fetch the next job from the entry queue. If the entire list is searched in vain, then the job is placed into a waiting queue. The Memory Manager then fetches the next job and repeats the process (Madnick & Donovan, 1974).

The algorithms for best-fit and first-fit are very different. Here's how first-fit is implemented:

First-Fit Algorithm

1 Set counter to 1
2 Do while counter <= number of blocks in memory
   If job_size > memory_size(counter)
     Then counter = counter + 1
   Else
     load job into memory_size(counter)
     adjust free/busy memory lists
     go to step 4
   End do
3 Put job in waiting queue
4 Go fetch next job

In Table 2.2 a request for a block of 200 spaces has just been given to the Memory Manager. (The spaces may be words, bytes, or any other unit the system handles.) Using the first-fit algorithm and starting from the top of the list, the Memory Manager locates the first block of memory large enough to accommodate the job, which is at location 6785. The job is then loaded, starting at location 6785 and occupying the next 200 spaces. The next step is to adjust the free list to indicate that the block of free memory now starts at location 6985 (not 6785 as before) and that it contains only 400 spaces (not 600 as before).

(table 2.2)

These two snapshots of memory show the status of each memory block before and after a request is made using the first-fit algorithm. (Note: All values are in decimal notation unless otherwise indicated.)

Before Request		After Request	
Beginning Address	Memory Block Size	Beginning Address	Memory Block Size
4075	105	4075	105
5225	5	5225	5
6785	600	*6985	400
7560	20	7560	20
7600	205	7600	205
10250	4050	10250	4050
15125	230	15125	230
24500	1000	24500	1000

The algorithm for best-fit is slightly more complex because the goal is to find the smallest memory block into which the job will fit (Madnick & Donovan, 1974):

Best-Fit Algorithm

1 Initialize memory_block(0) = 99999

2 Compute initial_memory_waste = memory_block(0) − job_size

3 Initialize subscript = 0

4 Set counter to 1

5 Do while counter <= number of blocks in memory

   If job_size > memory_size(counter)

     Then counter = counter + 1

   Else

     memory_waste = memory_size(counter) − job_size

  If initial_memory_waste > memory_waste

     Then subscript = counter

     initial_memory_waste = memory_waste

     counter = counter + 1

  End do

6 If subscript = 0

  Then put job in waiting queue

  Else

     Load job into memory_size(subscript)

     adjust free/busy memory lists

7 Go fetch next job

One of the problems with the best-fit algorithm is that the entire table must be searched before the allocation can be made because the memory blocks are physically stored in sequence according to their location in memory (and not by memory block sizes as shown in Figure 2.4). The system could execute an algorithm to continuously rearrange the list in ascending order by memory block size, but that would add more overhead and might not be an efficient use of processing time in the long run.

The best-fit algorithm is illustrated showing only the list of free memory blocks. Table 2.3 shows the free list before and after the best-fit block has been allocated to the same request presented in Table 2.2.

(table 2.3)

These two snapshots of memory show the status of each memory block before and after a request is made using the best-fit algorithm.

Before Request		After Request	
Beginning Address	**Memory Block Size**	**Beginning Address**	**Memory Block Size**
4075	105	4075	105
5225	5	5225	5
6785	600	6785	600
7560	20	7560	20
7600	205	*7800	5
10250	4050	10250	4050
15125	230	15125	230
24500	1000	24500	1000

In Table 2.3, a request for a block of 200 spaces has just been given to the Memory Manager. Using the best-fit algorithm and starting from the top of the list, the Memory Manager searches the entire list and locates a block of memory starting at location 7600, which is the smallest block that's large enough to accommodate the job. The choice of this block minimizes the wasted space (only 5 spaces are wasted, which is less than in the four alternative blocks). The job is then stored, starting at location 7600 and occupying the next 200 spaces. Now the free list must be adjusted to show that the block of free memory starts at location 7800 (not 7600 as before) and that it contains only 5 spaces (not 205 as before).

Which is best—first-fit or best-fit? For many years there was no way to answer such a general question because performance depends on the job mix. Note that while the best-fit resulted in a better fit, it also resulted (and does so in the general case) in a smaller free space (5 spaces), which is known as a sliver.

In the exercises at the end of this chapter, two other hypothetical allocation schemes are explored: next-fit, which starts searching from the last allocated block for the next available block when a new job arrives; and worst-fit, which allocates the largest free available block to the new job. Worst-fit is the opposite of best-fit. Although it's a good way to explore the theory of memory allocation, it might not be the best choice for an actual system.

In recent years access times have become so fast that the scheme that saves the more valuable resource, memory space, may be the best in some cases. Research continues to focus on finding the optimum allocation scheme. This includes optimum page size—a fixed allocation scheme we will cover in the next chapter, which is the key to improving the performance of the best-fit allocation scheme.

Deallocation

Until now, we've considered only the problem of how memory blocks are allocated, but eventually there comes a time when memory space must be released, or **deallocated**.

For a fixed partition system, the process is quite straightforward. When the job is completed, the Memory Manager resets the status of the memory block where the job was stored to "free." Any code—for example, binary values with 0 indicating free and 1 indicating busy—may be used so the mechanical task of deallocating a block of memory is relatively simple.

A dynamic partition system uses a more complex algorithm because the algorithm tries to combine free areas of memory whenever possible. Therefore, the system must be prepared for three alternative situations (Madnick & Donovan, 1974):

• Case 1. When the block to be deallocated is adjacent to another free block
• Case 2. When the block to be deallocated is between two free blocks
• Case 3. When the block to be deallocated is isolated from other free blocks

The deallocation algorithm must be prepared for all three eventualities with a set of nested conditionals. The following algorithm is based on the fact that memory locations are listed using a lowest-to-highest address scheme. The algorithm would have to be modified to accommodate a different organization of memory locations. In this algorithm, *job_size* is the amount of memory being released by the terminating job, and *beginning_address* is the location of the first instruction for the job.

Algorithm to Deallocate Memory Blocks

```
If job_location is adjacent to one or more free blocks
    Then
    If job_location is between two free blocks
        Then merge all three blocks into one block
        memory_size(counter-1) = memory_size(counter-1) + job_size
        + memory_size(counter+1)
        set status of memory_size(counter+1) to null entry
    Else
        merge both blocks into one
        memory_size(counter-1) = memory_size(counter-1) + job_size
    Else
    search for null entry in free memory list
    enter job_size and beginning_address in the entry slot
    set its status to "free"
```

Case 1: Joining Two Free Blocks

Table 2.4 shows how deallocation occurs in a dynamic memory allocation system when the job to be deallocated is next to one free memory block.

Beginning Address	Memory Block Size	Status
4075	105	Free
5225	5	Free
6785	600	Free
7560	20	Free
(7600)	(200)	(Busy)[1]
*7800	5	Free
10250	4050	Free
15125	230	Free
24500	1000	Free

[1]Although the numbers in parentheses don't appear in the free list, they've been inserted here for clarity. The job size is 200 and its beginning location is 7600.

After deallocation the free list looks like the one shown in Table 2.5.

Beginning Address	Memory Block Size	Status
4075	105	Free
5225	5	Free
6785	600	Free
7560	20	Free
*7600	205	Free
10250	4050	Free
15125	230	Free
24500	1000	Free

Using the deallocation algorithm, the system sees that the memory to be released is next to a free memory block, which starts at location 7800. Therefore the list must be changed to reflect the starting address of the new free block, 7600, which was the address of the first instruction of the job that just released this block. In addition, the memory block size for this new free space must be changed to show its new size; that is, the combined total of the two free partitions (200 + 5).

Case 2: Joining Three Free Blocks

When the deallocated memory space is between two free memory blocks, the process is similar, as shown in Table 2.6.

Using the deallocation algorithm, the system learns that the memory to be deallocated is between two free blocks of memory. Therefore, the sizes of the three free partitions (20 + 20 + 205) must be combined and the total stored with the smallest beginning address, 7560.

Beginning Address	Memory Block Size	Status
4075	105	Free
5225	5	Free
6785	600	Free
*7560	20	Free
(7580)	(20)	(Busy)[1]
*7600	205	Free
10250	4050	Free
15125	230	Free
24500	1000	Free

(table 2.6)

Case 2. This is the original free list before deallocation. The asterisks indicate the two free memory blocks that are adjacent to the soon-to-be-free memory block.

[1] Although the numbers in parentheses don't appear in the free list, they have been inserted here for clarity.

Because the entry at location 7600 has been combined with the previous entry, we must empty out this entry. We do that by changing the status to **null entry**, with no beginning address and no memory block size as indicated by an asterisk in Table 2.7. This negates the need to rearrange the list at the expense of memory.

Beginning Address	Memory Block Size	Status
4075	105	Free
5225	5	Free
6785	600	Free
7560	245	Free
*		(null entry)
10250	4050	Free
15125	230	Free
24500	1000	Free

(table 2.7)

Case 2. The free list after a job has released memory.

Case 3: Deallocating an Isolated Block

The third alternative is when the space to be deallocated is isolated from all other free areas.

For this example we need to know more about how the busy memory list is configured. To simplify matters let's look at the busy list for the memory area between locations 7560 and 10250. Remember that, starting at 7560, there's a free memory block of 245, so the busy memory area includes everything from location 7805 (7560 + 245) to 10250, which is the address of the next free block. The free list and busy list are shown in Table 2.8 and Table 2.9.

(table 2.8)

Case 3. Original free list before deallocation. The soon-to-be-free memory block is not adjacent to any blocks that are already free.

Beginning Address	Memory Block Size	Status
4075	105	Free
5225	5	Free
6785	600	Free
7560	245	Free
		(null entry)
10250	4050	Free
15125	230	Free
24500	1000	Free

(table 2.9)

Case 3. Busy memory list before deallocation. The job to be deallocated is of size 445 and begins at location 8805. The asterisk indicates the soon-to-be-free memory block.

Beginning Address	Memory Block Size	Status
7805	1000	Busy
*8805	445	Busy
9250	1000	Busy

Using the deallocation algorithm, the system learns that the memory block to be released is not adjacent to any free blocks of memory; it is between two other busy areas. Therefore it must search the table for a null entry.

The scheme presented in this example creates null entries in both the busy and the free lists during the process of allocation or deallocation of memory. An example of a null entry occurring as a result of deallocation was presented in Case 2. A null entry in the busy list occurs when a memory block between two other busy memory blocks is returned to the free list, as shown in Table 2.10. This mechanism ensures that all blocks are entered in the lists according to the beginning address of their memory location from smallest to largest.

Beginning Address	Memory Block Size	Status
7805	1000	Busy
*		(null entry)
9250	1000	Busy

(table 2.10)

Case 3. This is the busy list after the job has released its memory. The asterisk indicates the new null entry in the busy list.

When the null entry is found, the beginning memory location of the terminating job is entered in the beginning address column, the job size is entered under the memory block size column, and the status is changed from a null entry to free to indicate that a new block of memory is available, as shown in Table 2.11.

Beginning Address	Memory Block Size	Status
4075	105	Free
5225	5	Free
6785	600	Free
7560	245	Free
*8805	445	Free
10250	4050	Free
15125	230	Free
24500	1000	Free

(table 2.11)

Case 3. This is the free list after the job has released its memory. The asterisk indicates the new free block entry replacing the null entry.

Relocatable Dynamic Partitions

Both of the fixed and dynamic memory allocation schemes described thus far shared some unacceptable fragmentation characteristics that had to be resolved before the number of jobs waiting to be accepted became unwieldy. In addition, there was a growing need to use all the slivers of memory often left over.

The solution to both problems was the development of **relocatable dynamic partitions**. With this memory allocation scheme, the Memory Manager relocates programs to gather together all of the empty blocks and compact them to make one block of memory large enough to accommodate some or all of the jobs waiting to get in.

The **compaction** of memory, sometimes referred to as garbage collection or defragmentation, is performed by the operating system to reclaim fragmented sections of the memory space. Remember our earlier example of the makeshift lending library? If you stopped lending books for a few moments and rearranged the books in the most effective order, you would be compacting your collection. But this demonstrates its disadvantage—it's an overhead process, so that while compaction is being done everything else must wait.

Compaction isn't an easy task. First, every program in memory must be relocated so they're contiguous, and then every address, and every reference to an address, within each program must be adjusted to account for the program's new location in memory. However, all other values within the program (such as data values) must be left alone. In other words, the operating system must distinguish between addresses and data values, and the distinctions are not obvious once the program has been loaded into memory.

To appreciate the complexity of **relocation**, let's look at a typical program. Remember, all numbers are stored in memory as binary values, and in any given program instruction it's not uncommon to find addresses as well as data values. For example, an assembly language program might include the instruction to add the integer 1 to I. The source code instruction looks like this:

```
ADDI I, 1
```

However, after it has been translated into actual code it could look like this (for readability purposes the values are represented here in octal code, not binary code):

```
000007 271 01 0 00 000001
```

It's not immediately obvious which are addresses and which are instruction codes or data values. In fact, the address is the number on the left (000007). The instruction code is next (271), and the data value is on the right (000001).

The operating system can tell the function of each group of digits by its location in the line and the operation code. However, if the program is to be moved to another place in memory each address must be identified, or flagged. So later the amount of memory locations by which the program has been displaced must be added to (or subtracted from) all of the original addresses in the program.

This becomes particularly important when the program includes loop sequences, decision sequences, and branching sequences, as well as data references. If, by chance, every address was not adjusted by the same value, the program would branch to the wrong section of the program or to a section of another program, or it would reference the wrong data.

The program in Figures 2.5 and 2.6 shows how the operating system flags the addresses so they can be adjusted if and when a program is relocated.

Internally, the addresses are marked with a special symbol (indicated in Figure 2.6 by apostrophes) so the Memory Manager will know to adjust them by the value stored in the relocation register. All of the other values (data values) are not marked and won't

```
A          EXP 132, 144, 125, 110      ;the data values
BEGIN:     MOVEI              1,0       ;initialize register 1
           MOVEI              2,0       ;initialize register 2
LOOP:      ADD                2,A(1)    ;add (A + reg 1) to reg 2
           ADDI               1,1       ;add 1 to reg 1
           CAIG               1,4,-1    ;is reg 1.4-1?
           JUMPA              LOOP      ;if not, go to Loop
           MOVE               3,2       ;if so, move reg 2 to reg 3
           IDIVI              3,4       ;divide reg 3 by 4,
                                        ;remainder to register 4
           EXIT                         ;end
           END
```

(figure 2.5)

An assembly language program that performs a simple incremental operation. This is what the programmer submits to the assembler. The commands are shown on the left and the comments explaining each command are shown on the right after the semicolons.

```
000000'  000000 000132      A:          EXP132,144,125,110
000001'  000000 000144
000002'  000000 000125
000003'  000000 000110

000004'  201 01 0 00 000000  BEGIN:      MOVEI      1,0
000005'  201 02 0 00 000000              MOVEI      2,0
000006'  270 02 0 01 000000' LOOP:       ADD        2,A(1)
000007'  271 01 0 00 000001              ADDI       1,1
000008'  307 01 0 00 000003              CAIG       1,4-1
000009'  324 00 0 00 000006'             JUMPA      LOOP
000010'  200 03 0 00 000002              MOVE       3,2
000011'  231 03 0 00 000004              IDIVI      3,4
000012'  047 00 0 00 000012              EXIT

             000000                      END
```

(figure 2.6)

The original assembly language program after it has been processed by the assembler. To run the program, the assembler translates it into machine-readable code (shown on the left) with all addresses marked by a special symbol (shown here as an apostrophe) to distinguish addresses from data values.

be changed after relocation. Other numbers in the program, those indicating instructions, registers, or constants used in the instruction, are also left alone.

Figure 2.7 illustrates what happens to a program in memory during compaction and relocation.

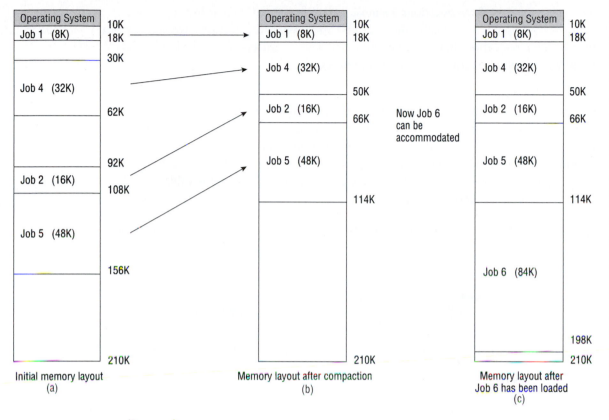

(figure 2.7)

Three snapshots of memory before and after compaction. When Job 6 arrives requiring 84K, the initial memory layout in (a) shows external fragmentation totaling 96K of space. Immediately after compaction (b), external fragmentation has been eliminated, making room for Job 6 (c).

This discussion of compaction raises three questions:

1. What goes on behind the scenes when relocation and compaction take place?
2. What keeps track of how far each job has moved from its original storage area?
3. What lists have to be updated?

The last question is easiest to answer. After relocation and compaction, both the free list and the busy list are updated. The free list is changed to show the partition for the new block of free memory: the one formed as a result of compaction that will be located in memory starting after the last location used by the last job. The busy list is changed to show the new locations for all of the jobs already in process that were relocated. Each job will have a new address except for those that were already residing at the lowest memory locations.

To answer the other two questions we must learn more about the hardware components of a computer, specifically the registers. Special-purpose registers are used to help with the relocation. In some computers two special registers are set aside for this purpose: the bounds register and the relocation register.

The **bounds register** is used to store the highest (or lowest, depending on the specific system) location in memory accessible by each program. This ensures that during execution, a program won't try to access memory locations that don't belong to it—that is, those that are out of bounds. The **relocation register** contains the value that must be added to each address referenced in the program so it will be able to access the correct memory addresses after relocation. If the program isn't relocated, the value stored in the program's relocation register is zero.

Figure 2.8 illustrates what happens during relocation by using the relocation register (all values are shown in decimal form).

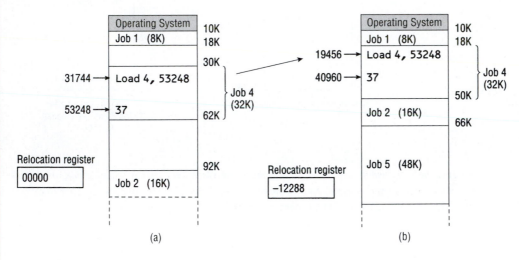

Contents of relocation register and close-up of Job 4 memory area (a) before relocation and (b) after relocation and compaction.

Originally, Job 4 was loaded into memory starting at memory location 30K. (1K equals 1,024 bytes. Therefore, the exact starting address is: 30 * 1024 = 30,720.) It required a block of memory of 32K (or 32 * 1024 = 32,768) addressable locations. Therefore, when it was originally loaded, the job occupied the space from memory location 30720 to memory location 63488-1. Now, suppose that within the program, at memory location 31744, there's an instruction that looks like this:

LOAD 4, ANSWER

This assembly language command asks that the data value known as ANSWER be loaded into Register 4 for later computation. ANSWER, the value 37, is stored at memory location 53248. (In this example Register 4 is a working/computation register, which is distinct from either the relocation or the bounds register.)

After relocation, Job 4 has been moved to a new starting memory address of 18K (actually 18 * 1024 = 18,432). Of course, the job still has its 32K addressable locations, so it now occupies memory from location 18432 to location 51200−1 and, thanks to the relocation register, all of the addresses will be adjusted accordingly.

What does the relocation register contain? In this example it contains the value −12288. As calculated previously, 12288 is the size of the free block that has been moved forward toward the high addressable end of memory. The sign is negative because Job 4 has been moved back, closer to the low addressable end of memory, as shown at the top of Figure 2.6(b).

However, the program instruction (LOAD 4, ANSWER) has not been changed. The original address 53248 where ANSWER had been stored remains the same in the program no matter how many times it is relocated. Before the instruction is executed, however, the true address must be computed by adding the value stored in the relocation register to the address found at that instruction. If the addresses are not adjusted by the value stored in the relocation register, then even though memory location 31744 is still part of the job's accessible set of memory locations, it would not contain the LOAD command. Not only that, but location 53248 is now out of bounds. The instruction that was originally at 31744 has been moved to location 19456. That's because all of the instructions in this program have been moved back by 12K (12 * 1024 = 12,288), which is the size of the free block. Therefore, location 53248 has been displaced by −12288 and ANSWER, the data value 37, is now located at address 40960.

In effect, by compacting and relocating, the Memory Manager optimizes the use of memory and thus improves throughput—one of the measures of system performance. An unfortunate side effect is that more overhead is incurred than with the two previous memory allocation schemes. The crucial factor here is the timing of the compaction—when and how often it should be done. There are three options.

One approach is to do it when a certain percentage of memory becomes busy, say 75 percent. The disadvantage of this approach is that the system would incur unnecessary overhead if no jobs were waiting to use the remaining 25 percent.

A second approach is to compact memory only when there are jobs waiting to get in. This would entail constant checking of the entry queue, which might result in unnecessary overhead and slow down the processing of jobs already in the system.

A third approach is to do it after a prescribed amount of time has elapsed. If the amount of time chosen is too small, however, then the system will spend more time on compaction than on processing. If it's too large, too many jobs will congregate in the waiting queue and the advantages of compaction are lost.

As you can see, each option has its good and bad points. The best choice for any system is decided by the operating system designer who, based on the job mix and other factors, tries to optimize both processing time and memory use while keeping overhead as low as possible.

Conclusion

Four memory management techniques were presented in this chapter: single-user systems, fixed partitions, dynamic partitions, and relocatable dynamic partitions. They have three things in common: they all require that the entire program (1) be loaded into memory, (2) be stored contiguously, and (3) remain in memory until the job is completed.

Consequently, each puts severe restrictions on the size of the jobs because they can only be as large as the biggest partitions in memory.

These schemes were sufficient for the first three generations of computers, which processed jobs in batch mode. Turnaround time was measured in hours, or sometimes days, but that was a period when users expected such delays between the submission of their jobs and pick up of output. As you'll see in the next chapter, a new trend emerged during the third-generation computers of the late 1960s and early 1970s: users were able to connect directly with the central processing unit via remote job entry stations, loading their jobs from online terminals that could interact more directly with the system. New methods of memory management were needed to accommodate them.

We'll see that the memory allocation schemes that followed had two new things in common. First, programs didn't have to be stored in contiguous memory locations—they could be divided into segments of variable sizes or pages of equal size. Each page, or segment, could be stored wherever there was an empty block big enough to hold it. Second, not all the pages, or segments, had to reside in memory during the execution of the job. These were significant advances for system designers, operators, and users alike.

Key Terms

address: a number that designates a particular memory location.

best-fit memory allocation: a main memory allocation scheme that considers all free blocks and selects for allocation the one that will result in the least amount of wasted space.

bounds register: a register used to store the highest location in memory legally accessible by each program.

compaction: the process of collecting fragments of available memory space into contiguous blocks by moving programs and data in a computer's memory or disk. Also called *garbage collection*.

deallocation: the process of freeing an allocated resource, whether memory space, a device, a file, or a CPU.

dynamic partitions: a memory allocation scheme in which jobs are given as much memory as they request when they are loaded for processing, thus creating their own partitions in main memory.

external fragmentation: a situation in which the dynamic allocation of memory creates unusable fragments of free memory between blocks of busy, or allocated, memory.

first-fit memory allocation: a main memory allocation scheme that searches from the beginning of the free block list and selects for allocation the first block of memory large enough to fulfill the request.

fixed partitions: a memory allocation scheme in which main memory is sectioned off, with portions assigned to each user.

internal fragmentation: a situation in which a fixed partition is only partially used by the program; the remaining space within the partition is unavailable to any other job and is therefore wasted.

kilobyte (K): a unit of memory or storage space equal to 1,024 bytes or 2^{10} bytes.

null entry: an empty entry in a list.

relocatable dynamic partitions: a memory allocation scheme in which the system relocates programs in memory to gather together all of the empty blocks and compact them to make one block of memory that's large enough to accommodate some or all of the jobs waiting for memory.

relocation: (1) the process of moving a program from one area of memory to another; or (2) the process of adjusting address references in a program, by either software or hardware means, to allow the program to execute correctly when loaded in different sections of memory.

relocation register: a register that contains the value that must be added to each address referenced in the program so that it will be able to access the correct memory addresses after relocation.

static partitions: another term for *fixed partitions*.

Exercises

Research Topic

The size of both main memory and secondary storage continues to grow rapidly. Complete the following table and explain how the first six names of units are derived. The first three units are shown. What are the next three?

Unit Name	Absolute Size	Exponential Form
byte	1 byte	2
kilobyte	1,024 bytes	2^{10}
megabyte	1,048,576 bytes	2^{20}
?	?	?
?	?	?
?	?	?

Exercises

1. Explain the following:

    a. Multiprogramming. Why is it used?

    b. Internal fragmentation. How does it occur?

    c. External fragmentation. How does it occur?

    d. Compaction. Why is it needed?

    e. Relocation. How often should it be performed?

2. Describe the major disadvantages for each of the four memory allocation schemes presented in the chapter.

3. Describe the major advantages for each of the memory allocation schemes presented in the chapter.

4. Given the following information:

Job list:

Job Number	Memory Requested
J1	740K
J2	500K
J3	700K

Memory list:

Memory Block	Size
Block 1	610K (low-order memory)
Block 2	850K
Block 3	700K (high-order memory)

    a. Use the best-fit algorithm to allocate the memory blocks to the three arriving jobs.

    b. Use the first-fit algorithm to allocate the memory blocks to the three arriving jobs.

5. Given the following information:

Job list:

Job Number	Memory Requested
J1	700K
J2	500K
J3	740K

Memory list:

Memory Block	Size
Block 1	610K (low-order memory)
Block 2	850K
Block 3	700K (high-order memory)

    a. Use the best-fit algorithm to allocate the memory blocks to the three arriving jobs.

    b. Use the first-fit algorithm to allocate the memory blocks to the three arriving jobs.

6. Next-fit is an allocation algorithm that keeps track of the last allocated partition and starts searching from that point on when a new job arrives.

    a. What might be an advantage of this algorithm?

    b. How would it compare to best-fit and first-fit for the conditions given in exercise 4?

    c. How would it compare to best-fit and first-fit for the conditions given in exercise 5?

7. Worst-fit is an allocation algorithm that is the opposite of best-fit. It allocates the largest free block to a new job.

    a. What might be an advantage of this algorithm?

b. How would it compare to best-fit and first-fit for the conditions given in exercise 4?

c. How would it compare to best-fit and first-fit for the conditions given in exercise 5?

8. The relocation example presented in the chapter implies that compaction is done entirely in memory, without secondary storage. Can all free sections of memory be merged into one contiguous block using this approach? Why or why not?

9. One way to compact memory is to copy all existing jobs to a secondary storage device and then reload them contiguously into main memory, thus creating one free block after all jobs have been recopied (and relocated) into memory. Is this viable? Could you devise a better way to compact memory? Write your algorithm and explain why it is better.

Advanced Exercises

10. Given the memory configuration in Figure 2.9, answer the following questions. At this point, Job 4 arrives requesting a block of 100K.

(figure 2.9)

Memory configuration for Exercise 10.

a. Can Job 4 be accommodated? Why or why not?

b. If relocation is used, what are the contents of the relocation registers for Job 1, Job 2, and Job 3 after recompaction?

c. What are the contents of the relocation register for Job 4 after it has been loaded into memory?

d. The instruction ADDI 4,10 is part of Job 1 and was originally loaded into memory location 22K. What is its new location after compaction?

e. The instruction MUL 4,NUMBER is part of Job 2 and was originally loaded into memory location 55K. What is its new location after compaction?

f. The instruction MOVE 3,SUM is part of Job 3 and was originally loaded into memory location 80K. What is its new location after compaction?

g. If SUM was originally loaded into memory location 110K, what is its new location after compaction?

h. If the instruction MOVE 3,SUM is stored as follows (this is in octal instead of binary for compactness):

200 03 00 334000

The rightmost value indicates the memory location where SUM is stored. What would that value be after compaction?

11. You have been given the job of determining whether the current fixed partition memory configuration in your computer system should be changed.

a. What information do you need to help you make that decision?

b. How would you go about collecting this information?

c. Once you had the information, how would you determine the best configuration for your system?

d. Could there be any consequences to reconfiguring such a system?

Programming Exercises

12. Here is a long-term programming project. Use the information that follows to complete this exercise.

Job List				Memory List	
Job Stream Number	Time	Job Size		Memory Block	Size
1	5	5760		1	9500
2	4	4190		2	7000
3	8	3290		3	4500
4	2	2030		4	8500
5	2	2550		5	3000
6	6	6990		6	9000
7	8	8940		7	1000
8	10	740		8	5500
9	7	3930		9	1500
10	6	6890		10	500
11	5	6580			
12	8	3820			
13	9	9140			
14	10	420			
15	10	220			

Job List		
Job Stream List	Time	Job Size
16	7	7540
17	3	3210
18	1	1380
19	9	9850
20	3	3610
21	7	7540
22	2	2710
23	8	8390
24	5	5950
25	10	760

At one large batch-processing computer installation the management wants to decide what storage placement strategy will yield the best possible performance. The installation runs a large real storage (as opposed to "virtual" storage, which will be covered in the following chapter) computer under fixed partition multiprogramming. Each user program runs in a single group of contiguous storage locations. Users state their storage requirements and time units for CPU usage on their Job Control Card (it used to, and still does, work this way, although cards may not be used). The operating system allocates to each user the appropriate partition and starts up the user's job. The job remains in memory until completion. A total of 50,000 memory locations are available, divided into blocks as indicated in the table above.

a. Write (or calculate) an event-driven simulation to help you decide which storage placement strategy should be used at this installation. Your program would use the job stream and memory partitioning as indicated previously. Run the program until all jobs have been executed with the memory as is (in order by address). This will give you the first-fit type performance results.

b. Sort the memory partitions by size and run the program a second time; this will give you the best-fit performance results. For both parts a. and b. you are investigating the performance of the system using a typical job stream by measuring:

1. Throughput (how many jobs are processed per given time unit)
2. Storage utilization (percentage of partitions never used, percentage of partitions heavily used, etc.)

3. Waiting queue length
4. Waiting time in queue
5. Internal fragmentation

Given that jobs are served on a first-come first-served basis:

c. Explain how the system handles conflicts when jobs are put into a waiting queue and there are still jobs entering the system—who goes first?

d. Explain how the system handles the "job clocks," which keep track of the amount of time each job has run, and the "wait clocks," which keep track of how long each job in the waiting queue has to wait.

e. Since this is an event-driven system, explain how you define "event" and what happens in your system when the event occurs.

f. Look at the results from the best-fit run and compare them with the results from the first-fit run. Explain what the results indicate about the performance of the system for this job mix and memory organization. Is one method of partitioning better than the other? Why or why not? Could you recommend one method over the other given your sample run? Would this hold in all cases? Write some conclusions and recommendations.

13. Suppose your system (as explained in exercise 12) now has a "spooler" (storage area in which to temporarily hold jobs) and the job scheduler can choose which will be served from among 25 resident jobs. Suppose also that the first-come first-served policy is replaced with a "faster-job first-served" policy. This would require that a sort by time be performed on the job list before running the program. Does this make a difference in the results? Does it make a difference in your analysis? Does it make a difference in your conclusions and recommendations? The program should be run twice to test this new policy with both best-fit and first-fit.

14. Suppose your spooler (as described in exercise 13) replaces the previous policy with one of "smallest-job first-served." This would require that a sort by job size be performed on the job list before running the program. How do the results compare to the previous two sets of results? Will your analysis change? Will your conclusions change? The program should be run twice to test this new policy with both best-fit and first-fit.

Chapter 3

Memory Management: Virtual Memory

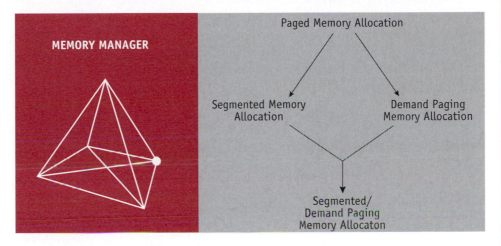

MEMORY MANAGER

Paged Memory Allocation

Segmented Memory Allocation

Demand Paging Memory Allocation

Segmented/ Demand Paging Memory Allocaton

"Nothing is so much strengthened by practice, or weakened by neglect, as memory." —Quintillian *(A.D. 35–100)*

Learning Objectives

After completing this chapter, you should be able to describe:

• The basic functionality of the memory allocation methods covered in this chapter: paged, demand paging, segmented, and segmented/demand paged memory allocation

• The influence that these page allocation methods have had on virtual memory

• The difference between a first-in first-out page replacement policy, a least-recently-used page replacement policy, and a clock page replacement policy

• The mechanics of paging and how a memory allocation scheme determines which pages should be swapped out of memory

• The concept of the working set and how it is used in memory allocation schemes

• The impact that virtual memory had on multiprogramming

• Cache memory and its role in improving system response time

In the previous chapter we looked at simple memory allocation schemes. Each one required that the Memory Manager store the entire program in main memory in contiguous locations, and as we pointed out each scheme solved some problems but created others, such as fragmentation or the overhead of relocation.

In this chapter we'll follow the evolution of virtual memory with four memory allocation schemes that first remove the restriction of storing the programs contiguously and then eliminate the requirement that the entire program reside in memory during its execution. These schemes are paged, demand paging, segmented, and segmented/demand paged allocation, which form the foundation for our current virtual memory methods. Our discussion of cache memory will show how its use improves the performance of the Memory Manager.

Paged Memory Allocation

Paged memory allocation is based on the concept of dividing each incoming job into **pages** of equal size. Some operating systems choose a page size that's the same as the memory block size and that is also the same size as the sections of the disk on which the job is stored.

The sections of a disk are called **sectors** (or sometimes blocks), and the sections of main memory are called **page frames.** The scheme works quite efficiently when the pages, sectors, and page frames are all the same size. The exact size (the number of bytes that can be stored in each of them) is usually determined by the disk's sector size. Therefore, one sector will hold one page of job instructions and fit into one page frame of memory.

Before executing a program, the Memory Manager prepares it by:

1. Determining the number of pages in the program;
2. Locating enough empty page frames in main memory;
3. Loading all of the program's pages into them (in static paging the pages need not be contiguous).

When the program is initially prepared for loading, its pages are in logical sequence— the first pages contain the first instructions of the program and the last page has the last instructions. To make our explanation as clear as possible, we'll refer to the program's instructions as lines of code, but they can also be thought of as bytes.

The loading process is different from the schemes we studied in Chapter 2 because the pages do not have to be loaded in adjacent memory blocks. In fact, each page can be stored in any available page frame anywhere in main memory (Madnick & Donovan, 1974).

The primary advantage of storing programs in noncontiguous locations is that main memory is used more efficiently because an empty page frame can be used by any page of any job. In addition, the compaction scheme used for relocatable partitions is eliminated because there is no external fragmentation between page frames (and no internal fragmentation in most pages).

However, with every new solution comes a new problem. Because a job's pages can be located anywhere in main memory, the Memory Manager now needs a mechanism to keep track of them—and that means enlarging the size and complexity of the operating system software, which increases overhead.

The example in Figure 3.1 shows how the Memory Manager keeps track of a program that's four pages long. To simplify the arithmetic, we've arbitrarily set the page size at 100 lines (or bytes). Job 1 is 350 lines (or bytes) long and is being readied for execution.

Notice in Figure 3.1 that the last page (Page 3) is not fully utilized because the job is less than 400 lines—the last page uses only 50 of the 100 lines available. In fact, very few jobs perfectly fill all of the pages, so internal fragmentation is still a problem (but only in the last page of a job).

In Figure 3.1 (with seven free page frames), the operating system can accommodate jobs that vary in size from 1 to 700 lines because they can be stored in the seven empty page frames. But a job that's larger than 700 lines can't be accommodated until Job 1 ends its execution and releases the four page frames it occupies. And a job that's larger than 1100 lines will never fit into memory. Therefore, although paged memory alloca-

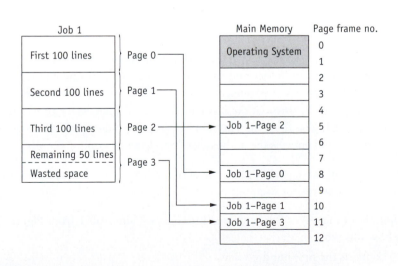

(figure 3.1)

Programs that are too long to fit on a single page are split into equal-sized pages that can be stored in free page frames. In this example each page frame can hold 100 lines. Job 1 is 350 lines long and is divided among four page frames, leaving internal fragmentation in the last page frame. (The Page Map Table for this job is shown later in Table 3.2.)

tion offers the advantage of noncontiguous storage, it still requires that the entire job be stored in memory during its execution.

Figure 3.1 uses arrows and lines to show how a job's pages fit into page frames in memory, but the Memory Manager uses tables to keep track of them. There are essentially three tables that perform this function: the Job Table, Page Map Table, and Memory Map Table. Although different operating systems may have different names for them, the tables provide the same service regardless of the names they're given. All three tables reside in the part of main memory that's reserved for the operating system.

As shown in Table 3.1, the **Job Table (JT)** contains two entries for each active job: the size of the job and the memory location where its Page Map Table is stored. This is a dynamic list that grows as jobs are loaded into the system and shrinks as they're later completed.

Job Table			Job Table			Job Table	
Job Size	PMT Location		Job Size	PMT Location		Job Size	PMT Location
400	3096		400	3096		400	3096
200	3100					700	3100
500	3150		500	3150		500	3150
(a)			(b)			(c)	

(table 3.1)

This section of the Job Table (a) initially has three entries, one for each job in process. When the second job (b) ends, its entry in the table is released and it is replaced by (c), information about the next job that is processed.

Each active job has its own **Page Map Table (PMT)** that contains the vital information for each page—the page number and its corresponding page frame memory address. Actually, the PMT includes only one entry per page. The page numbers are sequential (Page 0, Page 1, Page 2, through the last page), so it isn't necessary to list each page number in the PMT. The first entry in the PMT lists the page frame memory address for Page 0, the second entry is the address for Page 1, and so on.

The **Memory Map Table (MMT)** has one entry for each page frame listing the location and free/busy status for each one.

At compilation time, every job is divided into pages. Using Job 1 from Figure 3.1, we can see how this works:

• Page 0 contains the first hundred lines

• Page 1 contains the second hundred lines

• Page 2 contains the third hundred lines

• Page 3 contains the last fifty lines

As you can see, the program has 350 lines, but when they're stored, the system numbers them starting from 0 through 349, so the system refers to them as line 0 through line 349.

The **displacement**, or **offset**, of a line (that is, how far away a line is from the beginning of its page) is the factor used to locate that line within its page frame. It's a relative factor.

For example, lines 0, 100, 200, and 300 are the first lines for pages 0, 1, 2, and 3 respectively, so each has a displacement of zero. This is shown in Figure 3.2. Likewise, if the operating system needs to access line 214 it can first go to page 2 and then go to line 14 (the fifteenth line).

The first line of each page has a displacement of zero, the second line has a displacement of one, and so on to the last line (or byte), which has a displacement of 99. So

(figure 3.2)

Job 1 is 350 lines long and is divided into four pages of 100 lines each.

once the operating system finds the right page, it can access a line using the line's relative position within its page.

In this example, it's easy for us to see intuitively that all line numbers less than 100 will be on Page 0, all line numbers greater than or equal to 100 but less than 200 will be on Page 1, and so on. (That's the advantage of choosing a fixed page size, such as 100 lines.) The operating system uses an algorithm to calculate the page and displacement; it's a simple arithmetic calculation.

To find the address of a given program line, the line number is divided by the page size, keeping the remainder as an integer. The resulting quotient is the page number, and the remainder is the displacement within that page. When it's set up as a long division problem, it looks like this:

$$
\begin{array}{r}
\text{page number} \\
\hline
\text{page size)}\overline{\text{line number to be located}} \\
\underline{\text{xxx}} \\
\text{xxx} \\
\underline{\text{xxx}} \\
\text{displacement}
\end{array}
$$

For example, if we use 100 lines as the page size, the page number and the displacement (the location within that page) of Line 214 can be calculated like this:

$$
\begin{array}{r}
2 \\
\hline
100)\overline{214} \\
\underline{200} \\
14
\end{array}
$$

The quotient (2) is the page number, and the remainder (14) is the displacement. So the line is located on Page 2, 15 lines (Line 14) from the top of the page.

Let's try another example. We can calculate the page number and displacement of Line 36 by dividing 36 by 100. We find that the page number is 0 and the displacement is 36. So the line can be found on Page 0, Line 36, the 37th line from the top of the page.

Using the concepts just presented, and using the same parameters from the first example, answer these questions:

1. Could the operating system (or the hardware) get a page number that's greater than 3, if the program intended Line 214?
2. If it did, what should the operating system do?
3. Could the operating system get a remainder of more than 99?
4. What is the smallest remainder possible?

Here are the answers:

1. No, not if the application program was written correctly. (For the exception, see Exercise 14 at the end of this chapter.)
2. Send an error message and stop processing the program. (The page is out of bounds.)
3. Not if it divides correctly.
4. Zero.

Actually, the division is carried out in the hardware, but the operating system is responsible for maintaining the tables (allocating and deallocating storage).

This procedure gives the location of the line with respect to the job's pages. However, these pages are only relative; each page is actually stored in a page frame that can be located anywhere in available main memory. Therefore, the algorithm needs to be expanded to find the exact location of the line in main memory. To do so, we need to correlate each of the job's pages with its page frame number via the Page Map Table.

For example, if we look at the PMT for Job 1 from Figure 3.1, we see that it looks like the data in Table 3.2.

<table>
<tr><td>(table 3.2)</td><td>**Job Page Number**</td><td>**Page Frame Number**</td></tr>
<tr><td rowspan="4">*Page Map Table for Job 1 in Figure 3.1.*</td><td>0</td><td>8</td></tr>
<tr><td>1</td><td>10</td></tr>
<tr><td>2</td><td>5</td></tr>
<tr><td>3</td><td>11</td></tr>
</table>

In the first division example we were looking for an instruction with a displacement of 14 on Page 2. To find its exact location in memory, the operating system (or the hardware) has to perform the following four steps.

STEP 1 Do the arithmetic computation from the algorithm described previously to determine the page number and displacement of the line. (In actuality, the operating system identifies the lines, or data values and instructions, as addresses [bytes or words]. We refer to them here as lines to make it easier to explain.)

• Page number = the integer quotient from the division of the job space address by the page size

• Displacement = the remainder from the page number division

The computation shows that the page number is 2 and the displacement is 14.

STEP 2 Refer to this job's PMT and find out which page frame contains Page 2. According to Table 3.2, Page 2 is located in Page Frame 5.

STEP 3 Get the address of the beginning of the page frame by multiplying the page frame number by the page frame size.

```
ADDR_PAGE_FRAME = PAGE_FRAME_NUM * PAGE_SIZE
```

STEP 4 Now add the displacement (calculated in step 1) to the starting address of the page frame to compute the precise location in memory of the line:

```
INSTR_ADDR_IN_MEM = ADDR_PAGE_FRAME + DISPL
```

The result of this maneuver tells us exactly where Line 14 is located in main memory.

Figure 3.3 follows the hardware (and the operating system) as it runs an assembly language program that instructs the system to load into Register 1 the value found at Line 518.

In Figure 3.3 the page frame sizes in main memory are set at 512 bytes each and the page size is 512 bytes for this system. From the PMT we can see that this job has been divided into two pages. To find the exact location of Line 518 (where the system will find the value to load into Register 1), the system will do the following:

1. Compute the page number and displacement—the page number is 1, and the displacement is 6.
2. Go to the Page Map Table and retrieve the appropriate page frame number for Page 1. It's Page Frame 3.
3. Compute the starting address of the page frame by multiplying the page frame number times the page frame size: (3 * 512 = 1536).
4. Calculate the exact address of the instruction in main memory by adding the displacement to the starting address: (1536 + 6 = 1542). Therefore, memory address 1542 holds the value that should be loaded into Register 1.

Job 1

Line no.	Instruction/Data
001	BEGIN
⋮	⋮
025	LOAD R1, 518
⋮	⋮
518	3792
⋮	⋮

PMT for Job 1

Page no.	Page frame number
0	5
1	3

Main Memory		Page frame no.
0		0
512		1
1024		2
1536	Job 1 – Page 1	3
2048		4
2560	Job 1 – Page 0	5
3072		6
3584		7
⋮		8

(figure 3.3)

Job 1 with its Page Map Table. Main memory showing allocation of page frames to Job 1.

As you can see, this is a lengthy operation. Every time an instruction is executed, or a data value is used, the operating system (or the hardware) must translate the job space address, which is relative, into its physical address, which is absolute. This is called resolving the address, also called **address resolution**, also called address translation. Of course, all of this processing is overhead, which takes processing capability away from the jobs waiting to be completed. However, in most systems the hardware does the paging, although the operating system is involved in dynamic paging, which will be covered later.

The advantage of a paging scheme is that it allows jobs to be allocated in noncontiguous memory locations so that memory is used more efficiently and more jobs can fit in the main memory (which is synonymous). However, there are disadvantages—overhead is increased and internal fragmentation is still a problem, although only in the last page of each job. The key to the success of this scheme is the size of the page. A page size that is too small will generate very long PMTs while a page size that is too large will result in excessive internal fragmentation. Determining the best page size isn't easy—there are no hard and fast rules that will guarantee optimal use of resources—and it's a problem we'll see again as we examine other paging alternatives. The best size depends on the actual job environment, the nature of the jobs being processed, and the constraints placed on the system.

Demand Paging

Demand paging introduced the concept of loading only a part of the program into memory for processing. It was the first widely used scheme that removed the restriction of having the entire job in memory from the beginning to the end of its processing. With demand paging, jobs are still divided into equally sized pages that initially reside in secondary storage. When the job begins to run, its pages are brought into memory only as they are needed.

Demand paging takes advantage of the fact that programs are written sequentially so that while one section, or module, is processed all of the other modules are idle (Madnick & Donovan, 1974.) Not all the pages are necessary at once, for example:

• User-written error handling modules are processed only when a specific error is detected during execution. (For instance, they are often used to indicate to the operator that input data was incorrect or that a computation resulted in an invalid answer). If no error occurs, and we hope this is generally the case, these instructions are never processed.

• Many modules are mutually exclusive. For example, if the input module is active then the processing module is inactive. Similarly, if the processing module is active then the output module is idle.

- Certain program options are either mutually exclusive or not always accessible. This is easiest to visualize in menu-driven programs. For example, an application program that's used to maintain records in a data file may give the user four menu choices as shown in Figure 3.4. The system allows the operator to make only one selection at a time. If the user selects the first option then the module with the program instructions to move records to the file is the only one that's being used, so that's the only module that needs to be in memory. The other modules all remain in secondary storage until they're called from the menu.

- Many tables are assigned a large fixed amount of address space even though only a fraction of the table is actually used. For example, a symbol table for an assembler might be prepared to handle 100 symbols. If only 10 symbols are used then 90 percent of the table remains unused.

One of the most important innovations of demand paging was that it made virtual memory widely available. (Virtual memory will be discussed later in this chapter.) The demand paging scheme allows the user to run jobs with less main memory than is required if the operating system is using the paged memory allocation scheme described earlier. In fact, a demand paging scheme can give the appearance of an almost-infinite or nonfinite amount of physical memory when, in reality, physical memory is significantly less than infinite.

The key to the successful implementation of this scheme is the use of a high-speed direct access storage device (such as a hard drive) that can work directly with the CPU. That is vital because pages must be passed quickly from secondary storage to main memory and back again.

How and when the pages are passed (or swapped) depends on predefined policies that determine when to make room for needed pages and how to do so. The operating system relies on tables (the Job Table, the Page Map Table, and the Memory Map Table) to implement the algorithm. These tables are basically the same as for paged memory allocation but with the addition of three new fields for each page in the PMT: one to determine if the page being requested is already in memory; a second to determine if

(figure 3.4)

When users choose the first option from the menu of an application program, the other three modules that aren't currently required can be moved out of memory and reloaded later, when they're needed.

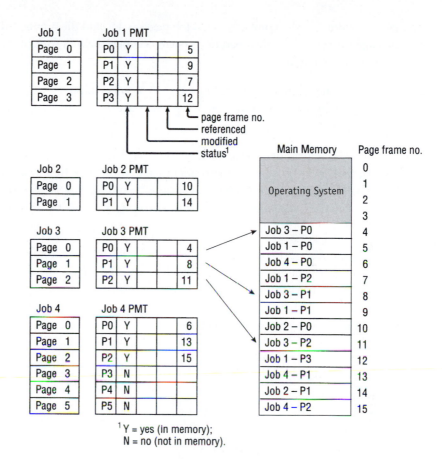

(figure 3.5)

Demand paging requires that the Page Map Table for each job keep track of each page as it is loaded or removed from main memory. Each PMT tracks the status of the page, whether it has been modified, whether it has been recently referenced, and the page frame number for each page currently in main memory. (Note: For this illustration the Page Map Tables have been simplified. See Table 3.3 for more detail.)

[1] Y = yes (in memory); N = no (not in memory).

the page contents have been modified; and a third to determine if the page has been referenced recently, as shown at the top of Figure 3.5.

The first field tells the system where to find each page. If it's already in memory, the system will be spared the time required to bring it from secondary storage. It's faster for the operating system to scan a table located in main memory than it is to retrieve a page from a disk.

The second field, noting if the page has been modified, is used to save time when pages are removed from main memory and returned to secondary storage. If the contents of the page haven't been modified then the page doesn't need to be rewritten to secondary storage. The original, already there, is correct.

The third field, which indicates any recent activity, is used to determine which pages show the most processing activity, and which are relatively inactive. This information is used by several page-swapping policy schemes to determine which pages should remain in main memory and which should be swapped out when the system needs to make room for other pages being requested.

For example, in Figure 3.5, the number of total job pages is 15, and the number of total available page frames is 12. (The operating system occupies the first four of the 16 page frames in main memory.)

Assuming the processing status illustrated in Figure 3.5, what happens when Job 4 requests that Page 3 be brought into memory if there are no empty page frames available?

To move in a new page, a resident page must be swapped back into secondary storage. Specifically, that includes copying the resident page to the disk (if it was modified), and writing the new page into the empty page frame. Such a swap requires close interaction between hardware components, software algorithms, and policy schemes.

The hardware components generate the address of the required page, find the page number, and determine whether it's already in memory. The following algorithm makes up the hardware instruction processing cycle.

Hardware Instruction Processing Algorithm

1 Start processing instruction
2 Generate data address
3 Compute page number
4 If page is in memory
        Then
        get data and finish instruction
        advance to next instruction
        return to step 1
    Else
        generate page interrupt
        call page fault handler
    End if

The same process is followed when fetching an instruction.

When the test fails (meaning that the page is in secondary storage but not in memory), the operating system software takes over. The section of the operating system that resolves these problems is called the **page fault handler**. It determines whether there are empty page frames in memory so the requested page can be immediately copied from secondary storage. If all page frames are busy, the page fault handler must decide which page will be swapped out. (This decision is directly dependent on the predefined policy for page removal.) Then the swap is made.

Page Fault Handler Algorithm

1 If there is no free page frame
    Then
    select page to be swapped out using page removal algorithm
    update job's Page Map Table
    If content of page had been changed then
       write page to disk
    End if
  End if
2 Use page number from step 3 from the Hardware Instruction Processing Algorithm to get disk address where the requested page is stored (the File Manager, to be discussed in Chapter 8, uses the page number to get the disk address)
3 Read page into memory
4 Update job's Page Map Table
5 Update Memory Map Table
6 Restart interrupted instruction

Before continuing, three tables must be updated: the Page Map Tables for both jobs (the PMT with the page that was swapped out and the PMT with the page that was swapped in) and the Memory Map Table. Finally, the instruction that was interrupted is resumed and processing continues.

Although demand paging is a solution to inefficient memory utilization, it's not free of problems. When there is an excessive amount of **page swapping** between main memory and secondary storage, the operation becomes inefficient. This phenomenon is called **thrashing**. It uses a great deal of the computer's energy but accomplishes very little, and it's caused when a page is removed from memory but is called back shortly thereafter. Thrashing can occur across jobs, when a large number of jobs are vying for a relatively few number of free pages (the ratio of job pages to free memory page frames is high), or it can happen within a job—for example, in loops that cross page boundaries. We can demonstrate this with a simple example. Suppose the beginning of a loop falls at the bottom of a page, and is completed at the top of the next page, as in the C program in Figure 3.6.

(figure 3.6)

An example of demand paging that results in a page swap each time the loop is executed and results in thrashing. If only a single page frame is available, this program will have one page fault each time the loop is executed.

The situation in Figure 3.6 assumes there's only one empty page frame available. The first page is loaded into memory and execution begins, but after executing the last command on Page 0, the page is swapped out to make room for Page 1. Now execution can continue with the first command on Page 1, but at the "}" symbol, Page 1 must be swapped out so Page 0 can be brought back in to continue the loop. Before this program is completed, swapping will have occurred 100 times (unless another page frame becomes free so both pages can reside in memory at the same time). A failure to find a page in memory is often called a **page fault** and this example would generate 100 page faults (and swaps).

In extreme cases, the rate of useful computation could be degraded by a factor of 100. Ideally, a demand paging scheme is most efficient when programmers are aware of the page size used by their operating system and are careful to design their programs to keep page faults to a minimum, but in reality this is not often feasible.

Page Replacement Policies and Concepts

As we just learned, the policy that selects the page to be removed, the **page replacement policy**, is crucial to the efficiency of the system, and the algorithm to do that must be carefully selected.

Several such algorithms exist and it's a subject that enjoys a great deal of theoretical attention and research. Two of the most well-known are first-in first-out and least-recently-used. The **first-in first-out (FIFO) policy** is based on the theory that the best page to remove is the one that has been in memory the longest. The **least-recently-used (LRU) policy** chooses the page least recently accessed to be swapped out.

To illustrate the difference between FIFO and LRU, let's imagine a dresser drawer filled with your favorite sweaters. The drawer is full, but that didn't stop you from buying a new sweater. Now you have to put it away. Obviously it won't fit in your sweater drawer unless you take something out, but which sweater should you remove to the storage closet? Your decision will be based on a sweater removal policy.

You could take out your oldest sweater (the one that was first in), figuring that you probably won't use it again—hoping you won't discover in the following days that it's your most used, most treasured possession. Or, you could remove the sweater that you haven't worn recently and has been idle for the longest amount of time (the one that was least recently used). It's readily identifiable because it's at the bottom of the drawer. But just because it hasn't been used recently doesn't mean that a once-a-year occasion won't demand its appearance soon.

What guarantee do you have that once you've made your choice you won't be trekking to the storage closet to retrieve the sweater you stored yesterday? You could become a victim of thrashing.

Which is the best policy? It depends on the weather, the wearer, and the wardrobe. Of course, one option is to get another drawer. For an operating system (or a computer), this is the equivalent of having more accessible memory, and we'll explore that option after we discover how to more effectively use the memory we already have.

The examples presented in the following sections related to FIFO and LRU have been adapted from Madnick & Donovan (1974).

First-In First-Out

The first-in first-out (FIFO) page replacement policy will remove the pages that have been in memory the longest. The process of swapping pages is illustrated in Figure 3.7.

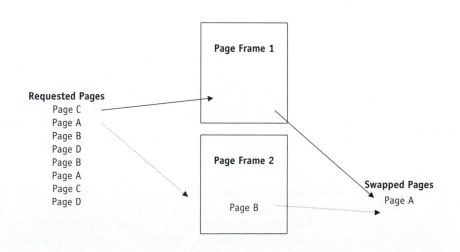

(figure 3.7)

The FIFO policy in action. When the program calls for Page C, Page A must be moved out of the first page frame to make room for it, as shown by the solid lines. When Page A is needed again, it will replace Page B in the second page frame, as shown by the dotted lines. The entire sequence is shown in Figure 3.8.

Requested Pages
Page C
Page A
Page B
Page D
Page B
Page A
Page C
Page D

Page Frame 1

Page Frame 2

Page B

Swapped Pages
Page A

Figure 3.8 shows how the FIFO algorithm works by following a job with four pages (A, B, C, D) as it's processed by a system with only two available page frames. Figure 3.8 displays how each page is swapped into and out of memory and marks each interrupt with an asterisk. We then count the number of page interrupts and compute the failure rate and the success rate. The job to be processed needs its pages in the following order: A, B, A, C, A, B, D, B, A, C, D.

When both page frames are occupied, each new page brought into memory will cause an existing one to be swapped out to secondary storage. A page interrupt, which we identify with an asterisk (*), is generated when a new page is brought into memory (whether a page is swapped out or not).

The efficiency of this configuration is dismal—there are 9 page interrupts out of 11 page requests due to the limited number of page frames available and the need for many new pages. To calculate the failure rate we divide the number of page requests into the number of interrupts. The failure rate of this system is 9/11, which is 82 percent. Stated another way, the success rate is 2/11, or 18 percent. A failure rate this high is usually unacceptable.

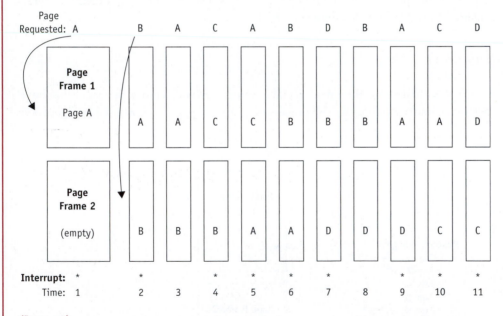

(figure 3.8)

Using a FIFO policy, each page requested is swapped into the two available page frames. When the program is ready to be processed all four pages are on secondary storage. Throughout the program, 11 page requests are issued. When the program calls a page that isn't already in memory, a page interrupt is issued, as shown by the asterisks. This program resulted in nine page interrupts.

We're not saying FIFO is bad. We chose this example to show how FIFO works, not to diminish its appeal as a swapping policy. The high failure rate here is caused by both the limited amount of memory available and the order in which pages are requested by the program. The page order can't be changed by the system, although the size of main memory can be changed. But buying more memory may not always be the best solution—especially when you have many users and each one wants an unlimited amount of memory. There is no guarantee that buying more memory will always result in better performance; this is known as the **FIFO anomaly** or **Belady's anomaly**.

Least Recently Used

The least recently used (LRU) page replacement policy swaps out the pages that show the least amount of recent activity, figuring that these pages are the least likely to be used again in the immediate future. Conversely, if a page is used, it's likely to be used again soon; this is based on the theory of locality, which will be explained later in this chapter.

To see how it works, let's follow the same job in Figure 3.8 but using the LRU policy. The results are shown in Figure 3.9. To implement this policy, a queue of the requests is kept in FIFO order, or a time stamp of when the job entered the system is saved, or a mark in the job's PMT is made periodically.

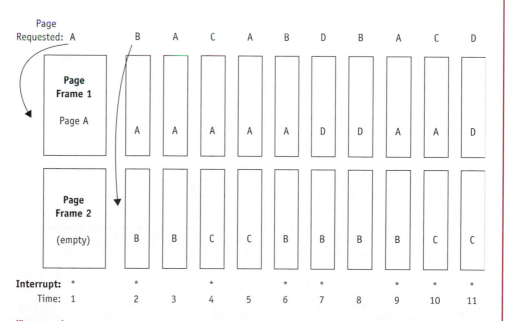

(figure 3.9)

Memory management using an LRU page removal policy for the program shown in Figure 3.8. Throughout the program, 11 page requests are issued, but they cause only 8 page interrupts.

The efficiency of this configuration is only slightly better than with FIFO. Here, there are 8 page interrupts out of 11 page requests, so the failure rate is 8/11, or 73 percent. In this example, an increase in main memory by one page frame would increase the success rate of both FIFO and LRU (you'll have the opportunity to calculate the exact increase in exercises 6 and 7 at the end of this chapter). However, we can't conclude on the basis of only one example that one policy is better than the others. In fact, LRU is a stack algorithm removal policy, which functions in such a way that increasing main memory will cause either a decrease in or the same number of page interrupts. In other words, an increase in memory will never cause an increase in the number of page interrupts.

On the other hand, it has been shown (Belady, Nelson, & Shelder, 1969) that under certain circumstances adding more memory can, in rare cases, actually cause an increase in page interrupts when using a FIFO policy. As noted before, it's called the FIFO anomaly. But although it's an unusual occurrence, the fact that it exists, coupled with the fact that pages are removed regardless of their activity (as was the case in Figure 3.8), has removed FIFO from the most favored policy position it held in some cases.

A variation of the LRU page replacement algorithm is known as the **clock page replacement policy** because it is implemented with a circular queue and uses a pointer to step through the reference bits of the active pages, simulating a clockwise motion. The algorithm is paced according to the computer's **clock cycle**, which is the time span between two ticks in its system clock. The algorithm selects a page for replacement if it has a reference bit of zero. However, if its reference bit is one, then the page is given a second chance, its reference bit is set to zero and the next page's reference bit is inspected. This process continues until a reference bit of zero is found. If all the reference bits are set to one, then the pointer must cycle through the entire circular queue again giving each page a second, and perhaps a third or fourth chance. Figure 3.10(a) shows the circular queue containing the reference bits for pages currently in memory. The pointer indicates the page that would be considered next for removal. Figure 3.10(b) shows what happens to the reference bits of the pages that have been given a

(a)

Reference Bits	0	0	1	1	1	0	1
Page Numbers	19	1	45	68	35	210	180

(b)

Reference Bits	0	0	0	0	0	1	1
Page Numbers	19	1	45	68	35	146	180

(figure 3.10)

Two views of the circular queue, which contains the page number and its reference bit. In (a), the pointer looks for the next candidate for removal. In (b), after the pointer has given pages 45, 68 and 35 a second chance and set their reference bits to zero, it replaces page 210 with a new page, 146.

second chance when a new page, 146, has to be allocated to a page frame, the space previously occupied by page 210 which had a reference bit of zero.

A second variation of LRU uses an 8-bit reference byte and a bit-shifting technique to track the usage of each page currently in memory. When the page is first copied into memory the leftmost bit of its reference byte is set to 1, all bits to the right of the one are set to zero, as shown in Figure 3.11. At specific time intervals of the clock cycle, the Memory Manager shifts every page's reference bytes to the right by one bit, dropping their rightmost bit. Meanwhile, each time a page is referenced the leftmost bit of its reference byte is set to 1.

This process of shifting bits to the right and resetting the leftmost bit to 1 when a page is referenced gives a history of each page's usage. For example, a page that has not been used for the last eight time ticks would have a reference byte of 00000000, while one that has been referenced once every time tick will have a reference byte of 11111111.

When a page fault occurs, the LRU policy selects the page with the smallest value in its reference byte because that would be the one least recently used. Figure 3.11 shows how the reference bytes for six active pages change during four snapshots of usage. In (a), the six pages have been initialized; this indicated that all of them have been referenced once. In (b), pages 1, 3, 5, and 6 have been referenced again (marked with 1), but pages 2 and 4 have not (now marked with 0 in the leftmost position). In (c), pages 1, 2, and 4 have been referenced. In (d), pages 1, 2, 4, and 6 have been referenced. In (e), pages 1 and 4 have been referenced.

As shown in Figure 3.11, the values stored in the reference bytes are not unique: page 3 and page 5 have the same value. In this case the LRU policy may opt to swap out all of the pages with the smallest value, or may select one among them based on other criteria such as FIFO, priority, or whether the contents of the page have been modified.

Other page removal algorithms, MRU (most recently used) and LFU (least frequently used), are discussed in exercises at the end of this chapter.

(figure 3.11)

Notice how the reference bit for each page is updated with every time tick. Arrows (a) through (e) show how the initial bit shifts to the right with every tick of the clock.

Page Number	Time 0	Time 1	Time 2	Time 3	Time 4
1	10000000	11000000	11100000	11110000	11111000
2	10000000	01000000	10100000	11010000	01101000
3	10000000	11000000	01100000	00110000	00011000
4	10000000	01000000	10100000	11010000	11101000
5	10000000	11000000	01100000	00110000	00011000
6	10000000	11000000	01100000	10110000	01011000

(a)   (b)   (c)   (d)   (e)

The Mechanics of Paging

Before the Memory Manager can determine which pages will be swapped out, it needs specific information about each page in memory—information included in the Page Map Tables.

For example, in Figure 3.5, the Page Map Table for Job 1 included three bits: the status bit, the referenced bit, and the modified bit (these were the three middle columns: the two empty columns and the Y/N column representing "in memory"). But the representation of the table shown in Figure 3.5 was simplified for illustration purposes. It actually looks something like the one shown in Table 3.3.

Page	Status Bit	Referenced Bit	Modified Bit	Page Frame
0	1	1	1	5
1	1	0	0	9
2	1	0	0	7
3	1	1	0	12

(table 3.3)

Page Map Table for Job 1 shown in Figure 3.5.

As we said before, the status bit indicates whether the page is currently in memory. The referenced bit indicates whether the page has been called (referenced) recently. This bit is important because it is used by the LRU algorithm to determine which pages should be swapped out.

The modified bit indicates whether the contents of the page have been altered and is used to determine if the page must be rewritten to secondary storage when it's swapped out before its page frame is released. (A page frame whose contents have not been modified can be overwritten directly.) That's because when a page is swapped into memory, it isn't removed from secondary storage. The page is merely copied—the original remains intact in secondary storage. Therefore, if the page isn't altered while it's in main memory (in which case the modified bit remains unchanged, zero), the page needn't be copied back to secondary storage when it's swapped out of memory—the page that's already there is correct. However, if modifications were made to the page, the new version of the page must be written over the older version—and that takes time.

Each bit can be either 0 or 1 as shown in Table 3.4.

(table 3.4)

The meaning of the bits used in the Page Map Table. As shown in Figure 3.5, each PMT must track the status of, and modifications and references to, its pages. It does so with three bits, each of which can be either 0 or 1.

Status Bit		Modified Bit		Referenced Bit	
Value	Meaning	Value	Meaning	Value	Meaning
0	not in memory	0	not modified	0	not called
1	resides in memory	1	was modified	1	was called

The status bit for all pages in memory is 1. A page must be in memory before it can be swapped out so all of the candidates for swapping have a 1 in this column. The other two bits can be either 0 or 1, so there are four possible combinations of the referenced and modified bits as shown in Table 3.5.

(table 3.5)

Four possible combinations of modified and referenced bits and the meaning of each.

	Modified	Referenced	Meaning
Case 1	0	0	Not modified AND not referenced
Case 2	0	1	Not modified BUT was referenced
Case 3	1	0	Was modified BUT not referenced [impossible?]
Case 4	1	1	Was modified AND was referenced

The FIFO algorithm uses only the modified and status bits when swapping pages, but the LRU looks at all three before deciding which pages to swap out.

Which page would the LRU policy choose first to swap? Of the four cases described in Table 3.5, it would choose pages in Case 1 as the ideal candidates for removal because they've been neither modified nor referenced. That means they wouldn't need to be rewritten to secondary storage, and they haven't been referenced recently. So the pages with zeros for these two bits would be the first to be swapped out.

What's the next most likely candidate? The LRU policy would choose Case 3 next because the other two, Case 2 and Case 4, were recently referenced. The bad news is that Case 3 pages have been modified, so it'll take more time to swap them out. By process of elimination, then, we can say that Case 2 is the third choice and Case 4 would be the pages least likely to be removed.

You may have noticed that Case 3 presents an interesting situation: apparently these pages have been modified without being referenced. How is that possible? The key lies in how the referenced bit is manipulated by the operating system. When the pages are brought into memory, they're all usually referenced at least once and that means that all of the pages soon have a referenced bit of 1. Of course the LRU algorithm would be defeated if every page indicated that it had been referenced. Therefore, to make sure the referenced bit actually indicates *recently* referenced, the operating system periodically resets it to 0. Then, as the pages are referenced during processing the bit is changed from 0 to 1 and the LRU policy is able to identify which pages actually are frequently referenced. As you can imagine, there's one brief instant, just after the bits are reset, in which all of the pages (even the active pages) have reference bits of 0 and are vulnerable. But as processing continues, the most-referenced pages soon have their bits reset to 1 so the risk is minimized.

The Working Set

One innovation that improved the performance of demand paging schemes was the concept of the **working set**. A job's working set is the set of pages residing in memory that can be accessed directly without incurring a page fault.

When a user requests execution of a program, the first page is loaded into memory and execution continues as more pages are loaded: those containing variable declarations, others containing instructions, others containing data, and so on. After a while, most programs reach a fairly stable state and processing continues smoothly with very few additional page faults. At this point the job's working set is in memory, and the program won't generate many page faults until it gets to another phase requiring a different set of pages to do the work—a different working set.

Of course, it's possible that a poorly structured program could require that every one of its pages be in memory before processing can begin.

Fortunately, most programmers structure their work, and this leads to a **locality of reference** during the program's execution, meaning that during any phase of its execution the program references only a small fraction of its pages. For example, if a job is executing a loop then the instructions within the loop are referenced extensively while those outside the loop aren't used at all until the loop is completed—that's locality of reference. The same applies to sequential instructions, subroutine calls (within the subroutine), stack implementations, or access to variables acting as counters or sums, or multidimensional variables such as arrays and tables (only a few of the pages are needed to handle the references).

It would be convenient if all of the pages in a job's working set were loaded into memory at one time to minimize the number of page faults and to speed up processing. But that's easier said than done. To do so the system needs definitive answers to some difficult questions: How many pages comprise the working set? What's the maximum number of pages the operating system will allow for a working set?

The second question is particularly important in time-sharing systems, which regularly swap jobs (or pages of jobs) into memory and back to secondary storage to accommodate the needs of many users. The problem is this: every time a job is reloaded back into memory (or has pages swapped) it has to generate several page faults until its working set is back in memory and processing can continue. It's a time-consuming task for the CPU, which can't be processing jobs during the time it takes to process each page fault, as shown in Figure 3.12.

One solution adopted by many paging systems is to begin by identifying each job's working set and then loading it into memory in its entirety before allowing execution to begin. This is difficult to do before a job is executed but can be identified as its execution proceeds.

In a time-sharing system this means the operating system must keep track of the size and identity of every working set, making sure that the jobs destined for processing at any one time won't exceed the available memory. Some operating systems use a variable working set size and either increase it when necessary (the job requires more processing) or decrease it when necessary. This may mean that the number of jobs in memory will need to be reduced if, by doing so, the system can ensure the completion of each job and the subsequent release of its memory space.

We've looked at several examples of demand paging memory allocation schemes. Demand paging had two advantages. It was the first scheme in which a job was no

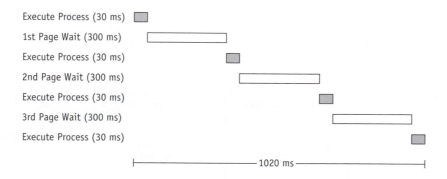

(figure 3.12)

Time line showing the amount of time required to process page faults. The program in this example takes 120 milliseconds (ms) to execute but an additional 900 ms to load the necessary pages into memory. Therefore, job turnaround is 1,020 ms.

longer constrained by the size of physical memory; it introduced the concept of virtual memory. The second advantage was that it utilized memory more efficiently than the previous schemes because the sections of a job that were used seldom or not at all (such as error routines) weren't loaded into memory unless they were specifically requested. Its disadvantage was the increased overhead caused by the tables and the page interrupts. The next allocation scheme built on the advantages of both paging and dynamic partitions.

Segmented Memory Allocation

The concept of segmentation is based on the common practice by programmers of structuring their programs in modules—logical groupings of code. With **segmented memory allocation**, each job is divided into several **segments** of different sizes, one for each module that contains pieces that perform related functions, and was designed to reduce page faults that resulted from having a segment's loop split over two or more pages. A **subroutine** is an example of one such logical group. This is fundamentally different from a paging scheme, which divides the job into several pages all of the same size, each of which often contains pieces from more than one program module.

A second important difference is that main memory is no longer divided into page frames because the size of each segment is different—some are large and some are small. Therefore, as with the dynamic partitions discussed in Chapter 2, memory is allocated in a dynamic manner.

When a program is compiled or assembled, the segments are set up according to the program's structural modules. Each segment is numbered and a **Segment Map Table** (**SMT**) is generated for each job; it contains the segment numbers, their lengths, access rights, status, and (when each is loaded into memory) its location in memory. Figures 3.13 and 3.14 show the same job, Job 1, composed of a main program and two subroutines, together with its Segment Map Table and actual main memory allocation.

(figure 3.13)

Segmented memory allocation. Job 1 includes a main program, Subroutine A, and Subroutine B. It's one job divided into three segments.

As in demand paging, the referenced, modified, and status bits are used in segmentation and appear in the SMT but they aren't shown in Figures 3.13 and 3.14.

The Memory Manager needs to keep track of the segments in memory. This is done with three tables combining aspects of both dynamic partitions and demand paging memory management:
- The Job Table lists every job in process (one for the whole system).
- The Segment Map Table lists details about each segment (one for each job).
- The Memory Map Table monitors the allocation of main memory (one for the whole system).

Like demand paging, the instructions within each segment are ordered sequentially, but the segments don't need to be stored contiguously in memory. We only need to know where each segment is stored. The contents of the segments themselves are contiguous in this scheme.

To access a specific location within a segment we can perform an operation similar to the one used for paged memory management. The only difference is that we work

(figure 3.14)

The Segment Map Table tracks each segment for Job 1.

Segment Map Table for Job 1

Segment no.	Size	Status[1]	Access[2]	Memory address
0	350	Y	E	4000
1	200	Y	E	7000
2	100	N	E	___

[1] Y = in memory;
N = not in memory.

[2] E = Execute only.

with segments instead of pages. The addressing scheme requires the segment number and the displacement within that segment, and, because the segments are of different sizes, the displacement must be verified to make sure it isn't outside of the segment's range.

In Figure 3.15, Segment 1 includes all of Subroutine A so the system finds the beginning address of Segment 1, address 7000, and it begins there.

If the instruction requested that processing begin at Line 100 of Subroutine A (which is possible in languages that support multiple entries into subroutines) then, to locate

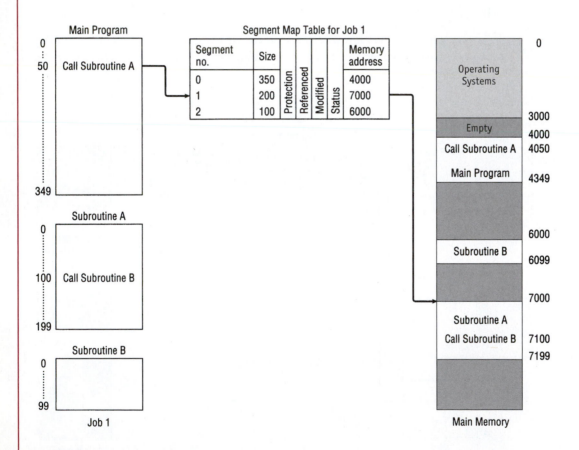

(figure 3.15)

During execution, the main program calls Subroutine A, which triggers the SMT to look up its location in memory.

that line in memory, the Memory Manager would need to add 100 (the displacement) to 7000 (the beginning address of Segment 1). Its code would look like this:

ACTUAL_MEM_LOC = BEGIN_MEM_LOC_OF_SEG + DISPLACEMENT

Can the displacement be larger than the size of the segment? No, not if the program is coded correctly; however, accidents do happen and the Memory Manager must always guard against this possibility by checking the displacement against the size of the segment, verifying that it's not out of bounds.

To access a location in memory when using either paged or segmented memory management, the address is composed of two entries: the page or segment number and the displacement. Therefore, it's a two-dimensional addressing scheme:

SEGMENT NUMBER—DISPLACEMENT

The disadvantage of any allocation scheme in which memory is partitioned dynamically is the return of external fragmentation. Therefore, recompaction of available memory is necessary from time to time (if that schema is used).

As you can see, there are many similarities between paging and segmentation, so they're often confused. The major difference is a conceptual one: pages are physical units that are invisible to the user's program and of fixed sizes; segments are logical units that are visible to the user's program and of variable sizes.

Segmented/Demand Paged Memory Allocation

The **segmented/demand paged memory allocation** scheme evolved from the two we've just discussed. It's a combination of segmentation and demand paging, and it offers the logical benefits of segmentation, as well as the physical benefits of paging. The logic isn't new. The algorithms used by the demand paging and segmented memory management schemes are applied here with only minor modifications.

This allocation scheme doesn't keep each segment as a single contiguous unit but subdivides it into pages of equal size, smaller than most segments, and more easily manipulated than whole segments. Therefore, many of the problems of segmentation (compaction, external fragmentation, and secondary storage handling) are removed because the pages are of fixed length.

This scheme, illustrated in Figure 3.16, requires four tables:
• The Job Table lists every job in process (one for the whole system).
• The Segment Map Table lists details about each segment (one for each job).
• The Page Map Table lists details about every page (one for each segment).
• The Memory Map Table monitors the allocation of the page frames in main memory (one for the whole system).

Note that the tables in Figure 3.16 have been simplified. The SMT actually includes additional information regarding protection (such as the authority to read, write, execute, and delete parts of the file), as well as which users have access to that segment (user only, group only, or everyone—some systems call these access categories owner, group, and world, respectively). In addition, the PMT includes the status, modified, and referenced bits.

To access a location in memory, the system must locate the address, which is composed of three entries: segment number, page number within that segment, and displacement within that page. It's a three-dimensional addressing scheme:

SEGMENT NUMBER–PAGE NUMBER–DISPLACEMENT

The major disadvantages of this memory allocation scheme are the overhead required for the extra tables and the time required to reference the segment table and the page

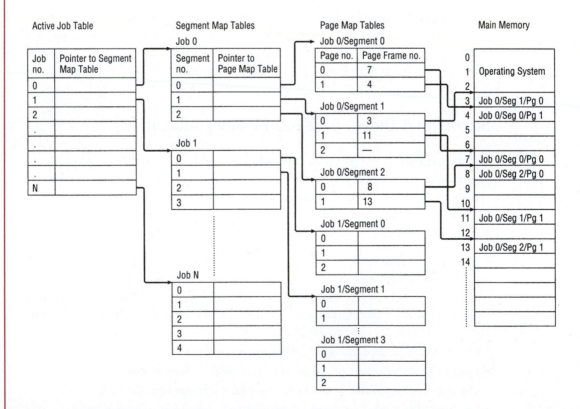

(figure 3.16)

How the Job Table, Segment Map Table, Page Map Table, and main memory interact in a segment/paging scheme.

table. To minimize the number of references, many systems use associative memory to speed up the process.

Associative memory is a name given to several registers that are allocated to each job that's active. Their task is to associate several segment and page numbers belonging to the job being processed with their main memory addresses. These associative registers reside in main memory, and the exact number of registers varies from system to system.

To appreciate the role of associative memory, it's important to understand how the system works with segments and pages. In general, when a job is allocated to the CPU its Segment Map Table is loaded into main memory while the Page Map Tables are loaded only as needed. As pages are swapped between main memory and secondary storage all tables are updated.

Here's a typical procedure: when a page is first requested, the job's SMT is searched to locate its PMT; then the PMT is loaded and searched to determine the page's location in memory. If the page isn't in memory, then a page interrupt is issued, the page is brought into memory, and the table is updated. (As the example indicates, loading the PMT can cause a page interrupt, or fault, as well.) This process is just as tedious as it sounds, but it gets easier. Since this segment's PMT (or part of it) now resides in memory, any other requests for pages within this segment can be quickly accommodated because there's no need to bring the PMT into memory. However, accessing these tables (SMT and PMT) is time-consuming.

That's the problem addressed by associative memory, which stores in memory the information related to the most-recently-used pages. Then, when a page request is issued, two searches begin—one through the segment and page tables and one through the contents of the associative registers.

If the search of the associative registers is successful, then the search through the tables is stopped (or eliminated) and the address translation is performed using the information in the associative registers. However, if the search of associative memory fails, no time is lost because the search through the SMTs and PMTs had already begun (in this schema). When this search is successful and the main memory address from the PMT has been determined, the address is used to continue execution of the program and the reference is also stored in one of the associative registers. If all of the associative registers are full, then an LRU (or other) algorithm is used and the least-recently-referenced associative register is used to hold the information on this requested page.

For example, a system with eight associative registers per job will use them to store the SMT and PMT for the last eight pages referenced by that job. When an address needs to be translated from segment and page numbers to a memory location, the system will look first in the eight associative registers. If a match is found the memory location is taken from the associative register; if there is no match then the SMTs and PMTs will continue to be searched and the new information will be stored in one of the eight registers as a result.

If a job is swapped out to secondary storage during its execution, then all of the information stored in its associative registers is saved, as well as the current PMT and SMT, so the displaced job can be resumed quickly when the CPU is reallocated to it. The primary advantage of a large associative memory is increased speed. The disadvantage is the high cost of the complex hardware required to perform the parallel searches. In some systems the searches do not run in parallel, but the search of the SMT and PMT follows the search of the associative registers.

Virtual Memory

Demand paging made it possible for a program to execute even though only a part of it was loaded into main memory. In effect it removed the restriction imposed on maximum program size. This capability of moving pages at will between main memory and secondary storage gave way to a new concept appropriately named **virtual memory**. Even though only a portion of each program is stored in memory, it gives users the appearance that their programs are being completely loaded in main memory during their entire processing time—a feat that would require an incredible amount of main memory.

Until the implementation of virtual memory, the problem of making programs fit into available memory was left to the users. In the early days, programmers had to limit the size of their programs to make sure they fit into main memory, but sometimes that wasn't possible because the amount of memory allocated to them was too small to get the job done. Clever programmers solved the problem by writing tight programs wherever possible. It was the size of the program that counted most—and the instructions for these tight programs were nearly impossible for anyone but their authors to understand or maintain. The useful life of the program was limited to the employment of its programmer.

During the second generation, programmers started dividing their programs into sections that resembled working sets, really segments, originally called roll in/roll out and now called **overlays**. The program could begin with only the first overlay loaded into memory. As the first section neared completion it would instruct the system to lay the second section of code over the first section already in memory. Then the second section would be processed. As that section finished, it would call in the third section to be overlaid, and so on until the program was finished. Some programs had multiple overlays in main memory at once.

Although the swapping of overlays between main memory and secondary storage was done by the system, the tedious task of dividing the program into sections was done by the programmer. It was the concept of overlays that suggested paging and segmentation and led to virtual memory, which was then implemented through demand paging and segmentation schemes. These schemes are compared in Table 3.6.

Virtual Memory with Paging	Virtual Memory with Segmentation
Allows internal fragmentation within page frames	Doesn't allow internal fragmentation
Doesn't allow external fragmentation	Allows external fragmentation
Programs are divided into equal-sized pages	Programs are divided into unequal-sized segments
Absolute address calculated using page number and displacement	Absolute address calculated using segment number and displacement
Requires PMT	Requires SMT

(table 3.6)

Comparison of virtual memory with paging and segmentation.

Segmentation allowed for sharing program code among users (see Exercise 12 for an example). This means that the shared segment contains: (1) an area where unchangeable code (called **reentrant code**) is stored, and (2) several data areas, one for each user. In this schema, users share the code, which cannot be modified, and can modify the information stored in their own data areas as needed without affecting the data stored in other users' data areas.

Before virtual memory, sharing meant that copies of files were stored in each user's account. This allowed them to load their own copy and work on it at any time. This kind of sharing created a great deal of unnecessary system cost—the I/O overhead in loading the copies and the extra secondary storage needed. With virtual memory, those costs are substantially reduced because shared programs and subroutines are loaded on demand, satisfactorily reducing the storage requirements of main memory (although this is accomplished at the expense of the Memory Map Table).

The use of virtual memory requires cooperation between the Memory Manager (which tracks each page or segment) and the processor hardware (which issues the interrupt and resolves the virtual address). For example, when a page is needed that's not already in memory, a page fault is issued and the Memory Manager chooses a page frame, loads the page, and updates entries in the memory map table and the page map tables.

Virtual memory works well in a multiprogramming environment because most programs spend a lot of time waiting—they wait for I/O to be performed; they wait for pages to be swapped in or out; and, in a time-sharing environment, they wait when their time slice is up (their turn to use the processor is expired). In a multiprogramming environment, the waiting time isn't lost, and the CPU simply moves to another job; this was the advantage of partitions.

Virtual memory has increased the use of several programming techniques. For instance, it aids the development of large software systems because individual pieces can be developed independently and linked later on.

Virtual memory management has several advantages:

• A job's size is no longer restricted to the size of main memory (or the free space within main memory).

• Memory is used more efficiently because the only sections of a job stored in memory are those needed immediately, while those not needed remain in secondary storage.

• It allows an unlimited amount of multiprogramming (which can apply to many jobs, as in dynamic and static partitioning, or many users in a time-sharing environment).

• It eliminates external fragmentation and minimizes internal fragmentation by combining segmentation and paging (internal fragmentation occurs in the program).

• It allows the sharing of code and data.

• It facilitates dynamic linking of program segments.

The advantages far outweigh these disadvantages:

• Increased processor hardware costs.

• Increased overhead for handling paging interrupts.

• Increased software complexity to prevent thrashing.

Cache Memory

As shown in Figure 3.17(a), the original architecture of a computer was such that data and instructions were transferred from secondary storage to main memory and then to special-purpose registers for processing, increasing the amount of time needed to complete a program. However, because in most programs the same instructions are used repeatedly, computer systems designers thought it would be more efficient if the system would not use a complete memory cycle every time an instruction or data value is required. Designers found that this could be done if they placed repeatedly used data in general-purpose registers instead of in main memory, but they found that this technique required extra work for the programmer. Moreover, from the point of view of

(figure 3.17)

Comparison of (a) traditional path used by early computers between main memory and the CPU and (b) path used by modern computers to connect the main memory and the CPU via cache memory

the system this use of general-purpose registers was not be an optimal solution because those registers are often needed to store temporary results from other calculations, and because the amount of instructions used repeatedly often exceeds the capacity of the general-purpose registers.

To solve this problem, modern computer systems have been designed so that data can be automatically stored in an intermediate memory unit called **cache memory**. This adds a middle layer to the original hierarchy. Cache memory can be thought of as being an intermediary between main memory and the special-purpose registers, which are the domain of the CPU, as shown in Figure 3.17(b). We must note that the transfer of data from cache to CPU and registers is a hardware function so it is transparent to the programmer. This is in contrast with the earlier practice of using general-purpose registers, which were directly manipulated by the programmer.

Cache memory is a small high-speed memory unit that a processor can access more rapidly than main memory. Its small size compared to main memory makes it a good candidate for implementing it using faster, more expensive memory chips. It is often five to ten times faster than main memory, matching the speed of the CPU. Therefore, when frequently used data, or instructions are stored in cache memory and memory access time can be cut down significantly, the CPU can execute instructions faster, and the overall performance of the computer system is raised.

A typical microprocessor has two levels of caches: Level 1 (L1) and Level 2 (L2). Information enters the processor through the bus interface unit, which immediately sends one copy to the L2 cache, which is an integral part of the microprocessor and is directly connected to the CPU. A second copy is sent to a pair of L1 caches, which are built directly into the CPU. One of these L1 caches is designed to store instructions, while the other stores data to be used by the instructions. If an instruction needs more data, it is put on hold while the processor looks for it first in the data L1 cache, and then in the larger L2 cache before looking for it in main memory.

Because the L2 cache is an integral part of the microprocessor, data moves at a rate between 2 to 4 times faster between the CPU and the L2 than between the CPU and main memory.

To understand the relationship between main memory and cache memory, consider the relationship between the size of the World Wide Web (WWW) and the size of your private bookmark file. In this case main memory is the WWW and cache memory is your private bookmark file where you collect your most frequently used Web addresses. Your bookmark file is small and may contain only 0.00001 percent of all the addresses in the Web, but the chance that you will soon visit a Web site that is in your bookmark file is high. Therefore, the purpose of your bookmark file is to keep your most recently accessed addresses so you can access them quickly, just as the purpose of cache memory is to keep handy the most recently accessed data and instructions so the CPU can access them repeatedly without wasting time.

Table 3.7 shows the wide range of speeds and sizes for all types of memory, main as well as secondary. As you can see the best, the smallest, access time is given by registers while the worst, longest, access time is given by magnetic tape.

Memory Type	Typical Capacity	Typical Access Time
CPU registers	~500 bytes	1 clock cycle
Cache memory	< 10 MB	1–2 clock cycles
Main memory	< 250 MB	1–4 clock cycles
Magnetic disk	< 10 GB (per device)	5–50 microseconds
Optical disc	< 15 GB (per device)	25 microseconds–1 second
Magnetic tape	< 5 GB (per tape)	Typically measured in seconds

(table 3.7)

A list of relative speeds and sizes for all types of memory. These are sample speeds to show how they compare. Actual speeds vary. The last three constitute secondary storage. Typical access times are used to provide a perspective of the range from the fastest to the slowest access. A clock cycle is the smallest unit of time for a processor.

The movement of data, or instructions, from main memory to cache memory uses a method similar to that used in paging algorithms. First cache memory is divided into blocks of equal size, called slots. Then, when the CPU first requests an instruction or data from a location in main memory, the requested instruction and several others around it are transferred from main memory to cache memory where they are stored in one of the free slots. Moving a block at a time is based on the principle of locality, which states that it is very likely that the next CPU request will be physically close to the one just requested. In addition to the block of data transferred, the slot also contains a label that indicates the main memory address from which the block was copied. When the CPU requests additional information from that location in main memory, cache memory is accessed first, and if the contents of one of the labels in a slot matches the address requested, then access to main memory is not required.

The algorithm to execute one of these "transfers from main memory" is simple to implement as follows:

Main Memory Transfer Algorithm

1 CPU puts the address of a memory location in the Memory Address Register and requests data or an instruction to be retrieved from that address
2 A test is performed to determine if the block containing this address is already in a cache slot:

    If YES, transfer the information to the CPU register – DONE

    If NO: Access main memory for the block containing the requested address

           Allocate a free cache slot to the block

           Perform these in parallel: Transfer the information to CPU

                                      Load the block into slot

    DONE

This algorithm becomes more complicated if there aren't any free slots, which can occur because the size of cache memory is smaller than that of main memory, which means that individual slots cannot be permanently allocated to blocks. To address this contingency the system needs a policy for block replacement, which could be one similar to those used in page replacement.

When designing cache memory one must take into consideration the following four factors:

• *Cache size.* Studies have shown that having any cache, even a small one, can substantially improve the performance of the computer system.
• *Block size.* Because of the principle of locality of reference, as block size increases, the ratio of number of references found in the cache to the total number of references will be high.
• *Block replacement algorithm.* When all the slots are busy and a new block has to be brought into cache, a block that is least likely to be used in the near future should be selected for replacement. However, as we saw in paging, this is nearly impossible to predict. A reasonable course of action is to select a block that has not been used for a long time. Therefore, LRU is the algorithm that's often chosen for block replacement, which requires a hardware mechanism to specify the least recently used slot.
• *Rewrite policy.* When the contents of a block residing in cache are changed, it must be written back to main memory before it is replaced by another block. A rewrite

policy must be in place to determine when this writing will take place. On the one hand, it could be done every time that a change occurs, which would increase the number of memory writes, increasing overhead. On the other hand, it could be done only when the block is replaced or the process is finished, which would minimize overhead but would leave the block in main memory in an inconsistent state. This would create problems in multiprocessor environments and in cases where I/O modules can access main memory directly.

The optimal selection of cache size and replacement algorithm can result in 80 to 90 percent of all requests being in the cache, making for a very efficient memory system. This measure of efficiency, called the cache hit ratio (h), is used to determine the performance of cache memory and represents the percentage of total memory requests that are found in the cache:

$$h = \frac{\texttt{number of requests found in the cache}}{\texttt{total number of requests}} \times 100$$

For example, if the total number of requests is 10 and 6 of those are found in cache memory, then the hit ratio is 60 percent.

```
h = (6 / 10) * 100 = 60%
```

On the other hand, if the total number of requests is 100 and 9 of those are found in cache memory then the hit ratio is only 9 percent.

```
h = (9 / 100) * 100 = 9%
```

Experimental studies have shown that the miss ratio $(1 - h)$, was minimized when cache size was between 8K and 16K, and block size was between 64 and 128 bytes.

Another way to measure the efficiency of a system with cache memory, assuming that the system always checks the cache first, is to compute the average memory access time, ta, using the following formula where tc is the average cache access time and tm is the average main memory access time:

```
ta =  tc + (1 - h) * tm
```

For example, if we know that the average cache access time is 200 nanoseconds (nsec) and the average main memory access time is 1000 nsec, then a system with a hit ratio of 60 percent will have an average memory access time of 600 nsec:

```
ta = 200 + (1 - 0.60) * 1000 = 600 nsec
```

A system with a hit ratio of 9 percent will show an average memory access time of 1110 nsec:

```
ta = 200 + (1 - 0.09) * 1000 = 1110 nsec
```

Case Study: Memory Management in Linux

To highlight the concepts presented in this chapter, we end with a more specific example of how memory is managed in the Linux operating system. Although Linux memory management has many features in common with UNIX, it has some unique characteristics, and it is quite complex.

Virtual memory in Linux is managed using a three-level table hierarchy, which accommodates both 64- and 32-bit architectures. For the example shown in Figure 3.18, each virtual address is made up of four fields, which are used by the Memory Manager to locate the instruction or data requested:

Main Directory   Middle Directory   Page Table Directory   Actual Page Offset

Figure 3.18 refers to the following virtual address:

Job: 1   Page Table: 3   Page: 2   Line: 214

Each job has its own entry in the main directory, which has pointers to each job's middle directory. A job's middle directory contains pointers to its corresponding page table directories. In turn, each page table directory has pointers to the actual pages, as shown in Figure 3.18. Finally, the page offset field is used to locate the instruction or data within the requested page (Line 214).

(figure 3.18)

In Linux virtual memory management, three levels of tables are used to locate a requested instruction or data within a job.

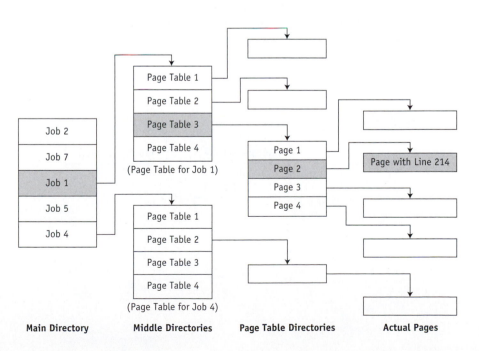

| Main Directory | Middle Directories | Page Table Directories | Actual Pages |

Page Table 1
Page Table 2
Page Table 3
Page Table 4
(Page Table for Job 1)

Page 1
Page 2
Page 3
Page 4

Page with Line 214

Job 2
Job 7
Job 1
Job 5
Job 4

Page Table 1
Page Table 2
Page Table 3
Page Table 4
(Page Table for Job 4)

Virtual memory is implemented in Linux through demand paging. Up to a total of 256 MB of usable memory can be configured into equal-sized page frames, which can be grouped to give more contiguous space to a job. These groups can also be split to accommodate smaller jobs. This process of grouping and splitting is known as the buddy algorithm, and it works as follows.

Let's consider the case where main memory consists of 64 page frames and Job 1 requests 15 page frames. The buddy algorithm first rounds up the request to a power of two (in this case 2^4, which is 16). The group of 64 page frames is divided into two groups of 32, and the lower section is then divided in half. Now there is a group of page frames that can satisfy the request, so the job's pages are copied into the page frames as shown in Figure 3.19(a). When Job 2 requests 8 page frames, the second group of 16 page frames is divided in two and the lower half is given to Job 2, as shown in Figure 3.19(b).

When Job 2 releases its page frames they are combined with the upper 8 page frames to form a group of 16 page frames, as shown in Figure 3.19(c).

The page replacement algorithm used by Linux is an expanded version of the clock algorithm presented in the page replacement policies section of this chapter. Instead of using a single reference bit, Linux uses an 8-bit byte to keep track of a page's activity, which is referred to as its age. Each time a page is referenced, this age variable is incremented. Behind the scenes, at specific intervals, the Memory Manager checks each of these age variables and decreases their value by one. The result of this interaction is that, if a page is not referenced frequently, then its age variable will drop to zero and will be a good candidate for replacement if a page swap is necessary. On the other

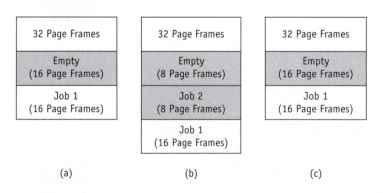

(a)   (b)   (c)

(figure 3.19)

Main memory is divided to accommodate jobs of different sizes. In (a) the original group of 64 page frames is divided to satisfy the request of Job 1 for 16 page frames. In (b) another group of 16 page frames is divided to accommodate Job 2, which needs 8 page frames. In (c), after Job 2 finishes, the two groups of 8 page frames are recombined into a group of 16, while Job 1 continues processing.

hand, a page that is frequently used will have a large age value and will not be a good choice for replacement. Therefore, we can say that Linux uses a form of least frequently used (LRU) replacement policy.

Conclusion

The Memory Manager has the task of allocating memory to each job to be executed, and reclaiming it when execution is completed.

Each scheme we discussed in Chapters 2 and 3 was designed to address a different set of pressing problems but, as we've seen, when some problems were solved, others were created. Table 3.8 shows how the various memory allocation schemes compare.

(table 3.8)

Comparison of memory allocation schemes discussed in Chapters 2 and 3.

Scheme	Problem Solved	Problem Created	Changes in Software
Single-user contiguous		Job size limited to physical memory size; CPU often idle	None
Fixed partitions	Idle CPU time	Internal fragmentation; Job size limited to partition size	Add Processor Scheduler; Add protection handler
Dynamic partitions	Internal fragmentation	External fragmentation	None
Relocatable dynamic partitions	Internal fragmentation	Compaction overhead; Job size limited to physical memory size	Compaction algorithm
Paged	Need for compaction	Memory needed for tables; Job size limited to physical memory size; Internal fragmentation returns	Algorithms to handle Page Map Tables
Demand paged	Job size no longer limited to memory size; More efficient memory use; Allows large-scale multiprogramming and time-sharing	Larger number of tables; Possibility of thrashing; Overhead required by page interrupts; Necessary paging hardware	Page replacement algorithm; Search algorithm for pages in secondary storage
Segmented	Internal fragmentation	Difficulty managing variable-length segments in secondary storage; External fragmentation	Dynamic linking package; Two-dimensional addressing scheme
Segmented/ demand paged	Large virtual memory; Segment loaded on demand	Table handling overhead; Memory needed for page and segment tables	Three-dimensional addressing scheme

The Memory Manager is only one of several managers that make up the operating system. Once the jobs are loaded into memory using a memory allocation scheme, the Processor Manager must allocate the processor to process each job in the most efficient manner possible. We'll see how that's done in the next chapter.

Key Terms

address resolution: the process of changing the address of an instruction or data item to the address in main memory at which it is to be loaded or relocated.

associative memory: the name given to several registers, allocated to each active process, whose contents associate several of the process segments and page numbers with their main memory addresses.

Belady's anomaly: see FIFO anomaly.

cache memory: a small, fast memory used to hold selected data and to provide faster access than would otherwise be possible.

clock cycle: the elapsed time between two ticks of the computer's system clock.

clock page replacement policy: a variation of the LRU policy that removes from main memory the pages that show the least amount of activity during recent clock cycles.

demand paging: a memory allocation scheme that loads a program's page into memory at the time it's needed for processing.

displacement: in a paged or segmented memory allocation environment, the difference between a page's relative address and the actual machine language address. Also called offset.

FIFO anomaly: an unusual circumstance through which adding more page frames causes an increase in page interrupts when using a FIFO page replacement policy. Also known as Belady's anomaly.

first-in first-out (FIFO) policy: a page replacement policy that removes from main memory the pages that were brought in first.

Job Table (JT): a table in main memory that contains two entries for each active job— the size of the job and the memory location where its page map table is stored.

least-recently-used (LRU) policy: a page-replacement policy that removes from main memory the pages that show the least amount of recent activity.

locality of reference: behavior observed in many executing programs in which memory locations recently referenced, and those near them, are likely to be referenced in the near future.

Memory Map Table (MMT): a table in main memory that contains as many entries as there are page frames and lists the location and free/busy status for each one.

offset: *see* displacement.

page: a fixed-size section of a user's job that corresponds to page frames in main memory.

page fault: a type of hardware interrupt caused by a reference to a page not residing in memory. The effect is to move a page out of main memory and into secondary storage so another page can be moved into memory.

page fault handler: the part of the Memory Manager that determines if there are empty page frames in memory so that the requested page can be immediately copied from secondary storage, or determines which page must be swapped out if all page frames are busy. Also known as a page interrupt handler.

page frame: an individual section of main memory of uniform size into which a single page may be loaded.

Page Map Table (PMT): a table in main memory with the vital information for each page including the page number and its corresponding page frame memory address.

page replacement policy: an algorithm used by virtual memory systems to decide which page or segment to remove from main memory when a page frame is needed and memory is full.

page swapping: the process of moving a page out of main memory and into secondary storage so another page can be moved into memory in its place.

paged memory allocation: a memory allocation scheme based on the concept of dividing a user's job into sections of equal size to allow for noncontiguous program storage during execution.

reentrant code: code that can be used by two or more processes at the same time; each shares the same copy of the executable code but has separate data areas.

sector: a division in a disk's track. Sometimes called a "block." The tracks are divided into sectors during the formatting process.

segment: a variable-size section of a user's job that contains a logical grouping of code.

Segment Map Table (SMT): a table in main memory with the vital information for each segment including the segment number and its corresponding memory address.

segmented/demand paged memory allocation: a memory allocation scheme based on the concept of dividing a user's job into logical groupings of code and loading them into memory as needed.

segmented memory allocation: a memory allocation scheme based on the concept of dividing a user's job into logical groupings of code to allow for noncontiguous program storage during execution.

subroutine: also called a "subprogram," a segment of a program that can perform a specific function. Subroutines can reduce programming time when a specific function is required at more than one point in a program.

thrashing: a phenomenon in a virtual memory system where an excessive amount of page swapping back and forth between main memory and secondary storage results in higher overhead and little useful work.

virtual memory: a technique that allows programs to be executed even though they are not stored entirely in memory.

working set: a collection of pages to be kept in main memory for each active process in a virtual memory environment.

Exercises

Research Topic

The key to using memory most efficiently is virtual memory management. Consider both Windows and UNIX operating systems. Compare and contrast how each implements virtual memory. Describe how each one handles page faults, working sets, and page sizes, and how it reconciles thrashing issues. Cite your sources.

Exercises

1. Explain the differences between a page and a segment.
2. List the advantages and disadvantages for each of the memory management schemes presented in this chapter. (Although this was done in Table 3.8, expand on it.)
3. What purpose does the modified bit serve in a demand paging system?
4. Answer these questions:
   a. What is the cause of thrashing?
   b. How does the operating system detect thrashing?
   c. Once thrashing is detected, what can the operating system do to eliminate it?
5. What purpose does the referenced bit serve in a demand paging system?
6. Given that main memory is composed of three page frames for public use and that a program requests pages in the following order:

   d c b a d c e d c b a e

   a. Using the FIFO page removal algorithm, do a page trace analysis indicating page faults with asterisks (*). Then compute the failure and success ratios.
   b. Increase the size of memory so it contains four page frames for public use. Using the same page requests as above and FIFO, do another page trace analysis and compute the failure and success ratios.

c. Did the result correspond with your intuition? Explain.

7. Given that main memory is composed of three page frames for public use and that a program requests pages in the following order:

a b a c a b d b a c d

a. Using the FIFO page removal algorithm, do a page trace analysis indicating page faults with asterisks (*). Then compute the failure and success ratios.

b. Using the LRU page removal algorithm do a page trace analysis and compute the failure and success ratios.

c. Which is better? Why do you think it's better? Can you make general statements from this example? Why or why not?

d. Let's define "most-recently-used" (MRU) as a page removal algorithm that removes from memory the most recently used page. Do a page trace analysis using the same page requests as before and compute the failure and success ratios.

e. Which of the three page removal algorithms is best, and why do you think so?

8. To implement LRU each page needs a referenced bit. If we wanted to implement a least-frequently-used (LFU) page removal algorithm, in which the page that was used the least would be removed from memory, what would we need to add to the tables? What software modifications would have to be made to support this new algorithm?

Advanced Exercises

9. Given that main memory is composed of four page frames for public use, use the following table to answer all parts of this problem:

Page Frame	Time When Loaded	Time When Last Referenced	Referenced Bit	Modified Bit
0	126	279	0	0
1	230	280	1	0
2	120	282	1	1
3	160	290	1	1

a. The contents of which page frame would be swapped out by FIFO?

b. The contents of which page frame would be swapped out by LRU?

c. The contents of which page frame would be swapped out by MRU?

d. The contents of which page frame would be swapped out by LFU?

10. Given that main memory is composed of four page frames and that a program has been divided into eight pages (numbered 0 through 7):

   a. How many page faults will occur using FIFO with a request list of: 0, 1, 7, 2, 3, 2, 7, 1, 0, 3 if the four page frames are initially empty?

   b. How many page faults will occur with the same conditions but using LRU?

11. Given three subroutines of 700, 200, and 500 words each, if segmentation is used then the total memory needed is the sum of the three sizes (if all three routines are loaded). However, if paging is used then some storage space is lost because subroutines rarely fill the last page completely, and that results in internal fragmentation. Determine the total amount of wasted memory due to internal fragmentation when the three subroutines are loaded into memory using each of the following page sizes:

   a. 200 words

   b. 500 words

   c. 600 words

   d. 700 words

12. Given the following Segment Map Tables for two jobs:

SMT for Job 1

Segment Number	Memory Location
0	4096
1	6144
2	9216
3	2048
4	7168

SMT for Job 2

Segment number	Memory location
0	2048
1	6144
2	9216

   a. Which segments, if any, are shared between the two jobs?

   b. If the segment now located at 7168 is swapped out and later reloaded at 8192, and the segment now at 2048 is swapped out and reloaded at 1024, what would the new segment tables look like?

13. Given a system with main memory and cache memory with the following characteristics:

    - Average main memory access time (tm) = 1200 nsec
    - Average cache memory access time (tc) = 100 nsec
    - Cost for cache memory (Cc) = .01 cents per bit
    - Cost for main memory (Cm) = .001 cents per bit

    Answer the following questions:

    a. What is the cost of 1 MB of main memory? (Give your answer in dollars and cents.)
    b. What is the cost of 1 MB of main memory if it is implemented using cache memory technology? (give your answer in dollars and cents)
    c. What is the hit ratio if the total number of requests is 200 and 130 of those are found in cache memory?
    d. What is the average memory access (ta) if the hit ratio is 80 percent? (Give your answer in nsec.)

14. Given a system with main memory and cache memory with the following characteristics:

    - Average main memory access time (tm) = 1000 nsec
    - Average cache memory access time (tc) = 200 nsec
    - Cost for cache memory (Cc) = .02 cents per bit
    - Cost for main memory (Cm) = .0001 cents per bit

    Answer the following questions:

    a. What is the cost of 1 MB of main memory? (Give your answer in dollars and cents.)
    b. What is the cost of 1 MB of main memory if it is implemented using cache memory technology? (Give your answer in dollars and cents.)
    c. What is the hit ratio if the total number of requests is 20 and 16 of those are found in cache memory?
    d. What is the average memory access (ta) if the hit ratio is 75 percent? (Give your answer in nsec.)

Programming Exercises

15. This problem studies the effect of changing page sizes in a demand paging system.

    The following sequence of requests for program words is taken from a 460-word program: 10, 11, 104, 170, 73, 309, 185, 245, 246, 434, 458, 364. Main memory can hold a total of 200 words for this program and the page frame size will match the size of the pages into which the program has been divided.

Calculate the page numbers according to the page size; divide by the page size, and the quotient gives the page number. The number of page frames in memory is the total number, 200, divided by the page size. For example, in problem (a) the page size is 100, which means that requests 10 and 11 are on Page 0, and requests 104 and 170 are on Page 1. The number of page frames is two.

a. Find the success frequency for the request list using a FIFO replacement algorithm and a page size of 100 words (there are two page frames).

b. Find the success frequency for the request list using a FIFO replacement algorithm and a page size of 20 words (10 pages, 0 through 9).

c. Find the success frequency for the request list using a FIFO replacement algorithm and a page size of 200 words.

d. What do your results indicate? Can you make any general statements about what happens when page sizes are halved or doubled?

e. Are there any overriding advantages in using smaller pages? What are the offsetting factors? Remember that transferring 200 words of information takes less than twice as long as transferring 100 words because of the way secondary storage devices operate (the transfer rate is higher than the access [search/find] rate).

f. Repeat (a) through (c) above, using a main memory of 400 words. The size of each page frame will again correspond to the size of the page.

g. What happened when more memory was given to the program? Can you make some general statements about this occurrence? What changes might you expect to see if the request list was much longer, as it would be in real life?

h. Could this request list happen during the execution of a real program? Explain.

i. Would you expect the success rate of an actual program under similar conditions to be higher or lower than the one in this problem?

16. Given the following information for an assembly language program:

Job size = 3126 bytes

Page size = 1042 bytes

instruction at memory location 532:   Load 1, 2098

instruction at memory location 1156:   Add 1, 2087

instruction at memory location 2086:   Sub 1, 1052

data at memory location 1052:   015672

data at memory location 2098:   114321

data at memory location 2087:   077435

a. How many pages are needed to store the entire job?

b. Compute the page number and displacement for each of the byte addresses where the data is stored. (Remember that page numbering starts at zero).

c. Determine whether the page number and displacements are legal for this job.

d. Explain why the page number and/or displacements may not be legal for this job.

e. Indicate what action the operating system might take when a page number or displacement is not legal.

Chapter 4 | Processor Management

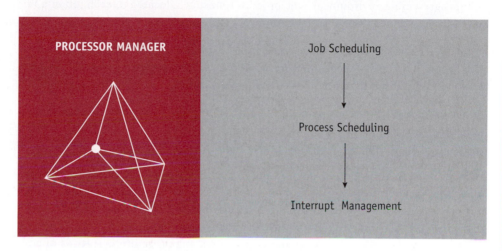

"*Nature acts by progress . . . It goes and returns, then advances further, then twice as much backward, then more forward than ever.*"

Blaise Pascal (1623–1662)

Learning Objectives

After completing this chapter, you should be able to describe:

- The difference between job scheduling and process scheduling, and how they relate
- The advantages and disadvantages of process scheduling algorithms that are preemptive versus those that are nonpreemptive
- The goals of process scheduling policies
- Up to six different process scheduling algorithms
- The role of internal interrupts and the tasks performed by the interrupt handler.

In the previous two chapters we explained how main memory is allocated to the system's users. In this chapter we'll see how the Processor Manager allocates a single CPU to execute the jobs of those users. Information on how operating systems manage processors can be found in the processor management sections of Chapters 13-15.

Overview

In a single-user system, the processor is busy only when the user is executing a job—at all other times it is idle. Processor management in this environment is simple. However, when there are many users with many jobs on the system (this is known as a **multiprogramming** environment), the processor must be allocated to each job in a fair and efficient manner, which can be a complex task, as we'll see in this chapter.

Before we begin, let's clearly define some terms. A **program** is an inactive unit, such as a file stored on a disk. A program is not a process. To an operating system, a program or job is a unit of work that has been submitted by the user.

On the other hand, a **process** is an active entity that requires a set of resources, including a processor and special registers, to perform its function. A process, also called a **task,** is a single instance of an executable program.

As mentioned in Chapter 1, a **thread** is a portion of a process that can run independently. For example, if your system allows processes to have a single thread of control and you want to see a series of pictures on a friend's Web site, you can instruct the browser to establish one connection between the two sites and download one picture at a time. However, if your system allows processes to have multiple threads of control, then you can request several pictures at the same time and the browser will set up multiple connections and download several pictures at once.

The **processor,** also known as the CPU (for central processing unit), is the part of the machine that performs the calculations and executes the programs.

Multiprogramming requires that the processor be allocated to each job or to each process for a period of time and deallocated at an appropriate moment. If the processor is deallocated during a program's execution, it must be done in such a way that it can be restarted later as easily as possible. It's a delicate procedure. To demonstrate, let's look at an everyday example.

Here you are, confident you can put together a toy despite the warning that some assembly is required. Armed with the instructions and lots of patience, you embark on your task—to read the directions, collect the necessary tools, follow each step in turn, and turn out the finished product.

The first step is to join Part A to Part B with a 2-inch screw, and as you complete it you check off Step 1. Inspired by your success, you move on to Step 2 and then Step 3. You've only just completed the third step when a neighbor is injured while working with a power tool and cries for help.

Quickly you check off Step 3 in the directions so you know where you left off, then you drop your tools and race to your neighbor's side. After all, someone's immediate need is more important than your eventual success with the toy. Now you find your-self engaged in a very different task: following the instructions in a first-aid book us-ing bandages and antiseptic.

Once the injury has been successfully treated you return to your previous job. As you pick up your tools you refer to the instructions and see that you should begin with Step 4. You then continue with this project until it is finally completed.

In operating system terminology, you played the part of the *CPU* or *processor*. There were two *programs*, or *jobs*—one was the mission to assemble the toy and the second was to bandage the injury. When you were assembling the toy (Job A), each step you performed was a *process*. The call for help was an *interrupt* and when you left the toy to treat your wounded friend, you left for a *higher priority program*. When you were interrupted, you performed a *context switch* when you marked Step 3 as the last com-pleted instruction and put down your tools. Attending to the neighbor's injury became Job B. While you were executing the first-aid instructions each of the steps you exe-cuted was again a *process*. And, of course, when each job was completed it was *fin-ished* or terminated.

The Processor Manager would identify the series of events as follows:

get the input for Job A	(find the instructions in the box)
identify resources	(collect the necessary tools)
execute the process	(follow each step in turn)
interrupt	(neighbor calls)
context switch to Job B	(mark your place in the instructions)
get the input for Job B	(find your first-aid book)
identify resources	(collect the medical supplies)
execute the process	(follow each first-aid step)
terminate Job B	(return home)
context switch to Job A	(prepare to resume assembly)
resume executing interrupted process	(follow remaining steps in turn)
terminate Job A	(turn out the finished toy)

As we've shown, a single processor can be shared by several jobs, or several processes, but if, and only if, the operating system has a scheduling policy, as well as a schedul-ing algorithm, to determine when to stop working on one job and proceed to another.

In this example, the scheduling algorithm was based on priority: you worked on the processes belonging to Job A until a higher priority job came along. Although this was a good algorithm in this case, a priority-based scheduling algorithm isn't always best, as we'll see later in this chapter.

113

Job Scheduling Versus Process Scheduling

The Processor Manager is a composite of two submanagers: one in charge of job scheduling and the other in charge of process scheduling. They're known as the **Job Scheduler** and the **Process Scheduler**.

Typically a user views a job either as a series of global job steps—compilation, loading, and execution—or as one all-encompassing step—execution. However, the scheduling of jobs is actually handled on two levels by most operating systems. If we return to the example presented earlier, we can see that a hierarchy exists between the Job Scheduler and the Process Scheduler.

The scheduling of the two jobs, to assemble the toy and to bandage the injury, was on a first-come, first-served and priority basis. Each job is initiated by the Job Scheduler based on certain criteria. Once a job is selected for execution, the Process Scheduler determines when each step, or set of steps, is executed—a decision that's also based on certain criteria. When you started assembling the toy, each step in the assembly instructions would have been selected for execution by the Process Scheduler.

Therefore, each job (or program) passes through a hierarchy of managers. Since the first one it encounters is the Job Scheduler, this is also called the **high-level scheduler.** It is only concerned with selecting jobs from a queue of incoming jobs and placing them in the process queue, whether batch or interactive, based on each job's characteristics. The Job Scheduler's goal is to put the jobs in a sequence that will use all of the system's resources as fully as possible.

This is an important function. For example, if the Job Scheduler selected several jobs to run consecutively and each had a lot of I/O, then the I/O devices would be kept very busy. The CPU might be busy handling the I/O (if an I/O controller were not used) so little computation might get done. On the other hand, if the Job Scheduler selected several consecutive jobs with a great deal of computation, then the CPU would be very busy. The I/O devices would be idle waiting for I/O requests. Therefore, the Job Scheduler strives for a balanced mix of jobs that require large amounts of I/O interaction and jobs that require large amounts of computation. Its goal is to keep most components of the computer system busy most of the time.

Process Scheduler

Most of this chapter is dedicated to the Process Scheduler because after a job has been placed on the READY queue by the Job Scheduler, the Process Scheduler takes over. It determines which jobs will get the CPU, when, and for how long. It also decides when processing should be interrupted, determines which queues the job should be moved to during its execution, and recognizes when a job has concluded and should be terminated.

The Process Scheduler is the **low-level scheduler** that assigns the CPU to execute the processes of those jobs placed on the ready queue by the Job Scheduler. This becomes a crucial function when the processing of several jobs has to be orchestrated—just as when you had to set aside your assembly and rush to help your neighbor.

To schedule the CPU, the Process Scheduler takes advantage of a common trait among most computer programs: they alternate between CPU cycles and I/O cycles. Notice that the following job has one relatively long CPU cycle and two very brief I/O cycles:

```
{
printf("\nEnter the first integer: ");
scanf("%d", &a);                           ⎫
printf("\nEnter the second integer: ");    ⎬  I/O cycle
scanf("%d", &b);                           ⎭

c = a+b                                    ⎫
d = (a*b)-c                                ⎬  CPU cycle
e = a-b                                    ⎭
f = d/e

printf("\n a+b= %d", c);                   ⎫
printf("\n (a*b)-c = %d", d);              ⎬  I/O cycle
printf("\n a-b = %d", e);                  ⎭
printf("\n d/e = %d", f);
}
```

Although the duration and frequency of CPU cycles vary from program to program, there are some general tendencies that can be exploited when selecting a scheduling algorithm. For example, **I/O-bound** jobs (such as printing a series of documents) have many brief CPU cycles and long I/O cycles, whereas **CPU-bound** jobs (such as finding the first 300 prime numbers) have long CPU cycles and shorter I/O cycles. The total effect of all CPU cycles, from both I/O-bound and CPU-bound jobs, approximates a Poisson distribution curve as shown in Figure 4.1.

In a highly interactive environment there's also a third layer of the Processor Manager called the **middle-level scheduler.** In some cases, especially when the system is overloaded, the middle-level scheduler finds it is advantageous to remove active jobs from memory to reduce the degree of multiprogramming and thus allow jobs to be completed faster. The jobs that are swapped out and eventually swapped back in are managed by the middle-level scheduler.

(figure 4.1)

Distribution of CPU cycle times. This distribution shows a greater number of jobs requesting short CPU cycles (the frequency peaks close to the low end of the CPU cycle axis), and fewer jobs requesting long CPU cycles.

In a single-user environment, there's no distinction made between job and process scheduling because only one job is active in the system at any given time. So the CPU and all other resources are dedicated to that job, and to each of its processes in turn, until the job is completed.

Job and Process Status

As a job moves through the system it's always in one of five states (or at least three) as it changes from HOLD to READY to RUNNING to WAITING and eventually to FINISHED as shown in Figure 4.2. These are called the **job status** or the **process status**.

Here's how the job status changes when a user submits a job to the system via batch or interactive mode. When the job is accepted by the system, it's put on HOLD and placed in a queue. In some systems the job spooler (or disk controller) creates a table with the characteristics of each job in the queue and notes the important features of

(figure 4.2)

A typical job (or process) changes status as it moves through the system from HOLD to FINISHED.

the job, such as an estimate of CPU time, priority, special I/O devices required, and maximum memory required. This table is used by the Job Scheduler to decide which job is to be run next.

From HOLD, the job moves to READY when it's ready to run but is waiting for the CPU. In some systems, the job (or process) might be placed on the READY list directly. RUNNING, of course, means that the job is being processed. In a single processor system this is one "job" or process. WAITING means that the job can't continue until a specific resource is allocated or an I/O operation has finished. Upon completion, the job is FINISHED and returned to the user.

The transition from one job or process status to another is initiated by either the Job Scheduler or the Process Scheduler:

• The transition from HOLD to READY is initiated by the Job Scheduler according to some predefined policy. At this point the availability of enough main memory and any requested devices are checked.

• The transition from READY to RUNNING is handled by the Process Scheduler according to some predefined algorithm (i.e., FCFS, SJN, priority scheduling, SRT, or round robin—all of which will be discussed shortly).

• The transition from RUNNING back to READY is handled by the Process Scheduler according to some predefined time limit or other criterion, for example a priority interrupt.

• The transition from RUNNING to WAITING is handled by the Process Scheduler and is initiated by an instruction in the job such as a command to READ, WRITE, or other I/O request, or one that requires a page fetch.

• The transition from WAITING to READY is handled by the Process Scheduler and is initiated by a signal from the I/O device manager that the I/O request has been satisfied and the job can continue. In the case of a page fetch, the page fault handler will signal that the page is now in memory and the process can be placed on the READY queue.

• Eventually, the transition from RUNNING to FINISHED is initiated by the Process Scheduler or the Job Scheduler either when (1) the job is successfully completed and it ends execution or (2) the operating system indicates that an error has occurred and the job is being terminated prematurely.

Process Control Blocks

Each process in the system is represented by a data structure called a **Process Control Block (PCB)** that performs the same function as a traveler's passport. The PCB (illustrated in Figure 4.3) contains the basic information about the job including what it is, where it's going, how much of its processing has been completed, where it's stored, and how much it has spent in using resources.

Process Identification
Process Status
Process State: ☐ Process Status Word   ☐ Register Contents   ☐ Main Memory   ☐ Resources   ☐ Process Priority
Accounting

(figure 4.3)

Contents of each job's Process Control Block.

Process Identification

Each job is uniquely identified by the user's identification and a pointer connecting it to its descriptor (supplied by the Job Scheduler when the job first enters the system and is placed on HOLD).

Process Status

This indicates the current status of the job—HOLD, READY, RUNNING, or WAIT-ING—and the resources responsible for that status.

Process State

This contains all of the information needed to indicate the current state of the job such as:

• *Process Status Word*—the current instruction counter and register contents when the job isn't running but is either on HOLD or is READY or WAITING. If the job is RUNNING this information is left undefined.

• *Register Contents*—the contents of the register if the job has been interrupted and is waiting to resume processing.

• *Main Memory*—pertinent information, including the address where the job is stored and, in the case of virtual memory, the mapping between virtual and physical memory locations.

• *Resources*—information about all resources allocated to this job. Each resource has an identification field listing its type and a field describing details of its allocation such as the sector address on a disk. These resources can be hardware units (disk drives or printers, for example) or files.

• *Process Priority*—used by systems using a priority scheduling algorithm to select which job will be run next.

Accounting

This contains information used mainly for billing purposes and performance measurement. It indicates what kind of resources the job used and for how long. Typical charges include:

- Amount of CPU time used from beginning to end of its execution.

- Total time the job was in the system until it exited.

- Main storage occupancy—how long the job stayed in memory until it finished execution. This is usually a combination of time and space used; for example, in a paging system it may be recorded in units of page-seconds.

- Secondary storage used during execution. This, too, is recorded as a combination of time and space used.

- System programs used such as compilers, editors, or utilities.

- Number and type of I/O operations, including I/O transmission time, that includes utilization of channels, control units, and devices.

- Time spent waiting for I/O completion.

- Number of input records read (specifically, those entered online or coming from optical scanners, card readers, or other input devices), and number of output records written (specifically, those sent to the line printer). This last one distinguishes between secondary storage devices and typical I/O devices.

PCBs and Queueing

A job's PCB is created when the Job Scheduler accepts the job and is updated as the job progresses from the beginning to the end of its execution.

Queues use PCBs to track jobs the same way customs officials use passports to track international visitors. The PCB contains all of the data about the job needed by the operating system to manage the processing of the job. As the job moves through the system its progress is noted in the PCB.

The PCBs, not the jobs, are linked to form the queues as shown in Figure 4.4. Although each PCB is not drawn in detail the reader should imagine each queue as a linked list of PCBs. The PCBs for every ready job are linked on the READY queue, and all of the PCBs for the jobs just entering the system are linked on the HOLD queue. The jobs that are WAITING, however, are linked together by "reason for waiting," so the PCBs for the jobs in this category are linked into several queues. For example, the PCBs for jobs that are waiting for I/O on a specific disk drive are linked together, while those waiting for the line printer are linked in a different queue. These queues need to be managed in an orderly fashion and that's determined by the process scheduling policies and algorithms.

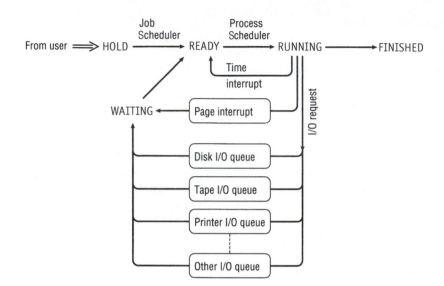

(figure 4.4)

Queuing paths from HOLD to FINISHED. The Job and Processor Schedulers release the resources when the job leaves the RUNNING state.

Process Scheduling Policies

In a multiprogramming environment there are usually more jobs to be executed than could possibly be run at one time. Before the operating system can schedule them, it needs to resolve three limitations of the system: (1) there are a finite number of resources (such as disk drives, printers, and tape drives); (2) some resources, once they're allocated, can't be shared with another job (e.g., printers); and (3) some resources require operator intervention—that is, they can't be reassigned automatically from job to job (such as tape drives).

What's a good **process scheduling policy**? Several criteria come to mind, but notice in the list below that some contradict each other:

• *Maximize throughput*. Run as many jobs as possible in a given amount of time. This could be accomplished easily by running only short jobs or by running jobs without interruptions.

• *Minimize response time*. Quickly turn around interactive requests. This could be done by running only interactive jobs and letting the batch jobs wait until the interactive load ceases.

• *Minimize turnaround time*. Move entire jobs in and out of the system quickly. This could be done by running all batch jobs first (because batch jobs can be grouped to run more efficiently than interactive jobs).

• *Minimize waiting time*. Move jobs out of the READY queue as quickly as possible. This could only be done by reducing the number of users allowed on the system so the CPU would be available immediately whenever a job entered the READY queue.

- *Maximize CPU efficiency*. Keep the CPU busy 100 percent of the time. This could be done by running only CPU-bound jobs (and not I/O-bound jobs).
- *Ensure fairness for all jobs*. Give everyone an equal amount of CPU and I/O time. This could be done by not giving special treatment to any job, regardless of its processing characteristics or priority.

As we can see from this list, if the system favors one type of user then it hurts another or doesn't efficiently use its resources. The final decision rests with the system designer, who must determine which criteria are most important for that specific system. For example, you might decide to "maximize CPU utilization while minimizing response time and balancing the use of all system components through a mix of I/O-bound and CPU-bound jobs." So you would select the scheduling policy that most closely satisfies your criteria.

Although the Job Scheduler selects jobs to ensure that the READY and I/O queues remain balanced, there are instances when a job claims the CPU for a very long time before issuing an I/O request. If I/O requests are being satisfied (this is done by an I/O controller and will be discussed later), this extensive use of the CPU will build up the READY queue while emptying out the I/O queues, which creates an unacceptable imbalance in the system.

To solve this problem, the Process Scheduler often uses a timing mechanism and periodically interrupts running processes when a predetermined slice of time has expired. When that happens, the scheduler suspends all activity on the job currently running and reschedules it into the READY queue; it will be continued later. The CPU is now allocated to another job that runs until one of three things happens: the timer goes off, the job issues an I/O command, or the job is finished. Then the job moves to the READY queue, the WAIT queue, or the FINISHED queue, respectively. An I/O request is called a **natural wait** in multiprogramming environments (it allows the processor to be allocated to another job).

A scheduling strategy that interrupts the processing of a job and transfers the CPU to another job is called a **preemptive scheduling policy;** it is widely used in time-sharing environments. The alternative, of course, is a **nonpreemptive scheduling policy,** which functions without external interrupts (interrupts external to the job). Therefore, once a job captures the processor and begins execution, it remains in the RUNNING state uninterrupted until it issues an I/O request (natural wait) or until it is finished (with exceptions made for infinite loops, which are interrupted by both preemptive and non-preemptive policies).

Process Scheduling Algorithms

The Process Scheduler relies on a **process scheduling algorithm,** based on a specific policy, to allocate the CPU and move jobs through the system. Early operating systems used nonpreemptive policies designed to move batch jobs through the system as efficiently as possible. Most current systems, with their emphasis on interactive use and **response time,** use an algorithm that takes care of the immediate requests of interactive users.

Here are six process scheduling algorithms that have been used extensively.

First-Come, First-Served

First-come, first-served (FCFS) is a nonpreemptive scheduling algorithm that handles jobs according to their arrival time: the earlier they arrive, the sooner they're served. It's a very simple algorithm to implement because it uses a FIFO queue. This algorithm is fine for most batch systems, but it is unacceptable for interactive systems because interactive users expect quick response times.

With FCFS, as a new job enters the system its PCB is linked to the end of the READY queue and it is removed from the front of the queue when the processor becomes available—that is, after it has processed all of the jobs before it in the queue.

In a strictly FCFS system there are no WAIT queues (each job is run to completion), although there may be systems in which control (context) is switched on a natural wait (I/O request) and then the job resumes on I/O completion.

The following examples presume a strictly FCFS environment (no multiprogramming). **Turnaround time** is unpredictable with the FCFS policy; consider the following three jobs:

- Job A has a CPU cycle of 15 milliseconds.
- Job B has a CPU cycle of 2 milliseconds.
- Job C has a CPU cycle of 1 millisecond.

For each job, the CPU cycle contains both the actual CPU usage and the I/O requests. That is, it is the total run time. Using an FCFS algorithm with an arrival sequence of A, B, C, the timeline (Gantt chart) is shown in Figure 4.5.

(figure 4.5)

Timeline for job sequence A, B, C using the FCFS algorithm

If all three jobs arrive almost simultaneously, we can calculate that the turnaround time for Job A is 15, for Job B is 17, and for Job C is 18. So the average turnaround time is:

$$\frac{15 + 17 + 18}{3} = 16.67$$

However, if the jobs arrived in a different order, say C, B, A, then the results using the same FCFS algorithm would be as shown in Figure 4.6.

(figure 4.6)

Timeline for job sequence
C, B, A using the FCFS
algorithm.

Job C	Job B	Job A	
0 1	3		18

In this example the turnaround time for Job A is 18, for Job B is 3, and for Job C is 1 and the average turnaround time is:

$$\frac{18 + 3 + 1}{3} = 7.3$$

That's quite an improvement over the first sequence. Unfortunately, these two examples illustrate the primary disadvantage of using the FCFS concept—the average turnaround times vary widely and are seldom minimized. In fact, when there are three jobs in the READY queue, the system has only a 1 in 6 chance of running the jobs in the most advantageous sequence (C, B, A). With four jobs the odds fall to 1 in 24, and so on.

If one job monopolizes the system, the extent of its overall effect on system performance depends on the scheduling policy and whether the job is CPU-bound or I/O-bound. While a job with a long CPU cycle (in this example, Job A) is using the CPU, the other jobs in the system are waiting for processing or finishing their I/O requests (if an I/O controller is used) and joining the READY queue to wait for their turn to use the processor. If the I/O requests are not being serviced, the I/O queues would remain stable while the READY list grew (with new arrivals). In extreme cases, the READY queue could fill to capacity while the I/O queues would be empty, or stable, and the I/O devices would sit idle.

On the other hand, if the job is processing a lengthy I/O cycle, the I/O queues quickly build to overflowing and the CPU could be sitting idle (if an I/O controller is used). This situation is eventually resolved when the I/O-bound job finishes its I/O cycle, the queues start moving again, and the system can recover from the bottleneck.

In a strictly FCFS algorithm, neither situation occurs. However, the turnaround time is variable (unpredictable). For this reason, FCFS is a less attractive algorithm than one that would serve the shortest job first, as the next scheduling algorithm does, even in a nonmultiprogramming environment.

Shortest Job Next

Shortest job next (SJN) is a nonpreemptive scheduling algorithm (also known as shortest job first, or SJF) that handles jobs based on the length of their CPU cycle time. It's easiest to implement in batch environments where the estimated CPU time required to run the job is given in advance by each user at the start of each job. However, it doesn't work in interactive systems because users don't estimate in advance the CPU time required to run their jobs.

For example, here are four batch jobs, all in the READY queue, for which the CPU cycle, or run time, is estimated as follows:

Job: A   B   C   D
CPU cycle: 5   2   6   4

The SJN algorithm would review the four jobs and schedule them for processing in this order: B, D, A, C. The timeline is shown in Figure 4.7.

(figure 4.7)

Timeline for job sequence B, D, A, C using the SJN algorithm.

The average turnaround time is:

$$\frac{2 + 6 + 11 + 17}{4} = 9.0$$

Let's take a minute to see why this algorithm can be proved to be optimal and will consistently give the minimum average turnaround time. We'll use the previous example to derive a general formula.

If we look at Figure 4.7, we can see that Job B finishes in its given time (2), Job D finishes in its given time plus the time it waited for B to run (4 + 2), Job A finishes in its given time plus D's time plus B's time (5 + 4 + 2), and Job C finishes in its given time plus that of the previous three (6 + 5 + 4 + 2). So when calculating the average we have:

$$\frac{[(2) + (4 + 2) + (5 + 4 + 2) + (6 + 5 + 4 + 2)]}{4} = 9.0$$

As you can see, the time for the first job appears in the equation four times—once for each job. Similarly, the time for the second job appears three times (the number of jobs minus one). The time for the third job appears twice (number of jobs minus 2) and the time for the fourth job appears only once (number of jobs minus 3).

So the above equation can be rewritten as:

$$\frac{[4*2 + 3*4 + 2*5 + 1*6]}{4} = 9.0$$

Because the time for the first job appears in the equation four times, it has four times the effect on the average time than does the length of the fourth job, which appears only once. Therefore, if the first job requires the shortest computation time, followed in turn by the other jobs, ordered from shortest to longest, then the result will be the smallest possible average. The formula for the average is as follows:

$$\frac{[t_1(n) + t_2(n-1) + t_3(n-2) + ... + t_n(1)]}{n}$$

where n is the number of jobs in the queue and $t_j (j = 1, 2, 3,...,n)$ is the length of the CPU cycle for each of the jobs.

However, the SJN algorithm is optimal only when all of the jobs are available at the same time and the CPU estimates are available and accurate.

Priority Scheduling

Priority scheduling is a nonpreemptive algorithm and one of the most common scheduling algorithms in batch systems, even though it may give slower turnaround to some users. This algorithm gives preferential treatment to important jobs. It allows the programs with the highest priority to be processed first, and they aren't interrupted until their CPU cycles (run times) are completed or a natural wait occurs. If two or more jobs with equal priority are present in the READY queue, the processor is allocated to the one that arrived first (first-come first-served within priority).

Priorities can be assigned by a system administrator using characteristics extrinsic to the jobs. For example, they can be assigned based on the position of the user (researchers first, students last) or, in commercial environments, they can be purchased by the users who pay more for higher priority to guarantee the fastest possible processing of their jobs. With a priority algorithm, jobs are usually linked to one of several READY queues by the Job Scheduler based on their priority so the Process Scheduler manages multiple READY queues instead of just one. Details about multiple queues are presented later in this chapter.

Priorities can also be determined by the Processor Manager based on characteristics intrinsic to the jobs such as:

• *Memory requirements*. Jobs requiring large amounts of memory could be allocated lower priorities than those requesting small amounts of memory, or vice versa.

- *Number and type of peripheral devices.* Jobs requiring many peripheral devices would be allocated lower priorities than those requesting fewer devices.
- *Total CPU time.* Jobs having a long CPU cycle, or estimated run time, would be given lower priorities than those having a brief estimated run time.
- *Amount of time already spent in the system.* This is the total amount of elapsed time since the job was accepted for processing. Some systems increase the priority of jobs that have been in the system for an unusually long time to expedite their exit. This is known as **aging**.

These criteria are used to determine default priorities in many systems. The default priorities can be overruled by specific priorities named by users.

There are also preemptive priority schemes. These will be discussed later in this chapter in the section on multiple queues.

Shortest Remaining Time

Shortest remaining time (SRT) is the preemptive version of the SJN algorithm. The processor is allocated to the job closest to completion—but even this job can be preempted if a newer job in the READY queue has a time to completion that's shorter.

This algorithm can't be implemented in an interactive system because it requires advance knowledge of the CPU time required to finish each job. It is often used in batch environments, when it is desirable to give preference to short jobs, even though SRT involves more overhead than SJN because the operating system has to frequently monitor the CPU time for all the jobs in the READY queue and must perform context switching for the jobs being swapped (switched) at preemption time (not necessarily swapped out to the disk, although this might occur as well).

The example in Figure 4.8 shows how the SRT algorithm works with four jobs that arrived in quick succession (1 CPU cycle apart).

Arrival time: 0   1   2   3

Job: A   B   C   D

CPU cycle: 6   3   1   4

In this case the turnaround time is the completion time of each job minus its arrival time:

Job: A   B   C   D

Turnaround: 14   4   1   6

So the average turnaround time is:

$$\frac{14 + 4 + 1 + 6}{4} = 6.25$$

Here Job A is preempted by Job B because Job B has less CPU time remaining.

Here Job B is preempted by Job C because Job C has less CPU time remaining.

Now Job B can resume because Job C has finished.

Job D runs next because it needs less CPU time to finish than does Job A.

Here Job A is finally allowed to finish.

Job A	Job B	Job C	Job B	Job D	Job A
0	1	2	3	5	9	14

How does that compare to the same problem using the nonpreemptive SJN policy? Figure 4.9 shows the same situation using SJN.

In this case the turnaround time is:

Job: A   B   C   D
Turnaround: 6   9   5   11

So the average turnaround time is:

$$\frac{6 + 9 + 5 + 11}{4} = 7.75$$

Job A	Job C	Job B	Job D
0	6	7	10	14

Note in Figure 4.9 that initially A is the only job in the READY queue so it runs first and continues until it's finished because SJN is a nonpreemptive algorithm. The next job to be run is C because when Job A is finished (at time 6), all of the other jobs (B, C, and D) have arrived. Of those three, C has the shortest CPU cycle, so it is the next one run, then B, and finally D.

Therefore, with this example, SRT at 6.25 is faster than SJN at 7.75. However, we neglected to include the time required by the SRT algorithm to do the context switching. **Context switching** is required by all preemptive algorithms. When Job A is preempted, all of its processing information must be saved in its PCB for later, when Job A's execution is to be continued, and the contents of Job B's PCB are loaded into the appropriate registers so it can start running again; this is a context switch. Later, when Job A is once again assigned to the processor, another context switch is performed. This time the information from the preempted job is stored in its PCB, and the contents of Job A's PCB are loaded into the appropriate registers.

How the context switching is actually done depends on the architecture of the CPU; in many systems there are special instructions that provide quick saving and restoring of information. The switching is designed to be performed efficiently but, no matter how fast it is, it still takes valuable CPU time. So although SRT appears to be faster, in a real operating environment its advantages are diminished by the time spent in context switching. A precise comparison of SRT and SJN would have to include the time required to do the context switching.

Round Robin

Round robin is a preemptive process scheduling algorithm that is used extensively in interactive systems because it's easy to implement and it isn't based on job characteristics but on a predetermined slice of time that's given to each job to ensure that the CPU is equally shared among all active processes and isn't monopolized by any one job.

This time slice is called a **time quantum** and its size is crucial to the performance of the system. It usually varies from 100 milliseconds to 1 or 2 seconds.

Jobs are placed in the READY queue using a first-come first-served scheme and the Process Scheduler selects the first job from the front of the queue, sets the timer to the time quantum, and allocates the CPU to this job. If processing isn't finished when time expires, the job is preempted and put at the end of the READY queue and its information is saved in its PCB.

In the event that the job's CPU cycle is shorter than the time quantum, one of two actions will take place: (1) if this is the job's last CPU cycle and the job is finished, then all resources allocated to it are released and the completed job is returned to the user; (2) if the CPU cycle has been interrupted by an I/O request, then information about the job is saved in its PCB and it is linked at the end of the appropriate I/O queue. Later, when the I/O request has been satisfied, it is returned to the end of the READY queue to await allocation of the CPU.

The example in Figure 4.10 illustrates a round robin algorithm with a time slice of 4 milliseconds (I/O requests are ignored):

Arrival time: 0   1   2   3

Job: A   B   C   D

CPU cycle: 8   4   9   5

(figure 4.10)

Timeline for job sequence A, B, C, D using the preemptive round robin algorithm with time slices of 4 ms.

Job A	Job B	Job C	Job D	Job A	Job C	Job D	Job C
0	4	8	12	16	20	24	25 26

(figure 4.10)

Timeline for job sequence A, B, C, D using the preemptive round robin algorithm with time slices of 4 ms.

The turnaround time is the completion time minus the arrival time:

Job: A   B   C   D
Turnaround: 20   7 24 22

So the average turnaround time is:

$$\frac{20 + 7 + 24 + 22}{4} = 18.25$$

Note that in Figure 4.10 Job A was preempted once because it needed eight milliseconds to complete its CPU cycle, while Job B terminated in one time quantum. Job C was preempted twice because it needed nine milliseconds to complete its CPU cycle, and Job D was preempted once because it needed five milliseconds. In their last execution or swap into memory, both Jobs D and C used the CPU for only 1 millisecond and terminated before their last time quantum expired, releasing the CPU sooner.

The efficiency of round robin depends on the size of the time quantum in relation to the average CPU cycle. If the quantum is too large—that is, if it's larger than most CPU cycles—then the algorithm reduces to the FCFS scheme. If the quantum is too small, then the amount of context switching slows down the execution of the jobs and the amount of overhead is dramatically increased, as the three examples in Figure 4.11 demonstrate. Job A has a CPU cycle of 8 milliseconds. The amount of context switching increases as the time quantum decreases in size.

In Figure 4.11 the first case (a) has a time quantum of 10 milliseconds and there is no context switching (and no overhead). The CPU cycle ends shortly before the time quantum expires and the job runs to completion. For this job with this time quantum, there is no difference between the round robin algorithm and the FCFS algorithm.

In the second case (b), with a time quantum of 5 milliseconds, there is one context switch. The job is preempted once when the time quantum expires, so there is some overhead for context switching and there would be a delayed turnaround based on the number of other jobs in the system.

In the third case (c), with a time quantum of 1 millisecond, there are seven context switches because the job is preempted every time the time quantum expires; overhead becomes costly and turnaround time suffers accordingly.

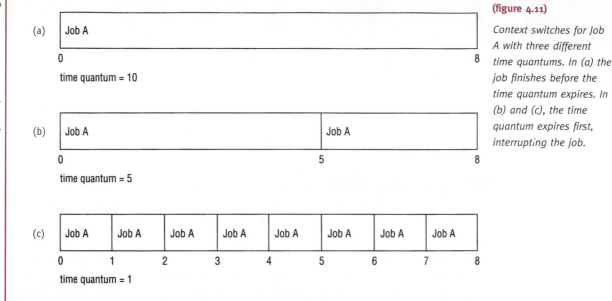

(figure 4.11)

Context switches for Job A with three different time quantums. In (a) the job finishes before the time quantum expires. In (b) and (c), the time quantum expires first, interrupting the job.

What's the best time quantum size? The answer should be predictable by now: it depends on the system. If it's an interactive environment the system is expected to respond quickly to its users, especially when they make simple requests. If it's a batch system, response time is not a factor (turnaround is) and overhead becomes very important.

Here are two general rules of thumb for selecting the proper time quantum: (1) it should be long enough to allow 80 percent of the CPU cycles to run to completion, and (2) it should be at least 100 times longer than the time required to perform one context switch. These rules are used in some systems, but they are not inflexible (Finkel, 1986).

Multiple-Level Queues

Multiple-level queues isn't really a separate scheduling algorithm but works in conjunction with several of the schemes already discussed and is found in systems with jobs that can be grouped according to a common characteristic. We've already introduced at least one kind of multiple-level queue—that of a priority-based system with different queues for each priority level.

Another kind of system might gather all of the CPU-bound jobs in one queue and all I/O-bound jobs in another. The Process Scheduler then alternately selects jobs from each queue to keep the system balanced.

A third common example is one used in a hybrid environment that supports both batch and interactive jobs. The batch jobs are put in one queue called the background queue while the interactive jobs are put in a foreground queue and are treated more favorably than those on the background queue.

All of these examples have one thing in common: the scheduling policy is based on some predetermined scheme that allocates special treatment to the jobs in each queue. Within each queue, the jobs are served in FCFS fashion.

Multiple-level queues raise some interesting questions:
• Is the processor allocated to the jobs in the first queue until it is empty before moving to the next queue or does it travel from queue to queue until the last job on the last queue has been served and then go back to serve the first job on the first queue, or something in between?
• Is this fair to those who have earned, or paid for, a higher priority?
• Is it fair to those in a low priority queue?
• If the processor is allocated to the jobs on the first queue and it never empties out, when will the jobs in the last queues be served?
• Can the jobs in the last queues get "time off for good behavior" and eventually move to better queues?

The answers depend on the policy used by the system to service the queues. There are four primary methods to the movement: not allowing movement between queues, moving jobs from queue to queue, moving jobs from queue to queue and increasing the time quantums for lower queues, and giving special treatment to jobs that have been in the system for a long time (aging). The following case examples are derived from Yourdon (1972).

Case 1: No Movement Between Queues

No movement between queues is a very simple policy that rewards those who have high-priority jobs. The processor is allocated to the jobs in the high-priority queue in FCFS fashion and it is allocated to jobs in lower priority queues only when the high-priority queues are empty. This policy can be justified if there are relatively few users with high-priority jobs so the top queues quickly empty out, allowing the processor to spend a fair amount of time running the low-priority jobs.

Case 2: Movement Between Queues

Movement between queues is a policy that adjusts the priorities assigned to each job: high-priority jobs are treated like all the others once they are in the system. (Their initial priority may be favorable.) When a time quantum interrupt occurs, the job is preempted and moved to the end of the next lower queue. A job may also have its priority increased; for example, when it issues an I/O request before its time quantum has expired.

This policy is fairest in a system in which the jobs are handled according to their computing cycle characteristics: CPU-bound or I/O-bound. This assumes that a job that exceeds its time quantum is CPU-bound and will require more CPU allocation than one that requests I/O before the time quantum expires. Therefore, the CPU-bound jobs are placed at the end of the next lower queue when they're preempted because of the expiration of the time quantum, while I/O-bound jobs are returned to the end of the next higher level queue once their I/O request has finished. This facilitates I/O-bound jobs and is good in interactive systems.

Case 3: Variable Time Quantum Per Queue

Variable time quantum per queue is a variation of the movement between queues policy, and it allows for faster turnaround of CPU-bound jobs.

In this scheme, each of the queues is given a time quantum twice as long as the previous queue. The highest queue might have a time quantum of 100 milliseconds. So the second-highest queue would have a time quantum of 200 milliseconds, the third would have 400 milliseconds, and so on. If there are enough queues, the lowest one might have a relatively long time quantum of 3 seconds or more.

If a job doesn't finish its CPU cycle in the first time quantum, it is moved to the end of the next lower level queue and when the processor is next allocated to it, the job executes for twice as long as before. With this scheme a CPU-bound job can execute for longer and longer periods of time, thus improving its chances of finishing faster.

Case 4: Aging

Aging is used to ensure that jobs in the lower-level queues will eventually complete their execution. The operating system keeps track of each job's waiting time and when a job gets too old—that is, when it reaches a certain time limit—the system moves the job to the next highest queue, and so on until it reaches the top queue. A more drastic aging policy is one that moves the old job directly from the lowest queue to the end of the topmost queue. Regardless of its actual implementation, an aging policy guards against the indefinite postponement of unwieldy jobs. As you might expect, **indefinite postponement** means that a job's execution is delayed for an undefined amount of time because it is repeatedly preempted so other jobs can be processed. (We all know examples of an unpleasant task that's been indefinitely postponed to make time for a more appealing pastime). Eventually the situation could lead to the old job's starvation. Indefinite postponement is a major problem when allocating resources and one that will be discussed in detail in Chapter 5.

A Word About Interrupts

We first encountered **interrupts** in Chapter 3 when the Memory Manager issued page interrupts to accommodate job requests. In this chapter we examined another type of interrupt that occurs when the time quantum expires and the processor is deallocated from the running job and allocated to another one.

There are other interrupts that are caused by events internal to the process. I/O interrupts are issued when a READ or WRITE command is issued. (We'll explain them in detail in Chapter 7.) Internal interrupts, or synchronous interrupts, also occur as a direct result of the arithmetic operation or job instruction currently being processed.

Illegal arithmetic operations such as the following can generate interrupts:
• Attempts to divide by zero
• Floating-point operations generating an overflow or underflow
• Fixed-point addition or subtraction that causes an arithmetic overflow

Illegal job instructions such as the following can also generate interrupts:
• Attempts to access protected or nonexistent storage locations
• Attempts to use an undefined operation code
• Operating on invalid data
• Attempts to make system changes, such as trying to change the size of the time quantum

The control program that handles the interruption sequence of events is called the **interrupt handler**. When the operating system detects a nonrecoverable error, the **interrupt handler** typically follows this sequence:

1. The type of interrupt is described and stored—to be passed on to the user as an error message.
2. The state of the interrupted process is saved, including the value of the program counter, the mode specification, and the contents of all registers.
3. The interrupt is processed: the error message and state of the interrupted process are sent to the user; program execution is halted; any resources allocated to the job are released; and the job exits the system.
4. The processor resumes normal operation.

If we're dealing with internal interrupts only, which are nonrecoverable, the job is terminated in Step 3. However, when the interrupt handler is working with an I/O interrupt, time quantum, or other recoverable interrupt, Step 3 simply halts the job and moves it to the appropriate I/O device queue, or READY queue (on time out). Later, when the I/O request is finished, the job is returned to the READY queue. If it was a time out (quantum interrupt), the job (or process) is already on the READY queue.

Conclusion

The Processor Manager must allocate the CPU among all the system's users. In this chapter we've made the distinction between job scheduling, the selection of incoming jobs based on their characteristics, and process scheduling, the instant-by-instant allocation of the CPU. We've also described how interrupts are generated and resolved by the interrupt handler.

Each scheduling algorithm presented in this chapter has unique characteristics, objectives, and applications. A system designer can choose the best policy and algorithm only after carefully evaluating their strengths and weaknesses. Table 4.1 shows how the algorithms presented in this chapter compare.

Algorithm	Policy Type	Best for	Disadvantages/*Advantages*
FCFS	Nonpreemptive	Batch	Unpredictable turnaround times/ *Easy to implement*
SJN	Nonpreemptive	Batch	Indefinite postponement of some jobs/ *Minimizes average waiting time*
Priority scheduling	Nonpreemptive	Batch	Indefinite postponement of some jobs/ *Ensures fast completion of important jobs*
SRT	Preemptive	Batch	Overhead incurred by context switching/ *Ensures fast completion of short jobs*
Round robin	Preemptive	Interactive	Requires selection of good time quantum/ *Provides reasonable response times to interactive users; provides fair CPU allocation*
Multiple-level queues	Preemptive/ Nonpreemptive	Batch/ interactive	Overhead incurred by monitoring of queues/ *Flexible scheme; counteracts indefinite postponement with aging or other queue movement; gives fair treatment to CPU-bound jobs by incrementing time quantums on lower priority queues or other queue movement*

(table 4.1)

Comparison of the scheduling algorithms discussed in this chapter.

In the next chapter we'll explore the demands placed on the Processor Manager as it attempts to synchronize execution of all the jobs in the system.

Key Terms

aging: a policy used to ensure that jobs that have been in the system for a long time in the lower level queues will eventually complete their execution.

context switching: the acts of saving a job's processing information in its PCB so the job can be swapped out of memory and of loading the processing information from the PCB of another job into the appropriate registers so the CPU can process it. Context switching occurs in all preemptive policies.

CPU-bound: a job that will perform a great deal of nonstop processing before issuing an interrupt.

first come, first-served (FCFS): a nonpreemptive process scheduling policy (or algorithm) that handles jobs according to their arrival time.

high-level scheduler: a synonym for the Job Scheduler.

I/O-bound: a job that requires a large number of input/output operations, resulting in much free time for the CPU.

indefinite postponement: signifies that a job's execution is delayed indefinitely because it is repeatedly preempted so other jobs can be processed.

interrupt: a hardware signal that suspends execution of a program and activates the execution of a special program known as the interrupt handler.

interrupt handler: the program that controls what action should be taken by the operating system when a sequence of events is interrupted.

Job Scheduler: the high-level scheduler of the Processor Manager that selects jobs from a queue of incoming jobs based on each job's characteristics.

job status: the condition of a job as it moves through the system from the beginning to the end of its execution.

low-level scheduler: a synonym for the Process Scheduler.

middle-level scheduler: a scheduler used by the Processor Manager to manage processes that have been interrupted because they have exceeded their allocated CPU time slice.

multiple-level queues: a process scheduling scheme (used with other scheduling algorithms) that groups jobs according to a common characteristic.

multiprogramming: a technique that allows a single processor to process several programs residing simultaneously in main memory and interleaving their execution by overlapping I/O requests with CPU requests.

natural wait: a common term used to identify an I/O request from a program in a multiprogramming environment that would cause a process to wait "naturally" before resuming execution.

nonpreemptive scheduling policy: a job scheduling strategy that functions without external interrupts so that once a job captures the processor and begins execution, it remains in the running state uninterrupted until it issues an I/O request or it's finished.

preemptive scheduling policy: any process scheduling strategy that, based on predetermined policies, interrupts the processing of a job and transfers the CPU to another job. It is widely used in time-sharing environments.

priority scheduling: a nonpreemptive process scheduling policy (or algorithm) that allows for the execution of high-priority jobs before low-priority jobs.

process: an instance of execution of a program that is identifiable and controllable by the operating system.

Process Control Block (PCB): a data structure that contains information about the current status and characteristics of a process.

Process Scheduler: the low-level scheduler of the Processor Manager that establishes the order in which processes in the ready queue will be served by the CPU.

process scheduling algorithm: an algorithm used by the Job Scheduler to allocate the CPU and move jobs through the system.

process scheduling policy: any policy used by the processor manager to select the order in which incoming jobs will be executed.

process status: information stored in the job's PCB that indicates the current position of the job and the resources responsible for that status.

processor: (1) a synonym for the CPU, or (2) any component in a computing system capable of performing a sequence of activities.

queue: a linked list of PCBs that indicates the order in which jobs or processes will be serviced.

response time: a measure of the efficiency of an interactive system that tracks the speed with which the system will respond to a user's command.

round robin: a preemptive process scheduling policy (or algorithm) that allocates to each job one unit of processing time per turn to ensure that the CPU is equally shared among all active processes and isn't monopolized by any one job.

shortest job next (SJN): a nonpreemptive process scheduling policy (or algorithm) that selects the waiting job with the shortest CPU cycle time.

shortest remaining time (SRT): a preemptive process scheduling policy (or algorithm) similar to the SJN algorithm that allocates the processor to the job closest to completion.

task: (1) the term used to describe a process, or (2) the basic unit of concurrent programming languages that defines a sequence of instructions that may be executed in parallel with other similar units.

thread: a portion of a program that can run independently of other portions. Multithreaded applications programs can have several threads running at one time with the same or different priorities.

time quantum: a period of time assigned to a process for execution before it is preempted.

turnaround time: a measure of a system's efficiency that tracks the time required to execute a job and return output to the user.

Exercises

Research Topic

Compare two processors currently being used in personal computers. Use standard industry benchmarks for your comparison and briefly list the advantages and disadvantages of each. You can compare different processors from the same manufacturer (such as two Intel processors) or different processors from different manufacturers (such as Intel and AMD).

Exercises

1. What information about a job needs to be kept in the PCB?

2. What information about a process needs to be saved, changed, or updated when context switching takes place?

3. Five jobs are in the READY queue waiting to be processed. Their estimated CPU cycles are as follows: 10, 3, 5, 6, and 2. Using SJN, in what order should they be processed to minimize average waiting time?

4. A job running in a system, with variable time quantums per queue, needs 30 milliseconds to run to completion. If the first queue has a time quantum of 5 milliseconds and each queue thereafter has a time quantum that is twice as large as the previous one, how many times will the job be interrupted and on which queue will it finish its execution?

5. Figure 4.12 (adapted from Madnick & Donovan, 1974) is a simplified process model of you, in which there are only two states: sleeping and waking. You make the transition from waking to sleeping when you are tired, and from sleeping to waking when the alarm clock goes off.

(figure 4.12)

Process model of two states for Exercise 5.

   a. Add three more states to the diagram (for example, one might be eating).

   b. State all of the possible transitions among the five states.

6. What is the relationship between turnaround time, CPU cycle time, and waiting time? Write an equation to express this relationship, if possible.

7. Given the following information:

Job Number	Arrival Time	CPU Cycle
1	0	10
2	1	2
3	2	3
4	3	1
5	4	5

Draw a timeline for each of the following scheduling algorithms. (It may be helpful to first compute a start and finish time for each job.)

a. FCFS

b. SJN

c. SRT

d. Round robin (using a time quantum of 2, ignore context switching and natural wait)

8. Using the same information given for Exercise 7, complete the chart by computing waiting time and turnaround time for every job for each of the following scheduling algorithms (ignoring context switching overhead).

a. FCFS

b. SJN

c. SRT

d. Round robin (using a time quantum of 2)

9. Using the same information given for Exercise 7, compute the average waiting time and average turnaround time for each of the following scheduling algorithms and determine which one gives the best results.

a. FCFS

b. SJN

c. SRT

d. Round robin (using a time quantum of 2)

Advanced Exercises

10. Consider a variation of round robin in which a process that has used its full time quantum is returned to the end of the READY queue, while one that has used half of its time quantum is returned to the middle of the queue and one that has used one-fourth of its time quantum goes to a place one-fourth of the distance away from the beginning of the queue.

a. What is the objective of this scheduling policy?

b. Discuss the advantage and disadvantage of its implementation.

11. In a single-user dedicated system, such as a personal computer, it's easy for the user to determine when a job is caught in an infinite loop. The typical solution to this problem is for the user to manually intervene and terminate the job. What mechanism would you implement in the Process Scheduler to automate the termination of a job that's in an infinite loop? Take into account jobs that legitimately use large amounts of CPU time; for example, one "finding the first 10,000 prime numbers."

12. Some guidelines for selecting the right time quantum were given in this chapter. As a system designer, how would you know when you have chosen the best time quantum? What factors would make this time quantum best from the user's point of view? What factors would make this time quantum best from the system's point of view?

13. Using the process state diagrams of Figure 4.2, explain why there's no transition:

    a. From the READY state to the WAITING state.

    b. From the WAITING state to the RUNNING state.

Programming Exercises

14. Write a program that will simulate FCFS, SJN, SRT, and round robin scheduling algorithms. For each algorithm, the program should compute waiting time and turnaround time of every job as well as the average waiting time and average turnaround time. The average values should be consolidated in a table for easy comparison. You may use the following data to test your program. The time quantum for round robin is 4 ms and the context switching time is 0.

Arrival Time	CPU Cycle (in milliseconds)
0	6
3	2
5	1
9	7
10	5
12	3
14	4
16	5
17	7
19	2

15. Using your program from Exercise 14, change the context switching time to 0.4 milliseconds. Compare outputs from both runs and discuss which would be the better policy. Describe any drastic changes encountered or a lack of changes and why.

Chapter 5

Process Management

> "We have all heard the story of the animal standing in doubt between two stacks of hay and starving to death." —Abraham Lincoln (1809–1865)

Learning Objectives

After completing this chapter, you should be able to describe:

- Several causes of system deadlock
- The difference between preventing and avoiding deadlocks
- How to detect and recover from deadlocks
- The concept of process starvation and how to detect and recover from it
- The concept of a race, and how to prevent it
- The difference between deadlock, starvation, and race

We've already looked at two aspects of resource sharing—memory management and processor sharing. In this chapter, we address the problems caused when many processes compete for relatively few resources and the system is unable to service all of the processes in the system.

A lack of **process synchronization** can result in two extreme conditions: deadlock or starvation.

In early operating systems, deadlock was known by the more descriptive phrase **"deadly embrace"**. It's a system-wide tangle of resource requests that begins when two or more jobs are put on hold, each waiting for a vital resource to become available. The problem builds when the resources needed by those jobs are the resources held by other jobs that are also waiting to run but cannot because they're waiting for other unavailable resources. The jobs come to a standstill. The deadlock is complete if the remainder of the system comes to a standstill as well. Usually the situation can't be resolved by the operating system and requires outside intervention by either operators or users who must take drastic actions, such as manually preempting or terminating a job.

A **deadlock** is most easily described with an example—a narrow staircase in a building (we'll return to this example throughout this chapter). The staircase was built as a fire escape route, but people working in the building often take the stairs instead of waiting for the slow elevators. Traffic on the staircase moves well unless two people, traveling in opposite directions, need to pass on the stairs— there's room for only one person on each step. In this example, the staircase is the system and the steps and landings are the resources. There's a landing between each floor and it's wide enough for people to share it, but the stairs are not and can be allocated to only one person at a time. Problems occur when someone going up the stairs meets someone coming down, and each refuses to retreat to a wider place. This creates a deadlock, which is the subject of much of our discussion on process synchronization.

On the other hand, if a few patient people wait on the landing for a break in the opposing traffic, and that break never comes, they could wait there forever. That's **starvation,** an extreme case of indefinite postponement, and it is discussed near the conclusion of this chapter.

Deadlock

Deadlock is more serious than indefinite postponement or starvation because it affects more than one job. Because resources are being tied up, the entire system (not just a few programs) is affected. The example most often used to illustrate deadlock is a traffic jam.

As shown in Figure 5.1, there's no simple and immediate solution to a deadlock; no one can move forward until someone moves out of the way, but no one can move out

(figure 5.1)

A classic case of traffic deadlock. This is "gridlock," where no vehicles can move forward to clear the traffic jam.

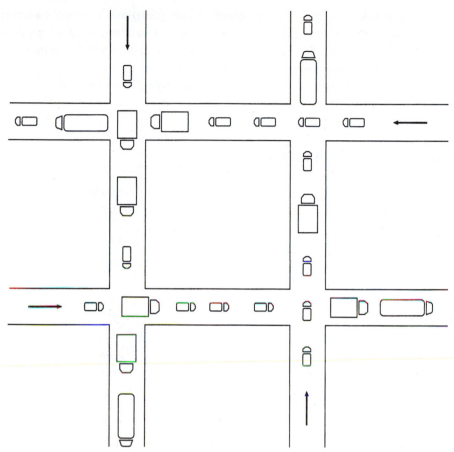

of the way until either someone advances or the rear of a line moves back. Obviously it requires an outside intervention to remove one of the four vehicles from an intersection or to make a line move back. Only then can the deadlock be resolved.

Deadlocks were infrequent in early batch systems because users would include in the job control cards that preceded the job a complete list of the specific system resources (tape drives, disks, printers, etc.) required to run the job. The operating system would then make sure that all requested resources were available and allocated to that job before moving the job to the READY queue; and then the system did not release these resources until the job was completed. If the resources weren't available, the job wasn't moved to the READY queue until they were.

Deadlocks became more prevalent with the growing use of interactive systems because such systems are more flexible than batch environments. Interactive systems generally improve the use of resources through dynamic resource sharing, but this resource-sharing capability also increases the possibility of deadlocks.

In general-purpose computer systems, deadlocks are sometimes regarded as a mere inconvenience that may cause delays. But for real-time systems, deadlocks quickly become critical situations. For example, a deadlock in a hospital's life support system or in the guidance system aboard a spacecraft could endanger lives. Regardless of the environment, the operating system must either prevent deadlocks or resolve them when they happen.

Seven Cases of Deadlock

A deadlock usually occurs when nonsharable, nonpreemptable resources, such as files, printers, or tape drives are allocated to jobs that eventually require other nonsharable, nonpreemptive resources—resources that have been locked by other jobs. However, deadlocks aren't restricted to files, printers, and tape drives. They can also occur on sharable resources such as disks and databases, as we'll see in the following examples:

Case 1: Deadlocks on File Requests

If jobs are allowed to request and hold files for the duration of their execution, a deadlock can occur. Figure 5.2 shows the deadlock using a modified representation of directed graphs that will be discussed in more detail in the "Modeling Deadlocks" section.

For example, consider the case of a home construction company with two application programs, purchasing (P1) and sales (P2), which are active at the same time. They each need to access two files, inventory (F1) and suppliers (F2), to update daily transactions. One day the system deadlocks when the following sequence of events takes place.

1. Purchasing (P1) accesses the supplier file (F2) to place an order for more lumber.
2. Sales (P2) accesses the inventory file (F1) to reserve the parts that will be required to build the home ordered that day.
3. Purchasing (P1) doesn't release the supplier file (F2) but requests the inventory file (F1) to verify the quantity of lumber on hand before placing its order for more, but P1 is blocked because F1 is being held by P2.

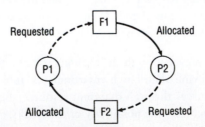

(figure 5.2)

Case 1. The two processes are shown as circles. Each process is waiting for a file that has already been allocated thus creating a system deadlock.

4. Meanwhile, sales (P2) doesn't release the inventory file (F1) but requests the supplier file (F2) to check the schedule of a subcontractor. At this point P2 is also blocked because F2 is being held by P1.

Any other programs that require F1 or F2 will be put on hold as long as this situation continues. This deadlock will remain until one of the two programs is withdrawn or forcibly removed and its file is released. Only then can the other program continue and the system return to normal.

Case 2: Deadlocks in Databases

A deadlock can also occur if two processes access and lock records in a database.

To appreciate the following scenario it is necessary to remember that database queries and transactions are often relatively brief processes that either search or modify parts of a database. Requests usually arrive at random and may be interleaved arbitrarily.

Locking is a technique used to guarantee the integrity of the data through which the user locks out all other users while working with the database. Locking can be done at three different levels: the entire database can be locked for the duration of the request; a subsection of the database can be locked; or only the individual record can be locked until the process is completed. If the entire database is locked (the most extreme and most successful solution) it prevents a deadlock from occurring but access to the database is restricted to one user at a time and, in a multiuser environment, response times are significantly slowed; this is normally an unacceptable solution. When the locking is performed on only part of the database, access time is improved but the possibility of a deadlock is increased because different processes sometimes need to work with several parts of the database at the same time.

Here's a system that locks each record when it is accessed until the process is completed. There are two processes (P1 and P2), each of which needs to update two records (R1 and R2) and the following sequence leads to a deadlock:

1. P1 accesses R1 and locks it.
2. P2 accesses R2 and locks it.
3. P1 requests R2, which is locked by P2.
4. P2 requests R1, which is locked by P1.

An alternative, of course, is to not use locks—but that leads to other difficulties. If locks are not used to preserve their integrity, the updated records in the database might include only some of the data—and their contents would depend on the order in which each process finishes its execution. This is known as a **race** between processes and is illustrated in the following example and Figure 5.3.

Original Record

Jones
GPA = 2.5
ADDR: 5th Ave.

P1 Grades Process
reads data

P2 Address Process
reads data

work
area

GPA
updated

Jones
GPA = 3.0
ADDR: 5th Ave.

Jones
GPA = 2.5
ADDR: Main St.

address
updated

P1 rewrites record
to database with
the new GPA

Jones
GPA = 3.0
ADDR: 5th Ave.

P2 rewrites record
to database with
the new address

Jones
GPA = 2.5
ADDR: Main St.

Final Record

(figure 5.3)

Case 2. If P1 finishes first it will win the race but its version of the record will soon be overwritten by P2. Regardless of which process wins the race, the final version of the data will be incorrect.

Let's say you are a veteran student of a university that maintains most of its files on a database that can be accessed by several different programs, including one for grades and another listing home addresses. Let's say you're a student on the move so you send the university a change of address form at the end of the fall term, shortly after grades are submitted. And one fateful day both programs race to access your record in the database:

1. The grades process (P1) is the first to access your record (R1) and it copies the record to its work area.
2. The address process (P2) accesses your record (R1) and copies it to its work area.
3. P1 changes R1 by entering your grades for the fall term and calculating your new grade average.
4. P2 changes R1 by updating the address field.
5. P1 finishes its work first and rewrites its version of your record back to the database. Your grades have been changed, but your address hasn't.
6. P2 finishes and rewrites its updated record back to the database. Your address has been changed, but your grades haven't. According to the database you didn't attend school this term.

If we reverse the order and say that P2 won the race, your grades will be updated but not your address. Depending on your success in the classroom you might prefer one mishap over the other, but from the operating system's point of view either alternative is unacceptable because incorrect data is allowed to pollute the database. The system can't allow the integrity of the database to depend on a random sequence of events.

Case 3: Deadlocks in Dedicated Device Allocation

The use of a group of dedicated devices can also deadlock the system.

Let's say two users from the local board of education are each running a program (P1 and P2), and both programs will eventually need two tape drives to copy files from one tape to another. The system is small, however, and when the two programs are begun, only two tape drives are available and they're allocated on an "as requested" basis. Soon the following sequence transpires:

1. P1 requests tape drive 1 and gets it.
2. P2 requests tape drive 2 and gets it.
3. P1 requests tape drive 2 but is blocked.
4. P2 requests tape drive 1 but is blocked.

Neither job can continue because each is waiting for the other to finish and release its tape drive—an event that will never occur. A similar series of events could deadlock any group of dedicated devices.

Case 4: Deadlocks in Multiple Device Allocation

Deadlocks aren't restricted to processes contending for the same type of device; they can happen when several processes request, and hold on to, dedicated devices while other processes act in a similar manner as shown in Figure 5.4.

(figure 5.4)

Case 4. Three processes, shown as circles, are each waiting for a device that has already been allocated to another process thus creating a deadlock.

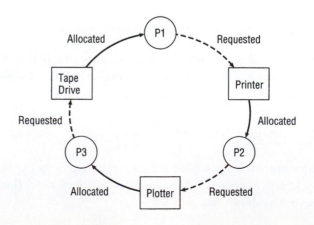

Consider the case of an engineering design firm with three programs (P1, P2, and P3) and three dedicated devices: tape drive, printer, and plotter. The following sequence of events will result in deadlock:

1. P1 requests and gets the tape drive.
2. P2 requests and gets the printer.
3. P3 requests and gets the plotter.
4. P1 requests the printer but is blocked.
5. P2 requests the plotter but is blocked.
6. P3 requests the tape drive but is blocked.

As in the earlier examples, none of the jobs can continue because each is waiting for a resource being held by another.

Case 5: Deadlocks in Spooling

Although in the previous example the printer was a dedicated device, most systems have transformed the printer into a sharable device (also known as a "virtual device") by installing a high-speed device, a disk, between it and the CPU. The disk accepts output from several users and acts as a temporary storage area for all output until the printer is ready to accept it. This process is called **spooling**. If the printer needs all of a job's output before it will begin printing, but the spooling system fills the available disk space with only partially completed output, then a deadlock can occur. It happens like this:

Let's say it's one hour before the big project is due for a computer class. Twenty-six frantic programmers key in their final changes and, with only minutes to spare, issue print commands. The spooler receives the pages one at a time from each of the students but the pages are received separately, several page one's, page two's, etc. The printer is ready to print the first completed program it gets, but as the spooler canvasses its files it has the first page for many programs but the last page for none of them. Alas, the spooler is full of partially completed output so no other pages can be accepted, but none of the jobs can be printed out (which would release their disk space) because the printer only accepts completed output files. An unfortunate state of affairs.

This scenario isn't limited to printers. Any part of the system that relies on spooling, such as one that handles incoming jobs or transfers files over a network, is vulnerable to such a deadlock.

Case 6: Deadlocks in a Network

A network that's congested or has filled a large percentage of its I/O buffer space can become deadlocked if it doesn't have protocols to control the flow of messages through the network as shown in Figure 5.5.

(figure 5.5)

Case 6, deadlocked network flow. Each circle represents a node and each line represents a communication line. Arrows indicate the direction of the flow of traffic.

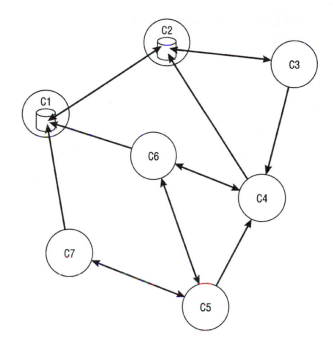

For example, a medium-sized word-processing center has seven computers on a network, each on different nodes. C1 receives messages from nodes C2, C6, and C7 and sends messages to only one: C2. C2 receives messages from nodes C1, C3, and C4 and sends messages only to C1 and C3. The direction of the arrows in Figure 5.5 indicates the flow of messages.

Messages received by C1 from C6 and C7 and destined for C2 are buffered in an output queue. Messages received by C2 from C3 and C4 and destined for C1 are buffered in an output queue. As the traffic increases, the length of each output queue increases until all of the available buffer space is filled. At this point C1 can't accept any more messages (from C2 or any other computer) because there's no more buffer space available to store them. For the same reason, C2 can't accept any messages from C1 or any other computer, not even a request to send. The communication path between C1 and C2 becomes deadlocked and since C1 can receive messages only from C6 and C7 those routes also become deadlocked. C1 can't send word to C2 about the problem and so the deadlock can't be resolved without outside intervention.

Case 7: Deadlocks in Disk Sharing

Disks are designed to be shared, so it's not uncommon for two processes to be accessing different areas of the same disk. This ability to share creates an active type of deadlock, known as **livelock** (Bic & Shaw, 2003). Processes use a form of busy-waiting that's different from a natural wait. In this case it's waiting to share a resource but never actually gains control of it. In Figure 5.6, two competing processes are sending conflicting commands causing livelock.

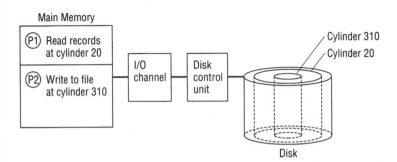

Main Memory

(figure 5.6)

Case 7. Two processes are each waiting for an I/O request to be filled: one at cylinder 20 and one at cylinder 310. Neither can be satisfied because the device puts each request on hold when it tries to fulfill the other.

For example, at an insurance company the system performs many daily transactions. One day the following series of events ties up the system:

1. Process P1 wishes to show a payment so it issues a command to read the balance, which is stored in cylinder 20 of a disk pack.

2. While the control unit is moving the arm to cylinder 20, P1 is put on hold and the I/O channel is free to process the next I/O request.

3. P2 gains control of the I/O channel and issues a command to write someone else's payment to a record stored in cylinder 310. If the command is not "locked out," P2 will be put on hold while the control unit moves the arm to cylinder 310.

4. Because P2 is "on hold," the channel is free to be captured again by P1, which reconfirms its command to "read from cylinder 20."

5. Since the last command from P2 had forced the arm mechanism to cylinder 310, the disk control unit begins to reposition the arm to cylinder 20 to satisfy P1. The I/O channel would be released because P1 is once again put on hold, so it could be captured by P2, which issues a WRITE command only to discover that the arm mechanism needs to be repositioned.

As a result, the arm is in a constant state of motion, moving back and forth between cylinder 20 and cylinder 310 as it responds to the two competing commands, but satisfies neither.

Conditions for Deadlock

In each of these seven cases, the deadlock (or livelock) involved the interaction of several processes and resources, but each deadlock was preceded by the simultaneous occurrence of four conditions that the operating system (or other systems) could have recognized: mutual exclusion, resource holding, no preemption, and circular wait. It's important to remember that each of these four conditions is necessary for the operating system to work smoothly. None of them can be removed easily without causing the system's overall functioning to suffer. Therefore, the system needs to recognize the combination of conditions before they occur and threaten to cause the system to lock up.

To illustrate these four conditions, let's review the staircase example from the beginning of the chapter and identify the four conditions required for a deadlock.

When two people meet between landings they can't pass because the steps can hold only one person at a time. **Mutual exclusion**, the act of allowing only one person (or process) to have access to a step (a dedicated resource), is the first condition for deadlock.

When two people meet on the stairs and each one holds ground and waits for the other to retreat, that is an example of **resource holding** (as opposed to resource sharing), the second condition for deadlock.

In this example, each step is dedicated to the climber (or the descender); it is allocated to the holder for as long as needed. This is called **no preemption**, the lack of temporary reallocation of resources, and is the third condition for deadlock.

These three lead to the fourth condition of **circular wait** in which each person (or process) involved in the impasse is waiting for another to voluntarily release the step (or resource) so that at least one will be able to continue on and eventually arrive at the destination.

All four conditions are required for the deadlock to occur and as long as all four conditions are present the deadlock will continue; but if one condition can be removed the deadlock will be resolved. In fact, if the four conditions can be prevented from ever occurring at the same time, deadlocks can be prevented. Although this concept is obvious it isn't easy to implement.

Modeling Deadlocks

Holt (1972) showed how the four conditions can be modeled using **directed graphs**. (We used modified directed graphs in Figures 5.2 and 5.4.) These graphs use two kinds of symbols: processes represented by circles and resources represented by squares. A solid arrow from a resource to a process (Figure 5.7(a)) means that the process is holding that resource. A solid arrow from a process to a resource (Figure 5.7(b)) means that the process is waiting for that resource. The direction of the arrow indicates the flow. If there's a cycle in the graph then there's a deadlock involving the processes and the resources in the cycle, as shown in Figure 5.7(c).

The following system has three processes—P1, P2, P3—and three resources—R1, R2, R3—each of a different type: printer, disk drive, and plotter. Because there is no specified order in which the requests are handled we'll look at three different possible scenarios using graphs to help us detect any deadlocks.

Scenario 1

The first scenario's sequence of events is shown in Table 5.1. The directed graph is shown in Figure 5.8.

Event	Action
1	P1 requests and is allocated the printer R1.
2	P1 releases the printer R1.
3	P2 requests and is allocated the disk drive R2.
4	P2 releases the disk R2.
5	P3 requests and is allocated the plotter R3.
6	P3 releases the plotter R3.

(table 5.1)

First scenario's sequence of events is shown in the directed graph in Figure 5.8.

Notice in the directed graph that there are no cycles. Therefore, we can safely conclude that a deadlock can't occur even if each process requests every resource *if* the resources are released before the next process requests them.

(figure 5.8)

First scenario. The system will stay free of deadlocks if all resources are released before they're requested by the next process.

Scenario 2

Now, consider a second scenario's sequence of events shown in Table 5.2. The directed graph is shown in Figure 5.9.

(table 5.2)	Event	Action
	1	P1 requests and is allocated R1.
	2	P2 requests and is allocated R2.
	3	P3 requests and is allocated R3.
	4	P1 requests R2.
	5	P2 requests R3.
	6	P3 requests R1.

The second scenario's sequence of events is shown in the directed graph in Figure 5.9.

In the directed graph, there *is* a deadlock because every process is waiting for a resource being held by another process, but none will be released without operator intervention.

(figure 5.9)

Second scenario. The system becomes deadlocked at event 6 when P3 requests R1. Notice the circular wait.

 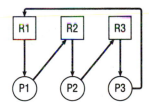

Scenario 3

The third scenario is shown in Table 5.3. As shown in Figure 5.10, the resources are released before deadlock can occur.

(table 5.3)	Event	Action
	1	P1 requests and is allocated R1.
	2	P1 requests and is allocated R2.
	3	P2 requests R1.
	4	P3 requests and is allocated R3.
	5	P1 releases R1, which is allocated to P2.
	6	P3 requests R2.
	7	P1 releases R2, which is allocated to P3.

The third scenario's sequence of events is shown in the directed graph in Figure 5.10.

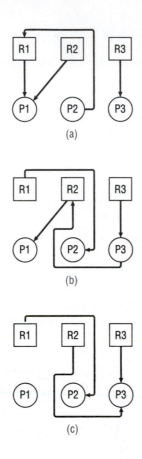

(a)

(b)

(c)

(figure 5.10)

The third scenario. After event 4 the directed graph looks like (a) and P2 is blocked because P1 is holding onto R1. However, event 5 breaks the deadlock and the graph soon looks like (b). Again there is a blocked process, P3, which must wait for the release of R2 in event 7 when the graph looks like (c).

Another Example

The examples presented so far have examined cases in which one or more resources of different types were allocated to a process. However, the graphs can be expanded to include several resources of the same type, such as tape drives, which can be allocated individually or in groups to the same process. These graphs cluster the devices of the same type into one entity, shown in Figure 5.11 as a rectangle, and the arrows show the links between the single resource and the processes using it.

Figure 5.11 gives an example of a cluster with three resources of the same type, such as three disk drives, each allocated to a different process. Although Figure 5.11(a) seems to be stable (no deadlock can occur), this is not the case because if all three processes request one more resource without releasing the one they are using, then deadlock will occur as shown in Figure 5.11(b).

(figure 5.11)

(a) A fully allocated cluster of resources. There are as many lines coming out of it as there are resources, units, in it. The state of (a) is uncertain because a request for another unit by all three processes would create a deadlock as shown in (b).

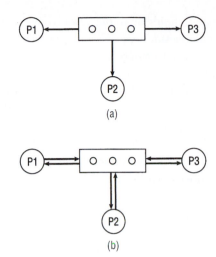

(a)

(b)

Strategies for Handling Deadlocks

As these examples show, the requests and releases are received in an unpredictable order, which makes it very difficult to design a foolproof preventive policy. In general, operating systems use one of three strategies to deal with deadlocks:

• Prevent one of the four conditions from occurring (**prevention**)

• Avoid the deadlock if it becomes probable (**avoidance**)

• Detect the deadlock when it occurs and recover from it gracefully (**detection**)

Prevention

To prevent a deadlock the operating system must eliminate one of the four necessary conditions, a task complicated by the fact that the same condition can't be eliminated from every resource.

Mutual exclusion is necessary in any computer system because some resources such as memory, CPU, and dedicated devices must be exclusively allocated to one user at a time. In the case of I/O devices such as printers the mutual exclusion may be bypassed by spooling so the output from many jobs may be stored into separate temporary spool files at the same time, and each complete output file is then selected for printing when the device is ready. However, we may be trading one type of deadlock (Case 3: Deadlocks in Dedicated Device Allocation) for another (Case 5: Deadlocks in Spooling).

Resource holding, where a job holds on to one resource while waiting for another one that's not yet available, could be sidestepped by forcing each job to request, at creation time, every resource it will need to run to completion. For example, if every job in a batch system is given as much memory as it needs, then the number of active jobs will be dictated by how many can fit in memory—a policy that would significantly decrease the degree of multiprogramming. In addition, peripheral devices would be idle because they would be allocated to a job even though they wouldn't be used all the time. As we've said before, this was used successfully in batch environments although it reduced the effective use of resources and restricted the amount of multiprogramming. But it doesn't work as well in interactive systems.

No preemption could be bypassed by allowing the operating system to deallocate resources from jobs. This can be done if the state of the job can be easily saved and restored, as when a job is preempted in a round robin environment or a page is swapped to secondary storage in a virtual memory system. On the other hand, preemption of a dedicated I/O device (printer, plotter, tape drive, and so on), or of files during the modification process, can require some extremely unpleasant recovery tasks.

Circular wait can be bypassed if the operating system prevents the formation of a circle. One such solution was proposed by Havender (1968) and is based on a numbering system for the resources such as: printer = 1, disk = 2, tape = 3, plotter = 4, and so on. The system forces each job to request its resources in ascending order: any "number one" devices required by the job would be requested first; any "number two" devices would be requested next; and so on. So if a job needed a printer and then a plotter, it would request them in this order: printer (#1) first and then the plotter (#4). If the job required the plotter first and then the printer, it would still request the printer first (which is a #1) even though it wouldn't be used right away. A job could request a printer (#1) and then a disk (#2) and then a tape (#3), but if it needed another printer (#1) late in its processing, it would still have to anticipate that need when it requested the first one, and before it requested the disk.

This scheme of "hierarchical ordering" removes the possibility of a circular wait and therefore guarantees the removal of deadlocks. It doesn't require that jobs state their maximum needs in advance, but it does require that the jobs anticipate the order in which they will request resources. From the perspective of a system designer, one of the difficulties of this scheme is discovering the best order for the resources so the needs of the majority of the users are satisfied. Another difficulty is that of assigning a ranking to nonphysical resources such as files or locked database records where there is no basis for assigning a higher number to one over another.

Avoidance

Even if the operating system can't remove one of the conditions for deadlock, it can avoid one if the system knows ahead of time the sequence of requests associated with each of the active processes. As was illustrated in the graphs presented in Figures 5.7 through 5.11, there exists at least one allocation of resources sequence that will allow jobs to continue without becoming deadlocked.

One such algorithm was proposed by Dijkstra (1965) to regulate resource allocation to avoid deadlocks. The Banker's Algorithm is based on a bank with a fixed amount of capital that operates on the following principles:

• No customer will be granted a loan exceeding the bank's total capital.

• All customers will be given a maximum credit limit when opening an account.

• No customer will be allowed to borrow over the limit.

• The sum of all loans won't exceed the bank's total capital.

Under these conditions the bank isn't required to have on hand the total of all maximum lending quotas before it can open up for business (we'll assume the bank will always have the same fixed total and we'll disregard interest charged on loans). For our example the bank has a total capital fund of $10,000 and has three customers, C1, C2, and C3, who have maximum credit limits of $4,000, $5,000, and $8,000, respectively. Table 5.4 illustrates the state of affairs of the bank after some loans have been granted to C2 and C3. This is called a **safe state** because the bank still has enough money left to satisfy the maximum requests of C1, C2, or C3.

(table 5.4)

The bank started with $10,000 and has remaining capital of $4,000 after these loans. Therefore it's in a "safe state."

Customer	Loan amount	Maximum credit	Remaining credit
C1	0	4,000	4,000
C2	2,000	5,000	3,000
C3	4,000	8,000	4,000

Total loaned: $6,000

Total capital fund: $10,000

A few weeks later after more loans have been made, and some have been repaid, the bank is in the **unsafe state** represented in Table 5.5.

(table 5.5)

The bank only has remaining capital of $1,000 after these loans and therefore is in an "unsafe state."

Customer	Loan amount	Maximum credit	Remaining credit
C1	2,000	4,000	2,000
C2	3,000	5,000	2,000
C3	4,000	8,000	4,000

Total loaned: $9,000

Total capital fund: $10,000

This is an unsafe state because with only $1,000 left, the bank can't satisfy anyone's maximum request and if the bank lent the $1,000 to anyone then it would be deadlocked (it can't make a loan). An unsafe state doesn't necessarily lead to deadlock, but it does indicate that the system is an excellent candidate for one. After all, none of the customers is required to request the maximum, but the bank doesn't know the exact amount that will eventually be requested, and as long as the bank's capital is less than the maximum amount available for individual loans it can't guarantee that it will be able to fill every loan request.

If we substitute jobs for customers and dedicated devices for dollars we can apply the same banking principles to an operating system. In this example the system has ten devices.

Table 5.6 shows our system in a safe state and Table 5.7 depicts the same system in an unsafe state. As before, a safe state is one in which at least one job can finish because there are enough available resources to satisfy its maximum needs. Then, using the resources released by the finished job, the maximum needs of another job can be filled and that job can be finished, and so on until all jobs are done.

Job No.	Devices Allocated	Maximum Required	Remaining Needs
1	0	4	4
2	2	5	3
3	4	8	4
Total number of devices allocated: 6			
Total number of devices in system: 10			

(table 5.6)

Resource assignments after initial allocations. A safe state: six devices are allocated and four units are still available.

Job No.	Devices Allocated	Maximum Required	Remaining Needs
1	2	4	2
2	3	5	2
3	4	8	4
Total number of devices allocated: 9			
Total number of devices in system: 10			

(table 5.7)

Resource assignments after later allocations. An unsafe state: only one unit is available but every job requires at least two to complete its execution.

The operating system must be sure never to satisfy a request that moves it from a safe state to an unsafe one. Therefore, as users' requests are satisfied, the operating system must identify the job with the smallest number of remaining resources and make sure that the number of available resources is always equal to, or greater than, the number needed for this job to run to completion. Requests that would place the safe state in jeopardy must be blocked by the operating system until they can be safely accommodated. If the system is always kept in a safe state, all requests will eventually be satisfied and a deadlock is avoided.

If this elegant solution is expanded to work with several classes of resources the system sets up a "resource assignment table" for each type of resource and tracks each table to keep the system in a safe state.

Although the Banker's Algorithm has been used to avoid deadlocks in systems with a few resources, it isn't always practical for most systems for several reasons (Tanenbaum, 1987):

- As they enter the system jobs must predict the maximum number of resources needed. As we've said before, this isn't practical in interactive systems.
- The number of total resources for each class must remain constant. If a device breaks and becomes suddenly unavailable the algorithm won't work (the system may already be in an unsafe state).
- The number of jobs must remain fixed, something that isn't possible in interactive systems where the number of active jobs is constantly changing.
- The overhead cost incurred by running the avoidance algorithm can be quite high when there are many active jobs and many devices because it has to be invoked for every request.
- Resources aren't well utilized because the algorithm assumes the worst case and, as a result, keeps vital resources unavailable to guard against unsafe states.
- Scheduling suffers as a result of the poor utilization and jobs are kept waiting for resource allocation. A steady stream of jobs asking for a few resources can cause the indefinite postponement of a more complex job requiring many resources.

Detection

The directed graphs presented earlier in this chapter showed how the existence of a circular wait indicated a deadlock, so it's reasonable to conclude that deadlocks can be detected by building directed resource graphs and looking for cycles. Unlike the avoidance algorithm, which must be performed every time there is a request, the algorithm used to detect circularity can be executed whenever it is appropriate: every hour, once a day, only when the operator notices that throughput has deteriorated, or when an angry user complains.

The detection algorithm can be explained by using directed resource graphs and "reducing" them. Begin with a system that is in use, as shown in Figure 5.12 (a). The steps to reduce a graph are these (Lane & Mooney, 1988):

1. Find a process that is currently using a resource and *not waiting* for one. This process can be removed from the graph (by disconnecting the link tying the resource to the process, such as P3 in Figure 5.12 (b)), and the resource can be

returned to the "available list." This is possible because the process would eventually finish and return the resource.

2. Find a process that's waiting only for resource classes that aren't fully allocated (such as P2 in Figure 5.12 (c)). This process isn't contributing to deadlock since it would eventually get the resource it's waiting for, finish its work, and return the resource to the "available list as shown in Figure 5.12(c)."

3. Go back to Step 1 and continue with Steps 1 and 2 until all lines connecting resources to processes have been removed, eventually reaching the stage shown in Figure 5.12 (d).

If there are any lines left, this indicates that the request of the process in question can't be satisfied and that a deadlock exists. Figure 5.12 illustrates a system in which three processes—P1, P2, and P3—and three resources—R1, R2, and R3—aren't deadlocked.

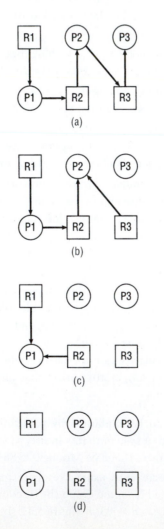

(figure 5.12)

This system is deadlock-free because the graph can be completely reduced, as shown in (d).

Figure 5.12 shows the stages of a graph reduction from (a), the original state. In (b), the link between P3 and R3 can be removed because P3 isn't waiting for any other resources to finish, so R3 is released and allocated to P2 (Step 1). In (c), the links between P2 and R3 and between P2 and R2 can be removed because P2 has all of its requested resources and can run to completion—and then R2 can be allocated to P1. Finally, in (d), the links between P1 and R2 and between P1 and R1 can be removed because P1 has all of its requested resources and can finish successfully. Therefore, the graph is completely resolved. However, Figure 5.13 shows a very similar situation which is deadlocked because of a key difference: P2 is linked to R1.

(figure 5.13)

This graph can't be reduced any further, indicating a deadlock.

(a)

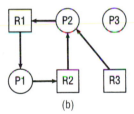

(b)

The deadlocked system in Figure 5.13 can't be reduced. In (a) the link between P3 and R3 can be removed because P3 isn't waiting for any other resource, so R3 is released and allocated to P2. But in (b) P2 has only two of the three resources it needs to finish and it is waiting for R1. But R1 can't be released by P1 because P1 is waiting for R2, which is held by P2; moreover, P1 can't finish because it is waiting for P2 to finish (and release R2), and P2 can't finish because it's waiting for R1. This is a circular wait.

Recovery

Once a deadlock has been detected it must be untangled and the system returned to normal as quickly as possible. There are several **recovery** algorithms, but they all have one feature in common: they all require at least one **victim**, an expendable job, which, when removed from the deadlock, will free the system. Unfortunately for the victim, removal generally requires that the job be restarted from the beginning or from a convenient midpoint.

The first and simplest recovery method, and the most drastic, is to terminate every job that's active in the system and restart them from the beginning.

The second method is to terminate only the jobs involved in the deadlock and ask their users to resubmit them.

The third method is to identify which jobs are involved in the deadlock and terminate them one at a time, checking to see if the deadlock is eliminated after each removal, until the deadlock has been resolved. Once the system is freed, the remaining jobs are allowed to complete their processing and later the halted jobs are started again from the beginning.

The fourth method can be put into effect only if the job keeps a record, a snapshot, of its progress so it can be interrupted and then continued without starting again from the beginning of its execution. The snapshot is like the landing in our staircase example: instead of forcing the deadlocked stair climbers to return to the bottom of the stairs, they need to retreat only to the nearest landing and wait until the others have passed. Then the climb can be resumed. In general, this method is favored for long-running jobs to help them make a speedy recovery.

Until now we've offered solutions involving the jobs caught in the deadlock. The next two methods concentrate on the nondeadlocked jobs and the resources they hold. One of them, the fifth method in our list, selects a nondeadlocked job, preempts the resources it's holding, and allocates them to a deadlocked process so it can resume execution, thus breaking the deadlock. The sixth method stops new jobs from entering the system, which allows the nondeadlocked jobs to run to completion so they'll release their resources. Eventually, with fewer jobs in the system, competition for resources is curtailed so the deadlocked processes get the resources they need to run to completion. This method is the only one listed here that doesn't rely on a victim, and it's not guaranteed to work unless the number of available resources surpasses that needed by at least one of the deadlocked jobs to run (this is possible with multiple resources).

Several factors must be considered to select the victim that will have the least-negative effect on the system. The most common are:

• The priority of the job under consideration—high-priority jobs are usually untouched

• CPU time used by job—jobs close to completion are usually left alone

• The number of other jobs that would be affected if this job were selected as the victim

In addition, programs working with databases also deserve special treatment because a database that is only partially updated is only partially correct. Therefore, jobs that are modifying data shouldn't be selected for termination because the consistency and validity of the database would be jeopardized. Fortunately, designers of many database systems have included sophisticated recovery mechanisms so damage to the database is minimized if a transaction is interrupted or terminated before completion (Finkel, 1986).

Starvation

So far we have concentrated on deadlocks, the result of liberal allocation of resources. At the opposite end is starvation, the result of conservative allocation of resources where a single job is prevented from execution because it's kept waiting for resources that never become available. To illustrate this, the case of "the dining philosophers" was introduced by Dijkstra (1968).

Five philosophers are sitting at a round table, each deep in thought, and in the center lies a bowl of spaghetti that is accessible to everyone. There are forks on the table—one between each philosopher, as illustrated in Figure 5.14. Local custom dictates that each philosopher must use two forks, the forks on either side of the plate, to eat the spaghetti, but there are only five forks—not the ten it would require for all five thinkers to eat at once—and that's unfortunate for Philosopher 2.

When they sit down to dinner, Philosopher 1 (P1) is the first to take the two forks (F1 and F5) on either side of the plate and begins to eat. Inspired by his colleague,

(figure 5.14)

The dining philosophers' table, before the meal begins.

Philosopher 3 (P3) does likewise, using F2 and F3. Now Philosopher 2 (P2) decides to begin the meal but is unable to start because no forks are available: F1 has been allocated to P1 and F2 has been allocated to P3, and the only remaining fork can be used only by P4 or P5. So Philosopher 2 must wait.

Soon, P3 finishes eating, puts down his two forks and resumes his pondering. Should the fork beside him (F2), that's now free, be allocated to the hungry philosopher (P2)? Although it's tempting, such a move would be a bad precedent because if the philosophers are allowed to tie up resources with only the hope that the other required resource will become available, the dinner could easily slip into an unsafe state; it would be only a matter of time before each philosopher held a single fork—and nobody could eat. So the resources are allocated to the philosophers only when both forks are available at the same time. The status of the "system" is illustrated in Figure 5.15.

P4 and P5 are quietly thinking and P1 is still eating when P3 (who should be full) decides to eat some more and because the resources are free he is able to take F2 and F3 once again. Soon thereafter, P1 finishes and releases F1 and F5, but P2 is still not

(figure 5.15)

Each philosopher must have both forks to begin eating, the one on the right and the one on the left. Unless the resources, the forks, are allocated fairly, some philosophers may starve.

F5   P1   F1

P5   P2   *Waiting for F1

F4   F2

P4   P3

F3

able to eat because F2 is now allocated. This scenario could continue forever, and as long as P1 and P3 alternate their use of the available resources P2 must wait. P1 and P3 can eat any time they wish while P2 starves—only inches from nourishment.

In a computer environment, the resources are like forks and the competing processes are like dining philosophers. If the resource manager doesn't watch for starving processes and jobs, and plan for their eventual completion, they could remain in the system forever waiting for the right combination of resources.

To address this problem, an algorithm designed to detect starving jobs can be implemented, which tracks how long each job has been waiting for resources (this is the same as aging, described in Chapter 4). Once starvation has been detected, the system can block new jobs until the starving jobs have been satisfied. This algorithm must be monitored closely: if it's done too often then new jobs will be blocked too frequently and throughput will be diminished. If it's not done often enough starving jobs will remain in the system for an unacceptably long period of time.

Conclusion

Every operating system must dynamically allocate a limited number of resources while avoiding the two extremes of deadlock and starvation.

In this chapter we discussed several methods of dealing with deadlocks: prevention, avoidance, and detection and recovery. Deadlocks can be prevented by not allowing the four conditions of a deadlock to occur in the system at the same time. By eliminating at least one of the four conditions (mutual exclusion, resource holding, no preemption, and circular wait) the system can be kept deadlock-free. As we've seen, the disadvantage of a preventive policy is that each of these conditions is vital to different parts of the system at least some of the time, so prevention algorithms are complex and to routinely execute them involves high overhead.

Deadlocks can be avoided by clearly identifying safe states and unsafe states and requiring the system to keep enough resources in reserve to guarantee that all jobs active in the system can run to completion. The disadvantage of an avoidance policy is that the system's resources aren't allocated to their fullest potential.

If a system doesn't support prevention or avoidance then it must be prepared to detect and recover from the deadlocks that occur. Unfortunately, this option usually relies on the selection of at least one "victim"—a job that must be terminated before it finishes execution and restarted from the beginning.

In the next chapter we'll look at problems related to the synchronization of processes in a multiprocessing environment.

Key Terms

avoidance: the dynamic strategy of deadlock avoidance that attempts to ensure that resources are never allocated in such a way as to place a system in an unsafe state.

circular wait: one of four conditions for deadlock through which each process involved is waiting for a resource being held by another; each process is blocked and can't continue, resulting in deadlock.

deadlock: a problem occurring when the resources needed by some jobs to finish execution are held by other jobs, which, in turn, are waiting for other resources to become available. Also called *deadly embrace*.

detection: the process of examining the state of an operating system to determine whether a deadlock exists.

directed graphs: a graphic model representing various states of resource allocations.

livelock: a locked system whereby two (or more) processes continually block the forward progress of the other without making any forward progress itself. It is similar to a deadlock except that neither process is blocked or waiting; both are in a continuous state of change.

locking: a technique used to guarantee the integrity of the data in a database through which the user locks out all other users while working with the database.

mutual exclusion: one of four conditions for deadlock in which only one process is allowed to have access to a resource.

no preemption: one of four conditions for deadlock in which a process is allowed to hold on to resources while it is waiting for other resources to finish execution.

prevention: a design strategy for an operating system where resources are managed in such a way that some of the necessary conditions for deadlock do not hold.

process synchronization: (1) the need for algorithms to resolve conflicts between processors in a multiprocessing environment; or (2) the need to ensure that events occur in the proper order even if they are carried out by several processes.

race: a synchronization problem between two processes vying for the same resource.

recovery: the steps that must be taken, when deadlock is detected, by breaking the circle of waiting processes.

resource holding: one of four conditions for deadlock in which each process refuses to relinquish the resources it holds until its execution is completed even though it isn't using them because it's waiting for other resources.

safe state: the situation in which the system has enough available resources to guarantee the completion of at least one job running on the system.

spooling: a technique developed to speed I/O by collecting in a disk file either input received from slow input devices or output going to slow output devices such as printers.

starvation: the result of conservative allocation of resources in which a single job is prevented from execution because it's kept waiting for resources that never become available.

unsafe state: a situation in which the system has too few available resources to guarantee the completion of at least one job running on the system. It can lead to deadlock.

victim: an expendable job that is selected for removal from a deadlocked system to provide more resources to the waiting jobs and resolve the deadlock.

Exercises

Research Topic

Research current literature for the name of the first operating system to power an electronic computer. Don't include manual computing machines. Attach a copy of the documentation from your research that supports your answer.

Exercises

1. What are the major differences between deadlock, starvation, and race?
2. Give some "real life" examples (not related to a computer system environment) of deadlock, starvation, and race.
3. Select one example of deadlock from Exercise 2 and list the four necessary conditions needed for the deadlock.
4. Suppose the narrow staircase (used as an example in the beginning of this chapter) has become a major source of aggravation. Design an algorithm for using it so that both deadlock and starvation are not possible.
5. Figure 5.16 shows a tunnel going through a mountain and two streets parallel to each other—one at each entrance/exit of the tunnel. Traffic lights are located at each end of the tunnel to control the crossflow of traffic through each intersection. Based on the figure, answer the following questions.
   a. Can deadlock occur? How can it happen and under what circumstances?
   b. How can deadlock be detected?
   c. Give a solution to prevent deadlock but watch out for starvation.

(Figure 5.16)

Traffic flow diagram for Exercise 5.

6. Consider the directed resource graph shown in Figure 5.17, and answer the following questions.

a. Is this system deadlocked?

b. Are there any blocked processes?

c. What is the resulting graph after reduction by P1?

d. What is the resulting graph after reduction by P2?

e. Both P1 and P2 have requested R2:

    1. What is the status of the system if P2's request is granted before P1's?

    2. What is the status of the system if P1's request is granted before P2's?

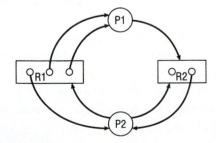

(Figure 5.17)

Directed resource graph for Exercise 6.

7. Consider the directed resource graph shown in Figure 5.18, and answer the following questions.

   a. Is this system, as a whole, deadlocked?

   b. Are there any deadlocked processes?

   c. Three processes—P1, P2, and P3—are requesting resources from R2.

      1. Which requests would you satisfy to minimize the number of processes involved in the deadlock?

      2. Which requests would you satisfy to maximize the number of processes involved in deadlock?

   d. Can the graph be reduced, partially or totally?

   e. Can the deadlock be resolved without selecting a victim?

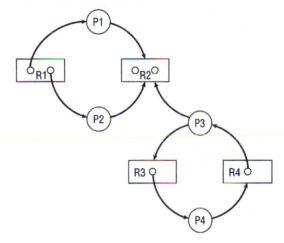

8. Consider a computing system with 13 tape drives. All jobs running on this system require a maximum of 5 tape drives to complete but they each run for long periods of time with just 4 drives and request the fifth one only at the very end of the run. The job stream is endless.

   a. If your operating system supports a very conservative device allocation policy no job will be started unless all tapes required have been allocated to it for the duration of its run:

      1. What is the maximum number of jobs that can be active at once?

      2. What are the minimum and maximum number of tape drives that may be idle as a result of this policy?

      3. Explain your answer.

   b. If your operating system supports the Banker's Algorithm:

      1. What is the maximum number of jobs that can be in progress at once?

      2. What are the minimum and maximum number of tape drives that may be idle as a result of this policy?

      3. Explain your answer.

9-11. For the three systems described in exercises 9 through 11, given that all of the devices are of the same type, and using the definitions presented in the discussion of the Banker's Algorithm, answer these questions.

    a. Determine the "remaining needs" for each job in each system.

    b. Determine whether each of the systems is safe or unsafe.

    c. If the system is in a safe state, list the sequence of requests and releases that will make it possible for all processes to run to completion.

    d. If the system is in an unsafe state, show how it's possible for deadlock to occur.

  9. System A has 12 devices; only 1 is available.

Job No.	Devices Allocated	Maximum Required	Remaining Needs
1	5	6	
2	4	7	
3	2	6	
4	0	2	

  10. System B has 14 devices; only 2 are available.

Job No.	Devices Allocated	Maximum Required	Remaining Needs
1	5	8	
2	3	9	
3	4	8	

  11. System C has 12 devices; only 2 are available.

Job No.	Devices Allocated	Maximum Required	Remaining Needs
1	5	8	
2	4	6	
3	1	4	

Advanced Exercises

12. Suppose you are an operating system designer and have been approached by the operator to help solve the recurring deadlock problem in your installation's spooling system. What features might you incorporate into the operating system so that deadlocks in the spooling system can be resolved without loss of work done by the processes involved?

13. A system in an unsafe state is not necessarily deadlocked. Explain why this is true. Give an example of a system in an unsafe state and show how all the processes could be completed without having deadlock occurring.

14. State how you would design and implement a mechanism to allow the operating system to detect which of the processes are starving.

15. Given the four primary types of resources—CPU, memory, storage devices, and files—select for each one the most suitable technique for fighting deadlock and briefly explain why it is your choice.

16. State the limitations imposed on programs (and on systems) that have to follow a hierarchical ordering of resources; for example, disks, printers, terminals, and files.

17. Consider a banking system with ten accounts. Transfer of funds between two of those accounts may occur by following these steps:

    lock A(i);   lock A(j);
    update A(i);   update A(j);
    unlock A(i);   unlock A(j);

    a. Can this system become deadlocked? If yes, show how. If no, explain why not.

    b. Could the numbering request policy (presented in the chapter discussion about detection) be implemented to prevent deadlock if the number of accounts is dynamic? Explain why or why not.

Chapter 6 | Concurrent Processes

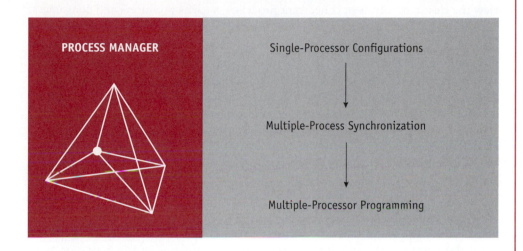

PROCESS MANAGER

Single-Processor Configurations

↓

Multiple-Process Synchronization

↓

Multiple-Processor Programming

> " *The measure of power is obstacles overcome.* "
>
> Oliver Wendell Holmes, Jr. *(1841–1935)*

Learning Objectives

After completing this chapter, you should be able to describe:

- The critical difference between processes and processors, and their connection
- The differences among common configurations of multiprocessing systems
- The significance of a critical region in process synchronization
- The basic concepts of process synchronization software: test-and-set, WAIT and SIGNAL, and semaphores
- The need for process cooperation when several processes work together
- How several processors, executing a single job, cooperate
- The similarities and differences between processes and threads
- The significance of concurrent programming languages and their applications

In Chapters 4 and 5, we described systems that use only one CPU. In this chapter we look at multiprocessing systems, those with more than one CPU. Discuss the reasons for their development, their advantages, and their problems.

As we will see in this chapter, the key to successful multiprocessing has been the object of extensive research. We'll examine several configurations of processors and review the classic problems of concurrent processes, such as producers and consumers, readers and writers, and the missed waiting customer. While the problems occur in single-processor systems, they are presented here because they apply to multiprocesses in general, whether they involve a single processor (with two or more processes) or more than one processor (hence, multiprocesses). The chapter concludes with a brief look at the Java programming language as well as a case study of process management strategies for Linux. Information on how other systems manage processors and processes is presented in the Processor Management sections of Chapters 13–15.

What Is Parallel Processing?

Parallel processing, also called **multiprocessing**, is a situation in which two or more processors operate in unison. That means two or more CPUs are executing instructions simultaneously. Therefore, with more than one process executing at the same time, each CPU can have a process in the RUNNING state at the same time. For multiprocessing systems, the Processor Manager has to coordinate the activity of each processor, as well as synchronize the interaction among the CPUs.

The complexities of the Processor Manager's task when dealing with multiple processors or multiple processes are easily illustrated with an example: You're late for an early afternoon appointment and you're in danger of missing lunch, so you get in line for the drive-through window of the local fast-food shop. When you place your order, the order clerk confirms your request, tells you how much it will cost, and asks you to drive to the pick-up window where a cashier collects your money and hands over your order. All's well and once again you're on your way—driving and thriving. You just witnessed a well-synchronized multiprocessing system. Although you came in contact with just two processors—the order clerk and the cashier—there were at least two other processors behind the scenes who cooperated to make the system work—the cook and the bagger.

The fast-food restaurant is similar to an information retrieval system. Processor 1 (the order clerk) accepts the query, checks for errors, and passes the request on to Processor 2 (the bagger). Processor 2 (the bagger) searches the database for the required information (the hamburger). Processor 3 (the cook) retrieves the data from the database (the meat to cook for the hamburger) if it's kept off-line in secondary storage. Once the data is gathered (the hamburger is cooked), it's placed where Processor 2 can get it (in the hamburger bin). Processor 2 (the bagger) passes it on to Processor 4 (the cashier). Processor 4 (the cashier) routes the response (your order) back to the originator of the request—you.

Synchronization is the key to the system's success because many things can go wrong in a multiprocessing system. For example, what if the communications system broke down and you couldn't speak with the order clerk? What if the cook produced hamburgers at full speed all day, even during slow periods? What would happen to the extra hamburgers? What if the cook became badly burned and couldn't cook anymore? What would the bagger do if there were no hamburgers? What if the cashier decided to take your money but didn't give you any food? Obviously, the system can't work properly unless every processor communicates and cooperates with every other processor.

Multiprocessors were developed for high-end models of IBM mainframes and VAX midrange computers where the operating system treated additional CPUs as additional resources that could be scheduled for work (Lane & Mooney, 1988).

Since the mid-1980s, when the costs of CPU hardware began to decline, multiprocessor systems with dozens of CPUs have found their way into business environments. Systems containing tens of thousands of CPUs (systems that had once been available only for research) could then be found in production environments. Today multiprocessor systems are available on systems of every size.

There are two major forces behind the development of multiprocessing: to enhance throughput and to increase computing power. And there are two primary benefits: increased reliability and faster processing.

The reliability stems from the availability of more than one CPU: if one processor fails, then the others can continue to operate and absorb the load. This isn't simple to do; the system must be carefully designed so that, first, the failing processor can inform the other processor(s) to take over and, second, the operating system can restructure its resource allocation strategies so the remaining processors don't become overloaded.

The increased processing speed is achieved because instructions can be processed in parallel, two or more at a time, in one of several ways. Some systems allocate a CPU to each program or job. Others allocate a CPU to each working set or parts of it. Still others subdivide individual instructions so each subdivision can be processed simultaneously. (This is called **concurrent programming** and will be discussed in detail later in this chapter.)

Increased flexibility brings increased complexity, however, and two major challenges remain: how to connect the processors into configurations and how to orchestrate their interaction, which applies to multiple interacting processes as well. (It might help if you think of each process as being run on a separate processor although, in reality, there is only one doing all the work.)

Typical Multiprocessing Configurations

Much depends on how the multiple processors are configured within the system. Three typical configurations are: master/slave, loosely coupled, and symmetric.

Master/Slave Configuration

The **master/slave** configuration is an asymmetric multiprocessing system. Conceptually, it's a single-processor system with additional slave processors, each of which is managed by the primary master processor as shown in Figure 6.1.

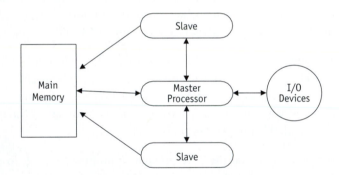

(figure 6.1)

In a master/slave multi-processing configuration, slave processors send all I/O requests through the master processor.

The master processor is responsible for managing the entire system—all files, devices, memory, and processors. Therefore it maintains the status of all processes in the system, performs storage management activities, schedules the work for the other processors, and executes all control programs. This configuration is well suited for computing environments in which processing time is divided between front-end and back-end processors; in these cases the front-end processor takes care of the interactive users and quick jobs, and the back-end processor takes care of those with long jobs using the batch mode.

The primary advantage of this configuration is its simplicity. However, it has three serious disadvantages:

- Its reliability is no higher than for a single processor system because if the master processor fails, the entire system fails.
- It can lead to poor use of resources because if a slave processor should become free while the master processor is busy, the slave must wait until the master becomes free and can assign more work to it.
- It increases the number of interrupts because all slave processors must interrupt the master processor every time they need operating system intervention, such as for I/O

requests. This creates long queues at the master processor level when there are many processors and many interrupts.

Loosely Coupled Configuration

The **loosely coupled configuration** features several complete computer systems, each with its own memory, I/O devices, CPU, and operating system, as shown in Figure 6.2.

(figure 6.2)

In a loosely coupled multiprocessing configuration, each processor has its own dedicated resources.

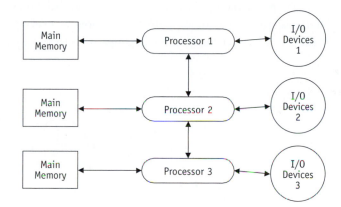

It is called loosely coupled because each processor controls its own resources—its own files and its own I/O devices—and that means that each processor maintains its own commands and I/O management tables. The only difference between a loosely coupled multiprocessing system and a collection of independent single-processing systems is that each processor can communicate and cooperate with the others.

When a job arrives for the first time, it's assigned to one processor. Once allocated, the job will remain with the same processor until it's finished. Therefore each processor must have global tables that indicate to which processor each job has been allocated.

To keep the system well-balanced and to ensure the best use of resources, job scheduling is based on several requirements and policies. For example, new jobs might be assigned to the processor with the lightest load or the best combination of output devices available.

This system isn't prone to catastrophic system failures because even when a single processor fails, the others can continue to work independently. However, it can be difficult to detect when a processor has failed.

Symmetric Configuration

The **symmetric configuration** is best implemented if the processors are all of the same type. It has four advantages over loosely coupled configuration:

• It's more reliable

• It uses resources effectively

• It can balance loads well

• It can degrade gracefully in the event of a failure

However, it is the most difficult configuration to implement because the processes must be well synchronized to avoid the problems of races and deadlocks that we discussed in Chapter 5.

In a symmetric configuration, processor scheduling is decentralized (as depicted in Figure 6.3). A single copy of the operating system and a global table listing each process and its status is stored in a common area of memory so every processor has access to it. Each processor uses the same scheduling algorithm to select which process it will run next.

(figure 6.3)

A symmetric multiprocessing configuration with homogeneous processors. Processes must be carefully synchronized to avoid deadlocks and starvation.

Whenever a process is interrupted, whether because of an I/O request or another type of interrupt, its processor updates the corresponding entry in the process list and finds another process to run. This means that the processors are kept quite busy. But it also means that any given job or task may be executed by several different processors during its run time. And because each processor has access to all I/O devices and can reference any storage unit, there are more conflicts as several processors try to access the same resource at the same time.

This presents the obvious need for algorithms to resolve conflicts between processors—that's **process synchronization**.

Process Synchronization Software

The success of process synchronization hinges on the capability of the operating system to make a resource unavailable to other processes while it is being used by one of them. These "resources" can include I/O devices, a location in storage, or a data file. In essence, the used resource must be locked away from other processes until it is released. Only when it is released is a waiting process allowed to use the resource. This is where synchronization is critical. A mistake could leave a job waiting indefinitely or, if it's a key resource, cause a deadlock.

It is the same thing that happens in a crowded ice cream parlor. Customers take a number to be served. The numbers on the wall are changed by the clerks who pull a chain to increment them as they attend to each customer. But what happens when there is no synchronization between serving the customers and changing the number? Chaos. This is the case of the missed waiting customer (Madnick & Donovan, 1974).

Let's say your number is 75. Clerk 1 is waiting on customer 73 and Clerk 2 is waiting on customer 74. The sign on the wall says "Now Serving #74" and you're ready with your order. Clerk 2 finishes with customer 74 and pulls the chain so the sign says "Now Serving #75." But just then the clerk is called to the telephone and leaves the building, never to return (an interrupt). Meanwhile, Clerk 1 pulls the chain and proceeds to wait on #76—and you've missed your turn. If you speak up quickly, you can correct the mistake gracefully, but when it happens in a computer system the outcome isn't as easily remedied.

Consider the scenario in which Processor 1 and Processor 2 finish with their current jobs at the same time. To run the next job each processor must:

1. Consult the list of jobs to see which one should be run next
2. Retrieve the job for execution
3. Increment the READY list to the next job
4. Execute it

Both go to the READY list to select a job. Processor 1 sees that Job 74 is the next job to be run and goes to retrieve it. A moment later, Processor 2 also selects Job 74 and goes to retrieve it. Shortly thereafter, Processor 1, having retrieved Job 74, returns to the READY list and increments it, moving Job 75 to the top. A moment later Processor 2 returns; it has also retrieved Job 74 and is ready to process it, so it increments the READY list and now Job 76 is moved to the top and becomes the next job in line to be processed. Job 75 has become the missed waiting customer and will never be processed, while Job 74 is being processed twice—an unacceptable state of affairs.

There are several other places where this problem can occur: memory and page allocation tables, I/O tables, application databases, and any shared resource.

Obviously, this situation calls for synchronization. Several synchronization mechanisms are available to provide cooperation and communication among processes. The common element in all synchronization schemes is to allow a process to finish work on a critical region of the program before other processes have access to it. This is applicable both to multiprocessors and to two or more processes in a single-processor (time-shared) processing system. It is called a **critical region** because its execution must be handled as a unit. As we've seen, the processes within a critical region can't be interleaved without threatening the integrity of the operation.

Synchronization is sometimes implemented as a lock-and-key arrangement: before a process can work on a critical region, it's required to get the key. And once it has the key, all other processes are locked out until it finishes, when it unlocks the entry to the critical region and returns the key so another process can get the key and begin work. This sequence consists of two actions: (1) the process must first see if the key is available and (2) if it is available, the process must pick it up and put it in the lock to make it unavailable to all other processes. For this scheme to work both actions must be performed in a single machine cycle; otherwise it is conceivable that while the first process is ready to pick up the key, another one would find the key available and prepare to pick up the key—and each could block the other from proceeding any further.

Several locking mechanisms have been developed including test-and-set, WAIT and SIGNAL, and semaphores.

Test-and-Set

Test-and-set is a single indivisible machine instruction known simply as **TS** and was introduced by IBM for its multiprocessing System 360/370 computers. In a single machine cycle it tests to see if the key is available and, if it is, sets it to unavailable.

The actual key is a single bit in a storage location that can contain a zero (if it's free) or a one (if busy). We can consider TS to be a function subprogram that has one parameter (the storage location) and returns one value (the condition code: busy/free), with the exception that it takes only one machine cycle.

Therefore, a process (P1) would test the condition code using the TS instruction before entering a critical region. If no other process was in this critical region, then P1 would be allowed to proceed and the condition code would be changed from zero to one. Later, when P1 exits the critical region, the condition code is reset to zero so another process can enter. On the other hand, if P1 finds a busy condition code, then it's placed in a waiting loop where it continues to test the condition code and waits until it's free (Calingaert, 1982).

Although it's a simple procedure to implement, and works well for a small number of processes, test-and-set has two major drawbacks. First, when many processes are waiting to enter a critical region, starvation could occur because the processes gain access in an arbitrary fashion. Unless a first-come, first-served policy were set up, some processes could be favored over others. A second drawback is that waiting processes remain in unproductive, resource-consuming wait loops. This is known as **busy waiting**—which not only consumes valuable processor time but also relies on the competing processes to test the key, something that is best handled by the operating system or the hardware.

WAIT and SIGNAL

WAIT and SIGNAL is a modification of test-and-set that's designed to remove busy waiting. Two new operations, which are mutually exclusive and become part of the process scheduler's set of operations, are WAIT and SIGNAL.

WAIT is activated when the process encounters a busy condition code. WAIT sets the process's process control block (PCB) to the blocked state and links it to the queue of processes waiting to enter this particular critical region. The Process Scheduler then selects another process for execution. SIGNAL is activated when a process exits the critical region and the condition code is set to "free." It checks the queue of processes waiting to enter this critical region and selects one, setting it to the READY state. Eventually the Process Scheduler will choose this process for running. The addition of the operations WAIT and SIGNAL frees the processes from the busy waiting dilemma and returns control to the operating system, which can then run other jobs while the waiting processes are idle (WAIT).

Semaphores

A **semaphore** is a nonnegative integer variable that's used as a flag. The most well-known semaphores are the flag-like signaling devices used by railroads to indicate whether a section of track is clear. When the arm of the semaphore is raised, the track is clear and the train can proceed. When the arm is lowered, the track is busy and the train must wait until the arm is raised, as shown in Figure 6.4.

In an operating system a semaphore performs a similar function: it signals if and when a resource is free and can be used by a process. Dijkstra (1965) introduced two operations to operate the semaphore to overcome the process synchronization problem we've discussed. Dijkstra called them P and V and that's how they're known today. The P stands for the Dutch word *proberen* (to test) and the V stands for *verhogen* (to increment). The P and V operations do just that: they test and increment.

(figure 6.4)

The semaphore used by railroads indicates whether the train can proceed. When it's lowered (a), an oncoming train is expected. If it is raised (b), the train can continue.

(a) Stop   (b) All Clear

Here's how they work. If we let s be a semaphore variable, then the V operation on s is simply to increment s by 1. The action can be stated as:

$$V(s): s: = s + 1$$

This in turn necessitates a fetch, increment, and store sequence. Like the test-and-set operation, the V operation must be performed as a single indivisible action to avoid deadlocks. And that means that s cannot be accessed by any other process during the operation.

The operation P on s is to test the value of s and, if it's not zero, to decrement it by one. The action can be stated as:

$$P(s): \text{If } s > 0 \text{ then } s: = s - 1$$

This involves a test, fetch, decrement, and store sequence. Again this sequence must be performed as an indivisible action in a single machine cycle or have it arranged that the process cannot take action until the operation (P or V) is finished.

The operations P and V are executed by the operating system in response to calls issued by any one process naming a semaphore as parameter (this alleviates the process from having control). If $s = 0$, it means that the critical region is busy and the process calling on the P operation must wait until the operation can be executed and that's not until $s > 0$.

As shown in Table 6.1, P3 is placed in the WAIT state (for the semaphore) on State 4. As also shown in Table 6.1, for States 6 and 8, when a process exits the critical region, the value of s is reset to 1 indicating that the critical region is free. This, in turn, triggers the awakening of one of the blocked processes, its entry into the critical region, and the resetting of s to zero. In State 7, P1 and P2 are not trying to do processing in that critical region and P4 is still blocked (Madnick & Donovan, 1974).

	Actions			Results		
State Number	Calling Process	Operation		Running in Critical Region	Blocked on s	Value of s
0						1
1	P1	P(s)		P1		0
2	P1	V(s)				1
3	P2	P(s)		P2		0
4	P3	P(s)		P2	P3	0
5	P4	P(s)		P2	P3, P4	0
6	P2	V(s)		P3	P4	0
7				P3	P4	0
8	P3	V(s)		P4		0
9	P4	V(s)				1

(table 6.1)

The sequence of states for four processes calling P and V operations on the binary semaphore s. (Note: the value of the semaphore before the operation is shown on the line preceding the operation. The current value is on the same line.)

After State 5 of Table 6.1, the longest waiting process, P3, was the one selected to enter the critical region, but that isn't necessarily the case unless the system is using a first-in first-out selection policy. In fact, the choice of which job will be processed next depends on the algorithm used by this portion of the Process Scheduler.

As you can see from Table 6.1, P and V operations on semaphore s enforce the concept of mutual exclusion, which is necessary to avoid having two operations attempt to execute at the same time. The name traditionally given to this semaphore in the literature is **mutex** and it stands for MUTual EXclusion. So the operations become:

```
P(mutex): if mutex > 0 then mutex: = mutex - 1
V(mutex): mutex: = mutex + 1
```

In Chapter 5 we talked about the requirement for mutual exclusion when several jobs were trying to access the same shared physical resources. The concept is the same here, but we have several processes trying to access the same shared critical region. The procedure can generalize to semaphores having values greater than zero and one.

Thus far we've looked at the problem of mutual exclusion presented by interacting parallel processes using the same shared data at different rates of execution. This can apply to several processes on more than one processor, or interacting (codependent) processes on a single processor. In this case the concept of a critical region becomes necessary because it ensures that parallel processes will modify shared data only while in the critical region.

In sequential computations mutual exclusion is achieved automatically because each operation is handled in order, one at a time. However, in parallel computations the order of execution can change, so mutual exclusion must be explicitly stated and maintained. In fact, the entire premise of parallel processes hinges on the requirement that all operations on common variables consistently exclude one another over time (Brinch Hansen, 1973).

Process Cooperation

There are occasions when several processes work directly together to complete a common task. Two famous examples are the problems of producers and consumers and of readers and writers. Each case requires both mutual exclusion and synchronization, and each is implemented by using semaphores.

Producers and Consumers

The classic problem of **producers and consumers** is one in which one process produces some data that another process consumes later. Although we'll describe the case with one producer and one consumer, it can be expanded to several pairs of producers and consumers.

Let's return for a moment to the fast-food framework at the beginning of this chapter because the synchronization between two of the processors (the cook and the bagger) represents a significant problem in operating systems. The cook *produces* hamburgers that are sent to the bagger *(consumed)*. Both processors have access to one common area, the hamburger bin, which can hold only a finite number of hamburgers (this is called a buffer area). The bin is a necessary storage area because the speed at which hamburgers are produced is independent from the speed at which they are consumed.

Problems arise at two extremes: when the producer attempts to add to an already full bin (as when the cook tries to put one more hamburger into a full bin) and when the consumer attempts to draw from an empty bin (as when the bagger tries to take a hamburger that hasn't been made yet). In real life, the people watch the bin and if it's empty or too full the problem is recognized and quickly resolved. However, in a computer system such resolution is not so easy.

Consider the case of the prolific CPU. The CPU can generate output data much faster than a line printer can print it. Therefore, since this involves a producer and a consumer of two different speeds, we need a buffer where the producer can temporarily store data that can be retrieved by the consumer at a more appropriate speed. Figure 6.5 shows three typical buffer states.

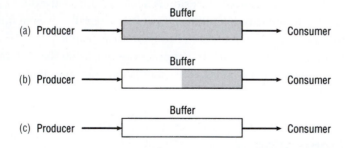

(figure 6.5)

The buffer can be in any one of these three states: (a) full buffer, (b) partially empty buffer, or (c) empty buffer.

Because the buffer can hold only a finite amount of data, the synchronization process must delay the producer from generating more data when the buffer is full. It must also be prepared to delay the consumer from retrieving data when the buffer is empty. This task can be implemented by two counting semaphores—one to indicate the number of full positions in the buffer and the other to indicate the number of empty positions in the buffer.

A third semaphore, mutex, will ensure mutual exclusion between processes.

Here are the definitions of the producer and consumer processes:

Producer	Consumer
produce data	P (full)
P (empty)	P (mutex)
P (mutex)	read data from buffer
write data into buffer	V (mutex)
V (mutex)	V (empty)
V (full)	consume data

The following list gives the definitions of the variables and functions used in the producers and consumers algorithm:

Given:	Full, Empty, Mutex defined as semaphores
n:	maximum number of positions in the buffer
V (x):	x: = x + 1 (x is any variable defined as a semaphore)
P (x):	if x > 0 then x: = x − 1
mutex = 1	means the process is allowed to enter the critical region

And here is the algorithm that implements the interaction between producer and consumer. **COBEGIN** and **COEND** are delimiters used to indicate sections of code to be done concurrently.

Producers and Consumers Algorithm

```
empty: = n
full: = 0
mutex: = 1
COBEGIN
      repeat until no more data PRODUCER
      repeat until buffer is empty CONSUMER
COEND
```

The processes (producer and consumer) then execute as described previously. You can try the code with $n = 3$ or try an alternate order of execution to see how it actually works.

The concept of producers and consumers can be extended to buffers that hold records or other data, as well as to other situations in which direct process-to-process communication of messages is required.

Readers and Writers

The problem of **readers and writers** was first formulated by Courtois, Heymans, and Parnas (1971) and arises when two types of processes need to access a shared resource such as a file or database. They called these processes readers and writers.

An airline reservation system is a good example. The readers are those who want flight information. They're called readers because they only read the existing data; they don't modify it. And because no one is changing the database, the system can allow many readers to be active at the same time—there's no need to enforce mutual exclusion among them.

The writers are those who are making reservations on a particular flight. Writers must be carefully accommodated because they are modifying existing data in the database. The system can't allow someone to be writing while someone else is reading (or writing). Therefore, it must enforce mutual exclusion if there are groups of readers and a writer, or if there are several writers, in the system. Of course the system must be fair when it enforces its policy to avoid indefinite postponement of readers or writers.

In the original paper, Courtois, Heymans, and Parnas offered two solutions using P and V operations. The first gives priority to readers over writers so readers are kept waiting only if a writer is actually modifying the data. However, this policy results in writer starvation if there is a continuous stream of readers. The second policy gives priority to the writers. In this case, as soon as a writer arrives, any readers that are already active are allowed to finish processing, but all additional readers are put on hold until the writer is done. Obviously this policy results in reader starvation if a continuous stream of writers is present. Either scenario is unacceptable.

To prevent either type of starvation, Hoare (1974) proposed the following combination priority policy. When a writer is finished, any and all readers who are waiting, or on hold, are allowed to read. Then, when that group of readers is finished, the writer who is on hold can begin, and any *new* readers who arrive in the meantime aren't allowed to start until the writer is finished.

The state of the system can be summarized by four counters initialized to zero:
- Number of readers who have *requested* a resource and haven't yet released it (R1 = 0)
- Number of readers who are *using* a resource and haven't yet released it (R2 = 0)
- Number of writers who have *requested* a resource and haven't yet released it (W1 = 0)
- Number of writers who are *using* a resource and haven't yet released it (W2 = 0)

This can be implemented using two semaphores to ensure mutual exclusion between readers and writers. A resource can be given to all readers, provided that no writers are processing (W2 = 0). A resource can be given to a writer, provided that no readers are reading (R2 = 0) and no writers are writing (W2 = 0).

Readers must always call two procedures: the first checks whether the resources can be immediately granted for reading; and then, when the resource is released, the second checks to see if there are any writers waiting. The same holds true for writers. The first procedure must determine if the resource can be immediately granted for writing, and then, upon releasing the resource, the second procedure will find out if any readers are waiting.

Concurrent Programming

Until now we've looked at multiprocessing as several jobs executing at the same time on a single processor (which interacts with I/O processors, for example) or on multiprocessors. Multiprocessing can also refer to one job using several processors to execute sets of instructions in parallel. The concept isn't new, but it requires a programming language and a computer system that can support this type of construct. This type of system is referred to as a **concurrent processing system**.

Applications of Concurrent Programming

Most programming languages are serial in nature—instructions are executed one at a time. Therefore, to resolve an arithmetic expression, every operation is done in sequence following the order prescribed by the programmer and compiler. Table 6.2 shows the steps to compute the following expression:

$$A = 3 * B * C + 4 / (D + E) ** (F - G)$$

(table 6.2)

The sequential computation of the expression requires several steps. (In this example, there are seven steps, but each step may involve more than one machine operation.)

Step No.	Operation	Result
1	(F − G)	Store difference in T1
2	(D + E)	Store sum in T2
3	(T2) ** (T1)	Store power in T1
4	4 / (T1)	Store quotient in T2
5	3 * B	Store product in T1
6	(T1) * C	Store product in T1
7	(T1) + (T2)	Store sum in A

For many computational purposes, serial processing is sufficient; it's easy to implement and fast enough for most users.

However, arithmetic expressions can be processed differently if we use a language that allows for concurrent processing. Let's define two terms—COBEGIN and COEND—that will indicate to the compiler which instructions can be processed concurrently. Then we'll rewrite our expression to take advantage of a concurrent processing compiler.

```
COBEGIN
    T1 = 3 * B
    T2 = D + E
    T3 = F - G
COEND
COBEGIN
    T4 = T1 * C
    T5 = T2 ** T3
COEND
    A = T4 + 4 / T5
```

As shown in Table 6.3, to solve $A = 3 * B * C + 4 / (D + E) ** (F - G)$, the first three operations can be done at the same time if our computer system has at least three processors. The next two operations are done at the same time, and the last expression is performed serially with the results of the first two steps.

Step No.	Processor	Operation	Result
1	1	3 * B	Store difference in T_1
	2	(D + E)	Store sum in T_2
	3	(F – G)	Store difference in T_3
2	1	(T_1) * C	Store product in T_4
	2	(T_2) ** (T_3)	Store power in T_5
3	1	4 / (T_5)	Store quotient in T_1
4	1	(T_4) + (T_1)	Store sum in A

(table 6.3)

With concurrent processing, the seven-step procedure can be processed in only four steps, which reduces execution time.

With this system we've increased the computation speed, but we've also increased the complexity of the programming language and the hardware (both machinery and communication among machines). In fact, we've also placed a large burden on the programmer—to explicitly state which instructions can be executed in parallel. This is **explicit parallelism**.

Early concurrent processing programs relied on the programmer to write the parallel instructions, but there were problems. Coding was a time-consuming task and led to missed opportunities for parallel processing. It also led to errors where parallel processing was mistakenly indicated. And from a maintenance standpoint the programs were difficult to modify. The solution: automatic detection by the *compiler* of instructions that can be performed in parallel. This is called **implicit parallelism**.

With a true concurrent processing system, the example presented in Tables 6.2 and 6.3 is coded as a single expression. It is the compiler that translates the algebraic expression into separate instructions and decides which can be performed in parallel and which in serial mode.

For example, the equation $Y = A + B * C + D$ could be rearranged by the compiler as $A + D + B * C$ so that two operations $A + D$ and $B * C$ would be done in parallel, leaving the final addition to be calculated last.

As shown in the four cases that follow, concurrent processing can also dramatically reduce the complexity of working with array operations within loops, of performing matrix multiplication, of conducting parallel searches in databases, and of sorting or merging files. Some of these systems use parallel processors that execute the same type of tasks (Ben-Ari, 1982).

Case 1: Array Operations

To perform an array operation within a loop in three steps, the instruction might say:

```
for(j = 1; j <= 3; j++)
    a(j) = b(j) + c(j);
```

If we use three processors, the instruction can be performed in a single step like this:

Processor #1 performs: $a(1) = b(1) + c(1)$
Processor #2 performs: $a(2) = b(2) + c(2)$
Processor #3 performs: $a(3) = b(3) + c(3)$

Case 2: Matrix Multiplication

To perform $C = A * B$ where A and B represent two matrices:

Matrix A

$$\begin{bmatrix} 1 & 2 & 3 \\ 4 & 5 & 6 \\ 7 & 8 & 9 \end{bmatrix}$$

Matrix B

$$\begin{bmatrix} 1 & 2 & 3 \\ 4 & 5 & 6 \\ 7 & 8 & 9 \end{bmatrix}$$

Several elements of the first row of matrix A could be multiplied by corresponding elements of the first column of matrix B. This process could be repeated until all of the products for the first element of matrix C would be computed and the result obtained by summing the products. The actual number of products that could be computed at the same time would depend on the number of processors available. Serially the answer can be computed in 45 steps. With three processors it takes only 27 steps by doing the multiplications in parallel.

Case 3: Searching Databases

Searching is a common nonmathematical application of concurrent processing. Each processor searches a different section of the database or file. It's a very fast way to find terms in a thesaurus, authors in a bibliographic database, or terms in inverted files. (Inverted files are generated from full document databases. Each record in an inverted file contains a subject term and the document numbers where that subject is found.)

Case 4: Sorting or Merging Files

By dividing a large file into sections, each with its own processor, every section can be sorted at the same time. Then pairs of sections can be merged together until the entire file is whole again—and sorted (Ben-Ari, 1982).

Threads and Concurrent Programming

So far we have considered the cooperation and synchronization of traditional-processes, also known as heavyweight processes, which have the following characteristics:

- They require space in main memory where they reside during their execution
- From time to time they require other resources such as data files or I/O devices
- They pass through several states from their initial entry into the computer system to their completion: ready, running, waiting, delayed, and blocked.

As we have seen in Chapters 3 and 4, these processes are often swapped between main memory and secondary storage during their execution to accommodate multiprogramming and to take advantage of virtual memory. Every time a swap occurs, overhead increases because of all the information that has to be saved.

To minimize this overhead time most current operating systems support the implementation of threads, or lightweight processes, which have become part of numerous application packages. Threads are supported at both the kernel and user level and can be managed by either the operating system or the application that created them.

A thread can be defined as a smaller unit within a process, which can be scheduled and executed (introduced in Chapter 1). Threads share the same resources as the process that created them, which now becomes a more passive element because the thread is the unit that uses the CPU and is scheduled for execution. Processes might have from one to several active threads, which can be created, scheduled and synchronized more efficiently because the amount of information needed is reduced. When running a process with multiple threads in a computer system with a single CPU, the processor switches very quickly from one thread to another, giving the impression that the threads are executing in parallel. However, it is only in systems with multiple CPUs that the multiple threads in a process are actually executed in parallel.

Each active thread in a process has its own processor registers, program counter, stack and status, but shares the data area and the resources allocated to its process. Each thread has its own program counter (PC) and stack, which is used to store variables dynamically created by a process. For example, function calls in C might create variables that are local to the function. These variables are stored in the stack when the function is invoked and are destroyed when the function is exited. Since threads within a process share the same space and resources they can communicate more efficiently, increasing processing performance.

A Web server can be used to show how the use of threads can improve performance and interactivity. When a Web server receives requests for images or pages, it serves each request with a different thread. For example, the process that receives all the requests may have one thread that accepts these requests and creates a new separate thread for each request received. This new thread retrieves the required information and sends it to the remote client. While this thread is doing its task, the original thread is free to accept more requests. Web servers are multiprocessor systems that allow for the concurrent completion of several requests, thus improving throughput and response time. Instead of creating and destroying threads to serve incoming requests, which would increase the overhead, Web servers keep a pool of threads that can be assigned to those requests. After a thread has completed its task, instead of being destroyed, it is returned to the pool to be assigned to another request (Deitel, 2004).

Thread States

As a thread moves through the system it is in one of five states, not counting its creation and finished states, as shown in Figure 6.6. When an application creates a thread it is made ready by allocating to it the needed resources and placing it in the READY queue. The thread state changes from READY to RUNNING when the Thread Scheduler, whose function is similar to that of the Process Scheduler, assigns it a processor.

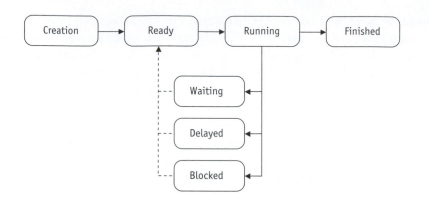

(figure 6.6)

A Typical thread changes states as it moves through the system.

A thread transitions from RUNNING to WAITING when it has to wait for an event outside its control to occur. For example, a mouse click can be the trigger event for a thread to change states, causing a transition from WAITING to READY. Alternatively, another thread, having completed its task, can send a signal indicating that the waiting thread can continue to execute. This is similar to the WAIT and SIGNAL process synchronization algorithm.

When an application such as a word processor has the capability of delaying the processing of a thread by a specified amount of time, it causes the thread to transition from RUNNING to DELAYED. When the prescribed time has elapsed, the thread transitions from DELAYED to READY. For example, the thread that periodically backs up a current document to disk will be delayed for a period of time after it has completed the backup. After the time has expired it performs the next backup and then is delayed again. If the delay was not built into the application, this thread would be forced into a loop that would continuously test to see if it was time to do a backup, wasting processor time and reducing system performance. Setting up a delay state avoids the problems of the test-and-set process synchronization algorithm.

A thread transitions from RUNNING to BLOCKED when an application issues an I/O request. After the I/O is completed the thread returns to the READY state. When a thread transitions from RUNNING to FINISHED all its resources are released and it can exit the system.

As you can see, the same operations are performed on both traditional processes and threads. Therefore the operating system must be able to support:

• Creating new threads

• Setting up a thread so it is ready to execute

• Delaying, or putting to sleep, threads for a specified amount of time

• Blocking, or suspending, threads that are waiting for I/O to complete

- Setting threads on a WAIT state until a specific event has occurred
- Scheduling threads for execution
- Synchronizing thread execution using semaphores, events, or conditional variables
- Terminating a thread and releasing its resources

To do so, the operating system needs to track the critical information for each thread.

Thread Control Block

Just as processes are represented in the computer system by Process Control Blocks (PCBs), so threads are represented by **Thread Control Blocks** (TCBs), which contain basic information about a thread such as its ID, state, and a pointer to the process that created it. Figure 6.7 shows the contents of a typical TCB:

- A thread ID, a unique identifier assigned by the operating system when the thread is created.
- The thread state, which changes as the thread progresses through its execution. State changes, as well as all other entries in the TCB, apply individually to each thread.
- CPU information, which contains everything that the operating system needs to know about how far the thread has executed, which instruction is currently being performed, and what data is being used.
- Thread priority, used to indicate the weight of this thread relative to other threads and used by the Thread Scheduler when determining which thread should be selected from the READY queue.
- A **pointer** to the process that created the thread
- Pointers to other threads created by this thread

(figure 6.7)

The contents of a typical Thread Control Block (TCB).

Thread ID
Thread state

CPU information:
    Program counter
    Register contents

Thread priority
Pointer to process that created this thread
Pointer(s) to other thread(s) that were created by this thread

Concurrent Programming Languages

Early programming languages such as FORTRAN did not support the creation of threads or the existence of concurrent processes. Typically, they gave programmers the possibility of creating a single process or thread of control. The Ada programming language was developed in the late 1970s and early 1980s and was one of the first languages to provide specific concurrency commands. Java, developed in 1995 at Sun Microsystems, Inc., was designed as a universal software platform for Internet applications and has been widely adopted in commercial as well as educational environments. We present a brief overview of both languages here.

Ada

In the early 1970s the U.S. Department of Defense (DOD) commissioned a programming language that could perform concurrent processing. At the time, half of the Department's applications were run on **embedded computer systems** requiring the use of numerous programming languages and many hours of custom programming. The DOD decided to fight the rising cost of software by commissioning the design of an original language suited for real-time and embedded systems.

Embedded systems are built into objects such as jet aircraft or ships and must be small and fast. They are usually required to work with real-time constraints, fail-safe execution, and nonstandard input and output devices. In addition, they must be able to manage concurrent activities, which requires parallel processing.

The software's requirements included efficiency, reliability, readability, simplicity, and implementability. It took 10 years to complete **Ada**, the final form of the high-level programming language made available to the public in 1980 (MacLennan, 1987).

The language was named after Augusta Ada Byron (1815-1852), the Countess of Lovelace and daughter of the renowned poet Lord Byron. She was a skilled mathematician and is regarded as the world's first programmer for her work on Charles Babbage's Analytical Engine in the 1830s. The Analytical Engine was an early prototype of a computer (Barnes, 1980).

The language was standardized by the American National Standards Institute (ANSI) in 1983 and nicknamed Ada83. It is the equivalent of the 1987 ISO standard issued by the International Standards Organization. The latest standard is ANSI/ISO/IEC-8652:1995 Ada 95.

Java

Java was developed at Sun Microsystems, Inc., and released in 1995 as the first software platform that promised to allow programmers to code an application once that would run on any computer. This type of universal software platform was an attempt to solve several issues: first, the high cost of developing software applications for each of the many incompatible computer architectures available in the world; second, the needs of distributed client-server environments; and third, the growth of the Internet and the World Wide Web, which added more complexity to program development.

In 1996 Sun licensed Java technology to all major hardware and software companies, and in 1998 a second generation of Java technology was introduced. By 2001 more than 2.5 million programmers were using Java to develop applications worldwide.

While other high-level programming languages are either compiled or interpreted, but not both, Java uses both a compiler and an interpreter. The source code of a Java program is first compiled into an intermediate language called Java bytecodes, which are platform-independent. This means that one can compile a Java program on any computer that has a Java compiler, and the bytecodes can then be run on any computer that has a Java interpreter.

The interpreter is designed to fit in with the hardware and operating system specifications of the computer that will run the Java bytecodes. Its function is to parse and run each bytecode instruction on that computer.

This combination of compiler and interpreter makes it easy to distribute Java applications because they don't have to be rewritten to accommodate the characteristics of every computer system. Once the program has been compiled it can be ported to and run on any system with a Java interpreter.

The Java Platform

Typically a computer platform contains the hardware and software where a program runs. The Java platform is a software-only platform that runs on top of other hardware-based platforms. It has two components: the Java Virtual Machine (Java VM), and the Java Application Programming Interface (Java API).

Java VM is the foundation for the Java platform and contains the Java interpreter, which runs the bytecodes provided by the compiler. Java VM sits on top of many different hardware-based platforms, as shown in Figure 6.8.

The Java API is a collection of software modules that programmers can use in their applications. The Java API is grouped into libraries of related classes and interfaces. These libraries, also known as packages, provide well-tested objects ranging from basic data types to I/O functions, from network interfaces to graphical user interface kits.

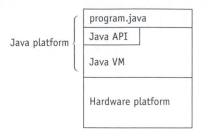

(figure 6.8)

A process used by the Java platform to shield a Java program from a computer's hardware.

The Java Language Environment

Java was designed to make it easy for experienced programmers to learn. Its syntax is familiar because it looks and feels like C++, which means that programmers can migrate easily to the Java platform and become productive very quickly. It is object-oriented, which means it takes advantage of modern software development methodologies and fits well into distributed client-server applications.

One of Java's features is that memory allocation is done at run time, unlike C and C++ where memory allocation is done at compilation time. Java's compiled code references memory via symbolic "handles" that are translated into real memory addresses at run time by the Java interpreter. This means that the memory allocation and referencing models are not visible to programmers, but are controlled entirely by the underlying run-time platform.

Because Java applications run in distributed environments, security is a very important built-in feature of the language and the run-time system. It provides compile-time checking and run-time checking, which helps programmers create very reliable software. For example, while a Java program is executing it can request particular classes to be loaded from anywhere in the network. In this case all incoming code is checked by the bytecode verifier, which ensures that the code is correct and can run safely without putting the Java interpreter at risk. Some of the checks performed by the bytecode verifier are to make sure that there are no operand stack overflows or underflows, or that the types of the parameters are correct.

With its sophisticated synchronization capabilities, Java supports multithreading at the language level. The language library provides the *thread* class, and the run-time system provides monitor and condition lock primitives. The thread class is a collection of methods used to start, run, stop, and check the status of a thread. Java's threads are preemptive and, depending on the platform on which the Java interpreter executes, can also be time-sliced.

When a programmer declares some methods within a class to be synchronized, they are not run concurrently. These synchronized methods are under the control of monitors that ensure that variables remain in a consistent state. When a synchronized method begins to run it is given a monitor for the current object. The monitor does not allow any other synchronized method in that object to execute. The monitor is released when a synchronized method exits, which allows other synchronized methods within the same object to run.

Java technology has gained in popularity among programmers since 1995 for several reasons:

- It can handle commercial, educational, and scientific applications
- It offers the capability of writing a program once and having it run on various platforms without having to make any changes
- It offers a robust set of features such as run-time memory allocation, security, and multithreading, which are important features in multimedia and distributed applications.
- It is used for many Web and Internet applications, and integrates well with browsers, such as HotJava, that can run Java applets with audio, video, and animation directly in a Web page.

Case Study: Process Management in Linux

To highlight the concepts in this chapter, here is an example of how processes are managed by Linux operating systems.

The Linux scheduler scans the list of processes in the READY state and, using predefined criteria chooses which process to execute. The scheduler has three different scheduling policies: two for real-time processes and one for normal processes. Each process has three attributes: an associated process type, a fixed priority, and a variable priority. The combination of type and priority are used by the scheduler to determine which scheduling policy will be used on the processes in the ready queue.

For example, each process is one of three types.

SCHED_FIFO	for non-preemtible "real time" processes
SCHED_RR	for preemptible "real time" processes
SCHED_OTHER	for "normal" processes

From among the processors of the first type (SCHED_FIFO), the scheduler selects the process with the highest priority and executes it in first in, first out order. This process is normally not preemptible and runs to completion unless one of the following situation occurs:

- Another process of the same type but having a higher priority becomes ready.
- The process is waiting for I/O to finish.
- The process voluntarily gives up the processor, in which case the process is moved to a waiting state and other processes are executed.

Only when all of the processes of the first type are completed, does the scheduler proceed to execute processes of the second and third types.

When a process of the second type (SCHED_RR) becomes ready, it is executed using a round robin algorithm with a small time quantum. Then, when the time quantum expires, other processes of the first type or processes of the second type with a higher priority, may be selected and executed before this process is allowed to run to completion.

Processes of the third type (SCHED_OTHER) are executed only when there are no processes of the first type in the ready queue. From among the processes in this group, the scheduler selects processes in order after considering their dynamic priorities (which are set by the level specified by the user using system calls and by a factor computed by the system). From among processes in this third group, the priority of all CPU-bound processes are lowered during execution, meaning that they may earn a lower priority than processes that are not executing or those whose priority has not been modified.

For more detail about how Linux manages processor resources, see Chapter 15.

Conclusion

Multiprocessing occurs in single-processor systems between interacting processes that obtain control of the one CPU at different times.

Multiprocessing also occurs in systems with two or more CPUs, each of which must be synchronized by the Processor Manager. Each processor must communicate and cooperate with the others. These systems can be configured in a variety of ways; from the simplest to the most complex they are master/slave, loosely coupled, and symmetric.

The success of any multiprocessing system depends on the ability of the system to synchronize the processors or processes and the system's other resources. The concept of mutual exclusion helps keep the processes with the allocated resources from becoming deadlocked. Mutual exclusion is maintained with a series of techniques including test-and-set, WAIT and SIGNAL, and semaphores (P, V, and mutex).

Hardware and software mechanisms are used to synchronize the many processes but care must be taken to avoid the typical problems of synchronization: missed waiting customers, the synchronization of producers and consumers, and the mutual exclusion of readers and writers.

In the next chapter we look at the module of the operating system that manages the printers, disk drives, tape drives, and terminals—the Device Manager.

Key Terms

Ada: a high-level concurrent programming language developed by the U.S. Department of Defense.

busy waiting: a method by which processes, waiting for an event to occur, continuously test to see if the condition has changed and remain in unproductive, resource-consuming wait loops.

COBEGIN: command used with COEND to indicate to a multiprocessing compiler the beginning of a section where instructions can be processed concurrently.

COEND: command used with COBEGIN to indicate to a multiprocessing compiler the end of a section where instructions can be processed concurrently.

concurrent processing: execution by a single processor of a set of processes in such a way that they appear to be happening at the same time.

concurrent programming: a programming technique that allows a single processor to simultaneously execute multiple sets of instructions.

critical region: a part of a program that must complete execution before other processes can have access to the resources being used.

embedded computer system: a dedicated computer system that must be small and fast and work with real-time constraints, fail-safe execution, and nonstandard I/O devices.

explicit parallelism: a type of concurrent programming that requires that the programmer explicitly state which instructions can be executed in parallel.

implicit parallelism: a type of concurrent programming in which the compiler automatically detects which instructions can be performed in parallel.

loosely coupled configuration: a multiprocessing configuration in which each processor has a copy of the operating system and controls its own resources.

master/slave: an asymmetric multiprocessing configuration consisting of a single processor system connected to "slave" processors each of which is managed by the primary "master" processor, which provides the scheduling functions and jobs.

multiprocessing: when two or more CPUs share the same main memory, most I/O devices, and the same control program routines.

mutex: a condition that specifies that only one process may use a shared resource at a time to ensure correct operation and results.

parallel processing: the process of operating two or more CPUs in parallel, with more than one CPU executing instructions simultaneously.

pointer: an address or other indicator of location.

process synchronization: (1) the need for algorithms to resolve conflicts between processors in a multiprocessing environment; or (2) the need to ensure that events occur in the proper order even if they are carried out by several processes.

producers and consumers: a classic problem in which a process produces data that will be consumed, or used, by another process.

readers and writers: a problem that arises when two types of processes need to access a shared resource such as a file or a database.

semaphore: a type of shared data item that may contain either binary or nonnegative integer values and is used to provide mutual exclusion.

symmetric configuration: a multiprocessing configuration in which processor scheduling is decentralized and each processor is of the same type.

test-and-set (TS): an indivisible machine instruction, which is executed in a single machine cycle to determine whether the processor is available.

Thread Control Block (TCB): a data structure that contains information about the current status and characteristics of a thread.

WAIT and SIGNAL: a modification of the test-and-set synchronization mechanism that's designed to remove busy waiting.

Exercises

Research Topic

Research current literature or the Internet to identify a supercomputer model with exceptional parallel processing ability. Identify the maximum number of processors the computer uses and how fast the machine can perform calculations. Cite your source. If your answer includes terms not used in this chapter (gigaflops, terabytes, etc.), be sure to define them.

Exercises

1. What is the central goal of most multiprocessing systems?
2. What is the meaning of the term busy waiting? Give an example.
3. Explain the need for mutual exclusion.
4. Describe explicit parallelism.
5. Describe implicit parallelism.
6. Rewrite each of the following arithmetic expressions to take advantage of concurrent processing and then code each. Use the terms COBEGIN and COEND to delimit the sections of concurrent code.
   a. $(X*(Y*Z*W*R) + M + N + P)$
   b. $((J+K*L*M*N)*I)$

7. Use the P and V semaphore operations to simulate the traffic flow at the intersection of two one-way streets. The following rules should be satisfied:
   - Only one car can be crossing at any given time.
   - A car should be allowed to cross the intersection only if there are no cars coming from the other street.
   - When cars are coming from both streets, they should take turns to prevent indefinite postponements in either street.

Advanced Exercises

8. Consider the following program segments for two different processes (P1, P2) executing concurrently and where B and A are not shared variables, but x starts at zero and is a shared variable.

P1	P2

   ```
   for(a = 1; a <= 3; a++)      for(b = 1; b <= 3; b++)
       x = x + 1;                   x = x + 1;
   ```

   If the processes P1 and P2 execute only once at any speed, what are the possible resulting values of x? Explain your answers.

9. Examine one of the programs you have written recently and indicate which operations could be executed concurrently. How long did it take you to do this? When might it be a good idea to write your programs in such a way that they can be run concurrently?

10. Consider the following segment taken from a C program:

    ```
    for(j = 1; j <= 12; j++)
    {
        printf("\nEnter an integer value:");
        scanf("%d", &x);
        if(x == 0)
                y(j)=0;
        if(x != 0)
                y(j)=10;
    }
    ```

    a. Recode it so it will run more efficiently in a single-processor system.

    b. Given that a multiprocessing environment with four symmetrical processors is available, recode the segment as an efficient concurrent program that performs the same function as the original C program.

    c. Given that all processors have identical capabilities, compare the execution speeds of the original C segment with the execution speeds of your segments for parts (a) and (b).

Programming Exercises

11. Dijkstra introduced the Sleeping Barber Problem (Dijkstra, 1965): A barbershop is divided into two rooms. The waiting room has n chairs and the work room only has the barber chair. When the waiting room is empty, the barber goes to sleep in the barber chair. If a customer comes in and the barber is asleep, he knows it's his turn to get his hair cut. So he wakes up the barber and takes his turn in the barber chair. But if the waiting room is not empty, the customer must take a seat in the waiting room and wait his turn. Write a program that will coordinate the barber and his customers.

12. Patil introduced the Cigarette Smokers Problem (Patil, 1971): Three smokers and a supplier make up this system. Each smoker wants to roll a cigarette and smoke it immediately. However, to smoke a cigarette the smoker needs three ingredients—paper, tobacco, and a match. To the great discomfort of everyone involved, each smoker has only one of the ingredients: Smoker 1 has lots of paper, Smoker 2 has lots of tobacco, and Smoker 3 has the matches. And, of course, the rules of the group don't allow hoarding, swapping, or sharing.

    All three ingredients are provided by the supplier, who doesn't smoke, and he has an infinite amount of all three items. But he only provides two of them at a time—and only when no one is smoking. Here's how it works. The supplier randomly selects and places two different items on the table (which is accessible to all three smokers), and the smoker with the remaining ingredient immediately takes them, rolls, and smokes a cigarette. When he's finished smoking he signals the supplier, who then places another two randomly selected items on the table, and so on.

    Write a program that will synchronize the supplier with the smokers. Keep track of how many cigarettes each smoker consumes. Is this a fair supplier? Why or why not?

| # Device Management

> " *If one takes care of the means, the end will take care of itself.*"

Mohandas K. Gandhi *(1869–1948)*

Learning Objectives

After completing this chapter, you should be able to describe:

- The features of dedicated, shared, and virtual devices
- The differences between sequential and direct access media
- The concepts of blocking and buffering and how they improve I/O performance
- The roles of seek time, search time, and transfer time in calculating access time
- The differences in access times in several types of devices
- The critical components of the input/output subsystem, and how they interact
- The strengths and weaknesses of common seek strategies, including FCFS, SSTF, SCAN/LOOK, C-SCAN/C-LOOK, and how they compare
- The different levels of RAID and what sets each one apart from the others

To put it simply: the Device Manager manages every peripheral device of the system. The Device Manager must maintain a delicate balance of supply and demand—balancing the system's finite supply of devices with users' infinite demand for them. Information on how specific operating systems manage devices is presented in the device management sections of Chapters 13–15.

Device management involves four basic functions; all are explained in this chapter:

- Tracking the status of each device, such as disk drives, printers, modems, and other peripheral devices
- Using preset policies to determine which process will get a device and for how long
- Allocating the devices
- Deallocating them at two levels—at the process level when an I/O command has been executed and the device is temporarily released, and at the job level when the job is finished and the device is permanently released

Types of Devices

The system's peripheral devices generally fall into one of three categories: dedicated, shared, and virtual. The differences are a function of the characteristics of the devices, as well as how they're managed by the Device Manager.

Dedicated devices are assigned to only one job at a time; they serve that job for the entire time it's active or until it releases them. Some devices, such as tape drives, printers, and plotters, demand this kind of allocation scheme, because it would be awkward to let several users share them. A shared plotter might produce half of one user's graph and half of another. The disadvantage of dedicated devices is that they must be allocated to a single user for the duration of a job's execution, which can be quite inefficient, especially when the device isn't used 100 percent of the time. Devices that are shared or virtual, described next, are generally preferred.

Shared devices can be assigned to several processes. For instance, a disk, or any other direct access storage device, can be shared by several processes at the same time by interleaving their requests, but this interleaving must be carefully controlled by the Device Manager. All conflicts—such as when Process A and Process B each need to read from the same disk—must be resolved based on predetermined policies to decide which request will be handled first. We'll examine some of these policies later in this chapter.

Virtual devices are a combination of the first two: they're dedicated devices that have been transformed into shared devices. For example, printers (which are dedicated devices) are converted into sharable devices through a spooling program that reroutes all print requests to a disk. Only when all of a job's output is complete, and the printer is ready to print out the entire document, is the output sent to the printer for printing. (This procedure has to be managed carefully to prevent deadlock, as we explained in Chapter 5.) Because disks are sharable devices, this technique can convert one printer into several virtual printers, thus improving both its performance and use. Spooling is a technique that is often used to speed up slow dedicated I/O devices.

For example, the **universal serial bus (USB) controller** is a virtual device that acts as an interface between the operating system, device drivers, and applications and the devices that are attached via the USB host. The USB host can accommodate up to 127 different devices, including flash memory, cameras, speakers, monitors, keyboards, etc. Each device is identified by the USB host controller with a unique identification number, which allows many devices to exchange data with the computer using the same USB connection (White, 2004).

The USB controller assigns bandwidth to each device depending on its priority:

- Highest priority is assigned to real-time exchanges where no interruption in the data flow is allowed, such a video or sound data.
- Medium priority is assigned to devices that can allow occasional interrupts without jeopardizing the use of the device, such as a keyboard or joystick.
- Lowest priority is assigned to bulk transfers or exchanges that can accommodate slower data flow, such as printers or scanners.

Regardless of the specific attributes of the device, the most important differences among them are speed and degree of sharability. By minimizing the variances among the devices, a system's overall efficiency can be dramatically improved.

Storage media are divided into two groups: **sequential access media**, which store records sequentially, one after the other; and **direct access storage devices (DASD)**, which can store either sequential or direct access files. There are vast differences in their speed and sharability.

Sequential Access Storage Media

The first storage medium was paper in the form of printouts, punch cards, and paper tape. However, the bulk and price of paper soon made this primitive medium unacceptable for large systems.

Magnetic tape was then developed for early computer systems for routine secondary storage; it is now used for routine archiving and for storing backup data.

Records on magnetic tapes are stored serially, one after the other, and each record can be of any length. The length is usually determined by the application program. Each record can be identified by its position on the tape. Therefore, to access a single record, the tape must be mounted and fast-forwarded from its beginning until the desired position is located. This is a time-consuming process because it can take several minutes to read the entire tape.

To see just how long it takes, let's consider a hypothetical computer system that uses a reel of tape ½ inch wide and 2400 feet long (see Figure 7.1). Data is recorded on eight of the nine parallel tracks that run the length of the tape. (The ninth track holds a **parity bit** which is used for routine error checking.)

(figure 7.1)

Nine-track magnetic tape with three characters recorded using odd parity. A 1/2-inch wide reel of tape, typically used to back up a mainframe computer, can store thousands of characters, or bytes, per inch.

The number of characters that can be recorded per inch is determined by the density of the tape, such as 1600 or 6250 bytes per inch (bpi). For example, if you had records of 160 characters each and were storing them on a tape with a density of 1600 bpi, then theoretically you could store ten records on one inch of tape. However, in actual practice, it would depend on how you decided to store the records: individually or grouped into blocks. If the records are stored individually, each record would need to be separated by a space to indicate its starting and ending places. If the records are stored in blocks, then the entire block is preceded by a space and followed by a space, but the individual records are stored sequentially within the block.

To appreciate the difference between storing individually or in blocks, let's take a minute to look at the mechanics of reading and writing on magnetic tape. Magnetic tape moves under the read/write head only when there's a need to access a record; at all other times it's standing still. So the tape moves in jerks: read a record and stop, read another record and stop again, and so on. Records would be written in the same way.

The tape needs time and space to stop, so a gap is inserted between each record. This **interrecord gap (IRG)** is about ½ inch long regardless of the sizes of the records it separates. Therefore, if ten records are stored individually, there will be nine ½-inch IRGs between each record. (In this example we assume the records are only ⅒ inch each.)

In Figure 7.2, 5½ inches of tape are required to store one inch of data—not a very efficient way to use the storage medium.

(figure 7.2)

IRGs in magnetic tape. Each record requires only 1/10 inch of tape, for a total of one inch. When ten records are stored individually on magnetic tape, they are separated by IRGs, which adds up to 4½ inches of tape. This totals 5½ inches of tape.

An alternative is to group the records into blocks before recording them on tape. This is called **blocking** and it's performed when the file is created. (Of course, you must take care to deblock them later.)

The number of records in a block is usually determined by the application program, and it's often set to take advantage of the **transfer rate,** which is the density of the tape (measured in bpi), multiplied by the tape drive speed, or transport speed, which is measured in inches per second (ips):

$$transfer\ rate = density * transport\ speed$$

Let's say that in our hypothetical system the transport speed is 200 inches per second. Therefore, at 1600 bpi, a total of 320,000 bytes can be transferred in one second, so theoretically the optimal size of a block is 320,000 bytes. But there's a catch: this technique requires that the *entire* block be read into a buffer, so the buffer must be at least as large as the block. In actual operating environments, buffers range from 1024 to 2048 bytes. For example, most blocks are 1K to 2K.

Notice in Figure 7.3 that the gap (now called an interblock gap or IBG) is still ½ inch long, but the data from each ten records is now stored on only one inch of tape—so we've used only 1½ inches of tape (instead of the 5½ inches used in Figure 7.2), and we've wasted only ½ inch of tape (instead of 4½ inches).

(figure 7.3)

Two blocks of records stored on magnetic tape, each preceded by an IBG of 1/2 inch. Each block holds ten records, each of which is still 1/10 inch. The block, however, is one inch, for a total of 1½ inches.

Blocking has two distinct advantages:

• Fewer I/O operations are needed because a single READ command can move an entire block, the physical record that includes several logical records, into main memory.

• Less tape is wasted because the size of the physical record exceeds the size of the gap.

The two disadvantages of blocking seem mild by comparison:
• Overhead and software routines are needed for blocking, deblocking, and record-keeping.
• Buffer space may be wasted if you need only one logical record but must read an entire block to get it.

How long does it take to access a block or record on magnetic tape? It depends on where the record is located, but we can make some general calculations. For example, our 2400-foot reel of tape with a tape transport speed of 200 inches per second can be read without stopping in approximately 2½ minutes. Therefore, it would take 2½ minutes to access the last record on the tape. On the average, then, it would take 1¼ minutes to access a record. And to access one record after another sequentially would take as long as it takes to start and stop a tape—which is 0.003 seconds, or 3 milliseconds (ms), for example.

As we can see from Table 7.1, **access times** can vary widely. That makes magnetic tape a poor medium for routine secondary storage except for files with very high sequential activity—that is, those requiring that 90 to 100 percent of the records be accessed sequentially during an application.

Benchmarks	Access Time
Maximum access	2.5 minutes
Average access	1.25 minutes
Sequential access	3 milliseconds

(table 7.1)

Access times for 2400-foot magnetic tape with a tape transport speed of 200 inches/second.

In addition to its low cost, an advantage of magnetic tape is its compact storage capabilities, so it is a good medium for backing up magnetic disks and for long-term archival file storage. Mainframe and server systems use tapes for off-site data storage in the event of disaster recovery. For interactive applications, a direct access medium is preferable.

Direct Access Storage Devices

Direct access storage devices (DASDs) are devices that can directly read or write to a specific place on a disk. (They're also called random access storage devices.) Although most of the disk drives used have one read/write head that floats across each recording surface, there are some that have several read/write heads per surface. They are fixed above each of the tracks on the recording surface. DASDs can be grouped into four categories: magnetic disks, optical discs, flash memory, and magneto-optical disks. Although the variance in DASD access times isn't as wide as with magnetic tape, the location of the specific record still has a direct effect on the amount of time required to access it.

Fixed-Head Magnetic Disk Storage

A fixed-head magnetic disk looks like a large CD or DVD covered with magnetic film that has been formatted, usually on both sides, into concentric circles. Each circle is a **track**. Data is recorded serially on each track by the fixed read/write head positioned over it.

A fixed-head disk, shown in Figure 7.4, is also very fast—faster than the movable-head disks we'll talk about in the next section. However, its major disadvantages are its high cost and its reduced storage space compared to a movable-head disk (because the tracks must be positioned farther apart to accommodate the width of the read/write heads). These devices are used when speed is of the utmost importance, such as space-craft monitoring or aircraft applications.

(figure 7.4)

A fixed-head disk with four read/write heads, one per track.

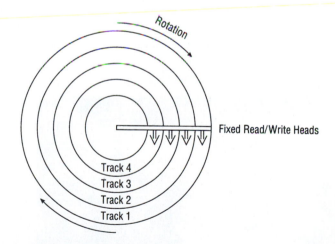

Movable-Head Magnetic Disk Storage

Movable-head magnetic disks, such as the hard drives found on PCs, have one read/write head that floats over the surface of each disk. Disks can be a single platter, or part of a disk pack, which is a stack of magnetic platters. Figure 7.5 shows a typical disk pack—several platters stacked on a common central spindle, separated by enough space to allow the read/write heads to move between each pair of disks.

As shown in Figure 7.5, each platter (except those at the top and bottom of the stack) has two surfaces for recording, and each surface is formatted with a specific number of concentric tracks where the data is recorded. The number of tracks varies from manufacturer to manufacturer, but typically they range from as few as 100 on a floppy disk to a thousand or more on a high-capacity hard disk. Each track on each surface is numbered: Track 0 identifies the outermost concentric circle on each surface; the highest-numbered track is in the center.

The arm, shown in Figure 7.6, moves two read/write heads between each pair of surfaces: one for the surface above it and one for the surface below. The arm moves all of the heads in unison, so if one head is on Track 36, then all of the heads are on Track 36—in other words, they're all positioned on the same track but on their respective surfaces.

© Courtesy Seagate Technology

This raises some interesting questions: Is it more efficient to write a series of records on surface one and, when that surface is full, to continue writing on surface two, and then on surface three, and so on? Or is it better to fill up every outside track of every surface before moving the heads inward to the next track position to continue writing?

It's slower to fill a disk pack surface-by-surface than it is to fill it up track-by-track— and this leads us to a valuable concept. If we fill Track 0 of all of the surfaces, we've got a virtual **cylinder** of data—this is the cylinder concept illustrated in Chapter 5, Figure 5.6. There are as many cylinders as there are tracks, and the cylinders are as tall as the disk pack. You could visualize the cylinders as a series of virtual coffee cans, one inside the other.

To access any given record, the system needs three things: its cylinder number, so the arm can move the read/write heads to it; a surface number, so the proper read/write head is activated; and a record number, so the read/write head knows the instant when it should begin reading or writing.

One clarification: we've used the term *surface* in this discussion because it makes the concepts easier to understand. However, conventional literature generally uses the term *track* to identify both the surface and the concentric track. Therefore, our use of *surface/track* coincides with the term *track* or *head* used in many other texts.

Optical Disc Storage

The advent of optical discs was made possible by developments in laser technology. Laserdiscs, developed in the early 1970s, were not a big success in the consumer market although they were used for industrial training purposes. On the other hand, the audio CD with its better-quality audio, convenience, and durability, became a great success when introduced in the early 1980s.

The success of the CD spurred the development of low-cost optical-disc storage technology for computer data storage. Optical storage devices are referred to as *discs*, to differentiate them from magnetic storage *disks*.

A fundamental difference between an optical disc and a magnetic disk is the track and sector design. A magnetic disk consists of concentric tracks of sectors, and it spins at a constant speed—this is called constant angular velocity (CAV). Because the sectors at the outside of the disk spin faster past the read/write head than the inner sectors, outside sectors are much larger than sectors located near the center of the disk, as you can see in Figure 7.7. This format wastes storage space but maximizes the speed with which data can be retrieved.

On the other hand, an optical disc consists of a single spiraling track of same-sized sectors running from the center to the rim of the disc, as shown in Figure 7.8. This design

(figure 7.7)

On a magnetic disk, the sectors are of different sizes: bigger at the rim and smaller at the center. The disk spins at a constant angular velocity (CAV) to compensate for this difference.

allows many more sectors, and much more data, to fit on an optical disc compared to a magnetic disk of the same size. If the track could be straightened, it would exceed three miles in length. The disc drive adjusts the speed of the disc's spin to compensate for the sector's location on the disc—this is called constant linear velocity (CLV). Therefore, the disc spins faster to read sectors located at the center of the disc, and slower to read sectors near the outer edge (White, 2004). If you listen to a CD drive in action, you can hear it change speeds as it makes these adjustments.

(figure 7.8)

On an optical disc, all sectors are of the same size throughout the disc. The disc drive changes speed to compensate, but it spins at a constant linear velocity (CLV).

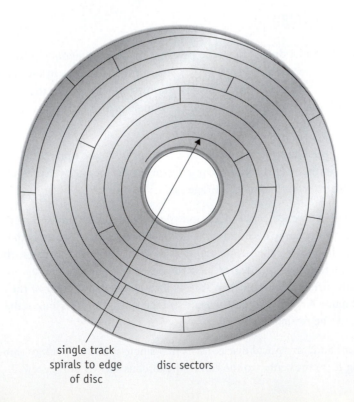

single track
spirals to edge
of disc   disc sectors

Two of the most important measures of optical disc drive performance are sustained data-transfer rate and average access time. The data-transfer rate is measured in megabytes per second (abbreviated as MBps) and refers to the speed at which massive amounts of data can be read from the disc. This factor is crucial for applications requiring sequential access, such as for audio and video playback. For example, a CD with a fast transfer rate will drop fewer frames when playing back a recorded video segment than will a unit with a slower transfer rate. This creates an image that's much smoother.

However, to retrieve data that is *not* stored sequentially, the drive's access time may be more important. Access time, which indicates the average time required to move the head to a specific place on the disc, is expressed in milliseconds (ms). The fastest units have the smallest average access time. Access time is most important when searching for information randomly, such as in an encyclopedia. Therefore, a fast data-transfer rate is most important for sequential disc access, such as for video playback, whereas fast access time is crucial when retrieving data that's widely dispersed on the disc.

A third important feature of optical disc drives is cache size. Although it's not a speed measurement, cache size has a substantial impact on perceived performance. A hardware cache acts as a buffer by transferring blocks of data from the disc, anticipating that the user may want to reread some recently retrieved information, which can be done quickly if the information remains in the cache. In some cases the cache can also act as a read-ahead buffer, looking for the next block of information on the disc. Read-ahead caches might appear to be most useful for multimedia playback, where a continuous stream of data is flowing. However, because they fill up quickly, read-ahead caches actually become more useful when paging through a database or electronic book. In these cases, the cache has time to recover while the user is reading the current piece of information.

There are several types of optical-disc systems, depending on the medium and the capacity of the discs: CDs, DVDs, and magneto-optical disks.

CD-ROM Technology

Compact disc read-only memory (CD-ROM) technology is very similar to that of an audio CD. The major difference is that CD-ROM drives are sturdier and have rigorous error-correction methods to make sure that data transferred from the disc to main memory is correct.

When making CDs for sale, such as music or software CDs, data is recorded on a master disc by means of a high-intensity laser beam, which burns indentations, called **pits,** and flat areas, called **lands.** The pits and lands represent ones and zeros, respectively. The master disc is then used to make an engraved mold from which copies are made.

In the CD player, data is read back by focusing a low-powered laser on it, which shines through the protective layer of the disc onto the track where data is recorded. Light striking a land is reflected into a photodetector while light striking a pit is scattered and absorbed. The photodetector then converts the intensity of the light into a digital signal of ones and zeros.

CD-ROM drives often feature a speed classification (such as 32x, 40x, or 75x) to indicate how fast they spin. For example, a 75x CD-ROM spins at a rate which is 75 times faster than that of the first commercial single-speed CD drive. Single-speed drives that operate at 75 sectors/second, and with a sector of 2048 bytes, therefore offer a rate of 153,600 bytes/second, or 150KB per second. CD-ROM players cannot read the CD-R or CD-RW discs that are described next.

Since CD-ROMs are a read-only media, they are appropriate for archival storage, and are primarily used for distribution of very large amounts of digital information.

According to market reports, the first major users of CD-ROMs were libraries and corporations that needed text-based information and reference works such as encyclopedias, system documentation and user training material. However, as more CD-ROM publishers began incorporating multimedia in their discs and marketing "edutainment" products, CD-ROMs became widespread in the microcomputer market, and the technology evolved to support CD-ROM jukeboxes (also called autochangers or libraries) capable of handling multiple discs and networked to distribute multimedia and reference works to distant users.

CD-Recordable Technology

CD-R drives require a more expensive disk controller than CD-ROM drives because the user can record data on optical discs using a write-once technique. Therefore, when data is written to the disc, it cannot be erased or modified. This technique, also known as WORM (write once, read many), first gave CD-R discs an edge for archiving data or creating audit trails.

The CD-R disc is made of several layers including a gold reflective layer and a dye layer, which is used to record the data. The write head uses a high-powered laser beam to record data. A permanent mark is made on the dye when the energy from the laser beam is absorbed into it. That is why a CD-R cannot be erased after it is recorded. It can be read only.

Data on a CD-R disc can be read by any ordinary CD drive, not just a CD-R drive, by using a low-power laser beam. If there is a mark on the dye, the beam is scattered and the light is not returned back to the read head. However, when there are no marks, the gold layer reflects the light right back to the read head. This is similar to the process of reading pits and lands. The software used to create a CD-R uses a standard format, such as ISO 9096, which automatically checks for errors and creates a table of contents, used to keep track of each file's location.

CD-Rewritable Technology

CD-RWs use a process called phase change technology to write, change, and erase data. The disc's recording layer uses an alloy of silver, indium, antimony, and tellurium. The recording layer has two different phase states: amorphous and crystalline. In the amorphous state, light is not reflected as well as in the crystalline state.

To record data, a laser beam heats up the disc and changes the state from crystalline to amorphous. When data is read by means of a low-power laser beam, the amorphous state scatters the light which does not get picked up by the read head. This is similar to what occurs when reading pits and is interpreted as a one. On the other hand, when the light hits the crystalline areas, light is reflected back to the read head, and this is similar to what occurs when reading lands and is interpreted as a zero.

To erase data, the CD-RW drive uses a low-energy beam to heat up the pits just enough to loosen the alloy and return it to its original crystalline state.

CD-RW drives can read a standard CD-ROM (which can't be written to or modified) as well as CD-R and CD-RW discs. This technology is useful for organizations that need to store large quantities of data as well as for sound, graphics, and multimedia applications.

DVD Technology

Although DVD-ROMs use the same design and are the same size and shape as CD-ROMs, they can store more data. A dual-layer, single-sided DVD (Digital Versatile Disc) can hold the equivalent of 13 CDs, because the pits are smaller and the spiral is wound tighter. These characteristics require that the laser beam used to read a DVD be of a shorter wavelength than the one used to read a CD. Therefore, DVD drives use the same red laser found in checkout registers, which means that DVDs cannot be read by CD or CD-ROM drives.

When the advantages of compression technology (discussed in the next chapter) are added to the high capacity of a DVD, such as MPEG video compression, a single-sided single-layer DVD can hold 4.7 GB, more than enough space to hold a two-hour movie with enhanced audio—soundtracks for up to eight languages and subtitles for thirty-two more. A double-sided, dual-layered disc (an opaque layer holding data covered by a transparent layer holding data) can accommodate 8.5 GB on each side of the disc. DVDs are used to store music, movies, and multimedia applications. Newer DVD technology known as DVD-RW, based on CD-RW technology, provides rewritable flexibility.

Magneto-Optical Storage

A **magneto-optical (MO) disk drive** combines the technology of magnetic disks with that of optical discs. The system can read and write to MO disks as it does to magnetic disks. MO disks can store up to several GB of data and their access rate is faster than that of a floppy disk but slower than that of hard drives. Their big advantage is that these disks are hardier than optical discs.

An MO disk is covered with a crystalline metal alloy that needs something more powerful than the magnetic field generated by the read/write head to change states. To record data, a narrow laser beam is focused on the surface of the disk. The beam heats up a small spot on the alloy until its metallic crystals become so loose that they can be changed by the write head's magnetic field. At this point the crystals are polarized one way to represent a zero and another way to represent a one. Unlike a CD, this process does not cause a physical change to the disk and, because the change is not permanent, changes can be made many times.

To read data, a weaker laser beam is focused on the tracks that had been created during the write operation. Its light is polarized by the crystals in the alloy and is reflected from the aluminum layer of the disk to a photodiode. The direction of the polarization of the light is sensed by the photodiode and interpreted as a stream of bits—zeros and ones (White, 1999).

A comparison of CD-RWs and MOs indicates that repeated writing to optical discs causes a slow but sure deterioration of the medium, which is not present in magneto-optical disks.

Flash Memory Storage

Flash memory is a removable medium that emulates random access memory, but, unlike RAM, stores data securely even when it's removed from its power source. Flash memory allows users to store data (including photos, music, documents, etc.) on a microchip card or "key" and move it from device to device, as they would magnetic or optical storage media. Flash memory is sold in a variety of configurations including compact flash, smart cards, and memory sticks, and they often connect to the computer through the USB port (White, 2004).

Flash memory is named for the ease and speed of erasing the microchip. To write data to the chip, an electric charge is sent through one transistor, called the floating gate, then through a metal oxide layer, and into a second transistor called the control gate where the charge is stored in a cell until it's erased. Each cell can contain one or two bits (as of 2005). Later, when it's time to reuse the card, a strong electrical field, a flash, is applied to the entire card to reset all values.

DASD Access Times

Depending on whether a DASD has fixed or movable heads, there can be as many as three factors that contribute to the time required to access a file: seek time, search time, and transfer time.

Seek time is usually the slowest of the three factors. It's the time required to position the read/write head on the proper track. Obviously, seek time doesn't apply to devices with fixed read/write heads because each track has its own read/write head. **Search time**, also known as rotational delay, is the time it takes to rotate the DASD until the requested record is moved under the read/write head. **Transfer time** is the fastest of the three; that's when the data is actually transferred from secondary storage to main memory.

Fixed-Head Devices

Fixed-head devices can access a record by knowing its track number and record number. The total amount of time required to access data depends on the rotational speed, which varies from device to device but is constant within each device, and the position of the record relative to the position of the read/write head. Therefore, total access time is the sum of search time plus transfer time.

$$
\begin{array}{l}
\quad\text{search time (rotational delay)} \\
+\quad\underline{\text{transfer time (data transfer)}} \\
\quad\text{access time}
\end{array}
$$

Because DASDs rotate continuously, there are three basic positions for the requested record in relation to the position of the read/write head. Figure 7.9(a) shows the best possible situation because the record is next to the read/write head when the I/O command is executed; this gives a rotational delay of zero. Figure 7.9(b) shows the average situation because the record is directly opposite the read/write head when the I/O command is executed; this gives a rotational delay of $t/2$ where t (time) is one full rotation. Figure 7.9(c) shows the worst situation because the record has just rotated past the read/write head when the I/O command is executed; this gives a rotational delay of t because it will take one full rotation for the record to reposition itself under the read/write head.

(figure 7.9)

As a disk rotates, Record 1 may be near the read/write head and ready to be scanned, as seen in (a); in the farthest position just past the head, (c); or somewhere in between, as in the average case, (b).

How long will it take to access a record? If one complete revolution takes 16.8 ms, then the average rotational delay, as shown in Figure 7.9(b), is 8.4 ms. The data transfer time varies from device to device, but a typical value is 0.00094 ms per byte—the size of the record dictates this value. For example, it takes 0.094 ms (almost 0.1 ms) to transfer a record with 100 bytes. Therefore, using these numbers, the resulting access times are shown in Table 7.2.

Benchmarks	Access Time
Maximum access	16.8 ms + 0.00094 ms/byte
Average access	8.4 ms + 0.00094 ms/byte
Sequential access	Depends on the length of the record; generally less than 1 ms (known as the transfer rate)

(table 7.2)

Access times for a fixed-head DASD at 16.8 ms/revolution.

Because there's little variance in access, DASDs are good for files with low activity (the percent of records accessed) or for users who access records in a random fashion.

Data recorded on DASDs may or may not be blocked at the discretion of the application programmer. With DASDs, blocking isn't used to save space because there are no IRGs between records. Instead, blocking is used to save time.

To illustrate the advantages of blocking the records, let's use the same values shown in Table 7.2 for a record containing 100 bytes and blocks containing ten records. If we were to read ten records individually, we would multiply the access time for a single record by ten:

$$\text{access time} = 8.4 + 0.094 \qquad = 8.494 \text{ ms for one record}$$
$$\text{total access time} = 10(8.4 + 0.094) = 84.940 \text{ ms for ten records}$$

On the other hand, to read one block of ten records we would make a single access, so we'd compute the access time only once, multiplying the transfer rate by ten:

$$\text{access time} = 8.4 + (0.094 * 10)$$
$$= 8.4 + 0.94$$
$$= 9.34 \text{ ms for ten records in one block}$$

Once the block is in memory the software that handles blocking and deblocking takes over. Of course, the amount of time used in deblocking must be less than what you saved in access time (75.6 ms) for this to be a productive move.

Movable-Head Devices

Movable-head DASDs add the third time element to the computation of access time. Seek time is the time required to move the arm into position over the proper track. So now the formula for access time is:

$$\begin{array}{l} \text{seek time (arm movement)} \\ \text{search time (rotational delay)} \\ + \quad \underline{\text{transfer time (data transfer)}} \\ \text{access time} \end{array}$$

Of the three components of access time in this equation, seek time is the longest. It has been the subject of many studies to find the seek strategy that will move the arm in the most efficient manner possible. We'll examine several seek strategies in a moment.

The calculations to figure search time (rotational delay) and transfer time are the same as those presented for fixed-head DASDs. The maximum seek time, which is the maximum time required to move the arm, is typically 50 ms. Table 7.3 compares typical access times for movable-head DASDs.

(table 7.3)

Typical access times for a movable-head DASD, such as the hard drive shown in Figure 7.6.

Benchmarks	Access Time
Maximum access	50 ms + 16.8 ms + 0.00094 ms/byte
Average access	25 ms + 8.4 ms + 0.00094 ms/byte
Sequential access	Depends on the length of the record, generally less than 1 ms

The variance in access time has increased in comparison to that of the fixed-head DASD, but it's relatively small—especially when compared to tape access, which varies from milliseconds to minutes. Again, blocking is a good way to minimize access time. If we use the same example as for fixed-head disks and consider the average case with ten seeks followed by ten searches, we would get:

$$\text{access time} = 25 + 8.4 + 0.094 = 33.494 \text{ ms for one record}$$
$$\text{total access time} = 10 * 33.494$$
$$= 334.94 \text{ ms for ten records}$$
$$(\text{about } \tfrac{1}{3} \text{ of a second})$$

But when we put the ten records into one block, the access time is significantly decreased:

$$\text{total access time} = 25 + 8.4 + (0.094 * 10)$$
$$= 33.4 + 0.94$$
$$= 34.34 \text{ ms for ten records}$$
$$(\text{about } \tfrac{1}{29} \text{ of a second})$$

We stress that these figures wouldn't apply in an actual operating environment. For instance, we haven't taken into consideration what else is happening in the system while I/O is taking place. Therefore, although we can show the comparable performance of these components of the system, we're not seeing the whole picture.

Exercises 7 and 8 at the end of this chapter show the interaction between I/O commands and processing of the data retrieved with those commands. In fact, Exercise 8 gives you the opportunity to design a more efficient order of data storage that will take advantage of this interaction.

Overall, movable-head DASDs are much more common than fixed-head DASDs because they're less costly and have larger capacities, even though retrieval time is longer. The system designer must make a choice: a less expensive movable-head unit with more storage and slower retrieval, or a more expensive fixed-head unit with less storage and faster retrieval.

Components of the I/O Subsystem

The pieces of the I/O subsystem all have to work harmoniously, and they work in a manner similar to the mythical "Flynn Taxicab Company" shown in Figure 7.10.

(figure 7.10)

The taxicab company works in a manner similar to an I/O subsystem. One mechanic can service several vehicles just as an I/O control unit can operate several devices, as shown in Figure 7.11.

Many requests come in from all over the city to the taxi company dispatcher. It's the dispatcher's job to handle the incoming calls as fast as they arrive and to find out who needs transportation, where they are, where they're going, and when. Then the dispatcher organizes the calls into an order that will use the company's resources as efficiently as possible. That's not easy, because the cab company has a variety of vehicles at its disposal: ordinary taxicabs, station wagons, vans, limos, and a minibus. These are serviced by specialized mechanics. A mechanic handles only one type of vehicle, which is made available to the drivers. Once the order is set, the dispatcher calls the mechanic who, ideally, has the vehicle ready for the driver who jumps into the appropriate vehicle, picks up the waiting passengers, and delivers them quickly to their respective destinations.

That's the ideal—but problems sometimes occur; rainy days mean too many phone calls, vehicles are not ready, and sometimes there are several calls for the minibus.

The **I/O subsystem**'s components perform similar functions. The channel plays the part of the dispatcher in this example. Its job is to keep up with the I/O requests from the CPU and pass them down the line to the appropriate control unit. The control units play the part of the mechanics. The I/O devices play the part of the vehicles.

I/O channels are programmable units placed between the CPU and the control units. Their job is to synchronize the fast speed of the CPU with the slow speed of the I/O device, and they make it possible to overlap I/O operations with processor operations so the CPU and I/O can process concurrently. Channels use **I/O channel programs**, which can range in size from one to many instructions. Each channel program specifies the action to be performed by the devices and controls the transmission of data between main memory and the control units (Calingaert, 1982).

The channel sends one signal for each function, and the **I/O control unit** interprets the signal, which might say "go to the top of the page" if the device is a printer or "rewind" if the device is a tape drive. Although a control unit is sometimes part of the device, in most systems a single control unit is attached to several similar devices, so we distinguish between the control unit and the device.

Some systems also have a disk controller, or disk drive interface, which is a special-purpose device used to link the disk drives with the system bus. Disk drive interfaces control the transfer of information between the disk drives and the rest of the computer system. The operating system normally deals with the controller, not the device.

At the start of an I/O command, the information passed from the CPU to the channel is this:

• I/O command (READ, WRITE, REWIND, etc.)
• Channel number

• Address of the physical record to be transferred (from or to secondary storage)

• Starting address of a memory buffer from which or into which the record is to be transferred

Because the channels are as fast as the CPU they work with, each channel can direct several control units by interleaving commands (just as we had several mechanics directed by a single dispatcher). In addition, each control unit can direct several devices (just as a single mechanic could repair several vehicles of the same type). A typical configuration might have one channel and up to eight control units, each of which communicates with up to eight I/O devices. Channels are often shared because they're the most expensive items in the entire I/O subsystem.

The system shown in Figure 7.11 requires that the entire path be available when an I/O command is initiated. However, there's some flexibility built into the system because each unit can end independently of the others, as will be explained in the next section. This figure also shows the hierarchical nature of the interconnection and the one-to-one correspondence between each device and its transmission path.

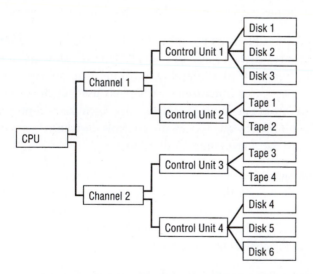

(figure 7.11)

Typical I/O subsystem configuration.

Additional flexibility can be built into the system by connecting more than one channel to a control unit or by connecting more than one control unit to a single device. That's the same as if the mechanics of the Flynn Taxicab Company could also make repairs for the ABC Taxicab Company, or if its vehicles could be used by ABC drivers (or if the drivers in our company could share vehicles).

These multiple paths increase the reliability of the I/O subsystem by keeping communication lines open even if a component malfunctions. Figure 7.12 shows the same system presented in Figure 7.11, but with one control unit connected to two channels and one device connected to two control units.

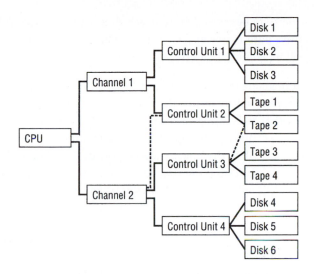

Communication Among Devices

The Device Manager relies on several auxiliary features to keep running efficiently under the demanding conditions of a busy computer system, and there are three problems that must be resolved:

• It needs to know which components are busy and which are free.

• It must be able to accommodate the requests that come in during heavy I/O traffic.

• It must accommodate the disparity of speeds between the CPU and the I/O devices.

The first is solved by structuring the interaction between units. The last two problems are handled by buffering records and queuing requests.

As we mentioned previously, each unit in the I/O subsystem can finish its operation independently from the others. For example, after a device has begun writing a record, and before it has completed the task, the connection between the device and its control unit can be cut off so the control unit can initiate another I/O task with another device. Meanwhile, at the other end of the system, the CPU is free to process data while I/O is being performed, which allows for concurrent processing and I/O.

The success of the operation depends on the system's ability to know when a device has completed an operation. This is done with a hardware flag that must be tested by the CPU. This flag is made up of three bits and resides in the **Channel Status Word (CSW)**, which is in a predefined location in main memory and contains information indicating the status of the channel. Each bit represents one of the components of the I/O subsystem, one each for the channel, control unit, and device. Each bit is changed from zero to one to indicate that the unit has changed from free to busy. Each component has access to the flag, which can be tested before proceeding with the next I/O operation to ensure that the entire path is free and vice versa. There are two common ways to perform this test—polling and using interrupts (Prasad, 1989).

Polling uses a special machine instruction to test the flag. For example, the CPU periodically tests the channel status bit (in the CSW). If the channel is still busy, the CPU performs some other processing task until the test shows that the channel is free; then the channel performs the I/O operation. The major disadvantage with this scheme is determining how often the flag should be polled. If polling is done too frequently, the CPU wastes time testing the flag just to find out that the channel is still busy. On the other hand, if polling is done too seldom, the channel could sit idle for long periods of time.

The use of **interrupts** is a more efficient way to test the flag. Instead of having the CPU test the flag, a hardware mechanism does the test as part of every machine instruction executed by the CPU. If the channel is busy the flag is set so that execution of the current sequence of instructions is automatically interrupted and control is transferred to the interrupt handler, which is part of the operating system and resides in a predefined location in memory (Bic & Shaw, 1988).

The interrupt handler's job is to determine the best course of action based on the current situation because it's not unusual for more than one unit to have caused the I/O interrupt. So the interrupt handler must find out which unit sent the signal, analyze its status, restart it when appropriate with the next operation, and finally return control to the interrupted process.

Some sophisticated systems are equipped with hardware that can distinguish between several types of interrupts. These interrupts are ordered by priority, and each one can transfer control to a corresponding location in memory. The memory locations are ranked in order according to the same priorities. So if the CPU is executing the interrupt-handler routine associated with a given priority, the hardware will automatically intercept all interrupts at the same or at lower priorities. This multiple-priority interrupt system helps improve resource utilization because each interrupt is handled according to its relative importance (Calingaert, 1982).

Direct memory access (DMA) is an I/O technique that allows a control unit to directly access main memory. This means that once reading or writing has begun, the remainder of the data can be transferred to and from memory without CPU intervention. However, it is possible that the DMA control unit and the CPU compete for the system bus if they happen to need it at the same time. To activate this process, the CPU sends enough information—such as the type of operation (read or write), the unit number of the I/O device needed, the location in memory where data is to be read from or written to, and the amount of data (bytes or words) to be transferred—to the DMA control unit to initiate the transfer of data; the CPU then can go on to another task while the control unit completes the transfer independently. The DMA controller sends an interrupt to the CPU to indicate that the operation is completed. This mode of data transfer is used for high-speed devices such as disks.

Without DMA, the CPU is responsible for the physical movement of data between main memory and the device—a time-consuming task that results in significant overhead and decreased CPU utilization.

Buffers are used extensively to better synchronize the movement of data between the relatively slow I/O devices and the very fast CPU. Buffers are temporary storage areas residing in three convenient locations throughout the system: main memory, channels, and control units. They're used to store data read from an input device before it's needed by the processor and to store data that will be written to an output device. A typical use of buffers (mentioned earlier in this chapter) occurs when blocked records are either read from, or written to, an I/O device. In this case, one physical record contains several logical records and must reside in memory while the processing of each individual record takes place. For example, if a block contains five records then a physical READ occurs with every six READ commands; all other READ requests are directed to retrieve information from the buffer (this buffer may be set by the application program).

To minimize the idle time for devices and, even more important, to maximize their throughput, the technique of double buffering is used, as shown in Figure 7.13. In this system, two buffers are present in main memory, channels, and control units. The objective is to have a record ready to be transferred to or from memory at any time to avoid any possible delay that might be caused by waiting for a buffer to fill up with data. Thus, while one record is being processed by the CPU, another can be read or written by the channel.

(figure 7.13)

Example of double buffering: (a) the CPU is reading from Buffer 1 as Buffer 2 is being filled; (b) once Buffer 2 is filled, it can be read quickly by the CPU while Buffer 1 is being filled again.

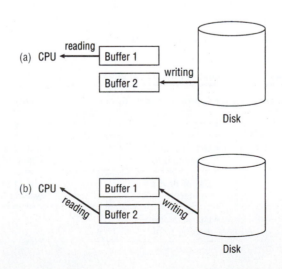

When using blocked records, upon receipt of the command to "READ last logical record," the channel can start reading the next physical record, which results in overlapped I/O and processing. When the first READ command is received, two records are transferred from the device to immediately fill both buffers. Then, as the data from one buffer has been processed, the second buffer is ready. As the second is being read, the first buffer is being filled with data from a third record, and so on.

Management of I/O Requests

Although most users think of an I/O request as an elementary machine action, the Device Manager actually divides the task into three parts with each one handled by a specific software component of the I/O subsystem. The I/O traffic controller watches the status of all devices, control units, and channels. The I/O scheduler implements the policies that determine the allocation of, and access to, the devices, control units, and channels. The I/O device handler performs the actual transfer of data and processes the device interrupts (Madnick & Donovan, 1974). Let's look at these in more detail.

The **I/O traffic controller** monitors the status of every device, control unit, and channel. It's a job that becomes more complex as the number of units in the I/O subsystem increases and as the number of paths between these units increases. The traffic controller has three main tasks: (1) it must determine if there's at least one path available; (2) if there's more than one path available, it must determine which to select; and (3) if the paths are all busy, it must determine when one will become available.

To do all this, the traffic controller maintains a database containing the status and connections for each unit in the I/O subsystem, grouped into Channel Control Blocks, Control Unit Control Blocks, and Device Control Blocks, as shown in Table 7.4.

Channel Control Block	Control Unit Control Block	Device Control Block
• Channel identification	• Control Unit identification	• Device identification
• Status	• Status	• Status
• List of control units connected to it	• List of channels connected to it	• List of control units connected to it
• List of processes waiting for it	• List of devices connected to it	• List of processes waiting for it
	• List of processes waiting for it	

(table 7.4)

Each control block contains the information it needs to manage its part of the I/O subsystem.

226

To choose a free path to satisfy an I/O request, the traffic controller traces backward from the control block of the requested device through the control units to the channels. If a path is not available, a common occurrence under heavy load conditions, the process (actually its Process Control Block, or PCB, as described in Chapter 4) is linked to the queues kept in the control blocks of the requested device, control unit, and channel. This creates multiple wait queues with one queue per path. Later, when a path becomes available, the traffic controller quickly selects the first PCB from the queue for that path.

The **I/O scheduler** performs the same job as the Process Scheduler described in Chapter 4 on processor management—that is, it allocates the devices, control units, and channels. Under heavy loads, when the number of requests is greater than the number of available paths, the I/O scheduler must decide which request to satisfy first. Many of the criteria and objectives discussed in Chapter 4 also apply here. In many systems, the major difference between I/O scheduling and process scheduling is that I/O requests are not preempted. Once the channel program has started, it's allowed to continue to completion even though I/O requests with higher priorities may have entered the queue. This is feasible because channel programs are relatively short, 50 to 100 ms. Other systems subdivide an I/O request into several stages and allow preemption of the I/O request at any one of these stages.

Some systems allow the I/O scheduler to give preferential treatment to I/O requests from high-priority programs. In that case, if a process has high priority then its I/O requests would also have high priority and would be satisfied before other I/O requests with lower priorities. The I/O scheduler must synchronize its work with the traffic controller to make sure that a path is available to satisfy the selected I/O requests.

The **I/O device handler** processes the I/O interrupts, handles error conditions, and provides detailed scheduling algorithms, which are extremely device dependent. Each type of I/O device has its own device handler algorithm.

Device Handler Seek Strategies

A **seek strategy** for the I/O device handler is the predetermined policy that the device handler uses to allocate access to the device among the many processes that may be waiting for it. It determines the order in which the processes get the device, and the goal is to keep seek time to a minimum. We'll look at some of the most commonly used seek strategies—first-come, first-served (FCFS); shortest seek time first (SSTF); and SCAN and its variations LOOK, N-Step SCAN, C-SCAN, and C-LOOK.

Every scheduling algorithm should do the following:
- Minimize arm movement
- Minimize mean response time
- Minimize the variance in response time

These goals are only a guide. In actual systems, the designer must choose the strategy that makes the system as fair as possible to the general user population while using the system's resources as efficiently as possible.

First-come, first-served (FCFS) is the simplest device-scheduling algorithm; it is easy to program and essentially fair to users. However, on average, it doesn't meet any of the three goals of a seek strategy. To illustrate, consider a single-sided disk with one recordable surface where the tracks are numbered from 0 to 49. It takes 1 ms to travel from one track to the next adjacent one. For this example, let's say that while retrieving data from Track 15, the following list of requests has arrived: Track 4, 40, 11, 35, 7, and 14. Let's also assume that once a requested track has been reached, the entire track is read into main memory. The path of the read/write head looks like the graph shown in Figure 7.14.

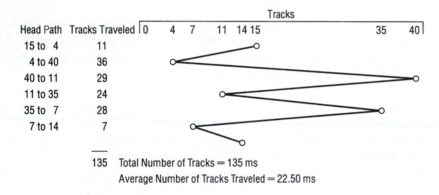

(figure 7.14)

The arm makes many time-consuming movements as it travels from track to track to satisfy all requests in FCFS order.

In Figure 7.14, it takes a long time, 135 ms, to satisfy the entire series of requests—and that's before considering the work to be done when the arm is finally in place—search time and data transfer.

FCFS has an obvious disadvantage of extreme arm movement: from 15 to 4, up to 40, back to 11, up to 35, back to 7, and, finally, up to 14. Remember, seek time is the most time-consuming of the three functions performed here, so any algorithm that can minimize it is preferable to FCFS.

Shortest seek time first (SSTF) uses the same underlying philosophy as shortest job next (described in Chapter 4), where the shortest jobs are processed first and longer jobs are made to wait. With SSTF, the request with the track closest to the one being served (that is, the one with the shortest distance to travel) is the next to be satisfied, thus minimizing overall seek time. Figure 7.15 shows what happens to the same track requests that took 135 ms to service using FCFS; in this example, all track requests are present and on the wait queue.

(figure 7.15)

Using the SSTF algorithm, with all track requests on the wait queue, arm movement is reduced by almost one third while satisfying the same requests shown in Figure 7.14 (using the FCFS algorithm).

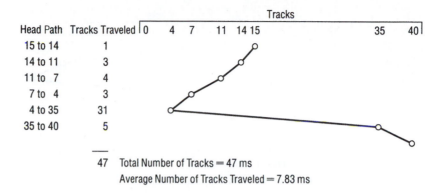

Head Path	Tracks Traveled
15 to 14	1
14 to 11	3
11 to 7	4
7 to 4	3
4 to 35	31
35 to 40	5
	47

Total Number of Tracks = 47 ms
Average Number of Tracks Traveled = 7.83 ms

Again, without considering search time and data transfer time, it took 47 ms to satisfy all requests—which is about one third of the time required by FCFS. That's a substantial improvement.

But SSTF has its disadvantages. Remember that the Shortest Job Next (SJN) process scheduling algorithm had a tendency to favor the short jobs and postpone the long, unwieldy jobs. The same holds true for SSTF. It favors easy-to-reach requests and postpones traveling to those that are out of the way.

For example, let's say that in the previous example the arm is at Track 11 and is preparing to go to Track 7 when the system suddenly gets a deluge of requests, including requests for Tracks 22, 13, 16, 29, 1, and 21. With SSTF, the system notes that Track 13 is closer to the arm's present position (only two tracks away) than the older request for Track 7 (five tracks away), so Track 13 is handled first. Of the requests now waiting, the next closest is Track 16, so off it goes—moving farther and farther away from Tracks 7 and 1. In fact, during periods of heavy loads, the arm stays in the center of the disk, where it can satisfy the majority of requests easily and it ignores (or indefinitely postpones) those on the outer edges of the disk. Therefore, this algorithm meets the first goal of seek strategies but fails to meet the other two.

SCAN uses a directional bit to indicate whether the arm is moving toward the center of the disk or away from it. The algorithm moves the arm methodically from the outer to the inner track, servicing every request in its path. When it reaches the innermost track, it reverses direction and moves toward the outer tracks, again servicing every request in its path. The most common variation of SCAN is LOOK, sometimes known as the elevator algorithm, in which the arm doesn't necessarily go all the way to either edge unless there are requests there. In effect, it "looks" ahead for a request before going to service it. In Figure 7.16, we assume that the arm is moving first toward the inner (higher-numbered) tracks before reversing direction. In this example all track requests are present and on the wait queue.

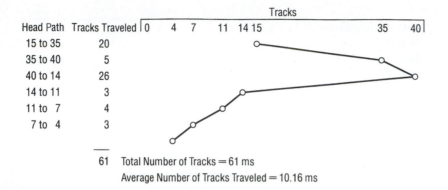

Head Path	Tracks Traveled
15 to 35	20
35 to 40	5
40 to 14	26
14 to 11	3
11 to 7	4
7 to 4	3
	61

Total Number of Tracks = 61 ms

Average Number of Tracks Traveled = 10.16 ms

(figure 7.16)

The LOOK algorithm makes the arm move systematically from the first requested track at one edge of the disk to the last requested track at the other edge. In this example, all track requests are on the wait queue.

Again, without adding search time and data transfer time, it took 61 ms to satisfy all requests, 14 ms more than with SSTF. Does this make SCAN a less attractive algorithm than SSTF? For this particular example, the answer is yes. But for the overall system, the answer is no because it eliminates the possibility of indefinite postponement of requests in out-of-the-way places—at either edge of the disk.

Also, as requests arrive, each is incorporated in its proper place in the queue and serviced when the arm reaches that track. Therefore, if Track 11 is being served when the request for Track 13 arrives, the arm continues on its way to Track 7 and then to Track 1. Track 13 must wait until the arm starts on its way back, as does the request for Track 16. This eliminates a great deal of arm movement and saves time in the end. In fact, SCAN meets all three goals for seek strategies.

Variations of SCAN, in addition to LOOK, are N-Step SCAN, C-SCAN, and C-LOOK.

N-Step SCAN doesn't incorporate requests into the arm's path as it travels, but holds all the requests until the arm starts on its way back. Any requests that arrive while the arm is in motion are grouped for the arm's next sweep.

With **C-SCAN** (an abbreviation for Circular SCAN), the arm picks up requests on its path during the inward sweep. When the innermost track has been reached, it immediately returns to the outermost track and starts servicing requests that arrived during its last inward sweep. With this modification, the system can provide quicker service to those requests that accumulated for the low-numbered tracks while the arm was moving inward. The theory here is that by the time the arm reaches the highest-numbered tracks there are few requests immediately behind it. However, there are many requests at the far end of the disk and these have been waiting the longest. Therefore, C-SCAN is designed to provide a more uniform wait time.

C-LOOK is an optimization of C-SCAN, just as LOOK is an optimization of SCAN. In this algorithm, the sweep inward stops at the last high-numbered track request, so the arm doesn't move all the way to the last track unless it's required to do so. In addition, the arm doesn't necessarily return to the lowest-numbered track; it returns only to the lowest-numbered track that's requested.

Which strategy is best? It's up to the system designer to select the best algorithm for each environment. It's a job that's complicated because the day-to-day performance of any scheduling algorithm depends on the load it must handle; but some broad generalizations can be made based on simulation studies:

- FCFS works well with light loads, but as soon as the load grows, service time becomes unacceptably long.
- SSTF is quite popular and intuitively appealing. It works well with moderate loads but has the problem of localization under heavy loads.
- SCAN works well with light to moderate loads and eliminates the problem of indefinite postponement. SCAN is similar to SSTF in throughput and mean service times.
- C-SCAN works well with moderate to heavy loads and has a very small variance in service times.

The best scheduling algorithm for a specific computing system may be a combination of more than one scheme. For instance, it might be a combination of two schemes: SCAN or LOOK during light to moderate loads, and C-SCAN or C-LOOK during heavy load times.

Search Strategies: Rotational Ordering

So far we've only tried to optimize seek times. To complete the picture, we'll now look at a way to optimize search times by ordering the requests once the read/write heads have been positioned. This **search strategy** is called **rotational ordering**.

To help illustrate the abstract concept of rotational ordering, let's consider a virtual cylinder with a movable read/write head.

Figure 7.17 illustrates the list of requests arriving at this cylinder for different sectors on different tracks. For this example we'll assume that the cylinder has only five tracks, numbered 0 through 4, and that each track contains five sectors, numbered 0 through 4. We'll take the requests in the order in which they arrive.

Each request is satisfied as it comes in. The results are shown in Table 7.5.

Request List	
Track	Sector
0	1
1	4
1	3
2	0
2	3
2	4
3	2
3	0

(figure 7.17)

This movable-head cylinder takes 5 ms to move the read/write head from one track to the next. The read/write head is initially positioned at Track 0, Sector 0. It takes 5 ms to rotate the cylinder from Sector 0 to Sector 4 and 1 ms to transfer one sector from the cylinder to main memory.

	Request (Track, Sector)	Seek time	Search time	Data transfer	Total time
1.	0,1	0	1	1	2
2.	1,4	5	2	1	8
3.	1,3	0	3	1	4
4.	2,0	5	1	1	7
5.	2,3	0	2	1	3
6.	2,4	0	0	1	1
7.	3,2	5	2	1	8
8.	3,0	0	2	1	3
	TOTALS	15 ms +	13 ms +	8 ms =	36 ms

(table 7.5)

It takes 36 ms to fill the eight requests on the movable-head cylinder shown in Figure 7.17.

Although nothing can be done to improve the time spent moving the read/write head because it's dependent on the hardware, the amount of time wasted due to rotational delay can be reduced. If the requests are ordered within each track so that the first sector requested on the second track is the next number higher than the one just served, rotational delay will be minimized, as shown in Table 7.6.

To properly implement this algorithm, the device controller must provide rotational sensing so the device driver can see which sector is currently under the read/write head. Under heavy I/O loads, this kind of ordering can significantly increase throughput, especially if the device has fixed read/write heads rather than movable heads.

Disk pack cylinders are an extension of the previous example. Once the heads are positioned on a cylinder each surface has its own read/write head shown in Figure 7.5. So rotational ordering can be accomplished on a surface-by-surface basis, and the read/write heads can be activated in turn with no additional movement required.

(table 7.6)

It takes 28 ms to fill the same eight requests shown in Table 7.5 after the requests are ordered to minimize search time, reducing it from 13 ms to 5 ms.

	Request (Track, Sector)	Seek time	Search time	Data transfer	Total time
1.	0,1	0	1	1	2
2.	1,3	5	1	1	7
3.	1,4	0	0	1	1
4.	2,0	5	0	1	6
5.	2,3	0	2	1	3
6.	2,4	0	0	1	1
7.	3,0	5	0	1	6
8.	3,2	0	1	1	2
	TOTALS	15 ms +	5 ms +	8 ms =	28 ms

Only one read/write head can be active at any one time, so the controller must be ready to handle mutually exclusive requests such as Request 2 and Request 5 in Table 7.6. They're mutually exclusive because both are requesting Sector 3, one at Track 1 and the other at Track 2, but only one of the two read/write heads can be transmitting at any given time. So the policy could state that the tracks will be processed from low-numbered to high-numbered and then from high-numbered to low-numbered in a sweeping motion such as that used in SCAN. Therefore, to handle requests on a disk pack, there would be two orderings of requests: one to handle the position of the read/write heads making up the cylinder and the other to handle the processing of each cylinder.

RAID

RAID is a set of physical disk drives that is viewed as a single logical unit by the operating system. It was introduced to close the widening gap between increasingly fast processors and slower disk drives. RAID assumes that several smaller-capacity disk drives are preferable to a few large-capacity disk drives because, by distributing the data among several smaller disks, the system can simultaneously access the requested data from the multiple drives, resulting in improved I/O performance and improved data recovery in the event of disk failure.

A typical disk array configuration may have five disk drives connected to a specialized controller, which houses the software that coordinates the transfer of data from the disks in the array to a large-capacity disk connected to the I/O subsystem, as shown in Figure 7.18. This configuration is viewed by the operating system as a single large-capacity disk, so that no software changes are needed.

(figure 7.18)

Data being transferred in parallel from a Level 0 RAID configuration to a large-capacity disk. The software in the controller ensures that the strips are stored in correct order.

Data is divided into segments called strips, which are distributed across the disks in the array. A set of consecutive strips across disks is called a **stripe** and the whole process is called striping. Figure 7.18 shows how data strips are distributed in an array of four disks.

While RAID introduces the much-needed concept of redundancy to help systems recover from hardware failure, it also requires more disk drives, which increases hardware costs.

RAID technology was originally proposed by researchers at the University of California at Berkeley, who created the acronym to stand for Redundant Array of Inexpensive Disks. The industry has since amended the acronym to represent Redundant Array of Independent Disks to emphasize the scheme's improved disk performance and reliability (Stallings, 2001).

To date there are seven levels of RAID, numbered from Level 0 through Level 6. It should be noted that the levels do not indicate a hierarchy but rather denote different types of configurations and error correction capabilities. Table 7.7 provides a summary of the seven levels including how error correction is implemented and the perceived quality of performance (Stallings, 2001).

	RAID Level	Error Correction Method	I/O Request Rate	Data Transfer Rate
(table 7.7)	0	None	Excellent	Excellent
The seven standard levels of RAID provide various degrees of error correction. Cost, speed, and the system's applications are significant factors to consider when choosing a system.	1	Mirroring	Read: Good Write: Fair	Read: Fair Write: Fair
	2	Hamming code	Poor	Excellent
	3	Word parity	Poor	Excellent
	4	Strip parity	Read: Excellent Write: Fair	Read: Fair Write: Poor
	5	Distributed strip parity	Read: Excellent Write: Fair	Read: Fair Write: Poor
	6	Distributed strip parity and independent data check	Read: Excellent Write: Poor	Read: Fair Write: Poor

Level 0

RAID Level 0 is the only one that does not provide error correction, or redundancy, and so it is not considered a true form of RAID because it cannot recover from hardware failure. However, it does offer the same significant benefit of all RAID systems—that this group of devices appears to the operating system as a single logical unit.

Raid Level 0 is well suited to transferring large quantities of non-critical data. In the configuration shown in Figure 7.19, when the operating system issues a read command for the first four strips, all four strips can be transferred in parallel, improving system performance.

(figure 7.19)

RAID Level 0 with four disks in the array. Strips 1, 2, 3, and 4 make up a stripe. Strips 5, 6, 7, and 8 make up another stripe, and so on.

RAID Level 0

Level 1

RAID Level 1 also uses striping, and is called a mirrored configuration because it provides redundancy by having a duplicate set of all data in a mirror array of disks, which acts as a backup system in the event of hardware failure. If one drive should fail, the system would immediately retrieve the data from its backup disk, making this a very reliable system. Figure 7.20 shows a RAID Level 1 configuration with three disks on each identical array: main and mirror.

(figure 7.20)

RAID Level 1 with three disks in the main array and three corresponding disks in the backup array, the mirrored array.

Using Level 1, read requests can be satisfied by either disk containing the requested data. The choice of disk could minimize seek time and rotational delay. The disadvantage is that write requests require twice as much *effort* because data must be written twice, once to each set of disks. However, this does not require twice the amount of *time* because both writes can be done in parallel.

Level 1 is an expensive system to construct because it requires at least twice the disk capacity of a Level 0 system, but its advantage of improved reliability makes it ideal for data-critical real-time systems.

Level 2

RAID Level 2 uses very small strips (often the size of a word or a byte) and uses a Hamming code to provide error detection and correction, or redundancy. The **Hamming code** is an algorithm that adds extra, redundant bits to the data and is therefore able to correct single-bit errors and detect double-bit errors.

Level 2 is an expensive and complex configuration to implement because the number of disks in the array depends on the size of the strip, and all drives must be highly synchronized in both rotational movement and arm positioning. For example, if each strip is 4 bits, then the Hamming code adds three parity bits in positions 1, 2, and 4 of the newly created 7-bit data item. In the example of RAID Level 2 shown in Figure 7.21, the array has seven disks, one for each bit. Its advantage is that, if a drive should malfunction, only one bit would be affected and the data could be quickly corrected.

(figure 7.21)

RAID Level 2 - Hamming Code

RAID Level 2. Seven disks are needed in the array to store a 4-bit data item, one for each bit and three for the parity bits. Each disk stores either a bit or a parity bit based on the Hamming code used for redundancy.

Level 3

RAID Level 3 is a modification of Level 2 that requires only one disk for redundancy. Only one parity bit is computed for each strip, and it is stored in the designated redundant disk. Figure 7.22 shows a five-disk array that can store 4-bit strips and their parity bit. If a drive malfunctions, the RAID controller considers all bits coming from that drive to be 0 and notes the location of the damaged bit. Therefore, if a data item being read has a parity error, then the controller knows that the bit from the faulty drive should have been a 1 and corrects it. If data is written to an array that has a malfunctioning disk, the controller keeps the parity consistent so data can be regenerated when the array is restored. The system returns to normal when the failed disk is replaced and its contents are regenerated on the new disk.

(figure 7.22)

RAID Level 3

RAID Level 3. A 4-bit data item is stored in the first 4 disks of the array. The fifth disk is used to store the parity for the stored data item.

Level 4

RAID Level 4 uses the same strip scheme found in Levels 0 and 1, but it computes a parity for each strip, and then it stores these parities in the corresponding strip in the designated parity disk. Figure 7.23 shows a Level 4 disk array with four disks; the first three hold data while the fourth stores the parities for the corresponding strips on the first three disks. The advantage of Level 4 is that if any one drive fails, data can be restored using the bits in the parity disk. Parity is computed every time a write command is executed. However, if data is rewritten, then the RAID controller must update both the data and parity strips. Therefore, the parity disk is accessed with every write, or rewrite, operation, sometimes causing a bottleneck in the system.

RAID Level 4

(figure 7.23)

RAID Level 4. The array contains four disks, the first three are used to store data strips, the fourth is used to store the parity of those strips.

Level 5

RAID Level 5 is a modification of Level 4. Instead of designating one disk for storing parities, it distributes the parity strips across the disks, which avoids the bottleneck created in Level 4. Its disadvantage is that regenerating data from a failed drive is more complicated. Figure 7.24 shows a Level 5 disk array with four disks.

RAID Level 5

(figure 7.24)

RAID Level 5 with four disks. Note how the parity strips are distributed among the disks.

Level 6

RAID Level 6 was introduced by the Berkeley research team in a paper that followed their original outline of RAID levels. This system provides an extra degree of error detection and correction because it requires two different parity calculations. One calculation is the same as that used in Levels 4 and 5; the other is an independent data-check algorithm. Both parities are distributed on separate disks across the array, and they are stored in the strip that corresponds to the data strips, as shown in Figure 7.25. The advantage is that the double parity allows for data restoration even if two disks fail.

However, the redundancy increases the time needed to write data because each write affects two parity strips. In addition, Level 6 requires that two disks become dedicated to parity strips and not data, which therefore reduces the number of data disks in the array.

(figure 7.25)

RAID Level 6. Note how parity strips and data check (DC) strips are distributed across the disks.

RAID Level 6

Case Study: Linux Device Management

The modular design of Linux lends itself well to the always changing variety of system devices because programmers can write device drivers, and amend them as necessary, to meet the unique needs of their systems.

Linux supports the standard classes of devices introduced by UNIX described below. In addition, Linux allows new device classes to support emerging devices such as USB drives, FireWire devices, and more. Device classes are not rigid in nature—programmers may choose to create large, complex device drivers to perform multiple functions, but such programming is discouraged for two reasons: (1) code can be shared among Linux users and there is a wider demand for several simple drivers than a single complex one, and (2) modular code is better able to support Linux's goals of system scalability and extendibility. Therefore, programmers are urged to write device drivers that maximize the system's ability to use the device effectively—no more, no less.

A popular feature of Linux is its ability to accept new device drivers on the fly, while the system is up and running. That means administrators can give the kernel additional functionality by loading and testing new drivers without having to reboot each time to reconfigure the kernel.

To understand the following discussion more fully, please remember that devices are treated in Linux (and UNIX) in the same way files are treated. (For details about this aspect, please see Chapter 15 on UNIX/Linux.) Although this might be a new concept to some readers, it is one reason for the flexibility that these operating systems and their derivatives offer.

Device Classes

The three standard classes of devices supported by Linux are character devices, block devices, and network interfaces.

Char Devices

Character devices (also known as *char devices*) are those that can be accessed as a stream of bytes, such as a serial port, monitor, or other byte-stream-fed device. At a minimum, drivers for these devices usually implement the *open*, *close*, *read*, and *write* system calls although additional calls are often added. Char devices are accessed by way of file system nodes and, from a functional standpoint, these devices look like an ordinary data area. Their drivers are treated the same way as ordinary files with the exception that char device drivers are data channels that must be accessed sequentially.

Block Devices

Block devices are similar to char devices except that they can host a file system, such as a hard disk. (Char devices cannot host a file system.) Like char devices, block devices are accessed by file system nodes in the /dev directory but these devices are transferred in blocks of data. Unlike most UNIX systems, data on a Linux system can be transferred in blocks of any size, from a few bytes to many. Like char device drivers, block device drivers appear as ordinary files with the exception that the block drivers can access a file system in connection with the device, something not possible with the char device.

Network Interfaces

Network interfaces are dissimilar from both char and block devices because their function is to send and receive packets of information as directed by the network subsystem of the kernel. So, instead of *read* and *write* calls, the network device functions relate to packet transmission.

Each system device is handled by a device driver which is, in turn, under the direction of a subsystem of Linux, as shown in Figure 7.26.

open and *release*

Two common functions of Linux device drivers are *open* and *release*, which essentially allocate and deallocate the appropriate device. For example, the operation to open a device should perform the following functions:

• Verify that the device is available and in working order
• Increase the usage counter for the device by one, so the subsystem knows that the module cannot be unloaded until its file is appropriately closed
• Initialize the device so old data is removed and it is ready to accept new data

(figure 7.26)

This example of the three primary classes of device drivers shows how device drivers receive direction from different subsystems of Linux.

- Identify the minor number and update the appropriate pointer if necessary. (major and minor numbers are explained in Chapter 15 on UNIX and Linux)
- Allocate any appropriate data structure

Likewise, the *release* function (called device_close or device_release) should perform these tasks. (It's important to remember that modules can be closed without ever releasing the device)

- Deallocate any resources that were allocated with the *open* function
- Shut down the device
- Reduce the usage counter by one so the device can be released to another module

Conclusion

The Device Manager's job is to manage every system device as effectively as possible despite the unique characteristics of each. The devices have varying speed and degrees of sharability; some can handle direct access and some only sequential access. For magnetic media, they can have one or many read/write heads, and the heads can be in a fixed position for optimum speed or able to move across the surface for optimum storage space. For optical media, the Device Manager tracks storage locations and adjusts the disc's speed accordingly so data is recorded and retrieved correctly. For flash memory, the Device Manager tracks every USB device and assures that data is sent and received correctly.

Balancing the demand for these devices is a complex task that's divided among several hardware components: channels, control units, and the devices themselves. The success of the I/O subsystem depends on the communications that link these parts.

In this chapter we reviewed several seek strategies, each with distinct advantages and disadvantages, as shown in Table 7.8.

Strategy	Advantages	Disadvantages
FCFS	• Easy to implement • Sufficient for light loads	• Doesn't provide best average service • Doesn't maximize throughput
SSTF	• Throughput better than FCFS • Tends to minimize arm movement • Tends to minimize response time	• May cause starvation of some requests • Localizes under heavy loads
SCAN/LOOK	• Eliminates starvation • Throughput similar to SSTF • Works well with light to moderate loads	• Needs directional bit • More complex algorithm to implement • Increased overhead
N-Step SCAN	• Easier to implement than SCAN	• The most recent requests wait longer than with SCAN
C-SCAN/C-LOOK	• Works well with moderate to heavy loads • No directional bit • Small variance in service time • C-LOOK doesn't travel to unused tracks	• May not be fair to recent requests for high-numbered tracks • More complex algorithm than N-Step SCAN, causing more overhead

(table 7.8)

Comparison of DASD seek strategies discussed in Chapter 7.

Our discussion of RAID included a comparison of the considerable strengths and weaknesses of each level as well as the potential boost to system reliability and error correction that each represents.

Thus far in this text we've reviewed three of the operating system's managers: the Memory Manager, the Processor Manager, and the Device Manager. In the next chapter, we'll meet the fourth, the File Manager, which is responsible for the health and well-being of every file used by the system, including the system's files, those submitted by users, and those generated as output.

Key Terms

access time: the total time required to access data in secondary storage.

blocking: a storage-saving and I/O-saving technique that groups individual records into a block that's stored and retrieved as a unit.

buffers: temporary storage areas residing in main memory, channels, and control units.

Channel Status Word (CSW): a data structure that contains information indicating the condition of the channel, including three bits for the three components of the I/O subsystem—one each for the channel, control unit, and device.

C-LOOK: a scheduling strategy for direct access storage devices that's an optimization of C-SCAN.

C-SCAN: a scheduling strategy for direct access storage devices that's used to optimize seek time. It's an abbreviation for circular-SCAN.

cylinder: a concept that describes a virtual tube that is formed when two or more read/write heads are positioned at the same track, at the same relative position, on their respective surfaces.

dedicated device: a device that can be assigned to only one job at a time; it serves that job for the entire time the job is active.

direct access storage device (DASD): any secondary storage device that can directly read or write to a specific place. Sometimes called a random access storage device.

direct memory access (DMA): an I/O technique that allows a control unit to access main memory directly and transfer data without the intervention of the CPU.

first-come, first-served (FCFS): the simplest scheduling algorithm for direct access storage devices that satisfies track requests in the order in which they are received.

flash memory: a type of nonvolatile memory used as a secondary storage device that can be erased and reprogrammed in blocks of data.

Hamming code: an error-detecting and error-correcting code that greatly improves the reliability of data, named after mathematician Richard Hamming, its inventor.

I/O channel: a specialized programmable unit placed between the CPU and the control units, which synchronizes the fast speed of the CPU with the slow speed of the I/O device and vice versa, making it possible to overlap I/O operations with CPU operations.

I/O channel program: the program that controls the channels.

I/O control unit: the hardware unit containing the electronic components common to one type of I/O device, such as a disk drive.

I/O device handler: the module that processes the I/O interrupts, handles error conditions, and provides detailed scheduling algorithms that are extremely device dependent.

I/O scheduler: one of the modules of the I/O subsystem that allocates the devices, control units, and channels.

I/O subsystem: a collection of modules within the operating system that controls all I/O requests.

I/O traffic controller: one of the modules of the I/O subsystem that monitors the status of every device, control unit, and channel.

interrecord gap (IRG): an unused space between records on a magnetic tape. It facilitates the tape's start/stop operations.

interrupt: a hardware signal that suspends execution of a program and activates the execution of a special program known as the interrupt handler.

lands: flat surface areas on the reflective layer of a CD or DVD. Each land is interpreted as a 1. Contrasts with pits, which are interpreted as 0s.

LOOK: a scheduling strategy for direct access storage devices that's used to optimize seek time. Sometimes known as the elevator algorithm.

magneto-optical (MO) disk drive: a data storage drive that uses a laser beam to read and/or write information recorded on magneto-optical disks.

N-step SCAN: a variation of the SCAN scheduling strategy for direct access storage devices that's used to optimize seek times.

parity bit: an extra bit added to a character, word, or other data unit and used for error checking. It is set to either 0 or 1 so that the sum of the one bits in the data unit is always even, for even parity, or odd for odd parity, according to the logic of the system.

pits: tiny depressions on the reflective layer of a CD or DVD. Each pit is interpreted as a 0. Contrasts with lands, which are interpreted as 1s.

RAID: acronym for redundant array of independent disks; a group of hard disks controlled in such a way that they speed read access of data on secondary storage devices and aid data recovery.

rotational ordering: an algorithm used to reorder record requests within tracks to optimize search time.

SCAN: a scheduling strategy for direct access storage devices that's used to optimize seek time. The most common variations are N-step SCAN and C-SCAN.

search: algorithm used to optimize search time in DASD.

search time: the time it takes to rotate the disk from the moment an I/O command is issued until the requested record is moved under the read/write head. Also known as rotational delay.

seek strategy: a predetermined policy used by the I/O device handler to optimize seek times.

seek time: the time required to position the read/write head on the proper track from the time the I/O request is issued.

sequential access medium: any medium that stores records only in a sequential manner, one after the other, such as magnetic tape.

shared device: a device that can be assigned to several active processes at the same time.

shortest seek time first (SSTF): a scheduling strategy for direct access storage devices that's used to optimize seek time. The track requests are ordered so the one closest to the currently active track is satisfied first and the ones farthest away are made to wait.

stripe: a set of consecutive strips across disks; the strips contain data bits and sometimes parity bits depending on the RAID level.

track: a path on a storage medium along which data is recorded.

transfer rate: the rate at which data is transferred from sequential access media.

transfer time: the time required for data to be transferred between secondary storage and main memory.

universal serial bus (USB) controller: the interface between the operating system, device drivers, and applications that read and write to devices connected to the computer through the USB port. Each USB port can accommodate up to 127 different devices.

virtual device: a dedicated device that has been transformed into a shared device through the use of spooling techniques.

Exercises

Research Topic

List two of the fastest devices available today for desktop computers or workstations that can be used to copy important files from the computer to a medium (paper, disk, flash memory, tape, etc.) that can be removed and stored in a safe place off-site. For both devices, explain in a short paragraph why you believe they are the best available. Include important benchmarks. Attach documentation from your research to substantiate your answer.

Exercises

1. What is the difference between buffering and blocking?
2. Given the following characteristics for a magnetic tape:

density =	1600 bpi
speed =	200 inches/second
size =	2,400 feet
start/stop time =	3 ms
number of records to be stored =	200,000 records
size of each record =	160 bytes
block size =	10 logical records
IBG =	0.5 inch

Find the following:

a. Number of blocks needed

b. Size of the block in bytes

c. Time required to read one block

d. Time required to write all of the blocks

e. Amount of tape used for data only, in inches

f. Total amount of tape used (data + IBGs), in inches

3. Given the following characteristics for a disk pack with 10 platters yielding 18 recordable surfaces:

rotational speed =	10 ms
transfer rate =	0.1 ms/track
density per track =	19,000 bytes
number of records to be stored =	200,000 records
size of each record =	160 bytes
block size =	10 logical records
number of tracks per surface =	500

Find the following:

a. Number of blocks per track

b. Waste per track

c. Number of tracks required to store the entire file

d. Total waste to store the entire file

e. Time to write all of the blocks (Use rotational speed; ignore the time it takes to move to the next track)

f. Time to write all of the records if they're not blocked (Use rotational speed; ignore the time it takes to move to the next track.)

g. Optimal blocking factor to minimize waste

h. What would be the answer to (e) if the time it takes to move to the next track were 5 ms?

i. What would be the answer to (f) if the time it takes to move to the next track were 5 ms?

4. Given that it takes 1 ms to travel from one track to the next, and that the arm is originally positioned at track 15 moving toward the low-numbered tracks, compute how long it will take to satisfy the following requests—4, 40, 11, 35, 7, and 14—using the LOOK scheduling policy. All requests are present in the wait queue. (Ignore rotational time and transfer time; just consider seek time.) How does your result compare to the one in Figure 7.16? Why do you think there is a difference between the two?

5. Interactive systems must respond quickly to users. Minimizing the variance of response time is an important goal, but it doesn't always prevent an occasional user from suffering indefinite postponement. What mechanism would you incorporate into a disk scheduling policy to counteract this problem and still provide reasonable response time to the user population as a whole?

Advanced Exercises

6. Under light loading conditions, every disk scheduling policy discussed in this chapter tends to behave like one of the policies discussed in this chapter. Which one is it and why?

7. Assume you have a file of ten records (identified as A, B, C, . . . J) to be stored on a disk that holds ten records per track. Once the file is stored, the records will be accessed sequentially: A, B, C, . . . J. It takes 2 ms to process each record once it has been transferred into memory. It takes 10 ms for the disk to complete one rotation. It takes 1 ms to transfer the record from the disk to main memory. Suppose you store the records in the order given: A, B, C, . . . J.
   Compute how long it will take to process all ten records. Break up your computation into (1) time to transfer a record, (2) time to process a record, and (3) time to access the next record.

8. Given the same situation described in Exercise 7:
   a. Organize the records so that they're stored in non-alphabetical order (not A, B, C, . . . J) to reduce the time it takes to process them sequentially in alphabetical order.
   b. Compute how long it will take to process all ten records using this new order. Break up your computation into (1) time to transfer a record, (2) time to process a record, and (3) time to access the next record.

9. Track requests are not usually equally or evenly distributed. For example, the tracks where the disk directory resides are accessed more often than those where the user's files reside. Suppose that you know that 50 percent of the requests are for a small, fixed number of cylinders.
   a. Which one of the scheduling policies presented in this chapter would be the best under these conditions?
   b. Can you design one that would be better?

10. Complete the following chart for magnetic disk storage devices. Cite your sources.

Type	Speed in Revolutions per Minute	Storage Capacity	Average Access Time	Cost in Dollars
Floppy				
Hard disk				
Other magnetic disk				

11. Complete the following chart for optical storage devices. Cite your sources.

Type	Transfer Rate in Bytes per Second	Storage Capacity	Average Access Time	Cost in Dollars
CD-ROM				
CD-R				
CD-RW				
DVD-ROM				
MO				

12. Complete the following chart for magnetic tape storage devices. Cite your sources.

Type	Storage Capacity	Platform Where Used (LAN, PC, Mainframe, etc.)	Manufacturer	Cost in Dollars
8mm Digital Audio Tape				
Digital Linear Tape				
Digital Tape Format				
3480/3490 Tape Storage				

13. Give an example of an environment or application that best matches the characteristics of each of the following RAID levels.
    a. Level 0
    b. Level 1
    c. Level 3
    d. Level 5
    e. Level 6

14. This chapter mentions CD-RWs and how information is stored in them. Use the Internet to find current information about CD-RWs and determine if all CD-RWs are exchangeable between readers and burners. Explain why or why not.

15. Search current articles about optical technology and find an illustration that shows how information is stored on CDs and CD-RWs. What are the differences and similarities?

Programming Exercise

16. Write a program that will simulate the FCFS, SSTF, LOOK, and C-LOOK seek optimization strategies. Assume that:

    a. The disk's outer track is the 0 track and the disk contains 200 tracks per surface. Each track holds eight sectors numbered 0 through 7.

    b. A seek takes $10 + 0.1 * T$ ms, where T is the number of tracks of motion from one request to the next, and 10 is a movement time constant.

    c. One full rotation takes 8 ms.

    d. Transfer time is 1 ms.

    Use the following data to test your program:

Arrival Time	Track Requested	Sector Requested
0	45	0
23	132	6
25	20	2
29	23	1
35	198	7
45	170	5
57	180	3
83	78	4
88	73	5
95	150	7

For comparison purposes, compute the average, variance, and standard deviation of the time required to accommodate all requests under each of the strategies. Consolidate your results into a table.

Optional: Run your program again with different data and compare your results. Recommend the best policy and explain why.

Chapter 8 | File Management

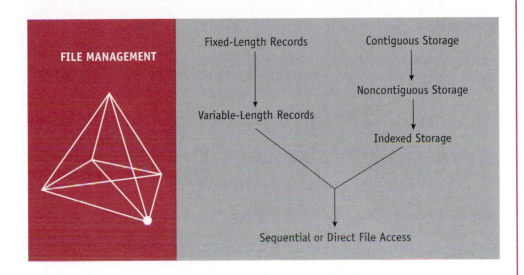

Learning Objectives

After completing this chapter, you should be able to describe:

- The fundamentals of file management and the structure of the file management system
- File-naming conventions, including the role of extensions
- The difference between fixed-length and variable-length record format
- The advantages and disadvantages of contiguous, noncontiguous, and indexed file storage techniques
- Comparisons of sequential and direct file access
- The security ramifications of access control techniques and how they compare
- The role of data compression in file storage

The File Manager controls every file in the system. In this chapter we'll learn how files are organized logically, how they're stored physically, how they're accessed, and who is allowed to access them. We'll also study the interaction between the File Manager and the Device Manager.

The efficiency of the File Manager depends on how the system's files are organized (sequential, direct, or indexed sequential); how they're stored (contiguously, noncontiguously, or indexed); how each file's records are structured (fixed-length or variable-length); and how access to these files is controlled. We'll look at each of these variables in this chapter. To see how today's operating systems manage files in detail, see the file management sections in chapters 13–15.

The File Manager

The File Manager (also called the file management system) is the software responsible for creating, deleting, modifying, and controlling access to files—as well as for managing the resources used by files. The File Manager provides support for libraries of programs and data to online users, for spooling operations, and for interactive computing. These functions are performed in collaboration with the Device Manager.

Responsibilities of the File Manager

The File Manager has a complex job. It's in charge of the system's physical components, its information resources, and the policies used to store and distribute the files. To carry out its responsibilities it must perform these four tasks:

1. Keep track of where each file is stored.
2. Use a policy that will determine where and how the files will be stored, making sure to efficiently use the available storage space and provide efficient access to the files.
3. Allocate each file when a user has been cleared for access to it, then record its use.
4. Deallocate the file when the file is to be returned to storage, and communicate its availability to others who may be waiting for it.

For example, the file system is like a library, with the File Manager playing the part of the librarian who performs the same four tasks:

1. A librarian uses the catalog to keep track of each item in the collection; each entry lists the call number and the details that help patrons find the books they want.
2. The library relies on a predetermined policy to store everything in the collection including oversized books, magazines, books-on-tape, DVDs, maps, and videos. And they must be physically arranged so people can find what they need.

3. When it's requested, the item is retrieved from its shelf and the borrower's name is noted in the circulation records.

4. When the item is returned, the librarian makes the appropriate notation in the circulation records and reshelves it.

In a computer system, the File Manager keeps track of its files with directories that contain the filename, its physical location in secondary storage, and important information about each file.

The File Manager's predetermined policy determines where each file is stored and how the system, and users, will be able to access them simply—via commands that are independent from device details. In addition, the policy must determine who will have access to what material, and this involves two factors: flexibility of access to the information and its subsequent protection. The File Manager does this by allowing access to shared files, providing distributed access, and allowing users to browse through public directories. Meanwhile, the operating system must protect its files against system malfunctions and provide security checks via account numbers, passwords, and lockwords to preserve the integrity of the data and safeguard against tampering. These protection techniques are explained later in this chapter.

The computer system *allocates* a file by activating the appropriate secondary storage device and loading the file into memory while updating its records of who is using what file.

Finally, the File Manager *deallocates* a file by updating the file tables and rewriting the file (if revised) to the secondary storage device. Any processes waiting to access the file are then notified of its availability.

Definitions

Before we continue, let's take a minute to review some basic definitions that relate to our discussion of the File Manager.

A **field** is a group of related bytes that can be identified by the user with a name, type, and size. A **record** is a group of related fields.

A **file** is a group of related records that contains information to be used by specific application programs to generate reports. This type of file contains data and is sometimes called a flat file because it has no connections to other files; unlike databases, it has no dimensionality.

A **database** appears to the File Manager to be a type of file, but databases are more complex because they're actually groups of related files that are interconnected at various levels to give users flexibility of access to the data stored. If the user's database requires a specific structure, the File Manager must be able to support it.

Program files contain instructions and **data files** contain data, but as far as storage is concerned, the File Manager treats them exactly the same way. **Directories** are listings of filenames and their attributes and are treated in a manner similar to files by the File Manager. Data collected to monitor system performance and provide for system accounting is collected into files. In fact, every program and data file accessed by the computer system, as well as every piece of computer software, is treated as a file.

Interacting with the File Manager

The user communicates with the File Manager via specific commands that may be either embedded in the user's program or submitted interactively by the user.

Examples of embedded commands are OPEN, CLOSE, READ, WRITE, and MODIFY. OPEN and CLOSE pertain to the availability of a file for the program invoking it. READ and WRITE are the I/O commands. MODIFY is a specialized WRITE command for existing data files that allows for appending records or for rewriting selected records in their original place in the file.

Examples of interactive commands are CREATE, DELETE, RENAME, and COPY. CREATE and DELETE deal with the system's knowledge of the file. Actually, files can be created with other system-specific terms: for example, the first time a user gives the command to SAVE a file, it's actually created. In other systems the OPEN NEW command within a program indicates to the File Manager that a file must be created. Likewise, an OPEN...FOR OUTPUT command instructs the File Manager to create a file by making an entry for it in the directory and to find space for it in secondary storage. RENAME allows users to change the name of an existing file, and COPY lets them make duplicate copies of existing files.

These commands and many more, which are the interface between the user and the hardware, were designed to be as simple as possible to use so they're devoid of the detailed instructions required to run the device where the file may be stored. That is, they're **device independent**. Therefore, to access a file, the user doesn't need to know its exact physical location on the disk pack (the cylinder, surface, and sector) or even the medium in which it's stored (tape, magnetic disk, optical disc, or flash storage). And that's fortunate because file access is a complex process. Each logical command is broken down into a sequence of low-level signals that trigger the step-by-step actions performed by the device and supervise the progress of the operation by testing the device's status. For example, when a user's program issues a command to read a record from a disk, the READ instruction has to be decomposed into the following steps:

1. Move the read/write heads to the cylinder where the record is to be found.
2. Wait for the rotational delay until the sector containing the desired record passes under the read/write head.

3. Activate the appropriate read/write head and read the record.

4. Transfer the record to main memory.

5. Send a flag to indicate that the device is free to satisfy another request.

While all this is going on, the system must check for possible error conditions.

The File Manager does all of this, freeing the user from including in each program the low-level instructions for every device to be used: the terminal, keyboard, printer, disk drive, etc. Without the File Manager every program would need to include instructions to operate all of the different types of devices, and all of the different models within each type. Considering the rapid development and increased sophistication of I/O devices it would be impractical, and certainly not very user friendly, to require each program to include these minute operational details.

Fortunately, with device independence, users can manipulate their files by using a simple set of commands such as OPEN, CLOSE, READ, WRITE, and MODIFY.

Typical Volume Configuration

Normally the active files for a computer system reside on secondary storage units. Some devices accommodate removable storage units—such as CDs, DVDs, floppy disks, USB devices, and other removable media—so files that aren't frequently used can be stored offline and mounted only when the user specifically requests them. Other devices feature integrated storage units, such as hard disks, and nonremovable disk packs.

Each storage unit, whether it's removable or not, is considered a **volume** and each volume can contain several files so they're called "multifile volumes." However, some files are extremely large and are contained in several volumes; not surprisingly these are called "multivolume files."

Generally, each volume in the system is given a name, just as files are named. The File Manager writes this name and other descriptive information, as shown in Figure 8.1, on an easy-to-access place on each unit: the innermost part of the CD or DVD, the beginning of the tape, or the first sector of the outermost track of the disk pack. Once identified, the operating system can interact with the storage unit.

(figure 8.1)

The volume descriptor, stored at the beginning of each volume, includes the volume name and other vital information about the storage unit.

Creation Date	← Date when volume was created
Pointer to Directory Area	← Indicates first sector where directory is stored
Pointer to File Area	← Indicates first sector where file is stored
File System Code	← Used to detect volumes with incorrect formats
Volume Name	← User-allocated name

255

The **master file directory (MFD)** is stored immediately after the volume descriptor and it lists the names and characteristics of every file contained in that volume. The filenames in the MFD can refer to program files, data files, and/or system files. And if the File Manager supports subdirectories, they're listed in the MFD as well. The remainder of the volume is used for file storage.

Early operating systems supported only a single directory per volume. This directory was created by the File Manager and contained the names of files, usually organized in alphabetical, spatial, or chronological order. Although it was simple to implement and maintain, this scheme had some major disadvantages.

• It would take a long time to search for an individual file, especially if the MFD was organized in an arbitrary order.

• If the user had many small files stored in the volume, the directory space would fill up before the disk storage space filled up. The user would then be told "disk full" when only the directory was full.

• Users couldn't create subdirectories to group the files that were related.

• Multiple users couldn't safeguard their files from other users browsing file lists because the entire directory was listed on request.

• Each program in the entire directory needed a unique name, even those directories serving many users, so only one person using that directory could have a program named PROG1.

For example, imagine the havoc in an introductory computer science class. The first person on the system would, as usual, name the first assignment PROG1, and the rest of the class would have an interesting choice: find unique names for their programs; write a new program and name it PROG1 (which would erase the original version); or simply modify PROG1 as it was most recently saved. Eventually, the entire class could end up with a single, though perhaps terrific, program.

About Subdirectories

Semi-sophisticated File Managers create an MFD for each volume that can contain entries for both files and for subdirectories. A **subdirectory** is created when a user opens an account to access the computer system. Although this user directory is treated as a file, its entry in the MFD is flagged to indicate to the File Manager that this file is really a subdirectory and has unique properties—in fact, its records are filenames pointing to files.

Although this is an improvement from the single directory scheme (now all of the students can name their first program PROG1), it doesn't solve the problems encountered by prolific users who want to group their files in a logical order to improve the accessibility and efficiency of the system.

Today's sophisticated File Managers allow their users to create their own subdirectories so related files can be grouped together. Many computer users call these subdirectories "folders." This structure is an extension of the previous two-level directory organization and it's implemented as an upside-down tree, as shown in Figure 8.2.

Tree structures allow the system to efficiently search individual directories because there are fewer entries in each directory. However, the path to the requested file may lead through several directories. For every file request the MFD is the point of entry. Actually, the MFD is usually transparent to the user—it's accessible only by the operating system. When the user wants to access a specific file, the filename is sent to the File Manager. The File Manager first searches the MFD for the user's directory and it then searches the user's directory and any subdirectories for the requested file and its location.

(figure 8.2)

File directory tree structure. The "root" is the MFD shown at the top, each node is a directory file, and each branch is a directory entry pointing to either another directory or to a real file. All program and data files subsequently added to the tree are the leaves, represented by circles.

Regardless of the complexity of the directory structure, each file entry in every directory contains information describing the file; it's called the **file descriptor**. Information typically included in a file descriptor includes the following:

• Filename—usually represented in ASCII code.

• File type—the organization and usage that are dependent on the system (for example, files and directories).

• File size—although it could be computed from other information, the size is kept here for convenience.

• File location—identification of the first physical block (or all blocks) where the file is stored.

• Date and time of creation.

• Owner.

• Protection information—access restrictions based on who is allowed to access the file and what type of access is allowed.

• Record size—its fixed size or its maximum size, depending on the type of record.

File Naming Conventions

A file's name can be much longer than the user thinks it is. Depending on the level of sophistication of the File Manager, it can have from two to many components.

Two components are common to most filenames: a **relative filename** and an **extension**. (In UNIX and Linux, the extension is sometimes called a "suffix," but it is not required.) To avoid confusion, in the following discussion we'll use the term "complete filename" to identify the file's **absolute filename** (that's the long name that includes all path information), and "relative name," to indicate the short name that appears in directory listings and folders.

The relative filename is the name that's selected by the user when the file is created, such as ACCOUNT ADDRESSES, TAXES_2737, or AUTOEXEC. Generally, the name can vary in length from one to many characters and can include letters of the alphabet as well as digits.

However, every operating system has specific rules that affect the length of the relative name and the types of characters allowed. For example, MS-DOS allows names from one to eight alphanumeric characters but without spaces. Most modern operating systems allow names with dozens of characters including spaces.

It's a good idea to select descriptive relative names that readily identify the contents or purpose of the file and are easy for other system users to remember and use correctly.

For example, PROG1 is a poor choice as a filename because it's easily confused with PROG7 and PROG11. If the file is used to run the hospital's inventory control program, then INVENTORY is a better name. INVENTORY FOR EMERGENCY SUITE is even better.

An extension is usually two or three characters long and is separated from the relative name by a period. Its purpose is to identify the type of file or its contents. For example, in a simple system, such as MS-DOS, a typical relative name with extension would be INVENTRY.FOR where the extension FOR indicates to the operating system that this file was written in FORTRAN. Similarly, TAXES.COB indicates a COBOL file. AUTOEXEC.BAT is a batch file that's automatically executed by some operating systems when they're booted up. INVENTRY.DAT indicates that this is a file that contains data to be used with another program, such as INVENTRY.FOR.

Some extensions, such as EXE, BAT, COB, and FOR, are recognized by certain operating systems because they constitute a standard set. Some of these extensions serve as a signal to the system to use a specific compiler or program to run these files. Other extensions, such as TXT, DOC, OUT, MIC, and KEY, are created by applications or by users for their own identification. Note that some file extensions are associated with more than one application.

The other components required for a file's complete name depend on the operating system. Here's how a filenamed INVENTRY.DOC is identified by three different operating systems:

1. Using the MS-DOS operating system and a personal computer with three disk drives, the file's complete name is composed of its relative name and extension preceded by the drive label and directory name:

    ```
    C:\IMFST.FLYNN\INVENTRY.DOC
    ```

    This indicates to the system that the file INVENTRY.DOC requires a word processing application program, and it can be found in the directory IMFST, subdirectory FLYNN in the volume residing on drive C.

2. In a networked environment using the OpenVMS Alpha operating system, its complete name could be:

    ```
    VAX2::USR3:[IMFST.FLYNN]INVENTRY.DOC;7
    ```

    The leftmost entry, VAX2, indicates which node in the computer network holds this particular user. The second entry, USR3, indicates the volume or storage device where the file will be retrieved and stored. This is followed by the directory, IMFST, and subdirectory, FLYNN, and then by the relative name and extension, INVENTRY.DOC. The final entry is this file's version number—7—which, in this case, indicates that the file had one original version and six revisions.

3. A UNIX or Linux system might identify the file as:

$$\texttt{/usr/imfst/flynn/inventry.doc}$$

The first entry is represented by the slash, /. It represents a special master directory called the *root*. Next is the name of the first subdirectory, usr/imfst, followed by a sub-subdirectory, /flynn, in this multiple directory system. The final entry is the file's relative name, inventry.doc. (Notice that UNIX and Linux filenames are generally expressed in lower case.)

As you can see, the names tend to grow in length as the file managers grow in flexibility. But very often, most files can be accessed simply by their short relative names.

The folders on a system with a graphical user interface, such as Windows or Macintosh, are actually directories or subdirectories. When someone creates a folder, the system creates a subdirectory in the current directory or folder. This can then be accessed by opening the folder when it is displayed, as shown in Figure 8.3.

Why don't command-driven operating systems require users to type in these extremely long names every time they access a file? Most operating systems provide a two-step solution. First, the File Manager selects a directory for the user when the interactive session begins, so all file operations requested by that user start from this "home" or "base" directory. Second, from this home directory, the user selects a subdirectory, which is called a **current directory or working directory**. Thereafter, the files are presumed to be located in this current directory. Whenever a file is accessed, the user types in the relative name and the File Manager adds the proper prefix. As long as users refer to files in the working directory, they can access their files without entering the complete name from the highest level to the lowest.

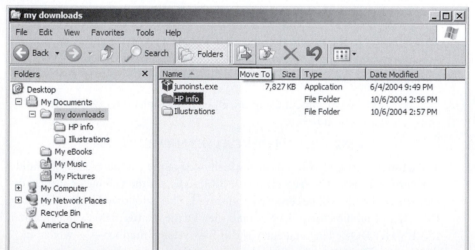

(figure 8.3)

In this example, Windows Explorer is used to see the directory tree on the left. On the right the contents of the subdirectory called "my downloads" are shown. From this screen users can copy, move, rename, and delete files.

The concept of a current directory is based on the underlying hierarchy present in a tree structure as shown in Figure 8.2 and allows programmers to retrieve a file by typing only the relative name INVENTRY.DOC, instead of its absolute name:

VAX2::USR3:[IMFST.FLYNN]INVENTRY.DOC;7

File Organization

When we discuss file organization, we are talking about the arrangement of records within a file because all files are composed of records. When a user gives a command to modify the contents of a file, it's actually a command to access records within the file.

Record Format

All files are composed of records. When a user gives a command to modify the contents of a file it's actually a command to access records within the file. Within each file the records are all presumed to have the same format: they can be of fixed length or of variable length, as shown in Figure 8.4. And these records, regardless of their format, can be blocked or not blocked.

Fixed-length records are the most common because they're the easiest to access directly. That's why they're ideal for data files. The critical aspect of fixed-length records is the size of the record. If it's too small—smaller than the number of characters to be stored in the record—the leftover characters are truncated. But if the record size is too large, larger than the number of characters to be stored, storage space is wasted.

(figure 8.4)

When data is stored in fixed-length fields (a), data that extends beyond the fixed size is truncated. When data is stored in a variable-length record format (b), the size expands to fit the contents, but it takes more time to access.

(a)

chair	steel desk with 4	file cabinet, 2	lamp

(b)

chair	steel desk with 4 file drawers	file cabinet, 2 drawers	lamp

Variable-length records don't leave empty storage space and don't truncate any characters, thus eliminating the two disadvantages of fixed-length records. But while they can easily be read, one after the other, they're difficult to access directly because it's hard to calculate exactly where the record is located. That's why they're used most frequently in files that are likely to be accessed sequentially, such as text files and program files, or files that use an index to access their records. The record format, how it's blocked, and other related information is kept in the file descriptor.

The amount of space that's actually used to store the supplementary information varies from system to system and it conforms to the physical limitations of the storage medium, as we'll see later in this chapter.

Physical File Organization

The physical organization of a file has to do with the way records are arranged and the characteristics of the medium used to store it.

On magnetic disks, files can be organized in one of three ways: sequential, direct, or indexed sequential. To select the best of these file organizations, the programmer or analyst usually considers these practical characteristics:

• Volatility of the data—the frequency with which additions and deletions are made

• Activity of the file—the percentage of records processed during a given run

• Size of the file

• Response time—the amount of time the user is willing to wait before the requested operation is completed. This is especially crucial when doing searches and retrieving information in an interactive environment.

Sequential record organization is by far the easiest to implement because records are stored and retrieved serially, one after the other. To find a specific record, the file is searched from its beginning until the requested record is found.

To speed the process some optimization features may be built into the system. One is to select a key field from the record and then sort the records by that field before storing them. Later, when a user requests a specific record, the system searches only the key field of each record in the file. The search is ended when either an exact match is found or the key field for the requested record is smaller than the value of the record last compared, in which case the message "record not found" is sent to the user and the search is terminated.

Although this technique aids the search process, it complicates the maintenance algorithms because the original order must be preserved every time records are added or deleted. And to preserve the physical order, the file must be completely rewritten or kept sorted dynamically every time it's updated.

A **direct record organization** uses direct access files, which, of course, can be implemented only on direct access storage devices. These files give users the flexibility of accessing any record in any order without having to begin a search from the beginning of the file to do so. It's also known as "random organization," and its files are called "random access files."

Records are identified by their **relative addresses**—their addresses relative to the beginning of the file. These **logical addresses** are computed when the records are stored and then again when the records are retrieved.

The method used is quite straightforward. The user identifies a field (or combination of fields) in the record format and designates it as the **key field** because it uniquely identifies each record. The program used to store the data follows a set of instructions, called a **hashing algorithm**, that transforms each key into a number, the record's logical address. This is given to the File Manager, which takes the necessary steps to translate the logical address into a physical address (cylinder, surface, and record numbers), preserving the file organization. The same procedure is used to retrieve a record.

Of course, a direct access file can be accessed sequentially by starting at the first relative address and incrementing it by one to get to the next record.

Direct access files can be updated more quickly than sequential files because records can be quickly rewritten to their original addresses after modifications have been made. And there's no need to preserve the order of the records, so adding or deleting them takes very little time.

For example, telephone mail order firms use hashing algorithms to directly access their customer information. Let's say you're placing an order and you're asked for your postal code and street number (let's say they are 15213 and 2727). The program that retrieves information from the data file uses that key in a hashing algorithm to calculate the logical address where your record is stored. So when the order clerk types 152132727 the screen soon shows a list of all current customers whose customer numbers generated the same logical address. If you're in the database the operator knows right away. If not, you will be soon.

The problem with hashing algorithms is that several records with unique keys (such as customer numbers) may generate the same logical address—and then there's a collision, as shown in Figure 8.5 When that happens the program must generate another logical address before presenting it to the File Manager for storage. Records that collide are stored in an overflow area that was set aside when the file was created. Although the program does all the work of linking the records from the overflow area to their corresponding logical address, the File Manager must handle the physical allocation of space.

The maximum size of the file is established when it's created, and eventually either the file might become completely full or the number of records stored in the overflow area

Records
2737 Highland Ave.
15212

2737 Anderson Ave.
15213

2737 Boyd Rd.
15213

2737 Glen St.
15213

2737 Balsam Way
15214

Logical Addresses
152122737

152132737

152142737

might become so large that the efficiency of retrieval is lost. In either case the file must be reorganized and rewritten, which requires intervention by the programmer.

Indexed sequential record organization combines the best of sequential and direct access. It's created and maintained through an Indexed Sequential Access Method (ISAM) software package, which removes the burden of handling overflows and preserving record order from the shoulders of the programmer.

This type of organization doesn't create collisions because it doesn't use the result of the hashing algorithm to generate a record's address. Instead, it uses this information to generate an index file through which the records are retrieved. This organization divides an ordered sequential file into blocks of equal size. Their size is determined by the File Manager to take advantage of physical storage devices and to optimize retrieval strategies. Each entry in the index file contains the highest record key and the physical location of the data block where this record, and the records with smaller keys, are stored.

Therefore, to access any record in the file, the system begins by searching the index file and then goes to the physical location indicated at that entry. We can say then that the index file acts as a pointer to the data file. An indexed sequential file also has overflow areas but they're spread throughout the file, perhaps every few records, so expansion of existing records can take place and new records can be located in close physical sequence as well as in logical sequence. Another overflow area is located apart from the main data area but is used only when the other overflow areas are completely filled. We call it the overflow of last resort.

This last-resort overflow area can store records added during the lifetime of the file. The records are kept in logical order by the software package without much effort on the part of the programmer. Of course, when too many records have been added here, the retrieval process slows down because the search for a record has to go from the index to the main data area and eventually to the overflow area.

When retrieval time becomes too slow, the file has to be reorganized. That's a job that, although it's not as tedious as reorganizing direct access files, is usually delegated to programmers or systems analysts.

For most dynamic files, indexed sequential is the organization of choice because it allows both direct access to a few requested records and sequential access to many. A variation of indexed sequential files is the B-tree.

Physical Storage Allocation

The File Manager must work with files not just as whole units but also as logical units or records. Records within a file must have the same format but they can vary in length, as shown in Figure 8.6.

(figure 8.6)

Every record in a file must have the same format but can be of different sizes, as shown in these five examples of the most common record formats. The supplementary information in (b), (c), (d), and (e) is provided by the File Manager when the record is stored.

265

In turn, records are subdivided into fields. In most cases their structure is managed by application programs and not the operating system. An exception is made for those systems that are heavily oriented to database applications, where the File Manager handles field structure.

So when we talk about file storage, we're actually referring to record storage. How are the records within a file stored? At this stage the File Manager and Device Manager have to cooperate to ensure successful storage and retrieval of records. In Chapter 7 on device management, we introduced the concept of logical versus physical records, and this theme recurs here from the point of view of the File Manager.

Contiguous Storage

When records use **contiguous storage** they're stored one after the other. This was the scheme used in early operating systems. It's very simple to implement and manage. Any record can be found and read once its starting address and size are known, so the directory is very streamlined. Its second advantage is its ease of direct access because every part of the file is stored in the same compact area.

The primary disadvantage is that a file can't be expanded unless there's empty space available immediately following it, as shown in Figure 8.7. Therefore, room for expansion must be provided when the file is created. If there's not enough room, the entire file must be recopied to a larger section of the disk every time records are added. The second disadvantage is fragmentation (slivers of unused storage space), which can be overcome by compacting and rearranging files. And, of course, the files can't be accessed while compaction is taking place.

The File Manager keeps track of the empty storage areas by treating them as files—they're entered in the directory but are flagged to differentiate them from real files. Usually the directory is kept in order by sector number so adjacent empty areas can be combined into one large free space.

Free Space	File 1 Record 1	File 1 Record 2	File 1 Record 3	File 1 Record 4	File 1 Record 5	File 1 Record 6	File 2 Record 1	File 2 Record 2	File 2 Record 3	File 2 Record 4	Free Space	File 3 Record 1	. . . . . .

(figure 8.7)

Using this example of contiguous file storage, File 1 can't be expanded without being rewritten to a larger storage area. File 2 can be expanded by only one record replacing the free space preceding File 3.

Noncontiguous Storage

Noncontiguous storage allocation allows files to use any storage space available on the disk. A file's records are stored in a contiguous manner only if there's enough empty space. Any remaining records, and all other additions to the file, are stored in other sections of the disk. In some systems these are called the **extents** of the file and are linked together with pointers. The physical size of each extent is determined by the operating system and is usually 256—or another power of two—bytes.

File extents are usually linked in one of two ways. Linking can take place at the storage level where each extent points to the next one in the sequence, as shown in Figure 8.8. The directory entry consists of the filename, the storage location of the first extent, the location of the last extent, and the total number of extents, not counting the first.

The alternative is for the linking to take place at the directory level, as shown in Figure 8.9. Each extent is listed with its physical address, its size, and a pointer to the next extent. A null pointer, shown here as a hyphen (-), indicates that it's the last one.

Although both noncontiguous allocation schemes eliminate external storage fragmentation and the need for compaction, they don't support direct access because there's no easy way to determine the exact location of a specific record.

(figure 8.8)

Noncontiguous file storage with linking taking place at the storage level. File 1 starts in address 2 and continues in addresses 8, 20, and 18. The directory lists the file's starting address and ending address, and the number of extents it uses. Each block of storage includes its address and a pointer to the next block for the file, as well as the data itself.

File No.	Start	End	No. extents
1	②	18	3
2	3	11	2

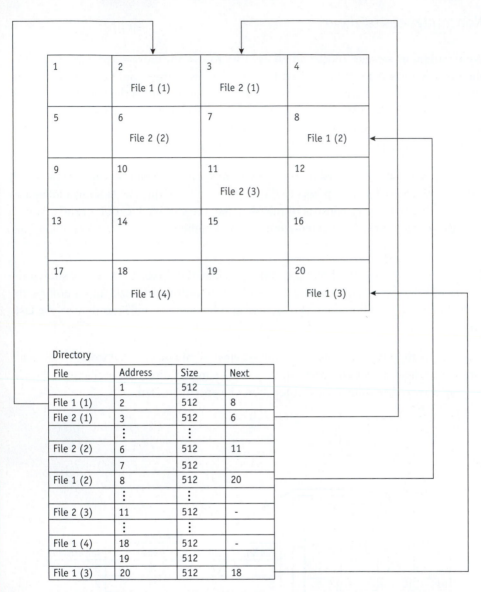

(figure 8.9)

Noncontiguous storage allocation with linking taking place at the directory level for the files shown in Figure 8.8.

Files are usually declared to be either sequential or direct when they're created so the File Manager can select the most efficient method of storage allocation: contiguous for direct files and noncontiguous for sequential. Operating systems must have the capability to support both storage allocation schemes.

Files can then be converted from one type to another by creating a file of the desired type and copying the contents of the old file into the new using a program designed for that specific purpose.

Indexed Storage

Indexed storage allocation allows direct record access by bringing together into an index block the pointers linking every extent of that file. Every file has its own index block, which consists of the addresses of each disk sector that make up the file. The index lists each entry in the same order in which the sectors are linked, as shown in Figure 8.10. For example, the third entry in the index block corresponds to the third sector making up the file.

When a file is created, the pointers in the index block are all set to null. Then, as each sector is filled, the pointer is set to the appropriate sector address—to be precise, the address is removed from the empty space list and copied into its position in the index block.

This scheme supports both sequential and direct access but it doesn't necessarily improve the use of storage space because each file must have an index block—usually the

(figure 8.10)

Indexed storage allocation with a one-level index allowing direct access to each record for the files shown in Figures 8.8 and 8.9.

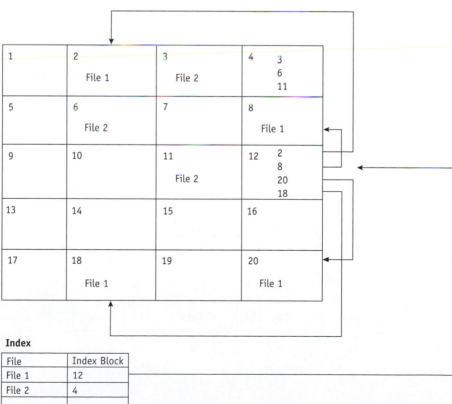

size of one disk sector. For larger files with more entries, several levels of indexes can be generated, in which case, to find a desired record, the File Manager accesses the first index (the highest level), which points to a second index (lower level), which points to an even lower level index and eventually to the data record.

Access Methods

Access methods are dictated by a file's organization; the most flexibility is allowed with indexed sequential files and the least with sequential.

A file that has been organized in sequential fashion can support only sequential access to its records, and these records can be of either fixed or variable length, as shown in Figure 8.4. The File Manager uses the address of the last byte read to access the next sequential record. Therefore, the **current byte address (CBA)** must be updated every time a record is accessed, such as when the READ command is executed (Madnick & Donovan, 1974).

Figure 8.11 shows the difference between storage of fixed-length and of variable-length records.

Sequential Access

For *sequential access of fixed-length records* the CBA is updated simply by incrementing it by the record length (RL), which is a constant:

$$CBA = CBA + RL$$

(figure 8.11)

Fixed-versus variable-length records. (a) Fixed-length records have the same number of bytes so record length (RL) is a constant. (b) With variable-length records RL_k isn't a constant. Therefore, it's recorded on the sequential media, such as magnetic tape, immediately preceding each record.

For *sequential access of variable-length records* the File Manager adds the length of the record (RLk) plus the number of bytes used to hold the record length (N) to the CBA.

$$CBA = CBA + N + RL_k$$

Direct Access

We've only looked at sequential access thus far. If a file is organized in direct fashion, it can be accessed easily in either direct or sequential order if the records are of fixed length. In the case of *direct access with fixed length records*, the CBA can be computed directly from the record length and the desired record number RN (information provided through the READ command) minus one:

$$CBA = (RN - 1) * RL$$

For example, if we're looking for the beginning of the eleventh record and the fixed record length is 25 bytes, the CBA would be:

$$(11 - 1) * 25 = 250$$

However, if the file is organized for *direct access with variable-length records*, it's virtually impossible to access a record directly because the address of the desired record can't be easily computed. Therefore, to access a record, the File Manager must do a sequential search through the records. In fact, it becomes a half-sequential read through the file because the File Manager could save the address of the last record accessed and when the next request arrives it could search forward from the CBA—if the address of the desired record was between the CBA and the end of the file. Otherwise the search would start from the beginning of the file. It could be said that this semi-sequential search is only semi-adequate.

An alternative is for the File Manager to keep a table of record numbers and their CBAs. Then, to fill a request, this table is searched for the exact storage location of the desired record so the direct access reduces to a table lookup.

To avoid dealing with this problem, many systems force users to have their files organized for fixed-length records if the records are to be accessed directly.

Records in an *indexed sequential file* can be accessed either sequentially or directly, so either of the procedures to compute the CBA presented in this section would apply but with one extra step: the index file must be searched for the pointer to the block where the data is stored. Because the index file is smaller than the data file, it can be kept in main memory and a quick search can be performed to locate the block where the desired record is located. Then the block can be retrieved from secondary storage and the beginning byte address of the record can be calculated. In systems that support several levels of indexing to improve access to very large files, the index at each level must be searched before the computation of the CBA can be done. The entry point to this type of data file is usually through the index file.

As we've shown, a file's organization and the methods used to access its records are very closely intertwined, so when one talks about a specific type of organization one is almost certainly implying a specific type of access.

Levels in a File Management System

The efficient management of files can't be separated from the efficient management of the devices that house them. This chapter and the previous one on device management have presented the wide range of functions that have to be organized for an I/O system to perform efficiently. In this section we'll outline one of the many hierarchies used to perform those functions.

The highest level module is called the "basic file system," and it passes information to the logical file system, which, in turn, notifies the physical file system, which works with the Device Manager. Figure 8.12 shows the hierarchy (Madnick & Donovan, 1974).

Each level of the file management system is implemented by using structured and modular programming techniques, which also set up a hierarchy—that is, the higher positioned modules pass information to the lower modules so that they, in turn, can perform the required service and continue the communication down the chain to the lowest module, which communicates with the physical device and interacts with the Device Manager. Only then is the record made available to the user's program.

Each of the modules can be further subdivided into more specific tasks, as we can see when we follow this I/O instruction through the file management system:

```
READ RECORD NUMBER 7 FROM FILE CLASSES INTO STUDENT
```

CLASSES is the name of a direct access file previously opened for input and STUDENT is a data record previously defined within the program and occupying specific memory locations.

Because the file has already been opened, the file directory has already been searched to verify the existence of CLASSES and pertinent information about the file has been brought into the operating system's active file table. This information includes its record size, the address of its first physical record, its protection, and access control information.

Figure 8.12

Typical modules of a file management system showing how information is passed from the File Manager at the top of the hierarchy to the Device Manager at the bottom.

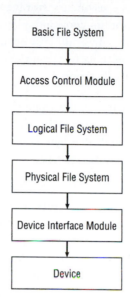

This information is used by the basic file system, which activates the access control verification module to verify that this user is permitted to perform this operation with this file. If access is allowed, information and control are passed along to the logical file system. If not, a message saying "access denied" is sent to the user.

Using the information passed down by the basic file system, the logical file system transforms the record number to its byte address using the familiar formula:

$$CBA = (RN - 1) * RL$$

This result, together with the address of the first physical record and, in the case where records are blocked, the physical block size, is passed down to the physical file system, which computes the location where the desired record physically resides. If there's more than one record in that block, it computes the record's offset within that block using these formulas:

$$\text{block number} = \text{integers}\left[\frac{\text{byte address}}{\text{physical block size}}\right] + \text{address of the first physical record}$$

$$\text{offset} = \text{remainder}\left[\frac{\text{byte address}}{\text{physical block size}}\right]$$

This information is passed on to the device interface module, which, in turn, transforms the block number to the actual cylinder/surface/record combination needed to retrieve the information from the secondary storage device. Once retrieved, here's where the device scheduling algorithms come into play as the information is placed in a buffer and control returns to the physical file system, which copies the information into the desired memory location. Finally, when the operation is complete, the "all clear" message is passed on to all other modules.

Although we used a READ command for our example, a WRITE command is handled in exactly the same way until the process reaches the device handler. At that point the portion of the device interface module that handles allocation of free space, the allocation module, is called into play because it's responsible for keeping track of unused areas in each storage device.

We need to note here that verification, the process of making sure that a request is valid, occurs at every level of the file management system. The first occurs at the directory level when the file system checks to see if the requested file exists. The second occurs when the access control verification module determines whether access is allowed. The third occurs when the logical file system checks to see if the requested byte address is within the file's limits. Finally, the device interface module checks to see whether the storage device exists.

Therefore, the correct operation of a simple user command requires the coordinated effort of every part of the file management system.

Access Control Verification Module

The first operating systems couldn't support file sharing among users. For instance, early systems needed ten copies of a compiler to serve ten users. Today's systems require only a single copy to serve everyone regardless of the number of active programs in the system. In fact, any file can be shared—from data files and user-owned program files to system files. The advantages of file sharing are numerous. In addition to saving space, it allows for synchronization of data updates, as when two applications are updating the same data file. It also improves the efficiency of the system's resources, because if files are shared in main memory then there's a reduction of I/O operations.

However, as often happens, progress brings problems. The disadvantage of file sharing is that the integrity of each file must be safeguarded; that calls for control over who is allowed to access the file and what type of access is permitted. There are five possible actions that can be performed on a file—the ability to READ only, WRITE only, EXECUTE only, DELETE only, or some combination of the four. Each file management system has its own method to control file access. The four with historical significance are the access control matrix, access control lists, capability lists, and lockword control.

Access Control Matrix

The **access control matrix** is intuitively appealing and easy to implement, but it works well only for systems with a few files and a few users. In the matrix each column identifies a user and each row identifies a file. The intersection of the row and column contains the access rights for that user to that file, as Table 8.1 illustrates.

(table 8.1)

The access control matrix showing access rights for each user for each file. User 1 is allowed unlimited access to File 1 but is allowed only to read and execute File 4 and is denied access to the three other files.

	User 1	User 2	User 3	User 4	User 5
File 1	RWED	R-E-	----	RWE-	-E-
File 2	----	R-E-	R-E-	-E-	----
File 3	----	RWED	----	-E-	----
File 4	R-E-	----	----	----	RWED
File 5	----	----	----	----	RWED

R = Read Access
W = Write Access
E = Execute Access
D = Delete Access
- = Access Not Allowed

(In the actual implementation, the letters RWED are represented by bits one and zero: a one indicates that access is allowed, and a zero indicates access is denied. Therefore, the code for User 4 for File 1 would read "1110" and not "RWE-.")

As you can see, it's a simple method, but as the numbers of files and users increase, the matrix becomes extremely large—sometimes too large to store in main memory. Another disadvantage is that a lot of space is wasted because many of the entries are all null, such as in Table 8.1, where User 3 isn't allowed into most of the files and File 5 is restricted to all but one user. A scheme that conserved space would have only one entry for User 3 or one for File 5, but that's incompatible with the matrix format.

Access Control Lists

The **access control list** is a modification of the access control matrix and was used in the MULTICS operating system (Madnick & Donovan, 1974). Each file is entered in the list and contains the names of the users who are allowed to access it and the type of access each is permitted. To shorten the list, only those who may use the file are named; those denied any access are grouped under a global heading such as WORLD, as shown in Table 8.2.

File	Access
File 1	USER1 (RWED), USER2 (R-E-), USER4 (RWE-), USER5 (-E-), WORLD (----)
File 2	USER2 (R-E-), USER3 (R-E-), USER4 (-E-), WORLD (----)
File 3	USER2 (RWED), USER4 (-E-), WORLD (----)
File 4	USER1 (R-E-), USER5 (RWED), WORLD(----)
File 5	USER5 (RWED), WORLD (----)

(table 8.2)

An access control list showing which users are allowed to access each file. This method requires less storage space than does an access control matrix and explicitly names each user allowed access to each file. WORLD indicates that access is allowed to all users.

Some systems shorten the access control list even more by putting every user into a category: system, owner, group, and world. SYSTEM is designated for system personnel who have unlimited access to all files in the system. The OWNER has absolute control over all files created in the owner's account. An owner may create a GROUP file so that all users belonging to the appropriate group have access to it. WORLD is composed of all other users in the system, that is, those who don't fall into any of the other three categories. In this system the File Manager designates default types of access to all files at creation time and it's the owner's responsibility to change them as needed.

Capability Lists

A **capability list** shows the access control information from a different perspective. It lists every user and the files to which each has access, as shown in Table 8.3.

User	Access
User 1	File 1 (RWED), File 4 (R-E-)
User 2	File 1 (R-E-), File 2 (R-E-), File 3 (RWED)
User 3	File 2 (R-E-)
User 4	File 1 (RWE-), File 2 (-E-), File 3 (-E-)
User 5	File 1 (-E-), File 4 (RWED), File 5 (RWED)

(table 8.3)

A capability list that shows files for each user requires less storage space than an access control matrix and is easier to maintain than an access control list when users are added or deleted from the system.

Of the three schemes described so far, the most commonly used is the access control list. However, capability lists, a more recent development, are gaining in popularity because they can control access to devices as well as to files.

Although both methods seem to be the same, there are some subtle differences best explained with an analogy. A capability list may be equated to a concert ticket, which allows the holder access to a seat in a specific part of the concert hall—orchestra, mezzanine, or rafters. On the other hand, an access control list can be equated to the reservation list in a restaurant; only those whose names appear on the list are allowed to be seated at a particular table (Bic & Shaw, 1988).

Lockwords

One of the first file protection techniques was the use of lockwords, or control words, to protect files. A **lockword** is similar to a password but protects a single file while a password protects access to a system. When the file is created, the owner can protect it by giving it a lockword, which is stored in the directory but isn't revealed when a listing of the directory is requested. Once it's protected, a user must provide the correct lockword to access the protected file.

The advantage of using lockwords is that they require the smallest amount of storage for file protection. But there are two disadvantages: lockwords can be guessed by hackers or passed on to unauthorized users. The second disadvantage is that a lockword generally doesn't control the type of access to the file: anyone who knows the lockword can read, write, execute, or delete the file—even if that wasn't the original intention of the owner.

Data Compression

Data compression is a technique used to save space in files. Here are three methods for compressing data in databases.

Records with repeated characters can be abbreviated. For example, data in a fixed-length field might include a short name followed by many blank characters; it can be replaced with a variable-length field and a special code to indicate how many blanks were truncated.

Let's say the original string, ADAMS, looks like this when it's stored in a field that's 15 characters wide (*b* stands for a blank character):

ADAMSbbbbbbbbbb

When it's encoded it looks like this:

ADAMSb10

Numbers with many zeros can be shortened too with a code to indicate how many zeros must be added to recreate the original number. For instance, if the original entry is a number:

300000000

the encoded entry is this:

3#8

Repeated terms can also be compressed. One method is to use symbols to represent each of the most commonly used words in the database. For example, in a university's student database, common words like student, course, teacher, classroom, grade, and department could each be represented with a single character. Of course, the system must be able to distinguish between compressed and uncompressed data.

Front-end compression is a third type that's used in database management systems for index compression. For example, the student database where the students' names are kept in alphabetical order could be compressed as shown in Table 8.4.

Original List	Compressed List
Smith, Betty	Smith, Betty
Smith, Gino	7Gino
Smith, Donald	7Donald
Smithberger, John	5berger, John
Smithbren, Ali	6ren, Ali
Smithco, Rachel	5co, Rachel
Smither, Kevin	5er, Kevin
Smithers, Renny	7s, Renny
Snyder, Katherine	1nyder, Katherine

(table 8.4)

With this compression scheme each piece of data builds on the previous piece of data. Each entry takes a given number of characters from the previous entry that they have in common and adds the characters that make it unique. So "Smithbren, Ali" uses the first six characters from "Smithberger, John" and adds "ren, Ali." Therefore, the entry is 6ren, Ali.

There is a trade-off: storage space is gained but processing time is lost. Remember, for all data compression schemes the system must be able to distinguish between compressed and uncompressed data.

Case Study: File Management in Linux

If there's a single feature that gives Linux its flexibility, it is its management of files.

All Linux files are organized in directories that are connected to each other in a tree-like structure. Linux specifies five types of files used by the system to determine what the file is to be used for, as shown in Table 8.5.

File Type	File Functions
Directory	A file that contains lists of filenames.
Ordinary file	A file containing data or programs belonging to users.
Symbolic link	A file that contains the path name of another file that it is linking to. (This is not a direct hard link. Rather it's information about how to locate a specific file and link it even if it's in the directories of different users. This is something that can't be done with hard links.)
Special file	A file that's assigned to a device controller located in the kernel. When this type of file is accessed, the physical device associated with it is activated and put into service.
Named pipe	A file that's used as a communication channel among several processes to exchange data. The creation of a named pipe is the same as the creation of any sort of file.

(table 8.5)

These five types of Linux files indicate to the system how each file is to be used.

FileNames

Filenames can be up to 255 characters long and contain alphabetic characters, underscores, and numbers. However, a filename can't start with a number or a period and can't contain slashes or quotes. Filenames can include a space, however this can cause complications if you're running programs from the command line because a program named *june invoice* would be viewed by the operating system as two files: *june* and *invoice*. To avoid confusion, join the new words with a hyphen or underscore, or enclose the two words in quotes: *"june invoice"*. (This is important only when using the command interpretive shell, and not when using a Linux desktop GUI. For more information about Linux user interfaces, see Chapter 15.)

File Directories

Linux users can obtain file directories either by opening the appropriate folder on their desktops or using the command shell interpreter and typing commands after the prompt.

File directories contain the same information, and in the same order, as UNIX, which is described in detail in Chapter 15.

As shown in Table 8.6, a "long listing" of files in a directory shows eight pieces of information for each file: the access control, the number of links, the name of the group and owner, the byte size of the file, the date and time of last modification, and, finally, the filename. Notice that the list is displayed in alphabetical order by filename.

Access Control	No. of Links	Group	Owner	No. of Bytes	Date	Time	File Name
drwxrwxr-x	2	journal	comp	12820	Jan 10	19:32	artwarehouse
drwxrwxr-x	2	journal	comp	12844	Jan 15	09:59	bus_transport
-rwxr-xr-x	1	journal	comp	11904	Jan 6	11:38	inventory
-rwxr----r----	1	journal	comp	12556	Jan 20	18:08	payroll
-rwx------	1	journal	comp	10362	Jan 17	07:32	supplier

(table 8.6)

The list of files stored in the directory called journal. The command ls -l (that's short for "listing-long") was used to generate this list from the command shell interpreter. The shorter command ls would show the list of filenames only, in alphabetical order.

Linux uses the same conventions as UNIX to show access control. For example, for each type of member (owner, group, or world), Linux allows three types of file permissions read (r), write (w), and execute (x), as shown in the first column of the directory listing in Table 8.6. These permissions are accessible to Linux desktop users who go to the folder's Properties and click Permissions.

Data Structures

Some Linux file types are unique to Linux and some are from other operating systems such as UNIX. Therefore, to allow processes to access files in a consistent manner, the kernel has a layer of software that maintains an interface between system calls related to files and the file management code. This layer is known as the Virtual File System (VFS).

Any process-initiated system call to files is directed to the VFS, which performs file operations independent of the format of the file system involved. VFS then redirects the request to the module managing the file.

Conclusion

The File Manager controls every file in the system and processes the user's commands to interact with (read, write, modify, create, delete, etc.) any file on the system. It also manages the access control procedures to maintain the integrity and security of the files under its control.

To achieve its goals, the File Manager must be able to accommodate a variety of file organizations, physical storage allocation schemes, record types, and access methods. And, as we've seen, this requires increasingly complex file management software.

In this chapter we discussed:

• Sequential, direct, and indexed sequential file organization
• Contiguous, noncontiguous, and indexed file storage allocation

- Fixed-length versus variable-length records
- Four methods of access control

To get the most from a File Manager, it's important for users to realize the strengths and weaknesses of its segments—which access methods are allowed on which devices and with which record structures—and the advantages and disadvantages of each in overall efficiency.

Chapter 9 introduces networking concepts, beginning with hardware and software components and the common topologies of networked systems.

Key Terms

absolute filename: a file's name, as given by the user, preceded by the directory (or directories) where the file is found and, when necessary, the specific device label.

access control list: an access control method that lists each file, the names of the users who are allowed to access it, and the type of access each is permitted.

access control matrix: an access control method that uses a matrix with every file, every user, and the type of access each user is permitted on each file.

capability list: an access control method that lists every user, the files to which each has access, and the type of access allowed to those files.

contiguous storage: a type of file storage in which all the information is stored in adjacent locations in a storage medium.

current byte address (CBA): the address of the last byte read. It is used by the File Manager to access records in secondary storage and must be updated every time a record is accessed.

current directory: the directory or subdirectory in which the user is working.

data compression: a procedure used to reduce the amount of space required to store data by reducing, encoding, or abbreviating repetitive terms or characters.

data file: a file that contains only data.

database: a group of related files that are interconnected at various levels to give users flexibility of access to the data stored.

device independent: programs that are devoid of the detailed instructions required to interact with any I/O device present in the computer system.

direct record organization: files stored in a direct access storage device and organized to give users the flexibility of accessing any record at random regardless of its position in the file.

directory: a storage area in a secondary storage volume (disk, disk pack, etc.) containing information about files stored in that volume.

extension: in some operating systems, it's the part of the filename that indicates which compiler or software package is needed to run the files. In UNIX and Linux, it is optional and called a *suffix*.

extents: any remaining records, and all other additions to the file, that are stored in other sections of the disk.

field: a group of related bytes that can be identified by the user with a name, type, and size. A record is made up of fields.

file: a group of related records that contains information to be used by specific application programs to generate reports.

file descriptor: information kept in the directory to describe a file or file extent.

fixed-length record: a record that always contains the same number of characters.

hashing algorithm: the set of instructions used to perform a key-to-address transformation in which a record's key field determines its location.

indexed sequential record organization: a way of organizing data in a direct access storage device. An index is created to show where the data records are stored. Any data record can be retrieved by consulting the index first.

key field: (1) a unique field or combination of fields in a record that uniquely identifies that record; or (2) the field that determines the position of a record in a sorted sequence.

lockword: a sequence of letters and/or numbers provided by users to prevent unauthorized tampering with their files.

logical address: the result of a key-to-address transformation.

master file directory (MFD): a file stored immediately after the volume descriptor. It lists the names and characteristics of every file contained in that volume.

noncontiguous storage: a type of file storage in which the information is stored in nonadjacent locations in a storage medium. Data records can be accessed directly by computing their relative addresses.

program file: a file that contains instructions for the computer.

record: a group of related fields treated as a unit. A file is a group of related records.

relative address: in a direct organization environment, it indicates the position of a record relative to the beginning of the file.

relative filename: a file's simple name and extension as given by the user.

sequential record organization: the organization of records in a specific sequence. Records in a sequential file must be processed one after another.

subdirectory: a directory created by the user within the boundaries of an existing directory. Some operating systems call this a folder.

variable-length record: a record that isn't of uniform length, doesn't leave empty storage space, and doesn't truncate any characters, thus eliminating the two disadvantages of fixed-length records.

volume: any secondary storage unit, such as hard disks, disk packs, CDs, DVDs, removable disks, or tapes.

working directory: the directory or subdirectory in which the user is currently working.

Exercises

Research Topic

Track the size of operating system software by researching the amount of disk space required by different versions of the same operating system. If the size is substantially different, explain why it changed. For example, how much hard disk space was required to install Windows NT versus the current Windows Server operating system? In addition, identify which features were added with the newer software. Cite your sources.

Exercises

1. Explain what is meant by device independence.
2. Design a file lookup algorithm for each of the following cases:
   a. Files are listed in a unique directory.
   b. Files are listed in a two-level directory.
   c. Files are listed in a hierarchical directory.
   Provide for a path to be taken if the file is *not* found.
3. Three types of file organization were presented in this chapter: sequential, direct, and indexed sequential. For each of the applications listed below, select the file organization best suited to it and explain why you selected it.
   a. A data file containing employee payroll records
   b. The circulation file in a library
   c. A data file containing student transcript records
   d. A bank's data file containing customers' checking account records
   e. An inventory file in a local supermarket
4. List the minimum information required in a directory to locate any one record in a file for each of the following cases:
   a. The file is stored in a simple contiguous form.
   b. The file is stored in a noncontiguous form with extents.
   c. The file is stored using the index method.

5. Some operating systems automatically open and close files for users so that OPEN and CLOSE commands are unnecessary. List some problems generated by this procedure.

6. Many operating systems use the file command RENAME to allow users to give a new name to an existing file. Suppose this command wasn't available and files could be renamed only by using a combination of other file commands such as LIST, COPY, DELETE, SAVE, and CREATE. Design a combination of commands that would perform the same function as RENAME and explain why you selected it.

7. Explain why it's difficult to support direct access to files with variable-length records. Suggest a method for handling this type of file if direct access is required.

8. As was done in the section on access control in this chapter, list the steps required to satisfy the following requests:

   a. READ RECORD NUMBER 10 FROM FILE INVENTORY INTO ITEM

   b. WRITE RECORD NUMBER 6 TO FILE ACCOUNT

   c. WRITE RECORD NUMBER 11 TO FILE ACCOUNT

Advanced Exercises

9. If you were designing the file access control for a highly secure environment and were given a choice between the establishment of many access categories and just a few access categories, which would you select and why?

10. Compare and contrast dynamic memory allocation and the allocation of files in secondary storage.

11. When is compaction of secondary storage beneficial from the file manager's perspective? Give several examples. List some problems that could be presented as a result of compaction and explain how they might be avoided.

12. While sophisticated file managers implement file sharing by allowing several users to access a single copy of a file at the same time, others implement file sharing by providing a copy of the file to each user. List the advantages and disadvantages of each method.

13. Indexed sequential files are widely used in business applications because of their versatility. However, as records are added to the file and blocks are filled to capacity they have to be stored in an overflow area.

   a. How does this affect performance?

   b. What can be done to improve performance?

Chapter 9 | Network Organization Concepts

> **" *Knowledge of the universe would somehow be … defective were no practical results to follow.* "**
>
> Cicero *(106-43 BC)*

Learning Objectives

After completing this chapter, you should be able to describe:

- Several different network topologies—including the star, ring, bus, tree, and hybrid—and how they connect numerous hosts to the network
- Three types of networks: LAN, MAN, and WAN
- The difference between circuit switching and packet switching, and examples of everyday use that favor each
- Conflict resolution procedures that allow a network to share common transmission hardware and software effecively
- The two transport protocol models (OSI and TCP/IP) and how the layers of each one compare

When computer facilities are connected together by data-communication components, they form a network of automated resources to support the many functions of business, education, healthcare, government, and other organizations. These networks provide an essential infrastructure for members of the information-based society to process, manipulate, and distribute data and information to each other. This chapter introduces the terminology and basic concepts of networks.

Basic Terminology

In general, a **network** is a collection of loosely coupled processors (as described in Chapter 6) interconnected by communication links using cables, wireless technology, or a combination of both.

A common goal of all networked systems is to provide a convenient way to share resources while controlling users' access to them. These resources include both hardware (such as a CPU, memory, printers, USB ports, and disk drives) and software (such as application programs and data files).

There are two general configurations for operating systems for networks. The oldest added a networking capability to a single-user operating system. This is called a **network operating system (NOS)**. With this configuration, users are aware of the specific assortment of computers and resources in the network and can access them by logging on to the appropriate remote host or by transferring data from the remote computer to their own.

With the second configuration, users don't need to be aware of every machine connected to the system; they can access remote resources as if they were local resources. A **distributed operating system (D/OS)** provides good control for distributed computing systems and allows their resources to be accessed in a unified way. A distributed operating system represents a total view across multiple computer systems for controlling and managing resources without local dependencies. Management is a cooperative process that encompasses every resource and involves every site.

A distributed operating system is comprised of the same four managers previously discussed but with a wider scope. At a minimum, it must provide the following components: process or object management, memory management, file management, device management, and network management, as shown in Figure 9.1. A distributed operating system offers several important advantages over traditional operating system environments including easy and reliable resource sharing, faster computation, adequate load balancing, good reliability, and dependable electronic communications among the network's users.

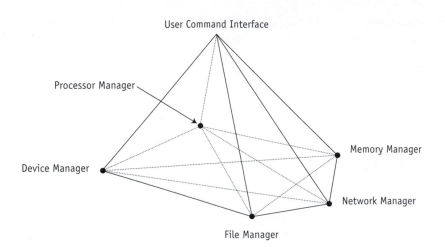

In a distributed system each processor classifies the other processors and their resources as **remote** and considers its own resources **local**. The size, type, and identification of processors varies. Processors are referred to as **sites**, **hosts**, and **nodes** depending on the context in which they're mentioned. Usually, the term "site" indicates a specific location in a network containing one or more computer systems, "host" indicates a specific computer system found at a site whose services and resources can be used from remote locations, and "node" (or, more formally, "node name") refers to the name assigned to a computer system connected to a network to identify it to other computers in the network.

Typically, a host at one site, called the server, has resources that a host at another site, called the client, wants to use. But the assignments aren't static. Hosts can alternate between being clients or servers depending on their requirements.

(figure 9.2)

Clients request data or services from the host server and wait for the response. If the client host has resources needed by the server host, the roles can be re-versed.

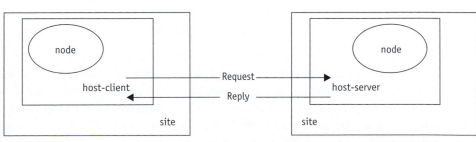

In this discussion, we've simplified the concept of client and server to represent static network software that's located at two different sites. That is, we've assumed that the host-client is a client all of the time, and that the host-server is always a server. However, the actual roles of client and server can alternate between two networked hosts depending on the application and the network configuration. In this text, we've chosen to use the simplest configuration to make our explanation as clear as possible.

Network Topologies

Sites in any networked system can be physically or logically connected to one another in a certain **topology**, the geometric arrangement of connections (cables, wireless, or both) that link the nodes . The most common geometric arrangements are star, ring, bus, tree, and hybrid. In each topology there are tradeoffs between the need for fast communication among all sites, the tolerance of failure at a site or communication link, the cost of long communication lines, and the difficulty of connecting one site to a large number of other sites. It's important to note that the physical topology of a network may not reflect its logical topology. For example, a network that is wired in a star configuration can be logically arranged to operate as if it is a ring. That is, it can be made to manipulate a token in a ring-like fashion even though its cables are arranged in a star topology. To keep our explanations in this chapter as simple as possible, whenever we discuss topologies we are assuming that the logical structure of the network is identical to the physical structure.

For the network designer, there are many alternatives available, all of which will probably solve the customer's requirements. When deciding which configuration to use, designers should keep in mind four criteria:

• Basic cost—the expense required to link the various sites in the system

• Communications cost—the time required to send a message from one site to another

• Reliability—the assurance that many sites can still communicate with each other even if a link or site in the system fails

• User's environment—the critical parameters that the network must meet to be a successful business investment

It's quite possible that there are several possible solutions for each customer. The best choice would need to consider all four criteria. For example, an international data retrieval company might consider the fastest communications and the most flexible hardware configuration to be a cost-effective investment. But a neighborhood word processing center might put the most emphasis on having a low cost networking solution. Over-engineering the neighborhood system could be just as big a mistake as under-engineering the international customer's network. The key to choosing the best design is to understand the available technology as well as the customer's business requirements and budget.

Star

A **star topology,** sometimes called a hub or centralized topology, is a traditional approach to interconnecting devices in which all transmitted data must pass through a central controller when going from a sender to a receiver, as shown in Figure 9.3.

(figure 9.3)

Star topology. Hosts are connected to each other through a central con- troller which assumes all responsibility for routing messages to the appropriate host. Data flow between the hosts and the central controller is represented by dotted lines. Direct host-to-host communication isn't permitted.

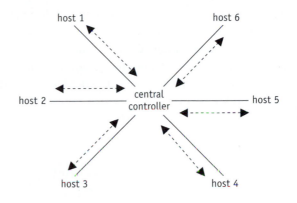

Star topology permits easy routing because the central station knows the path to all other sites and, because there is a central control point, access to the network can be controlled easily and priority status can be given to selected sites. However, this centralization of control requires that the central site be extremely reliable and able to handle all network traffic, no matter how heavy.

Ring

In the **ring topology** all sites are connected in a closed loop, as shown in Figure 9.4, with the first site connected to the last.

(figure 9.4)

Ring topology. Hosts are connected to each other in a circular fashion with data flowing in one direc- tion only, shown here as dotted lines. The network can be connected to other networks via a bridge or gateway. If the other net- work has the same proto- col, a bridge is used to connect the networks. If the other network has a different protocol, a gate- way is used.

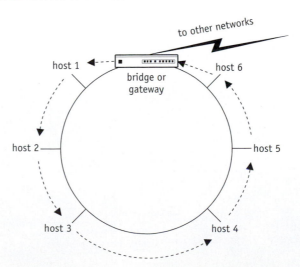

In a ring, the network can be connected to other networks via the bridge or gateway depending on the **protocol** used by each network. (The protocol is the specific set of rules used to control the flow of messages through the network.) If the other network has the same protocol then a bridge is used to connect the networks. If the other network has a different protocol, a gateway is used.

Data is transmitted in packets that also contain source and destination address fields. Each packet is passed from node to node in one direction only, and the destination station copies the data into a local buffer. Typically, the packet continues to circulate until it returns to the source station, where it's removed from the ring. There are some variations to this basic topology, such as the double loop network, shown in Figure 9.5, and a set of multiple rings bridged together, as shown in Figure 9.6. Both variations provide more flexibility, but at a cost.

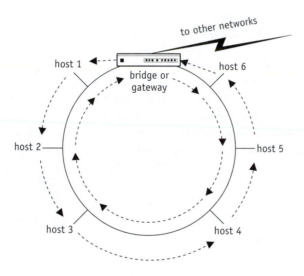

(figure 9.5)

Double loop computer network using a ring topology. Packets of data flow in both directions. The network can be connected to other networks via a bridge or gateway.

Multiple rings bridged together. Three rings connected to each other by two bridges. This variation of ring topology allows several networks with the same protocol to be linked together.

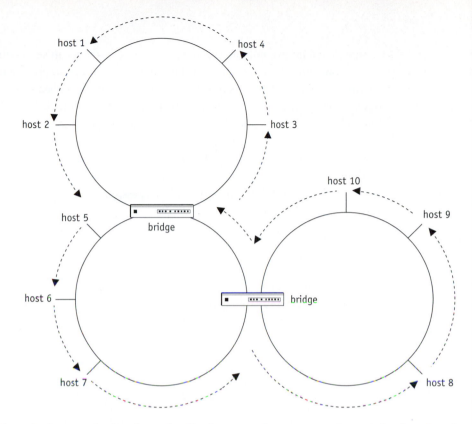

Although ring topologies share the disadvantage that every node must be functional for the network to perform properly, rings can be designed that allow failed nodes to be bypassed.

Bus

In the **bus topology** all sites are connected to a single communication line running the length of the network, as shown in Figure 9.7.

Bus topology. Hosts are connected to one another in a linear fashion. Data flows in both directions from host to host and is turned around when it reaches an end point controller.

Devices are physically connected by means of cables that run between them, but the cables don't pass through a centralized controller mechanism. Messages from any site circulate in both directions through the entire communication line and can be received by all other sites.

Because all sites share a common communication line, only one of them can successfully send messages at any one time. Therefore, a control mechanism is needed to prevent collisions. In this environment, data may pass directly from one device to another, or it may be routed to an end point controller at the end of the line. In a bus, if the data reaches an end point controller without being accepted by a host, the end point controller turns it around and sends it back so the message can be accepted by the appropriate node on the way to the other end point controller. With some busses each message must always go to the end of the line before going back down the communication line to the node to which it's addressed. However, other bus networks allow messages to be sent directly to the target node without reaching an end point controller.

Tree

The **tree topology** is a collection of busses. The communication line is a branching cable with no closed loops, as shown in Figure 9.8.

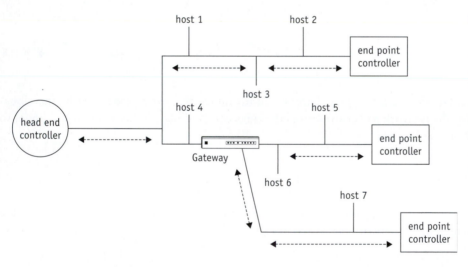

(figure 9.8)

Tree topology. Data flows up and down the branches of the trees and is absorbed by controllers at the end points. Gateways help minimize differences between different protocols used on the branches.

The tree layout begins at the head end, where one or more cables start. Each cable may have branches that may, in turn, have additional branches, potentially resulting in quite complex arrangements. Using bridges as special fitters between busses of the same protocol and as translators to those with different protocols allows designers to create networks that can operate at speeds more responsive to the hosts in the network. In a tree configuration a message from any site circulates through the communication line, and can be received by all other sites, until it reaches the end points. If a message reaches an end point controller without being accepted by a host, the end point controller absorbs it—it isn't turned around as it is when using a bus topology. One advantage of bus and tree topologies is that even if a single node fails, message traffic can still flow through the network.

Hybrid

A **hybrid topology** is some combination of any of the four topologies discussed here. For example, a hybrid can be made by replacing a single host in a star configuration with a ring, as shown in Figure 9.9. Or a star configuration could have a bus topology as one of the communication lines feeding its hub, as shown in Figure 9.10.

(figure 9.9)

Hybrid topology, version 1. This network combines a star and a ring, connected by a bridge. Hosts 5, 6, 7, and 8 are located on the ring.

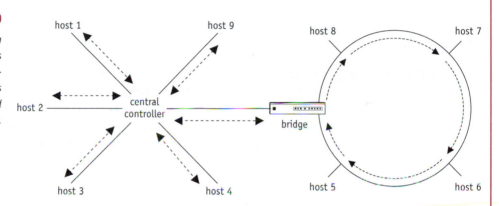

(figure 9.10)

Hybrid topology, version 2. This network combines star and bus topologies. Hosts 5, 6, 7, and 8 are located on the bus.

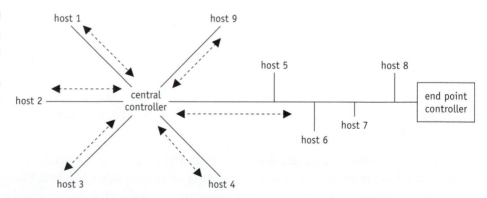

The objective of a hybrid configuration is to select among the strong points of each topology and combine them to meet that system's communications requirements most effectively.

Network Types

It's often useful to group networks according to the physical distances they cover. Although the characteristics that define each group are becoming increasingly blurred as communications technology advances, networks are generally divided into local area networks, metropolitan area networks, and wide area networks. In recent years, one type of local area network, the wireless local area network, has become increasingly popular.

Local Area Network

A **local area network** (**LAN**) defines a configuration found within a single office building, warehouse, campus, or similarly enclosed computing environment. Such a network is generally owned, used, and operated by a single organization and allows computers to communicate directly through a common communication line. Typically, it's a cluster of personal computers or workstations located in the same general area. Although a LAN is physically confined to a well-defined local area, its communications aren't limited to that area because the LAN can be a component of a larger communication network and can provide easy access to the outside through a bridge or a gateway.

A **bridge** is a device, and the software to operate it, that connects two or more geographically distant local area networks that use the same protocols. For example, a simple bridge could be used to connect two local area networks that use the Ethernet networking technology. (Ethernet is discussed later in this chapter.)

A **gateway**, on the other hand, is a more complex device, and software, used to connect two or more local area networks or systems that use different protocols. A gateway will translate one network's protocol into another, resolving hardware and software incompatibilities. For example, the systems network architecture (commonly called SNA) gateway can connect a microcomputer network to a mainframe host.

High-speed LANs have a data rate that varies from 100 megabits per second to more than 40 gigabits per second. Because the sites are close to each other, bandwidths are available to support very high-speed transmission for fully animated, full-color graphics and video, digital voice transmission, and other high data-rate analog or digital signals. The previously described topologies—star, ring, bus, tree, and hybrid— are normally used to construct local area networks. The transmission medium used may vary from one topology to another. Factors to be considered when selecting a transmission medium are cost, data rate, reliability, number of devices that can be supported, distance between units, and technical limitations.

Metropolitan Area Network

A **metropolitan area network** (**MAN**) defines a configuration spanning an area larger than a LAN, ranging from several blocks of buildings to an entire city but not exceeding a circumference of 100 kilometers. A metropolitan area network may be owned and operated by a single organization and usually is used by many individuals and organizations. In some instances MANs are owned and operated as public utilities, providing the means for internetworking several LANs.

A MAN is a high-speed network often configured as a logical ring. That means that ring depending on the protocol used, messages are either transmitted in one direction using only one ring, as illustrated in Figure 9.4, or in both directions using two counter-rotating rings, as illustrated in Figure 9.5. One ring always carries messages in one direction and the other always carries messages in the opposite direction.

Wide Area Network

A **wide area network** (**WAN**) defines a configuration that interconnects communication facilities in different parts of a country or even different parts of the world, or that's operated as part of a public utility. WANs use the communications lines of common carriers, which are government-regulated private companies such as telephone companies that already provide the general public with communication facilities. WANs use a broad range of communication media, including satellite and microwaves; in some cases the speed of transmission is limited by the capabilities of the communication line. WANs are generally slower than LANs.

The first WAN, ARPAnet, was developed in 1969 by the Advanced Research Projects Agency (ARPA); responsibility for its operation was transferred in 1975 to the Defense Communications Agency. Its successor, the **Internet**, is the most widely recognized WAN, but there exist other commercial WANs.

Wireless Local Area Network

A **wireless local area network** (**WLAN**) is a local area network that uses wireless technology to connect computers or workstations located within the range of the network. As shown in Table 9.1, the Institute of Electrical and Electronics Engineers (IEEE) has specified several standards for wireless networking, each with different ranges.

IEEE Standard	Speed	Range	Frequency	Compatibility
802.11a	54 Mbps	25-75 feet indoors	5 GHz	Found in corporate office areas
802.11b	11 Mbps	100-150 feet indoors	2.4 GHz	Not compatible with 802.11g
802.11g	54 Mbps	100-150 feet indoors	2.4 GHz	Compatible with 802.11b

(table 9.1)

Comparison of three IEEE standards for wireless networks (White, 2004).

For wireless nodes (workstations, laptops, etc.), a WLAN can provide easy access to a larger network or the Internet, as shown in Figure 9.11. Keep in mind that a WLAN typically poses security vulnerabilities because of its open architecture and the inherent difficulty of keeping out unauthorized intruders.

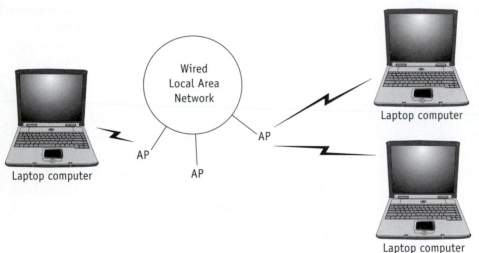

(figure 9.11)

In a WLAN, wireless-enabled nodes connect to the cabled LAN via access points (AP) if they are located within the range of the device sending the signal.

At this writing, a technology called WiMax is under development based on the IEEE 802.16 standard, which would enable wireless broadband connections over much greater ranges (up to 10 miles). Because of the fast-changing nature of this subject, we can provide only a brief introduction to wireless networks here, but we encourage you to refer to current research on the subject.

Software Design Issues

So far we've examined the configurations of a network's hardware components. In this section we'll examine four software issues that must be addressed by network designers:

• How do sites use addresses to locate other sites?

• How are messages routed and how are they sent?

• How do processes communicate with each other?

• How are conflicting demands for resources resolved?

Addressing Conventions

Network sites need to determine how to uniquely identify their users so they can communicate with each other and access each other's resources. Names, addresses, and routes are required because sites aren't directly connected to each other except over point-to-point links; therefore, addressing protocols are closely related to the network topology and geographic location of each site. In some cases (Pouzin & Zimmermann, 1978) a distinction is made between "local name," which refers to the name by which a unit is known within its own system, and "global name," the name by which a unit is known outside its own system. This distinction is useful because it allows each site the freedom to identify its units according to their own standards without imposing uniform naming rules, something that would be difficult to implement at the local level. On the other hand, a global name must follow standard name lengths, formats, and other global conventions.

Using an Internet address as a typical example, we can see that it follows a hierarchical organization, starting from left to right in the following sequence: from logical user to host machine, from host machine to net machine, from net machine to cluster, and from cluster to network. For example, in each Internet address—*someone@icarus.lis.pitt.edu* or *igss12@aber.ac.uk*—the periods are used to separate each component. These electronic mail addresses, which are fairly easy to remember, must be translated (or "resolved," using a concept similar to that described in Chapter 3) to corresponding hardware addresses. This conversion is done by the networking section of the computer's operation system.

The examples given above follow the **Domain Name Service (DNS)** protocol, a general-purpose distributed data query service whose principal function is the resolution of Internet addresses. If we dissect *someone@icarus.lis.pitt.edu* into its components, we have the following:

• *someone* is the logical user,

• *icarus* is the host for the user called someone,

• *lis* is the net machine for icarus,

• *pitt* is the cluster for lis, and

• *edu* is the network for the University of Pittsburgh.

Not all components need to be present in all Internet addresses. Nevertheless, the DNS is able to resolve them by examining each one in reverse order.

Routing Strategies

A **router** is an internetworking device, primarily software driven, which directs traffic between two different types of LANs or two network segments with different protocol addresses. It operates at the network layer, which is explained later in this chapter.

The role of routers changes as network designs change. Routers are used extensively for connecting sites to each other and to the Internet. They can be used for a variety of functions including securing the information that is generated in predefined areas, choosing the fastest route from one point to another, and providing redundant network connections so that a problem in one area will not degrade network operations in other areas.

Routing allows data to get from one point on a network to another. To do so, each destination must be uniquely identified. Once the data is at the proper network, the router makes sure that the correct node in the network receives it.

Routing protocols must consider addressing, address resolution, message format, and error reporting. Most routing protocols are based on an addressing format that uses a network and a node number to identify each node. When a network is powered on, each router records in a table the addresses of the networks that are directly connected. Because routing protocols permit interaction between routers, sharing network destinations that each router may have acquired as it performs its services becomes easy. At specified intervals each router in the internetwork broadcasts a copy of its entire routing table. Eventually all of the routers know how to get to each of the different destination networks (Dickie, 1994).

Although the addresses allow routers to send data from one network to another, they can't be used to get from one point in a network to another point in the *same* network. This must be done through address resolution, which allows a router to map the original address to a hardware address and store the mapping in a table to be used for future transmissions.

A variety of message formats are defined by routing protocols. These messages are used to allow the protocol to perform its functions, such as finding new nodes on a network, testing to determine whether they're working, reporting error conditions, exchanging routing information, establishing connections, and transmitting data.

Data transmission does not always run smoothly. For example, conditions may arise that cause errors such as inability to reach a destination because of a malfunctioning node or network. In cases such as this, routers and routing protocols would report the error condition although they would not attempt to correct the error; error correction is left to protocols at other levels of the network's architecture.

Two of the most widely used routing protocols in the Internet are routing information protocol and open shortest path first.

Routing Information Protocol

In **routing information protocol (RIP)**, selection of a path to transfer data from one network to another is based on the number of intermediate nodes, or hops, between the source and the destination. The path with the smallest number of hops is always chosen. This distance vector algorithm is easy to implement, but it may not be the best in today's networking environment because it does not take into consideration other important factors such as bandwidth, data priority, or type of network. That is, it can exclude faster or more reliable paths from being selected just because they have more hops. Another limitation of RIP relates to routing tables. The entire table is updated and reissued every 30 seconds, whether or not changes have occurred; this increases internetwork traffic and negatively affects the delivery of messages. In addition, the tables propagate from one router to another. Thus, in the case of an internetwork with 15 hops, it would take more than seven minutes for a change to be known at the other end of the internetwork. Because not all routers would have the same information about the internetwork, a failure at any one of the hops could create an unstable environment for all message traffic.

Open Shortest Path First

In **open shortest path first (OSPF)**, selection of a transmission path is made only after the state of a network has been determined, so that if an intermediate hop is malfunctioning, it's eliminated immediately from consideration until its services have been restored. Routing update messages are sent only when changes in the routing environment occur, thereby reducing the number of messages in the internetwork and reducing the size of the messages by not sending the entire routing table. However, memory usage is increased because OSPF keeps track of more information than RIP. In addition, the savings in bandwidth consumption are offset by the higher CPU usage needed for the calculation of the shortest path, which is based on Dijkstra's algorithm, simply stated as: find the shortest paths from a given source to all other destinations by proceeding in stages and developing the path in increasing path lengths (Stallings, 1994).

When a router uses Dijkstra's algorithm it computes all the different paths to get to each destination in the internetwork, creating what is known as a topological

299

database. This data structure is maintained by OSPF and is updated whenever failures occur. Therefore, a router would simply check its topological database to determine whether a path was available, and would then use Dijkstra's algorithm to generate a shortest path tree to get around the failed link.

Connection Models

A communication network isn't concerned with the content of data being transmitted but with moving the data from one point to another. Because it would be prohibitive to connect each node in a network to all other nodes, the nodes are connected to a communication network designed to minimize transmission costs and to provide full connectivity among all attached devices. Data entering the network at one point is routed to its destination by being switched from node to node, whether by circuit switching or by packet switching.

Circuit Switching

Circuit switching is a communication model in which a dedicated communication path is established between two hosts. The path is a connected sequence of links and the connection between the two points exists until one of them is disconnected. The connection path must be set up before data transmission begins; therefore, if the entire path becomes unavailable, messages can't be transmitted because the circuit would not be complete. The telephone system is a good example of a circuit-switched network.

In terms of performance, there is a delay before signal transfer begins while the connection is set up. However, once the circuit is completed, the network is transparent to users and information is transmitted at a fixed rate of speed with insignificant delays at intermediate nodes.

Packet Switching

Packet switching is basically a store-and-forward technique in which a message is divided into multiple equal-sized units called **packets**, which are then sent through the network to their destination, where they're reassembled into their original long format, as shown in Figure 9.12.

Packet switching is an effective technology for long-distance data transmission and provides more flexibility than circuit switching because it permits data transmission between devices that receive or transmit data at different rates. However, there is no guarantee that after a message has been divided into packets the packets will all travel along the same path to their destination, or that they will arrive in their physical

(figure 9.12)

A packet switching network does not require a dedicated connection. It sends packets using a three step procedure: (a) divide the data into addressed packets; (b) send each packet toward its destination; (c) and, at the destination, confirm receipt of all packets, place them in order, reassemble the data, and deliver it to the recipient.

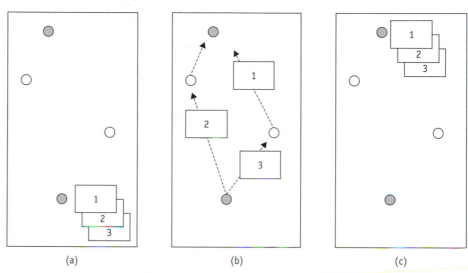

(a) (b) (c)

sequential order. In addition, packets from one message may be interspersed with those from other messages as they travel toward their destinations. Therefore, a header containing pertinent information about the packet is attached to each packet before it's transmitted. The information contained in the packet header varies according to the routing method used by the network.

The idea is similar to sending a series of 30 reference books through a package delivery system. Six boxes contain five volumes each, and each box is labeled with its sequence number (e.g., box 2 of 6), as well as its ultimate destination. As space on passing delivery trucks becomes available, each box is forwarded to a central switching center, where it's stored until space becomes available to send it to the next switching center closer to its destination. Eventually, when all six boxes arrive, they're put in their original order, the 30 volumes are unpacked, and the original sequence is restored.

As shown in Table 9.2, packet switching is fundamentally different from circuit switching, also a store-and-forward technique, in which an entire message is accepted by a central switching node and forwarded to its destination when one of two events occurs: all circuits are free to send the entire message at once, or the receiving node requests its stored messages.

Circuit Switching	Packet Switching
• Transmits in real time	• Transmits in batches
• Preferred in low volume networks	• Preferred in high volume networks
• Reduced line efficiency	• High line efficiency
• Dedicated to a single transmission	• Shared by many transmissions
• Preferred for voice communications	• Not good for voice communications
• Easily overloaded	• Accommodates varying priority among packets

(table 9.2)

Comparison of circuit and packet switching.

Packet switching provides greater line efficiency because a single node-to-node circuit can be shared by several packets and does not sit idle over long periods of time. Although delivery may be delayed as traffic increases, packets can still be accepted and transmitted.

That's also in contrast to circuit switching networks, which, when they become overloaded, refuse to accept new connections until the load decreases. Have you ever received a busy signal when trying to place a long distance telephone call during a major holiday? That problem is similar to a circuit switching network's overload response.

Packet switching allows users to allocate priorities to their messages so that a router with several packets queued for transmission can send the higher priority packets first. In addition, packet switching networks are more reliable than other types because most nodes are connected by more than one link, so that if one circuit should fail, a completely different path may be established between nodes.

There are two different methods of selecting the path: datagrams and virtual circuits. In the datagram approach, the destination and sequence number of the packet is added to the information uniquely identifying the message to which the packet belongs; each packet is then handled independently and a route is selected as each packet is accepted into the network. This is similar to the shipping label that's added to each package in the book shipment example. At their destination, all packets belonging to the same message are then reassembled by sequence number into one continuous message and finally are delivered to the addressee. Because the message can't be delivered until all packets have been accounted for, it's up to the receiving node to request retransmission of lost or damaged packets. This routing method has two distinct advantages: it helps diminish congestion by sending incoming packets through less heavily used paths, and it provides more reliability, because alternate paths may be set up when one node fails.

In the virtual circuit approach, the destination and packet sequence number aren't added to the information identifying the packet's message because a complete path from sender to receiver is established before transmission starts—all the packets belonging to that message use the same route. Although it's a similar concept, this is different from the dedicated path used in circuit switching because any node can have several virtual circuits to any other node. Its advantage over the datagram method is that its routing decision is made only once for all packets belonging to the same message—a feature that should speed up message transmission for long messages. On the other hand, it has a disadvantage in that if a node fails, all virtual circuits using that node become unavailable. In addition, when the circuit experiences heavy traffic, congestion is more difficult to resolve.

Conflict Resolution

Because a network consists of devices sharing a common transmission capability, some method to control access is necessary to facilitate equal and fair access to this common resource. First we will describe some access control techniques: round robin, reservation, and contention. Then we will briefly examine three common medium access control protocols used to implement access to resources: carrier sense multiple access (CSMA); token passing; and distributed-queue, dual bus (DQDB).

Access Control Techniques

Round robin access control follows the same principles as round robin processor management, described in Chapter 4. In networks, round robin allows each node on the network to use the communication medium. If the node has data to send, it's given a certain amount of time to complete the transmission, at the end of which the opportunity is passed to the next node. If the node has no data to send, or if it completes transmission before the time is up, then the next node begins its turn. Round robin is an efficient technique when there are many nodes transmitting over long periods of time. However, when there are few nodes transmitting over long periods of time, the overhead incurred in passing turns from node to node can be substantial, making other techniques preferable depending on whether transmissions are short and intermittent, as in interactive terminal-host sessions, or lengthy and continuous, as in massive file transfer sessions.

The reservation technique is well suited for lengthy and continuous traffic. Access time on the medium is divided into slots and a node can reserve future time slots for its use. The technique is similar to that found in synchronous time-division multiplexing, used for multiplexing digitized voice streams, where the time slots are fixed in length and preassigned to each node. This technique could be good for a configuration with several terminals connected to a host computer through a single I/O port.

The contention technique is better for short and intermittent traffic. No attempt is made to determine whose turn it is to transmit so nodes compete for access to the medium.

Therefore, it works well under light to moderate traffic, but performance tends to break down under heavy loads. This technique's major advantage is that it's easy to implement.

Access protocols currently in use are based on the previously mentioned techniques and are discussed here with regard to their role in LAN environments.

CSMA

Carrier sense multiple access (CSMA) is a contention-based protocol that's easy to implement. Carrier sense means that a node on the network will listen to, or test, the communication medium before transmitting any messages, thus preventing a collision with another node that's currently transmitting. Multiple access means that several nodes are connected to the same communication line as peers, on the same level, and with equal privileges.

Although a node will not transmit until the line is quiet, two or more nodes could come to that conclusion at the same instant. If more than one transmission is sent simultaneously, creating a collision, the data from all transmissions will be damaged and the line will remain unusable while the damaged messages are dissipated. When the receiving nodes fail to acknowledge receipt of their transmissions, the sending nodes will know that the messages did not reach their destinations successfully and both will be retransmitted. The probability of this happening increases if the nodes are farther apart, making CSMA a less appealing access protocol for large or complex networks.

Therefore, the original algorithm was modified to include collision detection and was named carrier sense multiple access with collision detection (CSMA/CD). **Ethernet** is the most widely known CSMA/CD protocol. Collision detection does not eliminate collisions but it does reduce them. When a collision occurs, a jamming signal is sent immediately to both sending nodes, which then wait a random period before trying again. With this protocol the amount of wasted transmission capacity is reduced to the time it takes to detect the collision.

A different modification is CSMA with collision avoidance (CSMA/CA). Collision avoidance means that the access method prevents multiple nodes from colliding during transmission. However, opinion on its efficiency is divided. Some claim it's more efficient than collision detection, whereas others contend that it lowers a network's performance when there are a large number of nodes. The CSMA/CA protocol is implemented in LocalTalk, Apple's cabling system, which uses a protocol called LocalTalk link access protocol. A terminal connected to an Apple CSMA/CA network would send out a three-byte packet to indicate that it wants to start transmitting. This packet tells all other terminals to wait until the first is finished transmitting before they initiate transmissions. If collisions do occur, they involve only the three-byte packets, not the actual data. This protocol does not guarantee the data will reach its destination, but it ensures that any data that's delivered will be error free.

Token Passing

In a token-passing network a special electronic message, called a "token," is generated when the network is turned on and is then passed along from node to node. Only the node with the token is allowed to transmit, and after it has done so, it must pass the token on to another node. These networks typically have either a bus or ring topology and are popular because access is fast and collisions are nonexistent.

In a **token-bus** network, the token is passed to each node in turn. Upon receipt of the token, a node attaches to it the data to be transmitted and sends the packet, containing both token and data, to its destination. The receiving node copies the data, adds the acknowledgment, and returns the packet to the sending node, which then passes the token on to the next node in logical sequence.

Initially, node order is determined by a cooperative decentralized algorithm. Once the network is up and running, turns are determined by priority based on node activity. A node requiring the token frequently will have a higher priority than one that seldom needs it. A table of node addresses is kept in priority order by the network. When a transmission is complete, the token passes from the node that just finished to the one having the next lower entry in the table. When the lowest priority node has been serviced, the token returns to the top of the table and the process is repeated.

This process is similar to a train engine pulling into the station. If the stationmaster has a delivery to send, those cars are attached to the engine and the train is dispatched to its destination with no intermediate stops. When it arrives, the cars are detached and the engine is sent back to the point of origin with the message that the shipment was successfully received. After delivering that message to the shipment's originator, the engine proceeds to the next station to pick up a delivery.

Implementation of this protocol dictates higher overhead at each node than does CSMA/CD, and nodes may have long waits under certain conditions before receiving the token.

Token ring is the most widely used protocol for ring topology; it became better known than token bus when IBM made its Token-Ring Network commercially available. It's based on the use of a token that moves between the nodes in turn and in one direction only. When it's not carrying a message, the token is called a "free" token. If a node wants to send a message it must wait for the free token to come by. It then changes the token from free to busy and sends its message immediately following the busy token. Meanwhile, all other nodes must wait for the token to become free and come to them again before they're able to transmit a message.

The receiving node copies the message in the packet and sets the copied bit to indicate it was successfully received; the packet then continues on its way, making a complete round trip back to the sending node, which then releases the new free token on the network. At this point, the next node down the line with data to send will be able to pick up the free token and repeat the process.

DQDB

The distributed-queue, dual bus (DQDB) protocol is intended for use with a dual-bus configuration, where each bus transports data in only one direction, and has been standardized by one of the IEEE committees as part of its MAN standards. Transmission on each bus consists of a steady stream of fixed-size slots, as shown in Figure 9.13. Slots generated at one end of each bus are marked free and sent downstream, where they're marked busy and written to by nodes that are ready to transmit data. Nodes read and copy data from the slots, which then continue to travel toward the end of the bus, where they dissipate.

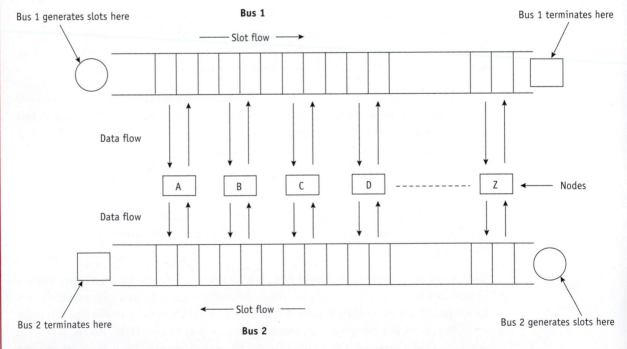

(figure 9.13)

Distributed-queue, dual bus protocol. Free slots are generated at one end of each bus and flow in only one direction. Using DQDB, if node C wants to send data to node D, it must wait for a free slot on Bus 1 because the slots are flowing toward node D on that bus.

The distributed access protocol is based on a distributed reservation scheme and can be summarized as follows. If node C in Figure 9.13 wants to send data to node D, it would use Bus 1 because the slots are flowing toward D on that bus. However, if the nodes before C monopolize the slots, then C would not be able to transmit its data to D. To solve the problem, C can use Bus 2 to send a reservation to its upstream neighbors. The protocol states that a node will allow free slots to go by until outstanding reservations from downstream nodes have been satisfied. Therefore, the protocol must provide a mechanism by which each station can keep track of the requests of its downstream peers.

This mechanism is handled by a pair of first-in, first-out queues and a pair of counters, one for each bus, at each of the nodes in the network. This is a very effective protocol providing negligible delays under light loads and predictable queuing under heavy loads. This combination makes the DQDB protocol suitable for MANs that manage large file transfers and able to satisfy the needs of interactive users.

Transport Protocol Standards

During the 1980s, network usage began to grow at a fast pace, as did the need to integrate dissimilar network devices from different vendors—a task that became increasingly difficult as the number and complexity of network devices increased. Soon the user community pressured the industry to create a single universally adopted network architecture that would allow true multivendor interoperability. We'll review two models, OSI and TCP/IP.

OSI Reference Model

The **International Organization for Standardization (ISO)**, which makes technical recommendations about data communication interfaces, took on the task of creating such a network architecture. Their efforts resulted in the **open systems interconnection (OSI) reference model**, which serves as a framework for defining the services that a network should provide to its users. This model provides the basis for connecting open systems for distributed applications processing. The word "open" means that any two systems that conform to the reference model and the related standards can be connected, regardless of the vendor.

Once all services were identified, similar functions were collected together into seven logical clusters known as layers. One of the main reasons used to define the seven layers was to group easily localized functions so that each layer could be redesigned and its protocols changed in any way to take advantage of new advances in architecture, hardware, or software without changing the services expected from, and provided to, the adjacent layers. Boundaries between layers were selected at points that past experience had revealed to be effective. The resulting seven-layer OSI model handles data transmission from one terminal or application program to another. Figure 9.14 shows how data pass through the seven layers and how they're organized: from the application layer, the one closest to the user, to the physical layer, the one closest to the cables, modems, and circuits. A brief description of each layer's function follows.

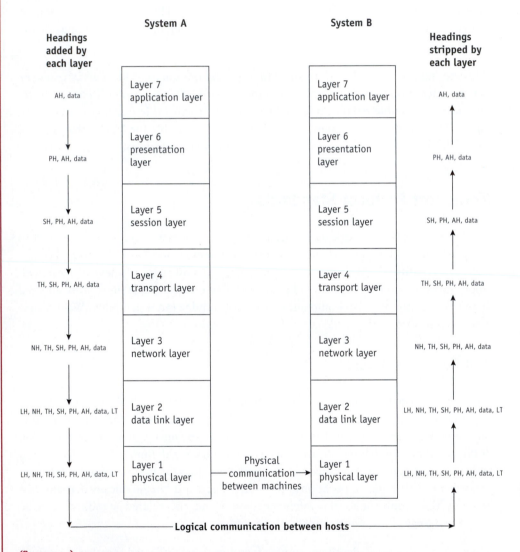

(figure 9.14)

The OSI transport protocol model. At every layer of the sending unit, System A, a new header is attached to the previous packet before it's passed on to the next lower layer. Finally, at the data link layer, a link trailer (LT) is added, completing the frame, which is passed to the physical layer for transmission. Then the receiving unit removes each header or trailer until it delivers the data to the application program at Layer 7 on System B.

Layer 1—The Physical Layer

Layer 1 is at the bottom of the model. This is where the mechanical, electrical, and functional specifications for connecting a device to a particular network are described. Layer 1 is primarily concerned with transmitting bits over communication lines, so voltages of electricity and timing factors are important. This is the only layer concerned with hardware, and all data must be passed down to it for actual data transfer between units to occur. (Layers 2 through 7 all are concerned with software, and communication between units at these levels is only virtual.) Examples of physical layer specifications are 100Base-T, RS449, and CCITT V.35.

Layer 2—The Data Link Layer

Because software is needed to implement Layer 2, this software must be stored in some type of programmable device such as a front-end processor, network node, or microcomputer. Bridging between two homogeneous networks occurs at this layer. On one side, the data link layer establishes and controls the physical path of communications before sending data to the physical layer below it. It takes the data, which have been divided into packets by the layers above it, and physically assembles the packet for transmission by completing its frame. Frames contain data combined with control and error detection characters so that Layer 1 can transmit a continuous stream of bits without concern for their format or meaning. On the other side, it checks for transmission errors and resolves problems caused by damaged, lost, or duplicate message frames so that Layer 3 can work with error-free messages. Typical data link level protocols are High-Level Data Link Control (HDLC) and Synchronous Data Link Control (SDLC).

Layer 3—The Network Layer

Layer 3 provides services such as addressing and routing that move data through the network to its destination. Basically, the software at this level accepts blocks of data from Layer 4, the transport layer, resizes them into shorter packets, and routes them to the proper destination. Addressing methods that allow a node and its network to be identified, as well as algorithms to handle address resolution, are specified in this layer. A database of routing tables keeps track of all possible routes a packet may take and determines how many different circuits exist between any two packet switching nodes. This database may be stored at this level to provide efficient packet routing and should be dynamically updated to include information about any failed circuit and the transmission volume present in the active circuits.

Layer 4—The Transport Layer

Layer 4 is also known as the host-to-host or end-to-end layer because it maintains reliable data transmission between end users. A program at the source computer can send a virtual communication to a similar program at a destination machine by using message headers and control messages. However, the physical path still goes to Layer 1 and across to the destination computer. Software for this layer contains facilities that handle user addressing and ensures that all the packets of data have been received and that none have been lost. This software may be stored in front-end processors, packet switching nodes, or host computers. In addition, this layer has a mechanism that regulates the flow of information so a fast host can't overrun a slower terminal or an overloaded host. A well-known transport layer protocol is Transmission Control Protocol (TCP).

Layer 5—The Session Layer

Layer 5 is responsible for providing a user-oriented connection service and transferring data over the communication lines. The transport layer is responsible for creating and maintaining a logical connection between end points. The session layer provides a user interface that adds value to the transport layer in the form of dialogue management and error recovery. Sometimes the session layer is known as the "data flow control" layer because it establishes the connection between two applications or processes, enforces the regulations for carrying on the session, controls the flow of data, and resets the connection if it fails. This layer might also perform some accounting functions to ensure that users receive their bills. The functions of the transport layer and session layer are very similar and, because the operating system of the host computer generally handles the session layer, it would be natural to combine both layers into one, as does TCP/IP.

Layer 6—The Presentation Layer

Layer 6 is responsible for data manipulation functions common to many applications, such as formatting, compression, and encryption. Data conversion, syntax conversion, and protocol conversion are common tasks performed in this layer. Gateways connecting networks with different protocols are presentation layer devices; one of their functions is to accommodate totally different interfaces as seen by a terminal in one node and expected by the application program at the host computer. For example, IBM's Customer Information Control System (CICS) teleprocessing monitor is a presentation layer service located in a host mainframe, although it provides additional functions beyond the presentation layer.

Layer 7—The Application Layer

At Layer 7, application programs, terminals, and computers access the network. This layer provides the interface to users and is responsible for formatting user data before passing it to the lower layers for transmission to a remote host. It contains network management functions and tools to support distributed applications. File transfer and e-mail are two of the most common application protocols and functions.

Once the OSI model is assembled, it allows nodes to communicate with each other. Each layer provides a completely different array of functions to the network, but all the layers work in unison to ensure that the network provides reliable transparent service to the users.

TCP/IP Model

The **Transmission Control Protocol/Internet Protocol (TCP/IP) reference model** is probably the oldest transport protocol standard. It's the basis for Internet communications and is the most widely used network layer protocol in use today. It was developed for the U.S. Department of Defense's ARPAnet and provides reasonably efficient and error-free transmission between different systems. Because it's a file-transfer protocol, large files can be sent across sometimes unreliable networks with a high probability that the data will arrive error free. Some differences between the TCP/IP model and the OSI reference model are the significance that TCP/IP places on internetworking and in providing connectionless services and its management of certain functions such as accounting for use of resources.

The TCP/IP model organizes a communication system with three main components: processes, hosts, and networks. Processes execute on hosts, which can often support multiple simultaneous processes that are defined as primary units that need to communicate. These processes communicate across the networks to which hosts are connected. Based on this hierarchy, the model can be roughly partitioned into two major tasks: one that manages the transfer of information to the host in which the process resides and one that ensures it gets to the correct process within the host. Therefore, a network needs to be concerned only with routing data between hosts, as long as the hosts can then direct the data to the appropriate processes. With this in mind, the TCP/IP model can be arranged into four layers instead of OSI's seven, as shown in Figure 9.15. A brief description of the layers' functions and how they relate to the OSI model follows.

Network Access Layer

The network access layer is equivalent to the physical, data link, and part of the network layers of the OSI model. Protocols at this layer provide access to a communication network. Some of the functions performed here are flow control, error control between hosts, security, and priority implementation.

Internet Layer

The Internet layer is equivalent to the portion of the network layer of the OSI model that isn't already included in the previous layer, specifically the mechanism that performs routing functions. Therefore, this protocol is usually implemented within gateways and hosts. An example of a standard set by the U.S. Department of Defense

OSI Model

TCP/IP Model

OSI Model	TCP/IP Model
Layer 7 application layer	Layer 4 process/ application layer
Layer 6 presentation layer	
Layer 5 session layer	Layer 3 host-host layer
Layer 4 transport layer	
Layer 3 network layer	Layer 2 Internet layer
Layer 2 data link layer	Layer 1 network access layer
Layer 1 physical layer	

(figure 9.15)

Comparison of OSI and TCP/IP models and their functional layers.

(DoD) is the Internet Protocol (IP), which provides connectionless service for end systems to communicate across one or more networks.

Host-Host Layer

The host-host layer is equivalent to the transport and session layers of the OSI model. As its name indicates, this layer supports mechanisms to transfer data between two processes on different host computers. Services provided in the host-host layer also include error checking, flow control, and an ability to manipulate connection control signals. An example of a standard set by the DoD is the Transmission Control Protocol (TCP), which provides a reliable end-to-end data transfer service.

Process/Application Layer

The process/application layer is equivalent to the presentation and application layers of the OSI model. It includes protocols for computer-to-computer resource sharing and terminal-to-computer remote access. Specific examples of standards set by the DoD for this layer are File Transfer Protocol (FTP), a simple application for transfer of ASCII, EBCDIC, and binary files; Simple Mail Transfer Protocol (SMTP), a simple electronic mail facility; and Telnet, a simple asynchronous terminal capability that provides remote log-on capabilities to users working at a terminal or a personal computer.

Conclusion

Although operating systems for networks necessarily include the functions of the four managers discussed so far in this textbook—the Memory Manager, Processor Manager, Device Manager, and File Manager—they also need to coordinate all those functions among the network's many varied pieces of hardware and software, no matter where they're physically located.

There is no single gauge by which we can measure the success of a network's operating system, but at a minimum it must meet the reliability requirements of its owners. That is, when a node fails—and all networks experience node failure from time to time—the operating system must detect the failure, change routing instructions to avoid that node, and make sure every lost message is retransmitted until it's successfully received.

In this chapter we've introduced the basic network organization concepts: common terminology, network topologies, types of networks, software design issues, and transport protocol standards. Bear in mind, however, that this is a complicated subject and we've only just touched the surface in these few pages. For more information about connecting topics discussed here, refer to the texts or listed as references at the end of the book.

Key Terms

bridge: a data-link layer device networks using the same protocol.

bus topology: network architecture to connect elements together along a single link.

circuit switching: a communication model in which a dedicated communication path is established between two hosts, and on which all messages travel.

distributed operating system (D/OS): an operating system that provides control for a distributed computing system, allowing its resources to be accessed in a unified way.

Domain Name Service (DNS): a general-purpose, distributed, replicated, data query service. Its principal function is the resolution of Internet addresses based on fully qualified domain names.

Ethernet: popular LAN network technology in which nodes contend for access to a network. Inexpensive, easy to install, maintain.

gateway: a communications device or program that passes data between networks having similar functions but different protocols.

host: (1) the Internet term for a network node that is capable of communicating at the application layer. Each Internet host has a unique IP address. (2) a networked computer with centralized program or data files that makes those resources available to other computers on the network.

hybrid topology: a network architecture that combines other types of network topologies to accommodate particular operating characteristics or traffic volumes.

Internet: the largest collection of networks interconnected with routers. The Internet is a multi-protocol internetwork.

International Organization for Standardization (ISO): a voluntary, non-treaty organization responsible for creating international standards in many areas, including computers and communications.

local: pertaining to the network node to which a user is attached.

local area network (LAN): a data network intended to serve an area covering only a few square kilometers or less.

metropolitan area network (MAN): a data network intended to serve an area approximating that of a large city.

Network: a collection of loosely coupled processors interconnected by communications links using cables, wireless technology, or a combination."

network operating system (NOS): the software that manages network resources for a node on a network and may provide security and access control.

node: a network-layer addressable device attached to a computer network.

open shortest path first (OSPF): a protocol designed for use in Internet Protocol (IP) networks, concerned with tracking the operational state of every network interface.

open systems interconnection (OSI) reference model: 7 layer conceptual structure describing computer network architectures and the ways in which data passes through them.

packet: a unit of data sent across a network.

packet switching: a communication model in which messages are individually routed between hosts, with no previously established communication path.

protocol: a set of rules to control the flow of messages through a network.

remote: pertaining to a node at the distant end of a network connection.

ring topology: network topology, each node is connected to two adjacent nodes.

router: a device that forwards traffic between networks.

routing information protocol (RIP): a routing protocol used by IP, based on a distance-vector algorithm.

site: a specific location on a network containing one or more computer systems.

star topology: a network topology in which multiple network nodes are connected through a single, central node.

token ring: a type of local area network with stations wired into a ring network.

token bus: a type of local area network with nodes connected to a common cable using a CSMA/CA protocol.

topology: in a network, the geometric arrangement of connections (cables, wireless, or both) that link the nodes.

Transmission Control Protocol/Internet Protocol (TCP/IP) reference model: a common acronym for the suite of transport-layer and application-layer protocols that operate over the Internet Protocol.

tree topology: a network architecture in which elements are connected in a hierarchical structure.

wide area network (WAN): a network usually constructed with long distance, point-to-point lines, covering a large geographic area.

wireless local area network (WLAN): a local area network with wireless nodes.

Exercises

Research Topic

Which operating systems are being used to run networks today? Research current literature and write down as many as possible. Don't include different versions of a single operating system unless the new version has a new name. For each operating system, list its name, the computer or network it operates, and its distributor or manufacturer. Cite your sources.

Exercises

1. Describe the primary functions of a network.
2. Compare the relative advantages and disadvantages of the five topologies discussed in this chapter.

3. Describe a hybrid topology and draw graphic illustrations of two examples.
4. Explain the major disadvantage of a star topology.
5. Describe the main differences between LANs, MANs, and WANs.
6. Discuss at least three advantages and disadvantages of WLANs.
7. Discuss the primary difference between a bridge and a gateway and give a real life example that uses each one.
8. Identify a network topology that would best suit each of the following environments and explain why.
   a. Dormitory floor
   b. University campus
   c. Airport
   d. State or province
   e. Nation
9. Explain the two ways in which packets can be routed and how they differ.
10. Although not explicitly discussed in the chapter, packet size would seem to have an impact on transmission time. Discuss whether or not this is true and explain why. Specifically compare the concept of the number of bits that constitute the data portion of the packet and the number of bits that constitute the address portion of the packet. Remember the address is overhead and impacts on transmission rates.

    Offer a comprehensive example comparing packet sizes and resulting transmission times. For example, look at some of your e-mail messages and compare the number of bytes that constitute the message with the number of bytes for the address. Compute the results for several e-mails and give your conclusions.
11. Name three commercially-available operating systems for LANs and their vendor names. Explain the topology that each is designed to manage and describe the access protocol it uses.

Advanced Exercises

12. Discuss what is wrong with the following logic: Packet switching requires control and address bits to be added to each packet, which causes considerable overhead in packet switching. In circuit switching a dedicated circuit is set up, and no extra bits are needed.
    a. Therefore, there is no overhead in circuit switching.
    b. Because there is no overhead in circuit switching, line utilization must be more efficient than in packet switching.
13. Describe the differences between CSMA/CD and CSMA/CA. Provide one real life example where CSMA/CD is used. Provide one real life example where CSMA/CA is used.

14. Explain the circumstances under which a token-ring network is more effective than an Ethernet network.

15. Contact the network expert at your school or place of work. Find out which topology, communication links, and configuration are used in that network. Is it a LAN, MAN, or WAN?

16. Even though the OSI model of networking specifies seven layers of functionality, most computer systems use fewer layers to implement a network. Why do they use fewer layers? What problems could be caused by the use of fewer layers?

17. Although security issues were not mentioned in this chapter, every network owner must consider them. Knowing that open networks allow all data to pass to every node, describe the possible security concerns of open network architectures. Include the implications of passing logon procedures, user IDs, and passwords openly on the network.

Chapter 10

Management of Network Functions

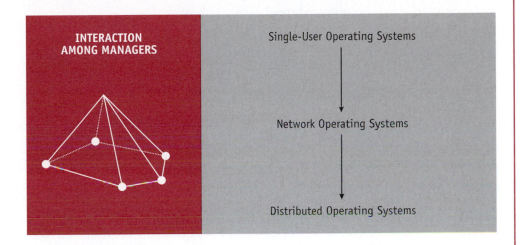

INTERACTION AMONG MANAGERS

Single-User Operating Systems

↓

Network Operating Systems

↓

Distributed Operating Systems

> **"** *As knowledge increases, wonder deepens.* **"**
>
> Charles Morgan *(1894–1958)*

Learning Objectives

After completing this chapter, you should be able to describe:

- The complexities introduced to operating systems by network capabilities
- Network operating systems (NOS) compared to distributed operating systems (DO/S)
- How a DO/S performs memory, process, device, and file management
- How a NOS performs memory, process, device, and file management
- Important features of DO/S and NOS

When organizations move toward completely decentralized systems, more and more computing devices are linked through complex networks of wireless communications, teleconferencing equipment, host computers, and other digital technologies. But there are two problems with this expansion. First, a tremendous demand is placed on data communication networks by the staggering number of hardware interconnections. Second, the user community places increasing pressure on these networks to operate with greater reliability, security, and speed.

In this chapter we'll explore the differences between network operating systems and distributed operating systems. We'll explain process-based and object-based operating system models and use them to define the roles of the Memory, Processor, Device, File, and Network Managers in distributed operating systems, and we'll discuss the role of network operating systems.

History of Networks

Networks were created initially to share expensive hardware resources such as large mainframes, laser printers, and sizable hard disks. These physical networks, with their network operating systems, allowed organizations to increase the availability of these resources and spread the cost among many users. However, the focus of technology changed when system owners realized that a network's most prized resource wasn't the hardware—it was the information stored on it. Soon many operating systems were enhanced with network capabilities to give users throughout an organization easy access to centralized information resources. The network operating system was developed first, followed by the more powerful distributed operating system.

Today, applications collectively known as computer-supported cooperative work, or **groupware**, use a set of technologies called **distributed processing** to allow even greater access to centralized information and to allow users to work together to complete common tasks.

Comparison of Network and Distributed Operating Systems

The **network operating system (NOS)** evolved from the need to give users global access to resources, globally manage the network's processes, and make the network almost completely transparent for users and their sites' operating systems, known as local operating systems. A typical NOS is shown in Figure 10.1.

A network operating system gives local operating systems extended powers. That is, it gives the local system new ability to accept a request to perform processing or to access data that's not available locally. It starts by determining where the resources are located. Then it initiates the operation and returns the appropriate data or service to the requester.

(figure 10.1)

In a NOS environment each node, shown here as a circle, is managed by its own local operating system, shown here as triangles. Their respective network operating systems, shown here as squares, come into play only when one site's system needs to work with another site's system.

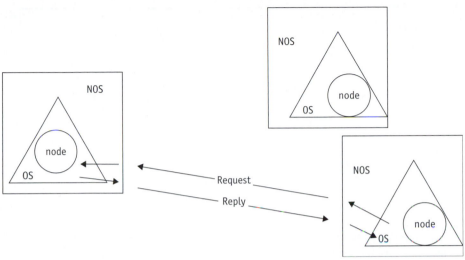

It's important that the NOS accomplish this transparently. The local operating system views the action as having been performed onsite. That's because the network operating system handles the interfacing details and coordinates the remote processing. It also coordinates communications between the local operating systems by tracking the status and location of all entities in the system.

The local operating systems are traditional operating systems designed to run a single computer. That means they can perform a task only if the process is part of their environment; otherwise, they must pass the request on to the network operating system to run it. To a local operating system, it appears that the NOS is the server performing the task, whereas in reality the NOS is only the facilitator.

The biggest limitation of a NOS is that it doesn't take global control over memory management, process management, device management, or file management. Rather, it sees them as autonomous *local* functions that must interact with each other. This limited view is problematic because an operating system can't achieve true distributed computing or processing functions without *global* control of all assets, not only assets at the network communication level. This need for global control led to the development of the **distributed operating system (DO/S)**. (Although they use a similar acronym, the DO/S described in this chapter must not be confused with DOS (disk operating system) for microcomputers or MS-DOS, described in Chapter 13.)

Distributed operating systems provide a unified environment designed to optimize operations for the network as a whole, not just for local sites, as illustrated in Figure 10.2.

The major difference between a NOS and a DO/S is how each views and manages the local and global resources. A NOS builds on capabilities provided by the local

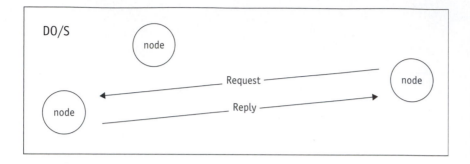

(figure 10.2)

In a DO/S environment all nodes are part of a globally managed operating system designed to optimize all system resources. Requests between nodes are handled entirely by the DO/S as well as every operation at every node.

operating system and extends it to satisfy new needs. It accesses resources by using local mechanisms and each system is controlled and managed locally based on that system's policy. On the other hand, the DO/S considers system resources to be globally owned and manages them as such. It accesses resources using *global* mechanisms rather than *local* mechanisms, with system control and management based on a single system-wide policy. A comparison of the two types of systems is shown in Table 10.1

Network Operating System (NOS)	Distributed Operating System (DO/S)
Resources owned by local nodes	Resources owned by global system
Local resources managed by local operating system	Local resources managed by a global DO/S
Access performed by a local operating system	Access performed by the DO/S
Requests passed from one local operating system to another via the NOS	Requests passed directly from node to node via the DO/S

(table 10.1)

Comparison of NOS and DO/S, two types of operating systems used to manage networked resources.

For example, in a typical NOS environment, a user who wants to run a local process at a remote site must (1) log on to the local network, (2) instruct the local system to migrate the process or data to the remote site, and then (3) send a request to the remote site to schedule the process on its system. Thereafter, the remote site views the process as a newly created process within its local operating system's environment and manages it without outside intervention. If the process needs to be synchronized with processes at remote sites, the process needs to have embedded calls to initiate action by the NOS. These calls are typically added on top of the local operating system to provide the communications link between the two processes on the different devices. This complicates the task of synchronization, a task that's the responsibility of the user and is only partially supported by the operating system.

On the other hand, a system managed by a DO/S handles the same example differently. If one site has a process that requires resources at another site, then the task is presented to the DO/S as just another process. The user acquires no additional responsibility. The DO/S examines the process control block to determine the specific requirements for this process. Then, using its process scheduler, the DO/S determines how to best execute the process based on the site's current knowledge of the state of the total system. The process scheduler then takes this process, along with all other processes ready to run on the network, and calculates their order of execution on each node while optimizing global run time and maintaining process priorities. The emphasis is on maintaining the operating system's global functionality, policies, and goals.

To globally manage the network's entire suite of resources, a DO/S is typically constructed with a replicated **kernel** operating system—low-level, hardware-control software (firmware) with system-level software for resource management. This software may be unique or duplicated throughout the system. Its purpose is to allocate and manage the system's resources so that global system policies, not local policies, are maximized. The DO/S also has a layer that hides the network and its intricacies from users so they can use the network as a single logical system and not as a collection of independent cooperating entities.

DO/S Development

Although the DO/S was developed after the NOS, its global management of network devices is the easiest to understand—so we'll explain it first.

Because a DO/S manages the entire group of resources within the network in a global fashion, resources are allocated based on negotiation and compromise among equally important peer sites in the distributed system. One advantage of this type of system is its ability to support file copying, electronic mail, and remote printing without requiring the user to install special server software on local machines. Here's how operating system management functions are performed by a DO/S.

Memory Management

For each node, the Memory Manager uses a kernel with a paging algorithm to track the amount of memory that's available. The algorithm is based on the goals of the local system but the policies and mechanisms that are used at the local sites are driven by the requirements of the global system. To accommodate both local and global needs, memory allocation and deallocation depend on scheduling and resource-sharing schemes that optimize the resources of the entire network.

The Memory Manager for a network works the same way as it does for a stand-alone operating system, but it's extended to accept requests for memory from both local and global sources. On a local level, the Memory Manager allocates pages based on the local policy. On a global level, it receives requests from the Process Manager to provide memory to new or expanding client or server processes. The Memory Manager also uses local resources to perform garbage collection in memory, perform compaction, decide which are the most and least active processes, and determine which processes to preempt to provide space for others.

To control the demand, the Memory Manager handles requests from the process manager to allocate and deallocate space based on the network's usage patterns. In a distributed environment, the combined memory for the entire network is made up of several subpools, one for each processor, and the Memory Manager has a subcomponent that exists on each processor.

When an application tries to access a page that's not in memory, a page fault occurs and the Memory Manager automatically brings that page into memory. If the page is changed while in memory, the Memory Manager writes the changed page back to the file when it's time to swap the page out of memory.

Before allocating space, the Memory Manager examines the total free memory table. If the request can be filled, the memory is allocated and the table is modified to show the location of the allocated space.

The Memory Manager also manages virtual memory. Specifically, it allocates and deallocates virtual memory, reads and writes to virtual memory, swaps virtual pages to disk, gets information about virtual pages, locks virtual pages in memory, and protects the pages that need to be protected.

Pages are protected using hardware or low-level memory management software in each site's kernel. This protection is summoned as pages are loaded into memory. Several protection checks are performed on the pages, as shown in Table 10.2.

Access Allowed	Protection
Read/write	Allows users to have full access to the page's contents, giving them the ability to read and write.
Read-only	Allows users to read the page but they're not allowed to modify it.
Execute-only	Allows users to use the page but they're not allowed to read or modify it. This means that, although a user's process can't read or write to the page, it can jump to an address within the page and start executing. This is appropriate for shared application software, editors, and compilers.
Guard-page	Used to facilitate automatic bounds-checking on stacks and other types of data structures.
No access	Prevents users from gaining access to the page. This is typically used by debugging or virus protection software to prevent a process from reading from or writing to a particular page.

(table 10.2)

Protection checks are performed on pages as they're loaded into memory. The last three controls shown in this table are needed to make sure processes don't write to pages that should be read-only.

Process Management

In a network, the Processor Manager provides the policies and mechanisms to create, delete, abort, name, rename, find, schedule, block, run, and synchronize processes, and to provide real-time priority execution if required. In addition, the Processor Manager manages the states of execution: READY, RUNNING, and WAIT as described in Chapter 4. To do this, each CPU in the network is required to have its own run-time kernel that manages the hardware—the lowest-level operation on the physical device, as shown in Figure 10.3.

(figure 10.3)

Each kernel controls each piece of hardware, including the CPU. Each kernel is operated by the DO/S which, in turn, is directed by the application software running on the host computer. In this way the most cumbersome functions are hidden from the user.

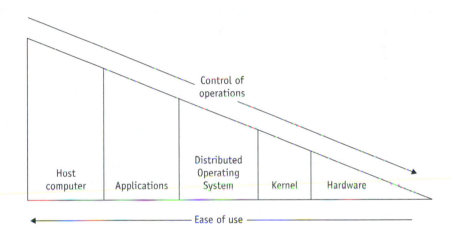

A kernel actually controls and operates the CPU and manages the queues used for states of execution, although upper-level system policies direct how process control blocks (PCBs) are stored in the queues and how they're selected to be run. Therefore, each kernel assumes the role of helping the system reach its operational goals.

The kernel's states are dependent on the global system's process scheduler and dispatcher, which organize the queues within the local CPU and choose the running policy that's used to execute the processes on those queues. Typically, the system's scheduling function has three parts: a decision mode, a priority function, and an arbitration rule.

The decision mode determines which policies are used when scheduling a resource. Options could include preemptive, nonpreemptive, round robin, etc.

The priority function gives the scheduling algorithm the policy that's used to assign an order to processes in the execution cycle. This priority is often determined using a calculation that's based on system characteristics such as, occurrence of events, task recurrence, system loading levels, or program run time characteristics. Examples of these run-time characteristics are most time remaining (MTR), least time remaining (LTR), and so on.

The arbitration rule is a policy that's used to resolve conflicts between jobs of equal priority. That is, it typically dictates the order in which jobs of the same priority are to be executed. Two examples of arbitration rules are last-in first-out (LIFO) and first-in first-out (FIFO).

Most advances in job scheduling rely on one of three theories: queuing theory, statistical decision theory, or estimation theory. (These queuing and statistical decision theories are the same as those discussed in statistics courses.) An example of estimation theory is a scheduler based on process priorities and durations. It maximizes the system's throughput by using durations to compute and schedule the optimal way to interleave process chunks. Distributed scheduling is better achieved when migration of the scheduling function and policies considers all aspects of the system, including I/O, devices, processes, and communications.

Processes are created, located, synchronized and deleted using specific procedures. To create a process, the Process Manager (which is part of the Processor Manager) starts by creating a PCB with information similar to the PCBs discussed in Chapter 4, but with additional information identifying the process's location in the network. To locate a process, the Process Manager uses a system directory or process that searches all kernel queue spaces—this requires system support for interprocess communications. To synchronize processes, the Process Manager uses message passing or remote procedure calls. To delete or terminate a process, the Process Manager finds the process control block, accesses it, and deletes it.

There are two ways to design a distributed operating system. The first is a **process-based DO/S** in which network resources are managed as a large heterogeneous collection. The second and more recent is an **object-based DO/S**, which clumps each type of hardware with its necessary operational software into discrete objects that are manipulated as a unit. Of the two, process-based DO/S most closely resembles the theory described in Chapter 4.

Process-Based DO/S

A process-based DO/S provides for process management through the use of client/server processes synchronized and linked together through messages and ports, also known as channels or pipes. The major emphasis is on processes and messages and how they provide the basic features essential to process management such as process creation, scheduling, pausing, communication, and identification, to name a few.

The issue of how to provide these features can be addressed in several ways. For example, the processes can be managed from a single copy of the operating system, from multiple cooperating peers, or from some combination of the two. Operating systems for distributed computers are typically configured as a kernel on each site. All other services, dependent on particular devices, are typically found on the sites where the devices are located. As users enter the system, they're given a unique process identifier and then assigned to a site for processing by the scheduling manager.

In a distributed system there is a high level of cooperation and sharing of actions and data maintained by the sites when determining which process should be loaded and where it should be run. This is done by exchanging messages between site operating systems. Once a process is scheduled for service, it must be initiated at the assigned site by a dispatcher. The dispatcher takes directions from the operating system's scheduler, allocates the device to the process, and initiates its execution. This procedure may necessitate moving a process from memory in one site to memory at another site; reorganizing a site's memory allocation; reorganizing a site's READY, RUNNING, and WAIT queues; and initiating the scheduled process. The Processor Manager only recognizes processes and their demands for service. It responds to them based on the established scheduling policy, which determines what must be done to manage the processes. As mentioned in earlier chapters, policies for scheduling must consider issues such as load balancing, overhead minimization, memory loading minimization, and first-come first-served and least-time-remaining.

Synchronization is a key issue in network process management. For example, processes can coordinate their activities by passing messages to each other. In addition, processes can pass synchronization parameters from one port to another using **primitives**, well-defined low-level operating system mechanisms such as "send and receive," to carry out the proper logistics to synchronize actions within a process. For instance, when a process reaches a point at which it needs service from an external source, such as an I/O request, it sends a message searching for the service. While it waits for a response, the processor server puts the process in a WAIT state.

Interrupts, which cause a processor to be assigned to another process, also are represented as messages that are sent to the proper process for service. For example, an interrupt may cause the active process to be blocked and moved into a WAIT state. Later, when the cause for the interruption ends, the processor server unblocks the interrupted process and restores it to a READY state.

Object-Based DO/S

An object-based DO/S has a different way of looking at the computer system. Instead of viewing the system as a collection of individual resources and processes, the system is viewed as a collection of **objects**. An object can represent hardware (such as CPUs and memory), software (such as files, programs, semaphores, and data), or a combination of the two (printers, scanners, tape drives, and disks—each bundled with the software required to operate it). Each object in the system has a unique identifier to differentiate it from all other objects in the system.

Objects are viewed as abstract entities, data types that can go through a change of state, act according to set patterns, be manipulated, or exist in relation to other objects in a manner appropriate to the object's semantics in the system. This means that objects have a set of unchanging properties that defines them and their behavior within the context of their defined parameters. For example, a writable CD drive has unchanging properties that include the following: data can be written to a disc, data can be read from a disc, reading and writing can't take place concurrently, and the data's beginning and ending points can't be compromised. If we use these simple rules to construct a simulation of a CD-R drive, we have created an accurate representation of this object.

To determine an object's state, one must perform an appropriate operation on it, such as reading or writing to a hard disk, because the object is identified by the set of operations one can send it. The combination of the operations with their internally defined data structures and computations represents an object's instantiation. Typically, systems using this concept have a large number of objects but a small number of operations on the objects. For example, a printer can have three operations: one to advance a full page, one to advance one line, and one to advance one character.

Therefore, in an object-based DO/S, process management becomes object management, with processes acting as discrete objects. Process management, in this case, deals with the policies and mechanisms for controlling the operations and the creation and destruction of objects. Therefore, process management has two components: the kernel level and the Process Manager.

The Kernel Level

The **kernel level** provides the basic mechanisms for building the operating system by creating, managing, scheduling, synchronizing, and deleting objects—and it does so dynamically. For example, when an object is created, it's assigned all the resources needed for its operation and is given control until the task is completed. Then the object returns control to the kernel, which selects the next object to be executed.

The kernel also has ultimate responsibility for the network's capability lists, discussed in Chapter 8. Each site has both a capability manager that maintains the capability list for its objects and a directory listing the location for all capabilities in the system. This directory guides local requests for capabilities to other sites on which they're located.

For example, if a process requests access to a region in memory, the capability manager first determines whether the requesting process has been previously granted rights. If so, then it can proceed. If not, it processes the request for access rights. When the requester has access rights, the capability manager grants the requester access to the named object, in this case the region in memory. If the named object is at a remote site, the local capability manager directs the requester, using a new address computation and message, to the remote capability manager.

The kernel is also responsible for process synchronization mechanisms and communication support. Typically, synchronization is implemented as some form of shared variable, such as the WAIT and SIGNAL codes discussed in Chapter 6. Communication between distributed objects can be in the form of shared data objects, message objects, or control interactions. Most systems provide different communications primitives to their objects, which are either synchronous (either the sender and receiver are linked and ready to send and receive) or asynchronous (there is some shareable area such as a mailbox, queue, or stack to which the communicated information is sent). In some cases, the receiver periodically checks to see if anyone has sent anything. In other cases, the communicated information arrives at the receiver's workstation without any effort on the part of the receiver; it just waits. There can also be a combination of these. An example of this communication model might have a mechanism that signals the receiver whenever a communication arrives at the sharable area so the information can be fetched whenever it's convenient. The advantage of this system is that it eliminates unnecessary checking when no messages are waiting.

Finally, the kernel environment for distributed systems must have a scheduler with a consistent and robust mechanism for scheduling objects within the system according to its operations goals.

The Process Manager

If the kernel doesn't already have primitives (test and set, P and V, etc.) to work with the hardware then the Process Manager has to create its own primitives before going on with its job. The Process Manager has responsibility for the following tasks: creating objects, dispatching objects, scheduling objects, synchronizing operations on objects, communicating among objects, and deleting objects. To perform these tasks, the Process Manager uses the kernel environment, which provides the primitives it needs to capture the low-level hardware in the system.

For example, to run a database object, the Process Manager must do the following steps in order:

1. Determine whether or not the object is in memory. If so, go to step 3.
2. If it's not in memory, find the object on secondary storage, allocate space in memory for it, and log it into the proper locations.
3. Provide the proper scheduling information for the object.
4. Once the object has been scheduled, wait for the kernel dispatcher to pull it out and place it into the RUNNING state.

Thus far we've discussed the similarities between the object-based and process-based managers. The major difference between them is that objects contain all of their state information. That means that the information is stored *with* the object, not separately in another part of the system such as in a process control block (PCB) or other data structure separate from the object.

Device Management

In all distributed systems, devices must be opened, read from, written to, and closed. In addition, device parameters must be initialized and status bits must be set or cleared—just as in stand-alone systems. All of this can be done on a global, cluster, or localized basis.

Usually users prefer to choose devices by name, and let the distributed operating system select and operate the best device from among those available. For example, if users need specific control of a device, then they should be able to call a device by name, such as DISK 12. When the choice is made, the DO/S takes control, allocating the unit when it's available, assigning it to the user when the OPEN command is issued, operating it, and then deallocating it when the job is finished.

The device can't be allocated until the Device Manager examines the device's status and, when it's free, sends the requesting process a unique device identifier—a name that's used for all communication between the process and the device. Later, when the process issues a CLOSE command, the device is released. That's when the DO/S resets the device's state information and returns its device control block to the device's READY queue. For example, when a user wants to print a file by executing a print command, the DO/S follows a process similar to this:

1. The user's File Manager places a copy of the file in the DO/S spooler directory.
2. The spooler selects the file from the spooler directory and initiates an open request to the DO/S File Manager.
3. When the open request is satisfied, the spooler initiates another open request to a networked line printer's device driver.
4. When the second open request is satisfied, the spooler sends the file to the printer's input buffer. This can be accomplished through a direct message transfer or a packet transfer, as described in Chapter 9.
5. When printing is complete, the DO/S File Manager deletes the copy of the file from the spooler.
6. Finally the device is reset and closed.

This system works only if the DO/S keeps a global accounting of each network device and its availability, maintaining each device's status record and control block, and distributing this information to all sites. As shown in Figure 10.4, the DO/S Device Manager is a collection of remote device drivers connected to and associated with the devices, but controlled by status data that's provided by the DO/S Device Manager.

Process-Based DO/S

All resources in the process-based DO/S are controlled by servers called "guardians" or "administrators." These servers are responsible for accepting requests for service on the individual devices they control, processing each request fairly, providing service to the requestor, and returning to serve others, as shown in Figure 10.5.

However, not all systems have a simple collection of resources. Many have clusters of printers, disk drives, tapes, and so on. To control these clusters as a group, most process-based systems are configured around complex **server processes**, which manage multiple resources or divide the work among subordinate processes. The administrator process is configured as a Device Manager and includes the software needed to accept local and remote requests for service, decipher their meaning, and act on them. Typically a server process is made up of one or more device drivers, a Device Manager, and a network server component.

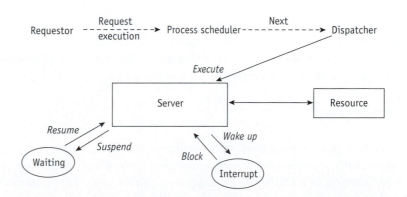

Object-Based DO/S

In an object-based DO/S, each device is managed the same way throughout the network. The physical device is considered an object, just like other network resources, and is surrounded by a layer of software that gives other objects a complete view of the device object.

The physical device is manipulated by a set of operations, explicit commands that mobilize the device to perform its designated functions. For example, an object to control a tape unit requires operations to rewind, fast forward, and scan. To use a tape drive, users issue an operation on a tape object such as this:

```
WITH TAPE 1 DO FAST FORWARD (N) RECORDS
```

This causes the tape drive to advance *N* records. This assumes, of course, that the operating system has already granted authorization to the user to use the tape object.

A disk drive works the same way. Users access the drive by sending operations to the Device Manager to create a new file, destroy an old file, open or close an existing file, read information from a file, or write to it. Users don't need to know the underlying mechanisms that implement the operations—they just need to know which operations work.

One advantage of object-based DO/S is that the objects can be assembled to communicate and synchronize with each other to provide a distributed network of resources, with each object knowing the location of its distributed peers. So, if the local device manager can't satisfy a user's request, the request is sent to another device manager, a peer. Again, users don't need to know if the network's resources are centralized or distributed—only that their requests are satisfied.

For this system to be successful, the Device Manager object at each site needs to maintain a current directory of device objects at all sites. Then, when a requesting object needs to use a printer, for example, the request is presented to its local device manager. If the local manager has the means and opportunity to provide the proper service, it prints the request. If it can't meet the request locally, it sends the request to a peer Device Manager that has the appropriate resources. It's this remote Device Manager that processes the request and performs the operation.

File Management

Distributed file management gives users the illusion that the network is a single logical file system that's implemented on an assortment of devices and computers. Therefore, the main function of a DO/S File Manager is to provide transparent mechanisms to find and open, read, write, close, create, and delete files, no matter where they're located in the network, as shown in Table 10.3.

(table 10.3)	Desired File Function	File Manager's Action
Typical file management functions and the necessary reactions of the File Manager.	Find and Open	It uses a master directory with information about all files stored anywhere on the system and sets up a channel to the file.
	Read	It sets up a channel to the file and attempts to read it using simple file access schemes. However, a read operation won't work if the file is currently being created or modified.
	Write	It sets up a channel to the file and attempts to write to it using simple file access schemes. To write to a file the requesting process must have exclusive access to it. This can be accomplished by locking the file, a technique frequently used in database systems. While a file is locked, all other requesting processes must wait until the file is unlocked before they can write to or read the file.
	Close	It sends a command to the remote server to unlock that file. This is typically accomplished by changing the information in the directory at the file's storage site.
	Create	It creates a unique file identifier in the network's master directory and assigns space for it on a storage device.
	Delete	It erases the unique file identifier in the master directory and deallocates the space reserved for it on the storage device.

File management systems are a subset of database managers, which provide more capabilities to user processes than file systems and are being implemented as distributed database management systems as part of local area network systems.

Therefore, the tasks required by a DO/S include those typically found in a distributed database environment. These involve a host of controls and mechanisms necessary to provide consistent, synchronized, and reliable management of system and user information assets, including the following:

• Concurrency control

• Data redundancy

• Location transparency and distributed directory

• Deadlock resolution or recovery

• Query processing

Concurrency Control

Concurrency control techniques give the system the ability to perform concurrent reads and writes, as long as the results of these actions don't jeopardize the contents of the database. That means that the results of all concurrent transactions are the same as if the transactions had been executed one at a time, in some arbitrary serial order, thereby providing the serial execution view on a database. The concurrency control mechanism keeps the database in a consistent state as the transactions are being processed.

For example, let's say a group of airline reservation agents are making flight arrangements for telephone callers. By using concurrency control techniques, the File Manager allows each agent to read and write to the airline's huge database if each read and write doesn't interfere with another that's already taking place. These techniques provide a serial execution view on a database.

Data Redundancy

Data redundancy can make files much faster and easier to read. That's because the File Manager can allow a process to read the copy that's closest or easiest to access. Or, if the file is very large, the read request can be split into several different requests, each of which is fulfilled at a different file location. For example, if an airline reservation system received a request for information about passengers on a certain flight, and the database was stored in three different locations, then one read request could search the passengers with last names beginning with A-K, the second read request could search L-R, and the third read request could search S-Z. The results of all three requests are combined before returning the results to the requester.

Data redundancy also has beneficial aspects from a disaster recovery standpoint because if one site fails, operations can be restarted at any another site with the same resources. Later, the failed site can be reinstated by copying all files that were updated since the failure. The disadvantage of redundant data is the task of keeping multiple copies of the same file up-to-date at all times. Every time a file is updated, every other copy of the file must be updated in the identical way and the update must be performed according to the system's reliability standards.

Based on the algorithm used and the method of recovery, the system can require that updates be performed at all sites before any reads occur to a master site or to a majority of sites. Some typically used update algorithms are: unanimous agreement, primary site copy, moving primary site, and majority site agreement.

Location Transparency and Distributed Directory

Location transparency means that users aren't concerned with the physical location of their files. Instead, they deal with the network as a single system. Location transparency is provided by mechanisms and directories that map logical data items to physical locations. The mechanisms usually use information about data that's stored at all sites in the form of directories.

The distributed directory manages transparency of data location and enhances data recovery for users. The directory contains definitions dealing with the physical and logical structure for the stored data, as well as the policies and mechanisms for mapping between the two. In addition, it contains the systemwide names of all resources and the addressing mechanisms for locating and accessing them.

Deadlock Resolution or Recovery

Deadlock detection and recovery, described in Chapter 5, are critical issues in distributed systems. The most important function is to detect and recover from a circular wait. This occurs when one process requests a resource (such as a file, disk drive, modem, or tape unit), which we'll call Resource B, while it keeps exclusive control over another resource, which we'll call Resource A. Meanwhile, a second process requests use of Resource A while it keeps exclusive control over Resource B. A directed graph for this example is shown in Figure 10.6.

However most real-life examples of circular wait are much more complex and difficult to detect because they involve multiple processes and multiple resources—all waiting for a resource that's held exclusively by another process.

(figure 10.6)

This example of circular wait was created when Process 1 requested Resource B without releasing its exclusive control over Resource A. Likewise, Process 2 requested Resource A without releasing Resource B.

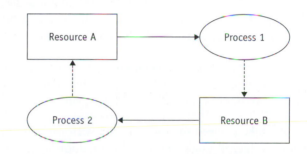

Detection, prevention, avoidance, and recovery are all strategies used by a distributed system. To recognize circular waits, the system uses directed resource graphs and looks for cycles. To prevent circular waits, the system tries to delay the start of a transaction until it has all the resources it will request during its execution. To avoid circular waits, the system tries to allow execution only when it knows that the transaction can run to completion. To recover from a deadlock caused by circular waits, the system selects the best victim—one that can be restarted without much difficulty and one that, when terminated, will free enough resources so the others can finish. Then the system kills the victim, forces that process to restart from the beginning, and reallocates its resources to the waiting processes.

Query Processing

Query processing is the function of processing requests for information. Query processing techniques try to increase the effectiveness of global query execution sequences, local site processing sequences, and device processing sequences. All of these relate directly to the network's global process scheduling problem. Therefore, to ensure consistency of the entire system's scheduling scheme, the query processing strategy must be an integral part of the processing scheduling strategy.

Network Management

The network management function is a communications function that's unique to networked systems because stand-alone operating systems don't need to communicate with other systems. For a DO/S, the Network Manager provides the policies and mechanisms necessary to provide intrasite and intersite communication among concurrent processes. For intrasite processes within the network, the Network Manager provides process identifiers and logical paths to other processes—in a one-to-one, one-to-few, one-to-many, or one-to-all manner—while dynamically managing these paths.

The Network Manager has many diverse responsibilities. It must be able to locate processes in the network, send messages throughout the network, and track media use. In addition, it must be able to reliably transfer data, code and decode messages, retransmit errors, perform parity checking, do cyclic redundancy checks, establish redundant links, and acknowledge messages and replies, if necessary.

The Network Manager begins by registering each network process as soon as it has been assigned a unique physical designator. It then sends this identifier to all other sites in the network. From that moment, the process is logged with all sites in the network.

When processes—or objects—need to communicate with each other, the Network Manager links them together through a port—a logical door on one process that can be linked with a port on another process, thus establishing a logical path for the two to communicate. Ports usually have physical buffers and I/O channels, and represent physical assets that must be used wisely by the Network Manager. Ports can be assigned to one process or to many.

Processes require routing because of the underlying network topology and the processes' location. Routing can be as simple as a process-device pair address that associates one logical process with one physical site. Or it can incorporate many levels traversing multiple links in either a direct or a hop count form, as described in Chapter 9.

In addition to routing, other functions required from the Network Manager are keeping statistics on network use (for use in message scheduling, fault localizations, and rerouting), and providing mechanisms to aid process time synchronization. This standardization mechanism is commonly known as a systemwide clock, a device that allows system components at various sites to compensate for time variations because of delays caused by the distributed communication system.

Process-Based DO/S

In a process-based DO/S, interprocess communication is transparent to users. The Network Manager assumes full responsibility for allocating ports to the processes that request them, identifying every process in the network, controlling the flow of messages, and guaranteeing the transmission and acceptance of messages without errors.

The Network Manager routinely acts as the interfacing mechanism for every process in the system and handles message traffic, relieving users of the need to know where their processes are physically located in the network. As traffic operator, the Network Manager accepts and interprets each process's commands to send and receive. Then it transforms those commands into low-level actions that actually transmit the messages over network communications links.

Object-Based DO/S

A Network Manager object makes both intermode and intramode communications among cooperative objects easy. A process, the active code elements within objects, can begin an operation at a specific instance of an object by sending a request message. The user doesn't need to know the location of the receiver. The user only needs to know the receiver's name and the Network Manager takes over, providing the message's proper routing to the receiver. A process can also invoke an operation that's part of its local object environment.

Generally, network communications allow some level of the following functions: send, receive, reply, and request, as described in Table 10.4.

(table 10.4)

Communications sent by the Network Manager allow objects to perform at least one of four functions.

Function	Purpose
Send	Allows objects to send a message with operations to any object in the system.
Receive	Warns objects of incoming communications from an object in the system.
Request	Provides a mechanism for objects to ask for particular services. For example, they can request that a message be sent.
Reply	Allows objects to do one of three things: • Respond to requests for communications from another object • Respond to a send command that they aren't prepared for • Indicate that they're ready to accept a send command; a message can now be sent knowing that the receiver is awaiting it

Network Manager services are usually provided at the kernel level to better accommodate the many objects that use them and to offer efficient service. However, depending on the system, the Network Manager may be a simple utility that handles only send and receive primitives. Or perhaps it's constructed using ports, or channels. A simple send-and-receive utility requires that users know the name of the objects they need to communicate with, whereas the port or channel system requires users to know only the name of the port or channel with which the object is associated. For example, if a communications facility is supported by a port-object type mechanism, then objects are grouped as senders, receivers, ports, and messages, and are linked together using capability lists.

NOS Development

A network operating system (NOS) typically runs on a computer called a **server** and performs services for network workstations called **clients**. Although computers can assume the role of clients most or all of the time, any given computer can assume the role of server (or client), depending on the requirements of the network. Client and server are not hardware-specific terms. Instead, they are role-specific terms.

Many modern network operating systems are true operating systems that include the four management functions: memory management, process scheduling, file management, and device management including disk and I/O operations. In addition, they have a network management function with responsibility for network communications, protocols, etc. In a NOS the network management functions come into play only when the system needs to use the network, as shown in Figure 10.7. At all other times, the Network Manager is dormant and the operating system operates as if it's a stand-alone system.

Although NOSs can run applications as well as other operating systems, their focus is on sharing resources instead of running programs. For example, a single-user operating system such as early versions of Windows, or even a multiuser system such as

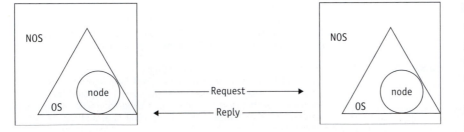

(figure 10.7)

In a NOS environment the four managers of the operating system manage all system resources at that site unless and until the node needs to communicate with another node on the network. When that happens the NOS of the first node opens communications with the NOS of the targeted network node.

UNIX or Linux, focuses on the user's ability to run applications. On the other hand, network operating systems focuses on the workstations' ability to share the server's resources including applications and data as well as expensive shared resources such as printers and high-speed modems.

In the following pages we describe some of the features commonly found in a network operating system without focusing on any one in particular. The best NOS choice depends on many factors including the applications to be run on the server, the technical support required, the user's level of training, and the compatibility of the hardware with other networking systems.

Important NOS Features

Most network operating systems are implemented as early versions of 32-bit or 64-bit software. However, more important than the processor is the support a NOS provides for standard local area network technologies and client desktop operating systems.

Networks are becoming increasingly heterogeneous. That is, they support workstations running a wide variety of operating systems. For example, a single network might include workstations running Windows, the Macintosh operating system, and Linux. For a NOS to serve as the networking glue, it must provide strong support for every operating system in the corporate information network, sustaining as many current standards as necessary. Therefore, it must have a robust architecture that adapts easily to new technologies.

For example, a NOS should preserve the user's expectations for a desktop system. That means that the network's resources should appear as simple extensions of that user's existing system. For example, on a Windows computer, a network drive should appear as just another hard disk but with a different volume name and a different drive letter. On a Macintosh computer, the network drive should appear as an icon for a volume on the desktop. And on a Linux system, the drive should appear as a mountable file system.

A NOS is designed to operate a wide range of third-party software applications and hardware devices including hard drives, modems, CD-ROM drives, and network interface cards. A NOS also supports software for multiusernetwork applications, such as electronic messaging, as well as networking expansions such as new protocol stacks.

Finally, the NOS must blend efficiency with security. Its constant goal is to provide network clients with quick and easy access to the network's data and resources without compromising network security. A compromised network instantly loses data integrity and the confidence of its users.

Major NOS Functions

An important NOS function is to allow users to access hardware or software at a re-mote site. One example is the Internet's **telnet** command, which allows users to log in from remote locations if they already have an authorized account at the connected site. So if authorized students need to access the computer at the University of Pittsburgh from home, they can issue a command like this:

```
telnet unixs.cis.pitt.edu
```

This telnet command establishes a connection between the student's home computer and the university's UNIX computer. Security is a critical function of the NOS by receiving the telnet command and confirming the student's current login name and password. It must verify every attempt to log in and have policies in place to handle unsuccessful at-tempts. Once the connection is established, the NOS creates a two-way communication line so that all commands sent by the student are executed by the UNIX operating sys-tem and all interactive output is displayed on the student's monitor.

Throughout the telnet session, typical operating system functions, such as memory management, file management, etc., are performed by the remote system, whereas the NOS handles the networking functions described in Chapter 9. When accessing telnet, the user must use the appropriate commands for the remote system. For example, whenever users working on a Windows system use telnet to reach a UNIX system, they must use UNIX commands exclusively while they're logged on to the UNIX computer. They use Windows commands only after ending the telnet session and returning to their own systems.

Another important function of a NOS is to let users transfer files from one computer to another. In this case, each system controls and manages its own file system. For ex-ample, the Internet provides the **File Transfer Protocol (FTP)** program. So, if students in a UNIX programming class need to copy a data file from the university computer to their home computers to complete an assignment, then each student begins by issu-ing the following command to create the FTP connection:

```
ftp unixs.cis.pitt.edu
```

This opens the FTP program, which then asks the student for a login name and password. Once this information has been verified by the UNIX operating system, each student is allowed to copy the file from the host computer by using this command:

```
get filename.ext
```

In this example, filename.ext is the absolute filename and extension of the required data file. That means the user must know *exactly* where the file is located—in which directory and subdirectory the file is stored. That's because the file location isn't transparent to the user.

This find-and-copy technique isn't considered true file sharing because all users wanting access to the data file must copy the file onto their own systems, thereby duplicating the code and wasting space. This practice also adds **version control** difficulties because when one user modifies the file in any way, those changes aren't reflected on other copies already stored in other directories unless each user replaces the old version with the new version.

For a collection of files to be available to the general public, the files must be placed in a public FTP directory on an FTP server. Then, anyone with an FTP client or a Web browser can download copies of the files on demand using a process called **anonymous FTP**. The advantage of an FTP connection is that it doesn't force files to pass through mail programs that might encode or decode the document. Therefore, all FTP documents usually download faster while retaining their necessary characteristics, including templates, formatting, fonts, and graphics.

Web visitors don't usually visit the FTP server until they want to download a file. When they click on the download link, they're transferred to the FTP server. These FTP sites aren't usually designed for easy browsing but Web browsers can be used to handle FTP files with some limitations. Most Web browsers display FTP directories using graphical icons to represent available files and directories. Typical Web browser commands and features can be used to download FTP files just as they do other Web objects. The advantage of using the Web for FTP is that most users already know how the Web browser works and don't need to learn new software.

Conclusion

The first operating systems for networks were NOS. Although they were adequate, they didn't take full advantage of the global resources available to all connected sites. The development of distributed operating systems (DO/S) specifically addressed that need.

Every networked system, whether a NOS or a DO/S, has specific requirements. Each must be secure from unauthorized access yet accessible to authorized users. Each must monitor its available system resources, including memory, processors, devices, and files (as described in Chapters 2 through 8), as well as its communications links. In addition, because it's a networking operating system, it must perform the required networking tasks described in Chapter 9.

Each of the technological advances we've discussed thus far has created security vulnerabilities. System security experts like to say that the only secure computer is one that is unplugged from its power source. In the next chapter we'll look at key elements of system security and ethics, and the role of the system administrator in safeguarding the network's most valuable resource—its data.

Key Terms

anonymous FTP: a use of File Transfer Protocol that allows a user to retrieve documents, files, programs, and other data from anywhere in the Internet without having to establish a user ID and password.

client: a user node that requests and makes use of various network services.

distributed operating system (DO/S): an operating system that provides control for a distributed computing system, allowing its resources to be accessed in a unified way.

distributed processing: a method of data processing in which files are stored at many different locations and in which processing takes place at different sites.

File Transfer Protocol (FTP): a protocol that allows a user on one host to access and transfer files to or from another host over a TCP/IP network.

groupware: software applications that support cooperative work over a network.

kernel: the part of the operating system that resides in main memory at all times and performs the most essential tasks, such as managing memory and handling disk input and output.

kernel level: in an object-based distributed operating system, provides the basic mechanisms for dynamically building parts of the operating system by creating, managing, scheduling, synchronizing, and deleting objects.

network operating system (NOS): the software that manages network resources for a node on a network and may provide security and access control.

object: any one of the many entities that constitute a computer system, such as CPUs, terminals, disk drives, files, or databases.

object-based DO/S: a view of distributed operating systems where each hardware unit is bundled with its required operational software, forming a discrete object to be handled as an entity.

primitives: well-defined, predictable, low-level operating system mechanisms that allow higher-level operating system components to perform their functions without considering direct hardware manipulation.

process-based DO/S: a view of distributed operating systems that encompasses all the system's processes and resources.

server: a node that provides to clients various network services such as file retrieval, printing, or database access services.

server process: a logical unit composed of one or more device drivers, a device manager, and a network server module needed to control clusters or similar devices in a process-based, distributed operating system environment.

telnet: an internet protocol that allows local users to access a remote computer via the Internet through a virtual network terminal.

version control: the tracking and updating of a specific release of a piece of hardware or software.

Exercises

Research Topic

Find five examples of software that's available over the Web using FTP (hint: watch for "ftp" instead of "http" in the site address). For each example, identify the software, the version or versions offered, the vendor or organization supplying the software, and the cost, if any. Briefly discuss the advantages and disadvantages of each file transfer opportunity to both the supplier and the user. Include any security concerns in your discussion.

Exercises

1. Compare the advantages and disadvantages of process-based DO/S.
2. Compare the advantages and disadvantages of object-based DO/S.
3. Name some of the advantages of distributed systems over centralized systems.
4. Name some of the disadvantages of distributed systems over centralized systems.
5. Give an example of a communications deadlock.
6. Give an example of a real-life situation in which each of the following access privileges are used: read-only, read/write, and execute-only.
7. Describe in detail how a DO/S protects a file from access or modification by an unauthorized user. Compare it to NOS file protection.

Advanced Exercises

8. If you were managing a hospital's network, what policies would you implement to protect your system? Keep in mind that, as system manager, your job is to provide the correct level of accessibility to authorized users while denying access to unauthorized users.

9. Remembering the discussion of deadlocks in Chapter 5, if you were designing a networked system, how would you manage the threat of deadlocks in your network? Consider all of the following: prevention, detection, avoidance, and recovery.

Chapter 11

Security and Ethics

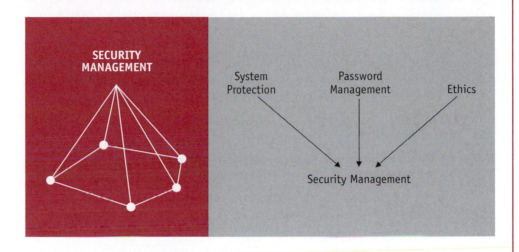

"Perfection of means and confusion of goals seem, in my opinion, to characterize our age. **"** —Albert Einstein (1879–1955)

Learning Objectives

After completing this chapter, you should be able to describe:

- The role of the operating system with regard to system security
- The effects of system security practices on overall system performance
- The levels of system security that can be implemented and the threats posed by evolving technologies
- The differences between computer viruses and worms, and how they spread
- The difficulties of teaching ethics to user groups and the role of education in system security

Every computing system has conflicting needs: To share resources and to protect them. In the early days, security consisted of a secure lock and a few keys. That is, the system was physically guarded and only authorized users were allowed in its vicinity, and that was sufficient when the user group was limited to several dozen individuals. However, with the advent of data communication, networking, the proliferation of personal computers, telecommunications software, Web sites, and e-mail, the user community has grown to include millions of people making computer security much more difficult.

System security is a vast and complex subject worthy of its own text. While we cannot do justice to the subject in a single chapter, we introduce the important concepts here and encourage the reader to review current research about the subject. Keep in mind that this subject changes with lightning speed and is well worth constant monitoring by system owners, operators, and users.

Role of the Operating System in Security

The operating system plays a key role in computer system security because it has access to every part of the system. Any vulnerability at the operating system level opens the entire system to attack. The more complex and powerful the operating system, the more likely it is to have vulnerabilities to attack. As a result, system administrators must be on guard to arm their operating systems with all available defenses against attack and possible failure.

System Survivability

System survivability is defined as: "the capability of a system to fulfill its mission, in a timely manner, in the presence of attacks, failures, or accidents" (Linger, 2002).

- The term *system* refers to any system. It's used here in the broadest possible sense, from laptop to distributed system to supercomputer.
- A *mission* is a very high-level set of requirements or goals.
- *In a timely manner* refers to system response time, a critical factor for most systems.
- The terms *attack*, *failure*, and *accident* refer to any potentially damaging incident, regardless of the cause, whether intentional or not.

Before a system can be considered survivable, it must meet all of these requirements, especially with respect to services that are considered essential to the organization in the face of adverse challenges. The four key properties of survivable systems are resistance to attacks, recognition of attacks and resulting damage, recovery of essential services after an attack, and adaptation and evolution of system defense mechanisms to mitigate future attacks.

With the elevated risks in recent years of system intrusion and compromise, system designers have recognized the critical need for system survivability that's incorporated into system development. It's no longer satisfactory to add survivability factors to the system only as an afterthought. Examples of sample strategies that can be built into systems to enhance their survivability are shown in Table 11.1.

(table 11.1)

Four key properties of a survivable system and strategies to achieve it (Linger, 2002). Details about the example strategies shown here can be found at www.cert.org.

Key Property	Description	Example Strategies
Resistance to attacks	Strategies for repelling attacks	Authentication Access controls Encryption Message filtering System diversification Functional isolation
Recognition of attacks and damage	Strategies for detecting attacks and evaluating damage	Intrusion detection Integrity checking
Recovery of essential and full services after attack	Strategies for limiting damage, restoring compromised information or functionality, maintaining or restoring essential services within mission time constraints, restoring full services	Redundant components Data replication System backup and restoration Contingency planning
Adaptation and evolution to reduce effectiveness of future attacks	Strategies for improving system survivability based on knowledge gained from intrusions	Intrusion recognition patterns

Levels of Protection

Any successful assault on a system poses a grave security risk because once a system is breached, the integrity of every file on the system, and the data in those files, can no longer be trusted. For each computer configuration, the system administrator must evaluate the risk of intrusion, which in turn depends on the level of connectivity given to the system, as shown in Table 11.2.

(table 11.2)

A simplified comparison of security protection required for three typical computer configurations. Notice that system vulnerabilities accumulate as the computer's level of connectivity increases.

Configuration	Ease of Protection	Relative Risk	Vulnerabilities
Single computer (without e-mail or Internet)	High	Low	Compromised passwords, viruses
LAN connected (without Internet)	Medium	Medium	Sniffers, spoofing (+passwords, viruses)
LAN connected (with Internet)	Low	High	E-mail, Web servers, FTP, Telnet (+sniffers, spoofing, passwords, viruses)

All of the vulnerabilities shown in Table 11.2 are discussed later in this chapter.

Backup and Recovery

Having sufficient **backup** and **recovery** policies in place and performing other archiving techniques is standard operating procedure for most computing systems. Many system managers use a layered backup schedule. That is, they back up the entire system once a week and back up daily only the files that were changed that day. As an extra measure of safety, copies of complete system backups are stored for three to six months in a safe off-site location.

Backups become significant when a computer virus infects your system. If you discover it early, you can run eradication software and reload damaged files from your backup copies. Of course, any changes made since the files were backed up will have to be regenerated.

Backups, with one set stored off-site, are also crucial to disaster recovery. The disaster could come from anywhere:

• water from a fire upstairs

• fire from an electrical connection

• malfunctioning server

• corrupted archival media

• intrusion from unauthorized users

Written policies and procedures and regular user training are essential elements of system management. Most system failures are caused by honest mistakes made by well-intentioned users—not by malicious intruders. Written security procedures should recommend frequent password changes, reliable backup procedures, guidelines for loading new software, compliance with software licenses, network safeguards, guidelines for monitoring network activity, and rules for terminal access.

Security Breaches

A gap in system security can be malicious or not. For instance, some intrusions are the result of an uneducated user and the unauthorized access to system resources. But others stem from the purposeful disruption of the system's operation, and still others are purely accidental such as hardware malfunctions, undetected errors in the operating system or applications, or natural disasters. Malicious or not, a breach of security severely damages the system's credibility. Following are some types of security breaks that can occur.

Unintentional Intrusions

An unintentional attack is defined as any breach of security or modification of data that was not the result of a planned intrusion.

When nonsynchronized processes access data records and modify some but not all of a record's fields, it's called "accidental incomplete modification of data." An example was given in Chapter 5 when we discussed the topic of a race in a database with two processes working on the same student record and writing different versions of it to the database.

Errors can occur when data values are incorrectly stored because the field isn't large enough to hold the numeric value stored there. For example, when a field is too small to hold a numeric value, FORTRAN replaces the number with a string of asterisks, and COBOL simply truncates the higher-order digits, as shown in Figure 11.1.

(figure 11.1)

The original data value is shown (a) in a field large enough to hold it. If the field is too small, FORTRAN (b) replaces the data with asterisks. COBOL (c) truncates the higher order digits (values to the left of the dotted line) and stores only the digits that remain.

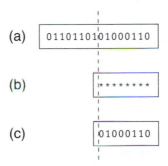

Neither error would be discovered at the time of storage—an error would be discovered only when the value is retrieved. Needless to say, that's an inconvenient time to make such an unpleasant discovery.

Intentional Attacks

Intentional unauthorized access includes denial of service attacks, browsing, wire tapping, repeated trials, trap doors, and trash collection. These attacks are fundamentally different from viruses and worms and the like (covered shortly), which inflict widespread damage to numerous companies and organizations—without specifying certain ones as targets.

Intentional Unauthorized Access

Denial of service (DoS) attacks are synchronized attempts to deny service to authorized users by causing a computer (usually a Web server), to perform a task (often an unproductive task) over and over, thereby making the system unavailable to perform the work it is designed to do. For example, if a Web server designed to accept orders from customers over the Internet is diverted from its appointed task with repeated commands to identify itself, then the computer becomes unavailable to serve the customers online.

Browsing is when unauthorized users gain the capability to search through storage, directories, or files for information they aren't privileged to read. The term "storage" refers to main memory or to unallocated space on disks or tapes. Sometimes the browsing occurs after the previous job has finished. When a section of main memory is allocated to a process, the data from a previous job often remains in memory—it isn't usually erased by the system—and so it's available to a browser. The same applies to data stored in secondary storage.

Wire tapping is nothing new. Just as telephone lines can be tapped, so can most data communication lines. When wire tapping is passive, the unauthorized user is just listening to the transmission but isn't changing the contents. There are two reasons for passive tapping: to copy data while bypassing any authorization procedures and to collect specific information (such as **passwords**) that will permit the tapper to enter the system at a later date. In an unsecured wireless network environment, wire tapping is not difficult.

Active wire tapping is when the data being sent is modified. Two methods of active wire tapping are "between lines transmission" and "piggyback entry." Between lines doesn't alter the messages sent by the legitimate user, but it inserts additional messages into the communication line while the legitimate user is pausing. Piggyback entry intercepts and modifies the original messages. This can be done by breaking the communication line and routing the message to another computer that acts as the host. For example, the tapper could intercept a log-off message, return the expected acknowledgment of the log-off to the user, and then continue the interactive session with all the privileges of the original user—without anyone knowing.

Repeated trials describes the method used to enter systems by guessing authentic passwords. If an intruder knows the basic scheme for creating passwords such as length of password and symbols allowed to create it, then the system can be compromised with a program that systematically goes through all possible combinations until a valid combination is found. This isn't as long a process as one might think if the passwords are short or if the intruder learns enough about the intended victim/user, as shown in Table 11.3. Because the intruder doesn't need to break a specific password, the guessing of any user's password allows entry to the system and access to its resources.

No. of Alphabetic Characters	Possible Combinations	Human Attempt avg. time to discovery at 1 try/second	Computer Attempt avg. time to discovery at 1 million tries/second
1	26	13 seconds	.000013 seconds
2	$26^2 = 676$	6 minutes	.000338 seconds
3	$26^3 = 17576$	2.5 hours	.008788 seconds
8	$26^8 = 208,827,064,576$	6640 years	58 hours
10	$26^{10} = (1.4 \times 10)^{14}$	4.5 million years	4.5 years

(table 11.3)

Average time required for a human and computer to guess passwords up to ten alphabetic characters (A-Z) using brute force.

Trap doors, including backdoor passwords, are defined as unspecified and undocumented entry points to the system. It's possible that trap doors can be caused by a flaw in the system design. More likely, they are installed by a system diagnostician or programmer for future use. Or, they are incorporated into the system code by a destructive virus or by a Trojan horse program—one that's seemingly innocuous but that executes hidden instructions. Regardless of the reason for its existence, a trap door leaves the system vulnerable to future intrusion.

Trash collection, also known as dumpster diving, is an evening pastime for those who enjoy perusing anything and everything thrown out by system users—the discarded disks, CDs, faxes, printer ribbons, as well as printouts of source code, programs, memory dumps, and notes. They all can yield important information that can be used to enter the system illegally. It's recommended that system administrators adopt a policy of routinely shredding all work that can conceivably contain data, code, passwords, access information, Web site development information, or clues to the organization's financial workings. The importance of this obvious precaution can't be overstated.

Legally, it's important for system defenders to know that malicious attacks on computers may violate state and federal law under the Federal Computer Fraud and Abuse Act of 1986. Those convicted have been sentenced to significant fines and jail terms, as well as confiscation of their computer equipment. In the U.S., attempts to intrude into your system should be reported to the Federal Bureau of Investigation.

Viruses

A **virus** is defined as a small program written to alter the way a computer operates, without the permission or knowledge of the user. A virus must meet two criteria:

- It must be self-executing. Often, this means placing its own code in the path of another program.

• It must be self-replicating. Usually, this is accomplished by copying itself from infected files to clean files as shown in Figure 11.2. Viruses can infect desktop computers and network servers alike and spread each time the host file is executed.

(a)   (b)

(figure 11.2)

A file infector virus attacks a clean file (a) by attaching a small program to it (b), which executes every time the infected file runs.

Viruses are usually written to attack a certain operating system. Therefore, it's unusual for the same virus code to successfully attack a Linux workstation and a Windows server. Writers of virus code usually exploit a known vulnerability in the operating system software, hence the need to keep it correctly updated with patches—something we discuss in Chapter 12.

Some viruses are designed to significantly damage the infected computer such as by deleting or corrupting files, or reformatting the hard disk. Others are not so malicious but merely make their presence known by delivering text, video, or audio messages to the computer's user. However, no virus can be considered benign because all viruses confiscate valuable memory and storage space required by legitimate programs, and often cause system failures and data loss. There are five recognized types of viruses, as shown in Table 11.4.

(table 11.4)	Type of Virus	Description
Five types of viruses	File infector virus	Infects files on the computer, normally executable files such as .exe and .com files commonly found on Microsoft operating systems. These viruses commonly become resident in memory and then infect any clean executable program that runs on that computer.
	Boot sector virus	Infects the boot record, the system area of a floppy disk or hard drive. These viruses activate whenever the user boots up (powers on) the computer. Most boot sector viruses were written for MS-DOS, but other operating systems are potential targets.
	Master boot record virus	Infects the boot record of a disk, saving a legitimate copy of the master boot record in a different location on the volume.
	Multipartite virus	Infects both the boot record and program files, making them especially difficult to repair. Successful removal requires that all instances of the virus be removed at once, on the boot records as well as all instances of files infected with the virus. Should any instance of the infection remain, the virus will infect the system again.
	Macro virus	Infects data files (such as word processing documents, spreadsheets, etc.), though newer versions now infect other program files as well. Computer users are advised to disable the automatic execution of macros on files they don't completely trust.

Viruses spread via a wide variety of applications and have even been found in legitimate shrink-wrapped software. In one case, a virus was inadvertently picked up at a trade show by a developer who unknowingly allowed it to infect the finished code of a completed commercial software package just before it was marketed. The package was quickly recalled.

In one bizarre example, a virus was distributed to tourists in the Middle East embedded in part of an illegally copied (and illegally bought) software package. Reportedly, the sellers told authorities that they did it to teach the buyers a lesson in ethics.

A macro virus works by attaching itself to the template (such as NORMAL.DOT) which in turn is attached to word processing documents. Once the template file is infected, every subsequent document created on that template is infected. The first reports of a macro virus attacking users of Microsoft Word date from 1995. Users of most word processing applications have the option of disabling automatic macros as a precaution against these intruders.

Worms

A **worm** is a memory-resident program that copies itself from one system to the next without requiring the aid of an infected program file. The immediate result of a worm is slower processing time of legitimate work because the worm siphons off processing time and memory space.

The first widely destructive worm infected more than 6,000 systems over several days in 1988. That program, called the Morris Worm, was installed from a university computer and spread overnight to hundreds of other universities. Worms are especially destructive on networks, where they hoard critical system resources such as main memory and processor time.

Trojan Horses

A **Trojan horse** is a virus that's disguised as a legitimate or harmless program that sometimes carries within itself the means to allow the program's creator to secretly access the user's system. Intruders have been known to capture user passwords by using a Trojan horse to replace the standard login program on the computer with an identical fake login that captures keystrokes. Once it's installed, it works like this:

1. The user sees a login prompt and types in the user ID.
2. The user sees a password prompt and types in the password.
3. The rogue program records both the user ID and password and sends a typical login failure message to the user. Then the program stops running and returns control to the legitimate program.
4. Now, the user sees the legitimate login prompt and retypes the user ID.
5. The user sees the legitimate password prompt and retypes the password.
6. Finally, the user gains access to the system, unaware that the rogue program has stored the first attempt and recorded the user ID and password.

This series of events would look something like the dialog shown in Figure 11.3. A similar technique using simulated Windows screens is also easy to program.

Later, at a convenient time, the Trojan horse owner retrieves the file with its list of valid user IDs and passwords, perhaps even a root password, which would allow access to sensitive administrative functions.

Rogue software doesn't need to be planted by someone outside the organization. In a California case, an employee planted a Trojan horse in his employer's system before quitting his job. The code, called Cleanup, was designed to erase a program he'd written on the job to track the availability and prices of parts for Atlas missiles. At its conclusion, the program was instructed to erase itself. Reportedly, the

(figure 11.3)

Two attempts by a legiti-mate user to access the system. The first attempt (shown shaded) shows a Trojan horse capturing the user's id and pass-word. The program then returns the user to the real system prompt (login:) to try again.

```
login: kat1422

password: ********

Error:login incorrect, please try again.

Login: kat1422

password: ********

Last login: Wed Nov 17 11:12:13
```

programmer hoped to become a consultant, and he planned to work for his former employer reconstructing the program he had written and then erased. The plan was foiled when another technician discovered the bad code and removed it before the scheduled date of operation. The programmer was indicted in federal court for his actions (Denning, 1999).

Bombs

A **logic bomb** is a destructive program with a fuse—a certain triggering event (such as a certain keystroke or connection with the Internet). A logic bomb often spreads un-noticed throughout a network until a predetermined event when it goes off and does its damage.

A **time bomb** is similar to a logic bomb but is triggered by a specific time, such as a day of the year. For example, the time bomb called the Michelangelo virus, first discovered in 1991, was one of the **first logic bombs** to prompt warnings to all computer users by the popular media. The code was designed to execute on the anniversary of the birth of the artist Michelangelo (March 6, 1475). The code was designed to execute when an infected computer was booted up on the trigger date (March 6 of any year) and overwrite the first 17 sectors on heads 0-3 on the first 256 tracks of the disk the infected machine's disk. Once infected, the bomb made subsequent boots very difficult.

Blended Threats

A **blended threat** combines into one program the characteristics of other attacks, including a virus, worm, Trojan Horse, **spyware**, and other malicious code. That is, this single program uses a variety of tools to attack systems and spread to others. Because the threat from these programs is so diverse, the only defense against them is a comprehensive security plan that includes multiple layers of protection. A blended threat shows the following characteristics:

- Harms the affected system. For example, it might launch a denial of service attack at a target IP address, deface a Web server, or plant Trojan horse programs for later execution.
- Spreads to other systems using multiple methods. For example, it might scan for vulnerabilities to compromise a system, such as embedding code in HTML files on a server, infect the systems of visitors who visit a compromised Web site, or send unauthorized e-mail from compromised servers with a worm attachment.
- Attacks other systems from multiple points. For example: inject malicious code into the .exe files on a system, raise the privilege level of an intruder's guest account, create world-readable and world-writeable access to private files, and add bogus script code to HTML files. (We discuss world access later in this chapter.)
- Propagates without human intervention. For example, it might continuously scan the Internet for vulnerable servers that are unpatched and open to attack.
- Exploits vulnerabilities of target systems. For example it might take advantage of operating system problems (such as buffer overflows), Web page validation vulnerabilities on input screens, and commonly known default passwords to gain unauthorized access.

When the threat includes all or many of these characteristics, no single tool can protect a system. Only a combination of defenses in combination with regular patch management (discussed in Chapter 12), can hope to protect the system adequately.

System Protection

There is no single guaranteed method of protecting your system from assault because invasive programs evolve over time, becoming more and more adept at evading the increasingly sophisticated system defenses. System vulnerabilities include file downloads, e-mail exchange, vulnerable firewalls, improperly configured Internet connections, etc. For that reason, system management responsibilities need to include continuous attention to security issues.

System protection is multifaceted. Four protection methods are discussed here: installing antivirus software (and running it regularly), using firewalls (and keeping them up-to-date), ensuring that only authorized individuals access the system, and taking advantage of encryption technology when the overhead required to implement it is mandated by the risk.

Antivirus Software

Antivirus software can be purchased to protect systems from attack by malicious software. The level of protection is usually in proportion to the importance of its data.

Medical data should be highly protected. Student-written computer programs probably don't deserve the same level of security.

Software to combat viruses can be preventive or diagnostic, or both. Preventive programs may calculate a checksum for each production program, putting the values in a master file. Later, before a program is executed, its checksum is compared with the master. Generally, diagnostic software compares file sizes (checking for added code when none is expected), looks for replicating instructions, and searches for unusual file activity. Some software may look for certain specific instructions and monitor the way the programs execute. But remember: soon after these packages are marketed, system intruders start looking for ways to thwart them. Hence, only the most current software can be expected to uncover the latest viruses. In other words, old software will find only old viruses.

Information about current viruses is available from vendors and government agencies dedicated to system security, such as those listed in Table 11.5.

<table>
<tr><td>(table 11.5)</td><td>Web Site</td><td>Organization</td></tr>
<tr><td>Systems security is a rapidly changing field. Current information can be found at these Web sites and many more. Sites are listed in alphabetical order.</td><td>http://csrc.nist.gov</td><td>Computer Security Division of the National Institute of Standards and Technology</td></tr>
<tr><td></td><td>www.cert.org</td><td>CERT Coordination Center</td></tr>
<tr><td></td><td>www.ciac.org</td><td>U.S. DOE Computer Incident Advisory Capability</td></tr>
<tr><td></td><td>www.mcafee.com</td><td>McAfee, Inc.</td></tr>
<tr><td></td><td>www.sans.org</td><td>SANS Institute</td></tr>
<tr><td></td><td>www.symantec.com</td><td>Symantec Corp.</td></tr>
<tr><td></td><td>www.us-cert.gov</td><td>U.S. Computer Emergency Readiness Team</td></tr>
</table>

While antivirus software is capable of repairing files infected with a virus, it is generally unable to repair worms, Trojan horses, or blended threats because of the structural differences between viruses and worms/Trojans. A virus works by infecting an otherwise clean file, as shown in Figure 11.4. Therefore, antivirus software can sometimes remove the infection and leave the remainder intact. On the other hand, a worm or Trojan horse is malicious code in its entirety. That is, the entire body of the software code contained in a worm or Trojan horse is threatening and must be removed as a whole.

The only way to remove a Trojan horse is to remove the entire body of the malicious program. For example, if a poker game, available for free download over the Internet, is a worm that steals system IDs and passwords, there is no way to cleanse the game of the bad code and save the rest. The poker game must go.

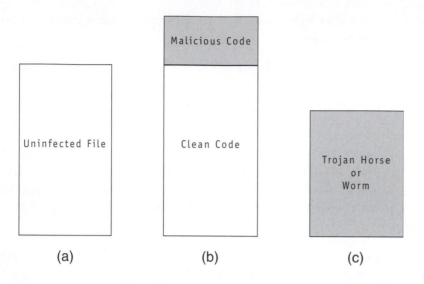

(figure 11.4)

The clean file (a) is unin-fected. After it's infected with a file infector virus (b), the file is larger and the virus is executed each time the program is exe-cuted. A Trojan horse or worm (c) consists entirely of malicious code.

Firewalls

Network assaults include compromised Web servers, circumvented firewalls, and FTP and Telnet sites accessed by unauthorized users, to name a few.

A **firewall** is a set of hardware and/or software designed to protect a system by disguising its IP address from outsiders who don't have authorization to access it or ask for information about it. A firewall sits between the Internet and the network, as shown in Figure 11.5, blocking curious inquiries and potentially dangerous intrusions from outside the system. The typical tasks of the firewall are to:

• log activities that access the Internet

• maintain **access control** based on the senders' or receivers' IP addresses

• maintain access control based on the services that are requested

• hide the internal network from unauthorized users requesting network information

• verify that virus protection is installed and being enforced

• perform authentication based on the source of a request from the Internet

The two fundamental mechanisms used by the firewall to perform these tasks are packet filtering and proxy servers. Using **packet filtering,** the firewall reviews the header information for incoming and outgoing Internet packets to verify that the source address, destination address, and protocol are all correct. For example, if a packet arrives from the Internet (outside the network) with an internal source address (which should be from inside the network), the firewall would be expected to refuse it entry (Gollmann, 1999).

A **proxy server** hides important network information from outsiders by making the network server invisible. To do so, the proxy server intercepts the request for access to the network, decides if it is a valid request and, if so, then passes the request to the appropriate server that can fulfill the request—all without revealing the makeup of the network, the servers, or other information that might reside on them. Likewise, if information is to be passed from the network to the Internet, the proxy server relays the transmission but without revealing anything about the network. Proxy servers are invisible to the users but are critical to the success of the firewall.

Authentication

Authentication is verification that an individual trying to access a system is authorized to do so. One popular authentication tool is **Kerberos**, a network authentication protocol developed as part of the Athena Project at MIT. The name is taken from the three-headed dog of Greek mythology that guarded the gates of Hades.

To answer the need for password encryption to improve network security, Kerberos was designed to provide strong authentication for client/server applications. A free open-source implementation of this protocol (under copyright permissions) is available from MIT (www.mit.edu/kerberos/) or for purchase from numerous distributors.

The Kerberos protocol uses strong **cryptography** (the science of coding messages) so that a client can prove its identity to a server, and vice versa, across an insecure network connection. Then, once authentication is completed, both client and server can encrypt all of their subsequent communications to assure privacy and data integrity.

In simplest form, here's how Kerberos works, as shown in Figure 11.6.

1. When you (the client) want to access a server that requires a Kerberos ticket, you request authentication from the Kerberos Authentication Server, which creates a session key based on your password. This key also serves as your encryption key.

2. Next, you are sent to a Ticket Granting Server (this can be the same physical server but a different logical unit) which creates a ticket valid for access to the server.

3. Next, your ticket is sent to the server where it can be rejected or accepted. Once accepted, you are free to interact with the server for the specified period of time. The ticket is time stamped so you can make additional requests using the same ticket within a certain time period but must be reauthenticated after the time period ends. This design feature is to limit the likelihood that someone will later use your ticket without your knowledge.

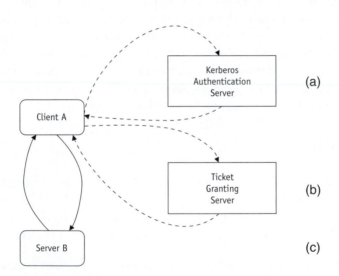

(figure 11.6)

Using Kerberos, when client A attempts to access server B, the user is authenticated (a) and receives a ticket for the session (b). Once the ticket is issued, client and server can communicate at will (c). Without the ticket, access is not granted.

Because the user gains access using a ticket, there's no need for the user's password to pass through the network, thus improving the protection of network passwords.

An essential part of maintaining a Kerberos protocol is the systematic revocation of access rights from clients who no longer deserve to have access. For this reason, the administrators of the Kerberos Authentication Server as well as the Ticket Granting Server must keep their databases updated and accurate. By keeping records of access revocation, the administrator can spot trends and anticipate the need for user education.

For example, if the organization hires new consultants in February of each year, which is followed by numerous calls of access revocation in March and April, as shown in Figure 11.7, then scheduling user education for new employees in February can be a proactive, cost effective move, thereby reducing the reason for revocation.

(figure 11.7)

Sample system adminis-trator report. By tracking the reasons for revoking user access, the adminis-trator can target activities to the user population, such as retraining and password management.

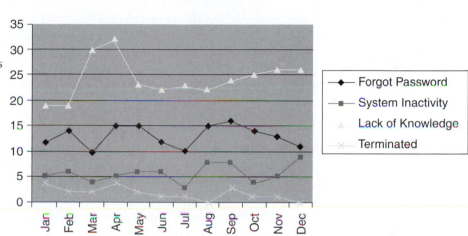

Encryption

The most extreme protection for sensitive data is with **encryption**—putting it into a secret code. Total network encryption, also called communications encryption, is the most extreme form—that's when all communications with the system are encrypted. The system then decrypts them for processing. To communicate with another system, the data is encrypted, transmitted, decrypted, and processed.

Partial encryption is less extreme and may be used between a network's entry and exit points or other vulnerable parts of its communication system. Storage encryption means that the information is stored in encrypted form and decrypted before it's read or used.

There are two disadvantages to encryption. It increases the system's overhead and the system becomes totally dependent on the encryption process itself—if you lose the key, you've lost the data forever. But if the system must be kept secure, then this procedure might be warranted.

How Encryption Works

The way to understand cryptography is to first understand the role of a public key and a private key. The **private key** is a pair of two prime numbers (usually with 75 or more digits each) chosen by the person who wants to receive a private message. The two prime numbers are multiplied together, forming a third number with 150 or more digits. The person who creates this private key is the only one who knows which two prime numbers were used to create it. What are the chances that someone else can guess the two prime numbers? Very slim, because there is no known formula for factoring large numbers greater than 80 digits, and this product has at least 150 digits. Even with brute force computation on a supercomputer, the task would take decades (as of this writing, at least).

Once the message receiver has the product, known as the **public key**, it can be posted in any public place, even an online directory, for anyone to see, because the private key can't be decoded from the public key.

Then, anyone who wants to send a confidential message to the receiver uses encryption software and inserts the public key as a variable. The software then scrambles the message before it's sent to the receiver. Once received, the receiver uses the private key in the encryption software and the confidential message is revealed. Should someone else receive the encrypted message and attempt to open it with a private key that is incorrect, the resulting message would be scrambled, unreadable code.

Sniffers and Spoofing

If sensitive data is sent over a network or the Internet in **cleartext**, without encryption, it becomes vulnerable at numerous sites across the network. **Packet sniffers**, also called sniffers, are programs that reside on computers attached to the network.

They peruse data packets as they pass by, examine each one for specific information, and log copies of interesting packets for more detailed examination. Sniffing is particularly problematic in wireless networks. Anyone with a wireless device can detect a wireless network that's within range. If the network is passing cleartext packets, it's quite easy to intercept, read, modify, and resend them. The information sought ranges from passwords, social security numbers, and credit card numbers to industrial secrets and marketing information. This vulnerability is a fundamental shortcoming of cleartext transmission over the Internet (Denning, 1999).

Wireless security is a special area of system security that is too vast to cover here. Readers are encouraged to pursue the subject in the current literature for the latest research, tools, and best practices.

Spoofing is a security threat that relies on cleartext transmission whereby the assailant falsifies the IP addresses of an Internet server by changing the address recorded in packets it sends over the Internet. This technique is useful when unauthorized users want to disguise themselves as friendly sites. For example, to guard confidential information on an internal network (intranet), some Web servers allow access only to users from certain sites; however, by spoofing the IP address, the server could inadvertently admit unauthorized users.

Password Management

The most basic techniques used to protect hardware and software investments are good passwords and careful user training, but this is not as simple as it might appear. Passwords are forgettable, unlikely to be changed often, commonly shared, and considered bothersome by many people.

Password Construction

Passwords are one of the easiest and most effective protection schemes to implement, but only if they're used correctly. A good password is unusual, memorable, and changed often, usually every 30 to 90 days. Ideally, the password should be a combination of characters and numbers, something that's easy for the user to remember but difficult for someone else to guess. The password should be committed to memory, never written down, and not included in a script file to log on to a network.

Password files are normally stored in encrypted form so they are not readable by casual browsers. To verify a password, the system will accept the user's entry in cleartext, encrypt it, and compare the encrypted version to the version stored in the password file for that user, as shown in Figure 11.8.

The length of the password has a direct effect on the ability of the password to survive password cracking attempts. The longer passwords are, the better. For example, if the system administrator mandates that all passwords must be exactly eight characters long and contain any lowercase letters such as "abcdefgh," the possible combinations number 26^8. Likewise, if the rule mandates ten characters of lowercase letters, the combinations total 26^{10}. However, if the rule allows eight characters from among 95 printable characters, the combinations jump to 95^8, as shown in Table 11.6.

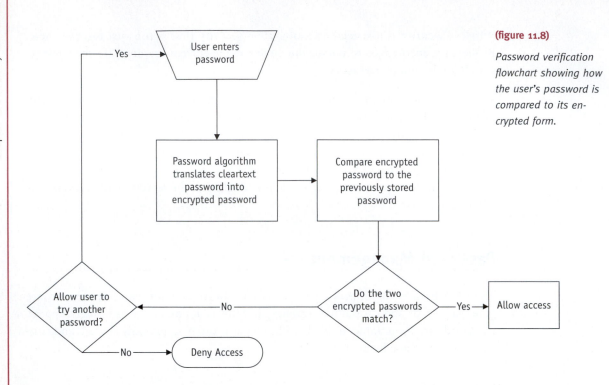

(figure 11.8)

Password verification flowchart showing how the user's password is compared to its encrypted form.

Length of Password in Characters

(table 11.6)

Number of combinations of passwords depending on their length and available character set.

	2	4	6	8	10	12
ASCII characters	128^2	128^4	128^6	128^8	128^{10}	128^{12}
Printable characters	95^2	95^4	95^6	95^8	95^{10}	95^{12}
Alphanumeric characters	62^2	62^4	62^6	62^8	62^{10}	62^{12}
Lowercase letters and numbers	36^2	36^4	36^6	36^8	36^{10}	36^{12}
Lowercase letters	26^2	26^4	26^6	26^8	26^{10}	26^{12}

There are several reliable techniques for generating a good password:

- Use a minimum of eight characters, including numbers and nonalphanumeric characters.
- Create a misspelled word or join bits of phrases into a word that's easy to remember.
- Follow a certain pattern on the keyboard, generating new passwords easily by starting your sequence with a different letter each time.
- Create acronyms from memorable sentences, such as MDWB4YOIA, which stands for: "My Dog Will Be 4 Years Old In April."

- If your operating system differentiates between upper- and lowercase characters (as UNIX and Linux do), take advantage of that feature by using both in the password: MDwb4YOia.
- Never use a word that's included in any dictionary.

Dictionary attack is the term used to describe a method of breaking encrypted passwords. Its requirements are simple: a copy of the encrypted password file and the algorithm used to encrypt the passwords. With these two tools, the intruder runs a software program that takes every word in the dictionary, runs it through the password encryption algorithm, and compares the encrypted result to the encrypted passwords contained in the file. If both encrypted versions match, then the intruder knows that this dictionary word was used as a legitimate password.

One technique used by some operating systems to make passwords harder to guess is to "salt" user passwords with extra random bits to make them less vulnerable to dictionary attacks. Here's how it works. The user enters the desired password, which is then encrypted. Then the system assigns the user a unique combination of bits (called the salt) which are tacked on the end of the encrypted password. That means, the stored combination of zeros and ones contains the encrypted password combined with a unique salt. Therefore, if an intruder downloads the list of encrypted passwords, the intruder will not only need to guess the password, but also needs to guess the random salt. This is something that's much more difficult and time consuming to do than merely guessing obvious passwords (Denning, 1999).

Password Alternatives

As an alternative to passwords, some systems have integrated use of a **smart card**—a credit card-sized calculator that requires both "something you have and something you know." The smart card displays a constantly changing multidigit number that's synchronized with an identical number generator in the system. To enter the correct password, the user must type in the number that appears at that moment on the smart card. For added protection, the user then enters a secret code. The user is admitted to the system only if both number and code are validated. Using this scheme, an intruder needs more than either the card or the code because unless both are valid, entry is denied.

Another alternative is **biometrics,** the science and technology of identifying individuals based on the unique biological characteristics of each person. Current research focuses on analysis of the human face, fingerprints, hand measurements, iris/retina, and voice prints. Biometric devices often consist of a scanner or other device to gather the necessary data about the user, software to convert the data into a form that can be compared and stored, and a database to keep the stored information from all authorized users. One of the strengths of biometrics is that it positively identifies the person being scanned.

For example, a fingerprint has about 35 discriminators—factors that set one person's fingerprint apart from someone else's. Even better, the iris has about 260 discriminators and is unique from right eye to left. Not even identical twins have the same iris pattern. A critical factor with biometrics is reducing the margin of error so authorized users are rarely turned away and those who are not authorized are caught at the door (Denning, 1999). At this writing, the technology to implement biometric authentication is expensive, but there's every indication that it will become widespread in the years to come.

Social Engineering

Historically, intruders gained access to systems by using innovative techniques to crack user passwords such as using default passwords, backdoor passwords, or trying words found in a file of dictionary terms. They also use a technique called **social engineering**, which means looking in and around the user's desk for a written reminder, trying the user logon ID as the password, searching logon scripts, and even telephoning friends and co-workers to learn the names of a user's family members, pets, vacation destinations, favorite hobbies, car model, etc.

It even works with military targets. One such instance involved a computer system in a remote location that was reported to be exceptionally secure. To test its security, a systems consultant was hired to try to break into the system. She started by opening an unprotected document that told her where the computer was located. Then she telephoned the base and learned the name of the base commanding officer. Then she learned the name of the commander's secretary. Then she called the data center, masquerading as the secretary, and informed them that the commander was having difficulty accessing the data. When the data center personnel were reluctant to help, the consultant got angry and demanded action. They responded with access so the "commander" could use the network. Soon the consultant was on the system with what appeared to be classified data. With that, the officers in charge of the exercise pulled the plug and sent the consultant on her way (Denning, 1999).

Phishing (pronounced fishing) is a form of social engineering whereby an intruder pretends to be a legitimate entity and contacts unwary users asking them to reconfirm their personal and/or financial information. In 2003, many customers of eBay, Inc. received an e-mail saying that their account had been compromised and would be closed. Attached to the e-mail was a link to a page that looked like a genuine eBay Web page where they could reenter their credit card data, ATM personal identification numbers, social security number, date of birth, and their mother's maiden name. The owner of the site then had all the information required to steal the identity of the people who responded (Computerworld, 2004).

Default passwords pose unique vulnerabilities because they are widely known among system attackers but are a necessary tool for vendors. Default passwords are routinely shipped with hardware or software. They're convenient for the manufacturer because they give field service workers supervisor-level access to fix problem equipment on site or using a telecommunications connection. System intruders also find them useful because if they have not been changed, they allow powerful access to the system. Lists of default passwords are routinely passed from one hacker to the next, often serving as a starting point for an attack. To protect the system, managers should periodically identify and change all default passwords on their hardware and software.

Ethics

What is ethical behavior? In briefest form it is this: Be good. Do good.

At least two professional associations have addressed the issue of **ethics**—the rules or standards of behavior that members of the computer-using community are expected to follow, demonstrating the principles of right and wrong. In 1992 the IEEE and the Association for Computing Machinery (ACM) issued a standard of ethics for the global computing community.

The apparent lack of ethics in computing is a significant departure from other professions. For example, we take for granted that our medical doctor will keep our records private, but many of us don't have the same confidence in the individuals working for companies that keep our credit records or the intruders who break into those systems. Although ethics is a subject that's not often addressed in computer science classes, the implications are so vast they can't be ignored by systems administrators or users.

At issue are the seemingly conflicting needs of users: the individual's need for privacy, the organization's need to protect its proprietary information, and the public's right to know as illustrated in freedom of information laws.

For the system's owner, ethical lapses by authorized or unauthorized users can have severe consequences:

- Illegally copied software can result in lawsuits and fines of several times the retail price of each product for each transgression. Several industry associations publish toll-free numbers encouraging disgruntled employees to turn in their employers who use illegal software.
- Plagiarism, the unauthorized copying of copyrighted work (including but not limited to music, movies, textbook material, databases), is illegal and punishable by law in the United States as well as in many other nations. When the original work is on paper, most users know the proper course of action, but when the original is in electronic form, some people don't recognize the ethical issues involved.

- Eavesdropping on e-mail, data, or voice communications is sometimes illegal and usually unwarranted, except under certain circumstances. If calls or messages must be monitored, the participants should always be notified before the monitoring begins.

- Cracking, sometimes called hacking, is gaining access to another computer system to monitor or change data, and it's seldom an ethical activity. Although it's seen as a sport by certain people, each break-in should cause the system's owner and users to question the validity of the system's data.

- Unethical use of technology, defined as unauthorized access to private or protected computer systems or electronic information, is a murky area of the law, but it's clearly the wrong thing to do. Legally, the justice system has great difficulty keeping up with each specific form of unauthorized access because the technology changes so quickly. Therefore, system owners can't rely on the law for guidance. Instead, they must aggressively teach their users about what is and is not ethical behavior.

How can users be taught to behave ethically? A continuing series of security awareness and ethics communications to computer users is more effective than a single announcement. Specific activities can include the following:

- Publish policies that clearly state which actions will and will not be condoned.

- Teach a regular seminar on the subject including real-life case histories.

- Conduct open discussions of ethical questions such as: Is it okay to read someone else's e-mail? Is it right for someone else to read your e-mail? Is it ethical for a competitor to read your data? Is it okay if someone scans your bank account? Is it right for someone to change the results of your medical test? Is it acceptable for someone to copy your software program and put it on the Internet? Is it acceptable for someone to copy a government document and put it on the Internet?

For a guide to ethical behavior, see excerpts from the ACM Code of Ethics and Professional Conduct in Appendix D of this book or visit www.acm.org.

Conclusion

We can't overemphasize the importance of keeping the system secure. After all, the system is only as good as the integrity of the data that's stored on it. A single breach of security—whether catastrophic or not, whether accidental or not—damages the system's integrity. And damaged integrity threatens the viability of the best-designed system, its managers, its designers, and its users. Therefore, vigilant security precautions are essential.

So far in this text we've discussed each manager and each operating system function in isolation, but in reality, system performance depends on the combined effort of each piece. In the next chapter we'll look at the system as a whole and examine how each piece contributes to, or detracts from, overall system performance.

Key Terms

access control: the control of user access to a network or computer system.

antivirus software: software that is designed to detect and recover from attacks by viruses and worms. It is usually part of a system protection software package.

authentication: the means by which a system verifies that the individual attempting to access the system is authorized to do so.

backup: the process of making long-term archival file storage copies of files on the system.

blended threat: a system threat that combines into one program the characteristics of other attacks, including a virus, worm, Trojan horse, spyware, and other malicious code.

biometrics: the science and technology of identifying authorized users based on their biological characteristics.

browsing: a system security violation in which unauthorized users are allowed to search through secondary storage directories or files for information they should not have the privilege to read.

cleartext: in cryptography, a method of transmitting data without encryption, in text that is readable by anyone who sees it.

cryptography: the science of coding messages or text so unauthorized users cannot read them.

denial of service (DoS) attack: an attack on a network that makes it unavailable to perform the functions it was designed to do. This can be done by flooding the server with meaningless requests or information.

dictionary attack: the technique by which an intruder attempts to guess user passwords by trying words found in a dictionary.

encryption: translation of a message or data item from its original form to an encoded form, thus hiding its meaning and making it unintelligible without the key to decode it. Used to improve system security and data protection.

ethics: the rules or standards of behavior that individuals are expected to follow demonstrating the principles of right and wrong.

firewall: a set of hardware and software that disguises the internal network address of a computer or network to control how clients from outside can access the organization's internal servers.

Kerberos: MIT-developed authentication system that allows network managers to administer and manage user authentication at the network level.

logic bomb: a virus with a trigger, usually an event, that causes it to execute.

packet filtering: reviewing incoming and outgoing Internet packets to verify that the source address, destination address, and protocol are correct. Usually a function of a firewall.

packet sniffer: software that intercepts Internet data packets sent in cleartext and searches them for information, such as passwords.

password: a user-defined access control method. Typically a word or character string that a user must specify in order to be allowed to log on to a computer system.

phishing: a technique used to trick consumers into revealing personal information by appearing as a legitimate entity.

private key: a tool that's used to decrypt a message that was encrypted using a public key.

proxy server: a server positioned between an internal network and an external network or the Internet to screen all requests for information and prevent unauthorized access to network resources.

public key: a tool that's used to encrypt a message, to be decoded later using a private key.

recovery: the steps that must be taken when a system is assaulted, to recover system operability and, in the best case, recover any lost data.

smart card: a small, credit-card-sized device that uses cryptographic technology to control access to computers and computer networks. Each smart card has its own personal identifier, which is known only to the user, as well as its own stored and encrypted password.

social engineering: a technique whereby system intruders gain access to information about a legitimate user to learn active passwords, sometimes by calling the user and posing as a system technician.

spoofing: the creation of false IP addresses in the headers of data packets sent over the Internet, sometimes with the intent of gaining access when it would not otherwise be granted.

spyware: a blended threat that covertly collects data about system users and sends it to a designated repository.

system survivability: the capability of a system to fulfill its mission, in a timely manner, in the presence of attacks, failures, or accidents.

time bomb: a virus with a trigger linked to a certain year, month, day, or time that causes it to execute.

trap door: an unspecified and undocumented entry point to the system, which represents a significant security risk.

Trojan horse: a malicious computer program with unintended side effects that are not intended by the user who executes the program.

virus: a program that replicates itself by incorporating itself into other programs, including those in secondary storage, that are shared among other computer systems.

wire tapping: a system security violation in which unauthorized users monitor or modify a user's transmission.

worm: a computer program that replicates itself and is self-propagating in main memory.

Exercises

Research Topic

Research current literature to find the status of research on biometric science and technology. List at least five commercially available products. How much do they cost? What industries are finding biometrics an attractive alternative to traditional authentication practices? Are they making money for the vendors who sell them? Cite your sources.

Exercises

1. Give three examples of excellent passwords and explain why each would be a good choice to protect a system from unauthorized users.

2. Give three examples of inadequate passwords and explain why each would be a poor choice to protect a system from unauthorized users.

3. Explain the similarities and differences between a file infector virus and a macro virus, including the types of files each infects.

4. System managers can't protect their resources without recognizing all threats and even learning to think like an intruder. Knowing that, and knowing that it's unethical to use a computer system without proper authorization, imagine that you are an unauthorized user who wants to break into your system. Describe how you might begin guessing the password of a legitimate user.

5. As a follow-up to the previous question, identify a friend who has chosen at least one computer password. On a piece of paper, list 20 possible passwords you might use if you were trying to access the friend's system. Then show the list to your friend and ask if any of your guesses were correct. You might try combinations of names of family members and friends, favorite hobbies, automobiles, pets, birthdays, slang terms, favorite sayings, etc.

6. Imagine that you are manager of a university computing center. List at least three reasons that you would give to convince a busy, reluctant staff member to

perform regular backups and manage your system's archives appropriately, and briefly elaborate.

7. Your medical records deserve privacy and yet, in an emergency, it's to your benefit if the attending healthcare professionals have access to your history, medications, etc. Acknowledging the need for privacy and the need for accessibility, discuss how you would like to have your medical records protected.

8. Many users are required to log into several networks and thus have multiple passwords, which are difficult to remember. One alternative is to use the same password on all networks. Another is to keep a master list showing each network and its current password. If the list is kept in a data file, it would be protected by its own password. Discuss the advantages and disadvantages of each course of action. Finally, discuss a third alternative to this dilemma.

Advanced Exercises

9. List 20 viruses and research three in detail, describing which files they infect, how they spread, and their intended effects.

10. Identify three sets of security parameters (one each for good, better, and best protection) for a computer that holds a university's registration information. Consider not only the operating system, but the protection software, access controls, and the room in which the computer is located. Then make a recommendation based on the need for security vs. the cost of that security.

11. Using information from the CERT Coordination Center (www.cert.org), identify the latest vulnerability for an operating system of your choice. List the threat, the criticality of the threat, the potential impact, the suggested solution, the systems that are affected, and the actions you would take as a system administrator.

12. The HIPAA (Health Insurance Portability and Accountability Act of 1996) imposed stringent security requirements on the U.S. health care industry. Identify the requirements for data transmissions between networks and the role of encryption, if any, in those transmissions.

13. Wireless LANs pose unique challenges for system operators because of their accessibility. Imagine that you are the systems administrator for a wireless network that is used in a scientific research setting. Identify the five biggest security challenges and how you would address each of them in spite of your a limited budget.

14. With identity theft becoming widespread, many organizations have moved to secure the social security numbers of their customers, suppliers, and employers. Discuss how you would change the system if you were the administrator for a college campus and student records were accessed using the student identification number that was identical to their social security number.

Chapter 12

System Management

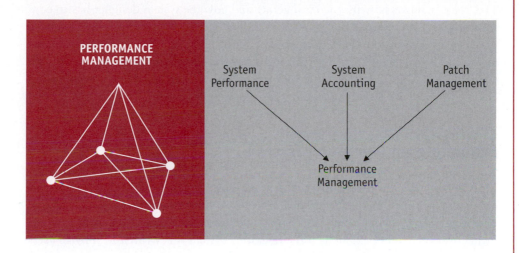

There is no such thing as a single problem; ... all problems are interrelated.

Saul D. Alinsky (1909-1972)

Learning Objectives

After completing this chapter, you should be able to describe:

• The tradeoffs to be considered when attempting to improve overall system performance

• The roles of system measurement tools such as positive and negative feedback loops

• Two system monitoring techniques

• The importance of sound accounting practices by system administrators

• The fundamentals of patch management

In Chapter 1 we introduced the overall operating system. In Chapters 2 through 8 we studied how each component works, and in Chapters 9 through 11 we discussed networking and security. In these chapters we examined each piece in isolation. In a real-life operating system, however, they don't work in isolation. Each component depends on the other components.

This chapter shows how they work together and how the system designer has to consider tradeoffs to improve the system's overall efficiency. We begin by showing how the designer can improve the performance of one component, the cost of that improvement, and how it might affect the performance of the remainder of the system. We conclude with some methods used to monitor and measure system performance, including the need to keep the operating system patched correctly.

Evaluating an Operating System

Most operating systems were designed to work with a certain piece of hardware, a category of processors, or specific groups of users. Although most evolved over time to operate multiple systems, most still favor some users and some computing environments over others. For example, if the operating system was written for novice users to meet basic requirements, it might not satisfy the demands of those more knowledgeable. Conversely, if it was written for programmers, then a business office's computer operator might find its commands obscure. If it serves the needs of a multiuser computer center, it might be inappropriate for a small computing center. Or, if it's written to provide rapid response time, it might provide poor throughput.

To evaluate an operating system, you need to understand its design goals, its history, how it communicates with its users, how its resources are managed, and what tradeoffs were made to achieve its goals. In other words, an operating system's strengths and weaknesses need to be weighed in relation to who will be using the operating system, on what hardware, and for what purpose.

Cooperation Among Components

The performance of any one resource depends on the performance of the other resources in the system. For example, memory management is intrinsically linked with device management when memory is used to buffer data between a very fast processor and slower secondary storage devices. Many other examples of interdependence have been shown throughout the preceding chapters.

If you managed an organization's computer system and were allocated money to upgrade it, where would you put the investment to best use? You might have several choices:

- More memory
- A faster CPU
- Additional processors
- More disk drives
- A RAID system
- New file management software

Or, if you bought a new system, what characteristics would you look for that would make it more efficient than the old one?

Any system improvement can be made only after extensive analysis of the needs of the system's resources, requirements, managers, and users. But whenever changes are made to a system, often you're trading one set of problems for another. The key is to consider the performance of the entire system and not just the individual components.

Role of Memory Management

Memory management schemes were discussed in Chapters 2 and 3. If you increase memory or change to another memory allocation scheme you must consider the actual operating environment in which the system will reside. There's a tradeoff between memory use and CPU overhead.

For example, if the system will be running student programs exclusively, and the average job is only three pages long, your decision to increase the size of virtual memory wouldn't speed up throughput because most jobs are too small to use virtual memory effectively. Remember, as the memory management algorithms grow more complex, the CPU overhead increases and overall performance can suffer. On the other hand, some operating systems perform remarkably better with additional memory.

Role of Processor Management

Processor management was covered in Chapters 4, 5, and 6. Let's say you decide to implement a multiprogramming system to increase your processor's utilization. If so, you'd have to remember that multiprogramming requires a great deal of synchronization between the Memory Manager, the Processor Manager, and the I/O devices. The tradeoff: better use of the CPU versus increased overhead, slower response time, and decreased throughput.

There are several problems to watch for, among them the following:

- A system could reach a saturation point if the CPU is fully utilized but is allowed to accept additional jobs—that would result in higher overhead and less time to run programs.
- Under heavy loads, the CPU time required to manage I/O queues (which under normal circumstances doesn't require a great deal of time) could dramatically increase the time required to run the jobs.
- With long queues forming at the channels, control units, and I/O devices, the CPU could be idle waiting for processes to finish their I/O.

Likewise, increasing the number of processors necessarily increases overhead required to manage multiple jobs among multiple processors. But under certain circumstances, the payoff can be faster turnaround time.

Role of Device Management

Device management, covered in Chapter 7, included several ways to improve I/O device utilization including buffering, blocking, and rescheduling I/O requests to optimize access times. But there are tradeoffs: each of these options also increases CPU overhead and uses additional memory space.

Blocking reduces the number of physical I/O requests, and that's good. But it's the CPU's responsibility to block and later deblock the records, and that's overhead.

Buffering helps the CPU match the slower speed of I/O devices, and vice versa, but it requires memory space for the buffers, either dedicated space or a temporarily allocated section of main memory, and this in turn reduces the level of processing that can take place. For example, if each buffer requires 64K of memory and the system requires two sets of double buffers, we've dedicated 256K of memory to the buffers. At a university this might equal, or exceed, the size of several student programs. The tradeoff is reduced multiprogramming versus better use of I/O devices.

Rescheduling requests is a technique that can help optimize I/O times; it's a queue reordering technique. But it's also an overhead function, so the speed of both the CPU and the I/O device must be weighed against the time it would take to execute the reordering algorithm. The following example illustrates this point. Table 12.1 lists three different CPUs with the speed for executing 1,000 instructions and four disk drives with their average access speeds.

(table 12.1)

A system with three CPUs and four disk drives of different speeds. Assuming the system requires 1,000 instructions to reorder I/O requests, the advantages of reordering vary depending on the combination of CPU and disk.

CPU	Time for 1000 Instructions
1	30.0 ms
2	1.2 ms
3	0.2 ms

Disk Drive	Access Speed
A	35 ms
B	10 ms
C	5 ms
D	50 ms

Using the data in Table 12.1 and assuming that a typical reordering module consists of 1,000 instructions, which combinations of one CPU and one disk drive warrant a reordering module? To learn the answer we need to compare disk access speeds before and after reordering.

For example, let's assume that a system consisting of CPU 1 and Disk Drive A has to access Track 1, Track 9, Track 1, and then Track 9, and that the arm is already located at Track 1. Without reordering, Drive A requires approximately 35 ms for each access: 35 + 35 + 35 = 105 ms, as shown in Figure 12.1.

(figure 12.1)

Using the combination of CPU 1 and Disk Drive A without reordering, data access requires 105 ms.

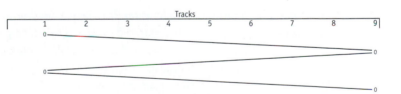

After reordering (which requires 30 ms), the arm can perform both accesses on Track 1 before traveling, in 35 ms, to Track 9 for the other two accesses, resulting in a speed nearly twice as fast: 30 + 35 = 65 ms, as shown in Figure 12.2. In this case, reordering would improve overall speed.

(figure 12.2)

Using CPU 1 and Disk Drive A after reordering (which takes 30ms), data access takes 35 ms.

However, when the same situation is faced by CPU 1 and the much faster Disk Drive C, we find the disk will again begin at Track 1 and make all four accesses in 15 ms (5 + 5 + 5) but, when it stops to reorder those accesses (which requires 30 ms), it takes 35 ms (30 + 5) to complete the task. Therefore, reordering requests isn't always warranted.

Remember, when the system is configured, the reordering algorithm is either always on or always off. It can't be changed by the systems operator without reconfiguration, so the initial setting, on or off, must be determined by evaluating the system on the average.

Role of File Management

The discussion of file management in Chapter 8 looked at how secondary storage allocation schemes help the user organize and access the files on the system. Almost every factor discussed in that chapter can affect overall system performance.

For example, file organization is an important consideration. If a file is stored noncontiguously and has several sections residing in widely separated cylinders of a disk pack, sequentially accessing all of its records could be a time-consuming task. Such a case would suggest that the files should be compacted, also called defragmented, so each section of the file resides near the others. However, recompaction takes CPU time and makes the files unavailable to users while it's being done.

Another file management issue that could affect retrieval time is the location of a volume's directory. For instance, some systems read the directory into main memory and hold it there until the user terminates the session. If we return to our example in Table 12.1 of the four disk drives of varying speeds, the first retrieval would take 35 ms when the system retrieves the directory for Drive A and loads it into memory. But every subsequent access would be performed at the CPU's much faster speed without the need to access the disk. Similar results would be achieved with each of the other disk drives, as shown in Table 12.2.

(table 12.2)

A system with four disk drives of different speeds and a CPU speed of 1.2 ms. If the file's directory is loaded into memory, access speed affects only the initial retrieval and none of the subsequent retrievals.

Disk Drive	Access Speed for First Retrieval	Subsequent Retrievals
A	35 ms	1.2 ms
B	10 ms	1.2 ms
C	5 ms	1.2 ms
D	50 ms	1.2 ms

This poses a problem if the system crashes before any modifications have been recorded permanently in secondary storage. In such a case, the I/O time that was saved by not having to access secondary storage every time the user requested to see the directory would be negated by not having current information in the user's directory.

Similarly, the location of a volume's directory on the disk might make a significant difference in the time it takes to access it. For example, if directories are stored on the outermost track, then, on average, the disk drive arm has to travel farther to access each file than it would if the directories were kept in the center tracks.

Overall, file management is closely related to the device on which the files are stored and designers must consider both issues at the same time when evaluating or modifying computer systems. Different schemes offer different flexibility, but the tradeoff for increased file flexibility is increased CPU overhead.

Role of Network Management

The discussion of network management in Chapters 9 and 10 examined the impact of adding networking capability to the operating system and the overall effect on system performance. The Network Manager routinely synchronizes the load among remote processors, determines message priorities, and tries to select the most efficient communication paths over multiple data communication lines

For example, when an application program requires data from a disk drive at a different location, the Network Manager attempts to provide this service seamlessly. When networked devices, such as printers, plotters, or disk drives, are required, the Network Manager has the responsibility of allocating and deallocating the required resources correctly.

In addition to the routine tasks handled by stand-alone operating systems, the Network Manager allows a network administrator to monitor the use of individual computers and shared hardware, and ensure compliance with software license agreements. The Network Manager also simplifies the process of updating data files and programs on networked computers by coordinating changes through a communications server instead of making the changes on each individual computer.

Measuring System Performance

Total system performance can be defined as the efficiency with which a computer system meets its goals—that is, how well it serves its users. However, system effciency is not easily measured because it's affected by three major components: user programs, operating system programs, and hardware. In addition, system performance can be very subjective and difficult to quantify—how, for instance, can anyone objectively gauge ease of use? While some aspects of ease of use can be quantified—for example, time to log in—the overall concept is difficult to quantify.

Even when performance is quantifiable, such as the number of disk accesses per minute, it isn't an absolute measure but a relative one based on the interactions of the three components and the workload being handled by the system.

Measurement Tools

Most designers and analysts rely on certain measures of system performance: throughput, capacity, response time, turnaround time, resource utilization, availability, and reliability.

Throughput is a composite measure that indicates the productivity of the system as a whole; the term is often used by system managers. Throughput is usually measured under steady-state conditions and reflects quantities such as "the number of jobs processed per day" or "the number of online transactions handled per hour." Throughput can also be a measure of the volume of work handled by one unit of the computer system, an isolation that's useful when analysts are looking for bottlenecks in the system.

Bottlenecks tend to develop when resources reach their **capacity**, or maximum throughput level; the resource becomes saturated and the processes in the system aren't being passed along. Thrashing is a result of a saturated disk drive. Bottlenecks also occur when main memory has been overcommitted and the level of multiprogramming has reached a peak point. That means the working sets for the active jobs can't be kept in main memory, so the Memory Manager is continuously swapping pages between main memory and secondary storage. The CPU processes the jobs at a snail's pace because it's very busy flipping pages.

Throughput and capacity can be monitored by either hardware or software. Bottlenecks can be detected by monitoring the queues forming at each resource: when a queue starts to grow rapidly, this is an indication that the arrival rate is greater than, or close to, the service rate and the resource is saturated. These are called feedback loops, and we'll discuss them later in this chapter. Once the bottleneck is detected the appropriate action can be taken to resolve the problem.

To online, interactive users, **response time** is an important measure of system performance. Response time is the interval required to process a user's request: from when the user presses the key to send the message until the system indicates receipt of the message. For batch jobs, this is known as **turnaround time**—the time from the submission of the job until its output is returned to the user. Whether in an online or batch context, this measure depends on both the workload being handled by the system at the time of the request and on the type of job or request being submitted. Some requests, for instance, are handled faster than others because they require fewer resources.

To be an accurate measure of the predictability of the system, measurement data showing response time and turnaround time should include not just their average values but also their variance.

Resource utilization is a measure of how much each unit is contributing to the overall operation. It's usually given as a percentage of time that a resource is actually in use. For example: Is the CPU busy 60 percent of the time? Is the line printer busy 90 percent of the time? How about each of the terminals? Or the seek mechanism on a disk? This data helps the analyst determine whether there is balance among the units of a system or whether a system is I/O-bound or CPU-bound.

Availability indicates the likelihood that a resource will be ready when a user needs it. For online users it may mean the probability that a port is free or a terminal is available when they attempt to log in. For those already on the system it may mean the probability that one or several specific resources, such as a plotter or a group of tape drives, will be ready when their programs make requests. Availability in its simplest form means that a unit will be operational and not out of service when a user needs it. A sample report showing the availability of several platforms is shown in Table 12.3.

(table 12.3)

Availability of certain platforms based on 24 hours, 365 days/year use [Lewis, 1999]. IBM's sysplex product allows a cluster of processors to behave like a multiprocessor system. Windows NT was a predecessor of Windows Server operating systems.

Type	Platform	Outages/Server/Year	Availability
Mainframe	IBM S/390 (sysplexed)	10 minutes	99.998
	AS/400	5.2 hours	99.94
	IBM S/390 (nonsysplexed)	8.9 hours	99.90
Midrange computer	Digital VAX	18.9 hours	99.78
	Unix-based (all types)	23.6 hours	99.73
PCs	Windows NT-based	224.5 hours	97.44

Availability is influenced by two factors: **mean time between failures (MTBF)** and **mean time to repair (MTTR)**. MTBF is the average time that a unit is operational before it breaks down, and MTTR is the average time needed to fix a failed unit and put it back in service. These values are calculated with simple arithmetic equations.

For example, if you buy a terminal with an MTBF of 4000 hours (the number is given by the manufacturer), and you plan to use it for 4 hours a day for 20 days a month (or 80 hours per month), then you would expect it to fail once every 50 months (4000/80)—not bad. The MTTR is the average time it would take to have a piece of hardware repaired and would depend on several factors: the seriousness of the damage, the location of the repair shop, how quickly you need it back, how much you are willing to pay, and so on. This is usually an approximate figure.

The formula used to compute the unit's availability (A) is:

$$A = \frac{\text{MTBF}}{\text{MTBF} + \text{MTTR}}$$

As indicated, availability is a ratio between the unit's MTBF and its total time (MTBF + MTTR). For our terminal, we could assume the MTTR is 2 hours; therefore:

$$A = \frac{4000}{4000 + 2} = 0.9995$$

So, on the average, this unit would be available 9,995 out of every 10,000 hours. In other words, you'd expect five failures out of 10,000 uses.

Reliability is similar to availability but it measures the probability that a unit will not fail *during a given time period* and it's a function of MTBF. The formula (Nickel, 1978) used to compute the unit's reliability (where *e* is the mathematical constant approximately equal to 2.71828) is:

$$R(t) = e^{-(1/\text{MTBF})(t)}$$

To illustrate how this equation works, let's say you absolutely need to use the terminal for the 10 minutes before your upcoming deadline. With time expressed in hours, the unit's reliability is given by:

$$R(t) = e^{-(1/4000)(10/60)}$$
$$= e^{-(1/24,000)}$$
$$= 0.9999584$$

This is the probability that it will be available (won't fail) during the critical 10-minute time period—and 0.9999584 is a very high number. Therefore, if the terminal was ready at the beginning of the transaction, it will probably remain in working order for the entire period of time.

These measures of performance can't be taken in isolation from the workload being handled by the system unless you're simply fine-tuning a specific portion of the system. Overall system performance varies from time to time, so it's important to define the actual working environment before making generalizations.

Feedback Loops

To prevent the processor from spending more time doing overhead than executing jobs, the operating system must continuously monitor the system and feed this information to the Job Scheduler. Then the Scheduler can either allow more jobs to enter the system or prevent new jobs from entering until some of the congestion has been relieved. This **feedback loop** has to be designed very carefully and can be either negative or positive.

A **negative feedback loop** mechanism monitors the system and, when it becomes too congested, signals the Job Scheduler to slow down the arrival rate of the processes, as shown in Figure 12.3.

(figure 12.3)

A simple negative feedback loop. It monitors system activity and goes into action only when the system is too busy.

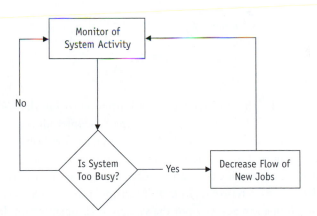

People on vacation use negative feedback loops all the time. For example, if you're looking for a gas station and the first one you find has too many cars waiting in line, you collect the data and you react negatively. Therefore your processor suggests that you drive on to another station (assuming, of course, that you haven't procrastinated too long and run out of gas).

In a computer system a negative feedback loop monitoring I/O devices would inform the Device Manager that Printer 1 has too many jobs in its queue, causing the Device Manager to direct all newly arriving jobs to Printer 2, which isn't as busy. The negative feedback helps stabilize the system and keep queue lengths close to their estimated mean values.

A **positive feedback loop** mechanism works in the opposite way: it monitors the system, and when the system becomes underutilized, the positive feedback loop causes the arrival rate to increase, as shown in Figure 12.4. Positive feedback loops are used in paged virtual memory systems, but they must be used cautiously because they're more difficult to implement than negative loops.

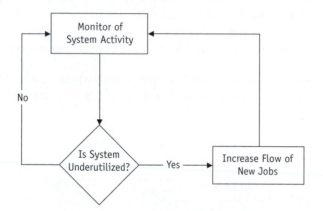

(figure 12.4)

A simple positive feedback loop. It monitors system activity and goes into action only when the system is not busy enough. System activity monitoring is critical here because the system can become unstable.

Here's how they work. The positive feedback loop monitoring the CPU informs the Job Scheduler that the CPU is underutilized, so the Scheduler allows more jobs to enter the system to give more work to the CPU. However, as more jobs enter, the amount of main memory allocated to each job decreases. If too many new jobs are allowed to enter the job stream, the result can be an increase in page faults. And this, in turn, may cause CPU utilization to deteriorate. In fact, if the operating system is poorly designed, positive feedback loops can actually put the system in an unstable mode of operation. Therefore, the monitoring mechanisms for positive feedback loops must be designed with great care.

As this example shows, an algorithm for a positive feedback loop should monitor the effect of new arrivals in two places: the Processor Manager's control of the CPU and the Device Manager's read and write operations. That's because both areas experience the most dynamic changes, which can lead to unstable conditions. Such an algorithm should check to see whether the arrival produces the anticipated result and whether system performance is actually improved. If the arrival causes performance to deteriorate then the monitoring algorithm could cause the operating system to adjust its allocation strategies until a stable mode of operation has been reached again.

Monitoring

Several techniques for measuring the performance of a working system have been developed as computer systems have evolved, and they can be implemented by either hardware or software components. Hardware monitors are more expensive but they have the advantage of having a minimum impact on the system because they're outside of it and attached electronically. They include hard-wired counters, clocks, and comparative elements.

Software monitors are relatively inexpensive but because they become part of the system they can distort the results of the analysis. After all, the software must use the resources it's trying to monitor. In addition, software tools must be developed for each specific system, so it's difficult to move them from system to system.

In early systems, performance was measured simply by timing the processing of specific instructions. The system analysts might have calculated the number of times an ADD instruction could be done in one second. Or they might have measured the processing time of a typical set of instructions (typical in the sense that they would represent the instructions common to the system). These measurements monitored only the CPU speed because in those days the CPU was the most important resource, so the remainder of the system was ignored.

Today, system measurements must include the other hardware units as well as the operating system, compilers, and other system software. Measurements are made in a variety of ways. Some are made using real programs, usually production programs that are used extensively by the users of the system, which are run with different configurations of CPUs, operating systems, and other components. The results are called **benchmarks** and are useful when comparing systems that have gone through extensive changes. Benchmarks are often used by vendors to demonstrate to prospective clients the specific advantages of a new CPU, operating system, compiler, or piece of hardware. A sample benchmark table is shown in Table 12.4.

Remember that benchmark results are highly dependent upon the system's workload, the system's design and implementation, as well as the specific requirements of the applications loaded on the system. Performance data is usually obtained in a rigorously controlled environment so results will probably differ in real-life operation. Still, benchmarks offer valuable comparison data—a place to begin a system evaluation.

(table 12.4)

Benchmarking results published by the Transaction Processing Performance Council on their website. This report includes transactions per minute (tpmC) as well as normalized price/performance ($/tpmC). This is only a sample report. For recent benchmark results and details of the testing conditions used to generate this report, please see the TPC website (www.tpc.org). Reprinted with permission of the Transaction Processing Performance Council.

Top Ten TPC-C by Performance, Version 5 Results (as of 1 Sept-2004)

Rank	Company	System	tpmC	Price/tpmC	System Availability	Database	Operating System	TP Monitor	Date Submitted	Cluster
1	HP	HP Integrity rx5670 Cluster 64P	1,184,893	5.52 US $	04/30/04	Oracle Database 10g Enterprise Edition	Red Hat Enterprise Linux AS 3	BEA Tuxedo 8.1	12/08/03	Y
2	IBM	IBM eServer pSeries 690 Model 7040-681	1,025,486	5.43 US $	08/16/04	IBM DB2 UDB 8.1	IBM AIX 5L V5.2	Microsoft COM+	02/17/04	N
3	HP	HP Integrity Superdome	1,008,144	8.33 US $	04/14/04	Oracle Database 10g Enterprise Edition	HP UX 11.iv2 64-Bit Base OS	BEA Tuxedo 8.0	11/04/03	N
4	IBM	IBM eServer p5 570 16P	809,144	4.95 US $	09/30/04	IBM DB2 UDB 8.1	IBM AIX 5L V5.3	Microsoft COM+	07/12/04	N
5	HP	HP Integrity Superdome	786,646	6.49 US $	10/23/03	Microsoft SQL Server 2000 Enterprise Ed. 64-bit	Microsoft Windows Server 2003 Datacenter Edition 64-bit	Microsoft COM+	08/27/03	N
6	IBM	IBM eServer pSeries 690 Turbo 7040-681	768,839	8.55 US $	02/29/04	Oracle Database 10g Enterprise Edition	IBM AIX 5L V5.2	TXSeries Developers for AIX V5	09/12/03	N
7	IBM	IBM eServer pSeries 690 Turbo 7040-681	763,898	8.25 US $	11/08/03	IBM DB2 UDB 8.1	IBM AIX 5L V5.2	BEA Tuxedo 8.0	06/30/03	N
8	HP	HP Integrity Superdome	707,102	7.16 US $	10/23/03	Microsoft SQL Server 2000 Enterprise Ed. 64-bit	Microsoft Windows Server 2003 Datacenter Edition	Microsoft COM+	05/20/03	N
9	NEC	NEC Express5800/1320Xd C/S w/ Express5800/120Rf-2	683,575	5.99 US $	10/05/04	Oracle Database 10g Enterprise Edition	SUSE LINUX Enterprise Server 9	BEA Tuxedo 8.1	06/28/04	N
10	IBM	IBM eServer pSeries 690 Turbo 7040-681	680,613	11.13 US $	11/08/03	IBM DB2 UDB 8.1	IBM AIX 5L V5.2	BEA Tuxedo 8.0	05/09/03	N

If it's not advisable or possible to experiment with the system itself, a simulation model can be used to measure performance. This is typically the case when new hardware is being developed. A simulation model is a computerized abstraction of what is represented in reality. The amount of detail built into the model is dictated by time and money—the time needed to develop the model and the cost of running it.

Designers of simulation models must be careful to avoid the extremes of too much detail, which becomes too expensive to run, or of too little detail, which doesn't produce enough useful information. If you'd like to write a program that's an example of a simulation model, see the first programming exercise in Chapter 2.

Accounting

The accounting function of the operating system might seem a mundane subject, but it's not; it pays the bills and keeps the system financially operable. From a practical standpoint, it might be one of the most important elements of the system.

Most computer system resources are paid for by the users. In the simplest case, that of a single user, it's easy to calculate the cost of the system. But in a multiuser environment, computer costs are usually distributed among users based on how much each one uses the system's resources. To do this distribution, the operating system must be able to set up user accounts, assign passwords, identify which resources are available to each user, and define quotas for available resources, such as disk space or maximum CPU time allowed per job. At a university, for example, students are sometimes given quotas that include maximum pages per job, maximum login time, and maximum number of jobs during a given period of time. To calculate the cost of the whole system, the accounting program must collect information on each active user.

Pricing policies vary from system to system. Typical measurements include some or all of the following:

- *Total amount of time* spent between job submission and completion. In interactive environments this is the time from login to logout, also known as connect time.
- *CPU time* is the time spent by the processor executing the job.
- *Main memory usage* is represented in units of time, bytes of storage, or bytes of storage multiplied by units of time—it all depends on the configuration of the operating system. For example, a job that requires 200K for 4 seconds followed by 120K for 2 seconds could be billed for 6 seconds of main memory usage, or 320K

of memory usage, or a combination of K/second of memory usage computed as follows:

$$[(200 * 4) + (120 * 2)] = 1040K/\text{second of memory usage}$$

- *Secondary storage used during program execution*, like main memory use, can be given in units of time or space, or both.
- *Secondary storage used during the billing period* is usually given in terms of the number of disk tracks allocated.
- *Use of system software* includes utility packages, compilers, and/or databases.
- *Number of I/O operations* is usually grouped by device class: line printer, terminal, and disks.
- *Time spent waiting for I/O completion.*
- *Number of input records read*, usually grouped by type of input device.
- *Number of output records printed*, usually grouped by type of output device.
- *Number of page faults* is reported in paging systems.

Pricing policies are often used as a way to achieve specific operational goals. For instance, by varying the price of system services, users can be convinced to distribute their workload to the system manager's advantage. Therefore, by offering reduced rates during off hours some users might be persuaded to run long jobs in batch mode inexpensively overnight instead of interactively during peak hours. Pricing incentives can also be used to encourage users to access more plentiful and cheap resources rather than those that are scarce and expensive. For example, by putting a high price on printer output, users might be encouraged to order a minimum of printouts.

Should the system give each user billing information at the end of each job or at the end of each online session? The answer depends on the environment. Some systems only give information on resource usage. Other systems also calculate the price of the most costly items, such as CPU utilization, disk storage use, and supplies (i.e., paper used on the printer) at the end of every job. This gives the user an up-to-date report of expenses and, if appropriate, calculates how much is left in the user's account. Some universities use this technique to warn paying students of impending disaster.

The advantage of maintaining billing records online is that the status of each user can be checked before the user's job is allowed to enter the READY queue. If the user's financial status is questionable, the job will be rejected until the account is corrected.

The disadvantage is overhead, of course. When billing records are kept online and an accounting program is kept active, memory space is used and CPU processing is increased. One compromise is to defer the accounting program until off-hours, when the system is lightly loaded.

Patch Management

Patch management is the systematic updating of the operating system and other system software. Typically, a **patch** is a piece of programming code that replaces or changes code that makes up the software. There are three primary reasons for the emphasis on software patches for sound system administration: the need for vigilant security precautions against constantly changing system threats; the need to assure system compliance with government regulations regarding privacy, and financial accountability; and the need to keep systems running at peak efficiency.

Patches aren't new—they've been written and distributed since programming code was first created. However, the task of keeping computing systems patched correctly has become a challenge because of the complexity of the entire system (including the operating system, network, various platforms, and remote users), and the speed with which software vulnerabilities are exploited by worms, viruses, and other system assaults described in the last chapter.

According to 2004 E-Crime Watch survey of security and law enforcement executives, manual and automatic patch management were among the eight technologies used most at their organizations, as shown in Table 12.5. The survey was conducted by CSO Online in cooperation with the U.S. Secret Service and the CERT Coordination Center.

(table 12.5)

Survey results show that patch management technologies were ranked by most respondents as being among the most effective tools used to detect and/or counter misuse or abuse of computer systems and networks (CSO Online, 2004).

Technologies in Use	Rank	Percentage
Firewalls	1	98.2%
Physical Security Systems	2	94.2%
Manual Patch Management	3	91.0%
Automated Patch Management	8	74.4%

Who has the overall responsibility of keeping an organization's up-to-date? It depends on the organization. For many, overall responsibility lies with the Chief Information Officer or Chief Security Officer. For others, it falls on the shoulders of the network administrator or system security officer. In still others, individual users assume that role. Regardless of which individual owns this job, it is only through rigorous patching that the system's resources can reach top performance, and its information can be best protected.

Patching Fundamentals

While the installation of the patch is the most public event, there are several essential steps that take place before that happens:

1. Identify the required patch
2. Verify the patch's source and integrity
3. Test the patch in a safe environment
4. Deploy the patch throughout the system
5. Audit the system to gauge the success of the patch deployment

Although this discussion is limited to managing operating system patches, all changes to the operating system or other critical system software must be undertaken in an environment that makes regular system backups, and tests the restoration from backups. Never patch your operating system without a recent data backup in hand.

Patch Availability

Let's say you receive notification that a patch is available for an operating system on your network. Your first task is to identify the criticality of the patch, information that is available from the vendor. To be on the forefront of patch information, we suggest that you enroll in automatic announcement services offered by government and industry groups or from your software vendors.

Should the patch be a critical one, plan to apply the patch as soon as possible. Remember that with every patch announcement, system attackers are also armed with this critical information, and they will move quickly to compromise your system. If the patch is not critical in nature, you might choose to delay installation until a regular patch cycle begins. Patch cycles will be discussed later in this chapter.

Patch Integrity

Once you've received a patch, be sure to validate its source and integrity. There's nothing more damaging than installing a system patch authored by a rogue programmer. To test the veracity of the new code, check the digital signature or validation tool that comes with the software. To be safe, and to assure the quality of the product, validate the digital signature used by the vendor to send the new software on a regular basis.

Patch Testing

Before installation on a live system, test the new patch on a sample system or an isolated machine to verify its worth. If a non-networked machine is not available, test the patch on a development system, instead of the operational system.

First, test to see if the system reboots after the patch is installed. Then, check to see if the patched software performs its assigned tasks—whether it's warding off intruders or improving system performance. While it's often not feasible to test the patch on a duplicate system, the tested system should resemble the complexity of the target network as closely as possible.

This is also the time to investigate what you'll do if something goes terribly wrong during installation. Test your contingency plans to uninstall the patch and recover the old software should it become necessary to do so.

Patch Deployment

Now it's time to install the patch. On a single-user computer, patch deployment is a simple task—install the software and reboot the computer. However, on a multi-platform system with hundreds or thousands of users, the task is exceptionally complicated.

To assure success, you should have an accurate inventory of all hardware and software on those computers that need the patch. On a large network, this information can be gleaned from network mapping software that peruses the network and takes a detailed inventory of the system (and this, in turn, assumes that all system hardware is connected to the network).

Finally, the deployment may be launched in stages to avoid overwhelming the help desk with telephone calls. Often, because it's impossible to use the system during the patching process, it is scheduled for times when system use will be low, such as evenings or weekends.

Audit the Finished System

Before announcing the deployment's success, you will need to confirm that the resulting system meets your expectations, by taking steps such as:

- verifying that all computers are patched correctly and perform fundamental tasks as expected
- verifying that no users had unauthorized versions of software on their computers and were thus ineligible for the patch
- verifying that no users are left with unpatched software on their computers

The process should include documentation of the changes made to the system and the success or failure of each stage of the process. Make sure you keep a log of all system changes for future reference. Finally, get feedback from the users to verify the deployment's success.

Software Options

Patches can be managed manually, one at a time, or via software that's written to perform the task automatically. Organizations that choose software can decide to build their own deployment software or buy ready-made software to perform the task for them. Deployment software falls into two groups: those programs that require an agent (called agent-based software), and those that do not (agentless software).

If the deployment software uses an agent, which is software that assists in patch installation, then the agent must be installed on all target computer systems before patches can be deployed. On a very large or dynamic system, this can be a daunting task. Therefore, for administrators of large, complex networks, agentless software offers attractive, time-saving efficiencies.

Timing the Patch Cycle

While critical system patches must be applied immediately, less-critical patches can be scheduled at the convenience of the systems group. These patch cycles can be based on calendar events or vendor events. For example, routine patches can be applied monthly or quarterly, or they can be timed to coincide with a vendor's **service pack** release. The advantage of routine patch cycles is that they allow for thorough review of the patch and testing cycles before deployment.

Conclusion

The operating system is more than the sum of its parts—it's the orchestrated cooperation of every piece of hardware and every piece of software. As we've shown, when one part of the system is favored, it's often at the expense of the others. So if a trade-off must be made, the system's managers must make sure they're using the appropriate measurement tools and techniques to verify the effectiveness of the system before and after modification, and then evaluate the degree of improvement.

With this chapter we conclude Part One of this book. Thus far we've seen how operating systems are alike. In Part Two we look at actual operating systems and show how they're different—and how each manages the components common to all operating systems. In other words, we see how close reality comes to the theory learned so far.

Key Terms

availability: a resource measurement tool that indicates the likelihood that the resource will be ready when a user needs it. It's influenced by mean time between failures and mean time to repair.

benchmarks: measurement tool used to objectively measure and evaluate a system's performance by running a set of jobs representative of the work normally done by a computer system.

capacity: the maximum throughput level of any one of the system's components.

feedback loop: a mechanism to monitor the system's resource utilization so adjustments can be made.

mean time between failures (MTBF): a resource measurement tool; the average time that a unit is operational before it breaks down.

mean time to repair (MTTR): a resource measurement tool; the average time needed to fix a failed unit and put it back in service.

negative feedback loop: a mechanism to monitor the system's resources and, when it becomes too congested, to signal the appropriate manager to slow down the arrival rate of the processes.

patch: executable software that repairs errors or omissions in another program or piece of software.

patch management: the rigorous application of software patches to make repairs and keep the operating system software up to the latest standard.

positive feedback loop: a mechanism used to monitor the system. When the system becomes underutilized, the feedback causes the arrival rate to increase.

reliability: a standard that measures the probability that a unit will not fail during a given time period. It's a function of mean time between failures.

resource utilization: a measure of how much each unit is contributing to the overall operation of the system.

response time: a measure of an interactive system's efficiency that tracks the speed with which the system will respond to a user's command.

service pack: a term used by some vendors to describe an update to customer software to repair existing problems and/or deliver enhancements.

throughput: a composite measure of a system's efficiency that counts the number of jobs served in a given unit of time.

turnaround time: a measure of a system's efficiency that tracks the time required to execute a job and return output to the user.

Exercises

Research Topic

Visit the Web site of a major operating system vendor and identify the patches that have been issued for that software in the last 12 months. Note for each patch its criticality and size. Then, as if you were assigned the task of installing these patches at one time, note if the patches are to be installed in a particular order and how many times the target computer must be rebooted throughout the patching process.

Exercises

1. Remembering that there's a tradeoff between memory use and CPU overhead, give an example where increasing the size of virtual memory will improve job throughput. Then give an example where doing so will cause throughput to suffer.

2. Discuss the financial and throughput implications of adding more processors to a university system that becomes CPU-bound at the conclusion of each school semester.

3. Using the information given in Table 12.1, calculate I/O access speed using CPU 1 and CPU 3 and each of the four disk drives as they evaluate the following track requests: 0, 31, 20, 15, 20, 31, 15. In each case, determine whether reordering the requests would be advantageous.

4. Describe how you would use a negative feedback loop to avoid eating too much food during each course of a very large meal.

5. Describe how a bank manager might use a positive feedback loop to direct waiting customers to five loan officers, being careful to minimize waiting time for customers and maximize the speed of loan processing. Include a description of how you would monitor the system and measure its success.

6. Describe how you would convince a university staff member to perform regular backups, manage archives appropriately, and keep the system patched.

Advanced Exercises

7. Calculate the availability of a magnetic tape cartridge with an MTBF of 80 hours and an MTTR of 3 days (72 hours).

8. Calculate the reliability of a hard disk drive with an MTBF of 1050 hours during the last 40 hours of this month. Assume e = 2.71828 and use Nickel's formula:

$$R(t) = e^{-(1/\text{MTBF})(t)}$$

9. Calculate the availability of a hard disk drive with an MTBF of 1050 and an MTTR of 8 hours.

10. Assuming you had sufficient funds to upgrade only one component for a system with which you are familiar, explain which component you would choose to upgrade to improve overall system performance, and why.

11. Perform a software inventory of your computer system to identify all applications resident on the computer. On a Windows machine, you might begin by exploring the Add or Remove Programs option on the Control Panel. If you have more than a dozen applications, choose twelve major vendors and check each for patches that are available for your software. For each vendor, identify how many patches are available for your software, the number of critical patches, and what patch cycle you would recommend for that vendor's patches: annual, quarterly, monthly, or weekly updates.

Part Two | Operating Systems in Practice

Thus far in this text we've explored how operating system software works in theory—the roles of the Memory Manager, Processor Manager, Device Manager, File Manager, and Network Manager. To do so, we've underplayed the intricate choreography required by all managers as they work together to accomplish even the simplest tasks. We've also described operating systems in their most basic form—operating systems running relatively simple hardware configurations.

In this part of the book, we explore operating systems in practice by becoming acquainted with a few of the most popular operating systems. Keep in mind that most operating systems are evolving into complex systems that can run applications written for many other operating systems—even several versions of other operating systems. For example, you'll notice that many operating systems have been adapted to accommodate UNIX and Linux commands and applications. Expect to see more of this as operating systems continue their inevitable evolution.

For each chapter in Part Two, our discourse includes the history of the operating system's development; its design goals; the unique properties of its submanagers; and its user interface, the portion of the operating system that interacts with users. The user interface commands and formats vary from system to system, as shown in the examples presented in this section. The user interface is probably the most unique component of an operating system, which is why it hasn't been presented until now.

The history of an operating system's development often illustrates its intrinsic strengths and weaknesses. For instance, a system that evolved from a rudimentary single-user system to a multifunctional multiuser system might perform simple tasks well but struggle when trying to meet the needs of a large computing environment. On the other hand, an elegant mainframe system that was later scaled down might excel at complex tasks but prove overdesigned and cumbersome when executing tasks in the smaller environment.

The goals of system designers often indicate which users will find the system appealing, and in which environments. For example, a system written to be appealing to programmers will find a favorable audience in an industrial computing environment, but it may not be as well received by a novice audience or business users.

The tasks of the submanagers are discussed briefly in light of the policies they follow and the tradeoffs they make to keep the system running smoothly. Unfortunately, a complete discussion of these tasks isn't possible in the limited space we have here, so for more detailed information we suggest that you read the technical documentation for the version of your operating system.

At the end of each chapter we review some user commands for each system. We've included only a few basic instructions—enough so you can compare, among the systems, the command structure, syntax, ease-of-use, and appropriateness to a given computing environment.

Our discussion in this part cannot serve as an in-depth evaluation of an operating system. But it does present each system in a standard format to help you compare them; and it's important that the comparison be made because every operating system has strengths and weaknesses.

Chapter 13 | MS-DOS Operating System

MS-DOS

Design Goals
Memory Management
Processor Management
Device Management
File Management
User Interface

" *Find a need and fill it.* **"**

Henry J. Kaiser *(1882–1967)*

Learning Objectives

After completing this chapter, you should be able to describe:

- The historical significance of MS-DOS
- How MS-DOS provided a foundation for early Microsoft Windows releases
- The basics of command-driven systems and how to construct simple batch files
- How one processor can be shared among multiple processes
- The limitations of MS-DOS for many of today's computer users

MS-DOS, also known simply as DOS, was developed to run single-user, stand-alone desktop computers. When the personal computer market exploded in the 1980s, MS-DOS was the standard operating system delivered with millions of these machines.

This operating system is one of the simplest to understand. In many ways, MS-DOS exemplifies early operating systems because it manages jobs sequentially from a single user. Its advantages are its fundamental operation and its straightforward user commands. With only a few hours of instruction a first-time user can learn to successfully manipulate a personal computer and its files and devices.

MS-DOS has two disadvantages. The first is its lack of flexibility and its limited ability to meet the needs of programmers and experienced users. The second stems from its roots; it was written for a single family of microprocessors: the Intel 8086, 8088, 80186, and 80286 chips. When those microprocessors dominated the personal computer market, MS-DOS did too. But newer chips made inroads. As a result, DOS lost its market advantage to more sophisticated operating systems. DOS has a historical significance as the primary operating system for a generation of microcomputers and is included in this text as such.

It's also worth noting that early versions of Windows (versions 1.0 through 3.1) were merely graphical user interfaces that ran on top of the MS-DOS operating system. See Chapter 14 on Windows for more information.

History

MS-DOS was the successor of the CP/M operating system. CP/M (for Control Program for Microcomputers) ran the first personal computers, 8-bit machines marketed by Apple Computer and Tandy Corporation. But when the 16-bit personal computers were developed in 1980, they required an operating system with more capability than CP/M, and many companies rushed to develop the operating system that would become the standard for the new generation of hardware.

IBM was the catalyst. When it searched for an operating system for its soon-to-be-released line of 16-bit personal computers, Digital Research offered the new CP/M-86 operating system and Softech offered their P-System. IBM looked carefully at both and began negotiations with Digital Research to buy the "new and improved CP/M" system. Meanwhile, Microsoft, a fledgling company started by Bill Gates and Paul Allen, discovered an innovative operating system, called 86-DOS, designed by Tim Patterson of Seattle Computer Products to run that company's line of 16-bit personal computers. Microsoft bought it, renamed it MS-DOS for Microsoft Disk Operating System, and made it available to IBM (Dettmann, 1988).

IBM chose MS-DOS in 1981, called it PC-DOS, and proclaimed it the standard for their line of personal computers. Eventually, with the weight of IBM's endorsement, MS-DOS became the standard operating system for most 16-bit personal computers.

This operating system has gone through many versions since its birth in Seattle. Some were needed to fix deficiencies; others were made to accommodate major hardware changes, such as increased disk drive capabilities or different formats. Table 13.1 lists some of the major versions.

Version No.	Release Date	Features
1.0	1981	CP/M compatible; supported only 1 directory
1.1	1982	Allowed double-sided 5¼ inch disks
2.0	1983	Eliminated some defects in Version 4
3.0	1984	Increased memory requirement to 36K, supported PC/AT
3.1	1984	First release to support networking
3.2	1986	Supported token ring and 3½ inch disks
3.3	1987	Supported the IBM PS/2 computer
4.0	1988	Supported hard disks larger than 32 MB
5.0	1991	Better use of extended memory
6.0	1993	Better use of conventional memory
6.22	1994	Provided users with capabilities previously available only as third-party applications

(table 13.1)

The evolution of MS-DOS.

Each version of MS-DOS is a standard version, so later versions of MS-DOS are compatible with earlier versions. Therefore, programs written to run on Version 5.0 can also be run on Version 6.2. It also means that, among different manufacturers, the same commands elicit the same response from the operating system regardless of who manufactured the hardware running it.

Although MS-DOS is no longer widely used, many Windows operating systems offer a DOS emulator to allow users who are comfortable with this operating system to use some DOS-like commands in a window. To find it in Windows XP, for example, click the Start button, then All Programs, Accessories, Command Prompt to see a screen similar to Figure 13.1.

Design Goals

MS-DOS was designed to accommodate a single novice user in a single-process environment, as shown in Figure 13.2. Its standard I/O support includes a keyboard, monitor, printer, and secondary storage unit. Its user commands are based on English words or phrases and are indicative of the action to be performed. Examples are shown in Appendix A. These commands are interpreted by the command processor, typically the only portion of the operating system with which most users interact.

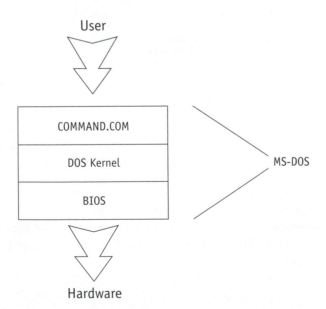

(figure 13.2)

The three layers of MS-DOS. The top layer is the command processor, a program called COMMAND.COM, that provides device independence. The DOS kernel software provides file management services. BIOS software provides device management services.

The layering approach is fundamental to the design of the whole MS-DOS system, which is to "protect" the user from having to work with the bits and bytes of the bare machine that make up the bottom layer—the hardware that includes the electrical circuits, registers, and other basic components of the computer. Each layer is built on the one that precedes it, starting from the bottom up.

The layer at the bottom of MS-DOS is **BIOS** (Basic Input/Output System). This layer of the operating system interfaces directly with the various I/O devices such as printers, keyboards, and monitors. BIOS contains the **device drivers** that control the flow of data to and from each device except the disk drives. It receives status information about the success or failure of each I/O operation and passes it on to the processor. BIOS takes care of the small differences among I/O units so the user can purchase a printer from any manufacturer without having to write a device driver for it—BIOS makes it perform as it should.

The middle layer, the DOS kernel, contains the routines needed to interface with the disk drives. It's read into memory at initialization time from the MSDOS.SYS file residing in the boot disk. The DOS kernel is a proprietary program supplied by Microsoft Corporation that implements MS-DOS. It's accessed by application programs and provides a collection of hardware-independent services, such as memory management, and file and record management. These are called system functions. Like BIOS, it compensates for variations from manufacturer to manufacturer so all disk drives perform in the same way. In other words, the kernel makes disk file management transparent to the user so you don't have to remember in which tracks and sectors your files are stored—and which sectors of the disk are damaged and must be avoided. The kernel does that for you; it manages the storage and retrieval of files and dynamically allocates and deallocates secondary storage as it's needed.

The third layer, the command processor, is sometimes called the shell. This is the part of the system that sends prompts to the user, accepts the commands that are typed in, executes the commands, and issues the appropriate responses. The command processor resides in a file called COMMAND.COM, which consists of two parts stored in two different sections of main memory. Some users mistakenly believe the COMMAND.COM file is the entire operating system because it's the only part that appears on the public directory. Actually, it's only one of several programs that make up MS-DOS; the rest are hidden.

It's the command processor's job to carry out the user's commands entered from the **system prompt** without having to wait for device-specific instructions. For example, when a user issues a PRINT command, the command processor directs the output to the line printer via BIOS. Similarly, with a user command to TYPE a file, the command processor directs the output to the monitor. In these cases the user doesn't need to compensate for the slow speed of the printer and the fast speed of the terminal; the user can interact with both devices and files in the same way.

The weakness of the command processor is that it isn't interpretive. That is, programmers can't take shortcuts by abbreviating the commands. And new users must learn to enter each command completely and correctly. It's unforgiving to those who can't type, spell, or construct commands perfectly.

MS-DOS Version 4.0 introduced a menu-driven DOS shell to ease user's interaction with the system, but it was not widely accepted. When Version 5.0 was released, IBM and Microsoft also released a new operating system, OS/2, which was designed to replace MS-DOS. Although OS/2 offered several advantages over MS-DOS, such as using all available memory and supporting multiprogramming, it failed to generate the interest that both companies expected.

In its heyday, MS-DOS ran an enormous collection of software packages, making it difficult to discontinue this operating system. Notable among these applications were Lotus 1-2-3 (a spreadsheet program) and WordPerfect (word processor). The widespread adoption of these two products helped novice users appreciate the power of a personal computer and spurred the growth of the industry.

To address the continuing demand for access to MS-DOS, Microsoft continues to incorporate access to a "DOS prompt," a DOS-like command capability, on many of its Windows products even though MS-DOS has been officially withdrawn from the market.

Memory Management

The Memory Manager has a relatively simple job because it's managing a single job for a single user. To run a second job, the user must close or pause the first file before opening the second. The Memory Manager uses a **first-fit memory allocation** scheme. First-fit was selected for early DOS versions because it's the most efficient strategy in a single-user environment. (Some versions accommodate extended memory capabilities and multitasking, features that are available with add-on hardware and software, but to keep our discussion succinct we won't include them here.)

Before we see how memory is allocated, let's see how it's structured. Main memory comes in two forms: Read Only Memory (ROM) and Random Access Memory (RAM).

ROM is usually very small in size and contains a program, a section of BIOS, with the sole task of starting up the system. The startup process is called **bootstrapping** because the system is effectively pulling itself up by its bootstraps. This program in ROM initializes the computer. It also retrieves the rest of the resident portion of the operating system from secondary storage and loads it into RAM.

RAM is the part of main memory where programs are loaded and executed. The RAM layout for a computer with 1 MB of memory is given in Figure 13.3.

(figure 13.3)

One megabyte of RAM main memory in MS-DOS. The interrupt vectors are located in low-addressable memory and the COMMAND.COM overlay is located in high-addressable memory.

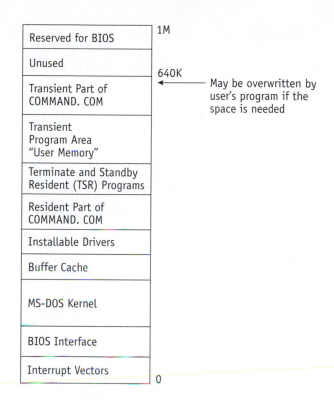

The lowest portion of RAM—known as low-addressable memory because this is where memory addressing starts: 0, 1, 2...—is occupied by 256 interrupt vectors and their tables. An interrupt vector specifies where the **interrupt handler** program for a specific interrupt type is located. The use of interrupt handlers was discussed in Chapter 4. This is followed by BIOS tables and DOS tables, and the DOS kernel with additional installable drivers, if any, which are specified in the system's configuration file called CONFIG.SYS. This is followed by the resident part of the COMMAND.COM command interpreter—the section that is required to run application programs.

Any user application programs can now be loaded into the transient program area (TPA). If more space is required, the COMMAND.COM overlay area, located at the high-numbered memory location, can be taken over by the application program as well. The COMMAND.COM programs in this area are considered transient because they are used to execute commands, such as FORMAT, that can't be executed by the user when an application program is running, so they can be overlayed (or overwritten) by other programs; thus, this space can be made available to large programs.

Main Memory Allocation

The first versions of MS-DOS gave all available memory to the resident application program, but that proved insufficient because the simple contiguous memory allocation scheme didn't allow application programs to dynamically allocate and deallocate memory blocks. With Version 2.0, MS-DOS began supporting dynamic allocation, modification, and release of main memory blocks by application programs.

The amount of memory each application program actually owns depends on both the type of file from which the program is loaded and the size of the TPA (Duncan, 1986).

Programs with the COM **extension** are given all of the TPA, whether or not they need it.

Programs with the EXE extension are only given the amount of memory they need. These files have a header that indicates the minimum and maximum amount of memory needed for the program to run. Ideally, MS-DOS gives the program the maximum amount of memory requested. If that isn't possible, it tries to satisfy the minimum requirement. If the minimum is more than the amount of main memory space available then the program cannot be run.

Except for COM files, there can be any number of files in the TPA at one time. But this raises an interesting question: Why would a system have two programs in memory when it can run only one at a time? Answer: by having several files in memory at once, the user can quickly open one and work on it and close it before starting on the next. They can't both be open at the same time but by alternately opening and closing them the user can use two programs quickly and easily.

For example, a word processing program might allow a user to display two files on the screen at once by opening a separate work area for each one. These work areas partition the screen into sections; in this example one would show the active file and the other the dormant file. If the user indicates that work should begin on the second (the dormant) file, then the first (the active) file is quickly closed and the second file is activated.

Here's a second example: Let's say your word processor's main program includes the code required to compose and print a document, but if you want to check your spelling, the spell checker program has to be loaded from the disk. When that's done, the main portion of the word processor is kept in memory and the second program is added without erasing the first one already there. Now you have two programs in memory but only one of them is executing at any given time. This is discussed in the section on Process Management later in this chapter.

If a program that is already running needs more memory, such as for additional I/O buffers, the Memory Manager checks to see whether enough memory remains. If so, it allocates it to the program while updating the memory block allocation table for that program. If not, then an error message is returned to the user and the program is stopped. Although initial memory allocation is handled automatically by programs written in BASIC, Pascal, or any other language supported by MS-DOS, the shrinking and expanding of memory allocation during execution can be done only from programs written in either assembly language or C.

Memory Block Allocation

The Memory Manager allocates memory by using a first-fit algorithm and a linked list of memory blocks. But with Version 3.3 and beyond, a best-fit or last-fit strategy can be selected. When using last-fit, DOS allocates the highest addressable memory block big enough to satisfy the program's request (Dettmann, 1988).

The size of a block can vary from as small as 16 bytes (called a "paragraph") to as large as the maximum available memory. When a block is formed its first five bytes contain the information shown in Table 13.2.

	Byte	Contents
(table 13.2) *The first five bytes of a memory block define the block's structural characteristics.*	Byte 0	ASCII 90h if it's the last block, or ASCII 77h if it's not.
	Bytes 1–2	Includes the number zero to indicate a busy block and the pointer to the Program Segment Prefix (PSP) that is created by the EXEC function when the program is loaded.
	Bytes 3–4	Gives the number of paragraphs contained in the block.

Therefore, if a block contains four paragraphs and is the first of two blocks then its code would be 7700000004h, which is explained in Table 13.3. (The letter h at the end indicates that the preceding value is in hexadecimal notation and is not recorded.)

	Byte	Contents	Meaning
(table 13.3) *A sample memory block with the first five bytes containing 7700000004h.*	Byte 0	77	Indicates that this is *not* the last block.
	Bytes 1–2	0000	Indicates that this is a busy block and its pointer to the PSP is zero.
	Bytes 3–4	0004	Indicates that this block contains four paragraphs.

Whenever a request for memory comes in, DOS looks through the free/busy block list, as shown in Figure 13.4, until it finds a free block that fits the request. If the list of blocks becomes disconnected, an error message is generated, and the system stops. To recover, the system must be rebooted (Dettmann, 1988).

A well-designed application program releases the memory block it no longer needs. If two free memory blocks are contiguous, they are merged immediately into one block and linked to the list. A program that isn't well designed, however, hoards its memory blocks until it stops running; only then can MS-DOS deallocate the memory blocks used by that program.

Processor Management

The Processor Manager has the relatively simple task of allocating the processor to the resident job when it's ready for execution.

Process Management

MS-DOS wasn't written in reentrant code, discussed in the section on Virtual Memory in Chapter 3, because it was designed for a single-user, single-task environment. Reentrant code is the basis for multitasking, and MS-DOS doesn't support it; therefore, programs can't break out of the middle of a DOS internal routine and then restart the routine from somewhere else (Dettmann, 1988).

In our word processing/spell checker example, the word processor's parent program called on the child spell checker program. The parent went to sleep, and remained asleep, while the child was running. There's no interleaving, so there's no need for sophisticated algorithms or policies to determine which job will run next or for how long. Each job runs in complete segments and is not interrupted midstream. In other words, there's no need to maintain a good job mix to balance system utilization.

However, although two jobs can't run together, some software programs give that illusion. Both Microsoft Windows and Borland's SideKick, for instance, appear to interrupt the parent program, change the screen displays, run unrelated programs, and then return to the parent—but this is not multitasking. (Multitasking is the microcomputer industry's synonym for multiprogramming.) These programs look and feel like multitasking operations because they retain their memory area and run executable programs, but they aren't both in the running state at the same time. In each case the parent program goes to sleep while the child runs along on its own. This synchronization is possible because the interrupt handlers built into MS-DOS give programmers the capability to save all information about the parent program that allows its proper restart after the child program has finished.

Interrupt Handlers

Interrupt handlers are a crucial part of the system. One might say they are responsible for synchronizing the processes. A personal computer has 256 interrupts and interrupt handlers, and they are accessed via the interrupt vector table residing in the lowest bytes of memory, as shown in Figure 13.3. Interrupts can be divided into three groups: internal hardware interrupts, external hardware interrupts, and software interrupts. Internal hardware interrupts are generated by certain events occurring during a program's execution, such as division by zero. The assignment of such events to specific interrupt numbers is electronically wired into the processor and isn't modifiable by software instructions.

External hardware interrupts are caused by peripheral device controllers or by coprocessors such as the 8087/80287 (Duncan, 1986). The assignment of the external devices to specific interrupt levels is done by the manufacturer of the computer system or the manufacturer of the peripheral device. These assignments can't be modified by software because they are hardwired—implemented as physical electrical connections.

Software interrupts are generated by system and application programs. They access DOS and BIOS functions, which, in turn, access the system resources.

Some software interrupts are used to activate specialized application programs that take over control of the computer. Borland's SideKick is one such program. This type of interrupt handler is called Terminate and Stay Resident (TSR). Its function is to terminate a process without releasing its memory, thus providing memory-resident programming facilities. The TSR is usually used by subroutine libraries that are called once from the MS-DOS command level and then are available to provide services to other applications through a software interrupt. When a TSR starts running it sets up its memory tables and prepares for execution by connecting to a DOS interrupt; when all is ready the program determines how much memory it needs to keep. Later, when the program exits, a return code is passed back to the parent.

How are these interrupts synchronized? When the CPU senses an interrupt it does two things: (1) it puts on a stack the contents of the PSW (Program Status Word), the code segment register, and the instruction pointer register; and (2) it disables the interrupt system so that other interrupts will be put off until the current one has been resolved. The CPU uses the 8-bit number placed on the system bus by the interrupting device to get the address of the appropriate interrupt handler from the interrupt vector table and picks up execution at that address.

Finally, the interrupt handler reenables the interrupt system to allow higher-priority interrupts to occur, saves any register it needs to use, and processes the interrupt as quickly as possible.

Obviously, this is a delicate procedure. The synchronization of TSR activities with DOS functions already in progress must be carefully designed and implemented to avoid either modifying things that shouldn't be modified or crashing the system.

Device Management

The ability to reorder requests to optimize seek and search time is not a feature of MS-DOS because it's designed for a single-user environment. All requests are handled on a first-come, first-served basis. But, since Version 3.0, BIOS can support spooling so users can schedule several files to be printed one after the other. To do this, BIOS continuously transfers data from a specified memory buffer to the printer until the buffer is empty (Duncan, 1986).

MS-DOS was written for simple systems that use a keyboard, monitor, printer, mouse, one or two serial ports, and maybe a second printer. For storage, most personal computer systems use direct access storage devices, usually floppy disks or hard disks. Some systems also support a magnetic tape sequential access archiving system. The MS-DOS Device Manager can work with all of them.

These systems use only one of each type of I/O device for each port, so device channels are not a part of MS-DOS. And because each device has its own dedicated control unit, the devices do not require special management from the operating system. Therefore, device drivers are the only items needed by the Device Manager to make the system work. A device driver is a software module that controls an I/O device but handles its interrupts. Each device has its own device driver. BIOS is the portion of the Device Manager that handles the device driver software.

BIOS is stored in both ROM and RAM. In many MS-DOS systems the most primitive parts of the device drivers are located in ROM so they can be used by stand-alone applications, diagnostics, and the system's bootstrapping program. A second section is loaded from the disk into RAM and extends the capabilities of the basic functions stored in ROM so BIOS can handle all of the system's input and output requests.

Normally BIOS is provided by the system manufacturer adhering to Microsoft's specifications for MS-DOS and, because it's the link between the hardware and DOS, it uses standard operating system kernels regardless of the hardware. This means that programs with the standard DOS and BIOS interfaces for their system-dependent functions can be used on every DOS machine regardless of the manufacturer.

BIOS responds to interrupts generated by either hardware or software. For example, a hardware interrupt is generated when a user presses the Print Screen key—this causes BIOS to activate a routine that sends the ASCII contents of the screen to the printer.

Likewise, a software interrupt is generated when a program issues a command to read something from a disk file. This causes the CPU to tell BIOS to activate a routine to read data from the disk and gives it the following: the number of sectors to transfer, track number, sector number, head number, and drive number. After the operation has been successfully completed it tells BIOS the number of sectors transferred and sends an all clear code. If an error should occur during the operation, an error code is returned so BIOS can display the appropriate error message on the screen.

Most device drivers are part of standard MS-DOS. Of course, you can always write your own device driver. All you need is knowledge of assembly language, information about the hardware, and some patience. This option might be necessary if you're using a system with an unusual combination of devices. For instance, in its early years of commercial availability, there was not a high demand for interfacing a computer with a videodisc player—so its device drivers were not incorporated into BIOS. Therefore, users who wanted to use a videodisc as an I/O device had to write or buy their own device drivers and load them when the system was booted up. These device drivers are called installable because they can be incorporated into the operating system as needed without having to patch or change the existing operating system. Installable device drivers are a salient feature of MS-DOS design.

File Management

MS-DOS supports sequential, direct, and indexed sequential file organizations. Sequential files can have either variable- or fixed-length records. However, direct and indexed sequential files can only have fixed-length records.

Filename Conventions

A filename contains no spaces and consists of the drive designation, the directory, any subdirectory, a primary name, and an optional extension. (DOS isn't case-sensitive so filenames and commands can be entered in uppercase, lowercase, or a combination of both.)

The drive name (usually A, B, C, or D) is followed by a colon (:). Directories or subdirectories can be from one to eight characters long and are preceded by a back-slash (\). The primary filename can be from one to eight characters long and the extension from one to three characters long. The primary name and extension are separated by a period. A file's extension can have a special meaning to DOS—the user should be aware of the standard extensions and their uses.

If no directories or subdirectories are included in the name, it's assumed that the file is in the current **working directory**. If no drive is designated, it's assumed the file is on the current drive. The root directory (see the next section, Managing Files, for a discussion of this) is called by a single backslash (\). The names of other directories are preceded by the backslash symbol. The backslash is also used as a delimiter between names.

A file's relative name consists of its primary name and extension, if used. A file's absolute name consists of its drive designation and directory location (called its **path**) followed by its relative name. When the user is working in a directory or subdirectory, it's called the working directory and any file in that directory can be accessed by its relative name. However, to access a file that's in another directory, the absolute name is required.

For example, if your working directory includes a file called JORDAN.DOC then you can identify that file by typing:

```
JORDAN.DOC
```

However, if you changed to another working directory, then you would have to include the directory name when you called the file:

```
\JOURNAL\CHAP9\JORDAN.DOC
```

And if you changed to another drive, such as drive A, and wanted to call the file, you would have to include the drive designation as well:

```
C:\JOURNAL\CHAP9\JORDAN.DOC
```

DOS file names can have no spaces within them. Therefore, to copy the file from drive C to drive B, the command would look like this:

```
COPY   C:\MEMO\DEAN.DOC   B:DEAN.DOC
```

A simpler way to access files is to select a working directory first and then access the files within that directory by their relative names. Later, when you're finished with one directory, you can issue the change directory command (see Table 13.4 later in this chapter) to move to another working directory.

Of course, there are many variations. For complete details, refer to a technical manual for your version of MS-DOS.

Managing Files

The earliest versions of MS-DOS kept every file in a single directory. This was slow and cumbersome, especially as users added more and more files. To retrieve a single file, the File Manager searched from the beginning of the list until either the file was found or the end of the list was reached. If a user forgot how the file was named there was a good chance that it would never be seen again.

To solve this problem, Microsoft implemented a hierarchical directory structure in Version 2.0—an inverted tree directory structure. (It's inverted because the root is at the top and the leaves are on the bottom.)

When a disk is formatted (using the FORMAT command) its tracks are divided into sectors of 512 bytes each. (This corresponds to a buffer size of 512 bytes.) Single-sided disks have one recording surface, double-sided disks have two recording surfaces, and hard disks have from two to four platters, each with two recording surfaces. The concept of *cylinders*, presented in Chapter 7, applies to these hard disks because the read/write heads move in unison.

The sectors (from two to eight) are grouped into clusters and that's how the File Manager allocates space to files. When a file needs additional space, DOS allocates more clusters to it. Besides dividing up the disk space, FORMAT creates three special areas on the disk: the boot record, the root directory, and the **FAT**, which stands for **file allocation table** (Dettmann, 1988).

The *boot record* is the first sector of every logical disk, whether it's an entire physical unit (such as a floppy disk or hard disk) or only a virtual disk (such as a RAM disk). Beginning with Version 2.0, the boot record contains the disk boot program and a table of the disk's characteristics.

The *root directory* is where the system begins its interaction with the user when it's booted up. The root directory contains a list of the system's primary subdirectories and files, including any system-generated configuration files and any user-generated booting instructions that may be included in an AUTOEXEC.BAT file. This is a **batch file** containing a series of commands defined by the user. Every time the CPU is powered up or is reset, the commands in this file are executed automatically by the system. A sample AUTOEXEC.BAT file is discussed later in this chapter.

The information kept in the root directory is: (1) the filename, (2) the file extension, (3) the file size in bytes, (4) the date and time of the file's last modification, (5) the starting cluster number for the file, and (6) the file attribute codes. The first four items are displayed in response to the DIR command, as shown in Figure 13.5.

The number of entries in a root directory is fixed. For instance, only 512 entries are allowed for a 20MB hard disk. The size of the root directory is limited because DOS needs to know where the disk's data area begins. Beginning with Version 2.0, users can avoid this limitation by creating subdirectories that have no size limit (Dettmann, 1988).

Volume in drive C is MINE				
Directory of C:\				
PROGRAMS		<DIR>	3-08-97	1:35p
MEMOS		<DIR>	3-08-97	1:36p
AUTOEXEC	BAT	45	8-22-98	10:12a
PHASES	DOC	210	2-12-96	5:15p
JOURNAL		<DIR>	12-18-98	11:27a
GEORGE	DOC	8644	10-15-99	3:00p
	6 File(s)		4077216 bytes free	

(figure 13.5)

Directory listing of a root directory, which includes three subdirectories and three files. Notice that the listing follows no particular order.

The directory listing shown in Figure 13.5 was generated by the user's command: DIR. Notice how the three subdirectories are distinguished from the three files. Notice, also, that the system maintains the date and time when it was most recently modified. Some software security programs use this data to detect any viruses or other unauthorized or unusual modifications of the system's software.

Each subdirectory can contain its own subdirectories and/or files, as shown in Figure 13.6.

(figure 13.6)

The directory system: the root directory listing has six entries, as shown in Figure 13.5. The directory listing for JOURNAL has four entries: its three files and its subdirectory CHAP9. The directory listing for CHAP9 has three entries for its three files.

MS-DOS supports hidden files—files that are executable but not displayed in response to DIR commands. Some of MS-DOS's system files are hidden files; they're used to run the operating system but they don't show up on the directory listings. COMMAND.COM is the only system file that isn't hidden and so it's always displayed on public directories.

The File Allocation Table (FAT) contains status information about the disk's sectors: which are allocated, which are free, and which can't be allocated because of formatting errors.

The directory notes the number of the first sector or cluster of the file—this number is recorded there when the file is created. All successive sectors or clusters allocated to that file are recorded in the FAT, and are linked together to form a chain, with each FAT entry giving the sector/cluster number of the next entry. The last entry for each chain contains the hexadecimal value FF to indicate the end of the chain. As you can see in Figure 13.7, a file's sectors don't have to be contiguous.

(figure 13.7)

For each file, the direc-
tory includes the first
sector/cluster location in
the File Allocation Table
so it can be accessed
quickly. The FAT links
every sector for each file.
Notice that the sectors
for the file PHASES.DOC
are not contiguous (the
arrows are a visual aid
to show their linking).

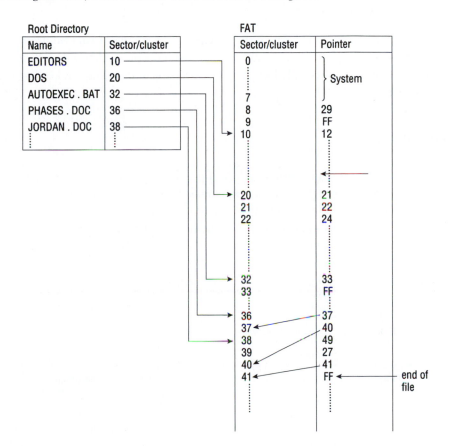

MS-DOS looks at data in a disk file as a continuous string of bytes. Therefore, I/O operations request data by relative byte (relative to the beginning of the file) rather than by relative sector. The transformation from physical sector (or cluster) to relative byte address is done by the File Manager so data on a disk appears to be accessed just like data in main memory.

As we mentioned a moment ago, MS-DOS supports noncontiguous file storage and dynamically allocates disk space to a file, provided there's enough room on the disk. Unfortunately, as files are added and deleted from the disk, a file may become quite fragmented, making it increasingly cumbersome and time-consuming to retrieve.

Compaction became a feature of MS-DOS Version 6.0 with the inclusion of DEFRAG.EXE, a utility used to defragment a disk by picking up the fragments of a file and repositioning them as a single piece in a contiguous space.

415

Another command can be used to determine the need for compaction. Given CHKDSK (filename) the system responds with the number of noncontiguous blocks in which the file is stored. It's up to the user to compact the file, if necessary, so it's stored in as few noncontiguous blocks as possible to speed access time and reduce maintenance on the seek mechanism.

Restricting user access to the computer system and its resources isn't built into MS-DOS. Add-on security software is available but, for most users, data is kept secure by keeping the computer physically locked up or by removing the disks and keeping them in a safe place.

User Interface

MS-DOS uses a **command-driven interface**. Table 13.4 shows some of the most common commands. Users type in their commands at the system prompt. The default prompt is the drive indicator and the > character; therefore, C> is the standard prompt for a hard drive system and A> is the prompt for a computer with one disk drive. The default prompt can be changed using the PROMPT command.

Command	Stands For	Action to be Performed
DIR	Directory	List what's in this directory.
CD or CHDIR	Change Directory	Change the working directory.
COPY	Copy	Copy a file. Append one to another.
DEL or ERASE	Delete	Delete the following file or files.
RENAME	Rename	Rename a file.
TYPE	Type	Display the text file on the screen.
PRINT	Print	Print one or more files on printer.
DATE	Date	Display and/or change the system date.
TIME	Time	Display and/or change the system time.
MD or MKDIR	Make Directory	Create a new directory or subdirectory.
FIND	Find	Find a string. Search files for a string.
FORMAT	Format Disk	Logically prepare a disk for file storage.
CHKDSK	Check Disk	Check disk for disk/file/directory status.
PROMPT	System Prompt	Change the system prompt symbol.
DEFRAG	Defragment Disk	Compact fragmented files.
(filename)		Run (execute) the file.

(table 13.4)

Some common MS-DOS user commands. Typically, commands are entered in either upper- or lowercase characters, although in this text we use all capital letters to make the notation consistent. Check the technical documentation for your system for proper spelling and syntax.

When the user presses the Enter key, the shell called COMMAND.COM interprets the command and calls on the next lower level routine to satisfy the request.

User commands include some or all of these elements in this order:

command   source-file   destination-file   switches

The command is any legal MS-DOS, command. The source-file and destination-file are included when applicable and, depending on the current drive and directory, might need to include the file's complete path name. The switches begin with a slash (i.e., /P /V /F) and are optional; they give specific details about how the command is to be carried out. Most commands require a space between each of their elements.

The commands are carried out by the COMMAND.COM file, which is part of MS-DOS, as shown in Figure 13.2. As we said before, when COMMAND.COM is loaded during the system's initialization, one section of it is stored in the low section of memory; this is the resident portion of the code. It contains the command interpreter and the routines needed to support an active program. In addition, it contains the routines needed to process CTRL-C, CTRL-BREAK, and critical errors.

The transient code, the second section of COMMAND.COM, is stored in the highest addresses of memory and can be overwritten by application programs if they need to use its memory space. Later, when the program terminates, the resident portion of COMMAND.COM checks to see if the transient code is still intact. If it isn't, it loads a new copy.

As a user types in a command, each character is stored in memory and displayed on the screen. When the Enter key is pressed, the operating system transfers control to the command interpreter portion of COMMAND.COM, which either accesses the routine that carries out the request or displays an error message. If the routine is residing in memory, then control is given to it directly. If the routine is residing on secondary storage, it's loaded into memory and then control is given to it.

Although we can't describe every command available in MS-DOS, some features are worth noting to show the flexibility of this operating system.

Batch Files

By creating customized batch files, users can quickly execute combinations of DOS commands to configure their systems, perform routine tasks, or make it easier for nontechnical users to run software.

For instance, if a user routinely checks the system date and time, loads a device driver for a mouse, moves to a certain subdirectory, and loads a program called MAIL.COM, then this program, called START.BAT, would perform each of those steps in turn as shown in Figure 13.8.

```
DATE
TIME
DEVICE=MOUSE.SYS
CD\FLYNN\BOOK
MAIL
```

(figure 13.8)

*Contents of the program
START.BAT.*

To run this program the user needs only to type START at the system prompt. To have this program run automatically every time the system is restarted, then the file should be renamed AUTOEXEC.BAT and loaded into the system's root directory. By using batch files, any tedious combinations of keystrokes can be reduced to a few easily remembered customized commands.

Redirection

MS-DOS can redirect output from one standard input or output device to another. For example, the DATE command sends output directly to the screen, but by using the **redirection** symbol (>) the output is redirected to another device or file instead.

The syntax is:

```
command > destination
```

For example, if you want to send a directory listing to the printer, you would type: DIR > PRN and the listing would appear on the printed page instead of the screen. Likewise, if you want the directory of the default drive to be redirected to a file on the disk in the B drive, you'd type: DIR > B:DIRFILE and a new file called DIRFILE would be created on drive B and it would contain a listing of the directory.

You can redirect and append new output to an existing file by using the append symbol (>>). For example, if you've already created the file DIRFILE with the redirection command and you wanted to generate a listing of the directory and append it to the previously created DIRFILE, you would type:

```
DIR >> B:DIRFILE
```

Now DIRFILE contains two listings of the same directory.

Redirection works in the opposite manner as well. If you want to change the source to a specific device or file, use the < symbol. For example, let's say you have a program called INVENTRY.EXE under development that expects input from the keyboard, but for testing and debugging purposes you want it to accept input from a test data file, then you would type:

```
INVENTRY < B:TEST.DAT
```

Filters

Filter commands accept input from the default device, manipulate the data in some fashion, and send the results to the default output device. A commonly used filter is SORT, which accepts input from the keyboard, sorts that data, and displays it on the screen. This filter command becomes even more useful if it can read data from a file and sort it to another file. This can be done by using the redirectional parameters. For example, if you wanted to sort a data file called STD.DAT and store it in another file called SORTSTD.DAT then you'd type:

```
SORT <STD.DAT> SORTSTD.DAT
```

The sorted file would be in ascending order (numerically or alphabetically) starting with the first character in each line of the file. If you wanted the file sorted in reverse order then you would type:

```
SORT /R  <STD.DAT> SORTSTD.DAT
```

You can sort the file by column. For example, let's say a file called EMPL has data that follows this format: the ID numbers start in Column 1, the phone numbers start in Column 6, and the last names start in Column 14. (A column is defined as characters delimited by one or more spaces.) To sort the file by last name the command would be:

```
SORT /+14  <EMPL.DAT> SORTEMPL.DAT
```

The file would be sorted in ascending order by the field starting at Column 14.

Another common filter is MORE, which causes output to be displayed on the screen in groups of 24 lines, one screen at a time, and waits until the user presses the Enter key before displaying the next 24 lines.

Pipes

A pipe can cause the standard output from one command to be used as standard input to another command; its symbol is a vertical bar (|). You can alphabetically sort your directory and display the sorted list on the screen by typing:

```
DIR | SORT
```

You can combine pipes and other filters, too. For example, to display on the screen the contents of the file INVENTRY.DAT one screen at a time, the command would be:

```
TYPE INVENTRY.DAT | MORE
```

You can achieve the same result using only redirection by typing:

```
MORE < INVENTRY.DAT
```

You can sort your directory and display it one screen at a time by using pipes with this command:

```
DIR | SORT | MORE
```

Or you can achieve the same result by using both pipes and filters with these two commands:

```
DIR | SORT > SORTFILE
```

```
MORE < SORTFILE
```

Additional Commands

Three additional commands often used in MS-DOS are FIND, PRINT, and TREE. Note that these are "traditional" MS-DOS commands, and some of the switches or options mentioned here might not work in Windows DOS-like emulators.

FIND

FIND is a filter command that searches for a specific string in a given file or files and displays all lines that contain the string from those files. The string must be enclosed in double quotes (" ") and must be typed exactly as it is to be searched; upper- and lowercase letters are taken as entered.

For example, the command to display all the lines in the file PAYROLL.COB that contain the string AMNT-PAID is this:

```
FIND "AMNT-PAID" PAYROLL.COB
```

The command to count the number of lines in the file PAYROLL.COB that contain the string AMNT-PAID and display the number on the screen is this:

```
FIND /C "AMNT-PAID" PAYROLL.COB
```

The command to display the relative line number, as well as the line in the file PAYROLL.COB that contains the string AMNT-PAID is this

```
FIND /N "AMNT-PAID" PAYROLL.COB
```

The command to display all of the lines in the file PAYROLL.COB that *do not* contain the string AMNT-PAID is this:

```
FIND /V "AMNT-PAID" PAYROLL.COB
```

The command to display the names of all files on the disk in drive B that *do not* contain the string SYS is this:

```
DIR B: | FIND /V "SYS"
```

PRINT

The PRINT command allows the user to set up a series of files for printing while freeing up COMMAND.COM to accept other commands. In effect, it's a spooler. As the printer prints your files, you can type other commands and work on other applications. The PRINT command has many options but to use the following two, they must be given the first time the PRINT command is used after booting the system:

The command PRINT /B allows you to change the size of the internal buffer. Its default is 512 bytes but increasing its value speeds up the PRINT process.

The command PRINT /Q specifies the number of files allowed in the print queue. The minimum value for Q is 4 and the maximum is 32.

TREE

The TREE command displays directories and subdirectories in a hierarchical and indented list. It also has options that allow the user to delete files while the tree is being generated. The display starts with the current or specified directory with the subdirectories indented under the directory that contains them. For example, if we issue the command TREE for the system illustrated in Figure 13.6, the response would be:

```
PROGRAMS

MEMOS

JOURNAL

CHAP9
```

To display the names of the files in each directory, add the switch /F:

```
TREE /F
```

The TREE command can also be used to delete a file that's duplicated on several different directories. For example, to delete the file PAYROLL.COB anywhere on the disk, the command would be:

```
TREE PAYROLL.COB /D /Q
```

The system displays the tree as usual but whenever it encounters a file called PAYROLL.COB, it pauses and asks if you want to delete it. If you type Y then it deletes the file and continues. If you type N then it continues as before.

For illustrative purposes, we've included only a few MS-DOS commands here, and a few in Appendix A. For a complete list of commands, their exact syntax, and more details about those we've discussed here, see a technical manual for the appropriate version of MS-DOS.

Conclusion

MS-DOS enjoyed years of popularity. It was written to serve users of several generations of personal computers, from the earliest IBM PCs to the more sophisticated stand-alone machines introduced in the late 1980s. As such, it was a huge success.

The strength of MS-DOS is that it was the first standard operating system to be adopted by many manufacturers of personal computing machines. As the standard, it also supported, and was supported by, legions of software design groups.

The weakness of MS-DOS is that it was designed for single-user/single-task systems and can't support multitasking, networking, and other sophisticated applications required of computers of every size.

Key Terms

batch file: a file that includes a series of commands that are executed in sequence without any input from the user. Contrasts with an interactive session.

BIOS: an acronym for basic input output system, a set of programs that are hard-coded on a chip to load into ROM at startup.

bootstrapping: the process of starting an inactive computer by using a small initialization program to load other programs.

command-driven interface: an interface that accepts typed commands, one line at a time, from the user. It contrasts with a menu-driven interface.

device driver: a device-specific program module that handles the interrupts and controls a particular type of device.

extension: the part of the filename that indicates which compiler or software package is needed to run the files.

file allocation table (FAT): the table used to track segments of a file.

filter command: a command that directs input from a device or file, changes it, and then sends the result to a printer or display.

first-fit memory allocation: a main memory allocation scheme that searches from the beginning of the free block list and selects for allocation the first block of memory large enough to fulfill the request. It contrasts with *best-fit memory allocation.*

interrupt handler: the program that controls what action should be taken by the operating system when a sequence of events is interrupted.

path: the sequence of directories and subdirectories the operating system must follow to find a specific file.

pipe: a symbol that directs the operating system to divert the output of one command so it becomes the input of another command. In MS-DOS the pipe symbol is |.

redirection: an instruction that directs the operating system to send the results of a command to or from a file or other device other than a keyboard or monitor. In MS-DOS the redirection symbols are < and >.

system prompt: the signal from the operating system that it is ready to accept a user's command, such as C:\> or C:\Documents>.

working directory: the directory or subdirectory which is currently the one being used; the home directory.

Chapter 14 | Windows Operating Systems

Design Goals

Memory Management

Processor Management

Device Management

File Management

Network Management

Security Management

User Interface

"What we learn to do, we learn by doing."

Aristotle *(384–322 BC)*

Learning Objectives

After completing this chapter, you should be able to describe:

- The importance of MS-DOS in early Windows releases
- The design goals for Windows operating systems
- The role of the Memory Manager, especially the Virtual Memory Manager
- The use of the Device, Processor, and Network Managers in recent versions of Windows
- The role of the NT file system in file management
- The challenges for Windows system security today
- How the current Windows user interface functions

The products now categorized as Windows® operating systems are descended from a series of graphical interfaces designed to work with or "on top of" Microsoft's MS-DOS operating system. Over time, Windows evolved into complex operating systems independent of MS-DOS. This chapter discusses Windows operating systems in general, though it covers in more depth the operating systems built on the Windows NT kernel, including Windows XP Professional and Windows Server.

Throughout this chapter we introduce many acronyms used to describe this networked operating system. When we introduce each one in this chapter, it's spelled out—thereafter we use the more commonly known acronym. A list of the Microsoft acronyms used in Chapters 13 and 14 can be found in Appendix B.

Windows Development

The first Windows product used a **graphical user interface (GUI)** as its primary method of communication with the user and needed an underlying operating system so it could translate the users' requests into system commands. (For a comparison of GUIs from several operating systems, see Appendix C.)

Early Windows Products

Windows 1.0, introduced in 1985, ran on PC-compatible microcomputers on top of MS-DOS. That is, the first Windows application was not a true operating system. It was merely an interface between the actual MS-DOS operating system and the user.

Windows 1.0 was followed by increasingly sophisticated GUIs designed to run increasingly powerful desktop computers, as shown in Table 14.1. The first widely adopted Windows product, Windows 3.0, featured a standardized look and feel, similar to the one made popular by Apple's Macintosh computer. Windows 3.0 became the entry-level product intended for single-user installations found in single-user or small-business environments.

Year	Product	Features
1985	Windows 1.0	First retail shipment of the first Windows product; required MS-DOS
1990	Windows 3.0	Improved performance and advanced ease-of-use; required MS-DOS
1992	Windows 3.1	Widely adopted, commercially successful GUI with more than 1,000 enhancements over 3.0; required MS-DOS
1992	Windows for Workgroups	GUI for small networks; required MS-DOS

(table 14.1)

Early Microsoft Windows GUI products ran "on top of" MS-DOS.

Notice in Table 14.1 that Windows for Workgroups was the first Windows product to accommodate the needs of network users by including programs and features for small LANs. For example, a Windows for Workgroups system could easily share directories, disks, and printers among several interconnected machines. It also allowed personal intercommunication through e-mail and chat programs. It was intended for small or mid-sized groups of PCs typically seen in small businesses or small departments of larger organizations.

Operating Systems for Single Users

Until the release of the Windows 95 operating system, Windows products for single users were built to run on top of the MS-DOS operating system. That is, MS-DOS was the true operating system but took its direction from the Windows program being run on it. However, this layering technique proved to be a disadvantage. Although it helped Windows gain market share among MS-DOS users, MS-DOS had little built-in security, couldn't perform multitasking, and had no interprocess communication capability. In addition, it was written to work closely with the microcomputer's hardware, making it difficult to move the operating system to other platforms.

To respond to these needs, Microsoft developed and released a succession of Windows operating systems (not mere GUIs) to appeal to home and office users, as shown in Table 14.2. (Parallel development of networking products is shown in Table 14.3.)

(table 14.2)			
	1995	Windows 95	True operating system designed to replace Windows 3.x, Windows for Workgroups, and MS-DOS for single-user desktop computers
The evolution of key Microsoft Windows operating systems for home and professional use.	1998	Windows 98	For PC users. Implemented many bug fixes to Windows 95, had more extended hardware support, and was fully 32 bit. Not directly related to Windows NT.
	2000	Windows Millennium Edition (ME)	Last Windows operating system built on the Windows 95 code.
	2001	Windows XP Home	For PC users. A 32-bit operating system built to succeed Windows 95 and 98, but built on the Windows NT kernel.
	2001	Windows XP Professional	For networking and power users, built on the Windows NT kernel. The Professional Edition, available in 32-bit and 64-bit versions, was intended for office and professional users who needed more computing power and extensive networking capabilities.

While Microsoft was courting the home and office environment with single user operating systems, the company also began developing more powerful networking products, beginning with Windows NT ("New Technology"). Unlike the single user operating systems, Windows NT never relied on MS-DOS for support.

Operating Systems for Networks

In the fall of 1988 Microsoft hired David Cutler to lead the development of the Windows NT operating system. An experienced architect of minicomputer systems, Cutler identified the primary market requirements for this new product: portability, multiprocessing capabilities, distributed computing support, compliance with government procurement requirements, and government security certification. The finished product was introduced in 1993, and evolved as shown in Table 14.3.

1993	Windows NT version 3.1	The first version of NT; featured true client/server operating system with support for Intel, RISC, and multiprocessor systems
1994	Windows NT version 3.5	Introduced BackOffice applications suite, required 4 MB less RAM, and offered tighter links to NetWare and UNIX networks through enhanced TCP/IP stack
1996	Windows NT version 4.0	Added popular interface from Windows 95, included support for DCOM, and integrated support for e-mail and Internet connectivity
1999	Windows 2000	Introduced X.500-style directory services, Kerberos security, and improved Distributed Component Object Model (DCOM)
2003	Windows Server 2003	Available in Standard Edition, Web Edition, Enterprise Edition, and Datacenter Edition, this operating system was designed as a server platform for Microsoft's .NET initiative
2005 (est.)	Windows Server 2005	Expected release of upgrade to Windows Server 2003

(table 14.3)

The evolution of key Microsoft Windows networking operating systems. All have evolved from Windows NT.

Microsoft offered Windows NT in several versions:

• Windows NT Workstation for individuals needing a desktop operating system
• Windows NT Server for small to medium-sized offices, Web servers, and off-site locations
• Windows NT Server Enterprise Edition for larger and more complex networks

In 1999, Microsoft changed the operating system's name from Windows NT to Windows 2000, which was also available in four packages: Windows 2000 Professional, Windows 2000 Server, Windows 2000 Advanced Server, and Windows 2000 Datacenter Server. The Datacenter Server was a new product designed to for large data warehouses and other data-intensive business applications and supported up to 64 GB of physical memory. Likewise, Windows Server 2003 was also released with these same four packages plus a Web edition.

The Server and Advanced Server editions of current versions of Windows make it easier to form collaborative work groups across departments. Some organizations use the operating system because it's easy to add new workstations and components, improve network systems, add new applications, and maintain the system as a whole. Others prefer its e-mail, conferencing, and collaboration tools and support for Web server software.

The rest of our discussion of Windows focuses primarily on the more recent NT-based networking releases of Windows.

Design Goals

For the system to fulfill its market requirements, certain features such as security had to be incorporated from the outset. Therefore, the designers of Windows assembled a set of software design goals to facilitate decision making as the coding process evolved. For example, if two design options conflicted, the design goals were used to help determine which was better.

When they were designed, Windows networking operating systems were influenced by several operating system models, so they used already-existing frameworks while introducing new features. For example, Windows Server uses a client/server model to provide a variety of operating system environments compatible (sometimes backwards compatible) with operating systems such as Windows, MS-DOS, OS/2, and POSIX (UNIX and Linux)to its users. It uses an object model to manage operating system resources and to allocate them to users in a consistent manner. It uses symmetric multiprocessing (SMP) to achieve maximum performance from multiprocessor computers.

To accommodate the various needs of its user community, and to optimize resources, the Windows team identified five design goals: extensibility, portability, reliability, compatibility, and performance.

Extensibility

Knowing that operating systems must change over time to support new hardware devices or new software technologies, the design team decided that the operating system had to be easily enhanced. This feature is called **extensibility**. To ensure the integrity of the Windows operating system code the designers separated operating system functions into a privileged executive process and a set of nonprivileged processes called "protected subsystems." The term "privileged" refers to a processor's mode of operation. Most processors have a privileged mode (in which all machine instructions are allowed and system memory is accessible), and a nonprivileged mode (in which certain instructions are not allowed and system memory isn't accessible). In Windows terminology, the privileged processor mode is called **kernel mode** and the nonprivileged processor mode is called **user mode**.

Usually operating systems execute in kernel mode only and application programs execute in user mode only, except when they call operating system services. In Windows the protected subsystems execute in user mode as if they were applications, which allows protected subsystems to be modified or added without affecting the integrity of the executive process.

In addition to protected subsystems, Windows designers included four features to ensure its extensibility:

- A modular structure so new components can be added to the executive process
- Objects, a group of abstract data types manipulated by a special set of services allowing system resources to be managed uniformly
- Drivers for new file systems, devices, and networks that can be added to the system at any time
- A remote procedure call that allows an application to call remote services regardless of their location on the network

Portability

Portability refers to the operating system's ability to operate on different machines that are based on different processors or configurations with a minimum amount of recoding. To achieve this goal, Windows system development followed certain guidelines. First, it was written in a standardized, high-level language available in all machines. Second, the system accommodated the hardware to which it was expected to be ported. For example, if the operating system was built on a 32-bit addressable machine, it couldn't be ported to a 16-bit addressable machine. Third, code that interacted directly with the hardware had to be minimized to reduce incompatibility errors. Fourth, all hardware-dependent code had to be isolated into modules that could be easily modified whenever the operating system was ported.

Windows NT and it successors were written for ease of porting to machines that use 32-bit linear addresses and provide virtual memory capabilities. These releases of Windows have the following features:

- The code is modular. That is, the code that must access processor-dependent data structures and registers is contained in small modules that can be replaced by similar modules for different processors.
- Much of Windows is written in C, a programming language that's standardized and readily available. The graphic component and some portions of the networking user interface are written in C++. Assembly language code (which generally is not portable) is used only for those parts of the system that must communicate directly with the hardware.

- It contains a hardware abstraction layer (HAL), a dynamic-link library that provides isolation from hardware dependencies furnished by different vendors. The HAL abstracts hardware, such as caches, with a layer of low-level software so that higher-level code need not change when moving from one platform to another.

Reliability

Reliability refers to the robustness of a system—that is, its predictability in responding to error conditions, even those caused by hardware failures. It also refers to the operating system's ability to protect itself and its users from accidental or deliberate damage by user programs.

Structured exception handling is one way to capture error conditions and respond to them uniformly. Whenever such an event occurs, either the operating system or the processor issues an exception call, which automatically invokes the exception handling code that's appropriate to handle the condition, ensuring that no harm is done to either user programs or the system. In addition, the following features strengthen the system:

- A modular design that divides the executive into individual system components that interact with each other through specified programming interfaces. For example, if it becomes necessary to replace the Memory Manager with a new one, then the new one will use the same interfaces.
- A file system called **NTFS (NT File System)** which can recover from all types of errors including those that occur in critical disk sectors. To ensure recoverability it uses redundant storage and a transaction-based scheme for storing data.
- U.S. government-certifiable security architecture that provides a variety of security mechanisms, such as user logon, resource quotas, and object protection.
- A virtual memory strategy that provides every program with a large set of memory addresses and prevents one user from reading or modifying memory that's occupied by another user unless the two are explicitly sharing memory.

Compatibility

Compatibility usually refers to an operating system's ability to execute programs written for other operating systems or for earlier versions of the same system. However, for Windows, compatibility is a more complicated topic.

Through the use of protected subsystems, Windows provides execution environments for applications that are different from its primary programming interface—the Win32 Application Programming Interface (API). When running on Intel processors, the protected subsystems supply binary compatibility with existing Microsoft applications.

Windows also provides source-level compatibility with POSIX applications that adhere to the POSIX operating system interfaces defined by IEEE. (**POSIX** is the Portable Operating System Interface for Computer Environments, an operating system API that's a set of calling conventions that define how a service is invoked through a software package developed by the IEEE to increase the portability of application software. POSIX is discussed in detail in the next chapter.)

In addition to compatibility with programming interfaces, recent versions of Windows support already-existing file systems, including the MS-DOS file allocation table (FAT), the CD-ROM file system (CDFS), and the NT file system (NTFS).

Windows comes with built-in verification of important hardware and software. That is, the upgrade setup procedures include a check-only mode that examines the system's hardware and software for potential problems and produces a report that lists them. The procedure stops when it can't find drivers for critical devices, such as hard-disk controllers, bus extensions, and other items necessary for a successful upgrade.

Performance

To give fast response times when dealing with CPU-bound applications, fast hardware isn't enough—the operating system's performance must be fast and efficient too. Several features help Windows achieve good performance levels.

- System calls, page faults, and other crucial processes are tested and optimized to ensure the fastest possible processing speeds.
- A mechanism called the local procedure call (LPC) is incorporated into the operating system to guarantee that communication among the protected subsystems is fast and doesn't restrain performance.
- The speed of frequently used system services is maximized by carefully designing the environment subsystem.
- Critical elements of Windows' networking software are built into the privileged portion of the operating system to gain the best possible performance. However, these components can also be loaded and unloaded from the system dynamically.

Memory Management

Every operating system uses its own view of physical memory and makes its application programs access memory in specified ways. In the example shown in Figure 14.1, each process's virtual address space is 4 GB, with 2 GB each allocated to program storage and system storage. When physical memory becomes full, the Virtual Memory Manager pages some of the memory contents to disk, freeing physical memory for other processes.

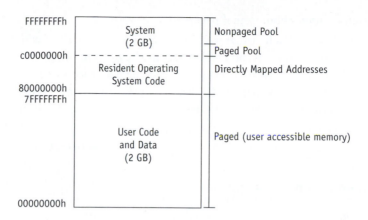

The challenge for all Windows operating systems, especially those running in a network, is to run application programs written for Windows, MS-DOS, or POSIX without crashing into each other in memory. Each of Windows's environment subsystems provides a view of memory that matches what its applications expect. The executive process has its own memory structure, which the subsystems access by calling the operating system's inherent services.

In recent versions of Windows the operating system resides in high virtual memory and the user's code and data reside in low virtual memory, as shown in Figure 14.1. A user process can't read or write to system memory directly. All user-accessible memory can be paged to disk, as can the segment of system memory labeled *paged pool*. However, the segment of system memory labeled *nonpaged pool* is never paged to disk because it's used to store critical NT objects, such as the code that does the paging, as well as major data structures.

User-Mode Features

The Virtual Memory (VM) Manager allows user-mode subsystems to share memory efficiently and provides a set of native services that a process can use to manage its virtual memory in the following ways:

• Allocate memory in two stages. First by reserving memory and then by committing memory, as needed. This two-step procedure allows a process to reserve a large section of virtual memory without being charged for it until it's actually needed.

• Read and/or write protection for virtual memory, allowing processes to share memory when needed.

• Lock virtual pages in physical memory. This ensures that a critical page won't be removed from memory while a process is using it. For example, a database application that uses a tree structure to update its data may lock the root of the tree in memory, thus minimizing page faults while accessing the database.

- Retrieve information about virtual pages.
- Protect virtual pages. Each virtual page has a set of flags associated with it that determines the types of access allowed in user mode. In addition, Windows provides object-based memory protection. Therefore, each time a process opens a section object, a block of memory that can be shared by two or more processes, the security reference monitor checks whether the process is allowed to access the object.
- Rewrite virtual pages to disk. If an application modifies a page, the VM Manager writes the changes back to the file during its normal paging operations.

Virtual Memory Implementation

The Virtual Memory Manager relies on address space management and paging techniques.

Address Space Management

As shown in Figure 14.1, the upper half of the virtual address space is accessible only to kernel-mode processes. Code in the lower part of this section, kernel code and data, is never paged out of memory. In addition, the addresses in this range are translated by the hardware, providing exceedingly fast data access. Therefore, the lower part of the resident operating system code is used for sections of the kernel that require maximum performance, such as the code that dispatches units of execution, called "threads of execution," in a processor.

When users create a new process they can specify that the VM Manager initialize their virtual address space by duplicating the virtual address space of another process. Therefore, environment subsystems can present to their client processes views of memory that don't correspond to the virtual address space of a native NT process.

Paging

The pager is the part of the VM Manager that transfers pages between page frames in memory and disk storage. As such, it's a complex combination of both software policies and hardware mechanisms. Software policies determine *when* to bring a page into memory and *where* to put it. Hardware mechanisms include the exact manner in which the VM Manager translates virtual addresses into physical addresses.

Because the hardware features of each system directly affect the success of the VM Manager, implementation of virtual memory varies from processor to processor. Therefore, this portion of the operating system isn't portable and must be modified for each new hardware platform. To ease transition, Windows keeps this code small and well isolated. The processor chip that handles address translation and exception handling looks at each address generated by a program and translates it into a physical address. If the page containing the address isn't in memory, then the hardware generates a page fault and issues a call to the pager. The translation look-aside buffer (TLB) is a hardware array of associative memory (explained in Chapter 3) used by the processor to speed memory access. As pages are brought into memory by the VM Manager, it creates entries for them in the TLB. If a virtual address isn't in the TLB, it may still be in memory. In that case, virtual software rather than hardware is used to find the address, resulting in slower access times.

Paging policies in a virtual memory system dictate *how* and *when* paging is done and are composed of fetch, placement, and replacement policies.

- The **fetch policy** determines when the pager copies a page from disk to memory. Several fetch policies were presented in Chapter 3. The VM Manager uses a demand paging algorithm with locality of reference, called "clustering," to load pages into memory. This strategy attempts to minimize the number of page faults that a process encounters.

- The **placement policy** is the set of rules that determines where the virtual page is loaded in memory. If memory isn't full, the VM Manager selects the first page frame from a list of free page frames. This list is called the page frame database, and is an array of entries numbered from zero through $n - 1$, with n equaling the number of page frames of memory in the system. Each entry contains information about the corresponding page frame, which can be in one of six states at any given time: valid, zeroed, free, standby, modified, or bad. Valid and modified page frames are those currently in use. Those zeroed, free, or on standby represent available page frames; bad frames can't be used.

  Of the available page frames, the page frame database links together those that are in the same state, thus creating five separate homogeneous lists. Whenever the number of pages in the zeroed, free, and standby lists reaches a preset minimum, the modified page writer process is activated to write the contents of the modified pages to disk and link them to the standby list. On the other hand, if the modified page list becomes too short, the VM Manager shrinks each process's working set to its minimum working set size and adds the newly freed pages to the modified or standby lists to be reused.

- The **replacement policy** determines which virtual page must be removed from memory to make room for a new page. Of the replacement policies considered in Chapter 3, the VM Manager uses a local FIFO replacement policy and keeps track of the pages currently in memory for each process—the process's working set. The FIFO algorithm is local to each process, so that when a page fault occurs, only page frames owned by a process can be freed. When it's created, each process is assigned a minimum working-set size, which is the number of pages the process is guaranteed to have in memory while it's executing. If memory isn't very full, the VM Manager allows the process to have the pages it needs up to its working set maximum. If the process requires even more pages, the VM Manager removes one of the process's pages for each new page fault the process generates.

Certain parts of the VM Manager are dependent on the processor running the operating system and must be modified for each platform. These platform-specific features include page table entries, page size, page-based protection, and virtual address translation.

Processor Management

In general, a process is the combination of an executable program, a private memory area, and system resources allocated by the operating system as the program executes. However, a process in Windows NT-derived operating systems requires a fourth component before it can do any work: at least one thread of execution. A thread is the entity within a process that the kernel schedules for execution; it could be roughly equated to a task. Using multiple threads, also called multithreading, allows a programmer to break up a single process into several executable segments and also to take advantage of the extra CPU power available in computers with multiple processors.

To explain how Microsoft developed multithreading for Windows operating systems, let's look at the evolution of its products.

Microsoft Windows 3.1 is a cooperative multitasking operating environment. This means that several processes appear to be running at the same time, so a word processor can function in one window while a spreadsheet appears to run in another. The word "cooperative" indicates that each program controls the resources and their releases, which presents problems if one program monopolizes a resource for a long time, to the detriment of other programs. A major problem of cooperative systems is that if one program becomes deadlocked, it can't release its resources, resulting in a deadlocked system.

Windows is a preemptive-multitasking, multithreaded operating system. It enhances the smoothness of operation and process independence of UNIX by allowing a process to break up into several threads of execution. By default, a process contains one thread, which is composed of the following:

• a unique identifier
• the contents of a volatile set of registers indicating the processor's state
• two stacks used during the thread's execution
• a private storage area used by subsystems and dynamic-link libraries

These components are called the thread's context; the actual data forming this context varies from one processor to another. The kernel schedules threads for execution on a processor. For example, when you use the mouse to double-click an icon in the Program Manager, the operating system creates a process, and that process has one thread that runs the icon's code. The process is like a container for the global variables, the environment strings, the heap owned by the application, and the thread. The thread is what actually executes the code. Figure 14.2 shows a diagram of a process with a single thread.

(figure 14.2)

Unitasking in Windows. Here's how a process with a single thread is scheduled for execution on a system with a single processor.

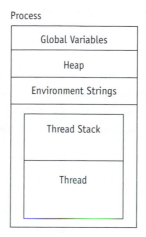

For systems with multiple processors, a process can have as many threads as there are CPUs available. The overhead incurred by a thread is minimal. In some cases, it's actually advantageous to split a single application into multiple threads because the entire program is then much easier to understand. The creation of threads isn't as complicated as it may seem. Although each thread has its own stack, all threads belonging to one process share its global variables, heap, and environment strings, as shown in Figure 14.3.

(figure 14.3)

Multitasking using multi-threading. Here's how a process with four threads can be scheduled for execution on a system with four processors.

Multiple threads can present problems because it's possible for several different threads to modify the same global variables independently of each other. To prevent this, versions of Windows since NT include some synchronization mechanisms to give exclusive access to global variables as these multithreaded processes are executed.

For example, let's say the user is modifying a database application. When the user enters a series of records into the database, the cursor changes into a combination of hourglass and arrow pointer, indicating that a thread is writing the last record to the disk while another thread is accepting new data. Therefore, even as processing is going on, the user can perform other tasks. The concept of overlapped I/O is now occurring on the user's end, as well as on the computer's end.

Multithreading is advantageous when doing database searches because data is retrieved faster when the system has several threads of execution that are searching an array simultaneously, especially if each thread has its own CPU. Programs written to take advantage of these features must be designed very carefully to minimize contention, such as when two CPUs attempt to access the same memory location at the same time, or when two threads compete for single shared resources, such as a hard disk.

Client/server applications tend to be CPU-intensive for the server because, although queries on the database are received as requests from a client computer, the actual query is managed by the server's processor. Therefore, if ten users send their database queries at the same time, the system will have difficulty searching for the data and transmitting it from disk to memory. A Windows multiprocessing environment can satisfy those requests by allocating additional CPU resources.

Device Management

The I/O system must accommodate the needs of existing devices—from a simple mouse and keyboard to printers, display terminals, disk drives, CD-ROM drives, multimedia devices, and networks. In addition, it must consider future storage and input technologies. The I/O system provides a uniform high-level interface for executive-level I/O operations and protects application programs from differences among physical devices. It shields the rest of the operating system from the details of device manipulation and thus minimizes and isolates hardware-dependent code.

The I/O system in Windows NT and its networking descendents was designed to provide the following:
• Multiple installable file systems including FAT, the CD-ROM file system, and NTFS
• Services to make device-driver development as easy as possible yet workable on multiprocessor systems
• Ability for system administrators to add drivers to the system or remove them from the system dynamically
• Fast I/O processing while allowing drivers to be written in high-level language
• Mapped file I/O capabilities for image activation, file caching, and application use

The I/O system is packet driven. That is, every I/O request is represented by an I/O request packet (IRP) as it moves from one I/O system component to another. An IRP is a data structure that controls how the I/O operation is processed at each step. The

I/O Manager creates an IRP that represents each I/O operation, passes the IRP to the appropriate driver, and disposes of the packet when the operation is complete. On the other hand, when a driver receives the IRP, it performs the specified operation and then either passes it back to the I/O Manager or passes it through the I/O Manager to another driver for further processing.

In addition to creating and disposing of IRPs, the I/O Manager supplies code, common to different drivers, that they call to carry out their I/O processing. It also manages buffers for I/O requests, provides time-out support for drivers, and records which installable file systems are loaded into the operating system. It provides flexible I/O facilities that allow subsystems such as POSIX to implement their respective I/O application programming interfaces. Finally, the I/O Manager allows device drivers and file systems, which it perceives as device drivers, to be loaded dynamically based on the needs of the user.

To make sure the operating system works with a wide range of hardware peripherals, Windows provides a device-independent model for I/O services. This model takes advantage of a concept called a "multilayered device driver" that's not found in operating systems, such as MS-DOS, with monolithic device drivers. These drivers provide a large and complex set of services that are understood by an intermediate layer of the operating system.

Each device driver is made up of a standard set of routines including the following:
- Initialization routine, which creates system objects used by the I/O Manager to recognize and access the driver.
- Dispatch routine, functions performed by the driver, such as READ or WRITE. This is used by the I/O Manager to communicate with the driver when it generates an IRP after an I/O request.
- Start I/O routine, used by the driver to initiate data transfer to or from a device.
- Completion routine, used to notify a driver that a lower-level driver has finished processing an IRP.
- Unload routine, which releases any system resources used by the driver so that the I/O Manager can remove them from memory.
- Error logging routine, used when unexpected hardware errors occur such as a bad sector on a disk; the information is passed to the I/O Manager, which writes all this information to an error log file.

When a process needs to access a file, the I/O Manager must determine from the file object's name which driver should be called to process the request, and it must be able to locate this information the next time a process uses the same file. This is accomplished by a driver object, which represents an individual driver in the system and a device object, which represents a physical, logical, or virtual device on the system and describes its characteristics.

The I/O Manager creates a driver object when a driver is loaded into the system and then calls the driver's initialization routine, which records the driver entry points in the driver object and creates one device object for each device to be handled by this driver. An example showing how an application instruction results in disk access is shown in Table 14.4 and graphically illustrated in Figure 14.4.

Event	Result
Instruction: READ "MYFILE.TXT"	READ = FUNCTION CODE 1 "MYFILE.TXT" = DISK SECTOR 10
Actions:	1. Access DRIVER OBJECT (1)
	2. Activate READ routine
	3. Access DISK SECTOR 10

(table 14.4)

Example showing how a device object is created from an instruction to read a file. The actual instruction is translated as illustrated in Figure 14.4.

Figure 14.4 illustrates how the last device object points back to its driver object, telling the I/O Manager which driver routine to call when it receives an I/O request. It works in the following manner: When a process requests access to a file it uses a filename, which includes the device object where the file is stored. When the file is opened the I/O Manager creates a file object and then returns a file handle to the process. Whenever the process uses the file handle, the I/O Manager can immediately find the device object, which points to the driver object representing the driver that services the device. Using the function code supplied in the original request the I/O Manager indexes into the driver object and activates the appropriate routine because each function code corresponds to a driver routine entry point.

(figure 14.4)

The driver object from Table 14.4 is connected to several device objects. The last device object points back to the driver object.

A driver object may have multiple device objects connected to it. The list of device objects represents the physical, logical, and virtual devices that are controlled by the driver.

For example, each sector of a hard disk has a separate device object with sector-specific information. However, the same hard disk driver is used to access all sectors. When a driver is unloaded from the system, the I/O Manager uses the queue of device objects to determine which devices will be affected by the removal of the driver.

Using objects to keep track of information about drivers frees the I/O Manager from having to know details about individual drivers—it just follows a pointer to locate a driver. This provides portability and allows new drivers to be easily loaded. Another advantage to representing devices and drivers with different objects is that it's easier to assign drivers to control additional or different devices if the system configuration changes.

Figure 14.5 shows how the I/O Manager interacts with a layered device driver to write data to a file on a hard disk by following these steps in order:

1. An application issues a command to write to a disk file at a specified byte off-set within the file.
2. The I/O Manager passes the file handle to the file system driver.

(figure 14.5)

Details of the layering of a file system driver and a disk driver first shown in Figure 14.4. These are the five steps that take place when the I/O Manager needs to access a secondary storage device to satisfy the user command shown here as number 1.

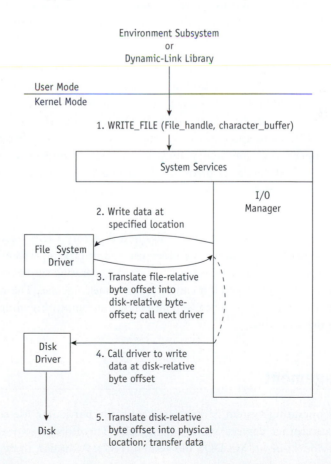

445

3. The I/O Manager translates the file-relative byte offset into a disk-relative byte offset and calls the next driver.
4. The function code and the disk-relative byte offset are passed to the disk driver.
5. The disk-relative byte offset is translated into the physical location and data is transferred.

This process parallels the discussion in Chapter 8 about levels in a file management system.

The I/O Manager knows nothing about the file system. The process described in this example works exactly the same if an NTFS driver is replaced by a FAT driver, a UNIX file system driver, a CD-ROM driver, a Macintosh file system driver, or any other driver.

Keep in mind that there is overhead involved when the I/O Manager passes requests for information back and forth. So for simple devices, such as serial and parallel printer ports, the operating system provides a single-layer device driver approach in which the I/O Manager can communicate with the device driver, which, in turn, returns information directly. But for more complicated devices, particularly for devices such as hard drives that depend on a file system, a multilayered approach is a better choice.

Another device driver feature that's unique to current Windows operating systems is that almost all low-level I/O operations are asynchronous. That means that when an application issues an I/O request it doesn't have to wait for data to be transferred, but it can continue to perform other work while data transfer is taking place. Asynchronous I/O must be specified by the process when it opens a file handle. During asynchronous operations, the process must be careful not to access any data from the I/O operation until the device driver has finished data transfer. Asynchronous I/O is useful for operations that take a long time to complete or for which completion time is variable.

For example, the time it takes to list the files in a directory varies according to the number of files. Because Windows is a preemptive multitasking system that may be running many tasks at the same time, it's vital that the operating system not waste time waiting for a request to be filled if it can be doing something else. The various layers in the operating system use preemptive multitasking and multithreading to get more work done in the same time.

File Management

Typically, an operating system is associated with the particular file structure that it uses for mass storage devices, such as hard disks. Therefore, we speak of a UNIX file system (i-nodes) or an MS-DOS file system (FAT). Although there is a resident

NT file system (NTFS), current versions of Windows are designed to be independent of the file system on which they operate.

Windows supports multiple file systems for hard disks including MS-DOS's FAT file system and a 32-bit FAT file system, as well as NTFS. NTFS extends the capabilities of the FAT and FAT32 file systems by adding:

- File system recovery that allows for quick restoration of disk-based data after a system failure
- The ability to handle large storage media, on the order of approximately 17 billion gigabytes in size
- Security features, including execute-only files
- Unicode filenames, which allow documents to be transferred from one computer to another internationally without distorting their file names or path names
- Support for the POSIX operating system environment, including hard links, case-sensitive names, and information about when a file was last opened
- Features for future extensibility, such as transaction-based operations to support fault-tolerant applications, user-controlled version numbers for files, multiple data streams per file, flexible options for file naming and file attributes, and support for popular file servers.

The primary file handling concept in current versions of Windows, first introduced in UNIX, is the virtual file—that's any I/O source or destination—and it's treated as if it were a file. In Windows, programs perform I/O on virtual files, manipulating them by using file handles. Although not a new concept, in Windows a file handle actually refers to an executive file object that represents all sources and destinations of I/O. Processes call native file object services such as those to read from or write to a file. The I/O Manager directs these virtual file requests to real files, file directories, physical devices, or any other destination supported by the system. File objects have hierarchical names, are protected by object-based security, support synchronization, and are handled by object services.

When opening a file, a process supplies the file's name and the type of access required. This request moves to an environment subsystem that in turn calls a system service. The Object Manager starts an object name lookup and turns control over to the I/O Manager to find the file object. The I/O Manager checks the security subsystem to determine whether or not access can be granted. The I/O Manager also uses the file object to determine whether asynchronous I/O operations are requested.

The creation of file objects helps bridge the gap between the characteristics of physical devices and directory structures, file system structures, and data formats. File objects provide a memory-based representation of shareable physical resources. When a file is opened the I/O Manager returns a handle to a file object. The Object Manager treats file objects like all other objects until the time comes to

443

write to, or read from, a device, at which point the Object Manager calls the I/O Manager for assistance to access the device. Figure 14.6 illustrates the contents of file objects and the services that operate on them. Table 14.5 describes in detail the object body attributes.

Object Type — File

Object Body Attributes:
- Filename
- Device Type
- Byte Offset
- Share Mode
- Open Mode
- File Disposition

Services:
- Create File
- Open File
- Read File
- Write File
- Query File Information
- Set File Information
- Query Extended Attributes
- Set Extended Attributes
- Lock Byte Range
- Unlock Byte Range
- Cancel I/O
- Flush Buffers
- Query Directory File
- Notify Caller When Directory Changes
- Get Volume Information
- Set Volume Information

(figure 14.6)

Illustration of a file object, its attributes, and the services that operate on them. The attributes are explained in Table 14.5.

Attribute	Purpose
Filename	Identifies the physical file to which the file object refers
Device type	Indicates the type of device on which the file resides
Byte offset	Identifies the current location in the file (valid only for synchronous I/O)
Share mode	Indicates whether other callers can open the file for read, write, or delete operations while this caller is using it
Open mode	Indicates whether I/O is synchronous or asynchronous, cached or noncached, sequential or random, etc.
File disposition	Indicates whether to delete the file after closing it

(table 14.5)

Description of the attributes shown in Figure 14.6.

Let's make a distinction between a file object, a memory-based representation of a shareable resource that contains only data unique to an object handle, and the file itself, which contains the data to be shared. Each time a process opens a handle, a new file object is created with a new set of handle-specific attributes. For example, the attribute byte offset refers to the location in the file where the next READ or WRITE operation using that handle will occur. It might help if you think of file object attributes as being specific to a single handle.

Although a file handle is unique to a process, the physical resource isn't. Therefore, processes must synchronize their access to shareable files, directories, and devices. For example, if a process is writing to a file, it should specify exclusive write-access or lock portions of the file while writing to it, to prevent other processes from writing to that file at the same time.

Mapped file I/O is an important feature of the I/O system and is achieved through the cooperation of the I/O system and the VM Manager. At the operating system level, file mapping is typically used for file caching, loading, and running executable programs. The VM Manager allows user processes to have mapped file I/O capabilities through native services. Memory-mapped files exploit virtual memory capabilities by allowing an application to open a file of arbitrary size and treat it as a single contiguous array of memory locations without buffering data or performing disk I/O.

For example, a file of 100 MB can be opened and treated as an array in a system with only 20 MB of memory. At any one time only a portion of the file data is physically present in memory—the rest is paged out to the disk. When the application requests data that's not currently stored in memory, the VM Manager uses its paging mechanism to load the correct page from the disk file. When the application writes to its virtual memory space, the VM Manager writes the changes back to the file as part of the normal paging. Because the VM Manager optimizes its disk accesses, applications that are I/O bound can speed up their execution by using mapped I/O—writing to memory is faster than writing to a secondary storage device.

A component of the I/O system called the **cache manager** uses mapped I/O to manage its memory-based cache. The cache expands or shrinks dynamically depending on the amount of memory available. Using normal working-set strategies, the VM Manager expands the size of the cache when there is memory available to accommodate the application's needs, and reduces the cache when it needs free pages. The cache manager takes advantage of the VM Manager's paging system, avoiding duplication of effort.

NTFS supports long filenames that can include spaces and special characters. Therefore, users can name a file "Spring 2005 Student Grades" instead of something cryptic like S05STD.GRD. Because the use of long filenames could create compatibility problems with older operating systems that might reside on the network, NTFS automatically converts long filenames to the standard eight-character filename and three-character extension required by MS-DOS and 16-bit Windows applications. NTFS does this by keeping a table that lists each long filename and relates it to the corresponding short filename.

Network Management

In Windows NT-based operating systems, networking isn't an add-on layer to the existing operating system. Rather, it's an integral part of the operating system executive, providing services such as user accounts, resource security, and mechanisms used to implement communication between computers, such as with named pipes and mailslots. **Named pipes** provide a high-level interface for passing data between two processes regardless of their locations. **Mailslots** provide one-to-many and many-to-one communication mechanisms useful for broadcasting messages to any number of processes.

MS-NET

Microsoft Networks, informally known as "MS-NET," was released in 1984 and became the model for the NT Network Manager (Custer, 1993). Three MS-NET components—the redirector, the server message block (SMB) protocol, and the network server—were extensively refurbished and incorporated into Windows NT and later versions.

The redirector, coded in the C programming language, is implemented as a loadable file system driver and isn't dependent on the system's hardware architecture. Its function is to direct an I/O request from a user or application to the remote server that has the appropriate file or resource needed to satisfy the request. A network can incorporate multiple redirectors, each of which directs I/O requests to remote file systems or devices. A typical remote I/O request might result in the following progression:

1. The user-mode software issues a remote I/O request by calling local I/O services.
2. After some initial processing, the I/O Manager creates an I/O request packet (IRP) and passes the request to the Windows redirector, which forwards the IRP to the transport drivers.
3. Finally, the transport drivers process the request and place it on the network. The reverse sequence is observed when the request reaches its destination.

The SMB protocol is a high-level specification for formatting messages to be sent across the network and correlates to the application layer (layer 7), and the presentation layer (layer 6) of the OSI model described in Chapter 9. An API called NetBIOS interface is used to pass I/O requests structured in the SMB format to a remote computer. Both the SMB protocols and the NetBIOS API were adopted in several networking products before appearing in Windows.

The Windows Server operating systems are written in C for complete compatibility with existing MS-NET and LAN Manager SMB protocols, are implemented as loadable file system drivers, and have no dependency on the hardware architecture on which the operating system is running.

Figure 14.7 (adapted from Custer, 1993) shows how the seven layers of the OSI reference model are implemented in current Windows network management. As discussed

(figure 14.7)

Implementation of the seven layers of the OSI reference model in the Windows network manager. (Adapted from Custer, 1993.)

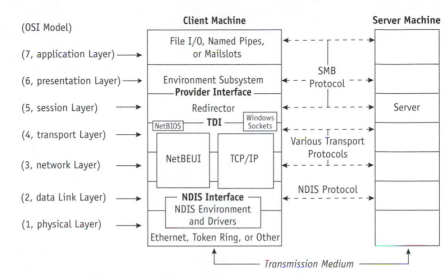

in Chapter 9, each layer of the hierarchy assumes that it's communicating to the same layer on another machine and uses a common protocol. In reality, however, a message must pass *down* each layer on the client machine, be transmitted across the network, and then pass *up* each layer of the destination machine until the request is satisfied.

Directory Services

The **Active Directory** database, implemented beginning with Windows 2000, stores all types of information so it can be a general-purpose directory service for a heterogeneous network.

Microsoft built the Active Directory entirely around the **Domain Name Service or Domain Name System (DNS)** and **Lightweight Directory Access Protocol (LDAP)**. DNS is the hierarchical replicated naming service on which the Internet is built. However, although DNS is the backbone directory protocol for one of the largest data networks, it doesn't provide enough flexibility to act as an enterprise directory by itself. That is, DNS is primarily a service for mapping machine names to IP addresses which is not enough for a full directory service, which must be able to map names of arbitrary objects (such as machines and applications) to any kind of information about those objects.

Active Directory groups machines into administrative units called domains, each of which gets a DNS domain name (such as pitt.edu). Each domain must have at least one domain controller which is a machine running the Active Directory server.

For improved fault tolerance and performance, a domain can have more than one domain controller with each holding a complete copy of that domain's directory database.

Current versions of Windows network operating systems eliminate the distinction between primary domain controllers and backup domain controllers making the

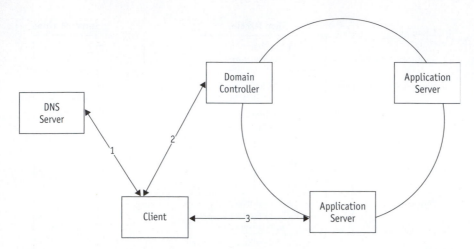

(figure 14.8)

Active Directory clients use standard DNS and LDAP protocols to locate objects on the network.

network simpler to administer because it doesn't have multiple hierarchies. Active Directory clients use standard DNS and LDAP protocols to locate objects on the network. As shown in Figure 14.8, here's how it works.

1. A client that needs to look up an Active Directory name first passes the DNS part of the name to a standard DNS server. The DNS server returns the network address of the domain controller responsible for that name.

2. Next, the client uses LDAP to query the domain controller to find the address of the system that holds the service the client needs.

3. Finally, the client establishes a direct connection with the requested service using the correct protocol required by that service.

Security Management

Today's Windows network operating systems provide an object-based security model. That is, a security object can represent any resource in the system: a file, device, process, program, or user. This allows system administrators to give precise security access to specific objects in the system while allowing them to monitor and record how objects are used.

One of the biggest concerns about Windows operating systems in general is the need for aggressive patch management (discussed in Chapter 12) to combat the many viruses and worms that target these systems.

Security Basics

The U.S. Department of Defense has identified and categorized into seven levels of security certain features that make an operating system secure. Early versions of Windows targeted Class C2 level with a plan to evolve to Class B2 level—a more stringent level of security in which each user must be assigned a specific security level clearance and is thwarted from giving lower-level users access to protected resources.

To comply with the Class C2 level of security, Windows 2000 and above include the following features:

- A secure logon facility requiring users to identify themselves by entering a unique logon identifier and a password before they're allowed access to the system
- Discretionary access control allowing the owner of a resource to determine who else can access the resource and what they can do to it
- Auditing ability to detect and record important security-related events or any attempt to create, access, or delete system resources
- Memory protection preventing anyone from reading information written by someone else after a data structure has been released back to the operating system

Windows strives to prevent access by unauthorized users while allowing entry to legitimate users by supporting a multilayered security system. Password management is the first layer of security.

If a hard disk is formatted with the NTFS, users encounter a second layer of security that deals directly with file access security. At this level, the user can create a file and establish various combinations of individuals to have access to it because the operating system makes distinctions between owners and groups. The creator of a file is its owner. The owner can designate a set of users as belonging to a group and allow all the members of the group to have access to that file. Conversely, the owner could prevent some of the members from accessing that file.

In addition to determining who is allowed to access a file, users can decide what type of operations a person is allowed to perform on a file. For example, one may have read-only access, while another may have read-and-write privileges. As a final measure, the operating system gives the user auditing capabilities that automatically keep track of who uses files and how.

Security Terminology

The built-in security for recent Windows network operating systems is a necessary element for managers of Web servers and networks. Its directory service lets users find what they need and a communications protocol lets users interact with it. However, because not everyone should be able to find or interact with everything in the network, controlling access is the job of distributed security services.

Effective distributed security requires an authentication mechanism that allows a client to prove its identity to a server. Then the client needs to supply authorization information that the server uses to determine which specific access rights have been given to this client. Finally, it needs to provide data integrity using a variety of methods ranging from a cryptographic checksum for all transmitted data to completely encrypting all transmitted data.

Recent Windows operating systems provide this with **Kerberos** security, as described in Chapter 11. Kerberos provides authentication, data integrity, and data privacy. In addition, it provides mutual authentication, which means that both the client and server can verify the identity of the other. (Other security systems require only that the clients prove their identity. Servers are automatically authenticated.)

Each domain has its own Kerberos server, which shares the database used by Active Directory. This means that the Kerberos server must execute on the domain-controller machine and, like the Active Directory server, it can be replicated within a domain. Every user who wants to securely access remote services must log on to a Kerberos server. Figure 14.9 shows the path followed by a request from an application to a service provided on the network.

(figure 14.9)

Requests from an application flow through a series of security providers, as do the responses from the network back to the application.

A successful login returns a **ticket granting ticket** to the user, which can be handed back to the Kerberos server to request tickets to specific applications servers.

If the Kerberos server determines that a user is presenting a valid ticket, it returns the requested ticket to the user with no questions asked. The user sends this ticket to the remote applications server, which can examine it to verify the user's identity and authenticate the user. All of these tickets are encrypted in different ways, and various keys are used to perform the encryption.

Different implementations of Kerberos send different authorization information. Microsoft has implemented the standard Kerberos protocol to make the product more compatible with other Kerberos implementations.

Different security protocols can have very different APIs, creating problems for applications that might want to use more than one of them. Microsoft has addressed this problem by separating the users of distributed security services from their providers, allowing support for many options without creating unusable complexity.

User Interface

Users already familiar with previous Windows products often find each release of Windows familiar because the products share the same look and feel. The desktop contains the icons for the tools and applications one can use to get work done. Users move around the desktop using a pointing device such as mouse, light pen, or stylus. Most novice users prefer pointing devices, while some experienced users prefer keyboard shortcuts to access both menus and commands quickly.

To start an application, users double-click an application icon or select it from the Start menu. To quit an application, they can select Exit from the File menu or click the "x" in the top-right corner of the window.

Although a detailed description of the tools present on the desktop is beyond the scope of this chapter, we'll take a brief look at the Start Menu because it's the key application of the Windows desktop. Figure 14.10 shows a typical Start Menu. Windows XP Professional is used for all of the examples and screenshots in this section.

(figure 14.10)

A typical Windows Start Menu divides functions into logical groups and it lists the applications most recently used.

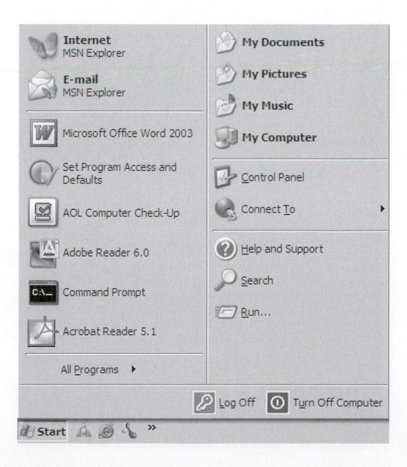

The Start Menu organizes files and programs into logical groups. From here users perform common functions including the following:

- *All Programs* goes to a list of many available applications. The applications listed above were recently used. To open one again, click the icon.
- *My Documents*, *My Pictures*, and *My Music*, and *My Computer* open folders with applications and files relating to a user's documents, pictures, music and computer setup. Launch applications through a recently-used data file.
- *Control Panel* directly accesses key system settings.
- *Help and Support* goes directly to the help file.
- *Search* initiates a searching routine.
- *Run* can be used to run an application from a command-line screen or a browse function.
- *Log Off* logs this user out of the system
- *Turn Off Computer* shuts down or restarts the operating system.

(figure 14.11)

Priority management in the Windows XP Professional Task Manager.

The Windows Task Manager, opened by pressing and holding the Ctrl, Alt, and Delete keys, offers users the chance to view running applications and processes, and set the priorities of each, as shown in Figure 14.11. From this window, users can also view information about performance, networking, and other users logged into the system.

A standard utility program called Windows Explorer (not to be confused with Microsoft's Web browser called Internet Explorer) contains directory and file display tools and a file finding tool, as shown in Figure 14.12.

(figure 14.12)

Windows Explorer is a file management tool that displays directories (folders) on the left and its contents on the right. In this example, the default configuration has been customized to show the files' attributes.

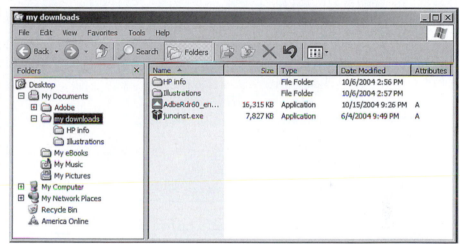

Windows Explorer features a series of pull-down menus along the top that are used to complete specific tasks:

- *File* contains menu items for creating new folders and creating shortcuts to applications.
- *Edit* contains menu items for undoing, cutting, pasting, and selecting files and directories.
- *View* shows options used to customize the way the page looks.
- *Favorites* shows a list of favorite Web sites, customizable by the user.
- *Tools* contains helpful tools, including a file or folder search capability and a network mapping function.
- *Help* opens the hypertext help tools.

For example, to add a new folder to an existing directory, open Windows Explorer and use the mouse pointer to open the existing folder for the directory that will house the new folder. While the existing folder is highlighted, click File, New, Folder. Then type in the name of the new folder and press the Enter key. Figure 14.13 shows the pull-down menu for the File option.

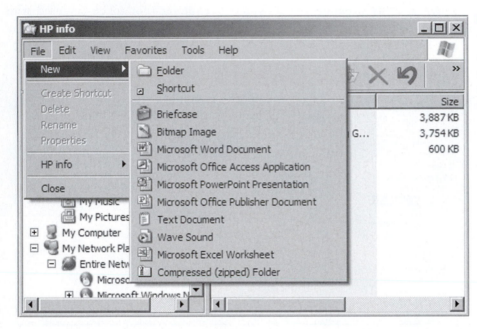

(figure 14.13)

To create a new folder in an existing folder, make sure the parent folder is open, then click File, New, Folder.

Program items can also be data files. The easiest way to add a data file to a program group is to drag it from the Explorer file manager window and the file appears with the icon of its parent application. For example, a file with the extension ".doc" has the icon identifying it as requiring the default word processing program. If the file isn't associated with any applications, it has a generic icon.

For networked systems, there are tools to help users identify and access network re-sources, such as folders, printers, and connections to other nodes. To identify them, go to My Network Places and click the option to map a network drive, as shown in Figure 14.14.

You can also use the commands within the File menu to move, copy, and delete icons from the desktop. This is a bonus to users who learned their first applications on UNIX, DOS, or another command-driven operating system.

(figure 14.14)

Users on a network can map a network drive to identify available resources.

Some people are so familiar with the command line that they can type commands faster than the system can execute them. A command interface that resembles MS-DOS is available from most Windows desktops, as shown in Figure 13.1 in the last chapter. Using this feature, almost anything that can be done from MS-DOS can be done in Windows.

For users who are faster with the keyboard than with a pointing device, Windows provides many keyboard shortcuts. For a guide, look for keyboard shortcuts on the pull-down menus, such as the one shown in Figure 14.15, which identifies Ctrl+C as the keyboard shortcut to make a copy of the selected object. To do so, press and hold the control (Ctrl) key and then press the "c" key.

A powerful feature of recent versions of Windows is their accommodation for users working in non-English languages. Windows has built-in input methods and fonts for many languages including double-byte languages such as Japanese. During installation, the system administrator can select one or several languages for the system, even adding different language support for specific individuals. For example, one user can work in Chinese while another can work in Hindi. Even better, the system's own resources also become multilingual, which means that the operating system changes its dialog boxes, prompts, and menus to support the user's preferred language.

(figure 14.15)

Keyboard shortcuts are shown on the right next to the menu items. For example, Ctrl+X is the keyboard shortcut for Cut.

For users who need enhanced accessibility options or who have difficulty using a standard keyboard, but who need its functionality, Windows offers an on-screen keyboard, as shown in Figure 14.16. This and other helpful tools (a magnifier, reader, and more) can be found from the Start button under Accessories, Accessibility.

(figure 14.16)

From the Accessories folder, Accessibility tools, such as an on-screen keyboard, are available to provide enhanced user interface tools.

Details about the system's hardware and software can be found from the Start, as shown in Figure 14.17.

(figure 14.17)

From the Accessories folder, System Information is available for hardware, software, and network components.

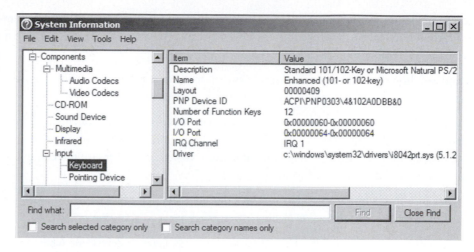

Conclusion

Current Windows operating systems such as Windows XP Professional and Windows Server 2003 incorporate ease-of-use with the technical power to operate a network across several existing platforms. Because these systems were designed to evolve modularly and consistently over time, their portability eases the difficulty of migrating it to new hardware platforms.

The introduction of significant security controls in Windows in recent operating systems has helped them gain inroads with organizations requiring consistent protection for their data and applications. Their authentication models support new user interfaces from bank teller machines to fingerprint or retinal scanners. They also allow the implementation of different security architectures such as the Kerberos model on top of the operating system, further extending the reach of Windows into the market.

That said, Windows operating systems require aggressive patch management because Windows has been targeted by viruses and worms designed to take advantage of security flaws as soon as they're discovered. That is an issue shared by UNIX and Linux, which we discuss in the next chapter.

Key Terms

Active Directory: Microsoft Windows directory service that offers centralized administration of application serving, authentication, and user registration for distributed networking systems.

cache manager: a component of the I/O system that manages the part of virtual memory known as cache. The cache expands or shrinks dynamically depending on the amount of memory available.

compatibility: the ability of an operating system to execute programs written for other operating systems or for earlier versions of the same system.

Domain Name Service or Domain Name System (DNS): a general-purpose, distributed, replicated, data query service. Its principal function is the resolution of Internet addresses based on fully qualified domain names such as .com (for commercial entity) or .edu (for educational institution).

extensibility: one of an operating system's design goals that allows it to be easily enhanced as market requirements change.

fetch policy: the rules used by the Virtual Memory Manager to determine when a page is copied from disk to memory.

graphical user interface (GUI): a user interface that allows the user to activate operating system commands by clicking on desktop icons or menus using a pointing device such as a mouse or touch screen. GUI evolved from command-driven user interfaces.

Kerberos: MIT-developed authentication system that allows network managers to administer and manage user authentication at the network level.

kernel mode: name given to indicate that processes are granted privileged access to the processor. Therefore, all machine instructions are allowed and system memory is accessible. Contrasts with the more restrictive user mode.

Lightweight Directory Access Protocol (LDAP): a protocol that defines a method for creating searchable directories of resources on a network. It's called "lightweight" because it is a simplified and TCP/IP-enabled version of the X.500 directory protocol.

mailslots: a high-level network software interface for passing data among processes in a one-to-many and many-to-one communication mechanism. Mailslots are useful for broadcasting messages to any number of processes.

named pipes: a high-level software interface to NetBIOS, which represents the hardware in network applications as abstract objects. Named pipes are represented as file objects in Windows NT and later and operate under the same security mechanisms as other executive objects.

NT file system (NTFS): The file system introduced with Windows NT that offers file management services, such as permission management, compression, transaction logs, and the ability to create a single volume spanning two or more physical disks.

placement policy: the rules used by the Virtual Memory Manager to determine where the virtual page is to be loaded in memory.

portability: the ability to move an entire operating system to a machine based on a different processor or configuration with as little recoding as possible.

POSIX: Portable Operating System Interface for Computer Environments, an operating system application program interface developed by IEEE to increase the portability of application software.

reliability: the ability of an operating system to respond predictably to error conditions, even those caused by hardware failures; or the ability of an operating system to actively protect itself and its users from accidental or deliberate damage by user programs.

replacement policy: the rules used by the Virtual Memory Manager to determine which virtual page must be removed from memory to make room for a new page.

ticket granting ticket: a virtual "ticket" given by a Kerberos server indicating that the user holding the ticket can be granted access to specific applications servers. The user sends this encrypted ticket to the remote applications server, which can then examine it to verify the user's identity and authenticate the user.

user mode: name given to indicate that processes are not granted privileged access to the processor. Therefore, certain instructions are not allowed and system memory isn't accessible. Contrasts with the less restrictive kernel mode.

Chapter 15 | UNIX and Linux Operating Systems

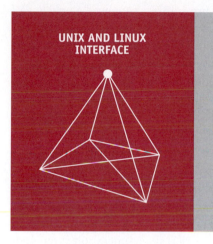

UNIX AND LINUX
INTERFACE

Design Goals

Memory Management

Processor Management

Device Management

File Management

User Interface

"All things are difficult before they are easy."

Thomas Fuller *(1654-1734)*

Learning Objectives

After completing this chapter, you should be able to describe:

• The similarities between UNIX and Linux
• The design goals for both operating systems
• The significance of using files to manipulate devices
• The differences between command-driven and menu-driven interfaces
• The roles of the Memory, Device, and Processor Managers

Unlike many operating systems, UNIX and Linux aren't limited to specific computers using a particular microprocessor as a CPU. Instead, they run on all sizes of computers using a wide range of microprocessors. In addition, current versions of many other operating systems have been revised to include the capability to run UNIX applications and connect smoothly with UNIX networks.

While Linux and UNIX are different operating systems, they strongly resemble each other in many ways. And while UNIX has enjoyed a dominant market role for decades, indications are that Linux and UNIX are now challenging each other as peers in every market. For example, as this text goes to press, IBM announced a new line of supercomputers that run on Linux in addition to its version of UNIX, called AIX. The same week, Sun Microsystems announced that it was releasing a free version of its UNIX-based Solaris operating system, presumably to compete with Linux for the small and midrange computer users. The competition between the two operating systems is one that's sure to play out in the marketplace for years to come.

Overview

UNIX and Linux share three major advantages: they are portable from large systems to small systems, they have very powerful utilities, and they are device independent. Their portability is attributed to the fact that both are written in a high-level language, C, instead of assembly language. Their utilities are brief, single-operation commands that can be combined in a single command line to achieve almost any desired result— a feature that many programmers find endearing. And because both include device drivers as part of the operating system, and not as part of the devices, both UNIX and Linux can be configured to run any device.

UNIX has the disadvantage of having no single standardized version of the operating system. (Linux is standardized.) Both share the disadvantage of having very brief, cryptic commands that novice users find unfriendly (see Appendix A for a comparison of UNIX commands with those from other operating systems).

Throughout our discussion of UNIX we'll describe AT&T's version unless otherwise specified. Note: UNIX and Linux are case-sensitive and strongly oriented toward lower-case characters which are faster and easier to type. Therefore, throughout this chapter all filenames and commands are shown in lower case.

History

The story of UNIX and Linux starts with a research project begun in 1965. It was a joint venture between Bell Laboratories (the research and development group of AT&T),

General Electric, and MIT (Massachusetts Institute of Technology) with a goal to develop the MULTICS operating system for the large and powerful GE-645 mainframe computer. MULTICS had a grand ambition: to serve the needs of a diverse group of users, but its ambition proved its undoing—it soon became too intricate, too complex, and too large to be of commercial value.

Bell Laboratories withdrew from the project in 1969, and AT&T management decided not to undertake the development of any more operating systems. But that didn't stop two young veterans of the MULTICS project, Ken Thompson and Dennis Ritchie. Some people say they needed a new operating system to support their favorite computer game. Regardless of their reasons for developing it, UNIX grew to become one of the most widely used operating systems in history.

The Evolution of UNIX

Thompson and Ritchie originally wrote UNIX in assembly language for a Digital Equipment Corporation PDP-7 computer. It was named "UNIX" by a colleague, Brian Kerninghan, as a play on words from MULTICS (Seyer & Mills, 1986).

The first official version, presented in 1971 by Thompson and Ritchie, was designed to run on the DEC PDP-11 minicomputer and included all of the features found in current versions, with the exception of pipes and filters, which were added with Version 2. Before long, UNIX became known as a major operating system. Table 15.1 shows how UNIX evolved in the early days. Note: Berkeley UNIX isn't included in Table 15.1; it was originally developed from Version 7, although some features from Berkeley versions were later integrated into System V.

(table 15.1)

The historical roots of UNIX, its features, and modifications. For current information about the history of UNIX, see www.theopengroup.org.

Year	Release	Features
1971	UNIX V1	Based on MULTICS; introduced shell concept, written in assembly language
1972	UNIX V2	Added pipes and filters
1973	UNIX V3	Kernel and I/O, first version written in C
1973	UNIX V4	
1975	UNIX V6	First version to become commercially available
1979	UNIX V7	More powerful shell added: string variables, structured programming, trap handling
1980	UNIX System III	First version used in 16-bit microcomputers

1981	UNIX System IV	First version available for a mainframe
1983	UNIX System V Release 1	Added small general-purpose programs
1984	UNIX System V Release 2	Added features from Berkeley version: shared memory, more commands, vi editor, termcap database, flex filenames
1988		The Open Group founded
1991	UNIX System V Release 4	Combined features from BSD, SunOS, and Xenix
1991	Solaris 1.0	Sun's version designed to run on Sun workstations, derived from AT&T's UNIX System V, Release 4
1993	Novell UnixWare	Novell's version of System V release 4 designed to work with NetWare
1994	Single UNIX Specification 1	Separates the UNIX trademark from actual code stream, opening the door to standardization
1997	Single UNIX Specification 2	Adds support for realtime processing, threads, and 64-bit processors
2001	Single UNIX Specification 3	Unites IEEE POSIX and industry efforts to standardize
2003	ISO/IEC 9945:2003	International standard approved for the core volumes of Single UNIX Specification Version 3

For Version 3, Ritchie took the innovative step of developing a new programming language, C, and wrote a compiler for the C language so UNIX could be rewritten in this faster, high-level language. C was specifically designed to meet the needs of systems designers who weren't familiar with writing programs in assembly language code.

As UNIX grew in fame and popularity, AT&T found itself in a difficult situation. At the time it was forbidden by government antitrust regulations to sell software—but it could, for a nominal fee, make the operating system available first to universities and later to independent developers who, in turn, transformed it into a commercial product. Between 1973 and 1975 several improved versions were developed—the most popular version was developed at the University of California at Berkeley and it became known as BSD. Its popularity in universities created a demand for it in business and industry—a demand AT&T was able to meet beginning in 1984 with the federal government's deregulation of its business.

AT&T entered the computer industry by offering a line of personal computers powered by UNIX System V—their version of UNIX with additional features from the Berkeley version. At that time, AT&T tried to promote their version of UNIX as the standard version, but by then UNIX had already been adopted and adapted by too many designers for too many machines.

By 1990, there were about two dozen versions of UNIX, among them AT&T's UNIX System V; A/UX (UNIX System V for the Macintosh II); Ultrix (UNIX for DEC's VAX system); Microsoft's XENIX (a UNIX-based operating system for microcomputers using Intel processors); and the University of California at Berkeley's UNIX Versions 4.1 bsd, 4.2 bsd, and 4.3 bsd. Berkeley UNIX is an expanded version of AT&T's Version 7. It was designed originally to run on VAX computers and became quite popular in many academic circles. Although it's a UNIX derivative, in some areas, such as file store structure and communications, it's very different from AT&T's System V.

In 1991, AT&T's Unix System Laboratories developed System V release 4 which incorporated almost all the features found in System V release 3 plus BSD release 4.3, SunOS, and Xenix. Other companies, including IBM and Hewlett-Packard, responded by establishing the The Open Group, which owns the trademark to the name UNIX, to create a standard version of the operating system.

By 1993 Berkeley released 4.4BSD based on AT&T's UNIX, requiring customers to obtain licenses from AT&T to use it. Shortly thereafter, Novell acquired UNIX from AT&T and released its own version called UNIX Ware designed to interact with Novell's NetWare system.

The original "do one thing well" position of the early commands has been modified in current releases, and recent commands offer many options and controls. This factor has pros and cons—although commands become more difficult to use, they can be adapted to new situations with relative ease. In essence, the key features of the early systems, such as pipelines, have been preserved, while the potential of the commands has increased to meet new needs.

The new releases offer full support for local area networks, and comply with international operating system standards. In addition, system security has been greatly improved and meets many of the U.S. government security requirements. Most UNIX systems feature the Common Desktop Environment (CDE) which is a uniform graphical user interface designed to give UNIX systems a standard look.

To resolve the issue of multiple standards, a problem that has plagued UNIX from its beginnings, the industry is attempting to standardize to improve portability of programs from one system to another. The release of ISO/IEC 9945:2003 is a big step in that direction, with more progress expected in the years to come.

The Evolution of Linux

Linux was developed in Finland by Linus Torvalds who wanted an operating system that could maximize the capabilities of the Intel 80386 microprocessor. He started with Minix (a miniature UNIX system developed primarily by Andrew Tanenbaum)

465

and rewrote certain parts to add more functionality. When he had a working operating system, he announced his achievement on an Internet usegroup with this message:

```
Hello everybody out there using minix.
I'm doing a (free) operating system (just a hobby, won't be
big and professional like gnu) for 386(486)AT clones.
```

It was August 1991, and Torvalds was 21. (Linux is a contraction of Linus and UNIX that when pronounced rhymes with "mimics.") The first version of Linux performed many of the same functions as MS-DOS and Windows but displayed impressive power and flexibility. Linux was based on a powerful multiplatform operating system, UNIX, unlike other microcomputer operating systems that began their development within the limits of small personal computers and had to be upgraded to keep up with the demands of ever-changing hardware. In other words, Linux brought the speed, efficiency, and flexibility of UNIX to a PC environment, taking advantage of all the capabilities built into personal computers (Horvath, 1998).

Table 15.2 shows the development of the Red Hat distribution of Linux since 1994. Other popular distributions of Linux include Mandrake, Debian, and SUSE.

Year	Release	Features
1994	Beta versions	First Red Hat Linux product available to the public in a series of beta versions.
1994	RHL 1.0	First non-beta release of Red Hat Linux.
1995	RHL 2.0	Written in Perl for quick development.
1996	RHL 3.0.3	The first approximately concurrent multi-architecture release; supported the Digital Alpha platform.
1996	RHL 4.0	Based on the 2.0.18 kernel and the first release to include documentation freely available in electronic form.
1997	RHL 5.0	Named 1997 InfoWorld Product of the Year.
1999	RHL 6.0	Integrated GNOME desktop GUI.
2000	RHL 7.0	First release that supported Red Hat Network out of the box.
2001	RHL 7.1	Introduced the 2.4 kernel.
2002	RHEL 2.1 AS (Advanced Server)	Launch of Red Hat Enterprise Linux, the first commercial enterprise computing offering, based on RHL 7.2.
2002	RHL 8.0	Designed to provide a unified look across RHL and RHEL desktops.

(table 15.2)

The major releases of Linux by Red Hat, Inc., one of several distributors of the Linux operating system. RHL is an acronym for Red Hat Linux. RHEL is an acronym for Red Hat Enterprise Linux. Fedora is a trademark of Red Hat, Inc.

2003	RHL 9	First release to include Native POSIX Thread Library (NPTL) support.
2003	RHEL 3	The first Red Hat product made to run on seven chip architectures (by Intel, AMD, and IBM).
2003	Fedora Core 1	Product based on RHL 9 for individual users; created by the Fedora Project in cooperation with Red Hat.
2004	Fedora Core 2	Introduced Security Enhanced Linux (SELinux) an implementation of Mandatory Access Control (MAC) in the kernel.
2004	Fedora Core 3	Supported the 2.6.9 Linux kernel, updated SELinux, and support for the latest popular GUIs including KDE and Gnome.

Linux is an open-source program. That is, the source code is freely available to anyone for improvement. If a programmer sends improved programming code to Torvalds, and if it's accepted as a universal improvement to the operating system, it's added to the current version that's made available to the computing world. In this way, Linux is under constant development by uncounted people around the world who, for the most part, have never met.

Linux is not UNIX. It's a clone. UNIX is a registered trademark and use of the term requires the developer to meet expensive certification criteria. Linux is a registered trademark of Linus Torvalds.

Although the first Linux fans were programmers at universities and research environments, the operating system is becoming widely adopted in commercial, educational, and industrial markets around the world especially as its Windows-like graphical user interfaces become widespread. Linux GUI desktops are discussed later in this chapter.

Design Goals

Because Linux and UNIX share a similar history, the two operating systems also share design goals. From the beginning, Thompson and Ritchie envisioned UNIX as an operating system by programmers for programmers, and they had both short-term and long-term design goals for it.

The immediate goals were twofold, to develop an operating system that would support software development, and to keep its algorithms as simple as possible (without becoming rudimentary).

To achieve their first goal, they included utilities in the operating system for which programmers typically need to write code. Each utility was designed for simplicity—to perform only one function but to perform it very well. And they were designed to be used in combination with each other so that programmers could select and combine any appropriate utilities that might be needed to carry out specific jobs.

This concept of small manageable sections of code fit right in with the second goal: to keep the operating system simple. To do this, Thompson and Ritchie selected the system's algorithms based on simplicity instead of speed or sophistication. As a result, UNIX can be mastered by experienced programmers in a matter of weeks.

Their long-term goal was to make the operating system, and any application software developed for it, portable from machine to machine. The obvious advantage of portability is that it reduces conversion costs and doesn't cause application packages to become obsolete with every change in hardware. This goal was finally achieved with UNIX Version 4 because it was written entirely in C, a high-level language that's hardware independent, instead of assembly language that's hardware dependent.

Linux and UNIX accommodate numerous operating systems functions that exploit the capability of modern systems as shown in Table 15.3.

Function	Purpose
Multiple processes and multiple processors	Linux can run more than one program at a time using one or several processors.
Multiple platforms	Although it was originally developed to run on Intel's processors for microcomputers, it can now operate on many other platforms
Multiple users	Like all UNIX systems, Linux allows several users to work on the same machine at the same time.
Interprocess communications	Linux supports pipes, IPC, sockets, etc.
Terminal management	Terminal management conforms to POSIX standards and it also supports pseudo-terminals as well as process control systems.
Peripheral devices	Supports a wide range of devices including sound cards, graphics interfaces, networks, SCSI, USB, etc.
Buffer cache	Linux supports a memory area reserved to buffer the input and output from different processes.
Demand paging memory management	Linux loads pages into memory only when they're needed.
Dynamic and shared libraries	Dynamic libraries are loaded only when they're needed and their code is shared if several applications are using them.
Disk partitions	Linux allows disk partitions used by file systems such as Ext2 and partitions having other formats (MS-DOS, ISO 9660, etc.).
Network protocol	Supports TCP/IP and other network protocols.

(table 15.3)

Linux and UNIX support a wide variety of system functions.

Linux and popular versions of UNIX meet the additional design element of conforming to the specifications for **Portable Operating System Interface for Unix (POSIX)** (a registered trademark of the IEEE). POSIX is a family of IEEE standards that define a portable operating system interface to enhance the portability of programs from one operating system to another. At this writing, the latest version is IEEE std. 1003.1, 2004 edition.

Memory Management

Both UNIX and Linux were originally designed for single users but eventually developed into powerful operating systems for multiuser environments as well.

UNIX Memory Management

For multiprogramming systems, most UNIX operating systems use either swapping or demand paging memory management techniques. The best choice depends on the kind of applications that will run on the system: if most jobs are small then swapping could be the best choice, but if the system will be running many large jobs then demand paging is best.

Swapping requires that the entire program be in main memory before it can be executed, and this imposes a size restriction on programs. For example, if there is 2MB of memory and the operating system takes up half of it (1MB), then the size of the programs must be less than one megabyte. Swapping uses a round robin policy—when a job's time slice is up, or when it generates an I/O interrupt, the entire job is swapped out to secondary storage to make room for other jobs waiting in the READY queue. That's fine when there are relatively few processes in the system, but when traffic is heavy this swapping back and forth can slow down the system.

Demand paging requires more complicated hardware configurations; it increases the system overhead and under heavy loads might lead to thrashing. But it has the advantage of implementing the concept of virtual memory.

Figure 15.1 shows the typical internal memory layout for a single user-memory part UNIX image. An "image" is an abstract concept that can be defined as a computer execution environment composed of a user-memory part (all of which is depicted in Figure 15.1), general register values, status of open files, and current directory. This image must remain in memory during execution of a process (Ritchie & Thompson, 1978).

In Figure 15.1, the segment called program code is the sharable portion of the program. Because this code will be physically shared by several processes it must be written in **reentrant code**. That means the code is protected so that its instructions

(figure 15.1)

This is how the user-memory part of an image is stored in main memory.

aren't modified in any way during its normal execution. In addition, all data references are made without use of absolute physical addresses.

The Memory Manager gives the program code special treatment. Because several processes will be sharing it, the space allocated to the program code can't be released until *all* of the processes using it have completed their execution. UNIX uses a text table to keep track of which processes are using which program code, and the memory isn't released until the program code is no longer needed. The text table is explained in more detail in the next section on Processor Management.

The data segment shown in Figure 15.1 starts after the program code and grows toward higher memory locations as needed by the program. The stack segment starts at the highest memory address and grows downward as subroutine calls and interrupts add information to it. A stack is a section of main memory where process information is saved when a process is interrupted. The data and stack are nonsharable sections of memory, so when the original program terminates the memory space is released.

Of course, while each process is in memory, the Memory Manager protects them from each other so they don't overlap.

The UNIX kernel, which permanently resides in memory, is the part of the operating system that implements the "system calls" to set up the memory boundaries so several processes can coexist in memory at the same time. The processes use these system calls to interact with the File Manager and to request I/O services.

The kernel is the set of programs that implements the most primitive of that system's functions, and it's the only part of the operating system to permanently reside in memory. The remaining sections of the operating system are handled in the same way as any large program. That is, pages of the operating system are brought into memory on demand, only when they're needed, and their memory space is released as other pages are called. UNIX uses the least recently used (LRU) page replacement algorithm.

Although we've directed this discussion to large multiuser computer systems, the same memory management concepts are used by UNIX systems for networked personal computers and single-user systems. For example, a single personal computer with a UNIX operating system, using a demand paging scheme, can support multiple users in a true **multitasking** environment.

Linux Memory Management

Linux allocates memory space to each process. For example, in the Intel x86 processor architecture for which it was originally written, Linux allocates 1 GB of high order memory to the kernel and 3 GB of memory to executing processes. This address space is divided among: process code, process data, code and shared library data used by the process, and the stack used by the process.

When a process begins execution its segments have a fixed size but there are cases when a process has to handle variables with an unknown number and size. Therefore, Linux has system calls that change the size of the process data segment, either by expanding it to accommodate extra data values or reducing it when certain values positioned at the end of the data segment are no longer needed.

Linux offers memory protection based on the type of information stored in each region belonging to the address space of a process. If a process modifies access authorization assigned to a memory region, the kernel changes the protection information assigned to the corresponding memory pages.

When a process requests pages, Linux loads them into memory. When the kernel needs the memory space, the pages are released using a least recently used (LRU) algorithm. Linux maintains a dynamically managed area in memory, a page cache, where new pages requested by processes are inserted, and from which pages are deleted when they're no longer needed. If any pages marked for deletion have been modified, they're rewritten to the disk—a page corresponding to a file mapped into memory is rewritten to the file and a page corresponding to the data is saved on a swap device. The swap device could be a partition on the disk or it could be a normal file. Linux shows added flexibility with swap devices because, if necessary, Linux can deactivate them without having to reboot the system. When this takes place, all pages saved on that device are reloaded into memory.

To keep track of free and busy pages, Linux uses a system of page tables. With certain chip architectures, memory access is carried out using segments, as described in Chapter 3. It uses the virtual memory mechanism provided by the processor on which it is executing, converting virtual addresses into physical addresses as discussed in the case study near the end of Chapter 3.

Processor Management

The Processor Manager of the UNIX system kernel handles the allocation of the CPU, process scheduling, and the satisfaction of process requests. To perform these tasks, the kernel maintains several important tables to coordinate the execution of processes and the allocation of devices.

Using a predefined policy, the Process Scheduler selects a process from the READY queue and begins its execution for a given time slice. Remember, as we discussed in Chapter 4, the processes in a time-sharing environment can be in any of five states: HOLD, READY, WAITING, RUNNING, or FINISHED.

The process scheduling algorithm picks the process with the highest priority to be run first. Since one of the values used to compute the priority is accumulated CPU time, any processes that have used a lot of CPU time will get a lower priority than those that have not. The system updates the compute-to-total-time ratio for each job every second. This ratio divides the amount of CPU time that a process has used up by the total time the same process has spent in the system. A result close to 1 would indicate that the process is CPU-bound. If several processes have the same computed priority, they're handled round-robin (low-priority processes are preempted by high-priority processes). Interactive processes typically have a low compute-to-total-time ratio, so interactive response is maintained without any special policies.

The overall effect of this negative feedback is that the system balances **I/O-bound** jobs with **CPU-bound** jobs to keep the processor busy and to minimize the overhead for waiting processes.

When the Processor Manager is deciding which process from the READY queue will be loaded into memory to be run first, it chooses the process with the longest time spent on the secondary storage.

When the Processor Manager is deciding which process, currently in memory and waiting or ready to be run, will be moved out temporarily to make room for a new arrival, it chooses the process that's either waiting for disk I/O or currently idle. If there are several processes to choose from, the one that has been in memory the longest is moved out first.

If a process is waiting for the completion of an I/O request and isn't ready to run when it's selected, UNIX will dynamically recalculate all process priorities to determine which inactive but ready process will begin execution when the processor becomes available. This is to avoid discrimination against I/O-bound jobs (Christian, 1983).

These policies seem to work well and don't impact on the running processes. However, if a disk is used for secondary file storage as well as a "swapping area," then heavy traffic can significantly slow disk I/O because job swapping may take precedence over file storage.

Process Table Versus User Table

UNIX uses several tables to keep the system running smoothly, as shown in Figure 15.2. Information on simple processes, those with nonsharable code, is stored in two sets of tables: the process table, which always resides in memory, and the user table, which resides in memory only while the process is active. In Figure 15.2, Processes P3 and P4 show the same program code indicated in the text table by the number 2. Their data areas and user tables are kept separate while the code area is being shared. Process P5 isn't sharing its code with another process; therefore it's not recorded in the text table, and its data and code area are kept together as a unit (Thompson, 1978).

(figure 15.2)

The process control structure showing how the process table and text table interact for processes with sharable code, as well as for those without sharable code.

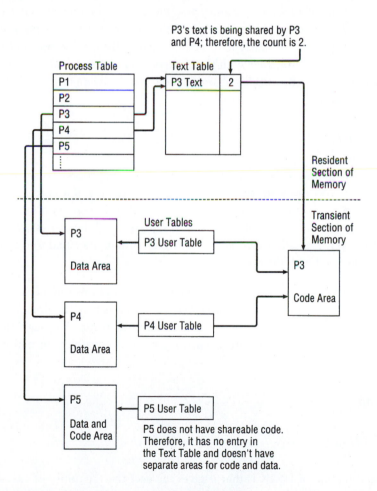

Each entry in the process table contains the following information: process identification number, user identification number, process memory address or secondary storage address, size of the process, and scheduling information. This table is set up when the process is created and is deleted when the process terminates.

For processes with sharable code, the process table maintains a subtable, called the text table, which contains the following information: memory address or secondary storage address of the text segment (sharable code) and a count to keep track of the number of processes using this code. Every time a process starts using this code, the count is increased by one; and every time a process stops using this code, the count is decreased by one. When the count is equal to zero the code is no longer needed and the table entry is released together with any memory locations that had been allocated to the code segment.

A user table is allocated to each active process. It's kept in the transient area of memory and contains information that must be accessible when the process is running. This information includes the user and group identification numbers to determine file access privileges; pointers to the system's file table for every file being used by the process; a pointer to the current directory; and a list of responses for various interrupts. This table, together with the process data segment and its code segment (which is present if the process has sharable code), can be swapped into or out of main memory as needed.

Synchronization

UNIX is a true multitasking operating system. It achieves process synchronization by requiring that processes wait for certain events. For example, if a process needs more memory, it's required to wait for an event associated with memory allocation. Later, when memory becomes available, the event is signaled, and the process can continue. Each event is represented by integers that, by convention, are equal to the address of the table associated with the event.

A **race** may occur if an event happens during the process's transition between deciding to wait for the event and entering the WAIT state. In this case the process is waiting for an event that has already occurred and may not recur. Although this isn't a problem in single-processor environments, it may pose a problem in multiprocessor environments.

fork, wait, and exec

fork

An unusual feature of UNIX is that it gives the user the capability of executing one program from another program using the *fork* command. This command gives the second program all the attributes of the first program, such as any open files, and saves the first program in its original form.

The system command *fork* splits a program into two copies, which are both running from the statement after the fork command. When *fork* is executed a "process id" (called "pid," for short) is generated, which ensures that each process has its own unique ID number.

Figure 15.3 shows what happens after the *fork*. The original process (Process 1) is called the "parent" process and the resulting process (Process 2) is the "child" process. A child inherits the parent's open files and runs asynchronously with it unless the parent has been instructed to wait for the termination of the child process.

(figure 15.3)

When the fork command is received, the parent process shown in (a) begets the child process shown in (b) and Statement 2 is executed twice.

wait

A related command, *wait*, allows the programmer to synchronize process execution by suspending the parent until the child is finished, as shown in Figure 15.4.

In a program, the IF-THEN-ELSE structure is controlled by the value assigned to pid: a pid greater than zero indicates a parent process, a pid equal to zero indicates a child process, and a negative pid indicates an error in the fork call.

exec

The *exec* family of commands—*execl, execv, execls, execlp* and *execvp*—are used to start execution of a new program from another program. Unlike *fork*, which results in two programs being in memory, a successful *exec* call will overlay the second program

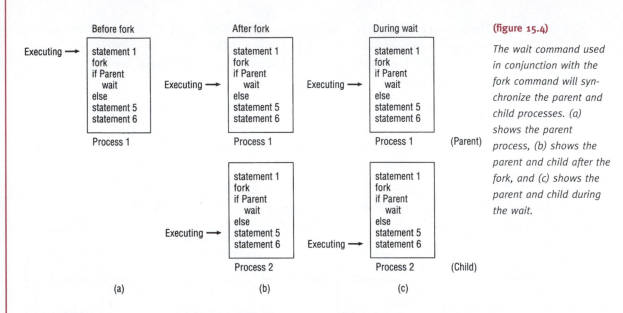

(figure 15.4)

The wait command used in conjunction with the fork command will synchronize the parent and child processes. (a) shows the parent process, (b) shows the parent and child after the fork, and (c) shows the parent and child during the wait.

over the first, leaving only the second program in memory. The second program can be considered a new process but, in fact, it takes on the pid of the first program.

It's important to note that there's no return from a successful *exec* call; therefore, the concept of parent-child doesn't hold here. However, a programmer can use the *fork*, *wait*, and *exec* commands in this order to create a parent-child relationship and then have the child be overlaid by another program that, when finished, awakens the parent so that it can continue its execution, as shown in Figure 15.5.

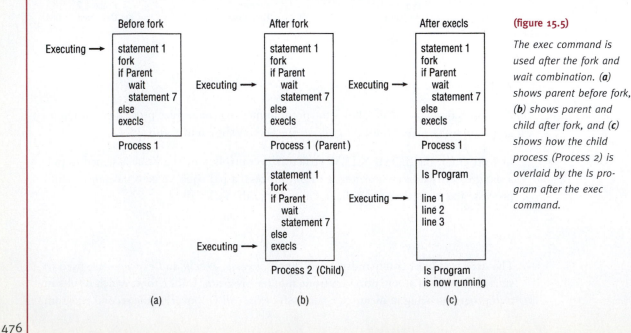

(figure 15.5)

*The exec command is used after the fork and wait combination. (**a**) shows parent before fork, (**b**) shows parent and child after fork, and (**c**) shows how the child process (Process 2) is overlaid by the ls program after the exec command.*

The *ls* command generates a listing of the current directory. When the *exec* call has been executed successfully, processing begins at the first line of the called program. Each *exec* call is followed by a test to ensure that it was completed successfully; if it was unsuccessful, the test would then indicate actions to be performed. Once the *ls* program is finished, control returns to the executable statement following *wait* in the parent process.

These commands illustrate the flexibility of UNIX that programmers find extremely useful. For example, a child process can be created to execute a procedure in the parent program, as was done in Figure 15.5, without having to load or find memory space for a separate program.

Linux Process Management

Linux supports the concept of "personality" to allow processes coming from other operating systems to be executed. This means that each process is assigned to an execution domain specifying the way in which system calls are carried out, and the way in which messages are sent to processes.

As with UNIX, Linux supports pipes to allow executing processes to exchange data. However, Linux has an extension, which permits process "clones" to be created. A clone process is created using the primitive "clone," by duplicating its parent process. Among other things, this allows both processes to share the same segment of code and data. Any modification of one is visible to the other, which is unlike classical processes. The ability to clone processes brings the possibility of implementing servers in which several threads may be executing. These operations may simply share data, without making use of the inter-process communication mechanisms.

Organization of Table of Processes

Each process is referenced by a descriptor, which contains approximately 70 fields describing the process attributes together with the information needed to manage the process. The kernel dynamically allocates these descriptors when processes begin execution. All process descriptors are organized in a doubly linked list, and the descriptors of processes that are ready or in execution are put in another doubly linked list with fields indicating "next run" and previously run." There are several macro instructions used by the scheduler to manage and update these process descriptor lists as needed.

Process Synchronization

Linux provides wait queues and semaphores to allow two processes to synchronize with each other. A wait queue is a linked circular list of process descriptors.

Semaphores, described in Chapter 6, are used to solve the problems of mutual exclusion and the problems of producers and consumers. In Linux the semaphore structure contains three fields: the semaphore counter, the number of waiting processes, and the list of processes waiting for the semaphore. The semaphore counter may contain only binary values, except in the case when several units of one resource are available, and the semaphore counter takes the value of the number of units which are accessible concurrently (Card, 1997).

A case study discussing Linux process management is included near the end of Chapter 6.

Device Management

An innovative feature of UNIX and Linux is their treatment of devices—they are truly device independent. They achieve this independence by treating each I/O device as a special type of file. (Other operating systems control devices with a "hard coded" program built into each device.) Every device that's installed in a UNIX or Linux system is assigned a name that's similar to the name given to any other file. But while device files are given "descriptors," other files are not. These descriptors identify the devices, contain information about them, and are stored in the device directory.

The subroutines that work with the operating system to supervise the transmission of data between main memory and a peripheral unit are called the **device drivers**. They're written in C and are part of the kernel.

UNIX and Linux operating systems come with device drivers to operate the most common peripheral devices. However, if the computer system should include peripherals that are not on the standard list, their device drivers must be written by an experienced programmer or obtained from a reliable source and installed on the operating system.

The actual incorporation of a device driver into the kernel is done during the system configuration. Recent versions of UNIX have a program called *config* that will automatically create a conf.c file for any given hardware configuration. This conf.c file contains the parameters that control resources such as the number of internal buffers for the kernel and the size of the swap space. In addition, the conf.c file contains two tables: bdevsw (short for "block I/O devices") and cdevsw (short for "character I/O devices"), which provide the UNIX system kernel with the ability to adapt easily to different hardware configurations by installing different driver modules.

Device Classifications

Both UNIX and Linux divide the I/O system into the "block I/O" system (sometimes called the "structured I/O" system) and the "character I/O" system (sometimes called the "unstructured I/O" system).

Each physical device is identified by a minor device number, a major device number, and a class—either block or character—as shown in Figure 15.6.

(figure 15.6)

The hierarchy of I/O devices in UNIX and Linux.

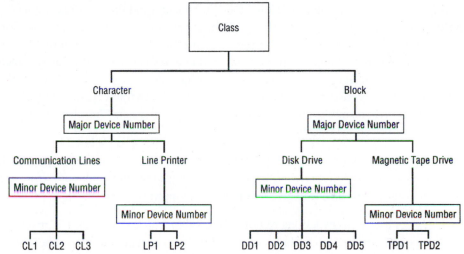

Each *class* has a Configuration Table that contains an array of entry points into the device drivers. This table is the only connection between the system code and the device drivers and it's an important feature of the operating system because it allows the systems programmers to create new device drivers quickly to accommodate differently configured systems (Thompson, 1978).

The *major device number* is used as an index to the array to access the appropriate code for a specific device driver.

The *minor device number* is passed to the device driver as an argument and is used to access one of several identical physical devices.

As its name implies, the block I/O system is used for devices that can be addressed as a sequence of 512-byte blocks. This allows the Device Manager to use buffering to reduce the I/O traffic. UNIX has from 10 to 70 buffers for I/O, and information related to these buffers is kept on a list.

Every time a read command is issued, the I/O buffer list is searched. If the requested data is already in a buffer then it's made available to the requesting process. If not, then it's physically moved from secondary storage to a buffer. If a buffer is available, the move is made. If all buffers are busy then one must be emptied out to make room for the new block. This is done by using an LRU policy, so the contents of frequently used buffers will be left intact, which, in turn, should reduce I/O traffic.

Devices in the character class are handled by device drivers that implement character lists. Here's how it operates: a subroutine puts a character on the list, or queue, and another subroutine retrieves the character from the list.

A terminal is a typical character device that has two input queues and one output queue. The two input queues are labeled the "raw queue" and the "canonical queue," and they're needed to synchronize the user's input speed with that of communication lines. It works like this. As the user types in each character, it's collected in the raw input queue. When the line is completed and the Enter key is pressed, the line is copied from the raw input queue to the canonical input queue, and the CPU interprets the line. Similarly, the section of the device driver that handles characters going to the output module of a terminal stores them in the "output queue" until it holds the maximum number of characters.

The I/O procedure is synchronized through hardware completion interrupts. Each time there's a completion interrupt, the device driver gets the next character from the queue and sends it to the hardware. This process continues until the queue is empty.

Some devices can actually belong to both classes: block and character. For instance, disk drives and tape drives can be accessed in block mode using buffers or the system can bypass the buffers when accessing the devices in character mode.

Device Drivers

In UNIX and Linux, each device has a special section in the kernel, called a device driver, which includes all the instructions necessary for the operating system to communicate with the device. Device drivers for disk drives use a seek strategy to minimize the arm movement, as explained in Chapter 7.

Device drivers are kept in a set of files that can be loaded as needed, in the case of seldom used devices, or can be kept in memory all the time when the operating system boots. When upgrades are made to peripherals, small changes to the device driver file can be linked into the kernel to keep the operating system appraised of the new features and capabilities.

Although device files may be kept anywhere on the file system, by default and convention they are kept in the /dev directory. Keeping them in this directory clearly marks them as device files.

A case study describing device management in Linux is included near the end of Chapter 7.

File Management

UNIX has three types of files: directories, ordinary files, and special files. (Linux has five types, which are discussed in Chapter 8.) In UNIX, each file enjoys certain privileges.

Directories are files used by the system to maintain the hierarchical structure of the file system. Users are allowed to read information in directory files, but only the system is allowed to modify directory files.

Ordinary files are those in which users store information. Their protection is based on a user's requests and related to the read, write, execute, and delete functions that can be performed on a file.

Special files are the device drivers that provide the interface to I/O hardware. Special files appear as entries in directories. They're part of the file system, and most of them reside in the /dev directory. The name of each special file indicates the type of device with which it's associated. For example, /dev/lp is for the line printer. Most users don't need to know much about special files, but system programmers should know where they are and how to use them.

UNIX stores files as sequences of bytes and doesn't impose any structure on them. Therefore, text files (those written using an editor) are strings of characters with lines delimited by the line feed, or new line, character. On the other hand, binary files (those containing executable code generated by a compiler or assembler) are sequences of binary digits grouped into words as they will appear in memory during execution of the program. Therefore, the structure of files is controlled by the programs that use them, not by the system.

The UNIX file management system organizes the disk into blocks of 512 bytes each and divides the disk into four basic regions: (1) the first region (address 0) is reserved for booting; (2) the second region contains the size of the disk and the boundaries of the other regions; (3) the third region includes a list of file definitions, called the "i-list," which uses a combination of major and minor device numbers and i-numbers to uniquely identify a file; and (4) the remaining region holds the free blocks available for file storage. The free blocks are kept in a linked list where each block points to the next available empty block. Then, as files grow, noncontiguous blocks are linked to the already existing chain.

Whenever possible files are stored in contiguous empty blocks. And since all disk allocation is based on fixed-size blocks, allocation is very simple and there's no need to compact the files until the files become large and more dispersed—so that file retrieval becomes cumbersome. When that happens, the system operator might choose **compaction** to bring retrieval time back to normal.

Each entry in the i-list is called an "i-node" (or inode) and contains 13 disk addresses. The first ten addresses point to the first ten blocks of a file. However, if a file is larger than ten blocks, the eleventh address points to a block that contains the addresses of the next 128 blocks of the file. For larger files, the twelfth address points to another set of 128 blocks, each one pointing to 128 blocks. For files larger than 8 MB there is a thirteenth address allowing for a maximum file size of over 100 MB (Thompson, 1978).

Each i-node contains information on a specific file, such as owner's identification, protection bits, physical address, file size, time of creation, last use and last update, number of links, and whether the file is a directory, an ordinary file, or a special file.

Filenames in UNIX and Linux

Filenames are case sensitive so they recognize capital letters in filenames. For example, these are legitimate names for four different files in a single directory: FIREWALL, firewall, FireWall, and fireWALL.

Linux and most versions of UNIX allow filenames to be of unlimited length, although some older versions of UNIX have a maximum of 14 characters, including any suffixes and the period. Although the operating systems don't impose any naming conventions on files, some system programs, such as compilers, expect files to have specific "suffixes" (they're the same as "extensions" described in Chapter 8). For example, prog1.bas would indicate the file to be a BASIC program because of its suffix .bas while the suffix in backup.sh would indicate the file to be a "shell" program.

Linux and UNIX support a hierarchical tree file structure. The root directory is identified by a slash (/); the names of other directories are preceded by the slash (/) symbol, which is used as a delimiter. A file is accessed by starting at a given point in the hierarchy and descending through the branches of the tree (subdirectories) until reaching the leaf (file). This path can become very long and it's sometimes advantageous to change directories before accessing a file. This can be done quickly by typing two periods ("..") if the file needed is in the parent directory of the current directory (which is the directory one level up from the present directory in the hierarchy). Typing ../.. will move you up two branches toward the root in the tree structure.

In multiuser systems the operating system assigns the user to an appropriate directory when logging on to the system. Thereafter, any file operations that are requested by this user are started from this home directory.

For instance, to access the file checks in the system illustrated in Figure 15.7, the user can type the following:

```
/programs/pay/checks
```

(figure 15.7)

The file hierarchy with (/) as the root, the directories as branches, and the files as leaves.

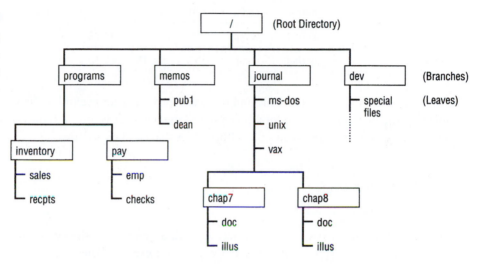

The first slash indicates that this is an absolute path name that starts at the root directory. On the other hand, a relative path name is one that doesn't start at the root directory. Two examples of relative path names from Figure 15.7 are:

```
pay/checks
journal/chap8/illus
```

A few rules apply to all path names:

1. If the path name starts with a slash, the path starts at the root directory.
2. A path name can be either one name or a list of names separated by slashes. The last name on the list is the name of the file requested.
3. Using two periods (..) in a path name will move you upward in the hierarchy (closer to the root). This is the only way to go up the hierarchy; all other path names go down the tree.
4. Spaces are not allowed within path names.

Directories in UNIX and Linux

As shown in Table 15.4, a "long listing" of files in a directory shows eight pieces of information for each file: the access control, the number of links, the name of the group and owner, the byte size of the file, the date and time of last modification, and, finally, the filename. Notice that the list is displayed in alphabetical order by filename.

Access Control	No. of Links	Group	Owner	No. of Bytes	Date	Time	Filename
drwxrwxr-x	2	journal	comp	128	Jan 10	19:32	chap7
drwxrwxr-x	2	journal	comp	128	Jan 15	09:59	chap8
-rwxr-xr-x	1	journal	comp	11904	Jan 6	11:38	ms-dos
-rwxr--r--	1	journal	comp	12556	Jan 20	18:08	unix
-rwx------	1	journal	comp	10362	Jan 17	07:32	vax

(table 15.4)

This table shows the list of files stored in the directory journal from the system illustrated in Figure 15.7. The command ls -l (short for "listing-long") was used to generate this list.

The first column shows the type of file and the access privileges for each file. The first character in the first column describes the nature of the file or directory; d indicates a directory and - indicates an ordinary file. Other codes that can be used are:

• b to indicate a block special file
• c to indicate a character special file
• p to indicate a named pipe file

The next three characters (rwx) show the access privileges granted to the owner of the file: r stands for read, w stands for write, and x stands for execute. Therefore if the list includes rwx the user can read, write, and/or execute that program.

Likewise, the following three characters describe the access privileges granted to other members of the user's group. (In UNIX, a "group" is defined as a set of users who have something in common: the same project, same class, same department, etc.) Therefore, rwx for characters 5–7 means other users can also read, write, and/or execute that file. However, a hyphen - indicates that access is denied for that operation. In Table 15.4 the r-- means that the file called unix can be read by other group members but can't be altered or executed.

Finally, the last three characters in column one describe the access privileges granted to users at large, those system-wide. Thus, at-large users can't modify the files listed in Table 15.4, nor can they modify or execute the file called unix. What's more, the vax file can't be read, modified, or executed by anyone other than the owner.

The second column in the directory listing indicates the number of links, also known as the number of aliases, that refer to the same physical file. Aliases are an important feature of UNIX; they support file sharing when several users work together on the same project. In this case it's convenient for the shared files to appear in different directories belonging to different users even though only one central file descriptor (containing information on the file) exists for that file. The filename may be different from directory to directory since these names aren't kept in the file descriptor, but the numbers of links kept there is updated so the system knows how many users are sharing this file. Eventually this number will indicate when the file is no longer needed and can be deleted.

The next three columns show, respectively, the name of the group, the name of the owner, and the file size in bytes. The sixth and seventh columns show the date and time of the last modification, and the last column lists the filename.

Data Structures in UNIX

The information presented in the directory isn't all kept in the same location. UNIX divides the file descriptors into parts, with the hierarchical directories containing only the name of the file and the "i-number," which is a pointer to another location, the "i-node," where the rest of the information is kept. Therefore, everything you see in Table 15.4, with the exception of the filename and the addition of the device's physical addresses for the file contents, is kept in the i-node. All i-nodes are stored in a reserved part of the device where the directory resides, usually in Block 1. This structure is illustrated in Figure 15.8, which uses the directory memos from Figure 15.7 as an example.

(figure 15.8)

Example of hierarchy for directories, i-nodes, and file blocks. Although the file blocks are represented here in physical serial order, they actually may be stored noncontiguously.

Each i-node has room for 13 pointers (0–12). The first ten block numbers stored in the i-node list relate to the first ten blocks of a file.

485

For the file called pub1 in Figure 15.8, only the first two entries have pointers to data blocks and all the others are zeros because this is a small file that occupies only two blocks of storage. If a file is larger than ten blocks, then the eleventh entry points to a block that contains a list of the next 128 blocks in the file. Because it's an extra step in the path to the data this block is called an "indirect block."

For files larger than 138 blocks, the twelfth entry points to a block that contains a list of 128 indirect blocks (each one containing pointers to 128 file blocks). Because this block introduces two extra steps in the path to the data it's called a "double indirect block." Finally, for extremely large files of more than 16,522 blocks, the thirteenth entry points to a "triple indirect block." This schema allows for 2,113,674 blocks to be allocated to a single file, for a total of 1,082,201,088 bytes (Christian, 1983).

Therefore, carrying this one step further, we can see that the bytes numbered below 5120 can be retrieved with a single disk access. Those in the range between 5120 and 70,656 require two disk accesses. Those in the range between 70,656 and 8,459,264 require three disk accesses; bytes beyond 8,459,264 require four disk accesses. This would give very slow access to large data files but, in reality, the system maintains a rather complicated buffering mechanism that considerably reduces the number of I/O operations required to access a file.

When a file is opened, its device, i-number, and read/write pointer are stored in the System File Table, residing in memory, and indexed by the i-node, so that during other read/write calls to the file the i-node information can be readily accessed.

When a file is created an i-node is allocated to it, and a directory entry with the filename and its i-node number is created.

When a file is linked (which happens when another user begins sharing the same file), a directory entry is created with the new name and the original i-node number, and the link-count field in the i-node is incremented by one.

When a shared file is deleted, the link-count field in the i-node is decremented by one. And when the count reaches zero, the directory entry is erased and all disk blocks allocated to the file, along with its i-node block, are deallocated.

An interesting note for system analysts is that linking files presents a problem to the accounting system, which must charge someone for the space occupied by the shared file. Should the file's owner, or those who used it, be charged? Charging the owner may not be fair because the owner may delete the file even though other users continue to share it. On the other hand, even though the user who created the file is still the registered owner, the space could be charged to those who are currently sharing it. Some installations divide the charges equally among every user with links to a file. Others avoid the issue by not charging any fees.

Data Structures in Linux

A case study discussing data structures in Linux is included near the end of Chapter 8.

User Interface

UNIX and Linux were created as command-driven systems and their virtually identical user commands (as shown in Table 15.5) are usually very short: either one character (usually the first letter of the command) or a group of characters (an acronym of the words that make up the command). In command mode, the system prompt is very economical, often only one character, such as a dollar sign ($) or percent sign (%). Error messages are also quite brief; they assume the user doesn't need much assistance from the system.

(table 15.5)

User commands can't be abbreviated or spelled out and must be in the correct case (usually, commands must be in lowercase letters). Many commands can be combined on a single line for additional power and flexibility. Check the technical documentation for your system for proper spelling and syntax.

Command	Stands For	Action to be Performed
(filename)	Run File	Run/Execute the file with that name.
ls	List Directory	Show a listing of the filenames in directory.
ls -l	Long List	Show a comprehensive directory list.
cd	Change Directory	Change working directory.
cp	Copy	Copy a file into another file or directory.
rm	Remove	Remove/delete a file or directory.
mv	Move	Move or rename a file or directory.
more	Show More	Type the file's contents to the screen.
lpr	Print	Print out a file.
date	Date	Show date and time.
date -u	Universal Date/Time	Show date and time in universal format (in Greenwich Mean Time).
mkdir	Make Directory	Make a new directory.
grep	"Global Regular Expression/Print"	Find a specified string in a file.
cat	Concatenate	Create a file or append to an existing file.
format	Format	Format a volume.
diff	Different	Compare two files.
pwd	Path Working Directory	Show the path name of this directory.

The general syntax of commands is this:

```
command arguments file_name
```

The "command" is any legal operating system command. The "arguments" are required for some commands and optional for others. The "file_name" can be a relative or absolute path name.

Commands are interpreted and executed by the shell, one of the two most widely used programs. The shell is technically known as the command interpreter, because that's its function. But it isn't only an interactive command interpreter, it's also the key to the coordination and combination of system programs. In fact, it's a sophisticated programming language in itself.

Script Files

Command files, often called shell files or script files, can be used to automate repetitious tasks. Each line of the file is a valid instruction and can be executed by the user simply by typing sh and the name of the script file. Another way to execute it is to define the file as an executable command and simply type the filename at the system prompt. (The default shell for Linux is called bash for Bourne Again Shell—a play on words honoring Steven Bourne (Wall, 1999).)

Other common shells are csh (the C shell, which was originally developed to support C language development environments at Berkeley and NASA) and ksh (the Korn shell, which was developed after the Bourne and C shells). The Korn shell is usually available as an unbundled product.

Script files are used to automate repetitive tasks and to simplify complex procedures. Here is an example of a simple script file that's designed to configure the system for a certain user:

```
setenv DBPATH /u/lumber:.:/zdlf/product/central/db
setenv TERMCAP $INFODIR/etc/termcap
stty erase `^H'
set savehistory
set history=20
alias h history
alias 4gen infogen -f
setenv PATH /usr/info/bin:/etc
```

In this example, the working directory paths are set, the history is set to 20 lines and is given an alias of "h" (so the user can perform the "history" command simply by typing h). Similarly, "4gen" is established as an alias for the command "infogen -f." Finally, the path is defined as: /usr/info/bin:/etc.

If this script file is included in the user's configuration file, it will be automatically executed every time the user logs on. The exact name of the user configuration file varies from system to system, but two common names are .profile and .login. See the documentation for your system for specifics.

Redirection

If you're an interactive user, most of the commands used to produce output will automatically send it to your screen and the editor will accept input from the keyboard. There are times when you may want to send output to a file or to another device. This is done by using the symbol > between the command and the destination to which the output should be directed. For example, to list the files in your current directory to the file named myfiles instead of listing them on the screen, use this command:

```
ls > myfiles
```

The following command will copy the contents of chapt1 and chapt2 into a file named sectiona:

```
cat chapt1 chapt2 > sectiona
```

The command *cat* is short for "concatenate." If sectiona is a new file then it's automatically created. If it already exists, the previous contents will be overwritten. (When cat is used with a single file and redirection is not indicated then it displays the contents of that file onto the screen.) Another way to achieve the same result is with the "wild card" symbol (*) like this:

```
cat chapt* > sectiona
```

The asterisk symbol (*) indicates that the command pertains to all files that begin with "chapt"—in this case that means chapt1 and chapt2.

The symbol >> will append the new file to an existing file. Therefore either of the following two commands will copy the contents of chapt1 and chapt2 onto the end of whatever already exists in the file called sectiona.

```
cat chapt1 chapt2 >> sectiona
cat chapt* >> sectiona
```

If sectiona doesn't exist then the file will be created as an empty file and will then be filled with chapt1 and chapt2, in that order.

The reverse redirection is to take input for a program from an existing file instead of from the keyboard. For example, if you have written a memo and need to mail to it several people, the following command will send the contents of the file memo to the people listed between the command mail and the symbol <.

```
mail ann roger < memo
```

By combining the power of redirection with system commands, you can achieve results not possible otherwise. For example, the following command will store in the file called temporary the names of all users logged on to the system:

```
who > temporary
```

And the command *sort* will sort the list stored in temporary and display the sorted list on the screen as it's generated.

In each of these examples, it's important to note that the interpretation of < and > is done by the shell and not by the individual program (such as *mail*, *who*, or *sort*). This means that input and output redirection can be used with any program because the program isn't aware that anything unusual is happening. This is one instance of the power of UNIX and Linux—the ability to combine many operations into a single brief command.

Pipes

Pipes and filters make it possible to redirect output or input to selected files or devices based on commands given to the command interpreter. UNIX and Linux do that by manipulating I/O devices as special files.

For the example just presented, we listed the number of users on-line into a file called temporary and we then sorted the file. There was no reason to create this file other than that we needed it to complete the two-step operation required to see the list in alphabetical order on the screen. However, a "pipe" can do the same thing in a single step.

A pipe is the operating system's way to connect the output from one program to the input of another without the need for temporary or intermediate files. A pipe is an open file connecting two programs; information written to it by one program may be read immediately by the other, with synchronization, scheduling, and buffering handled automatically by the system. In other words, the programs are executing concurrently, not one after the other. By using a pipe, indicated by the vertical symbol (|), the last example can be rewritten as:

```
who | sort
```

As a result, a sorted list of all users logged onto the system will be displayed on the screen.

A *pipeline* is several programs simultaneously processing the same I/O stream. For example, the following command is a pipeline that takes the output from who (a list of all logged-on users), sorts it, and prints it on the line printer.

```
who | sort | lpr
```

Filters

UNIX and Linux have many programs that read some input, manipulate it in some way, and generate output; they're called "filters." One example is *wc*, which stands for "word count" and counts the lines, words, and characters in a file. For example, the following command would execute the word count command on the file journal.

```
wc journal
```

As a result, the system would respond with: 10 140 700, meaning that the file journal has 10 lines, 140 words, and 700 characters. (A "word" is defined as a string of characters separated by blanks.) A shorter version (*wc -l*) counts just the number of lines in the file.

Another filter command is *sort* (the same command we used to demonstrate pipes). If a filename is given with the command, the contents of the file are sorted and displayed on the screen. If no filename is given with the command, sort accepts input from the keyboard and directs the output to the screen. When it's used with redirection, *sort* accepts input from a file and writes the output to another file. For example,

```
sort sortednames
```

will sort the contents of the file called names and send the output to the file sortednames. The data in names will be sorted in ASCII order, that is, using a standard collating sequence so lines with leading blanks come first (in sorted order), lines with lowercase characters follow, and lines beginning with uppercase characters come last. To sort the list in alphabetical order but ignore the case of letters the command is:

```
sort -f  sortednames
```

To obtain a numerical sort in ascending order the command is:

```
sort -n  sortednums
```

To obtain a numerical sort in descending order the command is:

```
sort -nr  sortednums
```

In every example presented here, *sort* uses each entire line of the file to conduct the sort. However, if the structure of the data stored in the file is known, then the sort can use other key fields.

For example, let's say a file called empl has data that follows the same column format: the ID numbers start in column 1, phone numbers start in column 10, and last names start in column 20. To sort the file by last name (the third "field") the command would be:

```
sort +2f  sortedempl
```

In this example, the file empl will be sorted alphabetically by the third field and the output will be sent to the file called sortedempl. (A field is defined as a group of characters separated by at least one blank). The +2 tells the *sort* command to skip the first two fields and the *f* says the list should be sorted in alphabetical order. The integrity of the file is preserved because the entire line is sorted—so each name keeps the correct phone and ID number.

Additional Commands

This section introduces several other commonly used UNIX/Linux commands.

man

This command displays the online manual supplied with the operating system. It's called with an argument that specifies which page of the online manual you are interested in seeing. For example, to display the page for the compare (*cmp*) command, the command would look like this:

```
man cmp
```

If the *cmp* entry appears more than once in the manual, all the pages are displayed, one after the other. You can redirect the output to a file, which can then be sent to a printer for future reference. The manual pages are usually formatted with *nroff* when they are displayed, so the *man* command may take a while to produce output.

grep

One of the most-used commands is *grep*—it stands for "global regular expression and print" and it looks for specific patterns of characters. It's one of the most helpful (and oddly named) commands. It's the equivalent of the FIND and SEARCH commands used in other operating systems. When the desired pattern of characters is found, the line containing it is displayed on the screen.

Here's a simple example: if you need to retrieve the names and addresses of everyone with a Pittsburgh address from a large file called maillist, the command would look like this:

```
grep Pittsburgh maillist
```

As a result, you see on your screen the lines from maillist for entries that included Pittsburgh. And if you want the output sent to a file for future use, you can add the redirection command.

This command, *grep*, can also be used to list all the lines that *do not* contain a certain string of characters. Using the same example, the following command displays on the screen the names and addresses of all those who don't have a Pittsburgh address:

```
grep -v Pittsburgh maillist
```

Similarly, the following command counts all the people who live in Pittsburgh and displays that number on the screen. But it doesn't print out each line:

```
grep -c Pittsburgh maillist
```

As we said before, the power of UNIX and Linux comes from their ability to combine commands. Here's how the *grep* command can be combined with the *who* command. Suppose you want to see if your friend Sam is logged on. The command to display Sam's name, device, and the date and time he logged in would be:

```
who | grep sam
```

Combinations of commands, though effective, can appear confusing to the casual observer. For example, if you wanted a list of all the subdirectories (but not the files) found in the root directory, the command would be:

```
ls -l / | grep '^d'
```

This command is the combination of several simpler commands:

• *ls* for list directory
• *-l*, which is the long option of ls and includes the information shown in Table 15.4
• / to indicate the root directory
• | to establish a pipe
• *grep* to find
• '^d', which says that d is the character we're looking for (because we only want the directories), the ^ indicates that the *d* is at the beginning of each line (and the quotes are required because we used the symbol ^)

nohup

If a program's execution is expected to take a long time, you can start its execution and then log off the system without having to wait for it to finish. This is done with the command *nohup*, which is short for "no hangup." Let's say, for example, you want to copy a very large file but you can't wait at the terminal until the job is finished. The command is:

```
nohup cp oldlargefile newlargefile &
```

The copy command (*cp*) will continue its execution copying oldlargefile to newlargefile in the background even though you've logged off the system. For this example, we've indicated that execution should continue in the background; the ampersand (&) is the symbol for running the program in "background" mode.

nice

If your program uses a large number of resources and you are not in a hurry for the results, you can be "nice" to other users by lowering its priority with the command nice. This will put the process in background mode and will free up your terminal for different work. For example, you want to copy oldlargefile to newlargefile and want to continue working on another project at the same time. To do that, use this command

```
nice cp oldlargefile newlargefile &
```

However, you may not log off when using the *nice* command until the copy is finished because the program execution would be stopped.

The command *nohup* automatically activates *nice* by lowering the process's priority. It assumes that since you've logged off the system, you're not in a hurry for the output. The opposite isn't true—when *nice* is issued it doesn't automatically activate *nohup*. Therefore, if you want to put a very long job on the background, work on some other jobs, and log out before the long job is finished, *nohup* is the command to use.

We've included only a few commands here. For a complete list of commands for a specific version of this operating system, their exact syntax, and more details about those we've discussed here, see a technical manual for the appropriate version.

Conclusion

UNIX and Linux were written by programmers for programmers, and both are quite popular among those fluent in the ways of programming.

Many of their proponents cite their advantages: the spare user interface, device independence, and portability. They like their lack of verbosity and the powerful combinations of commands. Both are extremely portable operating systems—there are versions of UNIX that can operate very large multiuser systems and single-user systems, and every size in between. And Linux is being adopted widely for single-user and enterprise-wide computing systems.

Those unfamiliar with these operating systems often have the opposite opinion. According to them, the commands are too brief and the system lacks a friendly human/computer interface that would make it easier to use for those with less-than-expert programming skills.

Linux, an increasingly popular adaptation of UNIX, is characterized by its power, flexibility, and constant maintenance by legions of programmers worldwide while maintaining its careful adherence to POSIX standards. It applies all the features of UNIX, including multitasking and multiuser capabilities, to desktop computers. Both operating systems are expected to increase in use and popularity for many years to come.

Key Terms

argument: in a command-driven operating system, a value or option placed in the command that modifies how the command is to be carried out.

child process: in UNIX-like operating systems, the subordinate processes that are controlled by a parent process.

command-driven interface: an interface that accepts typed commands, one line at a time, from the user. It contrasts with a menu-driven interface.

compaction: the process of collecting fragments of available memory space into contiguous blocks by moving programs and data in a computer's memory or secondary storage.

CPU-bound: a job that will perform a great deal of nonstop processing before issuing an interrupt. A CPU-bound job can tie up the CPU for long periods of time while all other jobs must wait.

device driver: a device-specific program module that handles the interrupts and controls a particular type of device.

device independent: programs that are devoid of the detailed instructions required to interact with any I/O device present in the computer system.

directory: a storage area in a secondary storage volume (disk, disk pack, CD, etc.) containing information about files stored in that volume. The information is used to access those files.

I/O-bound: a job that requires a large number of input/output operations, resulting in much free time for the CPU.

kernel: the part of the operating system that resides in main memory at all times and performs the most essential tasks, such as managing memory and handling disk input and output.

multitasking: a synonym for multiprogramming, a technique that allows a single processor to process several programs residing simultaneously in main memory and interleaving their execution by overlapping I/O requests with CPU requests.

parent process: in UNIX-like operating systems, a job that controls one or more child processes, which are subordinate to it.

Portable Operating System Interface for UNIX (POSIX): a set of IEEE standards that defines the standard user and programming interfaces for operating systems so developers can port programs from one operating system to another.

race: a synchronization problem between two processes vying for the same resource. In some cases it may result in data corruption because the order in which the processes will finish executing cannot be controlled.

reentrant code: code that can be used by two or more processes at the same time; each shares the same copy of the executable code but has separate data areas.

script: a series of executable commands written in plain text and executed by the operating system in sequence as a procedure.

sharable code: executable code in the operating system that can be shared by several processes.

Command Translation Table

Although each operating system has a unique collection of user commands, many are comparable across systems and perform approximately the same functions. Table A.1 compares several MS-DOS and UNIX/Linux operating system commands. (Microsoft Windows operating systems are not command-driven and so are not included here.)

Be aware that most commands require additional information, such as parameters, arguments, switches, and so on. And many UNIX/Linux commands are version- and vendor-specific. For complete command construction, see a technical manual for your system.

(table A.1)

MS-DOS and UNIX/Linux operating system commands

Command	MS-DOS	UNIX/Linux
Execute a file	(filename)	(filename)
List files in this directory	DIR	ls
Change directory	CD *or* CHDIR	cd
Copy a file	COPY	cp
Delete a file	DEL *or* ERASE	rm
Rename a file	RENAME *or* REN	mv
List the contents of a file to the screen	TYPE	more *or* cat
Print files on a printer	PRINT	lpr
Show system date	DATE	date
Show system time	TIME	date
Make a new directory	MD *or* MKDIR	mkdir
Search files for a string	FIND	grep
Append one file to another	COPY	cat
Format a volume	FORMAT	mkfs
Check the disk	CHKDSK	du *or* df
Compare two files	COMP	diff
Provide help	HELP	help

Notes:

1. MS-DOS commands can be in upper-or lowercase but cannot be abbreviated.
2. UNIX and Linux commands are case sensitive, and are usually in lowercase. Although filenames can be in upper-or lower case, names in lower case are the norm.

Guide to Microsoft Acronyms

Table B.1 gives the acronyms, in alphabetical order, and full names for terms used in this book describing Microsoft operating systems. For more detail refer to the technical documentation for your system.

Acronym	Spelled-Out Name
ACE	Access Control Entry
ACL	Access Control List
API	Application Programming Interface
BIOS	Basic Input/Output System
CDFS	CD-ROM File System
CP/M	Control Program for Microcomputers
DACL	Discretionary Access Control List
DLL	Dynamic-Link Library
DOS	Disk Operating System
DPC	Deferred Procedure Call
FAT	File Allocation Table
GUI	Graphical User Interface
HAL	Hardware Abstraction Layer
IFS	Installable File System
IOS	Input/Output Supervisor
IRP	I/O Request Packet
LPC	Local Procedure Call
NetBEUI	NetBIOS Extended User Interface
NDIS	Network Driver Interface Specification
NPI	Network Provider Interface
NT	New Technology
NTFS	New Technology File System

PSP	Program Segment Prefix
RAM	Random Access Memory
ROM	Read Only Memory
RPC	Remote Procedure Call
SACL	System Access Control List
SCSI	Small Computer System Interface
SMB	Server Message Block
SMP	Symmetric Multiprocessing
TCP/IP	Transmission Control Protocol/Internet Protocol
TDI	Transport Driver Interface
TLB	Translation Look-aside Buffer
TGT	Ticket-granting Ticket
TPA	Transient Program Area
UPS	Uninterruptible Power Supply
VFAT	Virtual File Allocation Table

Guide to Graphical User Interfaces

Many popular graphical user interfaces (GUIs) share several similarities in both appearance and operation. Figures C.1 through C.3 illustrate the interfaces of several popular operating systems: Windows, Macintosh, and Linux desktops.

(figure C.1)

Windows XP Professional desktop. To close the window, double-click the 'x' in the upper right corner. To minimize a window, click the minus sign in the upper right. To maximize a window, click the square (located between the 'x' and the minus sign) in the upper right. To run an application, double-click its icon or click once and press the Enter key.

(figure C.2)

Macintosh OS X desktop. To close a window, move the cursor over the red (leftmost) circle in the upper left corner. Doing so will cause the circle to become an x, which you can click to close the window. To resize a window, click the center circle in the upper left corner. To collapse a window, click the rightmost circle in the upper left corner.

(figure C.3)

A Red Hat Linux Gnome window. To close the window, double-click the 'x' in the upper right corner. To minimize the window, click the underscore in the upper right. To maximize a window, click the square (located between the 'x' and the underscore) in the upper right.

ACM Code of Ethics and Professional Conduct

The following passages are excerpted from the Code of Ethics and Professional Conduct adopted by the Association for Computing Machinery Council on October 16, 1992. They are reprinted here with permission. For the complete text, see *www.acm.org/constitution/code.html.*

Note: These imperatives are expressed in a general form to emphasize that ethical principles which apply to computer ethics are derived from more general ethical principles.

Preamble

Commitment to ethical professional conduct is expected of every member (voting members, associate members, and student members) of the Association for Computing Machinery (ACM).

This Code, consisting of 24 imperatives formulated as statements of personal responsibility, identifies the elements of such a commitment. It contains many, but not all, issues professionals are likely to face. Section 1 outlines fundamental ethical considerations, while Section 2 addresses additional, more specific considerations of professional conduct. Statements in Section 3 pertain more specifically to individuals who have a leadership role, whether in the workplace or in a volunteer capacity such as with organizations like ACM. Principles involving compliance with this Code are given in Section 4.

Section 1: GENERAL MORAL IMPERATIVES

As an ACM member I will ....

1.1 Contribute to society and human well-being.

This principle concerning the quality of life of all people affirms an obligation to protect fundamental human rights and to respect the diversity of all cultures. An essential aim of computing professionals is to minimize negative consequences of computing systems, including threats to health and safety. When designing or implementing systems, computing professionals must attempt to ensure that the products of their efforts will be used in socially responsible ways, will meet social needs, and will avoid harmful effects to health and welfare.

In addition to a safe social environment, human well-being includes a safe natural environment. Therefore, computing professionals who design and develop systems must be alert to, and make others aware of, any potential damage to the local or global environment.

1.2 Avoid harm to others.

"Harm" means injury or negative consequences, such as undesirable loss of information, loss of property, property damage, or unwanted environmental impacts. This principle prohibits use of computing technology in ways that result in harm to any of the following: users, the general public, employees, employers. Harmful actions include intentional destruction or modification of files and programs leading to serious loss of resources or unnecessary expenditure of human resources such as the time and effort required to purge systems of "computer viruses."

Well-intended actions, including those that accomplish assigned duties, may lead to harm unexpectedly. In such an event the responsible person or persons are obligated to undo or mitigate the negative consequences as much as possible. One way to avoid unintentional harm is to carefully consider potential impacts on all those affected by decisions made during design and implementation.

To minimize the possibility of indirectly harming others, computing professionals must minimize malfunctions by following generally accepted standards for system design and testing. Furthermore, it is often necessary to assess the social consequences of systems to project the likelihood of any serious harm to others. If system features are misrepresented to users, coworkers, or supervisors, the individual computing professional is responsible for any resulting injury.

In the work environment the computing professional has the additional obligation to report any signs of system dangers that might result in serious personal or social damage. If one's superiors do not act to curtail or mitigate such dangers, it may be necessary to "blow the whistle" to help correct the problem or reduce the risk. However, capricious or misguided reporting of violations can, itself, be harmful. Before reporting violations, all relevant aspects of the incident must be thoroughly assessed. In particular, the assessment of risk and responsibility must be credible. It is suggested that advice be sought from other computing professionals. See principle 2.5 regarding thorough evaluations.

1.3 Be honest and trustworthy.

Honesty is an essential component of trust. Without trust an organization cannot function effectively. The honest computing professional will not make deliberately false or deceptive claims about a system or system design, but will instead provide full disclosure of all pertinent system limitations and problems.

A computer professional has a duty to be honest about his or her own qualifications, and about any circumstances that might lead to conflicts of interest.

1.4 Be fair and take action not to discriminate.

The values of equality, tolerance, respect for others, and the principles of equal justice govern this imperative. Discrimination on the basis of race, sex, religion, age, disability, national origin, or other such factors is an explicit violation of ACM policy and will not be tolerated.

Inequities between different groups of people may result from the use or misuse of information and technology. In a fair society, all individuals would have equal opportunity to participate in, or benefit from, the use of computer resources regardless of race, sex, religion, age, disability, national origin or other such similar factors. However, these ideals do not justify unauthorized use of computer resources nor do they provide an adequate basis for violation of any other ethical imperatives of this code.

1.5 Honor property rights including copyrights and patent.

Violation of copyrights, patents, trade secrets and the terms of license agreements is prohibited by law in most circumstances. Even when software is not so protected, such violations are contrary to professional behavior. Copies of software should be made only with proper authorization. Unauthorized duplication of materials must not be condoned.

1.6 Give proper credit for intellectual property.

Computing professionals are obligated to protect the integrity of intellectual property. Specifically, one must not take credit for other's ideas or work, even in cases where the work has not been explicitly protected by copyright, patent, etc.

1.7 Respect the privacy of others.

Computing and communication technology enables the collection and exchange of personal information on a scale unprecedented in the history of civilization. Thus, there is increased potential for violating the privacy of individuals and groups. It is the responsibility of professionals to maintain the privacy and integrity of data describing individuals. This includes taking precautions to ensure the accuracy of data, as well as protecting it from unauthorized access or accidental disclosure to inappropriate individuals. Furthermore, procedures must be established to allow individuals to review their records and correct inaccuracies.

This imperative implies that only the necessary amount of personal information be collected in a system, that retention and disposal periods for that information be clearly defined and enforced, and that personal information gathered for a specific purpose not be used for other purposes without consent of the individual(s). These principles apply to electronic communications, including electronic mail, and prohibit procedures that capture or monitor electronic user data, including messages, without the permission of users or bona fide authorization related to system operation and maintenance. User data observed during the normal duties of system operation and maintenance must be treated with strictest confidentiality, except in cases where it is evidence for the violation of law, organizational regulations, or this Code. In these cases, the nature or contents of that information must be disclosed only to proper authorities.

1.8 Honor confidentiality.

The principle of honesty extends to issues of confidentiality of information whenever one has made an explicit promise to honor confidentiality or, implicitly, when private information not directly related to the performance of one's duties becomes available. The ethical concern is to respect all obligations of confidentiality to employers, clients, and users unless discharged from such obligations by requirements of the law or other principles of this Code.

This is an excerpt of the preamble and Section 1. For the entire ACM Code of Ethics and Professional Conduct, see www.acm.org/constitution/code.html.

Innovators

Improvements in operating systems, and computing in general, depend on the work and cooperation of numerous men and women around the world. While there are too many contributors to name, many individuals are recognized every year by industry organizations.

For example, the innovators listed here received the Koji Kobayashi Computers and Communications Award, which was established by the Institute of Electrical and Electronics Engineers (IEEE) Board of Directors for outstanding contributions to the integration of computers and communications.

The IEEE named the award in honor of Dr. Koji Kobayashi, "a leading force in advancing the integrated use of computers and communications." For more information about this and other IEEE awards, see *www.ieee.org*.

1988—STUART WECKER, Bell Atlantic Co., Sudbury, MA

"For contributions to distributed computer network architectures and protocol."

1989—ALEXANDER G. FRASER, AT&T Bell Labs, Murray Hill, NJ

"For contributions to computer communications and the invention of virtual-circuit switching."

1990—ELWYN R. BERLEKAMP, Cyclotomics, Inc., Berkeley, CA

"For profound contributions, in mathematical theory and engineering practice, to error-correcting codes for communications and data storage."

1991—STEPHEN S. LAVENBERG, IBM Corp., Yorktown Heights., NY: and **MARTIN REISER,** IBM Zürich, Switzerland

"For fundamental contributions to the theory and practice of computer and communications systems performance modeling."

1992—VINTON G. CERF and **ROBERT E. KAHN,** Corporation for National Research Initiatives, Reston, VA

"For the creation of the concept of the Transmission Control Protocol/Internet Protocol architecture for packet switched internetting."

1993—GOTTFRIED UNGERBOECK, IBM Zürich Research Lab, Rüschlikon, Switzerland

"For contributions to signal processing for data communications, specifically for pioneering trellis-coded modulation."

1994—JONATHAN SHIELDS TURNER, Washington University, St. Louis, MO. "For fundamental contributions to communications and computing through architectural innovation in high-speed packet networks."

1995—NORMAN ABRAMSON, Database Associates, Honolulu, HI. "For development of the concept of the Aloha System, which led to modern local area networks."

1996—KANIANTHRA (MANI) CHANDY, California Institute of Technology, Pasadena, CA. "For fundamental contributions to the theory and practice of computer and communications performance modeling."

1997—TIMOTHY JOHN BERNERS-LEE, Massachusetts Institute of Technology, Cambridge, MA. "For conceiving and pioneering the World-Wide Web."

1998—JACK K. WOLF, University of California, San Diego, CA. "For fundamental contributions to multi-user communications and applications of coding theory to magnetic data storage devices."

1999—WHITFIELD DIFFIE, Sun Microsystems, Palo Alto, CA; **MARTIN E. HELLMAN,** Stanford University, Stanford, CA; and **RALPH CHARLES MERKLE,** Xerox PARC, Sunnyvale, CA. "For the revolutionary invention of public key cryptosystems which form the foundation for privacy, integrity and authentication in modern communication systems."

2000—RONALD LINN RIVEST, Massachusetts Institute of Technology, Arlington, VA; **ADI SHAMIR,** Weizmann Institute of Science, Rehovot, Israel; and **LEONARD ADLEMAN,** University of Southern California, Northridge, CA. "For the revolutionary invention of the RSA public key cryptosystem which is the first to be widely adopted."

2001—JOHN M. CIOFFI, Stanford University, Stanford, CA. "For contributions to the development of asynchronous digital subscriber line technology, and supporting theory."

2002—VAN JACOBSON, Packet Design, Menlo Park, CA. "For major contributions to the understanding of network congestion, and the development of congestion control mechanisms, enabling the successful scaling of the Internet."

2003—BRUCE HAJEK, University of Illinois at Urbana-Champaign, Urbana, IL. "For the application of stochastic and probabilistic theory to improved understanding of computer-network behavior, particularly, the modeling and performance optimization of multiple-access channels."

2004—NOT AWARDED

2005—FRANK KELLY, Center for Mathematical Sciences, Univ. of Cambridge England. "For contributions to the development of fundamental theories for the understanding, performance, evaluation, and enhancement of telecommunications networks."

Timeline of Operating System Releases

Table F.1 is an overall timeline of operating system releases.

Operating System	Approximate Date	Comments
OS/PCP (IBM)	1964	Primary Control Program (PCP). Designed by IBM to run on the IBM 360 computer; it was a batch, single-task operating system.
OS/MFT (IBM)	1967	Descendant of IBM's OS/PCP; introduced multiprogramming with a fixed number of tasks (MFT). Used fixed partition memory management.
OS/MVT (IBM)	1967	Multiprogramming with a variable number of tasks (MVT). Descendant of IBM's PCP; introduced spooling; used dynamic memory management.
TSO (IBM)	1970	Built for the IBM 370, it incorporated MVT and introduced teleprocessing and time-sharing option (TSO) for the MVT operating system.
UNIX (AT&T)	1971	Based on MULTICS; introduced shell concept, written in assembly language to run on DEC's PDP-11 computer.
VM (DEC)	1973	IBM introduced the virtual machine (VM) concept. Built for the IBM 370 computer.
DOS/VS (IBM)	1973	IBM's disk operating system with virtual storage (DOS/VS) for large IBM computers. (Not related to Microsoft's DOS or IBM's PC DOS for microcomputers released in the 1980s.)
MVS (IBM)	1974	Multiple virtual storage system (MVS) for last IBM computers.
CP/M	1975	Control Program/Microcomputer (CP/M). First operating system that allowed serious business work on small personal computers.
VMS (DEC)	1978	Written specifically for the VAX-11 computer to take best advantage of its architecture.
UNIX System III (AT&T)	1980	First version of UNIX used in 16-bit microcomputers.
MS-DOS (Microsoft)	1981	First operating system for the very successful IBM PC family of computers. Version 1 was CP/M compatible and supported only one directory.
PC DOS (IBM)	1982	IBM's licensed version of Microsoft MS-DOS.

UNIX System III (AT&T)	1981	First version of UNIX available for use on a mainframe.
Mac OS (Apple)	1984	The first widely distributed operating system that was totally graphical in its user interface. Also, the Mac OS introduced the use of a mouse to PC-based systems.
Windows 3.0 (Microsoft)	1990	For PC users. First usable version of a Windows graphical user interface for the PC. Required MS-DOS operating system.
Windows for Workgroups (Microsoft)	1992	For networks. First version of Microsoft Windows with peer-to-peer networking support for the PC. Required MS-DOS.
OpenVMS Alpha (DEC)	1992	Introduced 64-bit addressing, multiple compilers, and networks for the Alpha system.
Novell UnixWare	1993	Novell's version of UNIX System V release 4, designed to work with NetWare
Windows NT (Microsoft)	1993	For networks. Featured true client/server operating system with support for Intel, RISC, and multiprocessor systems.
Solaris (Sun Microsystems)	1994	Sun's version of UNIX designed to run on Sun workstations, derived from AT&T's UNIX System V, Release 4
Linux 1.0	1995	First non-beta release of Red Hat Linux
Windows 95 (Microsoft)	1995	For PC users, this was the first true Windows operating system designed to replace Windows 3.x, Windows for Workgroups, and MS-DOS. Technically, Windows 95 was not related to Windows NT, which had networking capabilities.
OS/390, ver 1 (IBM)	1996	MVS core capability but with easier installation and management functions; open system certified.
Linux 3.0.3 (Red Hat)	1996	The first approximately concurrent multi-architecture release; supported the Digital Alpha platform.
OS/390, ver 2 (IBM)	1997	Scalable transaction-processing capability, batch workload scheduler, firewall security, enhanced e-commerce capability.
OpenVMS Alpha, version 7 (DEC)	1997	Designed for very large memory applications on the Alpha computer system.
Windows 98 (Microsoft)	1998	For PC users. Implemented many bug fixes to Windows 95, more extended hardware support, and fully 32 bit. Not directly related to Windows NT.

Windows 2000 (Microsoft)	1999	For networks. A major revision of the Windows NT operating system; much faster and more reliable than Windows NT. The Windows 2000 kernel contained more than 45 million lines of code, compared to 15 million for Windows NT. Not directly related to Windows 9x.
Windows XP Home (Microsoft)	2001	For PC users. A 32-bit system; the successor to Windows 9x.
Windows XP Pro (Microsoft)	2001	For network and power users. The successor to Windows 2000. The Professional Edition, available in 32-bit and 64-bit versions, was intended for office and professional users who need more computing power and extensive networking capabilities.
RHEL 2.1 (Red Hat)	2002	Launch of Red Hat Enterprise Linux, the first enterprise computing offering, based on RHL 7.2.
Windows Server 2003 (Microsoft)	2003	Available in Standard Edition, Web Edition, Enterprise Edition, and Datacenter Edition, this operating system is designed as a server platform for Microsoft's .NET initiative.
Fedora Core Linux (Red Hat)	2003	Product based on Red Hat Linux 9 for individual users (downloadable for free); created by the Fedora Project in cooperation with Red Hat, Inc.
Windows Server 2005 (Microsoft)	2005	Expected release of upgrade to Windows Server 2003.

Glossary

absolute filename: a file's name, as given by the user, preceded by the directory (or directories) where the file is found and, when necessary, the specific device label.

access control: the control of user access to a network or computer system. See also *authentication*.

access control list: an access control method that lists each file, the names of the users who are allowed to access it, and the type of access each is permitted.

access control matrix: an access control method that uses a matrix with every file (listed in rows) and every user (listed in columns) and the type of access each user is permitted on each file, recorded in the cell at the intersection of that row and column.

access control verification module: the section of the File Manager that verifies which users are permitted to perform which operations with each file.

access time: the total time required to access data in secondary storage. For a direct access storage device with movable read/write heads, it's the sum of seek time (arm movement), search time (rotational delay), and transfer time (data transfer).

access token: an object that uniquely identifies a user who has logged on. An access token is appended to every process owned by the user. It contains the user's security identification, the names of the groups to which the user belongs, any privileges the user owns, the default owner of any objects the user's processes create, and the default access control list to be applied to any objects the user's processes create.

active multiprogramming: a term used to indicate that the operating system has more control over interrupts; designed to fairly distribute CPU utilization over several resident programs. It contrasts with *passive multiprogramming*.

Active Directory: Microsoft Windows directory service that offers centralized administration of application serving, authentication, and user registration for distributed networking systems.

address: a number that designates a particular memory location.

address resolution: the process of changing the address of an instruction or data item to the address in main memory at which it is to be loaded or relocated.

Advanced Research Projects Agency network (ARPAnet): a pioneering long-distance network funded by ARPA (now DARPA). It served as the basis for early networking research, as well as a central backbone during the development of the Internet. The ARPAnet consisted of individual packet switching computers interconnected by leased lines.

aging: a policy used to ensure that jobs that have been in the system for a long time in the lower level queues will eventually complete their execution.

algorithm: a set of step-by-step instructions used to solve a particular problem. It can be stated in any form, such as mathematical formulas, diagrams, or natural or programming languages.

allocation module: the section of the File Manager responsible for keeping track of unused areas in each storage device.

allocation scheme: the process of assigning specific resources to a job so it can execute.

anonymous ftp: a use of ftp that allows a user to retrieve documents, files, programs, and other data from anywhere on the Internet without having to establish a user ID and password. By using the special user ID of "anonymous" the network user is allowed to bypass local security checks and publicly accessible files on the remote system.

antivirus software: software that is designed to detect and recover from attacks by viruses and worms. It is usually part of a system protection software package.

argument: in a command-driven operating system, a value or option placed in the command that modifies how the command is to be carried out.

ARPAnet: see *Advanced Research Projects Agency network*.

assembler: a computer program that translates programs from assembly language to machine language.

assembly language: a programming language that allows users to write programs using mnemonic instructions that can be translated by an assembler. It is considered a low-level programming language and is very computer dependent.

associative memory: the name given to several registers, allocated to each active process, whose contents associate several of the process segments and page numbers with their main memory addresses.

authentication: the means by which a system verifies that the individual attempting to access the system is authorized to do so. Password protection is an authentication technique.

availability: a resource measurement tool that indicates the likelihood that the resource will be ready when a user needs it. It's influenced by mean time between failures and mean time to repair.

avoidance: the strategy of deadlock avoidance. It is a dynamic strategy, attempting to ensure that resources are never allocated in such a way as to place a system in an unsafe state.

backup: the process of making long-term archival file storage copies of files on the system.

batch system: a type of system developed for the earliest computers that used punched cards or tape for input. Each job was entered by assembling the cards together into a "deck" and several jobs were grouped, or "batched," together before being sent through the card reader.

Belady's anomaly: points to the fact that, for some paging algorithms, the page fault rate may increase as the number of allocated page frames increases. Also called *FIFO anomaly*.

benchmarks: a measurement tool used to objectively measure and evaluate a system's performance by running a set of jobs representative of the work normally done by a computer system.

best-fit memory allocation: a main memory allocation scheme that considers all free blocks and selects for allocation the one that will result in the least amount of wasted space. It contrasts with the *first-fit memory allocation*.

biometrics: the science and technology of identifying authorized users based on their biological characteristics.

BIOS: an acronym for basic input output system, a set of programs that are hard-coded on a chip to load into ROM at startup.

blocking: a storage-saving and I/O-saving technique that groups individual records into a block that's stored and retrieved as a unit. The size of the block is often set to take advantage of the transfer rate.

bootstrapping: the process of starting an inactive computer by using a small initialization program to load other programs.

bounds register: a register used to store the highest location in memory legally accessible by each program. It contrasts with *relocation register*.

bridge: a data-link layer device used to interconnect multiple networks using the same protocol. A bridge is used to create an extended network so that several individual networks can appear to be part of one larger network.

browsing: a system security violation in which unauthorized users are allowed to search through secondary storage directories or files for information they should not have the privilege to read.

B-tree: a special case of a binary tree structure used to locate and retrieve records stored in disk files. The qualifications imposed on a B-tree structure reduce the amount of time it takes to search through the B-tree, making it an ideal file organization for large files.

buffers: the temporary storage areas residing in main memory, channels, and control units. They're used to store data read from an input device before it's needed by the processor and to store data that will be written to an output device.

bus: (1) the physical channel that links the hardware components and allows for transfer of data and electrical signals; or (2) a shared communication link onto which multiple nodes may connect.

bus topology: a network architecture in which elements are connected together along a single link.

busy waiting: a method by which processes, waiting for an event to occur, continuously test to see if the condition has changed and remain in unproductive, resource-consuming wait loops.

cache manager: a component of the I/O system that manage the part of virtual memory known as cache. The cache expands or shrinks dynamically depending on the amount of memory available.

cache memory: a small, fast memory used to hold selected data and to provide faster access than would otherwise be possible.

capability list: an access control method that lists every user, the files to which each has access, and the type of access allowed to those files.

capacity: the maximum throughput level of any one of the system's components.

Carrier Sense Multiple Access with Collision Avoidance (CSMA/CA): a method used to avoid transmission collision on shared media such as networks. It usually prevents collisions by requiring token acquisition.

Carrier Sense Multiple Access with Collision Detection (CSMA/CD): a method used to detect transmission collision on shared media such as networks. It is used to detect transmission collision and require that the affected stations stop transmitting immediately and try again after delaying a random amount of time.

CD-R: a compact disc storage medium that can be read many times but can be written to once.

CD-ROM: compact disc read-only memory; a direct access optical storage medium that can store up to 650 megabytes of data including graphics, audio, and video. Because it's read-only, the contents of the disc can't be modified.

CD-RW: a compact disc storage medium that can be read many times and written to many times.

central processing unit (CPU): the component with the circuitry, the "chips," to control the interpretation and execution of instructions. In essence, it controls the operation of the entire computer system. All storage references, data manipulations, and I/O operations are initiated or performed by the CPU.

channel: see *I/O channel*.

channel program: see *I/O channel program*.

Channel Status Word (CSW): a data structure that contains information indicating the condition of the channel, including three bits for the three components of the I/O subsystem—one each for the channel, control unit, and device.

child process: in UNIX and Linux operating systems, the subordinate processes that are controlled by a parent process.

circuit switching: a communication model in which a dedicated communication path is established between two hosts, and on which all messages travel. The telephone system is an example of a circuit switched network.

circular wait: one of four conditions for deadlock through which each process involved is waiting for a resource being held by another; each process is blocked and can't continue, resulting in deadlock.

cleartext: in cryptography, a method of transmitting data without encryption, in text that is readable by anyone who sees it.

client: a user node that requests and makes use of various network services. A workstation requesting the contents of a file from a file server is a client of the file server.

clock cycle: the time span between two ticks of the computer's system clock.

clock policy: a variation of the LRU policy that removes from main memory the pages that show the least amount of activity during recent clock cycles.

C-LOOK: a scheduling strategy for direct access storage devices that's an optimization of C-SCAN.

COBEGIN: used with COEND to indicate to a multiprocessing compiler the beginning of a section where instructions can be processed concurrently.

COEND: used with COBEGIN to indicate to a multiprocessing compiler the end of a section where instructions can be processed concurrently.

collision: when a hashing algorithm generates the same logical address for two records with unique keys.

command-driven interface: an interface that accepts typed commands, one line at a time, from the user. It contrasts with a menu-driven interface.

compact disc: see *CD-ROM*.

compaction: the process of collecting fragments of available memory space into contiguous blocks by moving programs and data in a computer's memory or secondary storage. Also called *garbage collection*.

compatibility: the ability of an operating system to execute programs written for other operating systems or for earlier versions of the same system.

compiler: a computer program that translates programs from a high-level programming language (such as FORTRAN, COBOL, Pascal, C, or Ada) into machine language.

complete file name: see *absolute file name*.

compression: see *data compression*.

concurrent processing: execution by a single processor of a set of processes in such a way that they appear to be happening at the same time. It's typically achieved by interleaved execution. Also called *multiprocessing*.

concurrent programming: a programming technique that allows a single processor to simultaneously execute multiple sets of instructions. Also called *multiprogramming* or *multitasking*.

connect time: in time-sharing, the amount of time that a user is connected to a computer system. It is usually measured by the time elapsed between log on and log off.

contention: a situation that arises on shared resources in which multiple data sources compete for access to the resource.

context switching: the acts of saving a job's processing information in its PCB so the job can be swapped out of memory and of loading the processing information from the Process Control Block (PCB) of another job into the appropriate registers so the CPU can process it. Context switching occurs in all preemptive policies.

contiguous storage: a type of file storage in which all the information is stored in adjacent locations in a storage medium.

control cards: cards that define the exact nature of each program and its requirements. They contain information that direct the operating system to perform specific functions, such as initiating the execution of a particular job. See *job control language*.

control unit: see *I/O control unit*.

control word: a password given to a file by its creator.

C programming language: a general purpose programming language developed by D. M. Ritchie. It combines high-level statements with low-level machine controls to generate software that is both easy to use and highly efficient.

CPU: see *central processing unit*.

CPU-bound: a job that will perform a great deal of nonstop processing before issuing an interrupt. A CPU-bound job can tie up the CPU for long periods of time while all other jobs must wait. It contrasts with *I/O-bound*.

cracker: an individual who attempts to access computer systems without authorization. These individuals are often malicious, as opposed to "hackers," and have several means at their disposal for breaking into a system.

critical region: the parts of a program that must complete execution before other processes can have access to the resources being used. It's called a critical region because its execution must be handled as a unit.

C-SCAN: a scheduling strategy for direct access storage devices that's used to optimize seek time. It's an abbreviation for circular-SCAN.

CSMA/CA: see *Carrier Sense Multiple Access with Collision Avoidance*

CSMA/CD: see *Carrier Sense Multiple Access with Collision Detection*

cryptography: the science of coding a message or text so an unauthorized user cannot read it.

current byte address (CBA): the address of the last byte read. It is used by the File Manager to access records in secondary storage and must be updated every time a record is accessed, such as when the READ command is executed.

current directory: the directory or subdirectory in which the user is working.

cylinder: for a disk or disk pack, it's when two or more read/write heads are positioned at the same track, at the same relative position, on their respective surfaces.

DASD: see *direct access storage device*.

database: a group of related files that are interconnected at various levels to give users flexibility of access to the data stored.

data compression: a procedure used to reduce the amount of space required to store data by reducing encoding or abbreviating repetitive terms or characters.

data file: a file that contains only data.

deadlock: a problem occurring when the resources needed by some jobs to finish execution are held by other jobs, which, in turn, are waiting for other resources to become available. The deadlock is complete if the remainder of the system comes to a standstill as a result of the hold the processes have on the resource allocation scheme. Also called *deadly embrace*.

deadly embrace: a colorful synonym for *deadlock*.

deallocation: the process of freeing an allocated resource, whether memory space, a device, a file, or a CPU.

dedicated device: a device that can be assigned to only one job at a time; it serves that job for the entire time the job is active.

demand paging: a memory allocation scheme that loads into memory a program's page at the time it's needed for processing.

denial of service (DoS) attack: an attack on a network that makes it unavailable to perform the functions it was designed to do. This can be done by flooding the server with meaningless requests or information.

detection: the process of examining the state of an operating system to determine whether a deadlock exists.

device: a computer's peripheral unit such as printer, plotter, tape drive, disk drive, or terminal.

device driver: a device-specific program module that handles the interrupts and controls a particular type of device.

device independent: programs that are devoid of the detailed instructions required to interact with any I/O device present in the computer system. This is made possible because the operating system provides an I/O interface that supports uniform I/O regardless of the type of device being used.

device interface module: transforms the block number supplied by the physical file system into the actual cylinder/surface/record combination needed to retrieve the information from a specific secondary storage device.

Device Manager: the section of the operating system responsible for controlling the use of devices. It monitors every device, channel, and control unit and chooses the most efficient way to allocate all of the system's devices.

dictionary attack: the technique by which an intruder attempts to guess user passwords by trying words found in a dictionary.

Dijkstra's algorithm: a graph theory algorithm that has been used in various link state routing protocols. This allows a router to step through an internetwork and find the best path to each destination.

direct access file: see *direct record organization*.

direct access storage device (DASD): any secondary storage device that can directly read or write to a specific place. Also called a *random access storage device*. It contrasts with a *sequential access storage device*.

directed graphs: a graphic model representing various states of resource allocations. It consists of processes and resources connected by directed lines (lines with directional arrows).

direct memory access (DMA): an I/O technique that allows a control unit to access main memory directly and transfer data without the intervention of the CPU.

directory: a storage area in a secondary storage volume (disk, disk pack, etc.) containing information about files stored in that volume. The information is used to access those files.

direct record organization: files stored in a direct access storage device and organized to give users the flexibility of accessing any record at random regardless of its position in the file.

disc: an optical storage medium such as CD or DVD.

disk pack: a removable stack of disks mounted on a common central spindle with spaces between each pair of platters so read/write heads can move between them.

displacement: in a paged or segmented memory allocation environment, it's the difference between a page's relative address and the actual machine language address. It's used to locate an instruction or data value within its page frame. Also called *offset*.

distributed operating system (DO/S): an operating system that provides control for a distributed computing system (two or more computers interconnected for a specific purpose), allowing its resources to be accessed in a unified way.

distributed processing: a method of data processing in which files are stored at many different locations and in which processing takes place at different sites.

DNS: see *domain name service.*

Domain Name Service (DNS): is a general purpose, distributed, replicated, data query service. Its principal function is the resolution of Internet addresses based on fully qualified domain names such as .com (for commercial entity) or .edu (for educational institution).

DO/S: see *distributed operating system.*

double buffering: a technique used to speed I/O in which two buffers are present in main memory, channels, and control units.

DVD: digital video disc; a direct access optical storage medium that can store up to 17 gigabytes, enough to store a full-length movie.

dynamic partitions: a memory allocation scheme in which jobs are given as much memory as they request when they are loaded for processing, thus creating their own partitions in main memory. It contrasts with *static partitions,* or *fixed partitions.*

elevator algorithm: see *LOOK.*

embedded computer system: a dedicated computer system that often resides inside a larger physical system, such as jet aircraft or ships. It must be small and fast and work with real-time constraints, fail-safe execution, and nonstandard I/O devices. In some cases it must be able to manage concurrent activities, which requires parallel processing.

encryption: translation of a message or data item from its original form to an encoded form, thus hiding its meaning and making it unintelligible without the key to decode it. It's used to improve system security and data protection.

Ethernet: a 10 megabit, 100 megabit, 1 gigabit or more standard for LANs, initially developed by Xerox and later refined by Digital Equipment Corporation, Intel, and Xerox. All hosts are connected to a coaxial cable where they contend for network access using CSMA/CD.

ethics: the rules or standards of behavior that members of the computer using community are expected to follow, demonstrating the principles of right and wrong.

explicit parallelism: a type of concurrent programming that requires that the programmer explicitly state which instructions can be executed in parallel. It contrasts with *implicit parallelism.*

extensibility: one of an operating system's design goals that allows it to be easily enhanced as market requirements change.

extension: in some operating systems, it's the part of the file name that indicates which compiler or software package is needed to run the files. UNIX and Linux call it a *suffix.*

extents: any remaining records, and all other additions to the file, that are stored in other sections of the disk. The extents of the file are linked together with pointers.

external fragmentation: a situation in which the dynamic allocation of memory creates unusable fragments of free memory between blocks of busy, or allocated, memory. It contrasts with *internal fragmentation.*

external interrupts: interrupts that occur outside the normal flow of a program's execution. They are used in preemptive scheduling policies to ensure a fair use of the CPU in multiprogramming environments.

FCFS: see *first come first served.*

feedback loop: a mechanism to monitor the system's resource utilization so adjustments can be made.

fetch policy: the rules used by the virtual memory manager to determine when a page is copied from disk to memory.

field: a group of related bytes that can be identified by the user with a name, type, and size. A record is made up of fields.

FIFO: see *first in first out.*

FIFO anomaly: an unusual circumstance through which adding more page frames causes an increase in page interrupts when using a FIFO page replacement policy. Also called *Belady's anomaly.*

file: a group of related records that contains information to be used by specific application programs to generate reports.

file allocation table (FAT): the table used to track noncontiguous segments of a file.

file descriptor: information kept in the directory to describe a file or file extent. It contains the file's name, location, and attributes.

File Manager: the section of the operating system responsible for controlling the use of files. It tracks every file in the system including data files, assemblers, compilers, and application programs. By using predetermined access policies, it enforces access restrictions on each file.

file server: a dedicated network node that provides mass data storage for other nodes on the network.

File Transfer Protocol (FTP): a protocol that allows a user on one host to access and transfer files to or from another host over a TCP/IP network.

filter command: a command that directs input from a device or file, changes it, and then sends the result to a printer or display.

FINISHED: a job status that means that execution of the job has been completed.

firewall: a set of hardware and software that disguises the internal network address of a computer or network to control how clients from outside can access the organization's internal servers.

firmware: software instructions or data that are stored in a fixed or "firm" way, usually implemented on *Read Only Memory* (ROM). Firmware is built into the computer to make its operation simpler for the user to understand.

first come first served (FCFS): (1) the simplest scheduling algorithm for direct access storage devices that satisfies track requests in the order in which they are received; (2) a nonpreemptive process scheduling policy (or algorithm) that handles jobs according to their arrival time; the first job in the READY queue will be processed first by the CPU.

first-fit memory allocation: a main memory allocation scheme that searches from the beginning of the free block list and selects for allocation the first block of memory large enough to fulfill the request. It contrasts with *best-fit memory allocation.*

first generation (1940–1955): the era of the first computers, characterized by their use of vacuum tubes and their very large physical size.

first-in first-out (FIFO) policy: a page replacement policy that removes from main memory the pages that were brought in first. It's based on the assumption that these pages are the least likely to be used again in the near future.

fixed-length record: a record that always contains the same number of characters. It contrasts with *variable-length record.*

fixed partitions: a memory allocation scheme in which main memory is sectioned off, with portions assigned to each user. Also called *static partitions.* It contrasts with *dynamic partitions.*

flash memory: a type of nonvolatile memory used as a secondary storage device that can be erased and reprogrammed in blocks of data.

flop: a measure of processing speed meaning floating point operations per second (FLOP). See *megaflop, gigaflop, teraflop.*

floppy disk: a removable flexible disk that provides low-cost, direct access secondary storage for personal computer systems.

fragmentation: a condition in main memory where wasted memory space exists within partitions, called *internal fragmentation,* or between partitions, called *external fragmentation.*

ftp: the name of the program a user invokes to execute the File Transfer Protocol.

FTP: see *File Transfer Protocol.*

garbage collection: see *compaction.*

gateway: a communications device or program that passes data between networks having similar functions but different protocols. A gateway is used to create an extended network so that several individual networks appear to be part of one larger network.

gigabit: a measurement of data transmission speed equal to 1,073,741,824 bits per second.

gigabyte (GB): a unit of memory or storage space equal to 1,073,741,824 bytes or 2^{30} bytes. One gigabyte is approximately 1 billion bytes.

gigaflop: a benchmark used to measure processing speed. One gigaflop equals 1 billion floating point operations per second.

group: a property of operating systems that enables system administrators to create sets of users that share the same privileges. A group can share files or programs without allowing all system users access to those resources.

groupware: software applications that support cooperative work over a network. Groupware systems must support communications between users and information processing. For example, a system providing a shared editor must support not only the collective amendment of documents, but also discussions between the participants about what is to be amended and why.

graphical user interface (GUI): a user interface that allows the user to activate operating system commands by clicking on a desktop icon using a pointing device such as a mouse or touch screen. GUI evolved from command-driven user interfaces.

GUI: see *graphical user interface.*

hacker: a person who delights in having an intimate understanding of the internal workings of a system—computers and computer networks in particular. The term is often misused in a pejorative context, where "cracker" would be the correct term.

Hamming code: an error-detecting and error-correcting code that greatly improves the reliability of data, named after mathematician Richard Hamming.

hard disk: a direct access secondary storage device for personal computer systems. It's generally a high-density, nonremovable device.

hardware: the physical machine and its components, including main memory, I/O devices, I/O channels, direct access storage devices, and the central processing unit.

hashing algorithm: the set of instructions used to perform a key-to-address transformation in which a record's key field determines its location. See also *logical address.*

high-level scheduler: another term for the *Job Scheduler.*

HOLD: one of the process states. It is assigned to processes waiting to be let into the READY queue.

hop: a node network through which a packet passes on the path between the packet's source and destination nodes.

host: 1) the Internet term for a network node that is capable of communicating at the application layer. Each Internet host has a unique IP address. 2) a networked computer with centralized program or data files that makes them available to other computers on the network.

hybrid system: a computer system that supports both batch and interactive processes. It appears to be interactive because individual users can access the system via terminals and get fast responses, but it accepts and runs batch programs in the background when the interactive load is light.

hybrid topology: a network architecture that combines other types of network topologies, such as tree and star, to accommodate particular operating characteristics or traffic volumes.

impersonation: in Windows, the ability of a thread in one process to take on the security identity of a thread in another process and perform operations on that thread's behalf. Used by environment subsystems and network services when accessing remote resources for client applications.

implicit parallelism: a type of concurrent programming in which the compiler automatically detects which instructions can be performed in parallel. It contrasts with *explicit parallelism.*

indefinite postponement: means that a job's execution is delayed indefinitely because it's repeatedly preempted so other jobs can be processed.

index block: a data structure used with indexed storage allocation. It contains the addresses of each disk sector used by that file.

indexed sequential record organization: a way of organizing data in a direct access storage device. An index is created to show where the data records are stored. Any data record can be retrieved by consulting the index first.

indexed storage: the way in which the File Manager physically allocates space to an indexed sequentially organized file.

interactive system: a system that allows each user to interact directly with the operating system via commands entered from a keyboard. Also called *time-sharing system.*

interblock gap (IBG): an unused space between blocks of records on a magnetic tape.

internal fragmentation: a situation in which a fixed partition is only partially used by the program. The remaining space within the partition is unavailable to any other job and is therefore wasted. It contrasts with *external fragmentation.*

internal interrupts: also called "synchronous" interrupts, they occur as a direct result of the arithmetic operation or job instruction currently being processed. They contrast with *external interrupts.*

internal memory: see *main memory.*

International Organization for Standardization (ISO): a voluntary, non-treaty organization founded in 1946 that is responsible for creating international standards in many areas, including computers and communications. Its members are the national standards organizations of the 89 member countries, including ANSI for the United States.

Internet: the largest collection of networks interconnected with routers. It is a three-level hierarchy composed of backbone networks (e.g., NSFNET), mid-level networks (e.g., NEARnet), and local networks. The Internet is a multiprotocol internetwork.

Internet Protocol (IP): the network-layer protocol used to route data from one network to another. It was developed by the United States Department of Defense.

interrecord gap (IRG): an unused space between records on a magnetic tape. It facilitates the tape's start/stop operations.

interrupt: a hardware signal that suspends execution of a program and activates the execution of a special program known as the interrupt handler. It breaks the normal flow of the program being executed.

interrupt handler: the program that controls what action should be taken by the operating system when a sequence of events is interrupted.

inverted file: a file generated from full document databases. Each record in an inverted file contains a key subject and the document numbers where that subject is found. A book's index is an inverted file.

I/O: see input/output.

I/O-bound: a job that requires a large number of input/output operations, resulting in much free time for the CPU. It contrasts with *CPU-bound.*

I/O channel: a specialized programmable unit placed between the CPU and the control units. Its job is to synchronize the fast speed of the CPU with the slow speed of the I/O device and vice versa, making it possible to overlap I/O operations with CPU operations. I/O channels provide a path for the transmission of data between control units and main memory, and they control that transmission.

I/O channel program: the program that controls the channels. Each channel program specifies the action to be performed by the devices and controls the transmission of data between main memory and the control units.

I/O control unit: the hardware unit containing the electronic components common to one type of I/O device, such as a disk drive. It is used to control the operation of several I/O devices of the same type.

I/O device: any peripheral unit that allows communication with the CPU by users or programs, including terminals, line printers, plotters, card readers, tape drives, and direct access storage devices.

I/O device handler: the module that processes the I/O interrupts, handles error conditions, and provides detailed scheduling algorithms that are extremely device dependent. Each type of I/O device has its own device handler algorithm.

I/O scheduler: one of the modules of the I/O subsystem that allocates the devices, control units, and channels.

I/O subsystem: a collection of modules within the operating system that controls all I/O requests.

I/O traffic controller: one of the modules of the I/O subsystem that monitors the status of every device, control unit, and channel.

IP: see *Internet Protocol*.

ISO: see *International Organization for Standardization*.

job: a unit of work submitted by a user to an operating system.

job control language (JCL): a command language used in several computer systems to direct the operating system in the performance of its functions by identifying the users and their jobs and specifying the resources required to execute a job. The JCL helps the operating system better coordinate and manage the system's resources.

Job Scheduler: the high-level scheduler of the Processor Manager that selects jobs from a queue of incoming jobs based on each job's characteristics. The Job Scheduler's goal is to sequence the jobs in the READY queue so that the system's resources will be used efficiently.

job status: the condition of a job as it moves through the system from the beginning to the end of its execution: HOLD, READY, RUNNING, WAITING, or FINISHED.

job step: units of work executed sequentially by the operating system to satisfy the user's total request. A common example of three job steps is the compilation, linking, and execution of a user's program.

Job Table (JT): a table in main memory that contains two entries for each active job—the size of the job and the memory location where its page map table is stored. It's used for paged memory allocation schemes.

Kerberos: MIT-developed authentication system that allows network managers to administer and manage user authentication at the network level.

kernel: the part of the operating system that resides in main memory at all times and performs the most essential tasks, such as managing memory and handling disk input and output.

kernel level: in an object-based distributed operating system, provides the basic mechanisms for dynamically building the operating system by creating, managing, scheduling, synchronizing, and deleting objects.

kernel mode: name given to indicate that processes are granted privileged access to the processor. Therefore, all machine instructions are allowed and system memory is accessible. Contrasts with the more restrictive *user mode*.

kilobyte (K): a unit of memory or storage space equal to 1,024 bytes or 2^{10} bytes.

key field: (1) a unique field or combination of fields in a record that uniquely identifies that record; or (2) the field that determines the position of a record in a sorted sequence.

LAN: see *local area network*.

lands: flat surface areas on the reflective layer of a CD or DVD. Each land is interpreted as a 1. Contrasts with *pits*, which are interpreted as 0s.

leased line: a dedicated telephone circuit for which a subscriber pays a monthly fee, regardless of actual use.

least-frequently-used (LFU): a page-removal algorithm that removes from memory the least frequently used page.

least-recently-used (LRU) policy: a page-replacement policy that removes from main memory the pages that show the least amount of recent activity. It's based on the assumption that these pages are the least likely to be used again in the immediate future.

LFU: see *least-frequently-used*.

lightweight directory access protocol (LDAP): A protocol that defines a method for creating searchable directories of resources on a network. It's called "lightweight" because it is a simplified and TCP/IP-enabled version of the X.500 directory protocol.

link: a generic term for any data communications medium to which a network node is attached.

livelock: a locked system whereby two or more processes continually block the forward progress of the other without making any forward progress itself. It is similar to a deadlock except that neither process is blocked or waiting, they are both in a continuous state of change.

local area network (LAN): a data network intended to serve an area covering only a few square kilometers or less.

local station: the network node to which a user is attached.

locality of reference: behavior observed in many executing programs in which memory locations recently referenced, and those near them, are likely to be referenced in the near future.

locking: a technique used to guarantee the integrity of the data in a database through which the user locks out all other users while working with the database.

lockword: a sequence of letters and/or numbers provided by users to prevent unauthorized tampering with their files. The lockword serves as a secret "password" in that the system will deny access to the protected file unless the user supplies the correct lockword when accessing the file.

logic bomb: a virus with a trigger, usually an event, that causes it to execute.

logical address: the result of a key-to-address transformation. See also *hashing algorithm*.

LOOK: a scheduling strategy for direct access storage devices that's used to optimize seek time. Sometimes known as the elevator algorithm.

loosely coupled configuration: a multiprocessing configuration in which each processor has a copy of the operating system and controls its own resources.

low-level scheduler: a synonym for *Process Scheduler*.

LRU: see *least-recently-used*.

magnetic tape: linear secondary storage medium that was first developed for early computer systems. It allows only for sequential retrieval and storage of records.

magneto-optical (MO) disk drive: a data storage drive that uses a laser beam to read and/or write information recorded on magneto-optical disks.

mailslots: a high-level network software interface for passing data among processes in a one-to-many and many-to-one communication mechanism. Mailslots are useful for broadcasting messages to any number of processes.

main memory: the memory unit that works directly with the CPU and in which the data and instructions must reside in order to be processed. Also called *random access memory (RAM)*, *primary storage*, or *internal memory*.

mainframe: the historical name given to a large computer system. It was characterized by its large size, high cost, and high performance.

MAN: see *metropolitan area network*.

master file directory (MFD): a file stored immediately after the volume descriptor. It lists the names and characteristics of every file contained in that volume.

master/slave configuration: an asymmetric multiprocessing configuration consisting of a single processor system connected to "slave" processors, each of which is managed by the primary "master" processor, which provides the scheduling functions and jobs.

mean time between failures (MTBF): a resource measurement tool; the average time that a unit is operational before it breaks down.

mean time to repair (MTTR): a resource measurement tool; the average time needed to fix a failed unit and put it back in service.

megabyte (MB): a unit of memory or storage space equal to 1,048,576 bytes or 2^{20} bytes.

megaflop: a benchmark used to measure processing speed. One megaflop equals 1 million floating point operations per second.

megahertz (MHz): a speed measurement used to compare the clock speed of computers. One megahertz is equal to 1 million electrical cycles per second.

Memory Manager: the section of the operating system responsible for controlling the use of memory. It checks the validity of each request for memory space and, if it's a legal request, allocates the amount of memory needed to execute the job.

Memory Map Table (MMT): a table in main memory that contains as many entries as there are page frames and lists the location and free/busy status for each one.

menu-driven interface: an interface that accepts instructions that users choose from a menu of valid choices. Users often use a mouse to point and click on the chosen instruction. It contrasts with a *command-driven interface.*

metropolitan area network (MAN): a data network intended to serve an area approximating that of a large city.

microcomputer: a small computer equipped with all the hardware and software necessary to perform one or more tasks.

middle-level scheduler: a scheduler used by the Processor Manager to manage processes that have been interrupted because they have exceeded their allocated CPU time slice. It's used in some highly interactive environments.

midrange computer: a small to medium-sized computer system developed to meet the needs of smaller institutions. It was originally developed for sites with only a few dozen users. Also called minicomputer.

minicomputer: see *midrange computer.*

MIPS: a measure of processor speed that stands for million instructions per second. A mainframe system running at 100 MIPS can execute 100,000,000 instructions per second.

modem: an electronic device that connects a terminal or computer to a communication line. The word comes from MOdulation/DEModulation, which is what the modem does: it converts a binary bit pattern generated by a terminal or computer into electrical signals that can be transmitted over communication lines, and then reconverts them into binary bit patterns when they reach their destination.

module: a logical section of a program. A program may be divided into a number of logically self-contained modules that may be written and tested by a number of programmers.

monoprogramming system: a single-user computer system.

most-recently-used (MRU): a page-removal algorithm that removes from memory the most recently used page.

MTBF: see *mean time between failures.*

MTTR: see *mean time to repair.*

multiple-level queues: a process-scheduling scheme (used with other scheduling algorithms) that groups jobs according to a common characteristic. The processor is then allocated to serve the jobs in these queues in a predetermined manner.

multiprocessing: when two or more CPUs share the same main memory, most I/O devices, and the same control program routines. They service the same job stream and execute distinct processing programs concurrently.

multiprogramming: a technique that allows a single processor to process several programs residing simultaneously in main memory and interleaving their execution by overlapping I/O requests with CPU requests. Also called *concurrent programming* or *multitasking.*

multitasking: a synonym for multiprogramming.

mutex: from MUTual EXclusion, a condition that specifies that only one process may use a shared resource at a time to ensure correct operation and results.

mutual exclusion: one of four conditions for deadlock in which only one process is allowed to have access to a resource. It's typically shortened to "mutex" in algorithms describing synchronization between processes.

named pipes: a high-level software interface to NetBIOS, which represents the hardware in network applications as abstract objects. Named pipes are represented as file objects in Windows and operate under the same security mechanisms as other executive objects.

natural wait: common term used to identify an I/O request from a program in a multiprogramming environment that would cause a process to wait "naturally" before resuming execution.

negative feedback loop: a mechanism to monitor the system's resources and, when it becomes too congested, to signal the appropriate manager to slow down the arrival rate of the processes.

NetBIOS interface: a programming interface that allows I/O requests to be sent to and received from a remote computer. It hides networking hardware from applications.

network: a system of interconnected computer systems and peripheral devices that exchange information with one another.

network operating system (NOS): the software that manages network resources for a node on a network and may provide security and access control. These resources may include electronic mail, file servers, and print servers.

no preemption: one of four conditions for deadlock in which a process is allowed to hold on to resources while it is waiting for other resources to finish execution.

noncontiguous storage: a type of file storage in which the information is stored in nonadjacent locations in a storage medium. Data records can be accessed directly by computing their relative addresses.

nonpreemptive scheduling policy: a job scheduling strategy that functions without external interrupts so that, once a job captures the processor and begins execution, it remains in the RUNNING state uninterrupted until it issues an I/O request or it's finished.

NOS: see *network operating system.*

N-step SCAN: a variation of the SCAN scheduling strategy for direct access storage devices that's used to optimize seek times.

NT file system (NTFS): The file system introduced with Windows NT that offers file management services, such as permission management, compression, transaction logs, and the ability to create a single volume spanning two or more physical disks.

null entry: an empty entry in a list. It assumes different meanings based on the list's application.

object: any one of the many entities that constitute a computer system, such as CPUs, terminals, disk drives, files, or databases. Each object is called by a unique name and has a set of operations that can be carried out on it.

object-based DO/S: a view of distributed operating systems where each hardware unit is bundled with its required operational software, forming a discrete object to be handled as an entity.

object-oriented: a programming philosophy whereby programs consist of self-contained, reusable modules called objects, each of which supports a specific function, but which are categorized into classes of objects that share the same function.

offset: in a paged or segmented memory allocation environment, it's the difference between a page's address and the actual machine language address. It's used to locate an instruction or data value within its page frame. Also called *displacement*.

open shortest path first (OSPF): a protocol designed for use in Internet Protocol networks, it is concerned with tracking the operational state of every network interface. Any changes to the state of an interface will trigger a routing update message.

open systems interconnection (OSI) reference model: a seven-layer structure designed to describe computer network architectures and the ways in which data passes through them. This model was developed by the ISO in 1978 to clearly define the interfaces and protocols for multi-vendor networks, and to provide users of those networks with conceptual guidelines in the construction of such networks.

operating system: the software that manages all the resources of a computer system.

optical disc: a secondary storage device on which information is stored in the form of tiny holes called "pits" laid out in a spiral track (instead of a concentric track as for a magnetic disk). The data is read by focusing a laser beam onto the track.

optical disc drive: a drive that uses a laser beam to read and/or write information recorded on compact optical discs.

OSI reference model: see *open systems interconnection reference model*.

OSPF: see *open shortest path first*.

overlay: a technique used to increase the apparent size of main memory. This is accomplished by keeping in main memory only the programs or data that are currently active; the rest are kept in secondary storage. Overlay occurs when segments of a program are transferred from secondary storage to main memory for execution, so that two or more segments occupy the same storage locations at different times.

owner: one of the three types of users allowed to access a file. The owner is the one who created the file originally. The other two types are "group" and "everyone else," also known as "world" in some systems.

P: an operation performed on a semaphore, which may cause the calling process to wait. It stands for the Dutch word *proberen*, meaning "to test," and it's part of the P and V operations to test and increment.

packet: a unit of data sent across a network. Packet is a generic term used to describe units of data at all layers of the protocol stack, but it is most correctly used to describe application data units.

packet sniffer: software that intercepts network data packets sent in cleartext and searches them for information, such as passwords.

packet switching: a communication model in which messages are individually routed between hosts, with no previously established communication path.

page: a fixed-size section of a user's job that corresponds to page frames in main memory.

page fault: a type of hardware interrupt caused by a reference to a page not residing in memory. The effect is to move a page out of main memory and into secondary storage so another page can be moved into memory.

page fault handler: part of the Memory Manager that determines if there are empty page frames in memory so that the requested page can immediately be copied from secondary storage, or determines which page must be swapped out if all page frames are busy.

page frame: individual sections of main memory of uniform size into which a single page may be loaded.

Page Map Table (PMT): a table in main memory with the vital information for each page including the page number and its corresponding page frame memory address.

page replacement policy: an algorithm used by virtual memory systems to decide which page or segment to remove from main memory when a page frame is needed and memory is full. Two examples are FIFO and LRU.

page swap: the process of moving a page out of main memory and into secondary storage so another page can be moved into memory in its place.

paged memory allocation: a memory allocation scheme based on the concept of dividing a user's job into sections of equal size to allow for noncontiguous program storage during execution. This was implemented to further increase the level of multiprogramming. It contrasts with *segmented memory allocation.*

parallel processing: the process of operating two or more CPUs in parallel: that is, more than one CPU executing instructions simultaneously.

parent process: In UNIX and Linux operating systems, a job that controls one or more child processes, which are subordinate to it.

parity bit: an extra bit added to a character, word, or other data unit and used for error checking. It is set to either 0 or 1 so that the sum of the one bits in the data unit is always even, for even parity, or odd for odd parity, according to the logic of the system.

partition: a section of hard disk storage of arbitrary size. Partitions can be static or dynamic.

passive multiprogramming: a term used to indicate that the operating system doesn't control the amount of time the CPU is allocated to each job, but waits for each job to end an execution sequence before issuing an interrupt releasing the CPU and making it available to other jobs. It contrasts with *active multiprogramming.*

pass-through security: used to perform remote-validation activities in Windows 95. Logon information is passed to the appropriate networking protocol for processing that enables Windows 95 to use existing network hardware and software with all the security that is built into these external network servers.

password: a user-defined access control method. Typically a word or character string that a user must specify in order to be allowed to log on to a computer system.

patch: executable software that repairs errors or omissions in another program or piece of software.

patch management: the rigorous application of software patches to make repairs and keep the operating system software up to the latest standard.

path: (1) the sequence of routers and links through which a packet passes on its way from source to destination node; (2) the sequence of directories and subdirectories the operating system must follow to find a specific file.

PCB: see *Process Control Block*.

peer (hardware): a node on a network that is at the same level as other nodes on that network. For example, all nodes on a local area network are peers.

peer (software): a process that is communicating to another process residing at the same layer in the protocol stack on another node. For example, if the processes are application processes they are said to be application-layer peers.

performance: the ability of an operating system to give users good response times under heavy loads and CPU-bound applications such as graphic and financial analysis packages, both of which require rapid processing.

phishing: a technique used to trick consumers into revealing personal information by appearing as a legitimate entity.

pipe: a symbol that directs the operating system to divert the output of one command so it becomes the input of another command.

pirated software: illegally obtained software.

pits: tiny depressions on the reflective layer of a CD or DVD. Each pit is interpreted as a 0. Contrasts with *lands*, which are interpreted as 1s.

placement policy: the rules used by the virtual memory manager to determine where the virtual page is to be loaded in memory.

pointer: an address or other indicator of location.

polling: a software mechanism used to test the flag, which indicates when a device, control unit, or path is available.

portability: the ability to move an entire operating system to a machine based on a different processor or configuration with as little recoding as possible.

Portable Operating System Interface (POSIX): a set of IEEE standards that defines the standard user and programming interfaces for operating systems so developers can port programs from one operating system to another.

positive feedback loop: a mechanism used to monitor the system. When the system becomes underutilized, the feedback causes the arrival rate to increase.

preemptive scheduling policy: any process scheduling strategy that, based on predetermined policies, interrupts the processing of a job and transfers the CPU to another job. It is widely used in time-sharing environments.

prevention: a design strategy for an operating system where resources are managed in such a way that some of the necessary conditions for deadlock do not hold.

primary storage: see *main memory.*

primitives: well-defined, predictable, low-level operating system mechanisms that allow higher-level operating system components to perform their functions without considering direct hardware manipulation.

priority scheduling: a nonpreemptive process scheduling policy (or algorithm) that allows for the execution of high-priority jobs before low-priority jobs.

process: an instance of execution of a program that is identifiable and controllable by the operating system.

process control block (PCB): a data structure that contains information about the current status and characteristics of a process. Every process has a PCB.

process identification: a user-supplied unique identifier of the process and a pointer connecting it to its descriptor, which is stored in the PCB.

process scheduler: the low-level scheduler of the Processor Manager that sets up the order in which processes in the READY queue will be served by the CPU.

process scheduling algorithm: an algorithm used by the Job Scheduler to allocate the CPU and move jobs through the system. Examples are FCFS, SJN, priority, and round robin scheduling policies.

process scheduling policy: any policy used by the Processor Manager to select the order in which incoming jobs will be executed.

process state: information stored in the job's PCB that indicates the current condition of the process being executed.

process status: information stored in the job's PCB that indicates the current position of the job and the resources responsible for that status.

Process Status Word (PSW): information stored in a special CPU register including the current instruction counter and register contents. It is saved in the job's PCB when it isn't running but is on HOLD, READY, or WAITING.

process synchronization: (1) the need for algorithms to resolve conflicts between processors in a multiprocessing environment; (2) the need to ensure that events occur in the proper order even if they are carried out by several processes.

process-based DO/S: a view of distributed operating systems that encompasses all the system's processes and resources. Process management is provided through the use of client/server processes.

processor: (1) another term for the CPU (central processing unit); or (2) any component in a computing system capable of performing a sequence of activities. It controls the interpretation and execution of instructions.

Processor Manager: a composite of two submanagers, the Job Scheduler and the Process Scheduler. It decides how to allocate the CPU, monitors whether it's executing a process or waiting, and controls job entry to ensure balanced use of resources.

producers and consumers: a classic problem in which a process produces data that will be consumed, or used, by another process. It exhibits the need for process cooperation.

program: a sequence of instructions that provides a solution to a problem and directs the computer's actions. In an operating systems environment it can be equated with a job.

program file: a file that contains instructions for the computer.

protocol: a set of rules to control the flow of messages through a network.

proxy server: a server positioned between an internal network and an external network or the Internet to screen all requests for information and prevent unauthorized access to network resources.

PSW: see *process status word*.

queue: a linked list of PCBs that indicates the order in which jobs or processes will be serviced.

race: a synchronization problem between two processes vying for the same resource. In some cases it may result in data corruption because the order in which the processes will finish executing cannot be controlled.

RAID: redundant arrays of independent disks. A group of hard disks controlled in such a way that they speed read access of data on secondary storage devices and aid data recovery.

random access storage device: see *direct access storage device*.

read only memory (ROM): a type of primary storage in which programs and data are stored once by the manufacturer and later retrieved as many times as necessary. ROM does not allow storage of new programs or data.

readers and writers: a problem that arises when two types of processes need to access a shared resource such as a file or a database. Their access must be controlled to preserve data integrity.

read/write head: a small electromagnet used to read or write data on a magnetic storage medium, such as disk or tape.

READY: a job status that means the job is ready to run but is waiting for the CPU.

real-time system: an extremely fast computing system used in time-critical environments that require immediate decisions, such as navigation systems, rapid transit systems, and industrial control systems.

record: a group of related fields treated as a unit. A file is a group of related records.

recovery: (1) when a deadlock is detected, the steps that must be taken to break the deadlock by breaking the circle of waiting processes. (2) When a system is assaulted, the steps that must be taken to recover system operability and, in the best case, recover any lost data.

redirection: a symbol that directs the operating system to send the results of a command to or from a file or other device other than a keyboard or monitor.

reentrant code: code that can be used by two or more processes at the same time; each shares the same copy of the executable code but has separate data areas.

register: a hardware storage unit used in the CPU for temporary storage of a single data item.

relative address: in a direct organization environment, it indicates the position of a record relative to the beginning of the file.

relative filename: a file's simple name and extension as given by the user. It contrasts with *absolute filename*.

reliability: (1) a standard that measures the probability that a unit will not fail during a given time period. It's a function of MTBF; (2) the ability of an operating system to respond predictably to error conditions, even those caused by hardware failures; (3) the ability of an operating system to actively protect itself and its users from accidental or deliberate damage by user programs.

relocatable dynamic partitions: a memory allocation scheme in which the system relocates programs in memory to gather together all of the empty blocks and compact them to make one block of memory that's large enough to accommodate some or all of the jobs waiting for memory.

relocation: (1) the process of moving a program from one area of memory to another; (2) the process of adjusting address references in a program, by either software or hardware means, to allow the program to execute correctly when loaded in different sections of memory.

relocation register: a register that contains the value that must be added to each address referenced in the program so that it will be able to access the correct memory addresses after relocation. If the program hasn't been relocated, the value stored in the program's relocation register is zero. It contrasts with *bounds register*.

remote login: the ability to operate on a remote computer using a protocol over a computer network as though locally attached.

remote station: the node at the distant end of a network connection.

repeated trials: repeated guessing of a user's password by an unauthorized user. It's a method used to illegally enter systems that rely on passwords.

replacement policy: the rules used by the virtual memory manager to determine which virtual page must be removed from memory to make room for a new page.

resource holding: one of four conditions for deadlock in which each process refuses to relinquish the resources it holds until its execution is completed, even though it isn't using them because it's waiting for other resources. It's the opposite of *resource sharing*.

resource sharing: the use of a resource by two or more processes either at the same time or at different times.

resource utilization: a measure of how much each unit is contributing to the overall operation of the system. It's usually given as a percentage of time that a resource is actually in use.

response time: a measure of an interactive system's efficiency that tracks the speed with which the system will respond to a user's command.

ring topology: a network topology in which each node is connected to two adjacent nodes. Ring networks have the advantage of not needing routing because all packets are simply passed to a node's upstream neighbor.

RIP: see *routing information protocol*.

root directory: (1) for a disk, it's the directory accessed by default when booting up the computer; or (2) for a hierarchical directory structure, it's the first directory accessed by a user.

rotational delay: a synonym for *search time*.

rotational ordering: an algorithm used to reorder record requests within tracks to optimize search time.

round robin: a preemptive process scheduling policy (or algorithm) that allocates to each job one unit of processing time per turn to ensure that the CPU is equally shared among all active processes and isn't monopolized by any one job. It's used extensively in interactive systems.

router: a device that forwards traffic between networks. The routing decision is based on network-layer information and routing tables, often constructed by routing protocols.

routing: the process of selecting the correct interface and next hop for a packet being forwarded.

routing information protocol (RIP): a routing protocol used by IP. It is based on a distance-vector algorithm.

RUNNING: a job status that means that the job is executing.

safe state: the situation in which the system has enough available resources to guarantee the completion of at least one job running on the system.

SCAN: a scheduling strategy for direct access storage devices that's used to optimize seek time. The most common variations are *N-step SCAN* and *C-SCAN*.

scheduling algorithm: see *process scheduling algorithm*.

script file: A series of executable commands written in plain text and executed by the operating system in sequence as a procedure.

search strategies: algorithms used to optimize search time in direct access storage devices. See also *rotational ordering*.

search time: the time it takes to rotate the drum or disk from the moment an I/O command is issued until the requested record is moved under the read/write head. Also called *rotational delay*.

second generation (1955–1965): the second era of technological development of computers, when the transistor replaced the vacuum tube. Computers were smaller and faster and had larger storage capacity than first-generation computers and were developed to meet the needs of the business market.

sector: a division in a disk's track. Sometimes called a "block." The tracks are divided into sectors during the formatting process.

security descriptor: a Windows data structure appended to an object that protects the object from unauthorized access. It contains an access control list and controls auditing.

seek strategy: a predetermined policy used by the I/O device handler to optimize seek times.

seek time: the time required to position the read/write head on the proper track from the time the I/O request is issued.

segment: a variable-size section of a user's job that contains a logical grouping of code. It contrasts with *page*.

Segment Map Table (SMT): a table in main memory with the vital information for each segment including the segment number and its corresponding memory address.

segmented memory allocation: a memory allocation scheme based on the concept of dividing a user's job into logical groupings of code to allow for noncontiguous program storage during execution. It contrasts with *paged memory allocation.*

segmented/demand paged memory allocation: a memory allocation scheme based on the concept of dividing a user's job into logical groupings of code and loading them into memory as needed.

semaphore: a type of shared data item that may contain either binary or nonnegative integer values and is used to provide mutual exclusion.

sequential access medium: any medium that stores records only in a sequential manner, one after the other, such as magnetic tape. It contrasts with *direct access storage device.*

sequential record organization: the organization of records in a specific sequence. Records in a sequential file must be processed one after another.

server: a node that provides to clients various network services such as file retrieval, printing, or database access services.

server process: a logical unit composed of one or more device drivers, a device manager, and a network server module; needed to control clusters or similar devices, such as printers or disk drives, in a process-based distributed operating system environment.

service pack: a term used by some vendors to describe an update to customer software to repair existing problems and/or deliver enhancements.

sharable code: executable code in the operating system that can be shared by several processes.

shared device: a device that can be assigned to several active processes at the same time.

shortest job first (SJF): see *shortest job next.*

shortest job next (SJN): a nonpreemptive process scheduling policy (or algorithm) that selects the waiting job with the shortest CPU cycle time. Also called *shortest job first.*

shortest remaining time (SRT): a preemptive process scheduling policy (or algorithm), similar to the SJN algorithm, that allocates the processor to the job closest to completion.

shortest seek time first (SSTF): a scheduling strategy for direct access storage devices that's used to optimize seek time. The track requests are ordered so the one closest to the currently active track is satisfied first and the ones farthest away are made to wait.

site: a specific location on a network containing one or more computer systems.

SJF: see *shortest job first*.

SJN: see *shortest job next*.

smart card: a small, credit-card-sized device that uses cryptographic technology to control access to computers and computer networks. Each smart card has its own personal identifier, which is known only to the user, as well as its own stored and encrypted password.

sniffer: see *packet sniffer*.

social engineering: a technique whereby system intruders gain access to information about a legitimate user to learn active passwords, sometimes by calling the user and posing as a system technician.

socket: abstract communication interfaces that allow applications to communicate while hiding the actual communications from the applications.

software: a collection of programs used to perform certain tasks. They fall into three main categories: operating system programs, compilers and assemblers, and application programs.

spin lock: a Windows synchronization mechanism used by the kernel and parts of the executive that guarantees mutually exclusive access to a global system data structure across multiple processors.

spoofing: the creation of false IP addresses in the headers of data packets sent over the Internet, sometimes with the intent of gaining access when it would not otherwise be granted.

spooling: a technique developed to speed I/O by collecting in a disk file either input received from slow input devices or output going to slow output devices such as printers. Spooling minimizes the waiting done by the processes performing the I/O.

SRT: see *shortest remaining time*.

SSTF: see *shortest seek time first*.

stack: a sequential list kept in main memory. The items in the stack are retrieved from the top using a last-in first-out (LIFO) algorithm.

stack algorithm: an algorithm for which it can be shown that the set of pages in memory for n page frames is always a subset of the set of pages that would be in memory with $n + 1$ page frames. Therefore, increasing the number of page frames will not bring about Belady's anomaly.

star topology: a network topology in which multiple network nodes are connected through a single, central node. The central node is a device that manages the network. This topology has the disadvantage of depending on a central node, the failure of which would bring down the network.

starvation: the result of conservative allocation of resources in which a single job is prevented from execution because it's kept waiting for resources that never become available. It's an extreme case of *indefinite postponement*.

static partitions: another term for *fixed partitions*.

station: any device that can receive and transmit messages on a network.

store-and-forward: a network operational mode in which messages are received in their entirety before being transmitted to their destination, or to their next hop in the path to their destination.

stripe: a set of consecutive strips across disks; the strips contain data bits and sometimes parity bits depending on the RAID level.

subdirectory: a directory created by the user within the boundaries of an existing directory. Some operating systems call this a folder.

subroutine: also called a "subprogram," a segment of a program that can perform a specific function. Subroutines can reduce programming time when a specific function is required at more than one point in a program.

subsystem: see *I/O subsystem.*

suffix: see *extension.*

supercomputers: the fastest, most sophisticated computers made, used for complex calculations at the fastest speed permitted by current technology.

symmetric configuration: a multiprocessing configuration in which processor scheduling is decentralized and each processor is of the same type. A single copy of the operating system and a global table listing each process and its status is stored in a common area of memory so every processor has access to it. Each processor uses the same scheduling algorithm to select which process it will run next.

synchronous interrupts: another term for *internal interrupts.*

system prompt: the signal from the operating system that it is ready to accept a user's command, such as C:\>.

system survivability: the capability of a system to fulfill its mission, in a timely manner, in the presence of attacks, failures, or accidents.

task: (1) the term used to describe a process, or (2) the basic unit of concurrent programming languages that defines a sequence of instructions that may be executed in parallel with other similar units.

TCP/IP reference model: a common acronym for the suite of transport-layer and application-layer protocols that operate over the Internet Protocol.

terabyte (TB): a unit of memory or storage space equal to 1,099,511,627,776 bytes or 2^{40} bytes. One terabyte approximately equals 1 trillion bytes.

teraflop: a benchmark used to measure processing speed. One teraflop equals 1 trillion floating point operations per second.

test-and-set: an indivisible machine instruction known simply as "TS," which is executed in a single machine cycle and was first introduced by IBM for its multiprocessing System 360/370 computers to determine whether the processor was available.

third generation: the era of computer development beginning in the mid-1960s that introduced integrated circuits and miniaturization of components to replace transistors, reduce costs, work faster, and increase reliability.

thrashing: a phenomenon in a virtual memory system where an excessive amount of page swapping back and forth between main memory and secondary storage results in higher overhead and little useful work.

thread: a portion of a program that can run independently of other portions. Multithreaded applications programs can have several threads running at one time with the same or different priorities.

Thread Control Block (TCB): a data structure that contains information about the current status and characteristics of a thread.

throughput: a composite measure of a system's efficiency that counts the number of jobs served in a given unit of time.

ticket granting ticket: a virtual "ticket" given by a Kerberos server indicating that the user holding the ticket can be granted access to specific applications servers. The user sends this encrypted ticket to the remote applications server, which can then examine it to verify the user's identity and authenticate the user.

time bomb: a virus with a trigger linked to a certain year, month, day, or time that causes it to execute.

time quantum: a period of time assigned to a process for execution. When it expires the resource is preempted, and the process is assigned another time quantum for use in the future.

time-sharing system: a system that allows each user to interact directly with the operating system via commands entered from a keyboard. Also called *interactive system*.

time slice: another term for *time quantum*.

token: a unique bit pattern that all stations on the LAN recognize as a "permission to transmit" indicator.

token bus: a type of local area network with nodes connected to a common cable using a CSMA/CA protocol.

token ring: a type of local area network with stations wired into a ring network. Each station constantly passes a token on to the next. Only the station with the token may send a message.

track: a path along which data is recorded on a magnetic medium such as tape or disk.

transfer rate: the rate with which data is transferred from sequential access media. For magnetic tape, it is equal to the product of the tape's density and its transport speed.

transfer time: the time required for data to be transferred between secondary storage and main memory.

transport speed: the speed that magnetic tape must reach before data is either written to or read from it. A typical transport speed is 200 inches per second.

trap door: an unspecified and nondocumented entry point to the system. It represents a significant security risk.

Trojan horse: a malicious computer program with unintended side effects that are not intended by the user who executes the program.

turnaround time: a measure of a system's efficiency that tracks the time required to execute a job and return output to the user.

unsafe state: a situation in which the system has too few available resources to guarantee the completion of at least one job running on the system. It can lead to deadlock.

universal serial bus (USB) controller: the interface between the operating system, device drivers, and applications that read and write to devices connected to the computer through the USB port. Each USB port can accommodate up to 127 different devices.

user: anyone who requires the services of a computer system.

user mode: name given to indicate that processes are not granted privileged access to the processor. Therefore, certain instructions are not allowed and system memory isn't accessible. Contrasts with the less restrictive *kernel mode.*

V: an operation performed on a semaphore that may cause a waiting process to continue. It stands for the Dutch word *verhogen,* meaning "to increment," and it's part of the P and V operations to test and increment.

variable-length record: a record that isn't of uniform length, doesn't leave empty storage space, and doesn't truncate any characters, thus eliminating the two disadvantages of fixed-length records. It contrasts with a *fixed-length record.*

verification: the process of making sure that an access request is valid.

version control: the tracking and updating of a specific release of a piece of hardware or software.

victim: an expendable job that is selected for removal from a deadlocked system to provide more resources to the waiting jobs and resolve the deadlock.

virtual device: a dedicated device that has been transformed into a shared device through the use of spooling techniques.

virtual memory: a technique that allows programs to be executed even though they are not stored entirely in memory. It gives the user the illusion that a large amount of main memory is available when, in fact, it is not.

virus: a program that replicates itself on a computer system by incorporating itself into other programs, including those in secondary storage, that are shared among other computer systems.

volume: any secondary storage unit, such as hard disks, disk packs, CDs, DVDs, removable disks, or tapes. When a volume contains several files it's called a "multifile volume." When a file is extremely large and contained in several volumes it's called a "multivolume file."

WAIT and SIGNAL: a modification of the test-and-set synchronization mechanism that's designed to remove busy waiting.

WAITING: a job status that means that the job can't continue until a specific resource is allocated or an I/O operation has finished.

waiting time: the amount of time a process spends waiting for resources, primarily I/O devices. It affects throughput and utilization.

warm boot: a feature that allows the I/O system to recover I/O operations that were in progress when a power failure occurred.

wide area network (WAN): a network usually constructed with long distance, point-to-point lines, covering a large geographic area.

wire tapping: a system security violation in which unauthorized users monitor or modify a user's transmission.

working directory: the directory or subdirectory in which the user is currently working.

working set: a collection of pages to be kept in main memory for each active process in a virtual memory environment.

workstation: a desktop computer attached to a local area network that serves as an access point to that network.

worm: a computer program that replicates itself and is self-propagating in main memory. Worms, as opposed to viruses, are meant to spawn in network environments.

Bibliography

ACM. (1999). *Ada 95: the language for a complex world*. http://www.acm.org/sigada/ada_95/.

Anderson, R. E. (1991). ACM code of ethics and professional conduct: *Communications of the ACM. 35* (5), 94–99.

Bailes, L. (1999). Windows 2000: the upgrade guide. *Windows Magazine, 7*(1), 22–33.

Barnes, J. G. P. (1980). An overview of Ada. *Software Practice and Experience, 10*, 85187.

Belady, L. A., Nelson, R. A., & Shelder, G. S. (1969, June). An anomaly in space-time characteristics of certain programs running in a paging environment. *CACM, 12*(6), 349–353.

Ben-Ari, M. (1982). *Principles of concurrent programming*. Englewood Cliffs, NJ: Prentice-Hall.

Bhargava, R. (1995). *Open VMS: architecture, use, and migration*. New York: McGraw-Hill.

Bic, L., & Shaw, A. C. (1988). *The logical design of operating systems* (2nd ed.). Englewood Cliffs, NJ: Prentice-Hall.

Bic, L., & Shaw, A. C. (2003). *Operating system principles*. Upper Saddle River, NJ: Pearson Education, Inc.

Bourne, S. R. (1987). *The UNIX system V environment*. Reading, MA: Addison-Wesley.

Brain, M. (1994). *Win32 system services. The heart of Windows NT*. Englewood Cliffs, NJ: Prentice-Hall.

Brinch Hansen, P. (1973). *Operating system principles*. Englewood Cliffs, NJ: Prentice-Hall.

Brown, G. D. (1998). *System/390 JCL* (4th ed). New York: Wiley.

Calingaert, P. (1982). *Operating system elements: A user perspective*. Englewood Cliffs, NJ: Prentice-Hall.

Card, R., Dumas, E., & Mevel, F. (1997). *The Linux kernel book, translated by Chris Skrimshire*. New York, NY: John Wiley & Sons.

Christian, K. (1983). *The UNIX operating system*. New York: Wiley.

Columbus, L., & Simpson, N. (1995). *Windows NT for the technical professional*. Santa Fe: OnWord Press.

Cook, R., & Brandon, J. (1984, October). The Pick operating system: Part I: Information management. *BYTE, 9*(11), 177–198.

Courtois, P. J., Heymans, F., & Parnas, D. L. (1971, October). Concurrent control with readers and writers. *CACM, 14*(10), 667–668.

CSO Online (2004, May). 2004 E-Crime Watch survey www.csoonline.com.

Custer, H. (1993). *Inside Windows NT*. Redmond, WA: Microsoft Press.

Davis, W. S. & Rajkumar, T.M. (2001). *Operating systems—a systematic view* (5th ed.). Reading, MA: Addison-Wesley.

Deitel, H., Deitel, P., & Choffnes, D. (2004). *Operating systems* (3rd ed.). Upper Saddle River, NJ: Pearson Education, Inc.

Denning, D.E. (1999). *Information warfare and security*. Reading, MA: Addison-Wesley.

Dettmann, T. R. (1988). *DOS programmer's reference*. Indianapolis, IN: Que Corporation.

Dickie, M. (1994). *Routing in today's internetworks. The routing protocols of IP, DECnet, NetWare, and AppleTalk*. New York: Van Nostrand Reinhold.

Dijkstra, E. W. (1965). *Cooperating sequential processes*. Technical Report EWD-123, Technological University, Eindhoven, The Netherlands. Reprinted in Genuys (1968), 43–112.

Dijkstra, E. W. (1968, May). The structure of the T.H.E. multiprogramming system. *CACM, 11*(5), 341–346.

Duncan, R. (1986). *Advanced MS-DOS*. Redmond, WA: Microsoft Press.

Finkel, R. (1986). *An operating systems vade mecum*. Englewood Cliffs, NJ: Prentice-Hall.

FitzGerald, J. (1993). *Business data communications. Basic concepts, security, and design* (4th ed.). New York: Wiley.

Forinash, D. E. (1987). *An investigation of Ada run-times supportive of real-time multiprocessor systems*. Unpublished master's thesis, Department of Statistics & Computer Science, West Virginia University, Morgantown.

Fortier, P. J. (1986). *Design of distributed operating systems*. New York: McGraw-Hill.

Frank, L. R. (Ed.). (2001). Quotationary. New York: Random House.

Gollmann, D. (1999). Computer security. Chichester, England: Wiley.

Gosling, J., & McGilton, H. (1996). *The Java language environment: Contents*. Sun Microsystems, Inc. http://java.sun.com/docs/white/langenv/

Habermann, A. N. (1976). *Introduction to operating system design*. Chicago: Science Research Associates.

Harvey, M.S. & Szubowicz, L.S. (1996). Extending OpenVMS for 64-bit addressable virtual memory. *Digital Technical Journal. 8*(2), 57–70.

Havender, J. W. (1968). Avoiding deadlocks in multitasking systems. *IBMSJ, 7*(2), 74–84.

Haviland, K., & Salama, B. (1987). *UNIX system programming*. Reading, MA: Addison-Wesley.

Henderson, T. (1999). Windows 2000: are you ready to make the move?. *Windows Magazine. 10*(5), 156–166.

Hoare, C. A. R. (1974, October). Monitors: An operating system structuring concept. *CACM, 17*(10), 549–557. Erratum in (1975, February), *CACM, 18*(2), 95.

Holt, R. C. (1972, September). Some deadlock properties of computer systems. *ACM Computing Surveys, 4*(3), 179–196.

Howell, M.A. & Palmer, J.M. (1996). Integrating the Spiralog file system into the OpenVMS operating system. *Digital Technical Journal. 8*(2), 46–56.

Hugo, I. (1993). *Practical open systems. A guide for managers* (2nd ed.). Oxford, England: NCC Blackwell Ltd.

Horvath, D. B. (1998). *UNIX for the mainframer* (2nd ed.). Upper Saddle River, NJ: Prentice-Hall PTR.

Intel. (1999). *What is Moore's Law?*. http://www.pentium.de/intel/museum/25anniv/hof/moore.htm.

Johnson, J.E. & Laing, W.A. (1996). Overview of the Spiralog file system. *Digital Technical Journal. 8*(2), 5–14.

Lane, M. G., & Mooney, J. D. (1988). *A practical approach to operating systems.* Boston: Boyd & Fraser.

Lehnert, W. G. (1998). *Internet 101, a beginner's guide to the Internet and the World Wide Web.* Reading, MA: Addison-Wesley Longman.

Leonard, T. E. (Ed.). (1987). *VAX architecture reference manual.* Bedford, MA: Digital Equipment Corporation.

Lewis,T. (1999, August). Mainframes are dead, long live mainframes. *Computer, 32*(8), 102–104.

Linger, R.C. et al. (2002). Life-cycle models for survivable systems. (CMU/SEI-2002-TR-026). Pittsburgh, PA: Software Engineering Institute, Carnegie Mellon University.

MacLennan, B. J. (1987). *Principles of programming languages: design, evaluation, and implementation* (2nd ed.). New York: Holt, Rinehart & Winston.

Madnick, S. E., & Donovan, J. J. (1974). *Operating systems.* New York: McGraw-Hill.

Microsoft. (2000). *Windows 2000 technical specifications.* http://www.microsoft.com/windows2000/.

Nemeth, E., Snyder, G., Seebass, S., & Hein, T. R. (1995). *UNIX system administration handbook* (2nd ed.). Upper Saddle River, NJ: Prentice-Hall.

Nickel, W. E. (1978, November). Determining network effectiveness. *Mini-Micro Systems, 11.*

Noel, K.L. & Karkhamis, N.Y. (1997). OpenVMS Alpha 64-bit very large memory design. *Digital Technical Journal. 9*(4), 33–48.

Parker, T. (1998). *Linux unleashed.* Indianapolis, IN: Sams Publishing.

Patil, S. S. (1971, February). *Limitations and capabilities of Dijkstra's semaphore primitive for coordination among processes.* M.I.T. Proj. MAC Computational Structures Group Memo 57.

Peterson, J. L., & Silberschatz, A. (1987). *Operating system concepts* (2nd ed.). Reading, MA: Addison-Wesley.

Petersen, R. (1998). *Linux: the complete reference* (2nd ed.). Berkeley, CA: Osborne/McGraw-Hill.

Pfaffenberger, B. (Ed.). (2001). *Webster's new world computer dictionary (9th ed.).* New York: Hungry Minds.

Pinkert, J. R., & Wear, L. L. (1989). *Operating systems concepts, policies, and mechanisms.* Englewood Cliffs, NJ: Prentice-Hall.

Pouzin, L., & Zimmermann, H. (1978, November). A tutorial on protocols. *Proceedings of the IEEE.* 66(11), 1346–1370.

Prasad, N. S. (1989). *IBM mainframes: Architecture and design.* New York: McGraw-Hill.

Ritchie, D. M., & Thompson, K. (1978, July–August). The UNIX time-sharing system. *The Bell Systems Technical Journal, 57*(6), 1905–1929.

Rubini, A. & Corbet, J. (2001) *Linux Device Drivers (2nd ed.).* Sebastopol, CA: O'Reilly.

Ruley, J. D., et al. (1994). *Networking Windows NT.* New York: Wiley.

Seyer, M. D., & Mills, W. J. (1986). *DOS:UNIX systems becoming a super user.* Englewood Cliffs, NJ: Prentice-Hall.

Shah, J. (1991). *VAXclusters: architecture, programming, and management.* New York: McGraw-Hill.

Shah, J. (1991). *VAX/VMX concepts and facilities.* New York: McGraw-Hill.

Shelly, G. B., & Cashman, T J. (1984). *Computer fundamentals for an information age.* Brea, CA: Anaheim Publishing Company.

Silberschatz, A. & Galvin, P. B. (1994). *Operating systems concepts* (4th ed.). Reading, MA: Addison-Wesley.

Shoch, J. F., & Hupp, J. A. (1982, March). The "worm" programs—early experience with a distributed computation. *Communications of the ACM, 25*(3), 172–180.

Smith, B. (1989, May). The UNIX connection. *BYTE, 14*(5), 245–253.

Spencer, D. D. (1983). *The illustrated computer dictionary* (rev. ed.). Columbus, OH: Charles E. Merrill.

Stair, R.M. & Reynolds, G.W. (1999) *Principles of Information Systems* (4th ed.). Cambridge, MA: Course Technology-ITP.

Stallings, W. (1994). *Data and computer communications* (4th ed.). New York: Macmillan.

Stallings, W. (2001). *Operating systems: internals and design principles* (4th ed.). Upper Saddle River, NJ: Prentice-Hall.

Tanenbaum, A. S. (1987). *Operating systems: Design and implementation.* Englewood Cliffs, NJ: Prentice-Hall.

Tanenbaum, A. S. (1992). *Modern operating systems.* Englewood Cliffs, NJ: Prentice-Hall.

Teorey, T. J., & Pinkerton, T. B. (1972, March). A comparative analysis of disk scheduling policies. *CACM, 15*(3), 177–184.

Thompson, K. (1978, July–August). UNIX implementation. *The Bell Systems Technical Journal, 57*(6), 1905–1929.

Trobel, S., & Uhl, T. (1996). *The Linux universe, installation and configuration* (2nd ed.). New York, NY: Springer-Verlag.

U.S. Department of Defense. (1982, April). *Ada Programming Language.* (MIL-STD-1815), Washington, D.C.

Wall, K., Watson, M. & Whitis, M. (1999). *Linux programming unleashed.* Indianapolis, IN: Sams Publishing.

Whitaker, C.E., Bayley, J.S. & Widdowson, R.D.W. (1996). Design of the servers for the Spiralog file system. *Digital Technical Journal.* 8(2), 15–31.

White, R. (1999). *How computers work, millennium edition.* Indianapolis, IN: Que.

White, R. (2004). *How computers work, 7th edition.* Indianapolis, IN: Que.

Yourdon, E. (1972). *Design of on-line computer systems.* Englewood Cliffs, NJ: Prentice-Hall.

Index